THE PACKAGE AND THE DEAL
THE NEW NOSTALGIA
THE DEATH OF THE YOUTH CULT
WOMAN AS A MALE FANTASY
THE BLACKOUT OF BLACK MOVIES
THE ALL-POWERFUL CONGLOMERATES
THE CHARMED CIRCLE OF PEOPLE WITH CLOUT
THE NEW ART OF THE SUPER-HYPE

All are part of the fascinating scene in

American Film Now

JAMES MONACO, one of America's most renowned authorities on film, is author of *The New Wave, How to Read a Film, Media Culture, Celebrity,* and *Alain Resnais.* His journalism, criticism, and fiction have appeared in *The New York Times, The Village Voice, American Film, Sight and Sound,* and many other publications. He has served as a contributing editor of MORE and *Cineaste,* and is Associate Editor of *Take One.* In addition, he is a member of the faculty at The New School for Social Research, and has taught at Columbia University, the City University of New York, and New York University.

James Monaco

American Film Now
The People,
The Power,
The Money,
The Movies

with four maps of the Film Industry
by David Lindroth

A New York Zoetrope book
Published by arrangement with The New American Library, Inc.
Lyrics from "Annie Doesn't Live Here Anymore," music by Harold Spina, words
by Joe Young and Johnny Burke, copyright 1938 by Bourne Co. Copyright
renewed. Reprinted with permission.

Lyrics from "It Don't Worry Me," words and music by Keith Carradine, copyright 1975 by American Broadcasting Music Co. and Lion's Gate Music and
Easy Music. Reprinted with permission.

The commentary on *Interiors* which appears in Chapter 7 first appeared in
slightly different form in *Take One*, November 1978. The ten-best lists included
in the "Critics and Critical Choices" section first appeared in slightly different
form in *Take One* , July 1978, in "What's the Score? The Best of the Decade."
Both copyright 1978, James Monaco and Unicorn Publishing Corp.

The graph in Chapter 11 first appeared in *Variety* and is reproduced with their
permission.

Library of Congress catalog card number: 84–042789

ISBN 0-918432-64-2

Printed in the United States of America
Revised edition first printing, June 1984

For my brother George
with hopes for the nineties

Preface
to the Second Edition

The decade of the eighties is now nearly half over and nobody quite knows what it's all about. Culturally, we seem to be in a state of suspended animation. We worry about the bomb (as we did in the early sixties). We're concerned about the environment (just like in the late sixties). Some of us are still interested in women's rights (remember the early seventies?) Kids listen to rock 'n' roll of a sort, just as they have for thirty years. People write the same sort of novels they have been writing since the fifties: our literature is, mainly, a mix of genre blockbusters, with a seasoning of rather downbeat meditations on the way we live now. Even our clothing hasn't changed much in the last dozen years. Watching a movie of indeterminate date, for example, you can't really tell how old it is until you get back to 1971 or 1972, at which point the long collars and wide ties give it away.

Yes, some of our cultural technology has changed. Significantly, more people watch cable television and own VCRs than seven or eight years ago. But what do they watch? Exactly the same sort of television shows and movies that have been prevalent since the early 1970s. We do all own computers now (or are about to if IBM and Apple have their way), but computers are only tools. They haven't yet changed the way we produce our culture.

As far as the movies go, it seems, the more things change, the more they remain the same.

The first edition of *American Film Now* appeared five years ago, early in 1979. It seemed then like a good place to stop to take account of an important decade in American film history. Now, what should have been a long time later, we are seeing pretty much the same fare made by mostly the same people. At best it can be said that we are in a period of equilibrium. But there's a nagging doubt: what are we waiting for?

The films produced between 1979 and 1984 have not been significantly different in style or approach from the films of the 1970s. The industry is still focused on the youth market. Remakes still dominate. Horror films, kids' capers, and other genres that appeal to young people come down the assembly line at an increasingly fast pace. All this is punctuated, as it was five years ago, by occasional films for adults and once or twice a year, a film—blockbuster or melodrama—that catches the imagination of the country.

The industry as a business, however, is undergoing radical change. That change was forecast as early as 1977 and indeed dominated much of the discussion of the American film business in the first edition of *American Film Now*.

After celebrating its most financially successful season in many years during the summer of 1981, the American film industry turned right around to enter a period of considerable anxiety in 1982 and 1983 as it became apparent that the financial relationships between film and the developing home video industries were not yet clear.

For five years, from 1976 to 1981, film moguls had rested easy with the knowledge that even if theatrical film budgets were inflating at a pace three to four times that of the economy, even if theatrical film was barely holding its own in terms of revenues from year to year, nevertheless, the golden age of home video was just over the horizon. We've now met the horizon and it's not at all clear where that pot of gold everybody believes in is buried.

About the New Edition:

Additional chapters covering events in the 1980s have been added, but few changes have been made to the original text of *American Film Now*. For better or worse, not much has changed. More important, I never saw a remake that was as good as the original. While you're reading the first chapters, please be kind enough to make the necessary changes in tense, and do please check the update chapters for further information. When the book was first published, we used to joke that, after a year or two, we'd have to change the title to "American Film a Little While Ago." The plain fact is that, as of the spring of 1984, American Film *Now* is American Film *a Little While Ago*.

James Monaco
New York City
April 1984

Preface
You Talkin' To Me?

Alone with his guns practicing his fast draw in a rented room, *Taxi Driver*'s Travis Bickle imagines dramatic encounters. "Are you talkin' to me?" he demands. "You must be, 'cause I'm the only one here." The head twitches to the side in the now classic Robert De Niro manner. It's a gesture of defiance. But it is also, paradoxically, a gesture of recognition. De Niro admits the existence of this imaginary universe of others by challenging it: "You talkin' to me?"

While writing *American Film Now*, I had that scene (and that gesture) continually in mind. Movies are the imaginary guests, and while the relationship between filmmaker and filmgoer is not quite so ephemeral as Bickle's psychopathic rehearsal, nevertheless we are collectively alone in the room. Are contemporary American movies talking to us? On the whole, I think not. The current governing myth has it that we are undergoing a Hollywood Renaissance—a rebirth. Yet, it seems to me, that—for the most part—American film in the seventies and eighties has a better reputation than it deserves.

There's no gainsaying the technical quality of American film now. In this strict sense, it's true: movies have never been better. The problem lies rather with the subjects that are chosen as raw material for the brilliantly made movies that we see. It took the film industry ten years even to begin to catch up with the feminist revolution, for example. Throughout most of the seventies we were cinematically still mired in the sexual politics of the fifties. Black film, which was one of the brightest signs of the early seventies, has almost completely disappeared as the studios learned how to exploit the Black market without directly serving it. It's only occasionally that a movie comes along that presents the kinds of characters and situations that we know from everyday life. Instead, remakes of aged Hollywood products and endless (and tiring) sequels to recent financial successes seem to overwhelm the nation's screens. On analysis, the seventies have been a decade in which we've stayed comfortably put, or regressed—in film as well as in other areas of culture.

Yet the powerful and sophisticated hype machine which has driven conglomerated Hollywood on to ever higher levels of profit, has convinced us—perhaps against our better judgments—that things have never been better. It's true that the very real talents of contemporary actors and technical personnel have given deceptive artistic body to what are otherwise rather thin movies. Yet we are stuck with old forms and irrelevant subjects. Anthropologists unearthing *Jaws, Heaven Can Wait, Grease, Close Encounters of the Third Kind,* and other popular films of the seventies a thousand years from now will be hard-pressed to divine from this evidence just what the 1970s in America were all about.

If this seems a harsh judgment, remember that film (together with allied forms of popular culture) still has a profound effect on our lives. Movies may reflect our society, but they also mold our view of it. What we see on film takes on a special significance, like it or not. Film validates reality. This is why the quality of American movies is not just as esthetic question: it's a political and social problem, as well.

Once again, the number of truly talented people working in the film industry is not to be doubted. Yet these filmmakers work within a precise set of constricting rules that notably limit the kinds of projects they are allowed to undertake. Well before it is an art, film is a business. And the structure of the contemporary movie business to a large extent determines the kinds of movies we see. In the pages that follow I've tried to indicate some of the ways that business works to shape the art, and the conclusion to *American Film Now* makes a few modest suggestions for nominal reform. Other chapters discuss the films of some of the more interesting filmmakers of the seventies who might serve as models for the eighties. We tend to think of directors as the prime authors of American movies today. While it is certainly true that directors wield more power than they ever have before, it's good to remember that film is still a highly collaborative art. If anything is clear about contemporary movies it is that actors still hold pride of place in the Hollywood scheme of things. If we had to choose just one filmmaker to serve as an emblem of the seventies, it seems to me it would be Robert Niro rather than one of the admittedly talented directors he has worked with during the last ten years. In order to redress the balance somewhat, I've included brief commentaries on the work of actors, cinematographers, producers, designers, and numerous other personnel who support—and sometimes supersede—director/auteurs.

Space has also been a problem in regard to defining the very broad spectrum of American film in the seventies. I've concentrated on Hollywood movies because those are the films most of us see most often; they are therefore the most influential. But there is a thriving underground of independent film, all too briefly touched on. Let's hope that a similar review of the American film scene ten years hence will include television, documentaries, independent, regional, and other sorts of non-theatrical film on a basis of equality with the entertainment products of Hollywood.

Two directors you might expect to take a prominent place in a book about contemporary American film make only brief appearances in the pages that follow. Stanley Kubrick and Richard Lester are, to my mind, among the top rank of American-born filmmakers. Yet both seem to have reached peaks before the proper beginning of the subject of this book. And both have chosen to work outside a purely American context, in England, for the last twenty years.

Movies have always seemed to me more honest than books in one respect: movies list credits. Certainly a book isn't as collaborative as a film. Nevertheless numerous people help to produce a book. Their names, like those of filmmakers from editor to grip and best boy, deserve to be known. At the end of *American Film Now*, you'll find our credits. I take full responsibility, of course, for the opinions contained herein, but at the same time I'm sincerely grateful for the help of the "crew." John Thornton, the editor who made it possible for the book to be written (and produced in record time) deserves special mention, as does my wife, Susan Schenker, always a partner.

James Monaco
New York City
November 1978

Contents

CONTENTS

American Film Now

1
Properties and Packages

Getting Started: A Fable

Fred wants to make a movie. At thirty, he figures this may be his last chance. He's been to film school. (He likes to think of himself as the Coppola—or at least the Scorsese—of the eighties.) He learned a lot about Bergman, Godard, and semiology. He learned how to load an Arriflex, how to zoom smoothly without a motor, how to operate a double system projector, and how to write a budget. He also learned, degree in hand, that none of this knowledge had much bearing on a career in the film business.

After graduation, he thought he might write, produce, and direct his own low-budget feature. Wasn't this how Godard and Truffaut started back in the fifties? How Cassavetes and De Palma began in the sixties? It took twenty-two months, but by begging out-of-date film stock, borrowing old equipment, and stealing the services of a couple of young actors (he gave them points in the profits), Fred actually did shoot one hour of footage for *Hear Me Talkin' to Ya*. It was about jazz. But distributors weren't interested in jazz in 1972, especially an unprogrammable single hour of it. Roger Corman wouldn't return his calls. The New York State Council on the Arts insisted that he wasn't an artist, that he was a craftsperson. He couldn't get completion money. Eventually he let it drop.

Some of his friends in film school were lucky enough to get honest jobs on the fringes of the industry. Jane was cutting newsfilm for CBS and making good money (although now that the networks were switching over to minicams and tape she figured to be on unemployment again soon). Larry served as occasional assistant director (read gofer) for films shot in New York. He was quite successful; in a good year, he was drawing a paycheck five, maybe six, months. Martin had a position of responsibility in the publicity department at Paramount. In six years, he'd moved up to assistant head publicist in charge of the local college press.

But Fred didn't think these strategies would work for him. He had never heard of a publicist or gofer who had been able to break into directing.

Logical about such things, he had completed a survey of forty young directors who had shot their first films since 1970. A number had worked their way in from television. One or two had started in advertising. There was an ex-editor, a former producer whose regular director had abandoned him, and surprisingly, two hairdressers who had cultivated a couple of actresses with box-office clout. But by far the great majority of this new generation of filmmakers, Fred discovered, had begun by writing scripts.

Why buck the numbers, Fred figured. He turned out three passable scripts in six months. He started writing for film magazines. He got to interview producers. At the end of the session, he'd thank them, reach into his bag, pull out the script neatly mimeoed by Studio Duplicating: "Oh, by the way, maybe you'd like to take a look at this." They smiled tightly. Every interview, this happened. Seems everybody wants to write a movie. The Writers Guild alone registers 15,000 scripts and treatments a year. Yet, Fred was undaunted.

Fred's agent had no luck with the studios. It quickly became evident that the formal channels of submission were cannily devised to siphon off the torrents of material that flowed through them. The production heads passed the scripts on to the story departments. The story departments efficiently distributed them to freelance readers. Grossly overworked and underpaid, the readers skimmed the scripts, produced short synopses that had tangential relationships to the plots, and neatly checked a "no" or perhaps a "maybe" on the evaluation sheet. The evaluation sheets were filed, the scripts were returned. In an average year, a good reader might handle 300 scripts and proposals. Options on five of them might be bought. Maybe one would make it to neighborhood screens.

So Fred and his agent gradually came to realize that their properties were going to have to be presold. The easiest way to do this was by novelization. The Writers Guild minimum for a shootable script is $20,821. Few first novels bring anywhere near that from a publisher. In

2

fact, the average advance even for established writers hovers somewhere between $5000 and $10,000. Conclusion: novels might be more time-consuming to write than screenplays, but they're much easier to sell.

Screenings, the novelization of Fred's second script, was worth a $5000 advance. It was published in 1975 and did quite well for a first novel. Fred expects an additional $3000 or $4000 in royalties, eventually.

For a while, David Susskind was interested in it for a television movie, but the deal fell through. Some Yugoslavs inquired as to its availability at one point, but then Susskind was holding a $500 six-month option and by the time the option lapsed, so had the Yugoslavs.

For about six months in between the second and third screenplays, Fred was involved with a young assistant producer friend of his who had the ear of Paul Klein at NBC. They were developing a pilot for a series. "The Top Banana Gang" was going to be a really funny show about the cast and crew of . . . a contemporary sitcom. A little bit like *Mary Tyler Moore*, a little bit like *Dick Van Dyke*, but, you know, much fresher, hipper, shot in New York, with lots of location work, and a real satiric bite to it.

The people at NBC seemed to like Fred's script for the pilot. They didn't say yes, but they didn't say no. Jerry, the assistant producer friend, was hopeful. NBC decided to send it out to the Coast for a polish. They sent it to a couple of veteran comedy writers out there in L.A. NBC told Fred and Jerry that these old hands would know how to smooth out the rough edges, make it look more like, well, television. (It was too much like a movie, they said.)

When the script for the pilot for "The Top Banana Gang" came back, it bore no readily discernible resemblance to Fred's original. The veterans knew something Fred and Jerry didn't. They knew that if they did a simple polish, what they got was their $10,000 fee, but if they threw out Fred's script and wrote their own, and it was used, and the pilot was picked up, they had a piece of the show. They could retire.

The polish was lousy—hackneyed, trite. Everybody preferred Fred's script. But they shot the polish. You see, they'd paid twice as much for it. The show never got on the schedule.

So after seven years on the fringes of the movie business, Fred could list among his credits: three screenplays, one novelization, one television script. Total income: $14,500.

This is when Fred meets Harry. An independent producer of the old school, Harry was the subject of an interview Fred did for *Take One* magazine. This time, when he pulled out the script as he was shutting off the cassette, there was a surprising glimmer of interest. Harry read it overnight and called Fred the next morning. He couldn't offer much, he said, but he was writing a check for $500 and sending it down by messenger and he'd like a two-month option.

Harry wants to make a movie, too. This is his business. He's been at it more than thirty years. But recently it's been tough to put together a deal. Harry doesn't have a lot of capital. In fact, it's shrinking year by year. As a result, he can't afford first-class properties. He cultivates a lot of young writers like Fred. He reads a lot in the libraries. Older books, not the current bestsellers.

Once he sends Fred the check, he has two months to put together the package and convince someone to put up the money. An inexpensive American film now costs in the neighborhood of $2-$3 million—twice what it did only six or seven years ago. No individual producer (except an occasional crazy actor like George C. Scott) ever wants to risk that much, even if he has it. If Harry had an arrangement with one of the six major studios, the remnants of Hollywood that have been passed down to us, there would be no problem. A few minor hassles with agents, of course; the inevitable compromises, but chances are good Fred's film would be made. It has good characters, plenty of action, a solid starring role, it's not too downbeat, with just enough sex for an 'R'. Perfect. Harry has taste and savvy. He knows how to do his job. Fred genuinely likes him.

But Harry does not have an understanding with Universal, Warners, Paramount, Fox, Columbia, or UA. He is an independent working out of New York, and the action is elsewhere.

A few years back, when movie tax-shelter deals were still permissible in the U.S. (and Harry was younger), he might have tried to put together a consortium of upstate dentists, Florida realtors, or Seventh Avenue garment kings who were looking for a little protection from a fifty percent tax bite. But movie tax shelters in this country were ruled out in 1976, and there's no sense in going with this project to West Germany or Canada, as a number of his colleagues were doing now.

Anyway, eventually Harry, as an independent, will have to find someone to distribute the film. The choice is severely limited. With certain exceptions, there are at most a dozen companies in this country with the organization necessary to give a film a fair chance at nationwide distribution. There are the six major studios (who for the most part simply finance and distribute rather than produce films as they once did). There are also a couple of minors, basically successful producers of exploitation films in the sixties who have graduated to respectable distributor status: American International and Roger Corman's New World. Add to this list of potential distributors a handful of companies that are essentially importers, such as Allied Artists and Cinema 5. There are, too, a couple of dozen small firms which have handled a film or two in the past. They can finance a New York opening, maybe L.A. and Chicago too, but they haven't got the network of advertising and sales people necessary to place and exploit the film in one of the two or three houses still·remaining in most American towns and cities.

Harry is not interested in making a film that is not seen. Eventually he is going to have to become the reluctant partner of one of the dozen controlling distributors, so why not now? Their upfront investment will serve as a guarantee of distribution.

Harry also knows there is no way he is ever going to get more than an "expression of interest" from one of these firms with only a raw screenwriter like Fred in his package. He's going to have to have a star and a director in the package before he sees the cash.

Despite the rise of directors as powers in the film industry during the last ten years, Harry knows that for the most part one filmmaker has as much commercial value as another. Directors are seldom the focal point of a package. So, armed with his expression-of-interest from one of the major minor distributors, he sets off in quest of his star.

Fred's film is basically small-budget. (Fred designed it that way on purpose.) Harry figures he could bring it in for a million eight. But this will hold true only if he uses stars of second magnitude or less. Otherwise, actors' salaries could double or triple the cost of the movie.

If he goes after the second-magnitude actors, however, he has to trade off a portion of the desultory interest of the major minor distributor. If by some chance somebody with real box-office clout could be interested—a Redford or a Pacino—the film would then be immediately financible, no questions asked, at four to five times the current projected budget. Yet Harry knows he's likely to hit a brick wall with the superstars. They are booked up too far in advance. So he takes the safer gamble. The script is sent, in turn, to younger actors who've shown promise, and a few supporting players who Harry thinks could graduate to box-office power, given the right vehicle. He's not worried about talent—there's plenty of that around—but rather about the bankable image of the star.

This will be the linchpin of the precarious construction which he hopes will become a film. With a marketable name, he'll get the money; without one, he won't; so he can't play his instincts. It's best to be conservative in such matters.

He hopes the star won't demand rewrites by a better-known screenwriter than Fred. He hopes he'll be able to sign a director who's at least trustworthy, if not notably talented. He hopes shooting will go smoothly, that the actors will get along with each other and with the director and crew, that he won't have undue problems with the unions, that the

Marlon Brando, Susannah York, and their otherworldly child in *Superman,* a nice little film based on the popular comic book. Shot as part of a two-film package produced by Alexander and Ilya Salkind which reputedly cost in the neighborhood of $50 million, *Superman* must set box-office records in order to show a minimal profit. These are the economics Harry and Fred are up against.

weather will hold up for the location sequences, that he'll be able to hire a competent editor, that his distributor's cashflow position will be such that, when the film is ready to be released, they'll have the necessary financial impetus to put some muscle into advertising. He hopes that all the myriad details that go to make up a film will come together properly once more. Approaching sixty, Harry has begun to wonder how and why movies succeed at all in the face of such fickle economics.*

Fred is hopeful, too. He has already begun work on the novelization of the screenplay, and his agent, by stretching the truth just a bit, has sold it for five figures to a trade-paperback house. The plan is to come out with a conservative first edition in about eight months, let it run for a while, then hit the racks with a redesigned mass-market edition (including stills from the film) about the time the movie premieres. The book will sell the film, which will sell the book.

Fred's agent has called in all outstanding copies of the earlier scripts.

*For more of Harry's semifictional exploits, see Robert Alan Aurthur's informative "Harry Makes a Movie," in my collection *Media Culture* (New York: Delta Books, 1978), pp. 142-149.

She plans to let them rest for a while on the shelf. Then, assuming this one makes a few ripples, she figures to unload the least salable of them (the first) for whatever she can get to the first reputable producer who comes around looking for more product from this bright, young, instant success.

With a track record of two films—one out, one in production—Fred will be able to bargain for real money ($150,000 and up) for the better of the two earlier scripts—the one that was novelized. It's a win-place-show parlay.

Meanwhile, with the sharp scent of his first real movie in his nostrils, Fred amuses himself by dreaming up marketing strategies which he intends to pass on to Harry at the proper time. He has a friend set to do the book about the making of the film and an expression of more than mild interest from the publisher of the novelization. This will be the book that sells the book which sells the film which sells the book.

Since the movie has a sports background (Fred had analyzed *Variety's* list of top grossers for 1977; the conclusion: 18.5 percent of films grossing over $10 million had a sports element in them), Fred has asked Harry to inquire about the mechanics of renting stadium billboards. If they could pick up centerfield boards in strategic cities in time, they'd receive an entire summer's worth of product recognition from television cameras chasing flys and line drives. Since the film is planned as a midsummer release, teeshirts (known in the trade as walking billboards) are also a must. Fred has visions of special teeshirt days at the stadium—40,000 people advertising his film!

Fred thinks he may also be able to work a useful new twist on product endorsement. Of course, they'll use brand-name equipment in the film in return for a small consideration, but Fred theorizes that if they could franchise a line of goods with the film's name to the same company, they could multiply the income from merchandise by a significant factor. Aware of the famous *Star Wars* snafu of Christmas 1977, when millions of Wookie-crazed kids had to settle for empty boxes and promises because the licensed merchandisers were slow in getting the games and toys on the shelves, Fred is pushing Harry to begin license negotiations now, even before the film is cast.

With the help of his friend Martin the publicist, Fred has also worked out a detailed public-relations campaign. Although the closed-set gambit worked well for such blockbusters as *Close Encounters of the Third Kind,* Fred believes that even if Harry obtains the services of a major star and a well-known director, this film will require a wide-open set. Despite the planned novelization presell campaign, Fred himself as a heretofore unknown quantity will not be able to carry and build interest in the film without the usual press panoply during shooting. The film simply isn't mysterious enough.

He has suggested to Harry that very soon they engineer a regular series of press junkets, and include an elaborate interview clause in the major actors' contracts spelling out precisely the amount of time that they will be required to devote to publicity both on the set and off, during shooting and after. To this end, the shooting schedule will make allowances for journalists' junkets.

Looking ahead to the development of his own career, Fred has spent $2000 of his novelization advance to buy an option on a story that appeared in *High Times* that he thinks has significant potential. The concept is salable enough so that he may be able to direct this one himself. But he knows he'll have to develop a higher level of visibility before attempting this package, and therefore he's signed up with Lilyan Wilder (whose profession is to teach people these things) to develop a television personality and work on his camera—eye contact.

He has a small, very hip public-relations firm on retainer and they are mapping out a basic plan of attack for the talkshow circuit in the two-month period after the release of Harry's project. The concept is this: young filmmakers like Lucas and Spielberg have developed a strong potential image in the public mind, but they haven't exploited it properly. They hardly ever appear on talkshows, and as a result the character of the bright young filmmaker hasn't yet been fixed in the video pantheon. Fred, the theory goes, will be able to stand on their metaphorical shoulders, fill the vacant image, and trade on this to set up a solid expectation for his next film which will be, of course, a very "personal" project (along the lines of *Star Wars* or *Close Encounters*) written, directed, and novelized by Fred, with Fred perhaps in a walk-on à la Hitchcock.

I think Fred is going to make it.

Building "Projects"

You may have noticed during this semifictional fantasy that the actual subjects of Fred's various media endeavors seldom came up. There's a good reason. Within certain parameters, the subjects don't matter very much anymore, if they ever did. Films—feature films—aren't *about* nuclear reactors, or contemporary capitalism, or political chicanery, or sharks, or close encounters of the third kind, or baseball, or disco dancing, or even love. These are just the raw materials from which films are fashioned. We tend now to leave such thematic or subject-ridden projects to television docudrama. (Of course, there's the occasional small feature film that does make the mistake of thinking it has a subject, or a purpose other than to entertain for two hours or so and earn back triple its negative costs, but there are fewer and fewer of these every year.)

I don't mean to suggest that information doesn't sometimes get communicated, even in blockbusters; simply that the American post-Hollywood film craft—no longer organized on the assembly-line model of the thirties and forties—has become so sophisticated, both in technical and in marketing terms, that structure thoroughly dominates content. The elements of the film equation—character, action, plotting, sex, genre, humor, and so on—count for a good deal in the total mix, but the guts of the experience, what we used to call content, or theme, or subject, has been reduced to the status of raw material. And contemporary manufacturing techniques can do wonders with a surprising variety of raw materials, many of which were hitherto considered unsuitable.

It's not impossible these days to sell a film project on the basis of a one-paragraph outline, and the salable concepts of most recent blockbusters can be reduced to a simple declarative sentence or two. A *TV Guide* blurb can tell you all you need to know: mind over matter. "Cute young heroes smash intergalactic villains." "Big shark terrorizes small town, eats one star, gets blown up." "Little girl is possessed, vomits peasoup, gets exorcized (until the sequel)." "An office building burns down (up); some people die, some people don't." "Over-the-hill but likable boxer almost beats the champ and falls in love." "Boy meets girl, boy gets girl, girl dies." "Cute Walter Keane visitors from another planet arrive in magnificent flying juke box; they don't say much but they whistle a happy tune."

Do they sound egregiously dull? They are, if reduced to content. Never has it been clearer that the medium is the message. The message certainly isn't.

A certain moral tone has begun to creep in here. I suppose it was inevitable, but don't put too fine a point on it. There's no particular ethical problem with taking pleasure in pure craft. Let a thousand *Star Wars* bloom: there's nothing inherently dangerous about color and music and action and fantasy. The difficulty lies rather with the inverse corollary to this nascent supremacy of craft: a kind of Gresham's law of culture. As the craft becomes able to accomplish more with less, to realize record-setting profits with the flimsiest of raw materials, bad product drives out good, just as bad money supersedes good money in the sphere of monetary economics.

The definitive irony of film culture in the seventies (as in all contemporary media culture from television to records to books) is that the refinement of the craft results in less freedom rather than more for the "artists,"

9

the producers of the culture. Superficially, it may look as if the reverse is true: after all, the more sophisticated and effective the craft becomes, the better it can deal with inherent problems in the raw material which it uses. We can practically spin gold out of straw now.

For example, it used to be a Hollywood rule of thumb that "sports movies don't sell." Yet Fred's analysis of the top grossers of 1977 is true: six of the thirty-two highest-grossing films that year had sports backgrounds. Likewise, it was known that science fiction was a marginal enterprise, 2001 not withstanding. Until *Star Wars* and *Close Encounters*, that is.

Why this sudden success with film types which had been anathema to studio accountants for forty years? The real key to product salability has to do, not with genres themselves, but with qualities associated with genres. Now that filmmakers understand this, it's a simple matter to separate the salable characteristics from the narrative characteristics and transplant them. Narratives, in other words, can be genetically engineered: preserve the superficial aspects if you like, so long as you implant the energy-producing drive elements that generate cash flow.*

This new sophistication is at least as much economic as it is technical or esthetic. The result is that any attempt at real understanding of American film now must be rooted in a discussion of its economic structure.

The Rules of the Game

At this point we can outline a few rules by which contemporary media industries operate to process the raw material of properties into marketable packages:

1. Any medium, any form. The choice whether a property first appears as novel or film, television show, play, or nonfiction magazine article depends mainly on marketing strategies.

There are still a few narrative artists around who think of themselves as specialists—novelists, critics, screenwriters, television writers, journalists, and so forth. They are anachronisms. One good reason media companies are merging into conglomerates is that it has become clear in the last ten or fifteen years that form is, in marketing terms, arbitrary. Just as it matters little which genre within an art is chosen as the framework for the elements of the work, so the narrative form itself in which the work

---

*There is one important ethical consideration here: it concerns the manipulative nature of money-machine films, which seduce and produce passive audiences. We'll try to deal with this in Chapter 2.

The new hoke: The mouse and the bum from the neighborhood—Talia Shire and Sylvester Stallone in *Rocky*: simple emotions and clear-cut philosophy.

first appears now depends more on marketing strategies than on any particular affinity between form and content. There is still the occasional film or play, novel or article that seems to fit its form so precisely that it would seem a mistake to try to translate it into an alternative form. But these exceptions prove the rule. And their seemingly perfect realization of the form doesn't, finally, prevent exploitation in other media if that seems economically justifiable.

As our fabulous Fred learned quickly, novels are generally easier to sell than filmscripts. They are also less profitable. Yet there has been an interesting feedback from the more lucrative media of film and television to the ancient and respectable form of the novel. Although most book contracts still apportion one hundred percent of subsequent film sales to the author, publishers are ever more acutely aware of a book's potential as an eventual film or television series. The sales value of taglines like "now a major motion picture" and "as seen on TV" increases each year. And as book publishing becomes more concentrated, depending on blockbusters much as the film industry does for a major percentage of profits, saturation advertising of the sort only film and television can provide becomes almost a necessity. A property that works well only in one medium is at a distinct disadvantage.

There are few of these single-minded efforts being produced, however. Generally, the film that can't be successfully novelized and the novel that

11

can't be profitably filmed are limited to the elite level of high art. Publishers still indulge in this sort of profitless culture; the film industry hardly ever does. What sells in one medium will, the necessary changes being made, sell in another. The same basic attractions (sex, character, action, novelty) work across the media spectrum without regard to form. A story is a story, now matter how it's told. The differences between media are a matter of consumption rather than genre. Television is successful because you don't have to go out to do it. Film survives because it gives you more—in image, sound, and lack of censorship—than television, and because sometimes it's fun to go out and be with other people. You can't read a film on the subway, but then it's difficult to watch a book with your family after dinner. (Before movies and television, communal reading was not unknown.)

Far from destroying print media, the audiovisual media of film and television may have strengthened books and magazines. There are now more bookstores in the United States than cinemas. They may not have the variety or offer the personal service that used to characterize the local bookshop, but then neither do the cinemas.

Perhaps the most successful recycling project in media during the last twenty-five years has been *Cabaret*. It began life as an unassuming collection of short stories, *Goodbye to Berlin* (1939), was dramatized by John Van Druten as *I Am a Camera* (1951), which play was filmed by Jack Clayton and Henry Cornelius in 1955, and served as the source for the musical *Cabaret* by John Kander and Fred Ebb (1966), which was later itself filmed by Bob Fosse (1972). There were soundtrack albums of these last two, of course. As I write, it has not yet appeared as a television series, the only major medium it's missed.

No wonder then that with the prospect of doubling or tripling profits from one property, in the mid-sixties, film, television, and publishing companies began a mad rush to buy each other up. All six major film studios operate recording divisions. Indeed, Universal, the most productive of all the studios, is owned by MCA, Inc., the keystone of which was originally Decca Records, and Warners realizes twice as much income from records in any given year as from film.

All six also engage profitably in television production, although Universal is by far the leader, producing more hours of prime time television than the other five studios put together. Most also operate a broadcasting license or two.

The three most powerful film conglomerates—MCA, Warner Communications, and Gulf + Western (Paramount)—are also heavily involved in book and/or magazine publishing. MGM/UA, Twentieth Century-Fox, and Columbia Pictures, less diversified, are struggling to catch up. (See chart on pp. 36–37 for more on conglomerates.)

Meanwhile, all three television networks are also involved in publishing, perhaps against their better judgment. Despite modern management techniques, book publishing is still a business with a relatively small profit margin, and the feedback between books and television is considerably less valuable to the networks than the parallel phenomenon is to the film companies. Interestingly, both ABC and CBS tried in the late sixties to establish positions for themselves in film production. Both efforts failed within a few years. Perhaps monopolizing the distribution of television programs as they do had made them insensitive to the singular fact of life of the film industry: power rests with the distributor. They didn't fail as producers, they failed as distributors.

In general, the book industry, with considerably less capital at its disposal than either television or film, and with control spread over a much wider number of individual companies, has been slow to catch up. Only Time Inc. has been able to wrest a major position in film and television. They import BBC programs, occasionally coproduce, operate a successful 16-mm distribution company, and are heavily involved in cable TV. HBO, *Time's* cable arm, is the most powerful force operating in movies today. But once again it remains to be seen whether or not an outside company can break the effective control the six major studios exert over distribution channels.

If investors then cover their media bets by spreading the capital over several forms, so do writers. When Fitzgerald and Faulkner went Hollywood to earn better money writing screenplays, it was thought they were slumming. But the idea that a novel is inherently more prestigious esthetically than a film is entertained only in the few small pockets of retrogressive literary culture that still exist. For better or worse, film has come of age as an art, probably because television now receives the brunt of contempt from the remaining proponents of elite culture.

Despite the high prices some popular novels now regularly bring in from paperback sales and the occasional million-dollar advance to a superstar like Norman Mailer, the vast majority of novelists are still involved in an essentially uneconomical activity (ask Fred) and are as eager as the conglomerates for the increased profit potential from allied media. "Serious" novelists used to support themselves by taking jobs in academia. A few of the old school still do. But younger intellectuals, critics, and scholars move with ease from abstruse analysis to popular fiction and never consider pseudonyms.

Erich Segal, former Yale professor of classics, author not only of the scholarly tome *Roman Laughter* but also of *Love Story* and *Oliver's Story,* is perhaps the most notorious of this new breed, but there are numerous

13

others. Andrew Bergman received his Ph.D. from the University of Wisconsin with a dissertation on film which was later published as *We're in the Money: Depression America and Its Films*. A few years later, he wrote a treatment for a film called "Black Bart," which later became *Blazing Saddles*. From all reports, the income from the film could have allowed Bergman to retire. He has amused himself since with novels (*The Big Kiss-Off of 44*, *Hollywood and LeVine*), screenplays (*In-Laws*), and plays.

Within the film-buff world, Paul Schrader's career stands as a shining example to hundreds of serious film students. Schrader, former editor of a film magazine and UCLA film student, wrote the scholarly *Transcendental Style in Film: Ozu Bresson Dreyer* (1972), then turned his attention to screenplays. In short order, he had sold three of them, including *Obsession* and *Taxi Driver*. In 1978, he made his debut as a director with *Blue Collar*. Philip Rosenberg's Columbia dissertation *The Seventh Hero: Thomas Carlyle and the Theory of Radical Activism* was hailed as a brilliant contribution to political scholarship when it appeared in 1973. His next book was a police/mafia novel, *Contract on Cherry Street*, later filmed for television by Frank Sinatra. Rosenberg is now much in demand as a nonfiction novelist and screenwriter. Numerous other young novelists, journalists, and screenwriters have followed similar paths.

High culture and popular culture, academic inquiry and entertainment are now no longer separate and antagonistic endeavors. Neither are film and the novel, journalism and film, fiction and nonfiction. If the form fits, use it. Then recycle the property. The criterion of the Bauhaus was "form follows function." The criterion of the media world in the 1970s is "form follows finances."

Within this spectrum, continuous and reciprocal, certain other laws of properties operate.

2. Just like/completely different. If it isn't the precise form that draws attention to a particular product, what is it? Producers and publishers have only empirical knowledge with which to form an answer to that question. The result is a strict commercial conservatism, one of the groundrules of the media world. If each individual property is milked until utterly dry, so each financial success is parodied and paraphrased within an inch of its life.

In the early seventies, disaster ruled the screen. *Airport* (1970) had revived the genre, updating "group" movies like *The High and the Mighty* and *Grand Hotel*. Those earlier films had been built around the study of a group of people facing impending disaster. *Airport* upped the ante, moved the holocaust closer to the front of the film. For years we were confronted at every turn with a colorful variety of disasters, natural and otherwise.

14

Buildings burned, ships capsized, planes sank, or were otherwise disabled, earthquakes leveled California. The genre has quieted down somewhat now.

This propensity to spinoffs was perhaps best exemplified by the *Jaws* parlor game, the object of which was to come up with the most amusing animal terror title, on the model of *Paws* (bears), *Caws* (crows), and *Laws* (voracious attorneys).

The result is that the best way to sell a film or television concept is to prove that it's "just like" *Laverne and Shirley, Star Wars,* or *Bad News Bears in Breaking Training.* But since no producer wants to be accused of ripping off an already successful film or show, it is necessary to add the paradoxical caveat, "but, of course, it's completely different."

This mimickry is not necessarily bad for the medium. In one sense, it simply means filmmakers have been attracted to mythic structures; variations on the theme refine those myths. Yet originality is still given lip service.

While the majority of producers chase their own tales this way, there are exceptions. There's the occasional original production that begins a sequence of variations (although in most cases the film scholar can find a string of earlier antecedents). More significant is the work of a couple of new film production and distribution companies operating entirely outside the traditional Hollywood orbit. Applying all the latest techniques of contemporary marketing theory to the packaging and sale of film products, they make even the conglomerateurs of the New Hollywood look like madly romantic artists.

Thinking (rightly, as it turned out) that the Hollywood companies were letting significant sectors of the total potential audience for films slip through their fingers, the investors in such companies as Sunn International set out early in the seventies to see where there might be profit for them. They had no experience in film; they didn't figure they needed it; they knew marketing strategy thoroughly and didn't see why film as product couldn't be developed and sold just as efficiently as breakfast cereal or soap powder.

Using sophisticated marketing surveys, they immediately identified their target audience: working-class couples and families who had previously attended movies seldom or not at all. The next step was to produce a profile of the kind of film that would get these people to the theaters. They settled on two genres, not unknown in the past but never fully exploited: the nature adventure film (*Life and Times of Grizzly Adams*) and the quasi-scientific religious semidocumentary (*In Search of Noah's Ark*). Next, they rented theaters outright (a process called "four-walling") in strategic areas identified by computer studies. This way they could control every aspect of the exploitation of their product. The films were made with unbelievably low budgets; it was thought that the cash saved could be more productively spent on advertising. Each well-timed release was accompanied by saturation television advertising in the target communities. Result: $23 million in rentals in 1977 for *Noah's Ark*, for example, a film which received no critical attention to speak of and none of the usual Hollywood chic hype. The law of Just Like/Completely Different needn't govern the kinds of films that are chosen to be made. As an entertainment product, film is susceptible to most of the regular laws of the marketplace.

3. Preselling. The combination of similarity to a previously successful film and apparent novelty is a potent sales tool. An even stronger guarantee of a project's potential profit is an extensive preselling campaign of the sort that is usually provided by a property which has already achieved a "track record" in another medium.

Novels don't draw million-dollar prices from the film industry because of their intrinsic story value. They are worth this much money because they have been presold. They are, it is hoped, already indelibly etched in the public consciousness. *Love Story* was a script before it was a novel. Segal and Paramount gained an incalculable amount of publicity from the prerelease novelization. *The Godfather* was fairly sure to be profitable because of the huge success of the novel in paperback. When that film fulfilled its promise it made the sequel possible. *The Godfather, Part II* was also drawn from the novel but made use of episodes which were much less immediately dramatic (if also more interesting). Financially, the second film rested on the shoulders of the first. The two together made possible the recut television serialization (given the unwieldy title *Mario Puzo's The Godfather: The Complete Novel for Television*). Without the saturation of six years of publicity that had made Puzo's saga part of the modern mythos, NBC would not have been likely to take a chance on such an expensive nine-hour project, with its dark cinematography, downbeat subject matter, and large patches of dialogue in Italian with subtitles. Publicity can be pyramided.

In early 1978, Columbia set a record for initial payment for a property when they acquired film rights to the Broadway musical *Annie* for $9.5 million. Since the contract stipulated that the film could not be released before 1981, interest rates should be included. Columbia's upfront cost for the film thus exceeded $12 million. No matter how tight the rein on production costs, the film had to become the most profitable musical of all time in order to climb out of the red. In the late sixties, a number of studios mounted unusually expensive Broadway musicals, many of which

Instant docudrama: Robert Redford, Jack Warden, Jason Robards, and Dustin Hoffman in the *Washington Post* newsroom set meticulously reconstructed for *All the President's Men.*

failed to return their investments. Was *Annie* a gamble for Columbia? Perhaps it seemed a safe one. The film was preceded by four years of media attention to the stage production, as well as forty years of comic strips that have reached every town and hamlet in the country.

Novels and plays aren't the only ways to presell a film. At least three moderately successful movies of the past ten years have been based on popular songs—*Alice's Restaurant, Tommy* and *Ode to Billy Joe.* Furthermore, any exploitation of a popular music group is usually a safe bet.

More important during the mid-seventies has been the rush to fictionalize the news. Three years of constant television obsession (as well as the best-selling source book) made *All the President's Men* one of the very few movies with a political theme to turn a profit. *Dog Day Afternoon* moved straight from the pages of newspapers to the screen, then back to print, as at least one young man staged a bank-hostage siege in imitation of the film.

A current industry joke suggests it's only a matter of time before the first commissioned crime is staged as a pseudoevent to attract prepublicity for its own followup film. In July 1978, a struggling mystery writer was shot and killed by police in Columbus, Ohio, as he prepared to rob a bank as research for a novel in progress. Publishers had told him, "Real crime is in."[1]

New York State's "Dog Day" law decrees that any profit a convicted

The reality-film circuit: The late John Cazale and Al Pacino in *Dog Day Afternoon*.

felon makes from any written or dramatic reenactment of a crime must be channeled into a special fund and held in reserve for possible judgments in favor of the criminal's victims. While this seems like an effective step to prevent commissioned crimes, it's not impossible that it may have the reverse effect one day, as hostages, for example, agree to play out a more dramatic story with their captor in exchange for a cut of the profits.

In fact, feature films have been relatively conservative in merchandising the news—probably because it takes so long to produce a quality film. Television and publishing have been much more aggressive in this area.

The docudrama became a staple of seventies television. While it often focuses on historical personalities (Lee Harvey Oswald, the Roosevelts, Rudolph Valentino), the docudrama form is immediately adaptable to late-breaking news. The Israeli raid on Entebbe became the subject for at least two TV docudramas within months after it splashed across newspaper pages. The film version shuffled along, appearing finally more than a year later.

Publishers have become so enamored of news novels that "the source" has become an equal partner in many book contracts, one of the accepted participants in the negotiating process, along with editors, publishers, authors, and agents. Robin Moore (*The Green Berets, The French Connection,* and many others) is probably the hardest-working fictional journalist, efficiently churning other people's more or less true stories. Such

Peter Boyle reveling in Brinks loot. In the summer of 1978 offices of the *Brinks Job* company (the movie, not the armored-car people) were robbed of several crucial and expensive sequences from the film. The movie based on a "true story," becomes a "true story" itself.

respected artists as Truman Capote and Norman Mailer pioneered the form. There are so many excops and former assistant D.A.s at work as novelists, now, that the best advice for an aspiring writer might be to chuck that M.A. in Creative Writing and sign up immediately at the nearest police academy. It's the straightest path to bestsellerdom. Medical doctors, following the lead of Michael Crichton, are not far behind the cops.

Most cops and physicians who write separate their careers; first they do it, then they write about it. But what happens when a politician, for instance, knows while he is in office that his actions will form part of a continuing story that might make him rich in several years' time? Did it matter to the course of Egyptian-Israeli negotiations that Menachem Begin had an agent?

While most of the economic value of these semifictional efforts lies largely in their newsworthiness and the prepublicity it provides, a significant part has deeper roots. People seem starved for a touch of reality in the fictional media sea of images, sounds, and print that surrounds them. Certainly, the film industry does little to assuage this hunger. Television and publishing thus step into the breach with docudramas and nonfiction novels that at least provide a semblance of realism. Newspaper and magazine gossip, now in resurgence following the success of magazines

19

like *People,* is another evidence of this appetite for stories based in fact that deal with the way we live now.

4. LCD. There's a type of novel—you still see occasional examples of it—that's so thoroughly localized it deals only with the lives and experiences of perhaps 100,000 people: "Upper West Side New York Intellectuals." Now, there are maybe another 400,000 people scattered around the country in various academic communities who might understand and appreciate this sort of thing. The figures don't seem very salutary: the core audience for this genre—let's call it West End Avenue Existentialism—amounts to slightly more than two-hundredths of one percent of the population of the country. Yet these books are often moderate successes, all things considered. They get published in the first place because perhaps 80 percent of the New York publishing community identifies strongly with their subject matter. They sell satisfactorily, at least in hardcover (they seldom make it to paperback), because the target audience for perhaps 90 percent of hardcover books published in the U.S. consists of these 500,000 intellectuals.*

In the late sixties and early seventies, when filmmakers were interested in "small" movies, several of the West Sider novels were turned into films. (*Bye, Bye Braverman, Pigeons,* and *Move* are examples.) Not surprisingly, they failed. It takes considerably more than half a million people in the potential film audience before the corner can be turned financially.

By the mid-seventies, with costs escalating rapidly and the studios now solidly under the control of accountants and businessmen with a hard eye on the bottom line, minority pictures like these were ruled out.

Simply put, it's harder to make a profitable small picture than a profitable large one. The small picture has to be precisely tuned to its minority audience, costs have to be watched carefully, and even if it's a success, the profit margin is narrow. Blockbusters, on the other hand, made for a worldwide mass audience, costs be damned, often recoup their massive investments simply because of the size of the investment. (This is the film world corollary to the gambler's theory that if you double your bet each time you can't lose, assuming you have unlimited funds.) An eight-figure

---

*A hardcover sale of 100,000 for most fiction and nonfiction (we're not talking about cookbooks, religious books, and how-to books, which have a much wider appeal) means an enormous bestseller. A hundred thousand admissions to a film is next to nothing. The scales by which success is measured in the two media have no relation to each other.

Joseph Wiseman, George Segal, Sorrell Booke, Jack Warden, and the late Godfrey Cambridge in *Bye, Bye Braverman*, an Upper West Side movie.

production budget galvanizes promotional mechanisms; the cost alone often guarantees widespread publicity.

If a $10- or $20-million film is going to do better than simply recoup its investment, however, three factors are usually responsible. First, the film must be presold in some way. Hence the prevalence of remakes, sequels, ripoffs, and massive hype in the mid-seventies. Second, perhaps as much as a third of the whole budget must be devoted to saturation advertising. (I'll deal with this in the next section.) Finally, the structure of the film must be designed to appeal to the broadest possible mass audience, to offend the smallest number of people. Not only are minority tastes ruled out, so are films that appeal only to a thin majority. The target audience must be massive, on the largest possible scale.

In other words, the theory of the lowest common denominator is operating. As much as half a film's potential revenue comes from export sales. One of the reasons sports films never did well in the past is that Europeans didn't understand American football, much less baseball (the only export market for which is usually Japan).

Television sales are important as well. They can make the difference between success and failure. A potential blockbuster must at least be able to be edited so that it fits the constraints of network standards-and-practices rules. (More often than not this presents the dilemma of making a film that offers considerably more than the usual television fare, so as to draw audiences away from the box, but which is at the same time revisable for later network sale.)

Finally, the film must appeal to children. Seventy percent of the highest-grossing films in history were clearly aimed at the adolescent and preadolescent markets. This may change slightly as the nation's demographics change, but it has been a notable fact of movie life for the last ten years.

5. The complete package. Once the proper media form, or chain of forms, has been decided upon, once the concept has been engineered to fit the Just Like/Completely Different axiom, and the property has been properly presold and/or reduced to a sufficiently low common denominator, it's time to package it. Even relatively independent projects—such as those by hot directors—need a complete, well-designed package before they can become realities.

The package has become so much a part of American filmmaking procedure that we tend to ignore it. But a comparison of American films with European films reveals just how strongly our cinema is dominated by this marketing concept. It's not that European directors don't have just as much trouble raising capital—they do—but the amounts in most cases are so much smaller that the process is different in kind as well as degree.

This is changing rapidly as European film becomes Americanized, yet on the Continent there is still a discernible split between the so-called "art" film and the commercial movie. Commercial movies are constructed and packaged more or less like American films. But the "art" films that remain still have relatively more freedom. The reason is that the small film remains viable. If a movie can make back its investment plus a small profit in a relatively short space of time by appealing to a minority audience there is considerably less reluctance on the part of investors to throw in for a share or two. The stakes are lower; the gamble is smaller.

European producers, therefore, are likely to trust a "package" that includes only a director with a decent reputation, and perhaps a story outline. Moreover, it's common practice in Europe for financing to be split among a number of investors—as many as half a dozen on occasion—often even from different countries. Result: the common denominator is considerably higher; the director's name is usually sufficient to "presell" the film (people are going to see a new Truffaut or Bergman simply on the basis of their past records); and the director's past oeuvre satisfies the unstated requirement of Just Like/Completely Different.

In other words, at least a part of the European film industry still operates the way literature used to work in U.S. publishing. Producers and filmmakers develop ongoing relationships just as authors and publishers once did. There is a regularity to the procedure of filmmaking which results in incalculably greater freedom. The package is replaced by the team, and the eye of the accountant is on continued solvency, not massive immediate profits.

You will have already noticed that this description of the European system is rather idealized. Increasingly, the world film market is a unified whole, and Europeans must fit into the American system. A score of English filmmakers have moved to the United States during the past fifteen years, as has almost the entire group of directors responsible for the Czech Renaissance of the mid-sixties. French, Italian, and German filmmakers are increasingly eager for an opportunity to work in the U.S.

Meanwhile, every interesting movement in European film since the end of World War Two—Italian Neorealism, the French New Wave, English "Free Cinema," Das Neue Kino in Germany—has been at least partly the result of temporary economic conditions that allowed filmmakers to do their work cheaply and expect a return sufficient to cover expenses and provide seed money to go on.

This was true in its way of the Hollywood Renaissance of the 1960s. From Cassavetes to Coppola, from Scorsese to Mazursky to Ritchie, the generation of the sixties started with small, cheap films. It was only after they had broken into the industry establishment that the tide turned to blockbusters. The conclusion to be drawn is that as long as we continue to concentrate on high-rolling projects where tens of millions are at stake it's unlikely that we will be able to develop a new generation to replace the old. In twenty years, these men (and they are all *men*) may form a vaguely archaic establishment not unlike the one that dominated the old Hollywood through its decline in the fifties and early sixties.

It's true that there are occasional exceptions to the massive investment rule. Independent films do get made; a few even get shown; and at least once a year, one makes a little money. This has been, for example, the only path open to women who want to direct. The examples of Joan Micklin Silver, Barbara Kopple, and Claudia Weill come to mind. Kopple financed her admittedly noncommercial documentary, *Harlan County U.S.A.*, with grants from church funds and a MasterCharge card.

But these are the exceptions. I have no doubt Steven Spielberg will be able to continue making "personal" films like *Close Encounters*, but this is a special case too. Wouldn't you trust him with your money when two of his three first features are among the highest grossing films of all time? It's difficult to make a case for the blockbuster as personal statement. And disaster may lie ahead. After *The Exorcist*, William Friedkin didn't find it too difficult to raise $18 million or so for *Sorcerer*, his remake of Henri-

Georges Clouzot's *Wages of Fear*. It was a nice little film, if rather pointless, and a box-office disaster of gargantuan proportions. *The Godfather* allowed Coppola to shoot *The Conversation*. It's one of his most interesting films, but he's not likely to go that way again. Not when he's mortgaged everything he owned to finish the outrageously expensive *Apocalypse Now*.

So the package rules American cinema. You need a story that's Just Like but Completely Different, preferably presold, and designed to reach the broadest audience. You need a director and a screenwriter with "track records." Most of all, you need stars with clout, and if the script doesn't have a meaty starring role to attract one, you'll have to rewrite it.

With all this, your film has a chance to be made. Our Fred learned early on that simply writing a filmscript was an exercise in futility; the key is packaging. Consequently, successful young writers and directors are the ones with enough business sense to prepare properties that lend themselves to efficient packaging and then go ahead and put that construction together themselves.

6. Marketing. The first five rules of the American film business deal with preparation. Once the package is tied up prettily, shot, cut, and scored, it's time to go out and sell the hell out of it. Most of the American film industry may not know as much about contemporary marketing theory as do renegade companies like Sunn International, but they are often hip enough to be able, with the proper investment, to turn a sow's ear into a silk purse.

Saturation advertising is the prime tool. *Close Encounters* cost $18 million to shoot, edit, score, and print, according to Steven Spielberg. The advertising budget for the first month of release came to an additional $9 million, roughly half the "negative" cost of the film itself. Did it work? Here was a science-fiction movie, in a year when *Star Wars* had already smashed all box-office records, with only one star with any drawing power, with an exceptionally thin plot, flat characters, and a conclusion that's just a pause before the sequel. It wasn't based on an already successful property from another medium and therefore wasn't presold (although a nice aura of mystery had been created by the closed set). It's true that it was "just like" *2001: A Space Odyssey*, only "completely different." And it also had Spielberg's *Jaws* track record going for it. But the real secret to its success was the intense and pervasive advertising campaign that made it immediately part of the American consciousness.

It has been said that *Close Encounters* "saved" Columbia Pictures, of all the studios the most heavily indebted in the early seventies. It certainly didn't hurt it. But though the expectation of a blockbuster sent Columbia stock soaring from a low of 4½ in 1976 to a high of 20 7/8 in 1977, CPI stock dropped five points after the picture opened, despite excellent sales. No matter how profitable the film was going to be, it couldn't match the hype that had preceded it.

The real secret to Columbia's success in 1977 was not *Close Encounters* at all, it was *The Deep*, a more conventional package, presold by Peter Benchley's novel followup to *Jaws*. It had a couple of stars, some acceptable adolescent sex (Jackie Bisset in a wet teeshirt), and an outrageously racist plot, where not only are the villains all Black but they do strange voodoo sex things to our Jackie.

The Deep was the sixth highest-grossing film of 1977, with $31 million in the till (according to *Variety*) before the end of the year. And this remarkable financial performance was accomplished without much help from the film itself.

Producer Peter Guber simply did a remarkable job of selling. Reviews certainly didn't help. Vincent Canby in *The New York Times* called it "even sillier than the Peter Benchley novel . . . juvenile without being in any attractive way innocent."

Guber spent the better part of two years orchestrating *The Deep*'s marketing campaign. First came the hardcover book, then the paperback, along with magazine excerpts and condensations. On the set publicity was heavy, with the lure of a junket to Bermuda convincing many magazine and newspaper writers and editors that this was a film that should be covered. Guber himself wrote *Inside "The Deep"*, the gossipy behind-the-scenes book that went on sale in an edition of 124,000 copies two days before the film premiered. By the time *The Deep* opened June 17th, 1977 (that day was chosen because most workers get paid on the 15th), Guber's research showed that each potential moviegoer had been exposed to at least fifteen different media announcements or exploitations of the film.

Guber chose a saturation booking for *The Deep*: 800 theaters (approximately 6 percent of total cinemas in the United States) began playing the film the same day. A saturation booking protects against bad reviews and word of mouth. The theory is: get in quick, get the money, and get out before the bad news trickles down.

Guber, director Peter Yates, author Peter Benchley, and the stars blanketed the talkshow circuit in June. Meanwhile, the merchandising campaign was gearing up, as much to advertise the film as to make a profit from tie-ins. There was a see-through blue-vinyl soundtrack album, a treasure-chest contest at supermarkets and shopping malls, department store mannequins dressed in *The Deep* teeshirts, and tie-ins with boat, watch, and cosmetics manufacturers.

An interesting and talented actress named Jacqueline Bisset (pronounced "Bissay") completed her metamorphosis into the redoubtably proportioned star Jackie Bisset (pronounced "Bissitt") with *The Deep*. Here a popular publicity shot shows her as contemporary equivalent of the twenties bathing beauty. We know the teeshirt is enticing, but what is the psychosexual significance of the mask?

Columbia's original advertising budget included $1.5 million for print and $1.3 million for television. The aim was 2.5 billion visual advertising impressions during the month of June in the nation's top fifty markets.

There were the usual publicity stunts, contests and gimmicks, and a fat marketing manual which went to local exhibitors suggesting imaginative ways to exploit the film (such as "Deep" cocktails at local taverns).[2]

It worked.

There's an art to making money.

2

Products and Profits

Conglomeration

Film in America has always been better understood as industry rather than as art. The febrile business atmosphere surrounding movies, the hype and glitter, the cashflow structure and balance sheet have been in large part responsible for the vitality for which American movies are known. Let the Old World worry about art and auteurs, esthetics, levels of meaning, and deeper significance. Meanwhile, we make entertainment products. And a great deal of money. Three billion dollars now for theatrical films alone in an average year.

Lacking deep-rooted traditions of elite culture, America has excelled in the popular arts—music and film in particular—and in the process has helped to revolutionize the cultural spectrum. Despite occasional aberrations—Erich von Stroheim, Orson Welles, John Cassavetes—American filmmakers have been characterized as employees first, artists second. In the thirties, even stars, directors, and writers earning a couple of hundred thousand dollars a year checked in daily at the studio/factory, served their time, and collected weekly paychecks—just like workers in other industries.

Yet just as American industry in general has changed radically in structure during the last thirty years, so has the film business. It is no longer the assembly-line factory system it once was, but rather a gigantic "cottage" industry—a farrago of freelancers, who are just as beholden to the company as the $2500-a-week wage slaves once were, but who operate on their own, separate from the factory, and get paid piecework rates.

Throughout the twenties, thirties, and forties, Hollywood operated a quaint and rather charming parody of a classic American industrial system. The automobile industry had located in Detroit to be nearer the sources of raw material and labor. Likewise, filmmakers first journeyed west from New York and Chicago in search of their "raw materials"—an embarrassment of sunlight and a strange and awesome variety of location backgrounds. They brought a number of their specialists—actors, writers, designers—with them from the dying industry of the Broadway stage, and they discovered in California a vast pool of day laborers—extras and grips, stagehands and secretaries. Unions were formed, and professional societies. The "factories" were built: elaborate production facilities which borrowed the assembly-line principle from Detroit. A property was acquired. The production manager, or studio head, assigned writers to the project. In a matter of weeks, the finished script emerged from the writers' building (usually the shabbiest on the lot) to be delivered to the production unit. Cast and crew were chosen from the roster of available talent on the studio payroll. After shooting was completed, the footage was delivered to postproduction personnel, edited, scored, and approved by the studio head. In the majority of cases, a film's director had little say over how the film was eventually cut. In a strict sense, the auteur of a film was the studio head.

At their height in the late thirties, the major studios were completing one feature film a week each together with shorts, newsreels, and cartoons. Films emerged from the assembly line to feed the chains of movie houses owned by the studios.

This classic industrial system began to disintegrate in the late forties. An antitrust suit forced the studios to divest themselves of their exhibition divisions. They continued to maintain control over production and distribution, the two other essential links in the film-business chain. But immediately, the rules of the game began to change. Production at the studios had been constant and regular chiefly because there was the ever-hungry maw of studio-owned cinema screens to fill.

At about the same time the antitrust decision struck, so did television. Weekly attendance at cinemas fell precipitously in the early fifties as television spread across the country. Now, not only did the studios not own the exhibition branch of the industry but they also found it increasingly difficult to sell a regular line of product to the newly independent exhibitors. The downward spiral had begun.

Without a constant demand for the product, film-industry executives did what any other executives would: they laid off employees, let contracts lapse. Within ten years, the efficient studio production system of the thirties had collapsed entirely. Studio backlots became worth more as sites for real-estate development than they were as film locations.

It is one of the great mysteries of film history that studio moguls couldn't see the solution to their problems: their production organizations would be just as profitable if committed to television work. In a sense they couldn't understand, the antitrust decision was a godsend, forcing them to sell off their cinemas at just the time they were about to become white elephants. Television damaged movie exhibition, no doubt, but it needn't have hurt film production, if the moguls had not been so shortsighted.

By the late fifties, most of the moguls had departed. By the early sixties, only the names of the studios remained. By the early seventies, M-G-M had closed down, only to reopen again years later, and Warners, United Artists, Paramount, and Universal had become divisions of conglomerates involved in selling insurance, sugar, auto parts, records, and real estate as well as films. Fox and Columbia maintained a certain degree of independence, but were continually subject to conglomerate raids, and eventually came under control of investors from outside the industry in the eighties.

Economist Thorstein Veblen (1857-1929) made an important differentiation between "industry," which he saw as the basic mode of economic operation in the United States in the nineteenth century, and "business," which he predicted at the turn of the century—correctly, I think—would replace "industry" as the basic mode of the twentieth century. For Veblen, the contrast is striking and powerful: industrialists, he said, are primarily concerned with making a product; businessmen, on the other hand, are far more interested in profit than product.

Film used to be an industry: its aim was to make films first, money second. In other words, though its object was to make a profit, certainly, it was preoccupied by making as many films as possible. The studio factory system was set up to accomplish this. In order to be able to amortize continuing overhead and salary expenses, it was necessary to maintain a regular schedule. As a result, many films were made—just to fill the sound stages and studio-owned cinemas—that would not otherwise have had a chance.

Today, film is clearly a business, in Veblen's sense of the word. If studio land is more profitable as real estate than as backlot, so be it: sell it off. If the accountants' analysis shows the profit margin is markedly greater if, say, $10 million is spent on one blockbuster and its attendant publicity than it would be if spent on ten smaller films, then the block-

31

buster will be made, the smaller films won't. It's not that those smaller films wouldn't have made a profit. It's just that they wouldn't have made so great a profit.

If Warner Bros., an arm of Warner Communication Industries, Inc., had taken just half of its profits for the fiscal year 1976 and plowed it back into film production, they would have made twice as many films (and perhaps almost as much profit, assuming some of these extra films also made money). (The same is true for Warner Records, by the way.) But the aim of Warner Communications Industries, formerly Kinney Services, née Warner Brothers, is now to make money, not films (or records), and it does this with great efficiency and some élan. The same holds true for Paramount, Columbia, and Universal, divisions, respectively, of Gulf + Western, Coca-Cola, Inc., and MCA Inc.

On analysis, conglomeration makes more sense·in the film industry than most others—at least from a business point of view. Selling out to a conglomerate allows a company access to much greater amounts of cash. In effect, the holding company acts as the bank, shunting cashflow from one industrial subsidiary to another as needed. Diversification also tends to smooth out profit curves. If a conglomerate is involved in a dozen or so industries as disparate as film and insurance, records and sugar cane, television and resort hotels, it's less likely that all of those industries will have a bad year at the same time. So a record boom covers for the decline in the hotel market, and increased insurance revenues make up for a bad year at the box office.

Since film is a notoriously mercurial business, the conglomerate shelter is useful. Universal/MCA's profits ballooned almost painfully in 1975, the year *Jaws* captured the greatest share of the total film market that any film ever had. The cash inflow in 1975 was so out of proportion that, despite an excellent year in 1976, Universal/MCA's annual balance sheet showed a net loss in revenue by comparison.

In 1977, it was Fox and Columbia who had to find a place to use excess profits (from *Star Wars* and *Close Encounters*, respectively). Columbia had no problem. During the early seventies the company was heavily in debt to banks for operating capital. There was a real danger that it would have to fold. *The Deep* and *Close Encounters* helped restore Columbia to solvency. Fox, the least diversified of all six majors, plowed its *Star Wars* riches into acquisitions, picking up a Coca-Cola bottling company in the Midwest and Aspen Skiing Corp., which owns a few mountains.

Because blockbusters don't come along every year, and because film companies increasingly depend on them, the film industry has not yet become as centralized and concentrated as, for example, the television and recording industries. The three networks effectively divide the television pie each year; CBS and Warner account for a substantial majority of recording sales. But the six film distributors take turns leading the pack. In 1975, Universal, Fox, and Columbia controlled more than 50 percent of the market. In 1976, the triad at the top of the heap consisted of Warners, UA, and Fox. In 1977, it was UA, Fox, and Columbia, with one film, *Star Wars*, accounting for fully 10 percent of the entire market. Fox now appears to have the most consistent showing. Before 1977, however, Warners had been either first or second in four out of six years.

Warner Communications, Inc., is probably the strongest and best diversified of the film entertainment conglomerates. In 1977, 47 percent of WCI revenues came from recordings sales, 31 percent from motion picture and television, 5 percent from publishing, 5 percent from cable television, and 13 percent from electronic games. An abbreviated list of their holdings includes Electra, Atlantic, Nonesuch, and Asylum Records, The Wolper Organization (television producers), Panavision (makers of the standard 35-mm equipment for the industry), half of the Burbank Studios (which they share with Columbia and rent out), Atari, Inc. (television games), Knickerbocker Toy Co., pieces of Warner Fragrances (perfume), Coca-Cola Bottling Co. of New York, Bausch & Lomb Optical Co., and almost all of the Cosmos North American Soccer League Team, champions in the late seventies, as well as half of Warner-Amex, the major cable TV company.

Gulf + Western Industries, Inc., seemingly constructed out of nothing in the mid-sixties by Charles Bluhdorn, is certainly the most massive of the film-industry conglomerates. Only 11 percent of their income in 1977 came from their "Leisure Time" division. With over 300 subsidiaries in manufacturing, consumer and agricultural products, natural resources, apparel products, paper and building products, automotive replacement parts, and financial services divisions, Gulf + Western would hardly notice a disastrous year in "Leisure Time." Yet they exert strong influence not only in film, but also in publishing and sports. They own Simon & Schuster, Inc., one of the most aggressive marketers of print entertainment, Esquire Magazine Corp. (but no longer the magazine itself, which was sold to Clay Felker and associates in 1977), Madison Square Garden Corp. (which in turn owns Madison Square Garden, a number of racetracks, the New York Knicks, and the New York Rangers), Sega Enterprises (electronic games), and bits and pieces of a number of other companies.

MCA Inc. was the first of the film conglomerates to take shape. They dominate television production (but not distribution of course). Barring a year with a theatrical film like *Jaws*, they can expect to earn more from film production for television than from theatrical films. The company developed into a powerful force in the entertainment world in the 1950s by selling films to television (not Universal's but other studios'). Filmed entertainment of both sorts accounted for 60 precent of MCA's revenues in 1977. The remainder of their income was fairly evenly distributed among three categories: "Recordings," "Retail and Mail Order," and a group that includes "Recreation Services, Book Publishing, and Financial Services." They own several record companies, Spencer Gift stores, a tram manufacturer, a savings and loan association in Colorado, a computer service company, and three publishers: G. P. Putnam's Sons; Coward, MacCann, & Geoghegan; and Berkley; as well as magazines. They also operate several theme parks and at least one hotel. Their Universal Studio Tour, advertised at the end of most of their films, is a perennial money-maker. They recently announced that the studio tour is to become a road show, appearing at shopping centers, malls, and fairs. The traveling, self-contained unit includes a three-man stunt team, a studio makeup artist, an animal demonstration, and a mock Frankenstein. If you can't come to Hollywood, Hollywood will come to you.

United Artists, once the most independent of the "studios" because it depended on the work of independent producers and concentrated solely on distributing its films, was for more than ten years a subsidiary of Transamerica Corporation, a company chiefly involved in financial services. They own life insurance companies, a loan service, a capital fund, an investors' fund, a relocation service, a microfilm company, a moving-and-storage company, a title insurance company, Budget Rent-A-Car, a computer service, and Trans-International Airlines. In 1977, only 15% of Transamerica's revenues came from United Artists and its subsidiaries.

Columbia Pictures Industries, Inc., like Fox, has not yet become a conglomerate, although they are moving as quickly as possible in that direction. They are controlled (although not owned outright) by an investment banking firm, Allen and Co.* During fiscal 1977, Columbia realized only 46 percent of its revenues from film production. Twenty percent came from the production of television series, 11 percent from records, 5 percent from broadcasting, 8 percent from amusement games, and 10 percent from other activities. They own several television and radio stations, half the Burbank studio (with Warners), commercial production companies, record companies, and D. Gottlieb and Co., makers of pinball machines.

Twentieth Century-Fox Film Corporation, while the least diversified

---

* See Chapter 11 for more on this relationship.

of the six major companies and the most independent financially, still realized only 63 percent of its revenues in fiscal 1977 from feature film production. Ten percent of its income is derived from television program production, 8 percent from international film activities, 6 percent from film processing, 5 percent from television broadcasting, and 5 percent from records and music publishing. They own a pay cable operation, several chains of foreign cinemas, three VHF stations, a film processing company, a small record company, Coca-Cola Bottling Midwest, and Aspen Skiing Corp.[1]

The Cash Flow

Coca-Cola bottling plants have been the novelty acquisition of the last few years. (Universal bid on the Los Angeles company, Fox the Midwest; Warners already owned a controlling piece of the New York firm.) Before that, it was game companies. Reading the corporate annual reports of the film companies and their conglomerate owners, you get the feeling that if theatrical film disappeared within the next five years all of them would survive rather nicely. Metro-Goldwyn-Mayer was the most prestigious of the studios during Hollywood's halcyon years. It no longer distributes films (although it produces a few each year for old time's sake) and has moved aggressively into the hotel business. As a corporation, it's now at least as healthy as it once was as a film company.

Similarly, Universal, Paramount, Warners, UA, Fox, and Columbia could survive the end of movies relatively unscathed. No matter how you analyze it, the conclusion that must be drawn from such successful conglomerate diversification is a distinct lessening of commitment to film.

The numbers prove it. As we've already noted, there is more money to be made from fewer movies, but how much more? and from how few films? A comparison of some statistics reveals the radical change the film industry underwent in the 1970s.

In 1972, the ten most profitable films grossed a total of $123 million. That list was led by the The Godfather, with total revenues for the year of $43 million. It was far ahead of the second-place film on the list that year, and a record-shattering blockbuster at the time. In 1972, seventy films grossed $1 million or more each.*

Five years later, in 1977, the top ten films grossed a combined total of $424 million. One film, Star Wars, led the list with gross receipts of $127 million—by itself earning $4 million more than the entire list of ten highest grossing films just five years previously! In 1977, 118 films grossed

---

*All figures from Variety.

Spanish Theatrical Film Div.

Arista Records (Clive Davis)

Columbia Pictures Pay Television

George Gage Productions

Bill Alton Films

Video Services

Columbia Pictures

Columbia Pictures Television

Marshall Stone Productions

Columbia Pictures Industries, Inc.

Bob Abel & Assoc. (TV graphics)

Columbia Pictures Merchandising
(8 mm film division)

D. Gottlieb Co. (pinball machines)

EUE Screen Gems (commercials)

WNJU-TV; WWVA radio;
WYDE radio; WCPI-FM;
KCPX-AM and FM.

Columbia Pictures Publications

Editel, Inc.

Independent Artists

Fred Levinson and Assoc.   The Burbank Studios (with Warner Bros.)

Bostonian Shoes

Bonney Forge

The New Jersey Zinc Co.

Madison Square Garden Corp.
(includes Knicks and Rangers)

Sega Enterprises

Esquire, Inc.

Cinema International Corp.

Supp-Hose

Gulf + Western Industries, Inc.

Simon & Schuster, Pocket Books
Monarch Books

International Holiday on Ice

Paramount Pictures

Desilu

Paramount Pictures Television

Famous Music Corp.   Roosevelt Raceway

D. R. Willem Cigars

Peavey Paper Mills

La Romana Sugar Mill

Schrafft's Candies

Collyer Insulated Wire

+ 300 other companies

Yosemite Park and Curry Company

Universal City

Berkeley Paperbacks

MCA Music

Universal Films

MCA Records

MCA, Inc.

Universal Studio Tour

Universal Pioneer Corp.
(Video discs)

Universal Television

MCA Merchandising   New Times Magazine

Spencer Gifts

Coca Cola Bottling of L.A.

Coward, McCann

Cinema International Corp.

Mid-Continent Computer Services

G. P. Putnam's Sons (books)

The American Film Industry: 1978: Corporate conglomerates are often so elaborate and change so rapidly that these charts were nearly out of date when they were completed late in 1977. A number of changes have occurred since then. The significant shifts are discussed in Chapter 13.

Occidental Life Insurance

Cinegraphics, Inc.

United Artists

United Artists Music

Transamerica, Inc.

Hollywood Home Theatre

United Artists Television

United Artists Records   Transamerica Life Insurance

Budget Rent-a-Car

Twentieth-Century Records

Feature Film Division   International Theatres Div.

Twentieth Century-Fox Film Corporation

United Television (3 VHF Stations)   Television Program Division

Aspen Skiing Corp.

Coca-Cola Bottling Midwest

Deluxe General, Keith Cole Photography,
Fox Movietone News
(all film processors)

Independent News Co.   Knickerbocker Toy Co.

The Burbank Studios (with Columbia)

Warner Bros. Records

Warner Bros.   Orion Pictures Corp.

DC Comics, *MAD* Magazine

Warner Communications, Inc.

Panavision (equipment)   Warner Cable Corp.

Warner Bros. Television

The Wolper Organization

Warner Books

Warner Fragrances Ltd.
(with Ralph Lauren)

Cosmos Soccer (95%)   Atari, Inc.

Elektra, Asylum, Atlantic Records

Not only has Transamerica divested itself of United Artists, but UA has been absorbed into "MGM/UA." Twentieth Century-Fox was acquired by oilman Marvin Davis. A number of smaller companies— not conglomerates—should probably be added to this chart now: Orion, Embassy, The Ladd Company, for instance.

Big films . . . : Olivia Newton-John, a singer, and John Travolta, a popular television star, in *Grease*.

$1 million or more (this despite the fact that significantly fewer films were made in 1977 than in 1972).

In five years the number of $1-million films—a good index of the health of the industry—increased 53 percent while inflation pushed up the cost-of-living index only 45 percent. Yet during the same period, the share of the market represented by the ten most profitable films increased an astonishing 245 percent. A remarkable twenty-two films in 1977 grossed as well as or better than the number-two film in 1972.

The conclusion is inescapable: between *The Godfather*, the first real blockbuster of the seventies, and *Star Wars*, the champ at the end of the 70s, the complexion of the American film business drastically altered.

Uncontrollable market factors are not responsible, as one might expect, for this remarkable shift. With minor exceptions, the shape of film distribution is pretty much what it was in 1972—not so long ago, after all. The change took place because American film distribution is effectively controlled by six companies, and the men who ran those companies in the 1970s decided to devote money, time, and energy to large films and cut the small films from the schedule.

There are several hundred listed companies nominally involved in film distribution of one kind or another. Yet for most purposes only the six studios count. Twelve films took 20 percent of the total market gross for 1977. The leading film by itself was responsible for 5.5 percent of total industry revenues.

. . . and Small films: Christopher Guest and Melanie Mayron, both actors, in *Girl Friends*, financed by Claudia Weill with grants and credit. In absolute terms, *Grease* will earn far more than *Girl Friends*, but when profits are measured relatively, as a percentage of investment, Weill's shoestring independent project proves the more remunerative.

These figures are important for themselves, but they also tell us a good deal about the social and political value of American film. Box-office grosses are the best index we have of a film's popularity, and a film's popularity is directly related to its influence and clout. No matter how many hundreds of independent films actually get made, by hook or by crook, no matter how many dozens get some sort of formal distribution, the net result is that more than one in twenty filmgoers in 1977 were on their way to see *Star Wars*, one in five saw one of only twelve films.

The blockbuster market may, however, have reached a saturation point. Despite their success, blockbusters present difficulties to exhibitors. The studios often extort crippling terms for major films from theater owners, demanding (and getting) 90 percent of box-office net. (See box on p. 40.) In addition, exhibitors are often asked to bid "blind," without having a chance to see the film, many months in advance. A number of recent expensive projects—*King Kong*, for example—have broken even, or made a small profit, despite lukewarm public response because the distributor was able to twist enough exhibitors' arms in advance to extract guarantees to cover basic costs. The distributors came out relatively unscathed; it was the exhibitors who had to absorb the losses.

Exhibitors are beginning to revolt. The National Association of Theater Owners has been discussing the possibility of going into production itself. Individual theater operators now think twice about committing their houses to blockbusters many months in advance. They may stand a better chance on smaller films, with considerably better exhibitor/distributor splits, than with the high-stakes gamble. Given the choice between a "small film" with a 50–50 split, a medium-sized film with a 70–30 split, and a blockbuster with a 90–10 split, the theater owner may very well calculate that the odds lie with the smaller film. With the 50–50 split he has to sell only 20 percent as many admissions as he would with the 90–10 split to make an equal amount of profit.

The distributors, by cutting down significantly on the number of films they offer each year, created the notorious product shortage of the mid-seventies and a hot seller's market. The results have been various: theaters have closed for lack of product or turned to porno for easier terms; chains have increased their percentage of the total number of theaters as against independents; and blockbusters have benefited from feedback: moviegoers are more likely to attend the big films when there is less to choose from.

Slicing the Pie: Accounting

Film budgets are complex documents. Depending on the accounting, the quoted "cost" of a film can vary by as much as 50 percent. "Above the line" costs include all expenses relating to the period of preparation, before shooting begins, such as script price, cast salaries, music, royalties, and commissions. "Below the line" costs include expenses incurred during shooting and after: set construction, salaries of technical personnel, equipment rental, transportation, location costs, makeup, wardrobe, special effects and lab work, filmstock, editing, and so forth. "Negative cost"—that is, the cost of the completed film negative—is the sum of above- and below-the-line expenses, but part of this may be "deferred." Equipment-rental houses in effect lend some equipment to the filmmaker to be paid for at a later date out of revenues. Actors (and some major technicians) may work for deferred salaries and/or a percentage of the profits (called "points" in Hollywood jargon). Deferred expenses can lower the initial outlay a film requires considerably.

At the other end of the film process, box-office grosses are the total amounts taken in from consumers at the theaters where the film plays. In general, the exhibitor first deducts the "house nut," an agreed-upon lump sum which is supposed to represent basic operating expenses (although it is sometimes padded). Taxes are also deducted. The remaining figure is net box-office receipts. This is split with the distributor according to the contract. For a major film, the distributor often receives ninety cents on

But distributors, despite their mastery of the all-important pipeline between producers and exhibitors, can milk the industry only so far. A number of schemes have been tried to circumvent the major distributors. George C. Scott sold prints of his film *The Savage Is Loose* directly to exhibitors, outright. Once they'd bought the print, they could play it as many times as they liked, keeping whatever profits there were. The film was not a success. A small company based in Texas, Mulberry Square Productions, has done very well distributing its own series of *Benji* films. Some producers have tried to go back to the "states' rights" system prevalent in the teens, selling rights to their films to independent small distributors state by state.

In general, however, these are isolated instances. The American film business isn't going to change until the majors decide it should. There is some small evidence they may be forced to do just that. Picture "starts" continued to increase throughout the early 1980s. Most of this increase was attributable to independent producers, yet the studios may be beginning to understand that they can goose profitability out of the

the dollar.* For a second-run film, the split may be as low as 50–50.

Immediately, the distributor takes 30 percent (40 percent for foreign distribution) of the net income from exhibitors as a distribution fee. This fee covers sales, shipping, office expenses—and also softens the blow when a film doesn't do as well as expected.

The remaining money may be considered the film's gross profit and goes to the producer (who may be the distributor, as well). The producer now attempts to recoup four basic costs: the negative cost (the cost of actually making the film), interest, prints (which may run to $1 million for a saturation booking), and advertising and publicity (which may run to several million dollars). Whatever is left is net profit and is distributed to anyone who owns a piece of the project.

It doesn't take an accountant to see that exhibitors (through their nut), distributors (through their distribution fee), and to a certain extent producers as well are at least in theory protected against a loss on any film. It is also easy to see why a film that is known to have grossed, say, $10 million winds up returning relatively little of that to its investors.

Perhaps as much as half of a film's revenues may come from foreign distribution. A Hollywood rule of thumb declares that a film must gross about three times its negative cost in order to be considered profitable.

---

*It should be noted that with a popular film, an exhibitor's income from food concessions is substantial—and he gets to keep 100 percent of it.

industry only so far. The average cost of a film in 1972 was $1 million; in 1977, $5 million. This escalation eventually must topple of its own weight. Distributors have been protected so far from astronomical losses on failed blockbusters mainly through exhibitors' guarantees. Eventually, the exhibitors will have been stung often enough on big films to return to smaller efforts. (The ratio of return to investment can be greater with small films than with large ones, as *American Graffiti* showed.)

But perhaps this is wishful thinking. With the *Star Wars* series and the *Superman* series still going strong it's still too early to predict that the film industry will return to more rewarding systems of production and distribution. Remember that conglomerated studios have no particular vested interest in seeing the industry survive. At least partially, their stunning financial performances during the last few years have been the result of the liquidation of capital—not their own, the exhibitors'. This gives a false impression of profitability. And it can't continue forever.

Agenting

In a 1974 essay much remarked upon at the time, "On the Future of Movies," critic Pauline Kael sketched a cynical picture of the American film industry as a battleground between venal businessmen who control the studios and pusillanimous directors who would produce a cornucopia of brilliant, relevant, exciting movies if only it weren't for the businessmen. "There's a natural war in Hollywood between the businessmen and the artists," she wrote. "It's based on drives that may go deeper than politics or religion: on the need for status, and warring dreams."[2]

Kael recognized the fact that Hollywood has always been in the control of businessmen. But now, she pointed out, advertising had put them "finally, on top of public reaction as well" as production. "You don't hear anybody say, 'I saw the most wonderful movie you never heard of'; when you hear people talking, it's about the same blasted movie that everybody's going to—the one that's flooding the media. . ." Yet even the worst cynics, Kael noted, still like to think it's word of mouth that makes hits, not a media blitz. "And the executives who set up the machinery of manipulation love to believe that the public—the public that's sitting stone-dead in front of its TV sets—spontaneously discovered its wonderful movie."

Kael thought "artists" like Robert Altman, Martin Scorsese, and Francis Coppola could transcend this parlous state of affairs if only they would band together to seize control—not of the means of production, but of the means of distribution.

In the abstract, she was right. There's very little doubt that the majority of interesting filmmakers—the ones treated in greater detail later in this book—have better film instincts than the executives who generally decide which films will be made and which won't. Yet Kael personalized her case too much, I think. The people in positions of power in the film business are there, for the most part, because they are better at putting together the deals that eventually result in images on the local screen. There's an occasional director who is good at this too—Roger Corman, for one, or Blake Edwards, or even Steven Spielberg. But the product remains the same. Given the financial structure of American films, how could it be otherwise?

Conversely, most directors who work regularly find themselves learning to like the characteristic Hollywood product. They aren't being duplicitous, at least not entirely. It's a normal psychological reaction: they want to make movies, and they haven't the freedom the critic has to exercise undue amounts of taste. Then too, there's the occasional Cassavetes or Altman producing personal works within the system or just on the edge of it. They don't get rich, but they show everyone that it is possible to do your own work, if you really want to. These exceptions to the rule act as a pressure valve, like others in a liberal society, to prevent upheaval: a slice or two of the loaf is better than none.

Kael is right to put the finger on advertising and modern merchandising techniques. And she is perceptive enough to see that these create their own film style. The kind of movie best able to draw people out of the house, away from the tube (on which they saw the ads that told them that the movie exists) is a kind of machine of "pure visceral excitement." It doesn't have to have much sense to it; it just has to have the right kind of energy.

But Pauline Kael's tentative solution to this problem seems beside the point to me. At the end of "On the Future of Movies" she called for the formation of a directors' distribution collective. Again ideally, it seems as if this should work: a new version of United Artists, no? But in the real world this collective would find itself in head-to-head competition with the studios still operating under the old system. In order to fight for their proper share of the market, they would undoubtedly be reduced to similar tactics. There are few real individual villains in Hollywood; the problem rather is with the system, and the atmosphere it creates, which gradually turns otherwise intelligent, thoughtful, and purposeful people into the status-seeking, profit-hungry, eyes-only-on-the-bottom-line ogres Kael described.

Kael, the only widely read critic who ever pays serious attention to the business of film, is certainly to be supported in her call for a palace revolution, but these collectives just aren't ever going to form. And if by accident they do, they'll have relatively little effect on the industry as a whole. Altman alone has had some success in creating a group, with his production company, Lion's Gate Films. The heralded Directors Company formed at Paramount in the early seventies (Coppola, Bogdanovich, Friedkin) never got anywhere. And First Artists at Warner Brothers (founded by Newman, Poitier, Streisand) has metamorphosed into just another independent production company, controlled by major distributors. In general, filmmakers tend to fit in with the hip new liberal Hollywood establishment, where Jane Fonda can host the Academy Awards, and everything's cool. Kael may want a more vital American cinema. We may, too. But the young Hollywood of the eighties is more or less content with things as they are. It's not a bad life out there.

The major reason nothing is going to happen along the lines Pauline Kael suggests is that Hollywood—surprisingly, after the debacle of the fifties and sixties—has come to terms with television, successfully rid itself of aging leadership, and achieved a level of remarkable stability. The reorganization happened haphazardly. It certainly wasn't planned. But the result is a system which works smoothly and efficiently and—it must be said—remains open to new talent, so long as it behaves itself.

We have been talking about the six studios that control distribution channels as if they were separate entities. In the thirties this was sharply evident. Not only did filmmakers work under long-term contracts, but each studio impressed its corporate style on the films it distributed: M-G-M was noted for its entertaining gloss, Paramount for a European tinge, Warners for its gutsy, working-class realism (more the result of tight budgets than ideology), and RKO for its musicals and occasional serious and ambitious projects. None of those characteristics remain (although I have a strong suspicion that somebody at Warners remembers the old days: they still distribute more than their share of genre films and film noir).

Indeed, there is a continuum, with the spaces between the six studios evenly filled with dozens of independent production companies. Executives move from one to another of these essentially interchangeable units with regularity and ease. It doesn't matter much under whose auspices a film is made now.

In 1974, for example, it was news when Fox and Warners discovered they both owned similar properties and merged them to coproduce *The Towering Inferno*. Now, such deals hardly raise an eyebrow.

Increasingly, the studios are leaving more and more of the actual work of production to the independent companies. United Artists has been operating this way for many years. Yet even Universal, still the most highly structured of the six companies, with its own working studio and a large staff on payroll, has been moving in this direction. At any time,

John Travolta and Karen Gorney work out in *Saturday Night Fever*, the film that assured Robert Stigwood's position as a major force in Hollywood production in the seventies.

sixteen films are in various stages of production at Universal. Only two of these arrived by the traditional route—as properties offered to the story department. Two more are thoroughly in-house productions. The remainder are generally subcontracted to independents.

Nominal "outsiders" range from Julia Phillips and Michael Phillips (*The Sting, Close Encounters*) to Robert Chartoff and Irwin Winkler (*Valentino, Rocky*). Some filmmakers serve as their own producers— Robert Altman, Blake Edwards, Alan Pakula, Warren Beatty, and the team of Charles Joffe and Woody Allen. Dino De Laurentiis (*King Kong, Hurricane*) holds a unique position, having been a mogul in Italy before emigrating, first to New York, then to Hollywood.

The most successful of the independents in recent years is certainly Robert Stigwood, whose music-based packages—*Saturday Night Fever, Grease, Sergeant Pepper's Lonely Hearts Club Band*—have earned remarkable amounts of cash through sophisticated marketing techniques Stigwood had learned in the record business.

In order to make a film, any one of these independents—even Stigwood and De Laurentiis—must first convince the head of production of one of the studios that the project is worth supporting financially and worth distributing. As a result, the studios still hold a considerable balance of power, and the independents function basically as a second level of management.

The studio production chiefs now are almost all relatively young men—most of them are under 45. They are part, therefore, of the same new generation as the directors and actors with whom they work. They are also, quite often, former talent agents. There is a good reason for this. Since the early sixties when the old studio system disintegrated, the agent has been in a prime position of power. Representing writers, directors, and actors, he can put together the nucleus of a project even before the studio chief sees a treatment. It's natural, then, to choose production heads from among this crop of men (there are no women in positions of significant power at any of the studios, although there are a few token women executives). The agents serve as a third level of management, in effect, for the producers and studios, and it becomes increasingly difficult to distinguish between agents and producers since they serve essentially the same function.

Interestingly, four of five ex-agents now making production decisions at the studios once worked for one agency, Creative Management Associates (CMA), founded in 1960 by David Begelman and Freddie Fields. After an embezzlement scandal in 1977, Begelman, in his mid-fifties, lost his position as head of production at Columbia, becoming an independent producer for the company. In addition to Mike Medavoy (Orion), Alan Ladd, Jr. (Fox), Martin Elfand (Warners), and Richard Shepherd (M-G-M), all worked at CMA. Meanwhile, Daniel Melnick (Columbia) and Mike Eisner and Barry Diller (Paramount) came to motion pictures from television. Only Ned Tanen (Universal) has worked continuously in theatrical production.*

Perhaps wielding more real power in the film industry than any four of these men is Marvin Josephson, although he does not work for a film company at all. He is president and chief executive officer of a company called Marvin Josephson Associates, a budding conglomerate which began as a talent agency and in fiscal 1977 had gross revenues of $28 million and profits of $3.7 million. In addition to a radio station, the Sol Hurok organization, and a couple of minor agencies, the company owns International Creative Management (ICM), whose only substantial competitor in the field is the privately owned William Morris Agency. Josephson constructed ICM out of bank loans. In 1969, when his own company was valued at $1.5 million, Josephson borrowed $10 million to buy the much larger Ashley Famous Agency. (Ted Ashley wound up at Warners.) In 1974 he merged Ashley with Fields and Begelman's CMA.

While agencies are prohibited from direct investment in film projects

---

*In 1978 a new generation of even younger executives began to take over as these men moved up the executive chain of command. See Chapter 11 for more on the new "minimoguls."

(but not curiously from investment in videotape productions), ICM nevertheless has fingers in most pies through its vast stable of clients. It is currently collecting, for example, the traditional 10 percent of 53¾ percent of the profits from *Jaws*, since it represents not only the author of the book but also the author of the screenplay, the director, and the producers, each of whom owns a piece of the film.

Eventually, the agencies, the production companies, and the investment/distribution organizations may begin to merge in form as well as in fact. The lines separating one function from another are already blurred. In the recent past, individual executives have moved smoothly from the agencies through management levels at the studios and out into independent production. In the near future, it may not be necessary for them to leave one company to go to another. It's only a matter of time before one of the entertainment conglomerates makes a tender offer for one of the larger talent agencies.

Even though two major entertainment corporations have already failed to establish successful film-distribution companies (ABC's ABC Films and CBS's Cinema Center), this doesn't mean new companies can't still be formed. In 1977 Mobil Oil made some quiet inquiries about the availability of Twentieth Century-Fox. They apparently decided not to buy, but Herbert Schmertz, the aggressive vice president in charge of public relations at Mobil, may still find a way to move from sponsoring public television series to producing his own movies. Mobil is one company that assuredly has the cash to make such a venture work. Profits in the oil business dwarf those of the film business.

In the end, the film business looks more like a conglomerateur's hobby. It's too mercurial to be really attractive to conservative accountants. As the distributors are in the process of squeezing the exhibitors dry, so in the near future the conglomerates may decide to liquidate their "Leisure Time" acquisitions. It's happened before. Howard Hughes played around with RKO for a few years in the early fifties, then dumped a weakened company on the General Tire Company. Within a few years, RKO, once a major force in Hollywood, was dead. M-G-M no longer actively distributes films, and Transamerica's United Artists may have been seriously damaged by the exodus of its top management level en masse in early 1978 to form a new company, Orion Pictures.

Liquidation of the traditional studios might not be such a bad thing. While it may simply concentrate the economic power of the film industry in fewer hands, it might also have the effect of opening up channels of distribution to larger numbers of true independents.

Regional films, for example, have been growing rapidly in importance during the Hollywood product shortage, as states such as Georgia and Texas lure filmmakers to location sites.

Then there are AIP, Corman's New World, Allied Artists, and Avco-Embassy. These "minor" distributors could form nuclei for full-fledged, competitive investment/distribution firms if they could find the kind of cash a company like Mobil could deliver. Tax shelters may be outlawed (between 1973 and 1976, it is estimated, they helped finance 20 percent of film starts), but the Small Business Administration may become a source of capital for independent producers. In ten years, cable television may play a part.

These are all relatively unlikely possibilities. It's much more likely that the film business will become even more centralized in the future than it is now. Pauline Kael's directors are not going to revolt, and if they did they wouldn't have the capital to make a success of it. Major changes in the American film business are going to have to wait for legislation—broad legislation that affects not only film but other conglomerated businesses, and returns us to Thorstein Veblen's age of industry, when product counted more than profit.

3

The Entertainment Machine

"Eat, Swim, Play, *Not* Talk!"

George C. Scott is talking to his costar, an aquatic mammal by the name of Fa, in Mike Nichols's 1974 film *The Day of the Dolphin.* Fa, a remarkably intelligent and convincing nonhuman character, wants to continue the interspecies conversation that is the absorbing premise of the movie. But Scott, more cynically knowledgeable in such matters, is desperately trying to protect Fa from the sinister forces who wish to exploit him. "Eat, swim, play, *not* talk!" Scott earnestly insists.

Fa is disappointed, "Fa *love* Pa," he squeaks. Fa trust Pa. Fa naive and innocent. But now it looks to Fa like Pa don't love Fa. Little does Fa know. Pa Scott has been around. He knows a movie about dolphins talking to humans, about the scientific, ethnological, linguistic, ethical, and political ramifications of such an intellectual adventure, interesting though it may be, doesn't stand a chance. But a film about a presidential assassination attempt, with heroes and villains and chases—in which a dolphin happens to take a starring role—that's another matter. That film may get made, and perhaps along the way we can sneak in a little information about interspecies communication and its ecological import.

So *The Day of the Dolphin* takes an immediate wrong turn, evolving in a few minutes from a fascinating essay in human (and animal) possibilities into a second-rate thriller, mildly dotty, and ultimately pointless. In its paradoxical mixture of interesting premise and formulaic execution *The*

49

Day of the Dolphin is emblematic of the Hollywood movie of the seventies.

Within a year's time we were back at sea again. This time, not with a dolphin who talks but with a shark who eats. *Jaws's* mechanical Bruce voraciously devoured *The Day of the Dolphin's* living Fa and a thousand other likeminded characters as the Bruce esthetic superseded the Fa esthetic. Enough talk, thank you very much. Talk don't sell. Gimme a fish with teeth, dammit! Eat, swim, play, kill, *that* sell! The Bruce esthetic is visceral—mechanical rather than human. Films like *Jaws* that fit it are machines of entertainment, precisely calculated to achieve their effect— at the box office as well as inside the theater. Their model is the amuse-ment-park rollercoaster. Some of them are very beautiful, if you appreciate machines, and I do. But, following the cinematic equivalent of Gresham's Law, Bruce movie machines have effectively driven out smaller, more idiosyncratic film projects of the sort that would rather interest an audience than viscerally excite it.

In *How to Murder Your Wife*, a prescient film of the mid-sixties, Jack Albertson describes to Jack Lemmon the pills he's just given him:

> . . . "Alcadexabenzatherapotathalamine," as your doctor calls it (and since I happen to *be* your doctor, that's what *I* call it)—*Brrrripp!* Right up the wall! And then, *blapp!* right down again!

Valium, alcohol, grass, and TV are our drugs of choice for the blappp! these days. Cocaine, uppers, movies, and sports supply the brrrripp!

While the current myth of American film has it that contemporary filmmakers enjoy far more freedom than their predecessors on the Holly-wood assembly line, the fact is that that freedom is severly circumscribed. Yes, directors have become stars and often are allowed to exert control over the final cut of their films. But the filmmaker-stars, for the most part, have achieved their eminence in the business because they know how to build the machines that supply the brrripp!s that make the money. For a while in the late sixties, during the period of transition as the New Hollywood took over from the superannuated moguls who'd come of age twenty or thirty years earlier, it looked as if American movies were about to enter a new era. The rules of the game had changed, as had the players. And for a few years, since no one quite knew what the new rules were, there was a genuine sense of freshness. Stanley Kubrick, who had exiled himself to England in 1960, was able to find financing for the five-year project of *2001: A Space Odyssey*. To its surprise, M-G-M made money on the film. Richard Lester came home from his fifteen-year exile to make *Petulia*. Haskell Wexler was able to cajole Paramount into distributing *Medium Cool*. Most important, it seemed as if the rising generation was a different

Scott with Fa in his native habitat: clearly a linguistic romance.

breed entirely, half easy-rider renegades from the B-movie shops, half serious students from the film schools. Certainly, they had a kind of political-cultural commitment and an analytical intelligence that had been lacking in the old Hollywood. But films like *Bonnie and Clyde* (1967), *The Graduate* (1967), *Easy Rider* (1969), and *2001* (1968) turned out to be anomalies rather than models—or rather they *were* models for the entertainment machines of the seventies, but for the wrong reasons: it wasn't their intelligence and passion that was copied, but rather their visceral formulations.

It's now clear, too, that the film-student generation—Bogdanovich, Friedkin, Lucas, Spielberg, De Palma, Scorsese, and others—had learned everything about film, and nothing about life. The result has been a cinema that is formally extraordinarily sophisticated at the same time that it is intellectually preadolescent.

Does it matter? Well, yes, I'm afraid it does. To a limited but effective extent movies define our reality. They don't have the power of television, but they do feed TV, are allied with that medium, and provide the main mythogenic alternative to it. If it's true, as a number of recent commentators have put it, that television is raising generations of passive consumers with attention spans equal to the distance between two commercials, then film is an able ally in this endeavor. If TV is the plug-in drug, then movies are the walk-in, drive-in drug. And this is not just a metaphor. Anyone familiar with the film-buff subculture, composed of sallow-

George C. Scott with Shirley Knight and Roger Bowen in *their* native habitat in *Petulia*: the wife, the ex-husband, the future husband exchange Christmas presents. ("They *used* to think this place was impossible to escape from." "We know, Dad, Warren told us.")

complected, glazed-eyed, semi-paralytic addicts who consume twenty, thirty, and more movies week in and week out, knows the real effects of the drug at its worst. *Clockwork Orange* was not a fantasy.

There's nothing wrong with the new clockwork movie machines per se. After all, film is an abidingly passive enterprise for its consumers. The problem lies in the net effect of the movement of the industry/art/medium away from the type of film that leaves room for audiences' intellectual and emotional participation toward the type which deliberately and effectively manipulates emotions and suppresses intellect.

Variety's list of "All-Time Film Rental Champs" provides a good statistical model of the success of the Bruce esthetic. All ten of the highest-grossing films of all time were made since 1971. All ten hew closely to the axiom that visceral action sells best. Eight of them—*Star Wars*, *Grease*, *Tootsie*, *E.T.*, *Raiders*, and *Jaws*—are relatively innocuous entertainments. They are admittedly magnificent examples of the manipulative craft of filmmaking and, it must be said, a case can be made for each of them as something more (although I wouldn't make it). One of the ten, *The Exorcist*, is I think clearly contemnable on moral and ethical grounds: antihuman, with no redeeming social value, and subtly advertised for the damage it did to audiences—pure sadistic pornography. And one—*The Godfather*—manages to combine visceral excitement with insightful and intellectually involving commentary. A perfect bell curve.

Robert Forster and Harold Blankenship in *Medium Cool*, another major landmark of the late sixties, and a film that surprisingly showed a strong sense of humanity together with its advanced political theory.

Once again, there is nothing inherently wrong with the movie of visceral action, and in fact the ratio of good to bad films that pertains among the top five suggests a rather higher return on artistic investment than one might expect. The problem is that films like these drive out other films. The Bruce esthetic dominates and controls the industry, not only financially (the top five have grossed half a billion dollars in rentals) but structurally as well. Films that don't fit this rigid pattern don't get made, let alone seen; hence Mike Nichols's regrettable but necessary wrong turn halfway through *The Day of the Dolphin*.

Nichols's career is a paradigm in many respects. He began not with eat-swim-play but with talk. His duologues with Elaine May in the late fifties and early sixties rank as theatrical highpoints of those years, and still impress with their wit and perspicacity. He then moved cautiously into stage directing, guiding a number of rather safe comedies on Broadway. His first film project was Edward Albee's play *Who's Afraid of Virginia Woolf?* It was thought quite daring at the time (1966), but was nevertheless a presold product. *The Graduate* (1967) caught the mood of the times perfectly and remains probably Nichols's most influential film. He backtracked a bit with *Catch-22* (1970), a literary classic to be sure, but of an earlier era—and better as a book than a movie. He took another step forward in 1971 with *Carnal Knowledge*, from the script by Jules Feiffer, then directed the problematic *The Day of the Dolphin* (1974). Nichols's

53

next move was conservative: a return to comedy, *The Fortune* (1975), which didn't pay off as well as it should have. Then there was an abortive attempt at *Bogart Slept Here* with Robert De Niro. He co-produced *Family* for television. Then he returned to the stage, as producer this time, with *Annie*. He returned to film with *Silkwood* in 1983.

Nichols's film career describes a gradual downward spiral. So do the careers of numerous directors who started out in the late sixties during a period of professional exhilaration in the film world, then had to come to grips with the economic realities of conglomerate Hollywood in the seventies. There are a few exceptions, of course, and we'll deal with them later on.

The Family of Genres

We don't usually think of them that way, but the five most profitable movies of the seventies fit the pattern of genres established in the thirties rather well: a musical, a sci-fi movie, a gangster film, a horror film, and a thriller, *Jaws*, with a touch of fifties monster movie about it. The conclusion to be drawn is that the generic patterns of the Golden Age of Hollywood are still very much with us forty years later. However, they have undergone some changes.

Movie genres are simply formulaic patterns, some stricter than others. Within five years after the advent of sound (1926), they had become well established, and have remained the dominant models, with variations, until today. The musical and the western are perhaps most clearly defined. The lines which separate gangster from detective from mystery films are less sharp. Horror films and science fiction sometimes seem to merge, but the war film is always easily identified, as is the usually romantic historical adventure (a movie in which "people write with feathers" in a famous phrase). The "women's" film or "tearjerker" of the forties always clearly identified itself. But film noir in the late forties borrowed elements from the gangster, detective, and mystery genres, and forged them into a new cinematic form. Perhaps film noir is better described as a style than a genre. Meanwhile, comedy, the broadest of genres, continually throws off new variations—which on closer examination often reveal their roots in earlier screwball and slapstick comedies, the essential verbal and visual forms, respectively, of the thirties. Finally, there are the genres manqués, chief among them political and sports films. Everybody in the industry knows these don't sell. Except for Frank Capra. Except that 20% of the leading money-makers in 1977 had sports backgrounds. Except that *All the President's Men* earned $30 million in 1976 to lead the year. Then, of course, science fiction was a notoriously low-profit genre—until recently, that is.

Jack Nicholson, Art Garfunkel, and Carol Kane try to deal with midlife crises (years before they were so named) in *Carnal Knowledge*.

The rule of genres is that there are no rules. It isn't the particular genre of a film that accounts for its financial success, as I hope to show, but rather the structural elements which the genre nurtures. Once this is understood those attractive elements can be transplanted from one genre to another and—all of a sudden—science fiction, sports, and politics all become salable commodities.

During the fifties, as Hollywood came to uneasy terms with the new medium of television, most of the classic genres began to feed on themselves. Some of them even seemed to become self-parodic. Westerns flourished as never before thanks to the wide screen and widespread use of color. Swashbucklers and other historical adventure films thrived, too, for the same reasons. Other genres, however, deteriorated. The musical came to depend more and more on Broadway for source material for stagy adaptations, losing the cinematic originality which had made it one of the superior genres of the thirties. Comedy and the tearjerker met in the person of Doris Day, and we didn't know whether to laugh or cry. Film noir thrived for a while before fading into film gris. Science fiction turned paranoid; and the horror film metamorphosed into the preteen favorite, the monster movie.

Throughout the sixties, as the film industry began to recover its health, the pattern of genres expanded. Comedy was still slave to television sitcom models, and the musical still mimicked Broadway (although more profitably than before). But new variations were developing as filmmaking moved out of the studio on location. Detective films turned into secret-agent/spy films which usually depended on the conventions of the chase and caper movies. Road movies left Hope, Lamour, and Crosby in the studio dust and went in search of America. Youth films, which had had a short vogue during the fifties, returned. There were a couple of drug films. Both formulas were in response to the social revolution of the late sixties. Neither lasted very long.

The two most important formal developments of the sixties don't fit into the classic genre pattern at all; they cut across lines. The Buddy film shifted the decades-old tradition of attention on a single hero to a focus on a pair of heroes, perhaps in response to the lack of powerful male leads like Bogart, Cooper, Gable, or Wayne. Any one of the ill-defined genres listed above could accommodate a Buddy film—and often did. *Easy-Rider*, by all accounts one of the most significant movies of the decade, was a Chase-Caper-Road-Youth-Drug Buddy film.

Far more important than the vogue of the Buddy film (which seems to have subsided in the late seventies) was the rise of the Black film. The Black Power movement of the sixties may not have accomplished much politically—still less economically—but culturally it had a truly profound effect, and its reverberations are still being felt. For the first time in the nation's history, Black people—one-fifth of the nation—have been liberated from the cultural ghetto. They are no longer nonpersons in the media world, but seen and heard daily on television and cinema screens. More about this radical change later.

In the seventies, the lines of definition that separate one genre from another continued to disintegrate. The occasional western is still made. Pauline Kael has identified a new urban western—the cop film which is also an offshoot from detective stories. *Death Wish* and *Walking Tall* (both 1974) are the primary examples of the urban western. Most of the cop films have evolved from *The French Connection. Serpico, The Friends of Eddie Coyle, The Seven-ups, Hustle,* and *Report to the Commissioner* are among the best examples. The new cop films have a strong sense of docudrama to them, and much of the best work in this area has been done by cops and D.A.s turned writer/producers—Joseph Wambaugh, Sonny Grosso, and George V. Higgins.

Surprisingly, war movies are still with us. Vietnam, almost totally ignored by the film industry during its interminable duration, received some oblique attention in such films as *Who'll Stop the Rain, Coming Home,* and *Apocalypse Now.* World War II still provides grist for the mill, although the trend in such films as *Patton, MacArthur,* and *A Bridge Too Far* is as much analytical as it is action-oriented. Broadway musicals are still dutifully filmed—*The Wiz, Hair*—but music now plays an increasingly large part in other areas as well. *Woodstock* (1969) became the model for a long string of more or less profitable concert films, including *Gimme Shelter* and Martin Scorsese's notable *The Last Waltz*. In addition, records have served as source material for fiction films (*Alice's Restaurant, Tommy, Ode to Billy Joe, Sergeant Pepper's Lonely Hearts Club Band*), and there is increasing interest in films about music and the music industry (*Nashville, Saturday Night Fever, You Light up My Life*). Together these innovations constitute one of the more significant shifts in the landscape of film genres in the seventies. The musical as such is now best seen as a subcategory of the large genre of music films.

Two of the lesser genres of previous eras—horror and science fiction—have proven immensely profitable in the mid-seventies. No film was more imitated in the seventies than *The Exorcist* (1973), essentially a monster movie that preyed on pedophobia. People still make movies where people write with feathers, although you have to go pretty far down the list of "Big Rental Films of 1977" to find one. (It seems that most costume dramas these days—*The Man Who Would Be King, Three* and *Four Musketeers, Barry Lyndon*—are European-American coproductions.)

Sports films and, one continues to hope, political films have come of age. *Bang the Drum Slowly* (1973) breathed new life into sports, and in recent years, *Chariots of Fire, Rocky,* and *Slapshot* have proven the strength of the genre. The success of *All the President's Men* (1976) was perhaps anomalous, but the crude yet recognizable political underpinnings of films like *The Parallax View, Three Days of the Condor,* and *Network,* and more pedestrian thrillers such as *Twilight's Last Gleaming,* suggest real potential here, realized by *The China Syndrome* and *Missing.*

The tearjerker is still with us in all its glory—*The Other Side of Midnight, The Other Side of the Mountain.* But the new Women's film is moving up fast. *Diary of a Mad Housewife* (1970) was well ahead of its time, but the genre finally proved itself in 1977 with *Julia* and *The Turning Point.* Women's Buddy films? Perhaps, but for the first time in more than twenty-five years it began to look as if women were going to be permitted to share center stage on an equal and regular basis with men. We may even see the day when a woman plays a role in which sex isn't a determinant: the script says "cop" or "doctor" and the producers just happen to hire a woman.

It's interesting to note that it took the women's movement just about ten years to achieve this long-sought breakthrough in American film, while it had taken Blacks an equal amount of time in the sixties. The major, and ironic, difference between these two parallel accomplishments, however, is that women have only regained a position they once held, whereas Blacks moved forward to new, uncharted ground. One of

57

The sports film: Robert De Niro, Michael Moriarty, and manager Vincent Gardenia in *Bang the Drum Slowly;* Paul Newman argues with the ref in *Slapshot;* James Caan and teammate as futuristic rollerballers; and Warren Beatty interviewed in *Heaven Can Wait.* The genre provides the material, not the approach or the significance. These four sports films range from the sentimental realism of *Bang the Drum Slowly* and the satiric realism of *Slapshot* to the futuristic and archaic fantasies, respectively, of *Rollerball* and *Heaven Can Wait.*

the most striking discoveries a student of film history makes is how much further advanced women's roles were in the twenties, thirties, and forties. The advent of Marilyn Monroe in the early fifties marked the beginning of a dark age of sexual politics from which we are only now beginning to emerge. Of course, there were the occasional exceptions throughout the fifties and sixties: Audrey Hepburn, Shirley MacLaine, Anne Bancroft, Natalie Wood—and, I suppose, Debbie Reynolds, Doris Day, and Julie Andrews. But for the most part, women were relegated to the role of "the girl," third banana behind the buddies, throughout the fifties and sixties and for far too long into the seventies.

There have been some genre innovations in the seventies. Just as the development of lightweight equipment and faster filmstocks led in the sixties to the chase, caper, and road movies shot on location, so in the seventies a number of new special effects techniques have made hitherto unrealizable fantasies possible. Naturally, science fiction has benefitted most from the work of technicians like Douglas Trumbull, Albert Whitlock, and Carlo Rambaldi, but the disaster film could not exist without the innovations of studio "FX" teams.

They are still being made, though disaster movies, so popular in the early seventies, have rather quickly achieved the status of instant camp classics. There is something ineffably charming about a movie in which Los Angeles is inexorably reduced to rubble by a major heave of the San Andreas fault, or a film about a bunch of folks in an upside-down ocean liner. Disaster films seem to appeal to the same apocalyptic religious instincts that recent science fiction does. On the one hand, Hollywood giveth (a trip to the stars in an antigravity jukebox), on the other, it taketh away (the parable of *The Towering Inferno*). Fa love Pa, but Pa angry with Fa, and the wrath of Pa knows no bounds once the special-effects team has been called in.

If we are to believe the historical evidence of the acetate record, we

The Tearjerker: Marilyn Hassett as quadraplegic Jill Kinmont in *The Other Side of the Mountain*, a tearjerker as serious film. Jackie Bisset as the Jackie Onassis character in *The Greek Tycoon*, the tearjerker as pulp docudrama.

The late Robert Shaw makes a pirate's pass at Genevieve Bujold in *Swashbuckler*. Bujold played a fairly aggressive woman character, which gave the film its only spark of interest.

59

The film-buff composite genre: Goldie Hawn, Chevy Chase, Dudley Moore, and Marilyn Sokol in various scenes from *Foul Play*, a genre-genre film that provides a catalogue of old genre styles, from old-fashioned romance to satiric sex comedy to thriller with a few feminist asides.

have not been happy in the 1970s: any place but here, it says, anytime but now. A film about an obvious distant future begins with the legend: "A long time ago, in a galaxy far, far away." But the role of "the girl" is played by the daughter of two emblematic stars of the fifties, the home planet looks like the Western backlot of the fifties, the villains are straight out of forties serials, and the spaceships dogfight like F-84 Thunderjets in the Korean War. Not so long ago. Not so far away. Seems like only yesterday.

The main thing new about American movies today is what's old. The seventies and eighties have no culture of their own, no style, unless it's nostalgia. Yes, the punk rockers brought *Clockwork Orange* to life; yes, SM sex is reaching new depths of popularity; but despite the best efforts of critics nobody really cares about punk rock except kids, and kids no longer demographically dominate as they once did in the sixties.

The rest of us have plugged into earlier times for the duration. We started with the ever-popular twenties, moved quickly into the thirties and forties, then settled down for a nice wallow in the fifties (when most of us in the generation of the sixties at the top of the demographic bell curve came of age). The sixties have been threatening dominance ever since *American Graffiti* and may shortly supersede the *Grease*-y fifties as *Hair* and other attempts at instant nostalgia come to the screen. Then the seventies were over (there is no such thing as nostalgia for the seventies; it would be a tautology) and maybe we'll be able to get on with business, transcending nostalgia in the eighties.

Nostalgia is not so much a specific genre in film as it is a pervasive influence. It reveals itself in a number of ways. First, youth films are out. No more *Getting Straight*, no more *Strawberry Statement*—until they can be rephrased as nostalgia. *Saturday Night Fever*, the recent film that comes closest to the short-lived youth genre of the late sixties, has been popular at least as much for its evocation of *West Side Story-Blackboard Jungle* fifties style (its star, John Travolta, carries this persona with him from TV) as for its programmed disco score.

Second (it follows), middle-aged films are in. The genre hasn't yet been labeled: let's call it the "midlife-crisis" movie. At its best—*The Happy Ending, Loving, Lovers and Other Strangers, Husbands, Save the Tiger*—it provides absorbing portraits of real people with real lives. At its worst—*A Touch of Class, The Prisoner of Second Avenue, The Way We Were, House Calls*—it's a more or less cloying exercise in rationalization—comforting, but in bad faith.

The midlife-crisis movie shows up in strange places. Both *Julia* and *The Turning Point*, interestingly, fit the genre well. Three seventies westerns—*The Missouri Breaks, Buffalo Bill and The Indians*, and, most important, *The Shootist*—focused on middle-aged (and older) heroes. From *The Lion in Winter* to *Robin and Marian*, the "feather" movie has had a distinct elderly cast in the seventies. Robert Mitchum (*The Yakuza, Friends of Eddie Coyle*) and Art Carney (*Harry and Tonto, The Late Show*) have forged Indian-summer careers playing over-the-hill heroes. John Wayne (*The Shootist, True Grit*) has put a magnificent period to his long and distinguished career by commenting upon and affectionately parodying the persona he built up over so many years.

It's only a matter of time before we are treated to the spectacle of a forty-five-year-old rock star going to seed (Kris Kristofferson has been practicing for this role for years), or a former Weatherperson turned corporation ombudsman so that he can afford braces for the kid's teeth and a new roof for the suburban commune. Part of the reason for the success of the disaster movies is the *Grand Hotel* principle: they provide numerous roles for older stars. It's so nice to see Charlton Heston, Burt Lancaster, Ava Gardner, Olivia De Havilland, Bill Holden again, and aren't they looking good!

Nostalgia has also had a more general influence on American film in the seventies. The industry has turned in on itself: The Hollywood genre has discovered new life. String together *Nickelodeon, Valentino, Gable and*

Nostalgia: Gary Grimes carries packages and a torch for Jennifer O'Neill in the highly profitable *Summer of 42*. Art Carney and Lily Tomlin in *The Late Show*, a film about the way things used to be and are no more, and about the old movies for which it's named.

Lombard, Day of the Locust, and *The Last Tycoon* and you have a quick historical survey of the first forty years of the film business. Remarkably, however, contemporary Hollywood has elicited only a few cautious essays: *Shampoo* skirted the issue: Mazursky's *Alex in Wonderland* and the Corman factory's *Hollywood Boulevard* came closer, but without much success at the box office.

On a broader scale, this self-absorption has resulted in the most unusual genre of the seventies: the Genre genre. Increasingly, movies are about themselves as well as their ostensible subjects. Don Siegel's *The Shootist* begins with a film-clip survey of John Wayne's forty-year career. It is *about* westerns as well as being one. *The Late Show* begins with Art Carney at the typewriter beginning work on a novel entitled "Naked Girls and Machine Guns." In the background the TV delivers a late-show version of Carney's private eye. He's trying to cash in on the nostalgia.

The film-school filmmakers have concentrated on the Genre genre. Bogdanovich has produced a string of imitation thirties and forties movies from *What's Up, Doc?* to *Paper Moon* to *Daisy Miller* and *At Long Last Love,* the most egregious of genre movies so far. Paul Schrader began with a genre imported from Japan, *The Yakuza,* then moved on to a romance (*Obsession*) and a film noir (*Taxi Driver*) before attempting to deal with contemporary themes. Mel Brooks has tried his hand at a *Silent Movie,* a *Young Frankenstein,* a western (*Blazing Saddles*), and a Hitchcock thriller (*High Anxiety*) riddled with film-school in-jokes. His epigones, Gene Wilder and Marty Feldman, for their part, have revived Sherlock Holmes and Beau Geste.

Perhaps the best of the Genre films have come from English directors Mike Hodges and Stephen Frears, who have some esthetic distance from the phenomenon that their American counterparts don't have. Hodges's *Get Carter, Pulp,* and *Terminal Man* commented upon the private eye, the pulp novel, and film-noir science fiction. Frears's *Gumshoe* dealt with a hero who saw himself as a film character.

All of this is reminiscent of the early days of the French New Wave. Jean-Luc Godard, François Truffaut, Claude Chabrol, and Jacques Rivette were the first to turn movies in on themselves.[1] But the resemblance is at best superficial. The French filmmakers, unlike their American (and English) counterparts, saw the pervasive influence of the old Hollywood genres as a challenge: one which they could meet, then go beyond. Truffaut wanted to "explode genres by combining them"; Godard wanted to "return to zero." Genres for them were a barrier, not a goal. They quickly moved on to films that were more about people and ideas than about movies. The American film-student generation hasn't reached that stage yet, and possibly never will.

Even films that aren't about films naturally reveal a modicum of concern for the genre. Once the art becomes self-conscious, there's no turning back. That would be like *not* thinking about elephants. New westerns like *Little Big Man, Jr. Bonner, Bad Company, Jeremiah Johnson, Kid Blue,* and *McCabe and Mrs. Miller* must perforce comment on their genre even if they don't make it part of their subject. There's an unavoidable dialectical tension between them and their predecessors, now that the art of film has traditions to look back on.

Likewise, it's impossible to make a detective movie these days without reference to the models established by Dashiell Hammett and Raymond Chandler (see *The Long Goodbye, Farewell, My Lovely,* or *The Drowning Pool,* for example).

Nostalgia is probably the prime esthetic force in American film today. It pervades almost every genre, and it dominates production strategy, so much so that a nice little caper movie about a couple of con men—*The Sting*—can achieve the number-14 position on the list of most profitable films of all time simply by placing its popular stars in a quaint studio-constructed thirties setting while the soundtrack illogically but very effectively recalls turn-of-the-century ragtime.

As Hollywood has become more centralized and concentrated in its pursuit of the blockbuster, a new market has begun opening up to serve specialty interests. Made entirely "on location" (as if there were any other choice), regional in tone, financed by local businessmen and investors rather than international conglomerates, and strongly encouraged by state film development authorities (Georgia and Texas are among the most active), these new equivalents to the B movie are strongly generic. Unlike the B's of old, they don't fill double bills. They survive on their own, mainly in the 1500 drive-ins in rural and suburban areas of the

United States. The roots of this movement lie in the sixties, with the beach-blanket-bingo and Edgar Allan Poe fodder produced by American International. When Roger Corman went off on his own, the spectrum of the new B genres widened. By the mid-seventies, he had been joined by a score of independent regional producers. These films are seldom if ever seen in the urban centers; they are mostly ignored by the national critics; but when a major distribution organization puts some financial muscle behind them they can easily earn in the eight-figure range. In short, there is a clear market for "minority" films.

The most interesting of the new B genres is the Black film that doesn't "cross over" into white markets. (We'll discuss this in Chapter 6.) But the primary focus in the late seventies was on the "country" movie, most often shot in the South and earning most of its income there. The grandfather of the country movies is *Easy Rider* (which Corman's *Wild Angels* prefigured in 1966), but there are also elements of the teenager movies of the 1950s, and strong doses of chase, road, and occasionally caper films.

Like country music, country movies celebrate small-town self-reliance, everyday working-class life, and the ongoing struggle with the Man. Unlike country music, country movies tend to avoid romance (*Ode to Billy Joe* was a significant exception) and concentrate on action, most often on the road. This is the world of CB radio. It has the same raw ethic of survival that used to characterize American westerns. The genre came of age in 1974 with the filming of real-life folk hero Buford Pusser's more-or-less true story in *Walking Tall*. The film was characterized by an unusual mixture of political ethics and raw violence, and that combination has come to form a base for most country movie. *Macon County Line, Dirty Mary Crazy Larry,* and *Jackson County Jail* followed. By 1977, the genre had reached maturity: *Smokey and the Bandit* earned close to $40 million in rentals (without any of the usual media hype, but with the presence of star Burt Reynolds), while Jonathan Demme's *Citizen's Band* (*Handle with Care*), although not financially successful, achieved a spot in the New York Film Festival. By this time studios had caught on to the potential in this market.

Meanwhile, a genre imported from the overseas Chinese community centered in Hong Kong and Taiwan—the kung fu movie—was quickly becoming the urban equivalent to the country movie. *Variety*, characteristically, dubbed this genre "chop socky." Like its rural cinematic cousin, chop socky combines a strongly moral tone together with precisely choreographed sequences of violence. Vengeance, often of an almost religious quality, is usually the dominant motivation for the action, a state of affairs which has led several critics to compare martial-arts movies with

The country movie: Paul Le Mat, Candy Clark, and Roberts Blossom share a meal in *Citizen's Band* (*Handle With Care*), a film about community.

Elizabethan drama. (Revenge plays a smaller, but still significant role in country movies, which are in general more down to earth and less ideological than their urban opposite numbers.)

No filmmaker has yet forged a union between the urban and rural essays in righteousness, but it is worth noting that the opportunity exists. The essential difference between country and kung fu is structural rather than thematic. The violence in country films is expressed in terms of automobiles, while the action of their urban counterparts—as we should expect—avoids mechanical demolition derbies in favor of raw-handed, two-fisted (and footed), stylish martial arts.

Just as the country movie uses scenery and the idea of community to nurture its morality tales, so chop socky offers the sharply beautiful choreography of the martial arts set within a matrix of history and tradition to elicit a mythic response. Bruce Lee, the American director/star of several of the most popular chop socky films who died in 1973 at the age of thirty-two, was well aware of the mythic bases of martial-arts cinema. Directors King Hu and Chang Cheh have done some quite interesting work in this area, too. Kung fu films remain the one foreign film genre that has taken root among popular audiences in the United States.

Both country and kung fu genres serve an essentially young and restless audience. In part, the films act as liberal safety valves, allowing angry urban and rural kids to let off steam. But the mythic bases of both genres—the structure of social oppression which finally forces the hero to

65

take arms in defense of justice and freedom—suggest that these two genres have a more active political function, as well.

While working-class kids are into country movies and chop socky, the privileged children of the middle class are treated to their own private genre, the "cult" films generally offered at Friday and Saturday midnight screenings in college towns across the U.S. Made in such remarkable hotbeds of the cinematic art as Pittsburgh and Baltimore, these notably inexpensive movies earn a higher ratio of profits than the great majority of studio product.

The cult film started in the late sixties as camp interest developed in Roger Corman's various monster and motorcycle movies. George Romero's *Night of the Living Dead* (1968) was a landmark. *El Topo* (1970) established the connection between cult movies and drugs. Gradually, cult films have developed their own esthetic—not a very pretty one. While there are occasional mainstream films like Philippe De Broca's *King of Hearts* and Hal Ashby's *Harold and Maude* that find renewed life on the cult circuit, and there is at least one instance of a really important film, *The Harder They Come* (1973), achieving well-deserved popularity at midnight screenings, the general trend has been toward what we might call the trash esthetic in cult. It parallels the development of sadomasochism in contemporary adolescent bourgeois music. And while defenders of the trash esthetic will tell you that the films which fit it are viewed with ironic distancing, camp isn't the only reason for their attraction. There is a vivid element of SM (which doesn't speak well for the future of the ruling class). Tobe Hooper's *Texas Chain Saw Massacre* is the bloodiest; John Waters's *Pink Flamingos* is the shittiest, literally. Perhaps the psychological explanation for the trash esthetic lies in a reversion to a pre-anal stage of infantile freedom.

There are other important genres on the B-movie scene. Companies like Sunn International and Pacific Films have cornered a market that other companies—studios and independents—had avoided almost entirely: they serve the older brothers and sisters of the working-class young people who go to country movies and chop socky—people who live in larger towns and small cities and seldom venture out to the movies. They haven't the money for the babysitter, and anyway they aren't particularly interested in the Hollywood product. Sunn and its competitors have identified two genres that will attract this audience. They began in the early seventies with nature-adventure films such as *American Wilderness* and *Legend of Boggy Creek*, then segued smoothly into what we might call science-fiction docudrama—*In Search of Noah's Ark, Food of the Gods*. The nature-adventure films offered attractive scenery, manly adventure in the wilderness, a strong family image—and you could take the kids. In fact, the major studio competition for Sunn and Pacific (until American International climbed on the bandwagon) had been Disney's Buena Vista studio, which for years had been producing an endless stream of nature-oriented films ostensibly for children, and which now were obviously also calculated to get their fathers out of the house. Even the science-fiction docudramas were prefigured by Disney's nature documentaries of the fifties.

Made for the proverbial pittance, these demographically engineered movies have had an enormous profit potential. They are capable of earn-ing a hundred times their negative cost, a ratio ten times better than that enjoyed by *Star Wars* and *Close Encounters* and in recent years matched in the domain of the major studios only by *American Graffiti*.

At least formally, the science-fiction docudramas had something else besides the profit margin to recommend them. Perhaps more significant than any of the theatrical film genres of the seventies we have discussed so far has been the merger of fiction and documentary known as docu-drama, which has dominated the more interesting commercial television network product for several years now. In terms of form, such productions as *Roots*, or *Washington: Behind Closed Doors*, are fresher than anything Hollywood has attempted. And telefilms like *Fear on Trial*, *The Missiles of October*, *The Trial of Lee Harvey Oswald*, and *Tail-Gunner Joe* are more theoretically ambitious than anything the nostalgia-drenched movie industry has produced during the same time span.

In a number of genres—sports and politics in particular—television has led the way, Hollywood has followed. The same may eventually be true for the docudrama.

There's one other genre that has an exceedingly high investment/revenue ratio—and it doesn't need demographical studies: porn. During the seventies, "nudies," "beavers," and "blue movies" came of age and moved into the spotlight of the commercial mainstream, even as first homosexual, then heterosexual sex clubs began providing the real thing for anyone who had the price of admission. For the most part, such hard-core classics as *Behind the Green Door* and *Deep Throat* (1974) were more clinical than erotic, and porn seems to have detumesced back into the minor industry it was before the media paid it such lavish attention. Yet the effect has been felt on the art at large: witness Louis Malle's *Pretty Baby*—respectable child pornography.

Which brings us, by a circuitous but significant route back to children. For decades, Walt Disney's Buena Vista company has had this market almost entirely to itself. Animated or live, "children's film" meant Disney. The Disney films on the whole still tell popular fairy stories and nature tales, a situation that would be unexceptionable except that these films are practically all there is available for children on the nation's movie screens. Children are better served by movies than by television these days, but only slightly.

Disney does have some competition now. Mulberry Square, a Texas company, has had unusual success with its *Benji* films, and Paramount's *Bad News Bears* has turned into a pleasant series, but these are still in the Disney mold. Films that treat children without condescension are so rare that most kids are in danger of graduating from junior high school before another is released. The only really interesting kid's film of the seventies was *Bugsy Malone* (1976), written and directed by an Englishman, Alan Parker. With child actors playing at being adults, *Bugsy* had something to say about children's conception of grownups and explored the relationship between the two cultures—kids' and adults'. It was, therefore, just as interesting to the latter.

The Quarks of Film

Contemporary film theory—at least part of it—is increasingly concerned with how a film is put together: what are the irreducible elements? How do they relate to each other? How do they work on an audience?[2] Metaphorically, the structuralist enterprise is not unlike particle physics. And just as nuclear physicists find the number of elementary particles multiplying, seemingly without end, so do the basic forms of film, the genres. Yet if physicists can descend from muons and pions to the hyperelementary level of the three quarks (out of which all subatomic particles are theoretically composed), so maybe we too can abstract certain more or less fundamental movie quarks from the growing thicket of genres.

Ideally, after all, a movie is very simple: you are watching something and you are listening to something. What you watch is, abstractly: color, shape, form, and movement. What you listen to is: language and sound, with rhythms, harmonies, and melodies. Concretely, we watch people, either alone or together, objects, scenery, and events. We listen to monologues and conversation, narration and sound effects, music and silence. Simple, eh?

Films that succeed, either artistically, financially, or both, simply combine these elements, concrete and abstract, into pleasing patterns. But there's the rub. What makes one pattern pleasing and another not? What sells? The industry moguls certainly don't know, at least in the long run. The business is notoriously mercurial, and even the best efforts of conglomerate accountant vice-presidents haven't been able to bring order and stability to it.

What we realized in the seventies is that the value of a film doesn't lie so much in its particular genre as with elements that historically have been associated with that genre but can be abstracted, and grafted onto another subject entirely. Caper films (*Butch Cassidy, The Hot Rock, The Sting, The Anderson Tapes*), chase films (*The Rain People, Five Easy Pieces, Slither, Scarecrow,* and eminently, *Duel* and *Two-Lane Blacktop*) didn't last as pure genres much past 1975 simply because filmmakers learned to use the elements of suspense and myth inherent in those genres in other types of film. The hybrids had more going for them. *French Connection* had a superb chase in it; it also had elements of the caper; it was a Buddy film in part; but primarily it was a cop movie. *Black Sunday*'s limited appeal lay in its astute combination of suspenseful caper, chase, politics, and sports. It also had a healthy dollop of disaster. *All the President's Men* wasn't just a movie about politics; it was an intellectual chase (inexorable because we know the aftermath), a bit of a caper, with touches of docudrama à clef and an undercurrent of Buddy. Country movies are westerns on the road.

Literary texts used to list the basic elements of the novel as plot, character, setting, theme, and style. Despite all that we've learned recently about the semiotic structure of storytelling, this five-part model remains useful for an analysis of the *conscious* motivation of film, as well as other narrative arts. Psychologically, film may work in a much more complex manner, but practically—for both filmmaker and film viewer—movies remain stories, about various people, in certain locations, which present a number of ideas, and do so in a more or less recognizable esthetic mode.

More than anything else, American movies are passionately devoted to storytelling. A good yarn is the basis for most successful films, and it is told in the most conventional manner, despite what you may have heard about the new artistic freedom in Hollywood. It has a very clear beginning, middle, and end, divided into fairly equal thirds, and it moves in good order from exposition through development to denouement and conclusion. It is tightly knit (and then what happened? and then? and then?), but it often leaves space for other profitable enterprises, such as character and setting.

The best way to organize the telling of a yarn is through a proper balance of suspense and action. Hitchcock is fond of defining suspense as "the opposite of surprise." Surprise is when something happens and you don't expect it. Suspense is when you expect it and it doesn't happen. Any story upon which the elements of surprise, action, and suspense can be superimposed can be successful in the Hollywood format. Often, the suspense/action balance can be adjusted after the film is shot. Steven Spielberg owes much of his success to an instinctive understanding of this process (and in *Jaws*, he also owes it to Verna Fields's excellent help in

Technique: In *Jaws*, Spielberg intercuts the people on the beach with Scheider's pensive face as he strains to see what they're running from. The technique creates a purely cinematic tension.

editing). Spielberg began with a couple of road films, a genre that has a built-in suspense axis: the journey begins, it continues, until it ends.*

In both *Jaws* and *Close Encounters* he was confronted with rather thin stories. Not a lot happens in either. The films work because of what doesn't happen. The shark enters the bay, but he doesn't eat the children. The aliens give the signal, but they don't land until the end of the movie (nicely setting up the sequel). But Spielberg knows very well how to build on these nonevents by keeping the nervous tension of the characters at a high level from the beginning. He even went back after *Close Encounters* was supposedly finished to shoot new footage which now appears at the opening of the film. There's no reason for there to be a sandstorm in the desert when Lacombe goes to investigate the mysteriously returned airplanes. No reason except that a sandstorm is noisy and tense and dangerous. Likewise, there is no reason for Roy Neary to upset his wife and children, no reason for them in turn not to try to understand and help, except that the familial tension provides some necessary suspense in the otherwise empty middle of the film. It isn't inherent in the story, which is rather calm, after all, no essential dramatic conflict—even

---

*An exception is the most interesting of the road pictures, Monte Hellman's *Two-Lane Blacktop*, where much more meaningfully, if less satisfyingly, the action simply freezes when the film ends, the road goes on, and on. . . .

Character: Roy Scheider, Robert Shaw, and Richard Dreyfuss as the haggard trio of oddball characters which forms the nucleus of *Jaws*.

the disagreement between the saucer buffs and the government is handled perfunctorily. But the suspense doesn't have to be inherent for the entertainment machine to work.

The general run of American films is strongly plot-oriented, but the best of our movies depend heavily on character for their full effect, even at the expense of the story line. (All of the directors singled out in this book for intensive study—Allen, Cassavetes, Altman, Coppola, Ritchie, Mazursky—are more interested in character than action, so it's no secret where my sympathies lie.)

The suspense/action style is so widespread in the '70s and '80s that it is clearly too broad to be called a genre: it has consumed half a dozen genres. Yet while directors like Friedkin, Lucas, and Spielberg can supply the action, even when it isn't necessarily there, they must depend on actors to bring the action alive. The *French Connection* would not have worked without Gene Hackman's Popeye Doyle. *American Graffiti* hinged on Richard Dreyfuss's Curt as *Star Wars* found a proper center in Alec Guinness's Obi-wan Kenobi and the resonant voice, dubbed in after shooting, of James Earl Jones as Darth Vader. Without Dreyfuss and Robert Shaw (and to a lesser extent, Roy Scheider) *Jaws* wouldn't have been the film it was, and Dreyfuss once more together with François Truffaut breathed life into *Close Encounters*.

In the films just listed, it is the actor—the star—who brings character to the role. In films which are in the first place oriented toward character, the material is there to begin with. *The Godfather* made stars of a number of hitherto unknown actors because the roles themselves had power. Paul Mazursky's films are so devoted to character that they become almost static portraits. Meanwhile, Altman and Cassavetes have worked together with their ensembles of actors to produce thematic variations.

In a real sense, television has taken the Hollywood star system to its logical end. No longer is it necessary for star personas to attempt to act separate and distinct roles. We always gave them the benefit of the doubt in old Hollywood films. We would have been shocked if John Wayne or Clark Gable or Cary Grant appeared any differently; we would have demanded our money back. But the television format of the talkshow releases personalities from the demands of acting. We can spend as much time with them as we want in their star personas, then move them on down the couch. Variety shows offer the same relaxed potential, while comedy and dramatic series are precisely designed to come as close as possible to the star's persona. Mary Tyler Moore may play Mary Richards and Bob Newhart Bob Hartley, but it's the stars' names in the titles, not the characters'.

For a while in the late sixties and early seventies, it looked as if real acting—the sort associated with the stage—was going to make a comeback. Actors like Al Pacino, Robert De Niro, Richard Dreyfuss, Robert Redford, and Dustin Hoffman prided themselves on their stage work and seemed to want to act characters rather than star personas on the screen. The results have been mixed. Pacino and De Niro have maintained their reputations as varied actors, but most of the new generation of actors have been quite willing to fall into the comfortable and comforting roles of stars.

When the main aim of the filmmakers is action, it's so much easier to be able to leave the character to the star, to be able to plug in readymade personas after the script has been written. Character development always takes away valuable time that could more profitably be devoted to action, anyway. So much more efficient if the character has been established in half a dozen earlier movies.

This dialectic between character and star, actor and persona has been one of the main esthetic motive forces of the movies, abroad as well as at home. It's relatively easy to assume a new role on stage; the nearest spectator is ten feet away. It's not so easy, nor is it necessarily advisable, to play character on film, where the camera can focus on the pores on your face. The aim shouldn't be to eschew star personas in favor of stagy acted roles—not at all—but rather to meld star and character in new ways, and to give the actor strong material to work with and against.

72

People may go to the movies for the visceral excitement of professionally paced action, but they become moviegoers because of the people they see on the screen. They come back to see those people. You can make a quick splash with action, but character builds careers. It isn't smart to leave the whole job up to actors, no matter how good they are at it.

The third element of the narrative format, setting, is probably more important in film than in any other art. Moreover, it increases in importance with each passing year. People do go to movies to see places they haven't been, whether it's another galaxy, New York City, or Hollywood and Vine. (They also like to see places they *have* been.) The indoor movie, once a staple of the studios, prisoners of their huge and expensive arc lights, now often seems cramped and claustrophobic.

Locale alone can't make a commercially successful film, as the failures of *Islands in the Stream* and *Bobby Deerfield,* both essentially travelogues, proved once again. But location work adds immeasurably to a film with other things going for it. *Rocky* has a grit and texture in Philadelphia that it wouldn't have had on the back lot. New York sees more film-production activity every year because of the variety and urgency its settings can provide. And, in fact, some films are rooted in travelogues: the James Bond films, for example, or road films. William Friedkin's underrated *Sorcerer* may not have been worth the $20 million it cost to make, but it certainly did provide an interesting trip.

Since studios per se have been largely freed from reproducing New York streets and plantation mansions they are now able to devote their energies to the construction of fantasies. Hence the rise in science fiction and such sets as the wonderfully symbolic and mechanical Bond interiors.

But setting isn't a matter of locale alone. People are also fascinated by the way things work. One of the main pleasures of the caper film is figuring out how the puzzle will be solved. As the old television caper series *Mission Impossible* used to phrase it at the beginning of every show: "Your mission, should you choose to accept it, is . . . ." Here are the premises, what's the solution? François Truffaut thinks one of the main strengths of American movies has been that they showed how working people's jobs were done. Raoul Walsh was especially good at this. As a pedagogical tool, film can explain how to perform a task better than a book, better than a record, and better than a still photograph. This epistemological value should be recognized in fictional entertainment too. Operations, effects, and spectacle are part of setting.

What about the last two classical elements of narrative, theme and style? As we've already seen, theme is—perhaps surprisingly—a salable com-

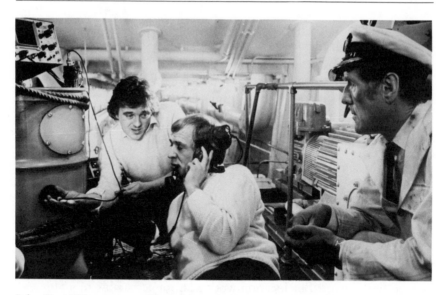

Jobs: David Hemmings and Richard Harris hard at work in *Juggernaut* defusing a bomb with professional gusto while Jack Watson looks on.

modity. People go to country films, to women's films, to chop socky and midlife-crisis movies at least partially for what those films have to say. *Network* wasn't a success because of Paddy Chayefsky's gassy dialogue. It wasn't Faye Dunaway or Bill Holden that lined them up around the block, it was the subject—television—and the attitude the film expressed toward it. *Network* didn't make the point very clearly, but people wanted to hear any critique of television.

Despite its generic components, *All the President's Men* attracted viewers mainly because it helped to explain how Watergate had happened, and people wanted to hear that too. There is a market for films about the way we live now, and the more it is catered to, the larger it will grow. The empty entertainment machines don't succeed because they are mindless, but in spite of that fact. Audiences have the creative power to read significance into otherwise perfunctory material. When the theme is missing, they supply it, albeit often unconsciously. Even preliterate stories told around the campfire had moral significance. People want to know the point of a story. If it isn't clear, they're puzzled, or they supply it themselves. Even television does this for its viewers, hence in part the popularity of docudramas—films which connect directly with known history. Certainly, audiences for blockbusters aren't rushing to the movies to escape the moral seriousness of television. If they choose movies over TV, it's often because they are searching for a much more complex and sophisticated thematic web of meaning. That they don't often get it

74

reflects more poorly on filmmakers than on filmgoers.

Movies have always been prized by critics and general audiences alike for the strong mythic base on which they are built. That is the chief reason for the perennial popularity of genres like the western, the gangster, and the detective story. All films *mean* something, whether or not the filmmaker intends it. Interpretation—supplying meaning—is the job of consumers as well as producers. The thematic spectrum runs from the direct and relatively simple lessons of realistic films that attempt to describe the way we live now (*Girl Friends*, for example, or any of the new feminist films), to the more complex and amorphous significances of the mythopoeic genres (such as *Rocky* or *Days of Heaven*). Far from being an intellectual's preoccupation, a fixation not shared by the general run of filmgoers, theme is the necessary skeleton on which action, character, and setting are arranged. If the bare bones aren't there, audiences will know it.

Indeed, occasionally a film enjoys a successful run simply because it carries with it the aura of "meaningfulness." American films that mean to be "serious" are often about outcasts or cripples (*Coming Home*, *The Other Side of the Mountain*). Partly audiences are attracted because such movies appeal to voyeurism and maudlin sentimentality, but basically people are interested in such downbeat films because seeing them becomes an act of moral commitment.

As for style, this last of the five elements of the cinematic equation is the least defensible. Only trained observers look for it or appreciate it. If it is blatantly evident, it is usually done in bad faith and audiences react with sensible contempt. In the early seventies, when the film-school graduates were laying siege to the Hollywood fortress and succeeding more often than they would have believed in their wildest fantasies because they were dealing with producers and businessmen who were confused and disoriented, scores of films were made with style and little else. *The Christian Licorice Store*, directed by James Frawley from a script by Floyd Mutrux, is a perfect example. About a successful tennis player (the title is never explained) who hangs out with a Swedish photographer for a while, then eventually dies in an auto accident, the film has vast expanses of rather interesting photography, a leisurely visit with Jean Renoir, a couple of tennis games, and little else. The characters are blank, there is little suspense and less action, some postcard scenery, and no discernible point. But it must have looked to executives at Cinema Center films (a company which didn't last very long) like just the ticket for the anomic youth market.

In European films, style usually plays a notably more significant part

Art: Diane Keaton, Kristin Griffith, and Marybeth Hurt as the "Three Sisters" in *Interiors* stare soulfully and significantly out the window at the sea. This is the last, portentous shot of the film.

than in American movies. Since European films are, on the whole, much more personal communications, the tone of voice of the author is an important element in the grand design. American films, however, can't rely on this established, intimate relationship between filmmaker and film viewer. They exist in the context of movies as powerful mass entertainment, so that personal style, when it makes itself evident, often seems intrusive. In terms of American movies, style is all too often defined as the residue that remains after action and character, locales and ideas have been subtracted. Some American filmmakers are still enamored of the personal European approach despite its inapplicability to the American situation. The most egregious recent example of this falsely placed faith has been Woody Allen's *Interiors*.

Technique, however, as opposed to style, often makes all the difference, as the new Hollywood generation of the seventies knows very well. Steven Spielberg's films are probably the best examples of this "high-tech" esthetic. *Jaws* is a precisely designed series of technical devices guaranteed to keep an audience in the proper state of anticipation. (See p. 177 for an analysis of one of *Jaws*'s most technically brilliant sequences.) *Close Encounters of the Third Kind* is, if anything, even more technically minded. The logic upon which the film is constructed has little to do with plot and less to do with character. The aim is simply to provide a well-timed series of technical frissons.

Art: A little more interesting because it's not so thickly allusive is Alan Rudolph's conception of the photographer played by Lauren Hutton in *Welcome to L.A.* She specializes in pictures of empty corners. O.K., I'll buy that.

Brian De Palma is also a master of cinematic high-tech. His earlier films, especially *Sisters*, employed split-screen editing in novel and effective ways. More recently, *Carrie* and *The Fury* have been designed around special effects climaxes, even if these grand-guignol ploys actually subtract from the narrative substances of the films. People went to see *Carrie* to watch the kitchen tools attack Piper Laurie, while the ultimately silly but nevertheless thrilling explosion of John Cassavetes put a loud period to *The Fury*.

To these five classic elements of narrative we should add two others, each of which is something more than a gimmick, but less than a basic component of construction: sex and music. They are hardly necessary and sufficient like the five basic "quarks" from which films are built, but they can often save a borderline case. There's a strong element of voyeurism to the film experience, so a judicious nude scene here or there can mean the margin between profit and loss, especially when feature films are in direct competition with puritan American network television. Even when a film contains no explicit sex, the very personas of the actors and actresses often work to provide a sexual subtext.

Music, on the other hand, may seem exterior to the film itself. Yet it's the mortar that fills in the cracks, even sometimes when they are large enough to push a dolly through. Prove it by turning down the sound on your television set. More often than not, it isn't the image that moves us, but the musical groundbase that tells us what to think and how to feel about that image.

How does all this work in practice? Let's use as an example *Coma* (1977), directed by Michael Crichton from a novel by Robin Cook, with Genevieve Bujold, Michael Douglas, and Richard Widmark. This film is a gimmick thriller. We already know that from the publicity the book and film have received. The idea is that doctors at a major hospital are quietly comatizing otherwise healthy patients in order to auction their organs for transplants at a healthy profit. The theme has exciting possibilities. It plays on a common fear of medical professionals, and it introduces a number of serious and interesting issues: When should a death certificate be issued? Who should decide? When should life-support systems be disconnected? Where will we get the organs to be used in transplant operations? What right (or duty) do we have to keep patients alive after "brain death"? And, finally, what should we do with a highly profitable private medical industry that spends billions on curative medicine and only a pittance on preventive medicine? These are issues many of which were raised by George Bernard Shaw seventy years ago in *The Doctor's Dilemma.* They are still with us.

Coma begins magnificently. Both Crichton and Cook are M.D.s and they therefore know the milieu well. The film rings with the truth of its setting. The plot is clean and direct: an absorbing mystery with a very cogent point to it. The dialogue is smart and rich and comes so fast that Crichton can afford almost to throw away a line like "I think we have to call this 'delayed return of consciousness of cryptogenic origin.'" Above all, however, the characters of *Coma* are joltingly real and contemporary, at least judged by current Hollywood standards. Bujold comes on early and strong. She is clearly the hero of the film: attractive, utterly self-assured, yet complex and human. Douglas tells her: "You don't want a goddam lover. You want a wife!" The plot is absorbing; the subplot is refreshing; and for about an hour, the film is exciting, resonant, evocative.

Then something strange happens. Of a sudden there is music on the soundtrack. It is by Jerry Goldsmith, one of the more prolific composer-hacks of the seventies. It doesn't belong in this film. This film doesn't need it. It's moving along just fine on its own. Next thing we know, the mystery has broken down, the subplot of sexual politics has been discarded, and hero Bujold is in danger of being transformed before our very eyes into a Hollywood heroine. There are several obligatory chase scenes. Nicely done, but the mystery was finished. The chases are superfluous. By the end, the film has sunk deep into its own coma, has in fact suffered

Woman as hero: Genevieve Bujold as Dr. Susan Wheeler purposefully scales the ladder in the hospital utilities shaft in hot pursuit of the villains. (There has already been a clue to her downfall: she's had to remove her slippery, feminine stockings.)

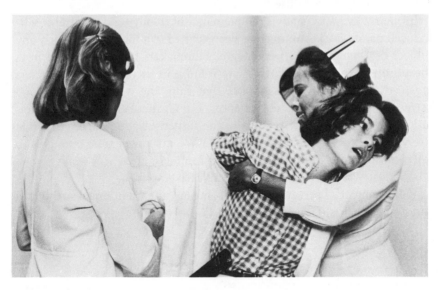

Woman as heroine: Susan gets prepared for surgery against her will at the end of *Coma.* Soon she will have to be rescued by the handsome Dr. husband.

cinematic brain death.

The remarkable character of Bujold has metamorphosed into a typical dumb broad who can't take care of herself. She falls for the oldest trick in the book—the old mickey finn routine. Next thing we know she's half paralyzed and being wheeled into an operating room. She actually gets cut up by Widmark the villain—sliced and stitched in her stupor. And, need it be said, she has to be saved by Douglas, formerly not such a nice character, who rises to the heroism the sexist plot demands.

The depth of ingrained misogyny can only be guessed at that can make an otherwise intelligent writer destroy a fascinating character before our eyes, put her under the knife, both literally and figuratively, and ignominiously subordinate her to a not too bright hospital politician.

The first half of *Coma* is extraordinary. The rest of it all the more disappointing because it begins so well. Maybe they can hang it up somewhere, use the good parts as transplants in some healthier film.

What has happened here? This is Cook's first novel, and Crichton's second opportunity at directing. They lost their nerve halfway through and gave in to some hoary old genre devices. Perhaps they thought the film would sell better with a couple of chases and an old-fashioned rescue. Maybe they were even right to think so. But that can't excuse the tyranny that rigid plot formulas exert over vital, fascinating characters in *Coma*, nor the cowardice that permits director and writer to allow this violence to be done to their characters.

In many ways, *Coma* is emblematic of Hollywood's current self-induced paralysis. Technique has been refined to a high state. Nearly any subject or theme is now permissible. Filmmakers have been freed from the prison of the studio: settings are infinite in their variety. Characters are ready and waiting: we can see that from the wealth of actors and actresses discussed in the next chapter. But all these elements are useless unless we can escape the tyranny of the suspense/action clichés that rule the vast majority of American movies. We no longer trust ourselves to tell our own stories. If it doesn't fit the formulas, audiences won't buy it. The industry suffers from a kind of collective aphasia.

We'll know it's been cured when, someday, the traditional starting call rings out: "Lights! Camera! *Character!*"

4

The People Who Make Movies

The Assets

Old Joe Kennedy, when he was wheeling and dealing at RKO, once commented bemusedly on the strangeness of the business of film. "It's the only industry," he remarked, "where the assets pick up their hats every afternoon and go home!" Despite the relatively large amounts of capital the art of film requires, it's still what we might call a labor-intensive enterprise. Kodak may have yearly revenues twice the size of the film-production industry (in 1977 Kodak's gross income amount to $6 billion from filmstock, chemicals, cameras, and other sources), but filmstock without people is useless. And while filmmakers are playing by a strict set of economic rules that often shape their work, within the circumscribed limits of the business/craft we've just outlined it is the people of the movie world who finally decide what films get made and how they get made.

Who are these people? Can anyone grow up to be a filmmaker in America? With certain reservations, the answer is yes. The film industry is a lot more open than more conventional industries. It was founded by a bunch of immigrants, and while of course it isn't immune to petty social and class prejudices, the roster of film talent on both sides of the camera often reads like those carefully ethnically mixed platoons in World War II epics. Blacks and Hispanics still have a tougher time than most, certainly, but even this situation is easing, and—except in supporting crafts, still dominated by father-son unions—minorities probably stand a better chance in the movie business than, say, in banking. A faint hope, no doubt, but one to build on.

Implicit here is the requirement that, in order to break into the industry, one has to be willing to conform to the accepted norms. They are looser than they were in the forties, fifties, and sixties, but not as liberal as they were around 1970. From a careerist point of view, that's not necessarily bad: it makes the game more interesting, as such new Hollywood powers as Francis Coppola, Steven Spielberg, or Paul Schrader might attest. From the point of view of art, naturally, such constricted norms cause problems, but they are not insurmountable, as we shall see.

For more than fifteen years, from the early fifties to the late sixties, the industry was in effect moribund. With the advent of television in the late forties, revenues for film were cut in half. It followed that the industry could then support far fewer workers. Those with executive positions clung to them tenaciously, while the craft unions battened down the hatches for a long siege. Until the late sixties, just about the only way you could become a cinematographer, for instance, was to be related to a member of the American Society of Cinematographers. The ASC roster is still overweighted with familiar names, sons and nephews who inherited their positions. Actors and actresses were better off. Television opened up a profitable new field for them, and many earned more from the residuals from one series than they might have from an entire career on the studio payroll.

By the late sixties most of the moguls had died off, and those that hadn't had been eased out of positions of power by the new conglomerate owners. The "assets," as Joe Kennedy called them—the technicians, producers, directors, actors, and actresses under contract—had been liquidated as the industry retrenched. The business was now essentially freelance. Nobody worked regularly, as they had in the golden years of the thirties and forties (actors began driving their Morgans and Mercedes to the unemployment office to collect the weekly checks), but opportunities for younger people were greatly increased.

The short-lived youth culture of the late sixties further enhanced opportunities. The new managers hadn't the slightest idea what would sell anymore; they were open to just about any cockamamie concept. Within five years, between 1968 and 1973, a new generation had taken over the reins of power. In their twenties and thirties, they were not one but two generations removed from the founding-father moguls.

This new generation is notably more versatile. They have to be. In the land of the hyphenates, the writer-producer-director-actor is king. The strict craft definitions and assembly-line system that divided the old Hollywood into categories of specialists no longer apply. This causes certain problems for auteurist critics. No doubt, the director of a film is still theoretically the prime creative mover, but the auteur policy was devised to treat a situation in which director and studio were in dialectical opposition. That situation no longer pertains. More often than not, now, it's the director versus the actor or the director versus the screenwriter that provides the creative tension. Anyway, auteurism was a moral imperative—a tool which critics who wanted to become directors (Truffaut, Godard, Chabrol, Rohmer) used to prepare their path to power.

Better to call everyone who works in movies "filmmakers," then assess the various contributions each makes on an ad hoc basis. In the past, studios may have constructed vehicles which fit their stars, so that it was proper to speak of a John Wayne movie or a Cary Grant film. Now the stars create their own vehicles; they have the power not only as personas but as producers (and sometimes directors) as well.

A partial list of actors and actresses who have directed or produced includes John Cassavetes, Paul Newman, Robert Redford, Alan Arkin, Jack Nicholson, Peter Fonda, Jack Lemmon, Burt Reynolds, George C. Scott, Barbra Streisand, Ellen Burstyn, Dyan Cannon, Shirley MacLaine, Joan Darling, Michael Douglas, Dennis Hopper, Robert Duvall, Ben Gazzara, Peter Falk, Sidney Poitier, Warren Beatty, Marlon Brando, Cliff Robertson, Ossie Davis, Bill Gunn, Ivan Dixon, and even young Robby Benson. In short, just about any actor with ambition and the economic power to realize it has tried his hand behind the camera.

Nearly all contemporary comedy directors star in their own films and began as performers. Mel Brooks, Woody Allen, Gene Wilder, Marty Feldman, and Elaine May are simply following in the tradition established by Charlie Chaplin, Buster Keaton, and Harold Lloyd many years ago.

Meanwhile, Clint Eastwood, Tom Laughlin, and, to a lesser extent, Charles Bronson and Burt Reynolds either produce or control their frequent and profitable appearances. They have concurrently established very strong screen personas, often in series of films about the same character—for example, Laughlin's Billy Jack, Eastwood's Dirty Harry. Eastwood, Laughlin, and Bronson are the three avenging angels of contemporary movies, and Reynolds (the tough Reynolds of the country movies, not the cute Burt of At Long Last Love) quite often plays an ironic parody of this role.

Other former actors—Robert Evans, Tony Bill, Max Baer, Jr.—have given up the boards completely in favor of production. Screenwriters and directors sometimes get the power to produce, but clearly actors dominate center stage, economically as well as theatrically. Any aspiring filmmaker might do well to start as an actor, no matter what his eventual aim.

That's assuming he wasn't born into the industry family. Dynasties are still strong, especially among actors, whose children carry with them a suspicion of their fathers' and mothers' screen personas. The leading clans at the present include: the Fondas, Jane and Peter, children of Henry; the Carradines, David, Keith, and Robert, sons of John; the Bridgeses, Beau and Jeff, sons of Lloyd; the Redgraves, Vanessa, Lynn, and Corin, children of Michael and Rachel Kempson; and the Masseys, Anna and Daniel, children of Raymond. (These last two families work mainly in England.)

Other star offspring who work regularly or occasionally in front of the camera include: Rob Reiner (son of Carl), James Mitchum (son of Robert), Michael Douglas (son of Kirk), Candice Bergen (daughter of Edgar), Susan Newman (daughter of Paul Newman and Joanne Woodward), Cathryn Harrison (daughter of Noel, granddaughter of Rex), Carrie Fisher (daughter of Eddie Fisher and Debbie Reynolds), Angelica Huston (daughter of John, granddaughter of Walter), Melanie Griffith (daughter of Tippi Hedren), Maria O'Brien (daughter of Edmund), Haley Mills (daughter of John), and of course Tatum O'Neal and Liza Minnelli. (And then there is the entire Cassavetes-Rowlands clan, whose members appear regularly in their films.)

Behind the camera, Hollywood bloodlines are less prominent; inherited personas don't matter here. Yet Alan Ladd, Jr., runs Twentieth Century–Fox and Richard Zanuck (son of Darryl) is a major independent producer, while Patrick Wayne (son of John), Michael Douglas, Jack Haley, Jr., David Niven, Jr., and Sam Goldwyn, Jr., have all tried their hand at producing films. Richard Fleisher (son of Max), and Gordon Parks, Jr., are directors, and Bruce Surtees (son of Robert), Chuck Rosher, Jr., and Gene Polito (son of Sol) have followed in their fathers' footsteps as cinematographers, while Bill Lancaster (son of Burt) has taken up screenwriting.

Now this doesn't mean all that much, except the obvious: that it's easier to get a job in an industry if you've grown up in it and your daddy knows people. It happens all the time.

What other paths are open? During the sixties, the easiest path for a director was through television. That medium was relatively open to new talent, and after guiding a number of productions satisfactorily to their conclusions, a television director had a track record to present to the film companies. Virtually the entire transitional generation of the sixties came out of TV production: Arthur Penn, John Frankenheimer, Martin Ritt, Franklin Schaffner, Robert Altman, Robert Mulligan, Norman

O'Neals Ryan and Tatum in *Paper Moon*, her first film. She actually won an Oscar for her performance.

Jewison, Irvin Kershner, Arthur Hiller, and Sidney Lumet, among others. With the rise of the made-for-television movie in the late sixties, however, a number of directors opted to continue in TV, with occasional forays into feature-film making. The new form apparently offered the needed prestige that series and specials hadn't. It was a kind of film, after all, and it certainly drew massively larger audiences than even the most popular theatrical films. Such filmmakers as Paul Bogart, Boris Sagal, John Korty, Tom Gries, Daniel Petrie, Paul Wendkos, Sam O'Steen, and David Greene are better known for their made-for-TV films than for their occasional theatrical enterprises.

The film schools (and repertory houses) replaced television as the prime source of directorial talent in the early seventies. Such leading trade schools as U.S.C., U.C.L.A., and N.Y.U., now offer real prospects to their students. Francis Coppola has been the most successful of film school graduates (U.C.L.A.); Martin Scorsese (N.Y.U.), Brian De Palma (N.Y.U.), Terrence Malick (A.F.I.), and George Lucas (U.S.C.) are other members of the group. Add to this list the self-educated film buffs Peter Bogdanovich and Steven Spielberg.

Often the road from film degree to director's chair includes a spell as screenwriter. Such was the case with Coppola, John Milius, and Paul Schrader. In fact, screenwriting seems to be second only to acting as an effective apprenticeship. Robert Benton and David Newman, the most famous screenwriters of the sixties, have both moved behind the camera, as have Michael Crichton, David Giler, Frank D. Gilroy, Frank R. Pierson, Thomas McGuane, Lewis John Carlino, Joseph Bologna and Renee Taylor, Charles Eastman, Walter Hill, Bill Gunn, Gloria Katz and Willard Huyck, Colin Higgins, Peter Hyams, Ernest Lehman, Joan Tewkesbury, and James Toback. A number of these people, however, had their shot and muffed it, only to return to the typewriter.*

Other industry crafts have been less productive as training grounds for directors. A few editors—Hal Ashby, Sam O'Steen—have been promoted; a number of producers have hired themselves—Lawrence Turman, Alan Pakula, and James B. Harris, for example. Only Pakula has had real success here. At least one designer, Paul Sylbert, has been given a chance to direct, and one special-effects expert, Douglas Trumbull. Neither, however, has been able to establish himself.

Broadway still provides useful training for a few directors: Gene Saks, Ulu Grosbard, Theodore Flicker, and more importantly Herb Ross, Bob Fosse, and Mike Nichols gained useful experience in the theater. A rather unique source of talent in the seventies was commercial advertising: Howard Zieff, Jerry Schatzberg, and Dick Richards were friends in the New York ad world of the 1960s. All went on to direct films with surprising similarity of approach. More recently Joseph Brooks parlayed an advertising career into a film career, and Stan Dragoti may still find fame as something other than Cheryl Tiegs's husband.

The handful of Black directors who have established a foothold in the film industry have had varied backgrounds, as might be expected. Melvin Van Peebles went to Europe to get his start. Ossie Davis, Ivan Dixon, and Sidney Poitier moved over from acting. Gordon Parks, Sr., was a successful photographer. Berry Gordy moved in from the music world. Only Michael Schultz took a traditional industry path.

We have effectively excluded the Black nation within the U.S. for the last ten years by offering token equal opportunity. Yet, during the same period of time, we have extended a warm welcome to foreigners. Half the filmmakers responsible for the brief Czechoslovak renaissance of the mid-sixties have moved to the United States, although in most cases it has been difficult for them to adjust to the new idiom. Ivan Passer, Jan Kadar, and Milos Forman certainly couldn't have maintained careers at home after the brutal counterrevolution of 1968. Roman Polanski has had more success emigrating from Poland, although he has never fulfilled his earlier promise, content instead to build a more colorful and dramatic persona in "real life" than any of his characters. A few French directors—Louis

---

*If you are interested in the credits for these people, and others mentioned in this section, you'll find them in "Who's Who", beginning on p. 475.

Malle, Claude Lelouch, Jacques Demy—have made attempts at American movies; Claude Chabrol has ventured as close as Canada.

By far the greatest number of immigrants to American film have come from Canada and England. They are economic rather than political refugees, and perhaps one of the reasons they have been welcomed is that the American film industry is responsible in part for their having to leave home. Canada has always been a cultural colony of the United States, and Canadians in film have a long tradition of moving south to find work when their own industry couldn't support them because Canadian screens were flooded with American product imported more cheaply than native films could be produced. But until the early seventies, the English cinema had survived rather well under similar pressures, thanks to an early quota law and a thriving national culture. Indeed, in the fifties, English filmmakers were able to export a fair number of home-grown comedies to the U.S. market.

In the late sixties, however, American producers flooded the English film industry with American dollars in the hopes that some of the interesting native talent—it was the era of "Swinging London," of the Beatles and the Rolling Stones—might return a profit commensurate with the investment. When the recession of 1969 hit, American capital pulled out of Britain quickly and disastrously. This, combined with the growth and health of British television (and perhaps the continuing malaise from which the former imperial power suffers) nearly destroyed British film. It is only now beginning to recover as television leads the way, infusing some much-needed capital back into film. Lord Lew Grade has been a central figure here. His company, ATC, is now the major producer of British films for export. Grade acquired his title for his work in television.

The large number of Canadians or former Canadians now directing in the United States includes Norman Jewison, Arthur Hiller, Ted Kotcheff (after a period in England), and Sidney Furie. There have also been American films by Darryl Duke, George Bloomfield, and Eric Till. The number of Canadian actors at work here, from Lorne Greene to Donald Sutherland, is incalculable.

The British migration counts among its members: John Boorman, Michael Anderson, Peter Yates, David Greene, John Guillermin, Michael Winner, Jack Clayton, Ronald Neame, Tony Richardson, and Marty Feldman, as well as Karel Reisz, Bryan Forbes, and John Schlesinger, who still keep one foot in Britain. In short, most of the English generation of the sixties has moved here. Of the familiar names, only Lindsay Anderson has stayed home. Of course, he works more, in theater than in film.

Most recently, Alan Parker, Ridley Scott, Michael Apted, and Adrian Lines have joined the British colony in Hollywood—all of them originally under the sponsorship of producer David Puttnam, himself an exile.

Meanwhile, British actors and actresses have been better able to combine careers in both countries, possibly because it is easier for them to move between television and film, film and theater. For a period around 1970 it looked as if British actresses might succeed where American actresses hadn't in breaking the sex line that had kept women in markedly inferior roles for twenty years. However, Julie Christie, Vanessa and Lynn Redgrave, Glenda Jackson, and others did not succeed. Fewer British actors were able to gain roles in entirely American films, although Alan Bates, Oliver Reed, Michael York, and others occasionally appear in American-financed coproductions. The majority, as with the women, has had to look to television and the stage for work. Only Sean Connery and Robert Shaw became Anglo-American stars with box-office appeal.

As for the rest of Europe, the wave of actor-immigrants which began in the early twenties subsided long ago. Not since World War I have there been so few European-born Hollywood players. Sophia Loren only visits. Marcello Mastroianni waited too long to learn English. A far greater number of Americans works in Europe, from Clint Eastwood and Charles Bronson, who began their careers there, to Burt Lancaster and Sterling Hayden. But as we enter the eighties, we can expect more European talent to make the move to southern California. Marie-France Pisier, a remarkable actress in her own language, has established a beachhead with a calculated role in *The Other Side of Midnight* and appearances on the talk shows. Isabelle Adjani took a limited part in Walter Hill's homage to Jean-Pierre Melville, *The Driver.* Other French actresses may well follow if the French industry doesn't revive. Their Canadian cousin Genevieve Bujold, bilingual but still with the faintest soupçon of an accent, has led the way with a canny series of moves the last few years designed to assure her of some economic power.

Native sources of new acting talent are varied. While a handful of directors may have made the move from advertising to feature films, actors and actresses have not had an easy time of it. They never did. Lauren Bacall achieved useful fame as a cover girl, but she had been thoroughly trained as an actress before she graced the nation's newsstands. Most ex-models suffer the fate of Suzy Parker, Jean Shrimpton, or Twiggy. Yet Farrah Fawcett-Majors, with the considerable help of her phenomenal if brief television career, may blaze a new trail. Ali McGraw, Maud Adams, and Lauren Hutton are still hanging in there, although the prognosis for their careers is not good. Carol Lynley and Jennifer O'Neill seem to me to be two ex-models with real potential as film actresses, although it has never been realized.

The transition from television to movies is equally difficult to make. Even such eminently successful television stars as Sid Caesar, Dick Van Dyke, and Mary Tyler Moore have been remarkably unpopular in theatrical films. Meanwhile, Joseph Campanella, Robert Culp, Jennifer Warren, and Larry Hagman have shown cinematic promise while not quite being able to establish healthy careers on the large screen. The reason may be that television demands rather colorless personalities, while film thrives on idiosyncratic character.

Yet the two mediums are not mutually exclusive: Art Carney has discovered a flourishing second career in film, and one program, *Laugh-In*, spawned two of the most interesting actresses of the seventies, Goldie Hawn and Lily Tomlin. Then we have Sally Field, who worked hard to make the switch. John Travolta and Tom Selleck have succeeded, at least for the moment, and so has Nick Nolte. Almost all successful film comedians started on TV.

The path in the other direction is considerably easier. Scores of second-level film stars (Jack Palance, Robert Stack) have had durable careers in television in the past, even if once again major stars like Doris Day and James Stewart have found the small screen relatively inhospitable. Cindy Williams and Lindsay Wagner are two eminent examples of interesting younger film actors who have found perhaps mitigated success in TV.

For Black actors, sports is still the major entree to acting, while records and stand-up comedy are close seconds. Jim Brown, Bernie Casey, O. J. Simpson, and Paul Winfield have all been able to graduate from football to films successfully. Richard Pryor and Bill Cosby have built increasingly interesting acting careers out of backgrounds as monologists. Meanwhile, few whites go the sports route—Burt Reynolds once played football, but he wasn't a star, Joe Namath tried films once and attempted a TV sitcom. Those whites who do move into the entertainment industry from its almost incestuously close relative, sports, usually prefer television sportscasting to films.

The stage remains by far the major training ground for film actors; in fact, it seems to be growing in importance. In the thirties and forties very few stage actors got to become major film stars, but now we can point to an entire generation of box-office balance-sheet heroes who began in the theater: Al Pacino, Robert Redford, Dustin Hoffman, Faye Dunaway, Barbra Streisand, and George C. Scott have followed the path Marlon Brando and Montgomery Clift blazed in the fifties. And Charles Durning, Robert Duvall, John Cazale, Ben Gazzara, Peter Falk, Cicely

Tyson, Jill Clayburgh, Carol Kane, Susan Anspach, Elizabeth Ashley, Barbara Harris, Rip Torn, Jason Robards, and Anne Bancroft have also successfully combined stage and screen careers. Dancers Rudolph Nureyev and Mikhail Baryshnikov have showed promise as contemporary heart-throbs, despite thick accents.

Music is not so productive a source of film talent as it once was during the days of Tin Pan Alley, despite the fact that all rock stars are actors for better or worse. Only Barbra Streisand, Diana Ross, and Kris Kristofferson have achieved any real success moving from music to acting. (Liza Minnelli acted before she had success as a singer.) Bob Dylan has attempted a role or two, as have David Bowie and Mick Jagger. Dylan has produced and directed his own film, as have a number of other rock stars, from the Beatles to Neil Young. (In general, wealthy musicians tend to make pretentious home movies.) Gladys Knight made an auspicious debut in *Pipe Dreams*, yet it's remarkable, considering the influence rock has had on popular culture, that so few contemporary musicians have developed auxiliary careers in the movies.

Obiter Dicta: Major Contributors

Scores of thousands of people make a living—or try to—in the film industry. Perhaps as many as a thousand have some prominence in the field and have done work recently that, for one reason or another, is worth discussion. Clearly, only an encyclopedia could handle the task adequately. But we can at least sketch out the geography of American film and add a few notes on major contributions and landmarks.

In the 1960s when Harold Hayes was editor of *Esquire* the magazine was famous for its wittily facetious maps of various media worlds. No doubt such attempts at blithe categorization leave themselves open to a number of criticisms, yet they provide a convenient way to organize great masses of information, and if we make allowances for a certain sardonic tone that inevitably creeps into such enterprises, such classifications may be no more arbitrary than any other attempt to impose order on chaos.

I must warn you not to expect anything more than capsule characterizations of the work of the hundreds of filmmakers discussed in the pages that follow. This may seem a superficial approach, yet I think the job of at least attempting passing comments on these numerous careers is well worth the effort. So often, film critics pretend that movies are personal works as private as poetry, as precise as painting, yet if there is one salient characteristic which sets film apart from other arts it is just this intensely collaborative and markedly communal nature. If nothing else, the obiter dicta that follow prove that point.[1]

Herewith, then, a map of the American film industry/art, circa 1978. The lists are far from complete, the classifications subject to immediate change ("What have you done for me lately?"). Comparisons with the landscape today seem to show surprisingly few changes.

Actresses: Two facts are apparent immediately. First, that even now that the first wave of new feminist films has arrived, precious few women in American movies can write their own tickets. Barbra Streisand and Liza Minnelli are alone in the "first magnitude" star category, and considering Minnelli's recent record of box-office flops, it could be said that Streisand rules by herself. For a while, in black films, Diana Ross was equally bankable. It's interesting that all three are singers, that two have strongly nostalgic personas harking back to the thirties and forties (and Ross had her greatest success playing Billie Holiday). In the early seventies, we weren't ready for a contemporary role model at the top. Outshining almost all women film stars of various magnitudes has been Mary Tyler Moore. Once again, television has led the way, and movies follow.

That women have been effectively excluded from equal participation in film is clear not only from the ratio of bankable male stars to bankable female stars, but also by the unusually long list of women "underachievers." The evaluations are idiosyncratic of course, but it seems to me that the actresses I've listed in this section were, in the late sixties and early seventies, all clearly capable of more. In 1966, Sidney Lumet's film of Mary McCarthy's novel *The Group* featured eight young actresses, each one more interesting than the next. At the time, the critical consensus was that seven of the eight had bright careers ahead of them. Yet the odd woman out, Candice Bergen, has had the most success since and didn't really come of age professionally until she started shilling for cameras and perfume on TV. Meanwhile, Shirley Knight, Joan Hackett, and Elizabeth Hartman have had to fight for the occasional role; Jessica Walter, Joanna Pettet, and Kathleen Widdoes have barely maintained visibility, and Mary Robin-Redd has totally dropped from sight. There's no better evidence of the disastrous waste of feminine resources which has characterized the last fifteen years of the American film industry.

And the actresses of *The Group* were not alone. A few years earlier two young nonprofessionals, Tippy Walker and Merri Spaeth, stole the show from Peter Sellers in *The World of Henry Orient*. They were each signed to five-picture contracts by producer Jerome Hellman. Nothing was ever heard of them again.

There were numerous stories like these in the sixties. If an actress did by chance gain a measure of box-office clout, she was soon put in her place. This is not to suggest a conspiracy; rather, the industry had simply

American Actresses: 1978.

ELDER STATESWOMEN (Red Giants)

☐ Katharine Hepburn ☐ Ruth Gordon

☐ Audrey Hepburn ☐

Shelley Winters ☐

☐ Joanne Woodward ☐ Lauren Bacall

C L O

FUTURES/RISING

Susan Sarandon •

Brooke Adams • Candice Bergen •

Carrie Fisher • Annette O'Toole • Blythe Danner •

Ellen Holly • Marta Heflin • Talia Shire •

Lindsay Crouse • Lily Tomlin •

Amy Irving • Jennifer Warren •

Susan Newman • Marilyn Hassett •

Melanie Mayron • Melanie Griffith • Gladys Knight •

Mary Steenburgen • Meryl Streep • Dianne Abbott •

Vonetta McGee • Ann Turkel •

Lauren Hutton •

CHARACTERS

Margot Kidde

Shirley Knight • Jane Alexander • • Lee Grant

• Verna Bloom • Estelle Parsons

• Susan Anspach • Teri Garr • Cicely Tyson

• Pam Grier • Beah Richar

• Viveca Lindfors

• Lee Remick

• Penelope Milford

WHITE DWARFS

Ali McGraw •

Farrah Fawcett-Majors •

UNDERACHIEVERS

Suzanne Pleshette • Carol Lynley •

Susan Blakely • Tuesday Weld •

Ann Prentiss • Jennifer O'Neill •

Carrie Snodgress • Katharine Ross •

Paula Prentiss • Valerie Perrine •

Lindsay Wagner • Cindy Williams • Natalie Wood •

Angie Dickenson • Janet Margolin • Ruby Dee •

Diahann Carroll • Elizabeth Ashley • Joanna Pettet •

BLACK HOLES

Raquel Welch • Jessica Walter • Jean Seberg •

• Elizabeth Taylor • Joan Hackett • Kathleen Widdoes •

Elizabeth Hartman • Jacqueline Bisset •

COMETS

Barbara Streisand ★

Ellen Burstyn

Shirley MacLaine

☆ Liza Minnelli

★

Jane Fonda

Margaux Hemingway

Olivia Hussey

Amy Robinson

STARS

U   T

Anne Bancroft

SAFE KOOKS

Sally Kellerman

Madeline Kahn

Diana Ross

Dyan Cannon

Jackie Bisset

Mia Farrow

Shelley Duvall

Carole Kane

Ann-Margret

Sally Struthers

Sissy Spacek

Sandy Dennis

Cybill Shepherd

Barbara Harris

Tatum O'Neal

Diane Keaton

Genevieve Bujold

Goldie Hawn

Jill Clayburgh

KIDS

Tatum O'Neal

NOVAS

Brooke Shields

Faye Dunaway

Quinn Cummings

Jodie Foster

&

CRAFTSWOMEN

Lisa Lucas

Geraldine Page

Linda Manz

Karen Black

Louise Fletcher

Elizabeth Ashley

Lee Remick

Stockard Channing

Brenda Vaccaro

Cloris Leachman

Pat Quinn

Anne Jackson

Marsha Mason

Sally Field

Eileen Brennan

IMMIGRANTS

Gena Rowlands

Liv Ullmann

Candy Clark

Sarah Miles

Glenda Jackson

Jeanne Moreau

Geraldine Chaplin

Geraldine Chaplin

Susannah York

Marthe Keller

Julie Christie

Isabelle Adjani

WAIFS

Vanessa Redgrave

Lynn Redgrave

Tisa Farrow

LOSSES

Marie-France Pisier

Gwen Wells

Camilla Sparv

Melinda Dillon

Johanna Shimkus

Stephanie Powers

decided collectively that interesting women wouldn't sell in starring roles. There were exceptions; these were written off as flukes. The decision against women became a self-fulfilling prophecy. It may not be much of an exaggeration to claim that an entire generation of women—the opposite numbers of Redford, Pacino, Hoffman, De Niro, et al.—has been suppressed. A few of these actresses are only now beginning to emerge from the exile into which Hollywood sent them.

At least they still have a chance to salvage their careers, an opportunity apparently lost to predecessors like Camilla Sparv, Johanna Shimkus, Joanna Barnes, and the remarkable Stephanie Powers, all interesting actresses who don't seem to have survived the 1960s.

The list of "underachievers," therefore, is unusually long. Tuesday Weld, an intelligent actress with considerable range, has settled for a string of kooky roles. Jacqueline Bisset hasn't been able to interest producers in her persona (although like many others she's able to sell her body). Models Carol Lynley and Jennifer O'Neill played "the girl" for a while, then gave up. Suzanne Pleshette, Angie Dickinson, Lindsay Wagner, and Cindy Williams, among others, were sensible enough to escape to television, where women sometimes star and occasionally are permitted to play relatively realistic roles. One of the interesting tensions of the *Bob Newhart Show,* for example, has been that between the intelligent, capable, and sardonic persona Pleshette projects, and the traditional, constricted role of the wife she must play.

The Prentisses, Paula and Ann, like the vast majority of interesting actresses in the sixties, have had to be content with very occasional roles to match their talents. Black actresses of the high caliber of Diahann Carroll and Ruby Dee have had two battles to fight.

There are some actresses with clout besides the lonely stars already mentioned. Ignoring for the moment "black holes," stars who like Elizabeth Taylor and Raquel Welch have collapsed into nothingness by enacting crude parodies of the worst misogynistic fantasies of womanhood, and "white dwarfs," the modern equivalent of starlets, there is (to complete the astronomical metaphor) an increasing number of "novas," potential stars of the first magnitude. Faye Dunaway has fought a canny battle for stardom for more than ten years, since *Bonnie and Clyde.* She has found a degree of acceptance in a sort of modern-day Bette Davis role—tough and a little bit nasty. The image carefully skirts misogynistic parody. Genevieve Bujold has been at work on the construction of a star persona just as long. She may be about to bring it off. Diane Keaton has succeeded through her association with Woody Allen, and by being in the right place at the right time in 1977, appearing in the contrasting roles of *Annie Hall* and *Looking For Mr. Goodbar* just at the time of the feminist revival. Jill Clayburgh may break through; again the secret is the right combination of consecutive roles: *Semi-Tough, An Unmarried Woman,* then *Luna.* Tatum O'Neal is on the list of novas because she is clearly the most successful of the children who collectively have been one of the brighter signs of the seventies. Goldie Hawn seems to be about to fulfill her early promise.

Meanwhile older veteran actresses—Ellen Burstyn, Anne Bancroft, Dyan Cannon, Jane Fonda, and Shirley MacLaine—enjoy some measure of economic power which they have gained partly simply by survival, partly because they have involved themselves in the business, and—in the cases of the latter two—partly for their political activities.

In the early seventies, just about the only roles really wide open for women were of four types: the Girl, fashionably cool and necessarily passive and pliant, usually made an appearance somewhere in the typical adventure or Buddy film. Most actresses played the Girl, or they didn't play at all. But the Kook and the Waif were safe, too. Both types are cute and unthreatening. Stage actresses of the sixties like Sandy Dennis and Barbara Harris found some work in films as kooks, as did Ann-Margret, a special type: the kook as sex object. Audrey Hepburn was not unfamiliar with the higher type of kook in the sixties, and Fonda, Cannon, and MacLaine began here. Later, Diane Keaton took the same path. At the same time, Robert Altman was giving work to a covey of the most egregious and talented kooks, from Sally Kellerman to Shelley Duvall and Sissy Spacek. Waifs have been less popular, but still common in the seventies. The function of the waif, as Mia Farrow, Carol Kane, and Elizabeth Hartman can attest, is to suffer at the hands of the macho hero. In this respect, the waif is simply an exaggeration of the girl.

The fourth safe category is the Child. Because it has an inherent validity, this role seems to have been more productive: Tatum O'Neal and her colleagues Jodie Foster, Brooke Shields, and Quinn Cummings have portrayed strong, no-nonsense kids—a considerable advance over the Shirley Temple type that prevailed from the thirties through the sixties. Yet we shouldn't overlook a possible subtext here. The strength of the little girls probably has something to do with their veiled sexual attraction. The role seems to have evolved in the direction of explicitness: see Shields in *Pretty Baby,* Foster in *Taxi Driver,* and even her vamp in the unusual children's film *Bugsy Malone.*

Immigrants like Liv Ullmann, Marie-France Pisier, and Marthe Keller, despite their realistic, powerful roles in European films, seem to have had very little success playing those types in the United States.

So much for types. Far more interesting is the full reservoir of talent that exists to draw on should Hollywood decide to let attractive, powerful, complex, interesting women characters back into the movies. There is no guarantee this is going to happen, but perhaps the sheer pressure of capable talent held in reserve will have some effect.

There is first a lengthy roster of capable craftswomen including Geral-

Kooks: Geraldine Chaplin (left), Sally Kellerman (center), and Sissy Spacek (right), with semikook Lauren Hutton and nonkook Viveca Lindfors in the Altman-produced *Welcome to L.A.*

Kids: Jodie Foster vamps mini-impresario John Cassisi in Alan Parker's unusual *Bugsy Malone.*

dine Chaplin (who has played kooks in American films, but not in European films), Elizabeth Ashley, and Louise Fletcher; and Shirley Knight, Jane Alexander, Verna Bloom, and Katharine Ross, anyone of whom has star potential if given the right roles.

Chances are, however, that the new stars will come from the "futures" category. There is a long list of younger actresses whose performances are often commented upon, but who until now have never been offered more than minimally interesting characters to play. Blythe Danner (*Hearts of the West*) is the perennial example of an actress who should be a star but isn't. Vonetta McGee (*Brothers*) could easily be the first Black actress to cross over to the white market. Diahnne Abbott as the Billie Holiday singer provided a bright spot in *New York, New York*. Marilyn Hassett has scored in the egregious tearjerker *The Other Side of the Mountain* and other romantic fables. She radiates an intelligence and appeal that could be much more effectively utilized in more interesting films. Lily Tomlin has raised the kook to a level of real interest in *The Late Show* and other films. She may have to write her own films, however. Meryl Streep (*Kramer vs. Kramer*) has been the first woman to follow Hoffman and Pacino from serious New York theater to film stardom. Younger actresses like Lindsay Crouse (*Between the Lines*) and Melanie Griffith (*Smile*) have begun to establish interesting personas. Jennifer Warren usually gets killed off in the first reel. If she can figure a way to last until the end of the movie, she

Futures: Jennifer Warren and Lindsay Crouse as rebellious and independent hockey wives in *Slapshot.* Both actresses project a sense of self, a strength of character, and an intelligence of the sort that would assure them of starring roles if the Equal Rights Amendment applied to film.

has a real chance to make a major contribution.

This list of actresses with significant unrealized potential suggests some exciting possibilities.

Actors: Perhaps just as important, we can discern some patterns in the map of actors that suggest a turning away from the macho type, which has dominated the male character of films for far too many years, toward a more complex type capable of realistic, human interactions with the new actresses.

Our chart of the male firmament reveals some striking if unsurprising dissimilarities with the Actress map. The number of stars with real box-office clout is greater in size by a factor of ten or more. In fact, it's necessary to divide it into subcategories. The macho hero still reigns supreme, from the mindless archetypes of Bronson, Eastwood, and Laughlin to the more thoughtful if still primarily tough and brawny personas like those created by Robert Shaw, Gene Hackman, and Kris Kristofferson. There are even real actors in this bunch, people who could if called upon play less stereotyped roles—Hackman, Scott, and Fonda, for example.

While the machos sell tickets, the new category of actor/star has received most of the attention during the seventies. First Hoffman, Redford, and Nicholson, then Pacino, De Niro, and Dreyfuss have played a series of characters each of which has, to be sure, included a fair number of macho roles, but each of which also covers a wider variety of types. The fact that such obviously introverted personalities as Hoffman, Pacino, and De Niro have achieved real stardom is remarkable in itself and suggests movement away from the lonely tough-guy stereotype established by John Wayne, Clark Gable, Humphrey Bogart, and a corralful of Western stars (as well as the fifties Brando), and toward the more thoughtful, human, and sensitive archetype prefigured by Jimmy Stewart, Spencer Tracy, Bing Crosby, and later Gregory Peck, Brando of the sixties, and Jack Lemmon.

It seemed in the sixties, with the advent of Lemmon and Paul Newman, that this new hero had superseded the macho loner, but Bronson, Eastwood, and friends represent a retrogression in kind as well as degree. They are notably colder and shallower than their predecessors Wayne, Bogart, and the generation of the thirties and forties.

Interestingly, too, the tradition of the romantic, good-looking hero with sensitivity, culture, and style seems to have died out. For a while, it looked as if Redford would continue it; he may still be a heart throb (with Newman before him, Kristofferson after), but neither he nor any other working actor could play the Fred Astaire or Cary Grant roles if they were being written today. As it happens, they aren't. Grant retired more than 15 years ago, and with him went the sort of sophisticated comedy at which he excelled. Perhaps Chevy Chase might be able to revive it, if allowed to develop beyond the pratfall.

There are at least as many "white dwarfs" among the men, but far fewer "black holes" and "losses." Male actors don't retire into grotesque parodies of the sex, because on the whole their sex is taken far more seriously. And any talented actor who gets a start in movies generally continues in the career; men have a far greater diversity as well as a greater whole number of roles to play. The category of kook doesn't really apply to male roles (although it's possible to think of at least one minor actor—Michael J. Pollard—who fits it), and the categories of the waif and the girl of course have no male equivalents. There are at present no male immigrants trying to establish a foothold in American film (except for dancers Nureyev and Baryshnikov), although as with the women there are a number of English actors who work here all or part of the time. European actors like Belmondo, Von Sydow, Delon, and Mastroianni don't have to work here for the simple reason that they've as much box-office power in their own national cinemas as our macho heroes do here. Giancarlo Giannini or Horst Buchholz may take the occasional role in a coproduction, but that's simply a result of the increasing internationalization of the film industry.

There is a small list of "underachievers," but it is arguable with each of

Lone kook: Fuzzy Michael J. Pollard hawks the rising underground *Back Bay Mainline* in Joan Micklin Silver's *Between the Lines*.

American Actors: 1978.

ELDER STATESMEN (Red Giants)

Henry Fonda
Melvyn Douglas
Kirk Douglas
John Wayne
Richard Widmark
Charlton Heston
Gregory Peck
Burt Lancaster
Marlon Brando
George Burns
Jack Lemmon
James Stewart
Yul Brynner
Lawrence Olivier
Robert Mitchum
Richard Burton
Stirling Hayden
William Holden

NOVAS

Sylvester Stallone
Richard Pryor
Nick Nolte
Richard Gere
Henry Winkler
Chevy Chase
John Travolta

FUTURES (Rising)

Ron Howard
Yaphet Kotto
Michael Moriarty
Chris Sarandon
Martin Sheen
William Atherton
Michael Douglas
Robbie Benson
John Belushi
Robert Daqui
John Considine
John Heard
Bernie Casey
William Katt
Michael Sacks
Jon Voight
Harvey Keitel
Sam Waterston
Billy Dee Williams
Robert Carradine
Paul Dooley
Richard Thomas
Alan Alda
Gary Busey
Kevin Conway
O.J. Simpson

UNDERACHIEVERS

Elliott Gould
Ron O'Neal
Robert Forster
Frank Langella
Joe Campanella
Rob Reiner
Robert Culp
Dennis Hopper
James Coburn
Jerry Orbach
Larry Hagman
Peter Fonda
Sid Caesar
Richard Mulligan
Robert Vaughn

CHARACTERS & CRAFTSMEN

Warren Oates
Rene Auberjonois
Rip Torn
Charles Cioffi
Michael V. Gazzo
Jeff Goldblum
Charles Durning
Randy Quaid
Ned Beatty
Bruce Davide
Allen Garfield (Goorwitz)
Harry Dean Stanton
Carmine Caridi
Peter Boyle
James Earl Jones
Ned Beatty
Alan Ark

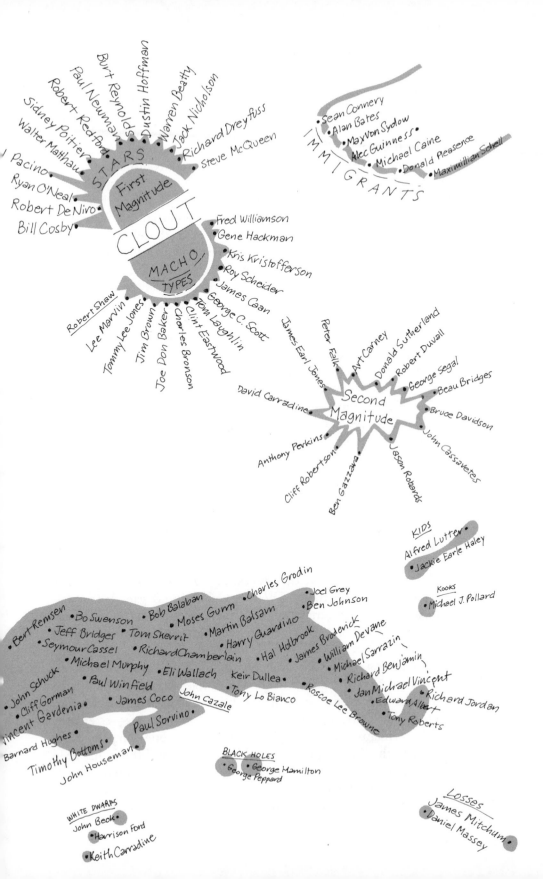

them that they have in fact realized their full potential, and if they haven't, the fault lies probably in themselves rather than in the star system. This is not true of the corresponding women's category.

As with the women, there is a large reservoir of general acting talent among the men, but here it is clearer that there is a continuum between stardom and the levels beneath. In addition to the twenty or more first-magnitude stars whose name on a contract is assurance that a film will be made, there are another dozen or so second-magnitude male stars, any one of whom can carry a film if the rest of the elements in the package are right. Another difference between men and women in this category is that the separation between "craftsmen of the second lead" (who tend to play sidekicks) and "character actors" (who take minor parts) is much more precise. The reason is that there is seldom a woman's part at the level of second lead, so actresses like Shirley Knight, Jane Alexander, or Verna Bloom, who could fill those rules admirably if they existed, are instead relegated to character parts, with the occasional female "lead" (always subsidiary to the male lead) in what passes for at least superficially heterosexual romances these days.

Many of the most interesting actors working today fit into this second-magnitude category: Sutherland, Duvall, and Carradine represent the role actors of the group. Beau Bridges, Ben Gazzara, and the irrepressible George Segal are good examples of the persona actors. As in the first-magnitude category, no inferences should be drawn regarding the separation of role actors from persona actors. Role acting—the ability to submerge personality beneath character—may be more admired by the critics, but film is still very much a matter of personas—transcendent images of personality created over a long series of particular roles. Among the first-magnitude stars, Newman, Poitier, Beatty, and especially Reynolds and Cosby are in the process of creating personas that may come close to matching those of Wayne, Gable, and Bogart. It's not fair to compare the earlier generation with the later yet. The actors of the seventies generation have just begun the lifelong work of developing personas.

It is interesting to see that a number of the actors listed as characters and craftsmen have specialized in the sort of roles that would have been played in the thirties and forties by, say, James Cagney, Fred MacMurray, or even Elisha Cook, Jr. These characters were—and are—essentially weak, often villains, always complex (if not always subtle). In part, this is a response to the rise of the antihero. More important, I think, has been the development of a political relationship of the sort Hitchcock has been studying for fifty years: a situation in which the response of the macho heroes of the twenties and thirties no longer seems justified. Just

The 1974 independent production *The Lords of Flatbush* not only heralded the arrival of the fifties esthetic, but also starred two of the three actors who were to benefit most from hood camp, Sylvester "Rocky" Stallone and Henry "Fonz" Winkler enjoy egg creams and lemon cokes with pals. (Vinnie Barberino was probably lurking in the next booth.)

because that response is no longer logical, the macho correlatives of the sixties and seventies—Bronson, Eastwood, Laughlin—were obvious exaggerations of the earlier models. They are no longer realistic, or even believeable; they are rather hysterical overreactions to the politics of paranoia. Perhaps the most sophisticated of these characters has been Gene Hackman's Harry Caul in Coppola's *The Conversation*. Hackman has always been exceptionally good at indicating the contradictions inherent in the contemporary macho role.

The macho response no longer suffices, so we have developed a cadre of actors whose personas are introverted, tense, anxious, and notably capable of failure: Keir Dullea, Bruce Davidson, Richard Chamberlain, Anthony Perkins, and William Devane are good examples. So are the slightly soiled personas of Warren Oates, John Cazale, Charles Cioffi, Rip Torn, and Peter Boyle. Pacino, Redford, and De Niro have played roles like these, but on the whole they, like all the first magnitude stars, are able to broadcast a sense of anger and inviolable selfhood at the same time that they play the repressed, haunted modern antihero.

By now, the antihero has become something of a cliché. Sylvester Stallone has built what is potentially a star's career purely from the reaction against that stereotype. Stallone is placed in the "nova" category—actors about to move up to full stardom—along with the remark-

Sex and age: Despite the dominance of buddy-adventure films in the seventies, men and women still had a few chances to get to know each other. Here are six representative pairs ranging in age from twenty to perhaps past fifty. John Heard and Lindsay Crouse in bed in *Between the Lines* deal with an ambiguous relationship of the sort most younger people understand. Richard Gere puts the make on Diane Keaton in *Looking for Mr. Goodbar*, a distorted view of people in their twenties by Richard Brooks, a director two generations removed from them. Genevieve Bujold gets bailed out by Jack Lemmon in John Korty's *Alex and the Gypsy*. These people are clearly approaching middle age, yet they're the subject of a romance, as are 41-year-old Jane Fonda and 40-year-old James Caan in Alan Pakula's neowestern *Comes a Horseman*. Elaine May and Walter Matthau made an effective comedy team of the sort we haven't seen since the thirties in *A New Leaf,* a film that also had something serious to say about love between unpretty people. Finally, Audrey Hepburn and Sean Connery share memories in Richard Lester's indian-summer ode *Robin and Marian.* Not since Tracy and Katharine Hepburn in the fifties have people this "old" been permitted a pleasant screen romance.

able Richard Pryor. (Robert Shaw led this group before his untimely death.) Of the group, Pryor is undoubtedly the most interesting. Stallone's reaction to the antihero stereotype is itself stereotypical, but Pryor's is witty, ironic, sensible, and ultimately more effective. With *Greased Lightning* and *Blue Collar*, he has begun moving away from stand-up comedy toward a really new type of hero for the eighties. Cosby could have done this if he hadn't essentially abandoned films for children's television. Henry Winkler and John Travolta, two decent actors successfully trying to parlay television careers into film stardom, are on the same track.

Among "futures"—those actors with exceptional potential—there are a number of Anthony Perkins types: Michael Moriarty, Martin Sheen, Jon Voight, Harvey Keitel. There are also a number of machos: Richard Gere, Nick Nolte, Michael Sarandon. But for the most part, the group reveals some interesting raw material for the new hero. Yaphet Kotto, William Atherton, Michael Douglas, Billy Dee Williams, John Considine, Michael Sacks, Robert Doqui, Christopher Walken, and especially Bernie Casey loom as potential new heroes. The archetype would combine elements of common sense, strength, irony, sensitivity, humor, and anger in equal parts. But before actors can play these roles, screenwriters must write them, producers must be convinced that they will sell. Don't hold your breath.

Screenwriters: If the media reports are to be believed, the seventies were kind years for screenwriters. Kids out of film school got a quarter of a million for their first and second scripts, and climbing from there. There may be some truth to this magazine-article version of reality, and it would be nice to report a new renaissance of screenwriting talent, but such sadly is not the case. No doubt, there are now a number of very sharp and sensitive young people plying the trade in Hollywood. No doubt, a goodly number are getting rich in the process. But the map of the screenwriters reveals very little in terms of really interesting contributions. No more than a dozen of the new generation (and some not so young at that) have been able to establish their own precise personalities as authors. Most begin auspiciously, then settle into a comfortable hack's life of adaptations, rewrites, and polishes. Lorenzo Semple, Jr., for example, made an auspicious debut with *Pretty Poison* in 1969, followed it up with the not uninteresting *Marriage of a Young Stockbroker* in 1971, then hit the bigtime: *Papillon*, *Parallax View*, and *King Kong*. His career is exemplary. Any number of "craftspeople" on the chart have enjoyed similar financial success—and a correlative artistic downward spiral. Ernest Tidyman can be counted on for a well-paced cop movie (*French*

American Screenwriters: 1978.

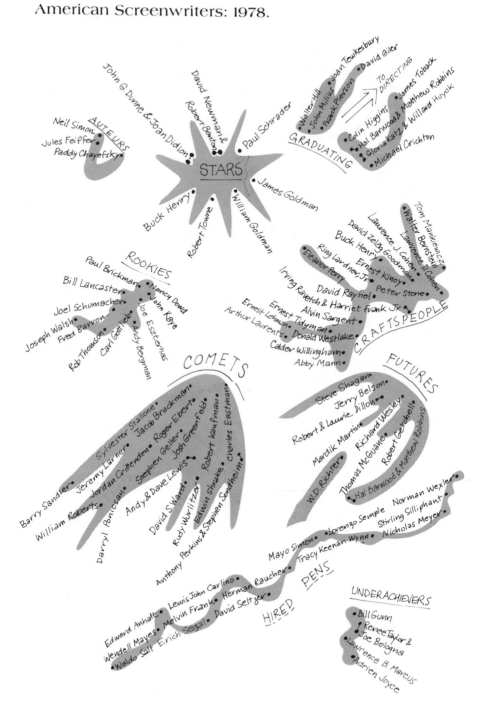

Connection, Shaft, Report to the Commissioner); Buck Henry is notoriously witty, although more so in his television appearances than in his scripts (*Catch-22, Day of the Dolphin*); David Zelag Goodman has what used to be called "taste" and a better than average sense of character (*Lovers and Other Strangers, Farewell My Lovely*) but is not beneath an occasional *Logan's Run*. Walter Bernstein has something to say, although it usually gets muddled (*Molly Maguires, The Front, Semi-Tough*). Arthur Laurents (*The Way We Were, The Turning Point*) has a nice sense of the problems of middle age. Ernest Lehman must be remembered for *North by Northwest* and *Family Plot*, if not for his direction of *Portnoy's Complaint*. Irving Ravetch and Harriet Frank, Jr., have certainly established an identifiable authorial personality with *The Reivers* and *Conrack*. And David Rayfiel is dependably unconventional (*Three Days of the Condor, Lipstick*). Equally arbitrary capsule evaluations could be made of the careers of any of the other hardworking screenwriters listed here.

So what? None of these well-known names has produced a body of work that demands critical attention. Split between adaptations and co-authorships, harried by revisionist producers and lackluster directors, they soon lose interest in the final product and are content to collect their very ample paychecks. Ironically, the old assembly-line Hollywood seems to have produced more interesting screenwriters than the current freelance market. More than any of the other craft contributors to the process, screenwriters seem to have suffered sometimes irreparable damage from the action plot which currently tyrannizes American movies.

Of the "hired pens," Edward Anhalt and Lewis John Carlino are notable for being facile, Peter Hyams and Wendell Mayes for their emptyheadedness, Herman Raucher and Erich Segal for dopey romanticism, and Waldo Salt and Norman Wexler for their insipid plotting and contempt for their characters. Tracy Keenan Wynn had a good start—*Autobiography of Miss Jane Pittman*. He now has a finger in many pies, most recently *The Deep*, a steep enough descent to cause the bends.

A number of the more intriguing contemporary screenwriters are in the process of graduating to direction. One hopes they will all have more success than Lehman and Carlino before them. In a few cases—Paul Schrader, Colin Higgins—this metamorphosis was calculated: screenwriting was only a means to an end. For most, however, it happened gradually. Walter Hill specialized in action with a recognizable sardonic twist (*The Getaway, The Thief Who Came to Dinner, The Drowning Pool*). His first effort as director was *Hard Times*, a classic Bronson vehicle raised above the ordinary by Hill's assured control and barely perceptible sense of humor. *The Driver* (1978) was an homage to French director Jean-Pierre Melville. John Milius, the leading champion of the new macho in

Hollywood, wrote such films as *Judge Roy Bean*, *Magnum Force*, *Jeremiah Johnson*, and *Apocalypse Now*. He has directed *Dillinger*, the silly but undeniably exuberant *Wind and the Lion*, and the pretentious surfing elegy, *Big Wednesday*. Milius is likely to fall into the Bogdanovich recycling mold.

Joan Tewkesbury has done fresh and powerful work for Robert Altman (*Thieves Like Us*, *Nashville*). She hasn't had any success so far as a director. On the evidence of *Blue Collar*, Paul Schrader is a more generous and assured director than he is a screenwriter. (More about the leading star of the screenwriter's guild in Chapter 5.) Frank Pierson rates attention for *The Anderson Tapes* and *Dog Day Afternoon*, both written for Sidney Lumet. His widely spaced attempts at direction, *The Looking Glass War* and *A Star Is Born*, were less successful if still promising. Colin Higgins (the most calculating of the bunch), David Giler, and James Toback are still relatively unknown quantities. Certainly Toback's script for *The Gambler* was not quite so portentous as Karel Reisz made it seem. Higgins's *Foul Play* ought to have been better than it was, considering the raw material—Goldie Hawn and Chevy Chase—Higgins had to work with.

There are a number of "comets" on this astronomical chart, writers who had some success with one or two scripts and then seemed to disappear. One hopes for further work from Josh Greenfeld (*Harry and Tonto*), Jeremy Larner (*Drive He Said*, *The Candidate*), William Roberts (*The Last American Hero*), Edwin Shrake (*Kid Blue*), and Darryl Ponicsan, whose service comedies *Cinderella Liberty* and *The Last Detail* (he wrote the novel, Robert Towne the script) breathed new life into the old genre. I myself would like to see Tony Perkins and Stephen Sondheim collaborate once again. Their British crossword puzzle of a movie, *The Last of Sheila*, is a uniquely tricky linguistic thriller.

Of all the comets listed here, Andy and Dave Lewis, authors of *Klute*, are undoubtedly the biggest loss. *Klute* remains one of the more important films of the seventies, and it is as fresh today as it was in 1971, so why haven't the Lewises been able to repeat?

David S. Ward, putative author of *The Sting*, is probably the richest of these one-time wonders, which is one reason he hasn't written since. Another may be the plagiarism suit that was instituted against Ward, the producers, and the distributor shortly after the film became a success. (It was later settled out of court.)

Of the screenwriting stars listed here, all have easily identifiable authorial personalities. The playwrights Jules Feiffer, Neil Simon, and Paddy Chayefsky all clearly control the films that are shot from their scripts, and writers like Joan Didion and John Gregory Dunne, David

Newman and Robert Benton have established literary personas outside of screenwriting. Former magazine writers Newman and Benton are god-fathers to the new corps of scribes. Their *Bonnie and Clyde* opened doors to new talent beginning in 1967. Buck Henry's adaptation the next year of *The Graduate* made it clear that the preceding generation of Hollywood writers was about to be replaced (but whatever happened to George Axelrod and Terry Southern after the sixties?). Newman and Benton have worked on such films as *What's Up, Doc?* and *Superman* during the seventies, while trying to establish separate careers as directors. Benton, with *Bad Company, The Late Show*, and *Kramer vs. Kramer*, has been more successful than Newman, whose unusual European-American hybrid, *The Crazy American Girl*, shot in 1975, is still unreleased.

Dunne and Didion have scripted *Panic in Needle Park, Play It as It Lays* (from Didion's novel), and *A Star Is Born* while maintaining careers as leading novelists. Perhaps the screenwriters with the most clout in Hollywood today are the middle-aged Goldman brothers, James and William. A generation older than most of the new breed, they both command respect because they are successful popular novelists as well as screenwriters. James has specialized in historical romances (*Lion in Winter, Nicholas and Alexandra, Robin and Marian*). William, the more prolific of the two, has been responsible for a variety of contemporary adventure/action movies from *Masquerade* (1965) and *Harper* (1966) to *Butch Cassidy and the Sundance Kid, The Hot Rock, The Great Waldo Pepper, Marathon Man*, and *A Bridge Too Far*. There's no question of Goldman's facility; in constructing an interesting yarn and providing a modicum of witty dialogue he's the Hollywood craftsman par excellence. But in only one film so far, *All the President's Men*, has he achieved any depth. (There are rumors that others made significant contributions to that script.) Generally, Goldman is best at generating a superficial buzz of interest. Yet it works.

If Goldman is the ultimate tale spinner, Robert Towne has the reputation of being Hollywood's most popular script doctor. His own films are relatively few, although they are important: *The Last Detail, Chinatown, Shampoo* (with Warren Beatty), and *The Yakuza* (with Paul Schrader). He has had a hand, however, in numerous recent scripts, usually uncredited. Like a number of contemporary filmmakers, he began with Roger Corman in the sixties. He certainly has built a substantial reputation on a relatively small number of credits.

For a while it looked as if Gloria Katz and Willard Huyck were going to join the seventies pantheon. *American Graffiti* is certainly one of the major films of the period in every sense. But *Lucky Lady* was a very expensive failure, with dismal casting and heavy-handed direction.

As we move to the categories of "rookies" and "futures," the scene begins to brighten considerably. It may yet turn out that these relatively new talents will peter out as they move into their careers, but their beginnings are certainly auspicious. Each of the writers listed as a "rookie" has brought a markedly fresh sensibility to debut scripts. The question is whether they can continue to fight the stereotypical patterns that constrict so much of Hollywood cinema. Paul Brickman's *Citizen's Band (Handle with Care)* evinced a rare sense of community and underlying politics. It was a human and humane comedy reminiscent of Frank Capra. Nancy Dowd's *Slapshot* had a manic intensity and furious sense of character and language that belies its classic construction. Dowd seems to have a rare sense of how people react in real situations, and she knows something about women and men, too. (Dowd is also credited with the original story for *Coming Home*, but rejects the film that was made from it.) John Kaye's *Rafferty and the Gold Dust Twins* was low-keyed and relied a bit too much on kooky characters, but it remains one of the most interesting road films of the seventies. Bill Lancaster's *Bad News Bears* was also a bit cute, but the construction was lithe, and the attitude sufficiently balanced. Joel Schumacher's *Carwash* was a very simple film, verging on exploitation, but it worked well enough. Judged against genre standards it had some of the same sense of community that marked *Citizen's Band*.

Rob Thompson's *Hearts of the West* was amusingly shaggy; Joseph Walsh's *California Split* revealed a fine balance betweeen character and structure. Andrew Bergman was responsible for the story of *Blazing Saddles*, a film whose script reads better than it finally played under Mel Brooks's direction (and without the aid of Richard Pryor, who was originally scheduled to play the lead). Caught in a bind that must be common for young screenwriters, Bergman has sold several more scripts and is patiently waiting for the films to be shot. Meanwhile, he has turned his hand to forties-style detective fiction.

In the "futures" category, Steve Shagan stands out as having achieved an identifiable authorial persona very quickly. *Save the Tiger* and *Hustle* gave us a vaguely liberal critique of Southern California lifestyles. Jerry Belson brings a television comedy writer's sensibility to feature films. *Smile* and *Fun with Dick and Jane* developed a comic attitude perhaps best characterized as slapstick/sketch/satire. Hal Barwood and Matthew Robbins have written two films that share a rather fresh vision, *Sugarland Express* and *The Bingo Long Traveling All-Stars and Motor Kings,* and one of the better historical sagas of recent years, *MacArthur.* Barwood produced and Robbins directed *Corvette Summer* (1978), which didn't do much to advance their reputations. Robert Getchell, W. D. Richter, and Mardik Martin gained some attention with *Alice Doesn't Live Here Anymore* and *Bound for Glory; Slither* and *Nickelodeon;* and *Mean Streets* and *New York, New York;* respectively. But all those films were markedly uneven; the jury is still out.

Robert Dillon and Thomas McGuane have exhibited perhaps the most unique—and writerly—sensibilities of the new generation. McGuane is well known as a novelist, and the films he has written—*Rancho Deluxe, 92 In the Shade* (which he also directed), and *Missouri Breaks*—are if anything too literarily mannered. As a colleague put it, he writes dialogue that's *too* good. The films are richly overblown, but McGuane may learn to tone them down. Dillon, for his part, has three unusual scripts to his credit—*Prime Cut* (which Michael Ritchie directed with just the right appreciation of Dillon's dark, unique humor), *99 44/100% Dead* (which John Frankenheimer mercilessly massacred), and *French Connection II,* a more conservative assignment lacking the humor of the earlier films, which Frankenheimer brought off successfully. Dillon may have to turn director to get his black satires filmed right.

Finally, playwright Richard Wesley has constructed some well-paced genre films (*Uptown Saturday Night*) and is capable of more, and under-achievers Bill Gunn (*The Landlord*), Joseph Bologna and Renee Taylor (*Lovers and Other Strangers, Made for Each Other*), Lawrence B. Marcus (the excellent *Petulia* and *Alex and the Gypsy*), and Adrien Joyce (*Five Easy Pieces, The Fortune*) deserve to work far more often than they do. Two of them, Gunn and Joyce (whose real name is Carol Eastman— Charles is her brother), have tried to direct; Bologna and Taylor, whose ethnic comedies are unique for their good sense, have apparently turned to television (*Woman of the Year*), and Marcus waits patiently for another director of the caliber of Richard Lester.

These capsule comments can only begin to indicate the shape of the best work being done by contemporary screenwriters. A few of the "stars" and "craftspeople" on the map, and all of the "underachievers," "rookies," and "futures" should really be accorded equal responsibility and billing with the directors of their films. But, despite the decline of the auteur policy, we still have no way to be sure that a screenwriter's script hasn't been distorted, modified, or otherwise significantly altered by the nominal director, who is, after all, still the person most likely to exert control over the content and style of the film. Eventually, the ideal of partnership may be recognized; for the present, screenwriters, despite their increasing visibility, must depend on directors. More often than you would think their faith is misplaced.

Directors: Most of the more interesting directors on this copious map receive comment in later chapters. For now, a few generalizations will suffice.

"Losers," first. These are people who have made one or two interesting films, then disappeared. A significant number of them worked out of New York, and that's one reason for their truncated careers. Only Frank and Eleanor Perry (in the sixties) and Sidney Lumet have had any ongoing success with the New York film, which is surprising at a time when other, lesser regional cinemas are flourishing.

"The fringe" includes a melange of styles from porn (softcore) to the Corman factory to the relatively precious, although occasionally attractive, films of independents like Susan Sontag and James Ivory. We verge here on the vast area of documentary film. Considered as a medium rather than as entertainment product, film is as far-reaching as print. Documentary and news film in the seventies is a subject large enough to demand a book of its own. (In chapter 8 I will only try to sketch out some of the relationships between documentary and fiction film.)

At the center of the map are the "leaders," those directors who have consistently produced the most interesting work, if not the most popular, and who have substantial track records. The choices are not so arbitrary as they might seem. Diane Jacobs in her sensible book *Hollywood Renaissance*[2] covers four of the five, leaving out Michael Ritchie (whom she has written about at length elsewhere) but including Martin Scorsese. A critical consensus would probably produce a similar list, possibly including a number of the directors I have listed in the "Whiz Kids" inner circle. The difference between the leaders and the Whiz Kids is simply that the first category seems more interested in what to *do* with the medium of film, while the second, a generation of cinematic techno-twirps if you will, is generally more interested in the medium than the uses to which it can be put. The two groups are closely interrelated—Scorsese could easily shift back into the leaders category, and there's a chance for Spielberg and Lucas, too; they are young. Still, I think the distinction is an important one.

Surrounding the "hot center" of leaders and whizzes are ever-widening circles of decreasing competence and interest. There are easily more than a dozen directors whose work demands close attention but who haven't made enough films to be spoken about in the same terms as the leaders. Call them "worth a detour." Closely associated with this group (together they offer real cause for hope for the future) are the "rookies with a future." Then there are the "underachievers"—mostly the BBS group— all of whom showed some promise in the early seventies but seem to have faded rapidly.

Certainly the most significant sociopolitical phenomenon of American film in the seventies has been the advent of the Black film. While a number of the directors in this category are increasingly crossing over into the nonracial market, it is still a disparate group, separate from the mainstream.

Women, by the way, are not listed separately here simply because they are united by nothing except their sex. They have been most successful in the documentary field, which is more fluid and open to new talent in general. Claudia Weill, Martha Coolidge, Barbara Kopple, Nell Cox, Julia Reichert, and Amalie Rothschild have done much of the most interesting work in documentary in the seventies. They are accompanied by scores of talented women documentarists not listed here. In feature films, however, only six women have been able to breech the sex barrier, so far, although another half dozen are close behind them. Stephanie Rothman makes exploitation films. Joan Darling (*First Love*) had her first success in television (*Mary Hartman, Mary Hartman*). Elaine May came out of cabaret and has more or less continued in that tradition. Renee Taylor with her husband Joseph Bologna has written some of the wiser ethnic films of the seventies and directed one. Joan Micklin Silver, an independent working out of New York, has probably attracted more attention than any of her colleagues, save May. Claudia Weill is the most recent addition to the club. Her first feature, *Girl Friends*, proved that independently financed films were still possible. Jane Wagner (*Moment to Moment*) and Joan Tewkesbury (*Old Boyfriends*) released their first features in 1979.

A couple of actresses have tried directing. Barbara Loden's *Wanda* (1971) garnered a lot of attention, but she hasn't followed it up. Jane Fonda and Shirley MacLaine have both been involved in documentaries with other filmmaker colleagues. While we're on the subject, it would be good to see Ida Lupino, godmother of them all, back behind a camera again.

Women have had just as little success as screenwriters in the seventies, despite the fact that this craft was always relatively open to women in the past. Only a handful of women appear on the screenwriting map: Carol Eastman thought it wise to write under the pseudonym Adrien Joyce; Joan Tewkesbury had valuable help from Robert Altman, who works outside the system. When Nancy Dowd wrote a script about some hockey players who talk dirty, the media were surprised—almost shocked: Where did a nice girl like Nancy *learn* such words? Aside from the evident absurdity of such a response in the late seventies, it was like praising a Black writer's grammatical use of the language! Jay Presson Allen still contributes an occasional romance. Aside from the infrequent contribu-

American Directors: 1978.

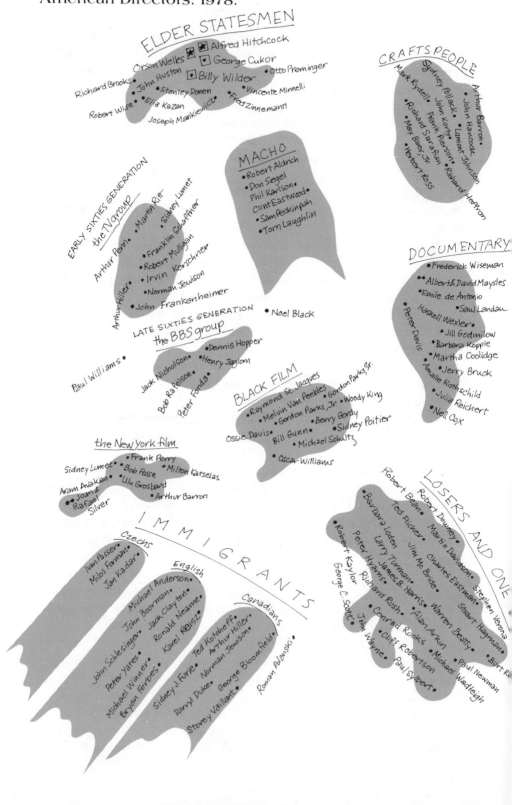

ANIMATION
• Ralph Bakshi

EXILES

Joseph Strick
Stanley Kubrick
Joseph Losey
Richard Lester
John Berry
Jules Dassin

WORTH A DETOUR

Rafael Silver
Joan Micklin Silver
Monte Hellman
Joseph Hellman
Jonathan Demme
Terrence Malick
Phillip Kaufman
Robert Benton
Elaine May
Mike Nichols
Howard Zieff
George Roy Hill
Alan Pakula
John Avildsen
Hal Ashby

COMIC ESTABLISHMENT

Mel Brooks
Gene Wilder
Woody Allen
Carl Reiner
Bud Yorkin
Marty Feldman
Blake Edwards

LEADERS

Robert Altman
John Cassavetes
Francis Ford Coppola
Michael Ritchie
Paul Mazursky

HIRED GUNS

Gene Saks
Jack Smight
John Sturges
James Goldstone
Richard Fleischer
Stanley Kramer
Rosenberg
John Guillermin
Frank
Larry Peerce
Peter Hyams
Robert Moore
Ted Post

WHIZ KIDS

Martin Scorsese
Steven Spielberg
Paul Schrader
Brian de Palma
William Friedkin
George Lucas
Peter Bogdanovich

QUESTION MARKS

Walter Hill
Thomas McGuane
Anthony Lover
James Frawley
Michael Campus
David Newman
Frank D. Gilroy
John Milius
David Giler
Alan Rudolph
Hal Needham
Susan Sontag
James Ivory

RISING
(ROOKIES WITH A FUTURE)

Joan Darling
Floyd Mutrux
Walter Hill
Alan Rudolph
Claudia Weill
Jane Wagner
Robert Zemeckis
Renee Taylor & Joseph Bologna
Steve Rash
Jim Bridges
John Badham
Joan Tewkesbury
Michael Pressman
Jonathan Kaplan
Randal Kleiser
Michael Crichton
John Byrum

THE INDEPENDENT FRINGE

Andy Warhol &
Paul Morrissey
Joe Dante
Stephanie Rothman
George Romero
Robert Kramer

ROCK
Frank Zappa

(B's) • Roger Corman
Paul Bartel

tions of novelists like Penelope Gilliatt, Lois Gould, and Anne Richardson Roiphe, these four are very lonely. The only other women who write commercial features work with their husbands in teams: Gloria Katz (with Willard Huyck), Joan Didion (with John Gregory Dunne), Harriet Frank, Jr. (with Irving Ravetch), Laurie Dillon (with Robert Dillon), and Leslie Newman (with David Newman). Eleanor Perry has had even less success than her husband Frank since their divorce.

Statistically, it is safe to conclude that women directors are no more numerous now than they ever were in American commercial film and that the number of women screenwriters has actually shrunk since the thirties. The new feminist wave ever recedes into the dim future.

Next comes the sixties generation, underachievers all, and centered around two production groups: BBS and Pressman-Williams. In the very early seventies Bert Schneider (BBS) and Edward R. Pressman looked as if they were about to remold at least a part of the Hollywood production process. But the stars of BBS and Pressman's directorial partner Paul Williams faded quickly, like the youth generation to which they were too closely tied. Dennis Hopper and Henry Jaglom are no losses. Bob Rafelson's most recent film, *Stay Hungry*, was of a piece with his earlier work—and revealed a consistent inadequacy: there's a kind of literary, forced quality to the BBS output, from *Five Easy Pieces* through Jaglom's *A Safe Place* to Hopper's *The Last Movie*. It no longer works, if it ever did. Jack Nicholson's *Drive, He Said* (from Jeremy Larner's novel) shares this quality, but it's more easygoing and less self-important and so survives better. *Going South,* his most recent film, is assured and stylish.

Paul Williams is the biggest loss. *Out of It* (1970), *The Revolutionary* (1970), and *Dealing* (1972) were indubitably youth films, but they revealed at least a modicum of critical intelligence.[3] Williams recently returned to work with *Nunzio*, a small film that disappeared quickly.

Interest drops off rapidly in the third circle. Among the craftsmen (there are no craftswomen) the generation of the sixties is perhaps more interesting than the generation of the seventies. Only two or three of the immigrants are worth discussion in an American context. Ivan Passer, the most interesting of the directors of the Czech Renaissance, has still to find the right key in his American films (*Born to Win, Law and Disorder*). Milos Forman has found it, but despite his box-office success with *One Flew Over the Cuckoo's Nest,* he hasn't matched the temper of his Czech films. The British contributions to American film range from Ronald Neame's hackwork (*Poseidon Adventure, Meteor*) to Karel Reisz's well-made *The Gambler* and *Who'll Stop the Rain* and John Schlesinger's *Marathon Man.* Peter Yates has turned out an entertaining movie or two (*Bullitt, The Hot Rock, The Friends of Eddie Coyle*), but most British

Visually, just about the only way to indicate what people who work behind the camera do is to show them pointing. Here, Alan Pakula directs his actors on the set of *All the President's Men*. (They are preparing for the shot in which the camera tracks up into the dome of the Library of Congress.)

directors in the States seem to develop pretensions: see Jack Clayton's *The Great Gatsby* or John Boorman's *Deliverance*.

Canadians have fared little better off native soil. Sidney J. Furie is responsible for the execrable *Sheila Levine Is Dead and Living in New York*. Arthur Hiller and Norman Jewison bumble along just keeping their heads above water; their reputations are inflated. Darryl Duke, George Bloomfield, and Eric Till haven't had much of a chance. Only Ted Kotcheff, from Canada by way of Britain, seems to have developed a viable style: it's febrile and testy, but it seems to work for such films as *The Apprenticeship of Duddy Kravitz* and *Fun with Dick and Jane*. It is certainly more attractive than the middlebrow pretensions of Hiller and Jewison.

Beyond this level we are deep in hackland. Only the more notable are listed here; each has a specialty; none is of interest.

Then there are the satellite systems. A number of American filmmakers have been able to stretch out careers through their fifties, even into their sixties and seventies. This is remarkable in itself in an industry that prizes youth. Even successful directors are usually in precipitous decline by their sixtieth birthdays. But Alfred Hitchcock is now approaching eighty; his career has spanned five decades; and if his films are perhaps a little too highly contrived these days, never mind. He is living history. George Cukor is just as old, and still producing. Fred Zinnemann, Orson Welles, and the other directors in the "elder statesman" column have also managed to maintain their careers.

Slightly younger is the macho generation that came of age in the fifties, ruled by the triumvirate of Siegel, Peckinpah, and Aldrich. Each of them is still capable of interesting work (*The Shootist, Junior Bonner,* and *Hustle,* respectively), but all seem to me to be clearly over the hill.

"Exiles" form another satellite. Losey, Lester, and Kubrick have been working in England for twenty years and more. Their films are no longer American, although they reveal their roots once in a while. They are certainly leading world filmmakers, but they no longer fit the American context. Losey's work is labored when he isn't associated with Harold Pinter. Kubrick is probably the most studied American-born filmmaker since Orson Welles. Richard Lester is in strong contention for the title of world's most underrated director. His one U.S. film, *Petulia,* is one of the three best American films of the sixties.

Finally, we have the special world of straight comedy—Mel Brooks and his epigones, Woody Allen, and the TV-trained Yorkin and Reiner (there's less here than meets the eye)—and the lone star of animation, the bitter, visionary Ralph Bakshi. On the whole, Bakshi's films have not been critically popular nor especially remunerative: *Coonskin* ran into criticism from Black organizations. (They were wrong, I think.) *Wizards* was both pretentious and dull. But there is an undeniable energy in Bakshi's work, and he has accomplished the prodigious feat of actually creating a new form: the adult animated feature film, drawing on the tradition of underground "comix" of the sixties. Disney beware. His only competition has come from the French filmmaker René Laloux, whose *Planète Fantastique* was widely seen in 1974. *Yellow Submarine* (1968, animation by Heinz Edelmann) was never followed up.

The Rest of the Crew

Writers, directors, actors, and actresses make evident, analyzable contributions to the complicated art of film. The work of other collaborators—producers, cinematographers, musicians, editors, designers—is much less easily recognized but deserves comment nevertheless. It is technical quality more than anything else which clearly separates contemporary film from earlier periods. The people who design, photograph, cut, and score a picture have new tools at their disposal. Overall, they've made excellent use of them.

Cinematographers: Nowhere is the difference between generations more evident than in cinematography. The "look" of a film counts for a great deal psychologically, and producers in the early seventies were quick to

Paul Schrader points for cinematographer Bobby Byrne. The film is *Blue Collar.*

discover the special talents of the new generation of cinematographers. There are still some older men shooting films more or less regularly— Joseph Biroc (*Hustle, The Longest Yard, Blazing Saddles*) and Robert Surtees (*The Graduate, The Sting, A Star Is Born, The Turning Point*), for example—but on the whole there has been a radical changing of the guard.

Haskell Wexler is the presiding genius of this new generation. He began shooting film in the late fifties in the days of black and white and quickly developed a reputation for what was known in those days as "gritty realism," which led to such assignments as *America, America, The Best Man, The Loved One,* and *Who's Afraid of Virginia Woolf?* When the massive changeover to color came in the late sixties because of the availability of new filmstocks and the increasing importance of sales for eventual broadcast on color television, Wexler was able quickly to translate "black and white realism" into color language (*In the Heat of the Night,* for example). Since directing (and photographing) *Medium Cool* in 1968, he has combined continued work as a documentarist with occasional assignments as cinematographer, often advising uncredited. *American Graffiti, The Conversation,* the almost too scenic *Bound for Glory,* and *Coming Home* are his major films of the seventies. Since he chooses his projects carefully—an advantage most working craftsmen don't have— he's been able to develop a strong persona. A Wexler film has some guts to it, and a cinematic precision which heightens his basically naturalistic style.

Immigrants Laszlo Kovacs and Vilmos Zsigmond were the first of the seventies generation to achieve some degree of celebrity. Kovacs established an early reputation for low-key lighting and relaxed composition with *Easy Rider, Targets,* and *Five Easy Pieces.* His later films (*Alex in Wonderland, Paper Moon, Shampoo*) continued in the realistic vein, while other assignments—notably *Slither, King of Marvin Gardens, New York, New York,* and *At Long Last Love*—were more highly stylized. Kovacs is among the most prolific of the present generation of cinematographers. Zsigmond can shoot realistically, too (*Sugarland Express, Cinderella Liberty*), but seems to prefer exaggerated styles. He experimented with three different approaches with Robert Altman: the flattened realism of *McCabe and Mrs. Miller,* the flashed pastels of *The Long Goodbye,* and the symbolic haze of *Images.* He has also shot mythic dreams like *Scarecrow, Deliverance,* and *Obsession.*

Two other "star" cinematographers with highly prized reputations are Conrad Hall and Gordon Willis. Hall, Wexler's age, hit his stride in the late sixties with *In Cold Blood* and *Butch Cassidy and the Sundance Kid,* proving he could handle a range of styles from downbeat realism to hazy romanticism. Like all cinematographers in the seventies he's essentially a realist: natural light is paramount, composition is fluid. It's the style of the age, not of the cinematographers particularly. They do it because it's required. But within that basic style, there is a range of approaches, and Hall—like Zsigmond and Kovacs—is essentially an expressionist. *Day of the Locust, Smile, Fat City, Marathon Man,* even *The Happy Ending*—each had a particular look to it. Hall's mark was evident.

Gordon Willis, on the other hand, has built a reputation as a highly opinionated photographer, but the style of his films is generally subdued. His greatest success (and cinematographically perhaps the most important film of the decade) was *The Godfather* (both parts), but from the rumors, Coppola may be more responsible for the influentially dark look of that film. Yet *Bad Company, Paper Chase, The Parallax View, All the President's Men,* and *Annie Hall* all share clean, assured, and well-balanced visuals. If nothing else, Willis certainly has excellent taste in projects.

Perhaps William A. Fraker has the most harshly naturalistic sensibility. He seems to choose (or get chosen for) the grittiest and funkiest movies, among them *Aloha Bobby and Rose* and *Looking for Mr. Goodbar,* as well as the live action sequences of *Coonskin.* He's also shot *Day of the Dolphin* and *Rancho Deluxe.*

For consistent achievement in downbeat realism we look, however, to the New York school for obvious reasons: a different city, a different light. Owen Roizman is probably best-known for this approach: *Pelham 1-2-3,*

Haskell Wexler points for Harold Blankenship during the shooting of *Medium Cool*.
Harold can point, too.

Three Days of the Condor, and *The Exorcist*. But he seems to be moving
away with films like *Play It Again Sam* and *Network*. Arthur J. Ornitz is
another accomplished cinematographer from New York: *Minnie and Moskowitz*, *Death Wish*, *Serpico*, and *Next Stop, Greenwich Village*.

Victor J. Kemper is the most prolific and to my mind the most talented
member of this school. A list of his best films fills a major part of the
roster of movies that have been cinematographically interesting during
the last eight years: *Husbands*, *The Candidate*, *The Friends of Eddie Coyle*,
Gordon's War, *Dog Day Afternoon*, *Mikey and Nicky*, and *Slapshot*, among
others. A Kemper film demands attention. It has a visual strength of
purpose undiluted by the gimmickry and manipulation that sometimes
marks even the best work of the Hollywood cameramen. Kemper's
movies are extraordinarily honest.

In this respect, Kemper's closest competitor is Michael Chapman (*The
Last Detail*, *White Dawn*, *The Front*, *Taxi Driver*). Again, there is a sense
that the photography is clean and direct: it brings the people and the
subject matter of the film closer to an audience and gives it a vitality it
might not otherwise have. Kent Wakeford, who like Chapman has
worked with Scorsese (*Mean Streets*, *Alice Doesn't Live Here Anymore*)
also has some of this quality.

Meanwhile, back at the studio backlot ranch, there are a number of
cinematographers moving up fast on celebrities Willis, Hall, Kovacs, and
Zsigmond. Paul Lohmann (*Buffalo Bill and the Indians*, *California Split*,

121

Nashville) and Chuck Rosher, Jr. (*The Late Show, Three Women, Semi-Tough*) have had experience in the Altman corral and carried away with them a sense of his attenuated realism. Lohmann, in a drastic contrast, has also worked closely with Mel Brooks (*Silent Movie, High Anxiety*), whose films are not so much shot as blasted.

The Butler brothers have each done some interesting work: Bill Butler is responsible for *The Conversation, Jaws,* and *Bingo Long*; Michael Butler for *Harry and Tonto, Missouri Breaks,* and *92 in the Shade.* David Butler (*Drive, He Said, The Christian Licorice Store*) is not related. Jordan Cronenweth is worth watching, on the evidence of *Play It As It Lays, Zandy's Bride,* and *Citizen's Band.* John Alonzo deserves mention for *Chinatown, The Fortune,* and *Farewell, My Lovely.*

But the Hollywood cinematographer most likely to join Wexler and Kemper in this idiosyncratic pantheon is Bruce Surtees. Once again, it's not easy to specify this filmmaker's contributions, but Surtees's films, among them *The Great Northfield Minnesota Raid, Lenny, Blume in Love, Night Moves, Leadbelly,* and *The Shootist,* show a range and honesty that are rare, even in this age of consistently effective and creative cinematography.

Finally, we must add to this list Nestor Almendros who has returned to the U.S. after a highly successful ten years in Europe to shoot the most visually astonishing American movie in recent memory—*Days of Heaven* —as well as the less publicized but equally thoughtful *Goin' South.*

Producers: In the hierarchy of the movie industry, producers rank as middle management. They undoubtedly exert greater control over product than anyone else in the Hollywood structure. Their job is to hire cast and crew, keep these workers within the budget, and even occasionally contribute directly to the style and substance of the film.[4]

During the last twenty years, the economic focus of Hollywood has shifted from its old center, production, to its new, distribution and finance. It may look as if producers more than anyone else would gain from the transition. No doubt they have. There is a far greater number of independent production companies operating now than ever before. But what is more remarkable is that producers haven't achieved even greater clout. In the old days, very few producers (David O. Selznick is the chief example) were able to establish industry personalities separate from the factory studios. The moguls—Mayer, Goldwyn, Cohn, Zukor, the Warners, even Thalberg—exerted iron control, and most producers were little more than powerful accountants.

The situation has changed, but not much. The studios may no longer have identifiable styles, but they still exert a pervasive control over the

Steven Spielberg on the set of *Close Encounters* points to the sky. To see the effect of this direction, turn to p. 179.

product flow of Hollywood. None of the current vested minimoguls has the colorful personality of a Harry Cohn or the style of a Thalberg. It might be interesting if we could analyze the particular contributions of men like Ted Ashley, John Calley, Arthur Krim, Mike Medavoy, Dan Melnick, Mike Eisner, Alan Ladd, Jr., Ned Tanen, Barry Diller, David Begelman. It would be interesting but it would be exceedingly difficult. Some of these men have reputations for being nicer guys than others, some are sharper businessmen than most of their colleagues, most project images of intelligence and good taste. But can anyone really tell the difference between an Alan Ladd, Jr., project and a film approved and financed by Dan Melnick?

Production chiefs hold their jobs as long as the movies they choose to finance and/or distribute make money. By contrast, independent producers, now that they operate in a context which is essentially freelance, reveal certain identifying traits despite their subservience to the distribution companies with their interchangeable executives.

The most powerful category among the producers consists of former studio executives: Frank Yablans (formerly of Paramount), Robert Evans (formerly Paramount), and Richard Zanuck and David Brown (Warners). They have clout not so much because of the deference that their successors at the studios show them (although it exists) as for their knowledge of just which pictures make money and how to engineer them. Yablans, who left Paramount under a cloud, has enjoyed the last laugh

123

with the high-grossing properties *Silver Streak* and *The Other Side of Midnight*. Zanuck and Brown, who have a comfortable relationship now with Universal, owe their status to *The Sting* and *Jaws*, and despite their more thoughtful productions of *Sugarland Express* and *MacArthur*. Evans has been the most vocal and public of this group. He desperately wants to project an image of the producer as a creative force (as they say in Hollywood). *Chinatown* worked, but *The Great Gatsby* didn't. *Marathon Man* made some money, but *Black Sunday* didn't live up to expectations. No doubt Evans really does pay close attention to details in his films; it shows. But he is a star producer for other reasons, not the least of which is his colorful private life. (The great real-life Hollywood romantic story of the early seventies wasn't between stars, it was Evans's courtship of Ali McGraw, and the consequent split.)

Add to this extended triumvirate of former studio heads Dino De Laurentiis, who once ran his own shop, Dinocittá, in Italy before emigrating and arrived on these shores with much old-fashioned hoopla. After *Serpico*, *Lipstick*, and *The Shootist*, he went for the prize with his remake of *King Kong*. He hasn't been the subject of many admiring magazine articles since.

Two longtime independent producers who have served as models for the new generation should also be included at this top level: Martin Ransohoff, who founded Filmways, one of the more successful independent companies of the sixties and seventies, obviously has some sense of his own worth. His productions include *Catch-22*, *The White Dawn*, and *Save the Tiger*, all films of some interest, as well as the moneymakers *Silver Streak* and *The Other Side of Midnight*. Joseph E. Levine started importing Italian spectacles in the late fifties. Ten years later, his Embassy Pictures was solvent enough to be sold to the Avco conglomerate, and recently Levine seemed to be trying to redeem his reputation (*The Carpetbaggers*, *Harlow*) with *A Bridge Too Far*. Sam Spiegel, close to eighty and a veteran independent producer, should also be cited in this category. His best years were the late fifties and early sixties—he made the majestic adventure films *Bridge on the River Kwai* and *Lawrence of Arabia*. But he has continued to work into the seventies: *Nicholas and Alexandra*, *The Last Tycoon*.

Then we have the specialists: Ray Stark (Rastar Productions) busies himself with product for the middle-aged market: *Funny Girl*, *The Way We Were*, and the Neil Simon films *Sunshine Boys*, *Murder by Death*, and *The Goodbye Girl*. (*Fat City* was also his.) Stark's main competition in this field comes from Melvin Frank, writer-producer-director: *Buona Sera, Mrs. Campbell*, *A Touch of Class*, *The Prisoner of Second Avenue*, *The Duchess and the Dirtwater Fox*. Irwin Allen is the chief angel of death of

Jerry Schatzberg points out something to Vilmos Zsigmond while shooting *Dandy, The All-American Girl*. Alas, the gesture was in vain. The film was never released.

the disaster-movie plague for his productions of *The Towering Inferno* and *The Poseidon Adventure*. Phil D'Antoni, the most interesting of these specialists, had some success in the early seventies with *Bullitt, The French Connection*, and *The Seven-ups*. Eventually D'Antoni seems to have run out of novel and exciting ways to stage chase sequences, his characteristic signature.

There is also a quite lengthy list of producers closely associated with a single director or star who are also specialists. Norman Lear used to produce his former associate Bud Yorkin's films (*Start the Revolution Without Me, The Thief Who Came to Dinner, Cold Turkey*). Now that he has decided to concentrate on film rather than television, we can expect some interesting projects. Edward Pressman formed a team with Paul Williams. Charles Joffe has been closely associated with Woody Allen (*Annie Hall, The Front, Sleeper, Love and Death*). Robert Daley is Clint Eastwood's resident producer. Gary Kurtz has worked with George Lucas on *American Graffiti* and *Star Wars*. Howard Gottfried works for Paddy Chayevsky (*Hospital, Network*).

Of all the established independents, Roger Corman has certainly been the most influential. It is hard to imagine the shape of the current industry without Corman. He has given starts to such directors as Coppola, Bogdanovich, and Demme, and his name is also linked with the careers of Scorsese (*Boxcar Bertha*), Peter Fonda (*The Wild Angels*), De Niro (*Bloody Mama*), Monte Hellman (*The Cockfighter*), and many others. Corman's B-movie style, established during his years as director for American-International Pictures, has served as a model for hosts of young directors looking for a way into the industry. It is all the more curious that he has chosen to stay with that style, as producer, rather than moving on to films of more general interest like so many of the people he has helped along the way. The Corman film has a leanness (the result of unbelievably limited budgets) and a sense of humor (the function of a necessarily ironic approach to the funkiness of the material) which stand it in good stead. But the camp attitudes it relies on can only go so far. Corman has performed a vital and notable function by proving that films don't have to have seven- or even six-figure budgets to be successful, and his own company, New World Pictures, is one of the more notable challenges to the distribution monopoly the major studios have enjoyed in the seventies. But one still wishes Corman had been able to break free of the camp and hoke that were necessary ingredients in his inexpensive films. Movies don't have to joke about themselves to be reasonably priced.

In the early seventies, there were a number of novel production setups that seemed at the time to offer some small hope for a revision of industry financing practices; none of them has survived intact. We've already noted the demise of BBS, whose presiding genius was Bert Schneider. Schneider still operates (*Stay Hungry, Days of Heaven*), as does his partner Steve Blauner. (The third member of the group was Bob Rafelson.) Bert and his brothers Stanley (who produced *Three Days of the Condor* before he died prematurely) and Harold (*Goin' South*) were film-industry brats, sons of Abe Schneider, long associated with Columbia. Abe and Stanley had presided over the most disastrous period in Columbia's history before being ousted in 1973.

The Pressman–Williams company also went into precipitous decline in the mid-seventies.

Meanwhile, two other attempts at new production strategies never got off the ground. The Directors Company, formed under the aegis of Paramount as a corporate shelter for prestigious directors Francis Coppola, Peter Bogdanovich, and William Friedkin, mounted a few films (*Daisy Miller, The Conversation*), then folded. And First Artists, a similar conjunction of stars under Warner Brothers' imprimatur (Barbra Streisand, Sidney Poitier, Paul Newman, Steve McQueen, Dustin Hoffman) was equally unsuccessful, although it still survives as a publicly-owned company and Poitier at least has made good use of the label (*Uptown Saturday Night*).

Michael and Julia Phillips have moved from strength to strength with *The Sting, Taxi Driver,* and *Close Encounters of the Third Kind.* Ex-actor

Producers know a thing or two, also. Here, Robert Evans makes a point, but incorrigible Dustin Hoffman returns it.

Tony Bill, who was associated with the Phillipses (and with Zanuck-Brown) on *The Sting,* has had less financial success with his succeeding films, *Hearts of the West* and *Harry and Walter Go to New York.*

Lawrence Turman, another influential producer-star in the late sixties (*The Graduate*), has had less luck with *First Love* and *Heroes* recently. Similarly, Al Ruddy (*The Godfather*) has been much less visible of late (*The Longest Yard, Coonskin, Matilda*). Blockbuster successes aren't necessarily repeated. James B. Harris, formerly associated with Stanley Kubrick, hasn't done well on his own, either as director (*Some Call It Loving*) or producer (*Telefon*).

The list of current producers doing generally ambitious and interesting films is surprisingly long. David Picker, formerly of United Artists, heads it. Unlike Evans, Zanuck, and company, Picker seems to have concentrated on films he likes rather than on potential blockbusters. He has at least two of the more admirable films of the seventies to his credit: *Juggernaut* and *Smile* (nor are *Royal Flash* and *Lenny* anything to be ashamed of). Picker has what commentators on the Old Hollywood like to call "taste." It's rather an elusive quality, but simply put, it means this: a producer with "taste" cares more about the movies than the money; he really enjoys his "product," and tends to produce films that are neither pretentious, on the one hand, nor exploitative, on the other.

Other current producers with taste include: Hannah Weinstein, who has struggled successfully to get nonexploitative Black pictures on the screen (*Claudine, Greased Lightning*); Joe Wizan (*Jeremiah Johnson, Junior Bonner, Prime Cut*), who has a sense of humor, at least; Gabe Katzka (*Pelham 1-2-3*); Stanley Jaffe (*Bad Company, The Bad News Bears*); Jerome Hellman (*Midnight Cowboy, Coming Home*); and Martin Bregman, who specializes in New York pictures (*Serpico, Dog Day Afternoon, The Next Man*).

Two established independents with taste stand out for their consistent track records: Edgar J. Scherick has a sentimental streak, but many of his movies are worth a close look (*Jenny, I Never Promised You a Rose Garden, The Heartbreak Kid, Sleuth, Gordon's War, Pelham 1-2-3*). Elliott Kastner has put together an unusually varied collection of films. Yes, he produced *Swashbuckler* (no one's perfect), but he also made *Cops and Robbers, The Missouri Breaks, The Long Goodbye, Rancho Deluxe, Farewell My Lovely, 92 in the Shade,* and *Love and Death.*

Robert M. Sherman was associated with Kastner on *Missouri Breaks* and *Love and Death,* and on his own has done *Night Moves* and *Scarecrow.* Robert Radnitz (*Sounder*) and Irving Ravetch/Harriet Frank, Jr. (*Hud, Conrack*) also have a sort of taste; the trouble is it's decidedly middle-brow.

The partnership of Robert Chartoff and Irwin Winkler is unusually prolific, yet surprisingly they've had only one real hit, *Rocky.* The rest of their list comprises a strange mélange, mostly films that should have been more interesting and more profitable than they were: *New York, New York, Valentino, The Gambler, Nickelodeon,* and earlier; *The Strawberry Statement, They Shoot Horses, Don't They?, The Gang that Couldn't Shoot Straight, Breakout,* and *The New Centurions* among others.

The rest of the producers map is composed of a couple of agents· who have moved directly into production without the tour of duty at the studios, a handful of actors, and a hairdresser or two. Agent Michael Grusskoff had some success with *Young Frankenstein,* and other Mel Brooks films, more trouble with *Silent Running, Rafferty and The Gold Dust Twins,* and *Lucky Lady,* an expensive failure. Freddie Fields, one of the most successful Hollywood agents before he turned producer, seems to have a penchant for mod sadomasochism—*Lipstick, Looking for Mr. Goodbar*—but on the other hand, he's also financed *Citizen's Band.*

Robert Redford's productions have been consistently interesting: *Downhill Racer, The Candidate,* and *All the President's Men.* He also seems to have imposed his own style on all of them. Warren Beatty has had more notoriety from his productions, *Bonnie & Clyde, Shampoo* and *Heaven Can Wait.* Jon Peters, a successful hairdresser and consort of Barbra Streisand, produced *A Star Is Born* for her. He met with considerable resistance: most of the Hollywood establishment figured him for a

Considering the extraordinary value of John Williams's contribution to *Close Encounters*, he has probably earned the right to out-point Spielberg.

gigolo (who better to produce *A Star Is Born?*), but Peters has gained a certain degree of believability with *Eyes of Laura Mars*, which fit the SM trend of the late seventies.

The youth market that BBS and Pressman-Williams once served still exists, even if it is smaller than it used to be. The Mel Brooks films have a large adolescent following. Young audiences are also attracted to the films of a couple of European producers, the father-and-son team of Alexander and Ilya Salkind, who have produced a string of romantic adventures: *Three Musketeers*, *Four Musketeers*, *Superman*, and *Crossed Swords*. The style of these films depends heavily on the special irony of novelist George Macdonald Fraser, who did the scripts for all save *Superman*. The financial bonanza depends more on the Salkinds' canny system of shooting the sequel (*Musketeers*, *Superman*) at the same time as the original.

Robert Stigwood made a lot of money in music, and is now duplicating his success in films exploiting the music: *Tommy*, *Jesus Christ Superstar*, *Saturday Night Fever*, *Grease*. In England, Lord Lew Grade is also posing a serious challenge to Hollywood centrism through international coproductions aimed at the American market.

And the future of film production? It's not likely to change much, although to a measurable extent the quality of the film types *offered* to the studios for distribution (although not necessarily those *chosen*) depends on an influx of fresh sensibilities among the ranks of producers. This is

129

not as impossible as you might think. The new freelance organization of the business leaves it open to outsiders. Established producers in other fields are not likely to prove an important source of new talent. David Susskind occasionally ventures into movies (*Lovers and Other Strangers, Buffalo Bill and the Indians, Alice Doesn't Live Here Anymore*), as does David Merrick (*The Great Gatsby, Semi-Tough*), but their films aren't noticeably different from the general stream of product. Moreover, few of their colleagues in stage and television have followed them.

More important have been the regional companies. William Girdler has produced and directed a skein of movies out of Detroit on a shoestring. Sunn International and Pacific Films are serving a significant audience Hollywood chooses to ignore. Mulberry Square Productions, operating out of Texas, has muscled in on Walt Disney's monopoly of the children's market with their *Benji* films. Max Baer, Jr. (*Macon County Line, Ode to Billie Joe*), leads a group of producers appealing to the southern country market.

The most hopeful sign of the late seventies has been the beginning of an influx of business talent from other fields. Journalist Peter Bart and industrialist Max Palevsky (Xerox) teamed up for *Islands in the Stream* and *Fun with Dick and Jane* before going their separate ways. Mel Simon, a developer of shopping centers out of Indianapolis, has set up what appears to be a major production office. It will be interesting to see whether or not he can crack the Hollywood establishment. His first acquisition was *Tilt*, a script Texan Rudy Durand had been trying to finance for nine years.

If Palevsky and Simon are successful, if other would-be producers with business sense acquired in other industries join them, if they prove they can make money on different kinds of films, then the spectrum of Hollywood production may widen. The only other possibility for immediate reform lies in Pauline Kael's suggestion that directors become more involved in production. Francis Coppola and Robert Altman are the only ones to take her seriously so far. A number of directors produce their own films (generally closely watched by studio accountants); it's prestigious. But Coppola and Altman are the only ones who have made enough money to finance other people's films and have the desire to do it. Altman's Lion's Gate Films is an important center of independence in Hollywood in the late seventies, mainly because the company gives Altman a real measure of freedom other directors, even successful ones, don't have. (Many of them probably don't want it.) But also because a film like Alan Rudolph's *Welcome to L.A.*, a throwback to the early-seventies self-indulgent film-freak genre, isn't going to get made by the studio-oriented producers. *The Late Show*, by Robert Benton, was more successful on all counts.

Coppola's company, American Zoetrope, was like the Directors Company and First Artists, an idea whose time had not yet come. Nevertheless Coppola's productions of films he hasn't himself directed—*THX 1138, American Graffiti,* and the upcoming *Hammett* and *The Black Stallion*—were influential. Moneymaker George Lucas is a Coppola present to the industry. Coppola now insists he will concentrate on his own films in the future, but that mindset may change if conditions improve—and if *Apocalypse Now* sets box-office records. You can't put all your profits into real estate! And maybe he and Altman will be joined by other new rich directors. In 1978, Spielberg "guaranteed" the production of *I Wanna Hold Your Hand* by some young friends of his. This, too, may prove a model arrangement for the future.

Editors: Editors should be discussed with the same specificity with which we surveyed cinematographers. After all, theoretically, they contribute at least as much to the sum effect of a movie. But the truth is that even film students have a hard time telling the work of one editor from another. The aim is always to be unobtrusive. Obvious editing is bad editing. As a result, we know editors best by their industry reputations.

Furthermore, most contemporary directors above the level of hack are involved very closely in the editing of their films. It's a much more intimate relationship—just two or three people in the cutting room weeks on end—than that between director and cinematographer, who are surrounded on the set by perhaps hundreds of other people. Directors, once they find editors they like and trust, tend to keep them close. Whatever separate personalities editors might have are usually submerged.[5]

Nevertheless, there are a dozen editors whose work clearly stands out.

Dede Allen is probably the most celebrated editor working today. She has cut most of Arthur Penn's films, including the recent *Missouri Breaks* and *Night Moves.* She has also established a strong independent reputation for herself with *Serpico, Dog Day Afternoon,* and *Slapshot.* These were three sharply cut action films whose style was in direct contrast to Penn's elegiac studies. The best way to describe the Allen style is to note that somehow there's no dead footage in one of her pictures. She is not frenetic, in the modern style, nor is she likely to remain for very long on a particular shot simply because it looks good. Her films move lightly but relentlessly, and with exceptional smoothness.

Verna Fields is second only to Allen in celebrity, and has a reputation for being able to help young directors find their métier. She has cut such films as *Targets, Medium Cool, What's Up, Doc?, Daisy Miller, Sugarland*

131

Express, and *American Graffiti.* Her cut of *Jaws* is nothing short of magnificent. In a film machine like the shark picture, editing really comes to the fore, and Fields enhanced nearly every foot of *Jaws* with sophisticated devices, most of which are indiscernible to audiences. Much of the tension of the film is in its editing rhythms. Moreover, Fields and Spielberg had to cut very carefully around the mechanical shark, Bruce, leaving him on the screen just long enough to be effective without becoming laughable. They succeeded. Because Fields has worked with relatively inexperienced directors (and possibly because she has directed herself), her style is more evident than most editors': she shows a tough, tight, no-nonsense hand.

Margaret Booth, in Hollywood since 1924, is the grand dame of film editing. Her recent films have been *The Way We Were, Fat City,* and *Murder by Death.* They are good examples of that seamless cutting that has become the hallmark of the Hollywood film, as much in the seventies as in the thirties.

Donn Cambern began with *Easy Rider* and developed a reputation for a looser, more easygoing and fluid style that was supposed to be a model for the future. As we've seen, it wasn't, but Cambern's laconic idiom added to such films as *Alex and the Gypsy, Blume in Love,* and *Cinderella Liberty.* He was less successful with more pedestrian commercial efforts like *The Hindenburg* and *The Other Side of Midnight,* both of which might have benefited from a more classical approach.

Lou Lombardo also has a loose enough style to tell a good shaggy yarn. He's worked almost exclusively for Robert Altman—*Brewster McCloud, McCabe and Mrs. Miller, The Long Goodbye, Thieves Like Us, California Split*—but also injected some of this confident yet restrained spirit into *The Black Bird* and *The Late Show.* Altman seems to owe him a good deal.

Ralph Rosenblum is best known for his work with Woody Allen: *Annie Hall, Sleeper, Love and Death, Interiors.* His style is restrained (he also cut *Bad Company*), and he has the reputation of being the top New York-based editor.

Richard Harris, for his part, has been associated for a long while with Michael Ritchie on *Smile, Bad News Bears,* and *Semi-Tough,* among other films. He certainly knows how to tell a sardonic Ritchie story. It will be interesting to see what he does with other directors.

Walter Murch and Marcia Lucas are members of the Coppola–Lucas–Scorsese group in good standing. Murch has cut films as disparate as *The Conversation* and *Julia,* while Lucas has worked with her husband on *American Graffiti* and *Star Wars* and with Scorsese on *Alice Doesn't Live Here Anymore* and *Taxi Driver.* Both have contributed significantly to the films they have worked on; Coppola gives much of the credit for *The*

Conversation to Murch's post-production supervision.

David Bretherton is an oldtimer who has worked steadily in the seventies. His recent films include *Slither*, *Harry and Walter Go to New York*, and *Winter Kills*. Sam O'Steen, who was associated with Mike Nichols for several years (*Day of the Dolphin*, *The Graduate*, *Catch-22*, *Carnal Knowledge*), has graduated to direction, as Hal Ashby did before him. In addition to *Sparkle*, he has guided a number of television films. He also edited *Chinatown*.

Gerald Greenberg is a relatively unknown editor who has been around for a while. His work is worth attending to. Like Dede Allen, he can move from action to contemplation with ease. He cut the breathless *Seven-Ups* and *The Taking of Pelham 1-2-3*, as well as *Bye Bye Braverman* and *Alice's Restaurant*. *Apocalypse Now* may mark his graduation to celebrity.

Finally, here are three editors whose reputations aren't yet clear, but whose records suggest potential for growth: Danford B. Green started with Altman (*That Cold Day in the Park*, M*A*S*H), and cut Brooks's *Blazing Saddles* and the very different *Aloha Bobby and Rose*. He also edited *Fun with Dick and Jane*. Frederic Steinkamp worked on *A New Leaf*, *Three Days of the Condor*, and *The Yakuza*, as well as *Bobby Deerfield*. Robert L. Wolfe has *The Terminal Man*, *The Deep*, and *The Wind and the Lion* to his credit, but his real promise was shown in *All the President's Men*, an extremely difficult film to pace. He succeeded.

The American style of filmmaking doesn't leave much room for editors. European cutters are not only better known to the people who watch the films they work on, but also have much more clearly defined artistic personalities. We've had nothing like the New Wave's revolution in cutting in the United States, despite the brief vogue in the late sixties for what we might call "hippy" editing.

Music: Also in the late sixties, when it looked as if American film were going to develop along the paths of realism and relevance, filmmakers' attitudes toward music changed briefly. Ever since the early thirties, music had been looked upon as a vital and influential groundbase which could guide—often force—audiences' emotions in the desired direction. Even a scene that seems to fail outright by itself can be saved by a lush and insistent score dubbed in afterward.

The majority of American films, therefore, relied heavily on musical scores right through the sixties. But late in that decade the attitude changed. *The Graduate* used music in a special way. Audiences already knew Simon and Garfunkel's songs, and brought with them to the theater attitudes and associations. *Easy Rider* and numerous other films used this same associative technique. Meanwhile, the number of films without any music track to speak of grew. The new attitude toward music seemed to be more narrowly verisimilitudinous. If there was no apparent reason for music in the film, it wouldn't be added later.

But this deprived filmmakers of a very effective tool. Once the industry began to flourish again and attention shifted back to the textbook entertainment machine, the score returned in force as a highly useful manipulative technique. Most films now rely heavily on music once again.

The difference between the Golden Age of the thirties and the seventies in filmscores is that while a number of composers and musicians who have established careers in recordings and concerts are often called to do service in film, those composers who make their living exclusively in film these days don't have anywhere near the idiosyncratic musical personalities of such predecessors as Max Steiner, Erich Wolfgang Korngold, and most important, Bernard Herrmann. The new scores are more or less interchangeable.

Herrmann himself before he died in 1976 discovered renewed popularity. The generation of film-school graduates knew very well how much responsibility he bore for the basic effect of the great Hitchcock thrillers. His last two scores were for Brian De Palma (*Obsession*) and Martin Scorsese (*Taxi Driver*). They were both a little self-parodic, overblown, and too insistent.

Meanwhile, younger musicians were learning the basic techniques that had been established by Herrmann and others many years before. A serious student of film music can compile a thick list of references and allusions, as well as direct ripoffs, in a weekend's moviegoing.

John Williams's career has been most instructive. In the early seventies he provided a couple of inventive scores for Robert Altman—*Images*, and particularly *The Long Goodbye*, the music for which was a complete set of variations on a torchy song Williams had composed. (The melody even appeared in a doorbell chime at one point.) But Williams soon discovered a new, more profitable talent. After *The Towering Inferno* and *The Poseidon Adventure*, two lackluster scores that seemed to work very well for the movies they accompanied, he quickly developed into the premiere composer for blockbusters. His credits now include not only *Jaws*, but also *Star Wars*, *Close Encounters*, and *Superman*. Each score is derivative (or an homage to the old Hollywood, if you prefer). And each works better than the one before. The result is that Williams can count three of the highest-grossing films of all time among his credits.

Each Williams score is built upon a simple idea. *Jaws* borrowed a few unsettling phrases on bass strings as a leitmotif from Bernard Herrmann. *Star Wars* rested on a nostalgic martial tune to underline the war-movie antecedents of the film. *Close Encounters* used a simple major melody as the musical correlative of the ecstatic quasireligious ending. Spielberg knows the value of film music well: that phrase is the hook on which the entire film is hung. It serves as climax, in story as well as emotional terms, and it is also the key to whatever mystery there is in the movie.

Marvin Hamlisch, who worked for Woody Allen on two early films, *Take the Money and Run* and *Bananas*, gained fame for his scores for *The Way We Were* and *The Sting*. The former was a derivative forties ballad which someone had the good sense to ask Barbra Streisand to sing; the latter simply "borrowed" the music of Scott Joplin. Joplin's reputation benefited from the attention. But the acclaim came a little late. Since *The Sting*, Hamlisch has relapsed into rather unmemorable work in film, while his music for *A Chorus Line* has enjoyed considerable success.

Richard Baskin and Paul Williams have been among the more imaginative film musicians, combining careers outside film with work on scores for movies which have music as their subjects. Williams (not the director) is responsible for *Phantom of the Paradise* and *Bugsy Malone*; Baskin was musical director for *Nashville*, and composed and acted in *Welcome to L.A.* The music in all of these films is considerably enhanced by the subject matter.

Most of the other composers of current Hollywood film music whose names one might recognize from credit rolls are unremarkable. Lalo Schifrin, who composes a great many TV themes, sets the style: this hip wallpaper music is vaguely jazzy, diffuse, and singularly uninvolving. It's not the kind of music you whistle leaving the theater. Quincy Jones and Jerry Goldsmith also work much too steadily. A rule seems to be operating here: the less interesting the music, the more often the composer works. Maybe there is some sense to that rule. If music in films is only a tool, then perhaps it really should be unexceptionable. There are, however, a few scorers of passing interest. John Addison, who has worked mainly in England (*A Bridge Too Far*), is capable of more than the usual pap. So is David Shire: *Drive, He Said, Farewell My Lovely, Harry and Walter Go to New York, The Conversation*, and *Saturday Night Fever*, an essentially musical film which curiously doesn't exploit its disco setting as well as it might. Dave Grusin has scored *The Friends of Eddie Coyle*, and *Bobby Deerfield*. And Michael Small has done interesting work: *Dealing, The Drowning Pool, Night Moves*.

Designers: Of film designers there is even less to say than of film editors and composers. As important as the work is, its aim is almost always to be as unobtrusive as possible—at least in American films. Few U.S. designers have the opportunity to work for visionaries like Fellini, Visconti,

135

Bergman, or Bertolucci.

Richard Sylbert is the dean of current designers. His credits include *Fat City*, *The Day of the Dolphin*, *Shampoo*, *The Fortune*, and *Carnal Knowledge*. Polly Platt is moving up fast: *Paper Moon*, *The Last Picture Show*, *The Bad News Bears*, and *A Star Is Born*. Pato Guzman has done good work for Paul Mazursky: *Alex in Wonderland*, *Blume in Love*. Gene Callahan's *The Friends of Eddie Coyle* is exemplary for its wan realism. Richard's twin, Paul Sylbert, has tried directing and designed *One Flew Over the Cuckoo's Nest*. Dean Tavoularis is probably the most precise and imaginative of current film designers, if we are to judge from the extraordinary evidence of *The Godfather* (both parts), *Farewell, My Lovely*, *The Conversation*, and *Apocalypse Now*.

John Barry's great work is *Star Wars*, a designer's dream—a big, abstract, science-fiction film that allows a production designer to realize long-repressed fantasies. During the last ten years, most films like this have gone not to Americans but to British designer Ken Adam, who is the master of the constructed caper film. He has been responsible for most of the Bond films as well as the landmark historical epic *Barry Lyndon* and the cryptic *The Last of Sheila*.

The work of costume designers is usually even more unobtrusive than the work of production designers. Once again, the contemporary realistic mode doesn't leave much room for these artists to make noticeable statements. Yet at least two costume designers stand out—Anthea Sylbert (Richard's wife) and Theoni V. Aldredge. Sylbert designed the clothes for *Chinatown* and *Julia* (two very fashion-conscious pictures), among many other films. As much as anyone in Hollywood, she has been responsible for the influence of 1930s style on contemporary fashions in movies, and thus in the real world, as well. Aldredge, who has recently been so prolific that she bids to become the next Edith Head, works on numerous films yet still designs for the New York stage, where she began. Her films have included *The Great Gatsby*, *Network*, and *Eyes of Laura Mars*. Both Sylbert and Aldredge have worked closely with Faye Dunaway, who is of all contemporary stars the most conscious of fashion, and apparently also the most desirous of setting styles as the stars of the old Hollywood used to do. Despite her obvious interest, however, Dunaway hasn't been nearly so influential as Diane Keaton. The clothes of *Annie Hall*, apparently based on Keaton's own personal style, have provided the one truly contemporary mode in seventies movies. The costume designer for *Annie Hall*, Ruth Morley, must be given some of the credit.

There are many other craftspeople who contribute significantly to the art of film. Special-effects designers Douglas Trumbull (*2001*, *Silent Running*,

Close Encounters) and Albert Whitlock (most disaster films) have had a profound influence on movies in the seventies. Sound is one half the medium of film, yet we seldom pay attention to the people who record, mix, and edit a film's soundtrack. Much interesting technical work is being done in this area now. Jim Webb and Chris McLaughlin of Lion's Gate Films, whose work with Dolby recording techniques has markedly increased the sophistication of contemporary soundtracks, certainly deserve mention.

As for the others, the gaffers and grips, the "best boys" and "script girls," the executive producers and gofers, we only have space to note: they also serve who only stand and wait.

5

The Whiz Kids

It didn't turn out the way we expected.

In 1968, 1969, and 1970, the New American Wave broke on Malibu beaches. Its style was easily recognizable and thoroughly—as we used to say in those days—"hip": loose, personal, introspective, let-it-all-hang-out, laid-back, I-hear-ya-talkin-to-me, and, in retrospect, instantly nostalgic for its own precious time. Now, only 15 years later, such films as *Easy Rider, Five Easy Pieces, Drive, He Said, The Last Picture Show, A Safe Place* (all BBS productions), *Out of It, The Revolutionary, Dealing* (all Pressman-Williams productions), *The Christian Licorice Store, Move, The Landlord,* and *Brewster McCloud* are at best evocative of a very brief and rather self-indulgent period of our history. At worst, they now seem shallow, cramped exploitations of morbid adolescent fantasies.

The youth film died quicker than the revolution it aspired to describe, and its hasty passing left filmmakers like Bob Rafelson, Dennis Hopper, Paul Williams, and Henry Jaglom high and dry, while Altman, Ashby, Nicholson, and Bogdanovich—who had only been visitors in the land of youth, anyway—struggled to catch the next tide.

As it turned out, it wasn't such auteurs, such personal film artists, who set the tone for the seventies; it was an even younger generation of whiz kids, who may have had some of the same fantasies of making meaningful, personal films as their immediate predecessors (although we have little evidence of this) but who also understood how to make popular entertainments and were eager and anxious to do so. Perhaps it was all for

139

Bruno Ganz and Dennis Hopper in *The American Friend,* a film about the Americanization of European movies and culture.

the best. We still get the occasional, typically self-centered "youth" film—Alan Rudolph's *Welcome to L.A.* is egregious evidence of the emptiness of the style—and Wim Wenders has transformed it into something more in such films as *Kings of the Road* and *The American Friend,* but generally speaking, commercial pressures have spared us movies by people who don't have anything much to say but want very much to say it anyway.

The problem is that the new Hollywood system has also made it much more difficult for filmmakers who *do* have something to say, whose voices we *do* want to hear more of. We've settled for a middle road, dominated by directors who've become star celebrities—interviewed, photographed, and gossiped about—of a magnitude never envisioned by Hawks or Ford, and achieved in the past only by Welles and Hitchcock, who had to become actors or television personalities to achieve it.

There's nothing really wrong with the work of the whiz kids individually. Indeed, Scorsese, De Palma, Lucas, and Spielberg have made a number of fascinating films, and the general attitude toward Bogdanovich, who used to be the bête noir of the film magazines, is mellowing now that he's received his comeuppance with three flops in a row. Schrader may yet conquer his fears and inadequacies. Only Billy Friedkin seems a lost cause, and even he has his defenders.

There are a number of ties among members of this group that suggest a certain camaraderie as well as a consistent attitude toward the business.

140

Bogdanovich and Friedkin are a little older than the others, but Scorsese, De Palma, Lucas, and Spielberg all arrived on the scene at about the same time. Schrader has written for Scorsese and De Palma. Lucas and Spielberg are planning a film together. Coppola, Bogdanovich, and Scorsese all worked for Roger Corman. Coppola, Lucas, and Scorsese are friendly. They give each other "points" in their films.

As divergent as their backgrounds are, all seven have followed a basic career pattern, as well. Bogdanovich, Scorsese, and De Palma are out of New York. Friedkin started in television in Chicago. Schrader comes from Michigan, Spielberg from Arizona. Lucas grew up in California. Scorsese and Lucas are film-school graduates; Schrader also has an academic background. Friedkin and Spielberg got their start in television. Bogdanovich and Schrader were journalists. But each of them had his major breakthrough within a year of his thirtieth birthday, and the older three have been around long enough to have directed chastening failures after the warm glow of the popular and successful films which made their careers. Bogdanovich, Friedkin, and Scorsese have each spent fortunes on box-office bombs. Lucas and Spielberg have been luckier the second time around. Bogdanovich and Friedkin were both born in 1939, Scorsese in 1942, De Palma and Lucas in 1944, and Spielberg and Schrader in 1946.

The Bogdanovich Syndrome

The first of the whiz kids to hit the big time was Peter Bogdanovich. He did not respond well to the celebrity that followed in the wake of *The Last Picture Show* (which was, by the way, the last picture show produced by BBS to make a profit). As a journalist for the film magazines, and later *Esquire* in the sixties, he'd developed an auteurist star complex, always dropping names ("as Duke told me the other day . . . as Orson puts it . . .") and generally insinuated himself into the Hollywood pantheon. Now, as a real filmmaker with a real track record, he played on his success in an embarrassingly egotistical fashion. He made a fool of himself on talkshows with chatty celebrity banter. The film magazines came to despise him as an ideological turncoat. Hadn't they been fighting the system of Hollywood royalty for years? Now one of their own had made it and immediately began talking as if the people he'd interviewed over the years were his coequals. (Bogdanovich had published monographs on Hawks, Hitchcock, Ford, Lang, and Allan Dwan.) It was rumored that his next film was going to be *The Peter Bogdanovich Story*—starring George Hamilton. Alternately, it was suggested that he was really the George Plimpton of the movies, that he was only making movies in order to have something to chat about on talkshows.

141

This exercise in celebrity reached a disastrous climax with Bog-danovich's well-publicized romance with Cybill Shepherd. She was properly icy in *The Last Picture Show,* but when Bogdanovich tried desperately to turn her into an actress in *Daisy Miller* and *At Long Last Love,* the result was ludicrous. *Cybill Does It to Cole,* her off-key album, produced by mentor Peter, was even more humiliating. Bogdanovich seemingly had infinite tolerance for self-mortification. The film journalists hated him for even more personal reasons. He had been one of their own, and since each of them carried a script in his bag, ready to be proffered to the next interview victim, they were worried that Peter would ruin it for all of them. They were all hoping for an American version of the New Wave.

But Bogdanovich was much more a reporter than a critic. (The first real critic to break the Hollywood line was to be Paul Schrader.) He had never been to college; he went to the movies instead on the West Side of New York where he grew up, son of a Serbian painter and an Austrian-Jewish mother. By the time he was fifteen he was studying acting with Stella Adler. He did a few off-Broadway productions, then hung out with Dan Talbot, whose New Yorker theater was the most exciting repertory house in those days, and Andrew Sarris and Eugene Archer, seminal critics of the sixties. The French New Wave, the most exciting development in cinema in twenty years, was just beginning to break in New York, but according to Talbot, Bogdanovich could never quite figure out what Godard and his colleagues were up to. Dan sent Peter to see *Breathless* twice, but it didn't take.

In 1964, at the age of twenty-five, young Peter set out for the Coast with his wife, designer Polly Platt. He was going to be a director. At the time, the idea must have seemed pure folly. At the time, nobody broke into the Hollywood system from the outside. Peter would have been far better advised to work his way into live television in New York. Within five years he might have been directing. Ten years of television and then he might have had a chance at Hollywood. That was the way it was done. But four years after arriving in L.A., Bogdanovich had done it his way, with a little help from Roger Corman.

His debut movie, *Targets* (1968), wasn't a financial success, but word got around. He had handled a tricky Corman puzzle with some aplomb. The problem Roger set for Peter was this: You can write and direct your own film, but you must do it for less than $125,000; you must use Boris Karloff, because he owes me a few days' work from another movie; and you must use eighteen minutes of outtakes from a previous Corman-engineered Karloff vehicle, *The Terror.* Peter's elegant solution was to construct the film around Karloff himself, adding the useful element of

Cybill Shepherd teases Timothy Bottoms in *The Last Picture Show*.

suspense by cross-cutting between the old actor and a young potential assassin. The concluding sequence, a shoot-out at a drive-in, was handled masterfully, even if some critics now see symbolic parallelism in the assassin's attack on the screen itself, and the movie being projected on it.

Peter's next project was also an obvious outgrowth of the work he had done as critic. His book-length monographs had been partially responsible for the new attention that was beginning to be paid to venerable American directors. The American Film Institute decided to pay homage to John Ford with a film about his films, and Peter spent three years off and on putting together *Directed by John Ford* (1971). The result is uneven, alternating between chatty and relatively uninformative interviews with the actors who had worked with Ford, and breathtaking, newly struck prints of footage from some of the films. If we never really get a sense of the importance of Ford in American film history we nevertheless must give Bogdanovich credit for leaving in the old man's abrupt and contemptuous answers to the kid's often fatuous questions.

The Last Picture Show (1971), from Larry McMurtry's novel, remains the only Bogdanovich film that has been both a critical and a commercial success. The movies are once again a subject, but this time operating as the moody subtext of this elegy on a country town in Texas twenty years before. As David Thomson has put it, "Few American films take so many clearly defined characters and manage to like them all. It is something we know from Renoir, and in Bogdanovich it seems to be the first profound sign of character. . . . "[1]

Bogdanovich with hero John Ford at John Ford Point, Monument Valley.

Sadly, Bogdanovich never developed that sense of character. His next film, *What's Up, Doc?* (1972), was the first of four consecutive attempts to mimic genres and periods. It was also the only one to garner decent reviews and good receipts at the box office. The idea was to shoot a classic screwball comedy in the style of Hawks, starring Barbra Streisand. Since Streisand is a throwback to the thirties, a chanteuse born out of her time, the conception wasn't half bad. With considerable help from screenwriters Buck Henry, Robert Benton, and David Newman, Bogdanovich came close to bringing it off. At least he caught the frenzy. The good humor and the groundbase of character eluded him, however. He was beginning to betray, in his third fiction film, a rather snide and coldly distant personality which has marked all of his films since.

Hard on the heels of *What's Up, Doc?* came *Paper Moon* (1973), an attempt to do for the thirties what *The Last Picture Show* had done for the early fifties. It was less successful. In black and white again, a medium fast becoming a Bogdanovich hallmark, *Paper Moon* was betrayed by its own cuteness, although Tatum O'Neal proved to be such a remarkable screen presence that the film survived.

Bogdanovich had left Polly Platt in 1971 to move in with ex-covergirl Cybill Shepherd. By the time his string of flops began in 1974 with *Daisy Miller*, a number of critics were beginning to make a correlation between his early success and his collaboration with Platt. When she disappeared, so it seemed did his sense of humor and character, traits which he has never evinced in his writing or his public utterances, and which were

O'Neal and Streisand spend a quiet evening with Madeline Kahn in *What's Up, Doc?*

therefore surprising to discover in *Targets* and *The Last Picture Show*. Peter cannily chose Frederic Raphael to do the script of the Henry James novel which he hoped would make Cybill a star, and the film does as well as can be expected in transfering the novel to the screen. The problems—insurmountable, as it happened—were twofold: first, Shepherd, decent in contemporary roles (as her work with directors other than Bogdanovich—May and Scorsese—has shown), found an historical role way above her head, especially one with Jamesian nuances. Second, although Bogdanovich made all the right textbook moves in the film, they seemed to telegraph themselves. Watching the film was like watching a magician who couldn't quite hide his tricks. He had chosen a proper role for Shepherd. She is definitely the contemporary equivalent of James's masterful character. But he couldn't make the proper translation, although Raphael's script worked and certain individual elements worked.

His next project was even more audacious: a real thirties musical. If there is one genre that is inevitably rooted in its time, it is this one. The film seemed doomed before shooting began. Ruby Keeler never pretended to be a great actress; consequently, Cybill could have played the part. But Ruby could dance; Cybill couldn't. Ruby could sing; Cybill couldn't. And Burt Reynolds, for all his qualities, was achingly removed from the class that made Fred Astaire a star. *At Long Last Love* (1975) was one of the more embarrassing displays since the advent of talkies.

Moving on the momentum from his earlier films, Bogdanovich was able to shrug off the $6-million-plus loss of *At Long Last Love* to complete one more film before the drought set in. *Nickelodeon* (1976) is a safer, and therefore more esthetically successful, project, but it did no better at the box office than its recent predecessors. Forbidden by contract from using Shepherd, Bogdanovich returned to the O'Neal team, Ryan and Tatum, who had worked so well for him in the past, and Burt Reynolds, who although he had flopped for Peter had certainly succeeded for other directors. The script by W. D. Richter was a pleasant tale of the early days of moviemaking. The style of the film, because it was historically about movies, required none of the distancing that had injured the genre movies which were parodies of themselves. Everything looked good. Yet the coldness of tone that Bogdanovich had developed over the last few years lapped over into *Nickelodeon* and what was basically a pleasant and thoughtful entertainment somehow never took off.

Peter Bogdanovich clearly knows a lot about moviemaking. He's talked with all the masters, and he seems to have assimilated their lessons. He's learned how they did what they did. What he doesn't know—has no apparent interest in knowing—is *why* they did it. He wants to make movies passionately. But he's not passionate about anything else. He is, in a word, magnificently shallow. That's the Bogdanovich syndrome. It's a strong argument for a return to the old studio system. In his beloved Hollywood of the thirties and forties, he could have carved a very respectable career for himself as a jack-of-all-trades metteur en scène. If only there were a studio to assign a writer and a property, choose the actors he had to work with, and make the final cut so as to eliminate some of his more egregious self-indulgences, Bogdanovich would be protected from himself and able to realize his talent.

But the studio factory exists no more, and Bogdanovich has been thrust into a position—as auteur—that he can't quite handle. The ideas aren't bad. They must have looked inviting on paper. But when Bogdanovich films them, they go all haywire. In future years, people will be returning to his films, no doubt, but they will be fascinated by them because they are strange, exaggerated efflorescences of a genre system that is no more.

They are the incontrovertible evidence that the Old Hollywood system is dead.

Billy The Kid

Billy Friedkin started working in the mailroom of Chicago station WGN when he was a teenager. Before he was seventeen, he was directing live TV. Before he was twenty he was no longer a cinematic virgin. He had directed a one-hour TV documentary, *The People vs. Paul Crump*. More than 2000 television shows, by his own count, followed. He also shot some documentaries for David Wolper. Then in 1966 he met Sonny Bono. The singer had had a hit record. He had a backer who wanted to put up some money for a film. Friedkin directed his first feature, *Good Times* (1967), starring Sonny and Cher. No one saw it, but once again the word got around. Here's someone who knows how to handle a camera. *The Night They Raided Minsky's* followed in 1968. It wasn't a bad movie, had some good New York mood to it, but Elliott Gould was not yet a star (at the time he was still Mr. Barbra Streisand), Jason Robards didn't draw at the box office, and Norman Wisdom was some English fellow. The film has a lot of nice bits, as befits a vaudeville movie, but it's perhaps a little too lackadaisical. The pieces don't come together. Norman Lear produced, and co-wrote the script. In retrospect, it's more a Lear film than a Friedkin movie.

Billy next turned his febrile attention to two stage adaptations, neither of which had any overriding reason to be filmed. *The Birthday Party* (1968) turns Harold Pinter's witty comedy of menace into a feral, darkly lit psychological suspense thriller. Perhaps it was a sign of the times. *The Boys in the Band* (1970) was next. Mart Crowley's unmemorable but at the time newsworthy play couldn't stand up under the bright lights of the film set. Friedkin's budding career was going nowhere. He looked like a television director.

Then he hit it big with *The French Connection* (1971), one of the major successes of the seventies. The film moved breathlessly, so quickly in fact that the gaping holes in the plot were smoothly skimmed over. The New York location photography gave the film some semblance of life. And Gene Hackman and Roy Scheider waded into the tough-guy cop roles with gusto. The film set a style for visceral excitement that has lasted ever since.

Give Friedkin full credit for pulling it all together, for having the good sense to eschew music and let the sounds of the city speak for themselves, for flashing with exciting abandon around New York locations in the dead of winter. But Owen Roizman's photography also counted for a lot; the two cops, Sonny Grosso and Eddie Egan, upon whose exploits the story was based, not only acted in the film but, as technical advisers, gave it the gritty authenticity for which it's famous. And the centerpiece scene, the chase, was producer Phil D'Antoni's signature. *The French Connection* set a style for seventies film noir, which was important, but it's unlikely Friedkin will be so lucky again.

The Exorcist (1973) was a logical outgrowth of *The French Connection*. Friedkin had established himself with the latter as a filmmaker who knew how to inject suspense and action into essentially static material. *The*

147

Sonny Grosso and Eddie Egan as Detective Phil Klein and Lieutenant Simonson in *The French Connection*. Grosso and Egan were the models for the roles played by Scheider and Hackman. They were still cops when the film was made. Now, they're actors.

French Connection, after all, was basically a story about two flatfoots standing around in the cold waiting. Similarly, *The Exorcist*, highly suspenseful, needed a director who could make that suspense visible. Otherwise it would have been campy. Friedkin knew how. He'd studied Hitchcock, of course, and Henri-Georges Clouzot, who has an even darker and more foreboding sense of suspense.

Here's Friedkin talking to an American Film Institute seminar in 1974:

> I figured [Hitchcock] had about 45 minutes in *Psycho* where absolutely nothing happened. It's a dull sort of story but the audience is expectant. The audience knows that they're coming in to see this horrific suspense film and they're not getting it. They're getting edgy and then suddenly, he whacks them with it and boom, you've got them in your back pocket.
>
> So I figured what I'm going to try and do is make this *Exorcist* go on for about an hour with nothing happening and then see how long I could pull the string.[2]

As an engine of manipulation, *The Exorcist* succeeds magnificently. What other film of recent years has had the medical, psychological effect it had? It is violently effective. For a while, people bought the thrills, but the new horror film lapsed rather quickly into a minor if occasionally profitable genre only a few years after *The Exorcist* was released. There was something cold and inhuman about the movie itself, not just its subject. Previously, horror had been done with a subtext of human concern; you had the feeling that a decent person was telling you the story. There is no such feeling supporting *The Exorcist*, which is one of the reasons, ironically, that it works so well.

From plot elements to special effects to the handling of sound (Friedkin has always been very conscious of the effect the level of the sound-track has) to the nervous cutting to the music, *The Exorcist* is a catalogue of devices that work. Friedkin could shoot the telephone book and make it exciting.

But to what end? Technique is admirable, but eventually audiences want to hear the voice of the person who's telling them this story. They may not like Bogdanovich's voice, but they can't even hear Friedkin's. For all his study of Hitchcock, he's missing precisely that quality that makes Hitchcock great: the wise, humorous, and ultimately friendly narrator we sense behind the film. There's no lasting pleasure in hearing the tale unless there is also an evident pleasure in the telling of it. Friedkin gets about as much pleasure totting up his far-too-numerous effects as a harried accountant around income-tax time.

But it's not too late for him to discover a sense of the telling. *Sorcerer* (1977), the gift he convinced two major studios to give him for hitting the bell with *The Exorcist*, cost upwards of $18 million, but it is more restrained than Billy's earlier films, even if the sum effect is a grandly naive gesture of self-indulgence. The kid, growing old, wanted to remake his hero Clouzot's *Wages of Fear*. It took him years; he shot on four continents (the trips are becoming a Friedkin trademark); and the film when released was a total writeoff.

Yet it's not a bad film in its way. In many ways it's his best so far. It's overblown, true, but one has the feeling Friedkin has a commitment to this story, for whatever reasons, and it is less pretentious in its parts than his earlier efforts. But to come to that positive conclusion, you have to make a few broad assumptions. You have to assume that *Wages of Fear* needed to be remade, which it didn't, thank you. You have to assume that a taut, lithe adventure movie deserves an inflated budget the size of the yearly expenditures for a dozen suburban school districts. And you have to forgive Friedkin the cheap trick of the title, meant to remind you not so subtly that this guy made *The Exorcist*, when in fact the movie has next to nothing to do with sorcerers of any kind.*

The Brinks Job (1979) was an expensive restaging of the famous 1950

---

*The truck which is the star of the film was once named "Sorcerer." The name on the door has almost faded away, but it is still observable in a few quick shots to those in the know. None of the characters ever mentions the name of the truck, and it's meaningless in the context of the film: perhaps a private joke.

Sorcerer is full of extraordinary shots like this, but somehow technique overwhelms meaning and emotion.

Boston robbery. Friedkin had assembled a superb cast including Peter Falk, Peter Boyle, Kevin O'Connor, Warren Oates, Paul Sorvino, and Allen Goorwitz. The rich possibilities of character in a gang like this suggest success that eluded Friedkin when the film was released. In late July 1978, in the middle of an extended shooting schedule on location in Boston, thieves broke into the *Brinks* movie editing room and lifted several reels of crucial footage. (They knew which scenes—those involving large numbers of extras—would be difficult to reshoot.) Now, when someone mentions the Brinks robbery, he may be referring to either of two classic heists. Friedkin insists it was not a publicity stunt.

Fear and Loathing in Hollywood

None of the new filmmakers has created as strong a public persona as Martin Scorsese. Hunted, haunted, asthmatic, diminutive, darkly bearded, a victim of religious nightmares, a mass of raging anxieties, Scorsese as we know him from interviews and photographs makes Paul Schrader, his only rival in film-noir paranoia, look by comparison like a happily adjusted Midwestern businessman. In fact, Scorsese's real success is to have made films at all. Each new project brings with it a baggage of stories about the director's agonies. The movies—even the ones with relatively pleasant atmospheres—seem rooted in this pain.

Peter Falk at work in *The Brinks Job.*

Perhaps this suffering need not be in vain: within Scorsese there may lie an Italian-American Bergman waiting for the right moment to show himself. Bergman himself made a dozen unremarkable films before he found the necessary key of objectivity to turn his own nightmares into art. Scorsese may, too. He's already shown evidence that he can in *Who's That Knocking at My Door?* and *Mean Streets.* But right now, he remains the most brilliant of the New Hollywood's disappointments, seemingly torn between two recurrent, obsessive dreams: his own childhood in New York's Little Italy, whose basic components were a malevolent Church and a (to him) frightening ethic of machismo, and the opiates that Hollywood offered as an alternative to that disturbing reality. When he sticks to the earlier set of compulsions, he produces brilliant, if slightly muddled, images of a complex reality. When he shifts to the later set, as he seems increasingly to feel it necessary to do, the results are at best disappointing.

Scorsese's genre homages—*Alice Doesn't Live Here Anymore, Taxi Driver,* and *New York, New York*—are certainly much more resonant and complex than Bogdanovich's similar efforts. They are felt variations on the basic themes rather than mechanistic parodies. But the ultimate effect is the same. Neither the cold and egotistical Bogdanovich nor the feverish, introverted Scorsese has been able to make those old genres actually come alive again. There is the smell of decay about them. It's as if they were refrains in a bad dream of the Old Hollywood: endless repetitions and regurgitations from phantoms of the Hollywood Hills. The children seem to have been possessed by the fathers. Maybe Hollywood should be closed down for twenty years, quarantined, or permitted to lie fallow. The weight of tradition oppresses.

Scorsese was a conscientious student of the movies long before he attended N.Y.U. in the sixties. As a sickly child, he used to draw sequences from his favorite films, analyzing sets, costumes, and structure. He did well enough at N.Y.U.'s film school to teach there for a while after graduating, while he was picking up odd jobs as a film editor in New York. One of his student efforts, a short called *It's Not Just You Murray*, (1964), was good enough to be picked up for commercial distribution. People who happened to catch it then (those were the days when features were still accompanied by shorts) still remember it well. Using student actors and his mother, Marty etched a vivid and loosely comic portrait of the sort of realistic city personalities one even now seldom sees on the screen. Another short, *The Big Shave* (1967), also got considerable festival exposure. It's a perfectly cinematic and simple exercise in black comedy. Accompanied by some Bunny Berigan music, the solitary shaver nicks himself once, then twice, then slashes a major artery or two. By the end of the six-minute film, the bright-red blood is flowing copiously into the clean white sink.

Scorsese worked as an editor for CBS around this time, shot some commercials in Britain in 1968, worked on a few scripts, and—Diane Jacobs reports in *Hollywood Renaissance*—began directing *The Honeymoon Killers* but was replaced by Leonard Kastle. In 1969, he completed his first feature, the independent production *Who's That Knocking at My Door?* starring the erstwhile television actress Zina Bethune and the unknown Harvey Keitel. He had been working on the film since his student days, and like *Mean Streets*, the script for which dates from at least this early, the film is essentially autobiographical: an interesting meld of sexual anxieties, Catholic guilt, religious symbolism, and tough street life. It had a freshness that was remarkable, especially in the context of the other independent films that were garnering a little publicity about the same time. Unlike the better-promoted BBS films, *Who's That Knocking?* dealt with a real urban environment. It was notably unself-conscious, and its people had histories—they lived for a while on the screen, rather than posing in the Hopper/Nicholson manner. The film was widely reviewed locally, but Scorsese was still an untried talent as far as the studios were concerned.

In 1969-70, he worked as assistant director and supervising editor on *Woodstock*, the most successful and still the best of concert music films. Michael Wadleigh (né Wadley) was credited as director, but the real honors ought to go to Martin Scorsese. Direction of *Woodstock* consisted simply of sending out ten or a dozen camerapeople with as much stock as they could carry and telling them to do their thing, shooting everything that happened during that historic weekend in upstate New York. The crew came back with an overwhelming amount of footage—more than one hundred hours by some accounts. The real creative job lay in reducing this amorphous mass of raw material to a running time of three hours and giving it shape and pace. Scorsese and his crew did a magnificent job, and *Woodstock* remains one of the most notable models of the craft of editing since the Steenbeck editing table was invented. Its thoughtful and moving use of the split screen (which allowed another hour or two of footage to be squeezed in) has never been equaled.

At about the same time, Scorsese became involved with a group of independent filmmakers known as the New York Cinetracts Collective. Hastily organized during the student strike of May 1970 in response to the Cambodia invasion, the group took its name from the short didactic newsreels produced anonymously in France two years earlier during the aborted rising of May—June 1968. Once again, Scorsese molded a bewildering amount of footage into a meaningful historical document. *Street Scenes 1970* was shown at the New York Film Festival in 1970, then dropped from sight.

Documentary work has provided Scorsese with a second, hidden career ever since. He acted as associate producer and supervising editor of *Medicine Ball Caravan* (1971), as supervisor of montages for *Elvis on Tour* (1972), and as supervising editor of *Unholy Rollers* (1973). More recently, he produced and directed *The Last Waltz* (1978). In all, a lot of energy has gone into these films. They may be less publicized than his Hollywood features, but they indicate an important second side to his personality as a filmmaker. There's no better example of a contemporary director seriously crippled by trying to accommodate himself to the system of commercial film production than Martin Scorsese. If he'd been left to his own devices, his films, I think, would be a lot more interesting than they are.

By 1971 it must have looked to Scorsese as if he were in serious danger of falling into the rut of the independent New York filmmaker: a documentary here, some editing work there, and maybe a gig as cameraman; long years between features which, when they were finally financed, shot, and distributed with much difficulty, earned perhaps a dollar or two, then sank without a trace. Instead, Scorsese decided to go Hollywood. Now he's free, at least geographically, from the mean streets of Little Italy, lives above the smog on Mulholland Drive, works with multimillion-dollar budgets, hangs out with the fast crowd. He's a name to conjure with, but at what price? It's a moralistic tale, which is touching and ironically fitting for the boy who thought that if he ate meat on Fridays he was going to burn in hell.

For a while, things went well. *Boxcar Bertha* (1972), an assignment from Roger Corman, is a good job of mise en scène. The well-mounted saga of "Sister of the Road" Boxcar Bertha Thompson during the Depression starred David Carradine, Barbara Hershey (Seagull), and Bernie Casey in early roles. Scorsese shows a good sense of locale (the South) and period. There's nothing special about the film. You can't tell from watching it that it was made by Martin Scorsese, but that was the whole point. This crazy auteur from New York showed the Hollywood establishment he could work within the system.

Mean Streets followed in 1973. Produced independently by young rock-concert promoter Jonathan T. Taplin for $350,000 cash and $150,000 in deferrals—a frugal sum even then—the film remains Scorsese's one great achievement so far. The script had been in preparation for seven years (there are obvious parallels with *Who's That Knocking at My Door?*), and the project was clearly an obsession. Scorsese later said he exorcised the demons of his childhood by making the film. Pauline Kael, ever on the lookout for new, anti-Hollywood talent, called it "a true original of our period, a triumph of personal filmmaking." It was that, no doubt, but it was also Scorsese's last "personal," "original" film. After the critical success of *Mean Streets* (the film did not make money for Warner Brothers), he settled down to work his way into the established Hollywood structure.

Like George Lucas's *American Graffiti*, Brian De Palma's *Greetings*, and Paul Mazursky's *Next Stop Greenwich Village*, *Mean Streets* is a *Bildungsfilm*. One of the axioms of American literary history in the twentieth century has been the difficulty of the second novel. Scores of writers, using their own childhood and adolescent experience, have produced critically acclaimed debuts. But they can't follow up. They know their own lives well; they can deal with them creatively; but they can't seem to put themselves in other people's places. Something like this ego block may be operating in film, as well.

In any event, Scorsese was careful in his next film to move as far away from the themes and subject matter of *Mean Streets* as possible. *Mean Streets* works because it is tremendously atmospheric (even though most of it was shot in and around Los Angeles, not where it supposedly takes place) and because Scorsese had at his disposal actors like Robert De Niro and Harvey Keitel who could add to the already strong characterizations he and old friend Mardik Martin had set up in the highly worked screenplay.

154

Scorsese couldn't do much with atmosphere in *Alice Doesn't Live Here Anymore*, but he could continue to develop in collaboration with superior actors the quirky, resonant characters which were fast becoming his trademark. No one can match him at this, not even Altman, Cassavetes, or Mazursky, who all seem to appreciate and depend on the work of actors to at least as great a degree as Scorsese. There are other things going on in Mazursky's films; Cassavetes doesn't know when to stop his people; and Altman focuses on theme-ridden kooks—they flash brightly for a while, but they don't have the staying power of Scorsese's people.

Apparently, his characters are at least as much the work of the actors themselves as they are of Scorsese, either as screenwriter or director. With *Alice*, he set up several weeks of rehearsal before shooting began, then had the actors do improvisations of a number of crucial scenes, while Robert Getchell observed and took notes, later reducing the material that was developed to its essence. The actors had an equal degree of freedom during shooting. Scorsese customarily shoots much more footage than he can use. *Mean Streets'* first cut lasted two hours and twenty minutes, then was brought down to 1:51; *Alice* started at three hours, sixteen minutes and was released at 1:53. And the first cut of *New York, New York*, now legendary, ran for four hours or more. It premiered at 2:34. For second runs, a further sixteen minutes was cut.

A great deal thus gets lost. According to Scorsese, these arduous trimming jobs were not simply a matter of tightening up scenes: whole sequences went, and with them characters. He himself feels *Alice* as it is now is simplistic. At more than three hours, "it was quite three-dimensional, let me put it that way."[3]

When it was released, *Alice Doesn't Live Here Anymore* was hailed as a feminist classic by a number of major critics. Scorsese had collaborated closely with Ellen Burstyn, who was the prime mover behind the film, the other actresses, associate producer Sandy Weintraub, designer Toby Carr Rafelson, and editor Marcia Lucas. This film about women was designed to be very far removed from the macho world of *Mean Streets*. Its failure is that it really isn't. It's a hip Doris Day film. In fact, Alice actually has less freedom, fewer opportunities, and a markedly weaker character than her professional-virgin predecessor had in the fifties. She makes no conscious decision to hit the road, she's forced into it when her husband dies. (Scorsese liked the fatalism: "The finger of God comes down. The truck crashes.") Director and screenwriter (did the women collaborate here too?) never allow her any success on the road. They do let her have a few interesting friendships with women, which form the heart of the film, but it's inevitable that she will sink back down into a complacent marriage before the film ends. The most dramatic sequences

Alice (Ellen Burstyn) is really more comfortable fixing a picnic lunch for her son (Alfred Lutter) and her man (Kris Kristofferson).

involve the macho character of Ben (Harvey Keitel), not the women's relationships. Alice is after all a klutz. It's rather charming in an old-fashioned way that she actually thinks to have a career of her own, such as it is, and it's interesting that she has a buddy-buddy relationship with her son, but after all she's really a dependent woman.

The filmmakers seem to think that they actually made a feminist film. They may have started out to do so. But *Alice* is more regressively chauvinist than a Russ Meyer softcore B simply because it pretends to be something it's not.

The preoccupations that Scorsese imposes on it don't help either. The quotes from old films and old music helped greatly to develop the atmosphere of *Mean Streets*. They belonged there. They don't belong here, unless the suggestion is meant that this is really a forties woman's movie which will teach the old lesson that you're nothing without a man. It's *Mildred Pierce* all over again, except that Mildred actually owned the restaurant. The title tells us what to think about Alice; it's an allusion to an old Carmen Lombardo standard.* But it's also a perhaps unconscious

*Annie doesn't live here any more/It must have been your picture that she tore/She said that I would know you by the smile in your eye/Your checkered vest, your fancy spats, your polkadot tie/You answer to that description, so I guess that you're the guy/No, Annie doesn't live here anymore. ["Annie Doesn't Live Here Anymore," music by Harold Spina, words by Joe Young and Johnny Burke, copyright 1938 by Bourne Co. Copyright renewed. Reprinted with permission.]

156

De Niro confronts genres: with Harvey Keitel in *Mean Streets,* a psychological, personal drama. . .

reference to a more recent Alice, she of the restaurant in Stockbridge, Massachusetts, the song by Arlo Guthrie, and the film by Arthur Penn. Alice Brock in song and story was emblematic of the new competent, independent woman of the late sixties. But Alice Hyatt doesn't live there anymore; she's the model for a TV sitcom. When *Alice Doesn't Live Here Anymore* isn't being repressive, it's camp. It likes *women,* and that sets it apart no doubt, but the women it likes are such harmless, cute kooks. What a relief! (They're no threat.)

Taxi Driver (1976) fails in similar ways. It was considered, like *Alice,* a great gamble on the part of producers Michael and Julia Phillips. Within the cramped Hollywood context of the seventies, perhaps it was. But it turned out to be an even greater critical and financial success than *Alice.* Meanwhile, the safer bet, *New York, New York,* which Scorsese wanted to shoot first, failed miserably at the box office.

Taxi Driver is a perfect match of the paranoid talents of writer Paul Schrader and director Scorsese, with the quirky persona of Robert De Niro as its anchor. It's an attempt to make a late-forties film noir more than twenty-five years later. At least on the film-buff level, it succeeds in recapturing that atmosphere. The Bernard Herrmann score, despite the fact that it's overblown and self-parodic, helps immeasurably in this respect. Once again, Scorsese gets great performances from his cast—even from himself in a remarkable cameo. He knows this mood, and has practiced with it in *Mean Streets,* so he's able to bathe the film in an effective wash of red and black fear.

157

. . . with Scorsese in *Taxi Driver*, a psychopathic gangster film. . .

The problem, and it is insurmountable, is that it is not 1948 anymore. It hasn't been for quite a while. So what's a film noir doing at a time like this? Mainly turning back the clock politically and artistically. In *Badlands*, a much better film about similar characters, Terrence Malick had the good sense not only to place the story in an historical context, but to stylize it, and set it on the Western plains. Scorsese's naked city is almost a joke: at best it's quaint. De Niro's Travis Bickle is certainly a magnificent construction within the crooked context of the film, but Scorsese and Schrader don't give us a point of view from which to get a handle on him. Before production began, Scorsese spoke of the film as being about Arthur Bremer, the would-be assassin of George Wallace. Bickle's diary has its source in Bremer's notebook (and cinematically in Malick's much more interesting narration for *Badlands*). But depriving a contemporary assassin of a context of contemporary sensibilities makes the film a hodgepodge. It's just as much an entertainment machine as *Rollercoaster* or *Meteor*; it's an individualist's disaster movie. But it has no mind of its own.

Schrader, to his credit, now considers *Taxi Driver* "a very rich piece of juvenilia, but it is juvenilia. It is an adolescent, immature mind, struggling to identify itself. It has no maturity except at the talent level."[4]

New York, New York seemed a much more promising project: a perfect film for Scorsese's unusual mix of talents and concerns. The archaic film style of forties musicals would fit a film about this subject. The period was

. . . and with Liza Minnelli in *New York, New York*, an attempt at a nostalgic forties musical drama.

an interesting one that deserved to be treated on film. And the music— that late efflorescence of Tin Pan Alley just before the advent of rock 'n' roll—was for any serious student of those times enormously attractive. In its parts, *New York, New York* fulfills its promise.

The major problem is that so many of its parts are missing. The first cut was twice as long as the final cut. The film moves fitfully, as if in a dream. The first sequence, introductory, lasts almost twenty-five minutes, about a fifth of the film. The fifteen-minute "Happy Endings" production number, which cost $350,000 to shoot, is reduced to a few seconds. (There were rumors, before the film bombed, that it would be released separately as a short.) Large chunks of plot have disappeared; the film moves jerkily into the fifties. We're getting only half the characters. Most people, including Scorsese, who were privileged to see early screenings of the four-hour-plus cut prefer it to the shorter release version. At its present length, *New York, New York* doesn't really have a chance to prove what it can do. It really ought to be recut into a five-part television serial.

But there are other conceptual problems with the film. Scorsese smartly is not trying to make an old musical, as Bogdanovich did, but the old music in the film is still a central focus. The parodies written by Liza Minnelli's friends John Kander and Fred Ebb simply don't jibe with the historical jive. One of the few brief moments when the film comes alive involves the remarkable Diahne Abbott's Lady Day rendition of "Hon-

159

eysuckle Rose." Another consists of Francine Evans (Minnelli) listening to an original recording of "Billet Doux" by the Hot Club of France, the only original recording in the film. Both sequences, ironically, were cut from the release version when the film went into its second run. If Scorsese was going to make a film about the music, he should have paid more attention to it.

A third brief but vital scene in the film consists of a short taxi ride down a rear-projected 1950 Fifth Avenue. All of a sudden, viewers are reminded forcibly of the hothouse atmosphere Scorsese has created. His original conception was to shoot the film entirely on stage sets, many of them purposely abstracted, to recall the sketchy studio milieus of forties musicals. This might have worked had the film been shot in black and white, but color is a lot more revealingly realistic. Now, it's simply a distraction. It might have been expensive to do a realistic film about the forties, but New York, New York, as is, cost $12 million. The budget was there.

Scorsese can't seem to keep his film-buff sensibility under control, even here in a movie where it should work positively. By the end of the film he is reduced to fitful starts and stops; he's lost the feel completely. Francine Evans, who started out as Doris Day, has nightmarishly metamorphosed into Liza Minnelli's mother. The mimickry is shameful. The film goes haywire. The romance subplot between Jimmy Doyle (De Niro) and Francine is a ripoff of A Star Is Born, a film that has already been remade more times than necessary. The music is used as decoration. There's no real feel for it, and there is no information about its history. Black musicians, for instance, were given lip service in the original release version. Now that a thirteen-minute sequence has been axed, they don't exist at all.

Scorsese and crew shot The Last Waltz, a filmed record of The Band's farewell concert, in November 1976. After an arduous editing and mixing job, the film was released eighteen months later. It was warmly received as the best concert music film since Woodstock—and probably deserved that accolade, if for no other reason than that it captures The Band's fine music with an honesty and straightforwardness that cinematically parallel that group's music.

Unlike other concert films, The Last Waltz was shot in standard-gauge 35 mm, which gives it a visual presence that is unusual in this genre. Scorsese carefully choreographed his eight cameramen (who included Laszlo Kovacs, Vilmos Zsigmond, and Michael Chapman), referring to a 300-page shooting script which listed all lyrics and chord changes. The soundtrack was mixed down to four Dolbyized tracks from an unprecedented twenty-four-track location "take." ("The longest mix in history," according to publicists.) Three of the musical numbers were filmed on a soundstage in Hollywood after the concert, where Scorsese indulged himself in complicated tracking shots of the kind he had used in New York, New York. The music—by Bob Dylan, Joni Mitchell, Eric Clapton, and others in addition to The Band—was punctuated by set-piece interviews in which Scorsese talks with the members of the group. Robbie Robertson, leader of the band and, in fact, producer of the movie, comes off pleasantly as a sort of undissipated Kristofferson. He shows himself to have star quality—which was one of the objects of the project.

Yet despite the inherent interest in The Last Waltz—the music, the memories of the sixties, the discovery of a new career for Robertson—and despite the admirable technical quality, there's a certain pretension to the film we wish weren't there. Scorsese himself does not come across as a star and his interview questions are rather beside the point; the studio numbers are superfluous, they break the rhythm of the concert. Once again, Scorsese's reach has exceeded his grasp, but only by a thin margin this time. Boiled down to pure concert performance, The Last Waltz would be a perfectly cut gem of a film.

There's no doubt Martin Scorsese is an exceptionally interesting and imaginative director, but for more than ten years now he's been setting self-destructive traps for himself, then stepping smartly right into them. He's capable of a great deal more, one surmises. In 1974 he shot a forty-eight-minute essay (originally meant to be part of a television series) called Italianamerican. Basically a documentary visit with his parents, it had many of the qualities missing from the feature films he has made since Mean Streets. The people weren't characters, they were people. The film wasn't a self-conscious parody of movies dead and gone, but honest and straightforward. Scorsese spoke for himself rather than hiding behind the pretentiously anxious film-noir mask. Italianamerican was relaxed, broadly humorous, not excessively ambitious, direct.

Phantom of the Roxy

Born in Philadelphia, Brian De Palma started making films when he was at Columbia University in the early sixties. As he tells it, they wouldn't let him direct the Columbia Players, so he went out and bought a Bolex and started making shorts. One of them, Woton's Wake, won a prize. By this time he was at Sarah Lawrence College, where he found a rich girl to finance a $100,000 black-and-white feature called The Wedding Party (1963-1968). He used Robert De Niro and Jill Clayburgh in it, showing remarkable foresight. But the film was never distributed (it played in one New York theater in 1968), and De Palma settled into the New York film

The Wedding Party: The groom and friends (the crew-cut young man at right is De Niro), the groom and bride (Jill Clayburgh). [Stills courtesy Brian De Palma.]

scene, doing occasional documentaries and picking up odd jobs. One of the documentaries, *The Responsive Eye*, made a large enough profit to enable De Palma to finance his second feature, *Murder à la Mod* (1967), but again it proved impossible to find a distributor.

With two complete feature films in the can, and on the shelf, De Palma was in a rather unusual position. His next step was to join forces with a young producer named Charles Hirsch. Together they sketched out a treatment for an improvisatory film about the draft, young people, sex, and other sundry concerns of the late sixties. *Greetings* (1968), starring De Niro, was shot for $43,100, according to Hirsch, only $15,000 of which was cash, the rest deferred. That figure even includes $4000 wasted on a false start in 16 mm. The third time out, De Palma hit the jackpot. *Greetings* was picked up for distribution and in fact became something of a minor hit, returning many times its cost. It was followed by a sequel, *Hi, Mom!* (1969), a gentle satire on television and contemporary concerns, and De Palma was set to graduate to Hollywood.

Both *Greetings* and *Hi, Mom!* would have been interesting movies even if they hadn't been shot for next to nothing. They were made so quickly and so informally that they had to mirror closely the world of their subjects, no matter how inexperienced the filmmakers may have been. Together, they made up an instant-feedback image of what it was like to be a member of the counterculture (although it hadn't yet been so named) living on the edge in New York in 1968 and 1969. They validated the existence of a lifestyle. And the conditions under which they were produced not only gave them a timeliness major studio productions could never hope to achieve, but also demanded a loose style that was further ingratiating. They were more like home movies than anything else. If there were stretches that were boring or that didn't develop anywhere, nevertheless you had a feeling that one of our own was telling the story. Even in the much more highly structured projects which have

162

Murder à la Mod: Ken Burrows, William Finley, Melanie Mander, and Margot Norton illustrate the catalogue. [Stills courtesy Brian De Palma.]

followed, De Palma still gives this impression of a rather likable directorial personality.

While finishing *Hi, Mom!* he made one last independent film, a record of a performance of Richard Schechner's stage production of *Dionysus in '69*, a landmark of the participatory total-theater style that was current in the late sixties. By 1970 De Palma was in Hollywood with a contract from Warner Brothers to direct Tommy Smothers and Orson Welles in a rather fey comedy by novelist Jordan Crittenden.

Get to Know Your Rabbit was shot in 1970, shelved, then dumped in 1973. It has become a minor cult film since, more because of the studio's treatment of it than for any intrinsic qualities. It must have seemed at the time a proper commercial industry debut for an idiosyncratic young filmmaker who had made a few bucks with loose, improvisational satire. Smothers plays a business executive who gets bored with the "rat race," enrolls in magician school, then hits the road performing. Katharine Ross plays "the girl," Orson Welles, the teacher. By the end of the film, Smothers discovers you can't really escape. His business manager has turned tap-dancing, the magician's dropout trick, into a minor industry, pushing a patented "17-day dropout plan." De Palma actually does rather well with this material. He doesn't take it too seriously.

But De Palma's Hollywood career was dying in the bud. He returned to New York to do an inexpensive thriller for Edward R. Pressman. *Sisters*

163

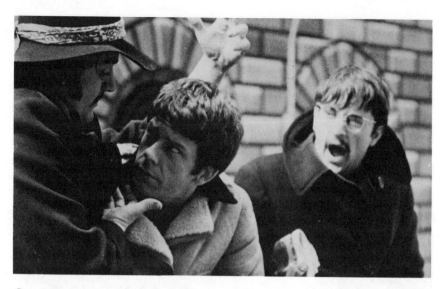

Greetings: De Niro, now with mustache, with Gerrit Graham and Jonathan Worden. Considering the range of films he has made with De Palma, Scorsese, and Coppola during the last fifteen years, Robert De Niro must be counted the most influential actor of his generation.

(1973), with Margot Kidder, is probably his best film to date. A guignol tour de force based on Siamese twins as a cinematic concept, it is lovingly mounted by De Palma, whose own pet device has always been the split screen. Once again, the inexpensive film proved highly profitable and the by now rapidly aging young director was a marketable commodity in Hollywood.

Sisters depended heavily on Hitchcock techniques for its effect, and even more heavily on Bernard Herrmann, Hitchcock's ex-composer, whom De Palma had coaxed into doing the score for the film. De Palma was beginning to find a marketable style as a distant Hitchcock epigone.

For his next film he thought to combine some of the occult mood that had worked in *Sisters* with the counterculture subject matter of his earlier movies. *Phantom of the Paradise* (1974), with Paul Williams (the musician, not the director) as composer and star, failed to find an audience and has joined *Get to Know Your Rabbit* as a midnight cult film.

Obsession (1976) was a more conservative variation on a Hitchcock theme. From a script by Paul Schrader, the film reprises the dream and romance of *Vertigo*, just as *Sisters* before it had played on *Psycho*. With a major middle-aged star, Cliff Robertson, it was aimed at a broader market, but it was too distanced and stylized. Once again, a Herrmann score helped, but as with the score from *Taxi Driver* (these were his last two

Donald (Tommy Smothers) and The Terrific-Looking Girl (Katharine Ross) perform the Incredible Sack Trick in *Get to Know Your Rabbit*.

compositions before his death), Herrmann lapsed into self-parody. Genevieve Bujold almost brings off the double role of wife and daughter but gets drowned eventually in the bathos of the script.

Carrie (1976) was more successful at the box offiice, but once again derivative without being creative. Again borrowing from *Psycho*, De Palma was able to create a highly effective thrill machine from Stephen King's novel about a lonesome high-school girl who discovers she has telekinetic powers. Whatever substance the film has centers around questions of adolescent womanhood, but *Carrie* is on the whole decidedly misogynistic. Despite *Sisters*, De Palma has never been able to cope successfully with woman characters. Yet there's some humor to the film, and that makes it more attractive than the enervatingly serious *Obsession*, even if the latter film is clearly a more ambitious product.

The Fury (1978) reprised some of *Carrie*'s telekinetic tricks, but on a larger budget. It's hard to tell what De Palma had in mind taking on a project so similar to the one he had just completed. *The Fury* has some of the same portentous quality that marked *Obsession*, a number of technically admirable scenes, and some better than satisfactory performances (especially from John Cassavetes and Kirk Douglas), but on the whole it seems ponderous. There is an interesting movie buried here somewhere —it has to do with the relationship between father and son and the curiously affecting ghostly romance between two young people (played by Amy Irving and Andrew Stevens) who have never met but who are

John Cassavetes attempts to cajole Amy Irving at the end of *The Fury*—just before she tires of him in a most cinematographically entertaining way.

nevertheless united and isolated by their shared telepathic gift. The trouble with the film is that these human relationships are overshadowed by the supernatural gimmicks.

De Palma may yet graduate from his conscientious study of Hitchcock. He seems to have the desire to do so. But commercially he's most valuable as a mimic of the master. Andrew Sarris once wrote of De Palma, "I always had the curious feeling that De Palma's sensibility was sweeter than the circumstances warranted. I never felt any malice or snideness in his work, only a cheerful lightheadedness. Could he ever pull it all together?"

We're still waiting to find out.

Where Were You in '62?

George Lucas has done more with less than any of the other young new star directors. He grew up in rural Modesto, California, and never thought much about movies. As a teenager, he was a car freak. So, as it happens, was Haskell Wexler. Lucas was working for a mechanic hired by Wexler when the two first met. Gradually, the interest in cars was transferred to film. After a spell in Junior College, Lucas enrolled in film school at U.S.C. He discovered an immediate facility for the medium, and one of the short films he made, *THX-1138*, later served as the model for his first feature, by the same name. Lucas was able to move directly from film school to the Warner Brothers lot mainly through the good

George Lucas's first attempt at science fiction was intellectual and distanced. It didn't make a profit. Robert Duvall *is* THX-1138.

offices of Francis Coppola, whom he had met while interning on *Finian's Rainbow.* The two became good friends, and have formed the nucleus of the unusually tight-knit community of the new generation in Hollywood. Neither lives in L.A., but rather near San Francisco, and like Michael Ritchie, who settled in Mill Valley, they like to think they preserve a perspective on the L.A.-centered industry not shared by filmmakers who live in Southern California.

THX-1138, completed in 1971, was a nicely built science-fiction fantasy, not unlike the Patrick MacGoohan television series *The Prisoner,* about a world under complete authoritarian control from which the hairless inmates try to escape. Completely subterranean in setting, it ends with a shocking shot of the sun. Lucas utilized the then-unfinished tunnels of the San Francisco BART transit system to create his abstract world for a very small investment, and the rest of the settings, inexpensive but effective, match the sterile milieu, but so do the characters. The film quickly became a cult object, but it also gave Lucas a reputation as a mechanical technotwirp director who couldn't handle human beings. The film is based on stale science-fiction concepts, but it has the advantage of ending on an optimistic note that is unusual for the genre.

Lucas consciously planned his next film to be diametrically opposed to *THX. American Graffiti* (1973) was his concept—indeed it's considerably autobiographical—worked out by neophyte screenwriters Willard Huyck and Gloria Katz. Made for $750,000, it grossed nearly $50 million; the

Ronny Howard, Candy Clark, and Charlie Martin Smith chug-a-lug some brews in *American Graffiti.* "Where were you in 62?" (I was living across the street from *Animal House*—see p. 225.)

most profitable feature-film investment of the seventies. It's also a worthwhile movie. Lucas sharply etched a portrait of a generation coming of age—or more precisely, of the fantasy image those of us in our thirties all hold of our adolescence. Cannily, Lucas analyzed the archetypes of fifties[*] teenagerhood. His four male leads cover the spectrum: Terry (Charlie Martin Smith) is the luckless schlemiel, the butt of most jokes, the class clown. His type is just barely accepted in the rigid high-school social hierarchy, usually because he plays the drums well, or his father owns the local diner, or his mother always feeds everybody. At Bayside High School, we used to call guys like Terry "nerds." John (Paul Le Mat) is only one level higher in the social structure. We used to call guys like this "rocks." They were slightly tougher than the rest of us, and often older. They managed to acquire a jalopy before anyone else, often grew up to be mechanics, wore the sleeves of their teeshirts rolled, with the cigarettes neatly tucked in, and sported D.A. haircuts. The "rocks" I knew swaggered more than John does—the difference I suppose between the country town of Modesto and New York City, the West Coast and the East. Their social standing was brief. Within a year or two, the rest of us had been accepted at colleges and class structure was beginning to

---

[*]Although the film is set in 1962, its milieu is much more closely associated with the late fifties.

develop. "Rocks," very simply, were working-class kids—and the rest of us weren't.

The middle classes in *American Graffiti* are represented by Steve (Ron Howard), the sociable type, president-of-his-class-and-all-the-girls-like-him, as we used to say, partly in envy, more in thinly veiled contempt, and Curt (Richard Dreyfuss), everyman, part nerd, would-be rock, never quite the personality kid that Steve was, but the one who gets to leave in the end; the one who later writes the book, makes the movie, immortalizes Steve and John and Terry. Usually, he wears glasses.

Lucas sketches these people with precision and feeling. And that's one major reason the film is not only popular but meaningful. Where he falls down—and it's not unexpected—is in his portrayal of the women. Cindy Williams, who plays Laurie, later went on to become a star in the television series *Laverne and Shirley*, which spins off from the girls in *American Graffiti.* * In the film, she plays the more sensitive of the two archetypes, Laurie the essence of middle-class girlhood, and the ideal girlfriend for Curt or Steve. Candy Clark plays Debbie, the working-class stereotype. But Lucas has chosen to ignore the numerous other feminine roles. Where are the bookworm, the best friend, and the talent? The blond fantasy makes a mysterious appearance, but where is the female equivalent of Curt? *American Graffiti* has a distinctly male point of view that is, moreover, adolescent. It gives us the nostalgia; it doesn't give us a more reasoned explication of our untenable situation at seventeen.

For all its attractiveness, it is also a very calculated film. It is masterfully photographed by Haskell Wexler. (Coppola guaranteed the production at Universal by acting as producer.) It is intelligently acted. But it was a success not for these reasons but because Lucas had the smart sense to mold the film around forty-one rock 'n' roll classics. They were written into the script, and $80,000—more than 10 percent of the budget—went to pay for music rights. It was worth it. Lucas discovered it didn't really matter where the songs went in the film. Every scene worked well with a number of them. Visually and textually, *American Graffiti* is a rather small and unambitious movie. Paul Williams (the director, not the musician) had done it as well or better several years earlier in *Out of It.* But the music track, incessant, releases great amounts of nostalgic energy: it makes the film what it is. Within a few years, rock 'n' roll would prove to be Hollywood's most financially valuable tool.

After only his second feature, Lucas was in a position to write his own

---

*The film actually spawned three television series. Ron Howard went on to star in *Happy Days*; Suzanne Somers (the mysterious blonde in the T-bird) later achieved a certain jiggly fame in *Three's Company*.

ticket. He was cynical about it. But he was smart, too. He wasn't about to jeopardize his position. Indeed, *Star Wars* (1977) made *Graffiti* look like a student exercise. Lucas crammed everything he knew about movies into the picture, and the result is a compendium of genre entertainment from the last thirty years. The overarching metaphor is science fiction, but there is little science in the film and still less of the philosophical structure that made such classics as *2001* and the television series *Star Trek* cult objects of furious devotion. There are, however, great gobs of fiction, almost all of it borrowed.

The desert planet and the sand people come from Frank Herbert's *Dune*, the moisture farm parodies John Ford's *The Searchers*. Hyperspace is borrowed from *Forbidden Planet* (and numerous novel predecessors), and photon torpedoes from *Star Trek*. The saloon is straight out of the western, as are most of the land-bound scenes; robots with personality have a tradition that stretches back through the magnificent HAL of *2001* to the granddaddy of them all, Robby of *Forbidden Planet*; R2D2 is clearly the product of the same factory that produced Huey, Dewey, and Louie of *Silent Running*; Chewbacca suggests a Cowardly Lion via *Planet of the Apes*; the character of Obi-Wan Kenobi also looks back on a long tradition stretching from Gandolph to the Wiz; C3PO is a Tin Man, even talks like Jack Haley. And the climactic attack on the death star has no basis in orbital physics: the mise en scène comes straight from any one of a dozen Korean War movie dogfights. The ships even look like F-84s and display surprisingly similar aerodynamic qualities. Finally, as film lovers know, the ultimate scene intentionally parodies Leni Riefenstahl's *Triumph of the Will*.[5]

The Force be with you, indeed!

The closest *Star Wars* gets to the mystery and intelligence usually associated with SF is a mildly apocalyptic quasi-religious belief in heroes, hero worship, and the heroic in history that some interpreters have labeled quasi-fascist. Quoting Leni Riefenstahl, apparently as a joke, doesn't help. *Star Wars* disappears into hyperspace. It's a black-hole neutron star sucking up everything in its wake. Whole genres of film disappear into it, from swashbucklers (the Kenobi-Vader battle) to Laurel and Hardy (R2D2-C3PO). Nor does it help that the arch-villain is all black and Lucas thought it advisable to hire James Earl Jones to re-dub Darth Vader's voice.

Star Wars is nothing short of stupendous—as a catalogue of Hollywood entertainment techniques. But it offers very little else to anyone old enough to be slightly familiar with them from other movies.

No one is suggesting that just because *Star Wars* comes to an orgasmic, operatic climax, the kid from Modesto is a secret Bircher. That's clearly

Robby is the prototype for contemporary cinematic robots, HAL, the sacrificial saint of the cybernetic performers. Here Robby serves Anne Francis and friend some refreshments in *Forbidden Planet*. He uses an Erlenmeyer flask: hi-tech in 1956. David Bowman (Keir Dullea) is reflected in the glass eye of HAL in Kubrick's *2001: A Space Odyssey*. The least anthropomorphic of cinematic robots (and therefore the most realistic) HAL was also the most intelligent and witty before his untimely demise. *2001* still dwarfs all other attempts at science fiction.

absurd. What he is, on the evidence we have so far, is a cool, calculating technician. In a revealing interview with Stephen Farber shortly before he began work on *Star Wars*, he smartly summarized his own directorial persona. Because what he says is so widely characteristic of the new Hollywood, it's worth quoting him at length.

"I like action, adventure, chases, things blowing up," he told Farber,

> and I have strong feelings about science fiction and comic books and that sort of world. Some of my friends are concerned about art and being considered a Fellini or an Orson Welles, but I've never really had that problem. I just like making movies. I was at a film-conference with George Cukor, and he detested the fact that everyone calls us film-makers. He said, "I'm not a film-maker. A film-maker is like a toy-

Close encounters of design: Woody Allen's *Sleeper* butler-robot and Huey and Dewey (or Dewey and Louie, or Louie and Huey) with Bruce Dern in *Silent Running* are clear models, respectively, for. . .

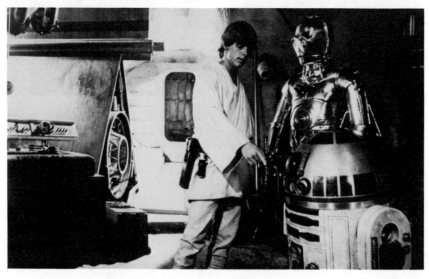

. . . C3PO and R2D2 (here shown with humanoid actor) in *Star Wars*.

maker, and I'm a director." Well, I'm a film-maker. I'm very much akin to a toy-maker. If I wasn't a film-maker, I'd probably *be* a toy-maker. I like to make things move and I like to make them myself. Just give me the tools and I'll make the toys. I can sit forever doodling on my movie. I don't think that much about whether it's going to be a great movie or a terrible movie, or whether it's going to be a piece of art or a piece of shit.[6]

The modesty is admirable. The trouble is that a talented craftsman like Lucas doesn't turn out a product any more absorbing than an arrogant would-be Orson Welles like Bogdanovich.

There are other reasons to make movies, George.

Son of Universal

Steven Spielberg decided to be a moviemaker at the age of 12 the way other kids in his hometown of Phoenix, Arizona, might have been deciding at the same time to be astronauts or jet pilots or firemen. "Some kids get involved in a Little League team or in music, in a band—or watching TV," he told Mitch Tuchman in a recent revealing interview, "I was always drowning in little home movies."[7] As a teenager he shot fifteen or twenty 8-mm films before graduating to 16 mm.

He had moved to L.A. before he was twenty, and one day in 1967 just sort of wandered onto the Universal lot. "I would get up at the crack of dawn," he explains, "wear a suit, and carry a briefcase, and for some reason Scotty at the gate waved me through each day. I just assumed that people assumed I was somebody's son, one of the executives in the Black Tower." In the last few years the Spielberg ploy has been used by a number of other would-be directors.

For three months, he watched professional directors making movies and television shows, but nobody seemed to want what he had to offer. The industry was still a preserve of the middle-aged. Francis Coppola, a film-school graduate who was then actually earning a living as director and screenwriter, was his idol. He first met George Lucas at a U.S.C. student-film retrospective. They became friends. John Milius was in the same U.S.C. group. A little while later he encountered Hal Barwood (U.S.C.) and Matthew Robbins (A.F.I.), who have collaborated, credited or uncredited, on all his feature films since. Over the years that followed the group expanded to include producer Rob Cohen, Brian De Palma, Philip Kaufman, Bill Huyck, Gloria Katz, Marcia Lucas, and Michael Ritchie, as well as godfather and role model Coppola.

The group is as close as the new Hollywood comes to a controlling clan, and Spielberg is at the center of it, not only because his three feature films have grossed more than the collected works of any of the others, but more important because Steve symbolizes best the prodigious but gloriously innocent talent that is the hallmark of this generation of whiz kids. The image he projects is like nothing so much as the wide-eyed wonder of Cary Guffey, the four-year-old at the hot center of *Close Encounters* who takes such pure pleasure in the phenomena that frighten and consternate the grownups. Spielberg is not unintelligent—far from it. On the contrary, he has an infectious sense of self-effacing humor and analytical Hollywood street smarts that are ingratiating. He's charming, modest, sharp, and kind—and these qualities come across strongly both in the characters of his films and their tone.

Spielberg's first effort in 35 mm, a short entitled *Amblin'*, was made in 1969 purely to demonstrate to producers that he had professional credentials. His esoteric 16-mm films were getting him nowhere. *Amblin'* did the trick. It proved he could "move the camera and compose nicely and deal with lighting and performances." He says he can't look at it now, it's "the slick by-product of a kid immersed up to his nose in film."

Within months, he was under contract to Universal, where he rose quickly. During 1970 and 1971 he shot a string of television programs and TV movies that included a *Night Gallery*, a *Marcus Welby*, two episodes of *The Psychiatrists* (he considers the second, in which Clu Gulager is dying of duodenal cancer, his best television work), a *Name of the Game*, an *Owen Marshall*, and the first regular episode (after two TV movies) of *Columbo*.

Then came the made-for-television films *Duel, Something Evil,* and *Savage* (made on loan to CBS). Of the three he considers *Something Evil* a personal work, and *Savage* an antipathetic assignment. But it was the first of the trio, *Duel,* that received most attention. The film was later released abroad as a theatrical film (as many TV movies are), where it achieved the status of a cult object. Basically, it's a simple metaphor of the American road: a chase film, with a mysterious truck pursuing Dennis Weaver across the country.

Soon after it was shown in 1971, offers to direct a feature began to pour in, but Spielberg, 24, was still under an exclusive contract to Universal.

His first feature assignment was to be the Burt Reynolds film *White Lightning.* He spent several months on the project before realizing that it was going to be a Burt Reynolds movie, not a Steven Spielberg film, and that he didn't want to make his debut as a hired hand. *Sugarland Express* (1974) was clearly his own project, with the script being written by old friends Hal Barwood and Matthew Robbins. Like *White Lightning,* it was meant to take advantage of his demonstrated strengths as a director of chase/road movies. It remains one of the most interesting of the genre. A

William Atherton and Goldie Hawn on the lam with hostage Michael Sacks in *Sugarland Express.*

convict's wife (Goldie Hawn) convinces her husband (William Atherton) to escape because their baby is being adopted. The chase that ensues is not only grandiose but essentially comic, and the film makes a number of interesting points. Hawn is a stronger character than her husband, which is still rare in the Hollywood scheme of things, and Ben Johnson as the sheriff is given a complex character which is almost as sympathetic as those of the convict and his wife. The relationship between Atherton and Hawn, and Michael Sacks as a police officer, is also rather unusual. Structurally, the chase is not only more exciting than most, but humorous as well. In all, quite an achievement. Since it leaves itself more time to deal with character, and since its people are complex, interesting, and rooted in reality, *Sugarland Express* is arguably a more interesting film than either of the two blockbusters that succeeded it. The chase draws us in, but it's the notoriety of the couple that is the real subject of the film, and that is a more interesting theme than either *Jaws* or *Close Encounters* has. If Spielberg had stuck closer to Barwood and Robbins we might have a far different image of him today.

Jaws and *E.T.*, two of the five most profitable films of all time, are surprisingly similar. Both present simple suspense stories with linear plots and make them exciting and absorbing through a continual, incessant panoply of cinematic effects. They are just the sort of films we should expect from a young man who has achieved breathless mastery of the medium. Not that character and human relationships aren't as freshly realized as they are in *Sugarland Express*; Spielberg doesn't owe his entire sense of people to Barwood and Robbins, but there's so little time to develop character in the two blockbusters that he only has space to sketch them in. Both films depend on machines more than human beings for their ultimate effect.

Close Encounters was apparently Spielberg's conception from the beginning, although Paul Schrader (and perhaps others) prepared early drafts of the script for him. Schrader at one point thought he was going to receive screen credit, but the final version lists only Spielberg as writer. In fact, he takes sole credit for the novelization of the film as well. He was at work on *Close Encounters* before he started shooting *Jaws*, so the parallel development of the projects may account for some of the structural similarities.

Far from being his own conception, *Jaws* was an assignment from producers David Brown and Richard Zanuck. It must have looked like a very appealing challenge. The book by writer Peter Benchley had started out as a very small novel—the original advance from the publisher was only $7500—but had been engineered by Doubleday editor Tom Congdon into one of the major popular successes of the seventies. Zanuck and Brown were intent on repeating that success with the film of the novel. The basic problem was simple: how to visualize the shark. Train one? Not likely. The producers eventually settled on a combination of documentary footage (shot off the Australian coast) and a shark-machine, nicknamed "Bruce."

There were technical problems with Bruce, as it turned out, and filming at sea was much more trying than Spielberg, Zanuck, or Brown had ever envisioned. Eventually the budget for the film ballooned to more than $8 million. The producers were seriously worried. It wasn't so much that they'd hired an extraordinarily young director. The real potential hazard lay in the material. The shark was everything. Benchley hadn't been able to come up with much of a plot: it's essentially borrowed from Ibsen's *Enemy of the People*—some of the townsfolk want to close the beaches, others are worried about the loss in tourist income if they do. Everything hung on the battle between the shark and the men. The men were controllable; the shark was not. If Bruce didn't perform up to expectations, the film would be a total failure.

To their credit, the special-effects staff of Universal under the direction of Robert A. Mattey managed to jiggle a satisfactory performance out of Bruce. But it was minimal at best. Spielberg saved the day by devising a series of much less complicated, more purely cinematic effects that make *Jaws* the most cleanly efficient and thoroughly effective entertainment machine of the decade. Next to *Jaws*, *Star Wars* looks like an idiosyncratic mood piece. John Williams, a friend of Spielberg's, provided a necessary groundbase of music keys. Verna Fields's editing earned her a position as vice president at Universal. But the major part of the credit must go to Spielberg.

Perhaps the best way to explain just what it is he does so well is to describe one scene. I think this one is exemplary. At one point, Brody (Roy Scheider) is sitting on the beach as people frolic in the surf. He is nervous. He wanted the beaches closed. He thinks he sees a fin. He panics. But it turns out to be a lady in a black swimming cap. In prose, as it must have appeared in the screenplay, it's not much of anything. But Spielberg films it this way:

The beach. A fat lady. Kid on raft. Dog. Lots of close shots and fast cutting. Brody sees something. We don't know what. In one very quick montage, three shots of Scheider worried, looking, interrupted and in effect cut by people walking between him and the camera. The effect is to interrupt our field of vision, just as his is being interrupted. Then, a climactic shot of Scheider, zooming in and tracking out at the same time to maintain the same frame while drastically increasing depth perception. The effect is quick and vertiginous. In fact, this is the shot Hitchcock spent twenty years devising and $20,000 shooting for the tower scene which is the climax of *Vertigo*. Spielberg has the confidence to throw it away on a minor scene. He knows there'll be better effects later.

The film is a catalogue of such devices. Someday, cinema Ph.D. candidates will be writing voluminous treatises on *Jaws*. At one point, Hooper (Richard Dreyfuss) describes the shark very nicely: "All this machine does," he explains, "is swim and eat and make little sharks and that's it." There's enticing purity there, and it's emblematic. *Jaws* is a shark of a movie.

But Spielberg is not only a technician. There's a sense of pleasure in people about his work as well as the characteristic joy in the execution of craft. Dreyfuss, who has starred in both blockbusters, perhaps comes closest to duplicating Spielberg's infectious enthusiasm on the screen. He's nervous, energetic, bright, ingratiating, impatient, sometimes silly. Although you don't notice it, and it only occurs to you when you think back on it, and it seems like carping, he's also, well, not very deep, perhaps even shallow. Everything happens on the surface. "I wouldn't be satisfied with my films," Spielberg told Tuchman, "if there weren't human beings functioning as your guide through this world of mechanized madness." The difficulty is we don't often get to know as much as we would like about the guides.

If *Jaws* is a lovely machine, *Close Encounters of the Third Kind* is a spacey tour de force. The tension between the characters and the machine of plot and effect was very much on Spielberg's mind. He says he finally wrote the film himself because he couldn't convince anyone else to do both the personal story of Roy Neary (Dreyfuss) and the larger narrative of the first meeting between humans and extraterrestrials. He wanted a balance between the macrocosm and the microcosm.

As it happened, the film that was shot concentrates strongly on the human stories that would have been minor subplots in most other versions of this archetypal SF plot. We learn extremely little about the official mystery of the potential encounter, and what little information we do get is filtered through François Truffaut's French and Bob Balaban's translations. Spielberg makes it especially difficult for us to follow the big story. In order to redirect our attention to the little stories, he has to contrive a very rickety MacGuffin (like the motivating red herrings by that name that power Hitchcock's films). The plot is shot through with false leads, gaping holes, and circuitous side trails, as a number of critics have noted. But it doesn't seem to matter, either, as a number of other critics have explained.

There may be no plausible reason for Neary or Jillian Guiler (Melinda Dillon) to be so teased by the extraterrestrials into making the trip to the landing site (just in the nick of time). Of course, it would have been easier just to pick them up—or at least imprint the whole plan more clearly in their consciousnesses. But Spielberg is saving the actual encounter for the climax. No film, in fact, has been more obviously designed to foster a sequel: it stops where we would expect it to begin. For most of the time, he wants to concentrate on Neary's obsession, and see how he can handle it on film. To keep us properly tense, he punctuates this modest enterprise with a string of devices almost as long as *Jaws*'s: the moving objects (out of *The Exorcist*), the bright lights, the strange sunburns, a few perfunctory chases, occasional shots of the ships (but not *the* ship!), a few quotes from *North by Northwest*, and most amusingly, the lovely little scene in which Jillian tries to keep The Force out of her house. (It's a classic nightmare and ends with the screws in the ventilator cover slowly twisting themselves out. Scary! So what, if it's pointless in terms of plot?)

People who take science fiction seriously are even angrier with this film than they are with *Star Wars*. It assiduously avoids all of the issues that should adhere to the basic plot. Spielberg has stolen the subject matter and carefully left the theme behind. He keeps us entertained with some nice effects while he goes about the business of playing with his own mountain: the character of obsession. Then he brings in a little lukewarm apocalyptic quasi-religious ecstasy at the end to let us feel we've completed the experience and drawn the moral.

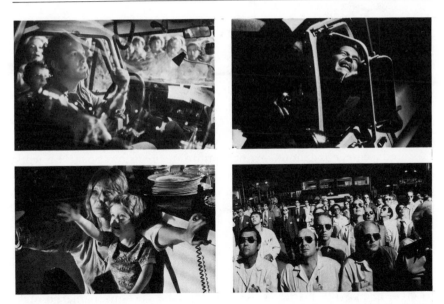

When You Wish Upon a Star: Richard Dreyfuss, Melinda Dillon, Carey Guffey, and a group of technicians follow directions. Far out.

Preview versions of the film included the original recording of "When You Wish Upon a Star" in the ultimate sequence. Spielberg cut it out because it seemed to cheapen the religious aura at the end of the film. In context, it was ironic, although Steven didn't mean it to be so. He's a born-again filmmaker and he takes his cinematic pleasures seriously. But it was a fitting comment for the boy whose first movie was *The Greatest Show on Earth* and who has been trying to top that three-ring circus ever since.

Does *Close Encounters* represent a conversion for Spielberg? Has he been touched by The Force? Does Neary's obsession parallel St. Paul's conversion on the road to Damascus, as Richard Corliss, an admirer of the pure energy of the film, has suggested? Janet Maslin spoke with this very likeable guy when the film was released. He told her, "I never believed in anything before I believed in movies, and it's just now that I'm realizing that there's an entire backlog, an intellectual and emotional gap, for me to begin filling in." How will he do that? Maslin queried. "Oh, living around. Growing up. Making movies."[8]

That may not be enough. Most of us begin to question religious faith long before we're thirty. That Steven has been able to preserve his belief in movies is perhaps novel, but it may be too late for him ever to feel comfortable with the world of ideas.

Careerist in the Naked City

Steve Spielberg brings us the uncluttered religious ecstasy of pure movies; Paul Schrader would make us pay for it. Spielberg turned movies into religion; Schrader brought religion to the movies. He has a vision so dark that he has brought new meaning to the phrase film noir. Yet, at the same time he has perhaps the most sharply analytical cinematic mind now operating in the greater Los Angeles area. He has planned and executed a career as a filmmaker with stunning precision. So far, his work has been crippled by an angst large enough to bring the wrath of God down on the City of Angels, and for all we know his scripts have been significantly modified by the people who directed them. But it seems more likely that Schrader will come to terms with his misanthropy than that Spielberg will undergo a crisis of faith. And when Schrader does pass through the stage he's currently in, he'll still be equipped with a steely intelligence—and where will Spielberg be? Without the faith, he's likely to give up making movies, maybe go into the auto-mechanic business with friend George Lucas.

Schrader was born and raised in Michigan, son of strict Calvinist parents. He didn't see a film until he was seventeen. His church wouldn't allow it. He was at Calvin College, a seminary, when he caught the disease. He was infected by European films—*The Seventh Seal*, *La Strada*—rather than American movies. While Spielberg was getting off on *The Greatest Show on Earth* and planning mischievous practical jokes with his buddies in the sun in Phoenix, Schrader was desperately pleading with his mother to see an educational film like Disney's *The Living Desert*, getting on his knees and crying, begging to be allowed to see *King Creole*, in the dark snows of Michigan. (*The Living Desert*, indeed!)

One summer while he was still in seminary he somehow convinced his parents to let him attend Columbia University. He took all the film courses he could find, and met Pauline Kael, who took a strong interest in his career as budding film critic. When he graduated from Calvin, she got him into film school at U.C.L.A.

He edited *Cinema* magazine for a while and wrote a serious and quite well-reviewed book called *Transcendental Style: Ozu Bresson Dreyer*. (Like most serious attempts at film criticism, it sold a few hundred copies.) He realized he'd rather join the industry than write about it. Schrader set about in earnest to create a career for himself as filmmaker. He talked to people who wrote scripts. He learned the tricks of the trade. He wrote a number of trial efforts. He went through personal troubles too detailed to go into here.[9] He learned how to "take a meeting," as they say. His marriage fell apart. The affair that caused that breakup fell through, too.

The sword versus the gun: Takakura Ken and Robert Mitchum in *The Yakuza*.

He wandered around at night. He drank. He ate. (No, this is not a movie.) He got an ulcer and was hospitalized.

He got the idea for *Taxi Driver*. He wrote the script in fifteen days. He bummed around the country. His brother Leonard wrote him from Japan with the idea for *The Yakuza*. He and Leonard wrote it between Thanksgiving and Christmas. It was sold two months later for $300,000.

Bingo.

The scripts rolled out of the typewriter after that. "Pipeliner" (written in 1971, permanently shelved) was an attempt at transcendental style in an American context. It was about a dying man returning to his home in northern Michigan, bringing the stench of death with him. It was clearly not what Hollywood was looking for.

But *Taxi Driver* (written in 1972, filmed in 1975–76) was on the money. Schrader the film scholar had decided that film noir was about to make a commercial comeback. In an article he wrote on the subject for *Film Comment* in 1972[10] he suggested that "as the current political mood hardens, filmgoers and filmmakers will find the film-noir style of the late forties increasingly attractive. The forties may be to the seventies what the thirties were to the sixties."

The Yakuza (written in 1973, shot by Sydney Pollack in 1974), however, traded on another trend. Schrader's first sale is still one of his most interesting films. It introduces the highly stylized Japanese yakuza gangster genre to American films in the person of Robert Mitchum. It's the best combination so far of the film critic's analytical sensibilities with the commercial requirements of action, blood, and guts. It works where, for example, *Taxi Driver* doesn't, because it's based on a foreign genre, not a domestic one, a current genre, not one from the past. Warner Brothers must have seen in it a chance to expand on the chop-socky violence craze which was quite popular at the time. For some reason, however, possibly because Schrader was writing better analysis than action, possibly because Pollack's sense of style slowed the film down too much, it didn't garner the hoped-for receipts at the box office.

But Schrader didn't care. By this time he was off and running. "Déjà Vu" (written in 1973) was sold, then resold. Brian De Palma made it as *Obsession* in 1976. *Rolling Thunder* (written in 1973) was sold, and filmed by John Flynn for AIP (1977). Schrader now disowns it, but the film had the by then characteristic touch of symbolic violence and the film-noir mise en scène. Again, he was just a few years ahead of his time. The cycle of returning-Vietnam-vet films didn't hit its stride until 1978.

"Québecois" (written 1973) was optioned to Lewis Allen. It still hasn't been made. Schrader thinks the gangster cycle is now at a low point, but he's sure the graph will start to rise again, and this story of a French–Italian gang war in Montreal will get to the screen.

He next worked on a first draft of *Close Encounters of the Third Kind*, but Spielberg wants to keep this one for himself, so we're unlikely to see Schrader's script. "The Havana Colony" (written 1975) was bought by Paramount, has been traded at least once since, but has not yet been shot. Schrader describes it as a cross between *Casablanca* and *Last Tango in Paris* set in Havana in 1959. *Hard Core* (also written 1975) Schrader directed himself. *Blue Collar*, written by Paul and his brother Leonard, "suggested by source material" by Sydney A. Glass, served as his directorial debut in 1978.

In seven years, Paul Schrader has thus written ten scripts, all originals, no adaptations, each of them contrasting strongly with the dominant mood of the industry. All but one have been sold for better than satisfactory prices, and six out of ten have been shot and released. Two have been major hits.

This record speaks for itself.

As a filmmaker, Schrader presents a difficult persona. His attitude toward the industry is cold, analytical, and rightfully cynical. But his attitude toward people is equally dark. His characters seldom succeed at anything, and they take no pleasure at all in daily life. Schrader presents a remarkably schizophrenic artistic personality. On the one hand, he is clearly the most mechanical of screenwriters. It's not that he has a talent for the thrill machine, like Friedkin, or De Palma, for example. He's

Harvey Keitel, Richard Pryor, and Yaphet Kotto on the line in *Blue Collar*.

actually thought all this out. He has constructed his films according to the principles he discovered as a critic. Yet at the same time, no one— not even Cassavetes, not Coppola, not Altman—makes more profoundly personal and revealing films. Schrader's anguish is apparent.

Blue Collar is possibly a sign of hope. For the first time in a Schrader script, the element of politics makes an appearance. The film gives us three workers in an auto factory (Yaphet Kotto, Richard Pryor, Harvey Keitel) in a Detroit with artificially darkened skies, who take on the system only to end up dead or compromised, and despising each other. The vision is just as dark as in any of the earlier films, but along the way, for a little while, the anomie, angst, contempt, and raw violence that are the basic Schrader elements are seen for the first time in context. These characters understand who's responsible. Paul Schrader, with the help of his brother Leonard, is in the process of graduating from religion to politics. He may turn out to be one of the most intellectually and emotionally interesting of the new generation. He already has the equipment and the material. He just has to want to learn to put it together in new ways. *Blue Collar*, while still debilitated by Schrader's own sense of paralysis, is a step in the right direction. If Schrader didn't have such contempt for the industry he's conquered, he might feel better about his own remarkable financial success, and let his characters win once in a while. Of course, if he doesn't come to terms with his own tortuous anxieties, he's not likely to remain a filmmaker for very long.

6

The Black Film
(and the Black Image)

ILSA: Hello, Sam.

SAM: Hello, Miss Ilsa. I never expected to see you again.

ILSA: It's been a long time.

SAM: Yes, Ma'am. A lot of water under the bridge.

ILSA: Some of the old songs, Sam.

SAM: Yes, Ma'am.

Sam begins to play a number. He is nervous, waiting for anything.

ILSA: Where is Rick?

SAM (*evading*): I don't know. I ain't seen him all night.

Sam looks very uncomfortable.

ILSA: When will he be back?

SAM: Not tonight no more. He ain't coming. He went home.

ILSA: Does he always leave so early?

SAM: Oh, he never... well... (*desperately*) He's got a girl up at the Blue
Parrot. He goes up there all the time.

ILSA: You used to be a much better liar, Sam.

SAM: Leave him alone, Miss Ilsa. You're bad luck to him.

ILSA (*softly*): Play it once, Sam, for old time's sake.

SAM: I don't know what you mean, Miss Ilsa.

ILSA: Play it, Sam. Play "As Time Goes By."

The film is *Casablanca*, of course. Ilsa is Ingrid Bergman. Sam is Dooley
Wilson. Sam is Black. It may not seem so now, but in 1942, when it was
produced, *Casablanca* was recognized as having rather advanced attitudes

toward race. Now, all we notice is that piano-player Sam treats the white characters in the film with proper respect; he knows his place. But then—you must remember this—the very fact that Sam could interact in extended scenes with a white woman, that they could reminisce about a mutually shared past, that Sam could take a part in the story of the great romance between Rick and Ilsa, and that no mention was ever made of his race—all these were remarkable elements in a film made only three years after Hattie McDaniel had won the Academy Award for her portrayal of the archetypal "Mammy" in Gone with the Wind.

Judging the painstaking, subtle advance of Black people in the overwhelmingly white world of film requires sensitive instruments to measure the often imperceptible shifts of balance in the collective racial unconscious. Impossible as it seems now, even Gone with the Wind was praised when it was released for "enlightened" attitudes toward race.

For the longest time, it was a triumph just to be seen, no matter how demeaning the role, no matter how outrageous the stereotype. Often, actors operated on two levels: the performance had one significance for white audiences, quite another for Blacks. Actors like Stepin Fetchit and Butterfly McQueen worked this way: the ironic exaggeration they brought to the stereotypes allowed them to salvage at least a modicum of self-respect, and Black audiences enjoyed this hidden critique of the demeaning roles.

Yet, with a few notable exceptions, Blacks simply did not exist as real people in American movies until at least half a century after the viciously racist "classic" *Birth of a Nation* marked the beginning of feature film.

Within the last 15 years that situation has changed. Black Americans have been validated by the media. They appear in television commercials and shows and on movie screens with some regularity, and the public in general is much more sensitive to the old stereotypes. The problem now is to increase the quality and quantity of the roles. Blacks' position in the industry is now best described as more than tokenism, but considerably less than full and equal participation. Sidney Poitier is no longer the only Black actor whose name comes readily to mind, yet it is still exceedingly rare when a film comes along that really evinces Black sensibility. As usual, liberal ideology has operated to allow a certain degree of improvement in the situation at the same time as it limits and attenuates the gains made. The operating motto is "half a loaf is better than none."

This carefully controlled change came about when Blacks opened up a second front in the struggle to gain power in the film industry. A parallel, underground Black film business had operated since the early years of movies but it was never strong—plagued by lack of capital and limited to ghetto theaters. Moreover, from the twenties to the fifties, this parallel Black cinema often aspired no higher than to mimic white films, and white entrepreneurs exerted considerable financial control. Only in the late sixties, with the rise of the militant Black Power movement, were Blacks able to gain a foothold in Hollywood, to take, on occasion, a serious share of power behind the camera as well as in front of it.

The birth of the Black film of the late sixties and early seventies—with Blacks, by Blacks, and for Blacks; written, directed, and acted by Blacks (and sometimes even produced and financed by Blacks)—was the major success of the Hollywood Renaissance of 1968-1970. Consequently, the virtual disappearance of the Black film in the mid-seventies has been the greatest failure of the American film business in recent years: strong evidence that the Hollywood Renaissance died in its infancy and that we have reverted to the historical norm, in which the industry is controlled by a relative handful of people, and propagates a prescribed and often distorted image of the American scene.

The Black struggle in film has been well chronicled in recent books by Donald Bogle, James Murray, Lindsay Patterson, and Thomas Cripps.* As James Murray put it: "The three goals of Black cinema are: correction of white distortions, the reflection of Black reality, and (as a propagandizing tool) the creation of a positive Black image."[1] There's no doubt this strug-

---

*Toms, Coons, Mulattoes, Mammies, & Bucks; To Find an Image; Black Films and Filmmakers; and Slow Fade to Black; respectively.

The published caption for this publicity photo reads in full: "OSCAR MICHEAUX's dynamic COLORED CAST production *Underworld* featuring Bee Freeman, Oscar Polk, Ethel Moses, Sol Johnson, 'Slick' Chester."

gle is now well established, but the battle continues. There are far more Blacks in American film now than there once were, but few have been able to maintain positions of power. None, for example, holds a major executive position at any studio.* Roles are more varied and sophisticated, but for the most part, they are still stereotypical. Moreover, even now, 36 years after *Casablanca*, it is still remarkable when a Black actor is cast for a role that a white actor could play, a role without a specifically racial dimension to it. Each of Murray's three goals has been nominally realized; none of them has been fully achieved. In short, Blacks in film, as elsewhere, have in a way been co-opted, and Black aspirations have been trimmed, modified, and channeled by the industry to serve its own ends.

There had always been (white) people in Hollywood with fairly sophisticated racial attitudes. The several drafts of Howard Koch's script for *Casablanca*, for example, reveal how carefully he engineered the role of Sam to make a statement. But commercial exigencies usually distorted

*As of 1984, the highest-ranking Black executives in Hollywood were Ashley Boone, President of Distribution and Marketing Group for Columbia Pictures, and Stanley Robertson, Vice-President for Production at Columbia.

While Blacks have lost considerable ground in Hollywood, Black independent cinema has achieved some success in the seventies, especially in documentaries. Here, a shot from William Miles's fascinating *Men of Bronze,* about the members of the 369th Regiment of Black Americans who fought with the French army in World War I.

statements like these.[2] The same old story. And producers and studios usually excused themselves by explaining their hands were tied by white Southern audiences who wouldn't accept a potentially strong Black character or theme. Of course, they never explained why ten million Southern whites could exert such veto power while fifteen million American Blacks couldn't exercise similar clout.

While occasional independent productions featured Blacks in starring roles throughout the forties and fifties, real change had to wait until the civil rights movement was at its height in the mid-sixties. Finally, it became clear that Black people not only exerted considerable economic power, but also that white audiences would accept Black actors as stars—under certain conditions. Of the several tentative attempts at racially conscious film in the mid-sixties, *Nothing But a Man* (1964), a simple chronical of Black family life, stands out as unpretentious, sensible, yet pointed. Written, produced, and directed by Michael Roemer and Robert Young, the film starred Ivan Dixon and Abbey Lincoln. Shirley Clarke's *The Cool World* (1964), a semidocumentary study of young people in Harlem, should also be mentioned among the more interesting Black-oriented films of the mid-sixties. (Roemer, Young, and Clarke are white.)

The box-office success of the liberally sentimental *Guess Who's Coming to Dinner?* in 1967 serves as a milestone. Sidney Poitier has been rightfully criticized over the years for projecting a white man's image of the Black man, and nowhere is this more painfully clear than in *Guess Who's Coming to Dinner?* but it must be remembered that for almost fifteen years those were the only roles open to Poitier (or any other Black actor). It is at least an arguable thesis that the careers of men like Poitier, Belafonte, and even Sammy Davis, Jr., were necessary steps before Blacks could even begin to think of playing roles devised by and aimed at Black people. Poitier's only other choice was to play roles that weren't Black at all. He did this once in James B. Harris's *The Bedford Incident* (1965), perhaps the first film to star a Black actor with no reference to race. *The Bedford Incident* remains a milestone, but it was not a model. It's now not uncommon to hire Blacks for minor, subsidiary roles without regard to race, but when a Black gets a starring role, race immediately becomes part of the thematic structure of the film even if it wasn't in the script. Of course, this limits severely the number of roles open to Black actors—they can't play doctors, lawyers, and generals, they can only play Black doctors, Black lawyers, and Black generals—but to a certain extent it is understandable, for during the last ten years race consciousness has been high and that, in general, has been a positive fact.

In 1968 and 1969, Poitier moved quickly to exploit his newfound influence. (So did other Black actors.) He worked out the story line for *For Love of Ivy*, in which he starred with Abbey Lincoln (Daniel Mann directed, Robert Alan Aurthur wrote the script)—a dull movie but influential: the first major Hollywood Black love story. He later turned to directing himself with *Buck and the Preacher* (1971), *A Warm December* (1972), and *Uptown Saturday Night* (1974). These films are unremarkable—Poitier still carries with him the dull earnestness that has led Black critics to see him as Hollywood's premiere modern Uncle Tom—but the last of them set a style for relaxed and pleasant Black film entertainment. Its sequel, *Let's Do It Again*, which Poitier also directed (in 1975), is the highest-grossing Black film of the seventies (and therefore of all time).

Very quickly, the contradictions that govern Black film became evident. If Black actors were successful box-office draws, as they increasingly were, then white directors moved to exploit their talents in essentially white films. If Black themes drew large audiences, white producers moved in to share in the receipts. Most important, the necessity of struggling on two fronts developed into an insoluble dilemma. For many Blacks in the film industry in the early seventies the main aim was to train Black technicians, writers, and directors, to get them union cards and establish them as working members of the industry. Very often, the best way to increase

Sidney Poitier (Clyde) and Bill Cosby (Billy) discuss a bet in *Let's Do It Again*, whose title referred as much to Poitier and Cosby's earlier success as to the story by Richard Wesley.

Black participation in the industry was to downplay the Black theme of a film. It's just as easy—perhaps even easier—to train a score of Black cinematographers, soundmen, grips, designers, set builders, and makeup artists on a general interest "white" film as on a Black film. Conversely, Black films were to a certain extent risky financial investments. Why increase the odds by using neophyte technicians? It was easier to get a "Black" film made with a white director and mainly white technicians (there were always a few token trainees on the set), just as it was much less of a hassle to get Blacks jobs on "white" films.

Moreover, it quickly became apparent that, for the most part, Black films per se were subject to the same box-office rules as white films. Black audiences were just as eager to buy the twin commodities of action and sex as white audiences were, and studios therefore were far more willing to finance such genre pictures. Some Black producers thus tried to raise money from the Black business establishment. It proved even more conservative than the Hollywood financial organizations. The Black film of the early seventies was soon dominated by what *Variety* quickly labeled "Blaxploitation." These followed the dominant patterns of white action genres—urban private eye, cop, drug, and caper movies, together with the occasional western or "biopic"—simply substituting Black actors for white, reversing racial stereotypes, and occasionally (at their best) even injecting a little Black sensibility.

Blaxploitation wasn't an entirely negative phenomenon: at least such films fulfilled one of James Murray's three aims—the correction of white distortions—even if they didn't reflect a Black reality. Moreover, the films gave work to Black actors. Most of the new generation moved into films from allied areas; few Black actors had not made their reputations outside of movies. Action heroes came mainly from sports: Jim Brown, first, then Rosey Grier, Fred Williamson, O.J. Simpson, Rafer Johnson, and others. Nightclub and television monologists also had an inside track: Godfrey Cambridge, Bill Cosby, Jimmie Walker, and most notably Richard Pryor.

Theater supplied not only the best trained of the Black actors of the late sixties and seventies, but also gave rise to the only genre to seriously challenge Blaxploitation. Diana Sands, Abbey Lincoln, Gloria Foster, Roscoe Lee Browne, James Earl Jones, Brock Peters, Moses Gunn, Al Freeman, Jr., and Cicely Tyson all had established reputations on the New York stage before they were able to find work in movies. Music was another source of talent, especially for women: Diana Ross, Gladys Knight, et cetera.

The Black revolution in film was foreshadowed and accompanied by the Black revolution in theater. On the whole, the latter has maintained its separate identity better—Black repertory companies seem to have more staying power than Black film-production companies, and the Black influence on Broadway has been prodigious. But Black theater seems to be subject to the same basic dilemma as Black film: there's little Blaxploitation theater, but then there's little white exploitation theater. The contradiction reveals itself in other ways: much of serious Black theater in the seventies has been too closely parallel to the white socially conscious domestic dramas of the thirties. There has also been too much Blackface—*The Wiz, Timbuktu,* for example. Yet, just as with Blaxploitation, this theatrical genre has had its positive effect: admitting Blacks to the "nomenclature," in Jean Genet's phrase, validating their existence on the stage.

Films made from Black plays have been one of the categories to challenge Blaxploitation in film. Oscar Williams's *Five on the Black Hand Side* (1973), from the play by Charlie L. Russell, is an example. Allied with the filmed plays have been the uplifting morality tales of the liberal esthetic, usually by whites: *Sounder* (1972) and *Conrack* (1974) are the most evident examples. Neither of these categories proved a serious threat to Blaxploitation.

While the Black film never really succeeded in escaping from the models of white movies upon which it was based, Blaxploitation did have a noticeable and apparently long-lasting effect on Hollywood. The phenomenon was surprisingly short-lived. By 1974 the number of Black movies had been reduced to a trickle. But thereafter, Blacks have been a significant factor in the general commercial economic equation. Ironically, the fall of Black film—as rapid as its rise—was in no small part a measure of its success.

As critic Clayton Riley points out, Black films helped significantly to stabilize the industry during the difficult period of 1968–72. But once producers realized the economic potential of the Black audience it was only a matter of time before they extrapolated this new data and came to the conclusion that they didn't have to make entirely Black films to exploit it. Surveys showed that as much as 35% of the audience for such blockbusters as *The Godfather* (1972) and *The Exorcist* (1973) was Black. If Black audiences were turning out in such numbers for essentially non-Black films, why cater specifically to this particular subculture? Moreover, if white people could be attracted to movies that were based on Black themes or that starred Black actors, revenues could easily double. The success of films like *Sounder* and *Lady Sings the Blues* in 1972, starring Blacks in Black stories, but directed and written by whites with an overlay of white sensibility, proved the workability of this theory. The "crossover" film essentially replaced the Black film, except for a few independent productions. Once again, the seemingly insoluble dilemma of the Black situation in America presented itself: how to make a significant and fair contribution to the general culture while at the same time maintaining a separate and thriving Black identity. It's the same dilemma that has characterized Black American politics since the end of the Civil War: integration and separatism are both necessary, but seemingly mutually exclusive.

There was a second reason for the decline in Black films in the seventies: television discovered the potential of Black culture. The enormous success of the television series based on Alex Haley's *Roots* is of such magnitude as to make recent movie blockbusters pale by comparison. The eight episodes of the series had ratings which garnered for them eight out of the top ten positions on Nielsen's list of most popular television programs of all time. Cicely Tyson had her first great financial success in the film *Sounder* (after a distinguished fifteen-year career in the theater), but her second coup, *The Autobiography of Miss Jane Pitman*, was produced for television and controlled by whites, like *Roots* itself, which Ossie Davis had dreamed of making long before Alex Haley's book was published.

Most television series starring Blacks are no better than their white counterparts, but Blacks have generally been more successful as television stars during the last few years than as movie stars. Co-optation by television and the crossover dilemma together have sapped Black film of much of its strength in the late seventies.

Ossie Davis

Actor and stage director Ossie Davis is perhaps the prototypical Black director of the seventies. Like Poitier, Raymond St. Jacques, Ivan Dixon, Robert Hooks, and numerous other Black directors, he was able to get financing for his first film mainly because he had already established a reputation as an actor. (For whites, too, acting has proved the quickest path to the director's chair in the seventies.) But unlike most of his contemporaries, Davis has at the same time been deeply involved in developing alternate systems of finance.

He has not made a great many films, and none of his projects has generated very wide critical support, but Davis's work during the last ten years serves as a model of strategy. He had written the script for *Gone Are the Days* (1963) from the play *Purlie Victorious* and had directed a number of plays before his first film, *Cotton Comes to Harlem*, was produced in 1969. Based on the Gravedigger Jones novels of Chester Himes, *Cotton* was the first commercially successful film by a Black director and set the style for the cycle that followed. Davis was able to put together an unusually good cast, including Godfrey Cambridge, Raymond St. Jacques, Calvin Lockhart, Cleavon Little, and Judy Pace, most of whom were relatively unknown at the time. Shot on location in Harlem, the film had a gritty realism that served to provide ironic emphasis to novelist Himes's particular brand of humor. *Cotton Comes to Harlem* has never been a critical favorite, but it remains the model for the more interesting Blaxploitation films that followed it, using basically white forms and giving them Black sensibility.

Having established a track record, Davis immediately began to seek ways to wrest the power of the purse from the Hollywood establishment. *Cotton* had been produced by Sam Goldwyn, Jr.; a series was planned, but Davis wasn't interested. He'd already proved that Black films could be financially profitable. Now it was time to find a way to channel that profit back into the community of Black artists.

Early in 1970, in conjunction with other Black actors, Davis announced the formation of Third World Cinema Corporation, designed to do just this. Third World would produce commercial films and documentaries "utilizing talents and providing jobs for Blacks, Puerto Ricans, and other minority groups" in New York. Davis had worked out some novel methods for financing these films. Since Third World was engaged in training minority talent, it was eligible for a grant from the U.S. Manpower Career and Development Administration of $200,000. A year later, Davis announced that he had agreed to give a 40 percent interest in the company to a community group in order to qualify for a federal Model Cities grant of $400,000.

194

Raymond St. Jacques and Godfrey Cambridge as detectives deal with the people in *Cotton Comes to Harlem.*

He knew this seed money would go only so far, however, and apparently was well aware of the necessity to produce films that made substantial profits at the box office, money which could then be recirculated through Third World. The company never quite succeeded in becoming a major force, though it still exists.* Davis's first project, a life story of Billie Holiday which was to star Diana Sands, was usurped by Berry Gordy's Motown Productions, a new filmmaking arm of the successful record company. Introducing Motown's leading singer Diana Ross to movies, *Lady Sings the Blues* was made for Paramount as a Hollywood, not an independent, film. Davis also had at least a dream of making a film of Alex Haley's *Roots*, years before the book was published. Again, the establishment had the financial power to outmaneuver him.

As a job-training organization, Third World was more successful, placing people on a number of Black films made in New York by the Hollywood studios. But it was 1974 before *Claudine*, Third World's first production, was completed. John Berry, white, and an exile from Hollywood who had been living in Europe for many years, directed. *Greased Lightning* followed in 1977.

Third World Cinema wasn't the only technique Ossie Davis developed for financing Black movies. The American Black business establishment

---

*It has now split its functions. Third World Cinema Productions produces films while the Institute of New Cinema Artists, Inc., handles the training programs.

was notoriously conservative in such matters, but African sources of capital might open up. Davis's second film, made in 1970 and released in 1971, followed this route. *Kongi's Harvest* was written by the Nigerian playwright and novelist Wole Soyinka. It was the first major English-language film produced by an African company. Davis had considerable trouble trying to get it released in the United States, even though producer/writer Soyinka's plays had often been staged here and his reputation as the leading English-language African playwright was unchallenged. Davis later returned to Africa for *Countdown at Kusini* financed by the Delta Sigma Theta Sorority. *Black Girl*, from the play by J. E. Franklin, followed in 1972. It, too, was all but ignored by the studios, and met the same fate as most films of Black stage productions.

Davis's next film, *Gordon's War* (1973), with Paul Winfield, was an attempt to turn the Blaxploitation action genre to some social utility. Gordon returns to Harlem from action in Vietnam to avenge the death of his wife by declaring all-out war on drug dealers. Gordon Parks, Jr.'s *Superfly* (1972) had been criticized for setting up a cocaine dealer as hero to a generation of Black youth. Davis's Gordon attempted to rechannel that energy to more productive political ends. It did not succeed. Ossie Davis has not been the most successful of Black filmmakers, in either commercial or artistic terms, but he has evinced a knowledge of how the system operates, which is rare. His experiments in production, even if they did not ultimately succeed, were important markers in the development of Black film.

Gordon Parks

Now in his sixties like Ossie Davis, Gordon Parks, Sr., had already achieved fame in one career, as photographer, mainly for *Life* magazine, and dabbled in two others successfully (as novelist and composer) before he turned to filmmaking in 1968. He had made a short, *Flavio*, about a boy in a Brazilian *favela*, in 1965. It was well received, but it took him more than three years to put together his first feature, *The Learning Tree*. "John Cassavetes kept after me," he says. Finally Hollywood was ready for its first prominent Black director.

The Learning Tree (1968), based on Parks's own memoirs, is a visually stunning evocation of his childhood in Kansas in the twenties. Because the setting is Midwestern, the story is also rather novel, successfully avoiding the clichés and truisms of growing up Black in the South, or in a Northern ghetto. Yet, Parks's childhood wasn't particularly dramatic—no great traumas—and so *Learning Tree* is rather static, a fact which would have caused no problems if the film had been European, but which did not do much for his reputation as a bankable director in late-sixties Hollywood.

The emphasis in the moving-picture industry had always been on "mov-

Parks's upbringing in Kansas was portrayed almost idyllically in *The Learning Tree.*

ing" rather than "picture," and Parks's superb training as a still photographer wasn't of much use to him commercially in 1968, when Hollywood was just learning, through the use of new filmstock and techniques, that movies didn't have to be breathlessly paced to be attractive; that audiences would buy the "picture," too.

So Parks set out to show he could do "movies." The proof, *Shaft* (1971), was irrefutable. *Cotton Comes to Harlem* had introduced the form of Blaxploitation action films; *Shaft* added the all-important tone. The film was tough, lean, cool, hip, angry, and in the end even wise. Black audiences understood immediately that Richard Roundtree's heroic exploits as private eye John Shaft were a commentary on decades of white detective films as well as being entertaining in themselves. Most important: at last there was a real Black hero on the screen. Parks did one sequel, *Shaft's Big Score*, in 1972 (*Shaft in Africa*, 1973, was directed by John Guillermin), and a more general urban cop film, *The Supercops* (1974), unusual in being one of extremely few non-Black films directed by a Black. Parks refused to be ghettoized as a filmmaker, just as he had refused to be ghettoized as a *Life* photographer.

Having paid his dues to the commercial film establishment, Parks was finally able to return to a more personal project. But the studios had the last laugh: *Leadbelly* (1975) was dumped by Paramount with an inefficient ad campaign and quick, perfunctory bookings. The film had been caught in a management switch, and like so many other movies signed by one studio head but completed under the reign of his successor, the film was

Shaft's urban world is diametrically opposed to Parks's memories of rural Kansas. Richard Roundtree directs traffic.

never really given a chance in the marketplace.

It remains, however, a magnificent telling of an historical episode with strong mythic overtones. *Leadbelly* was just the sort of film Parks was meant to make. His experiences as photographer, musician, and novelist combine to create a film that works well on all three levels.

Like most mythic stories, this biography of Huddie Ledbetter—"Leadbelly"—the master of the twelve-string guitar, potentially verges on cliché. It takes someone of Parks's particular talents to avoid those pitfalls. He does so by confronting the mythic material head-on rather than apologizing for it. The film has a classic narrative structure: strong, simple, direct, and pointed. In short, it's very much like Leadbelly's own music.

It's grounded in humiliation. (Texas Governor Pat Neff comments after Leadbelly has performed for him: "Ain't nothin' can sing like a darkie when he puts his mind to it!") It opposes that oppression with the elemental politics of survival. (Dicklikker, Leadbelly's prison buddy, explains: "Ya suit yerself to the situation. When they wants to kill ya, just livin' is winning.") Ultimately, *Leadbelly* is a triumph of will. After seven years on the chain gang, Huddie can rightly and righteously proclaim: "You ain't broke my body, you ain't broke my mind, you ain't broke my spirit!" And we know it's true. *Leadbelly* provides a legitimate historical high of the sort we seldom get any longer from mainstream American movies, made by people who have lost (or never had) a sense of the vitality and meaning of the politics of existence.

Performers: Roger E. Mosley as "Leadbelly."

Parks can bring it off because, first, he understands the strength of Lead-belly's music. He has also guided actors Roger E. Mosley, Madge Sinclair, Art Evans, and Alpert P. Hall to an extraordinary level of performance. Along with his cinematographer, Bruce Surtees, he has in addition created a breathtakingly elemental imagery for the film—full of earth, air, sun, sweat, and color—that's almost insolent it is so powerful.

Most important, perhaps, is the groundbase of the film. What gave Leadbelly's songs their special power was the people whose stories they told. The same must be said for Parks's film. He made a movie about people, and the people give *Leadbelly* its mythic energy.

Melvin Van Peebles

Van Peebles is a generation younger than both Davis and Parks and, as a result, his career has taken an entirely different path, altogether more in-souciant. While still very young, he had written a book about San Francisco cable cars with a photographer friend, then studied filmmaking. Watching a movie in a San Francisco theater (so legend has it), he decided he certainly could do better. He made three short films and, in 1954, took them to Hollywood. He was offered jobs as elevator operator and parking-lot attendant (according to James Murray). So he left for Europe.

After ten years in France painting and writing, he was able to make his first feature there, *The Story of a Three Day Pass* (1967). It was a very European film, but with an American hero: a romance between a soldier and a

199

French girl. The film had some critical success in the United States, and Van Peebles immediately had offers from the studios. Parks had already made his first film and Davis was about to begin his. Van Peebles accepted an offer to direct *Watermelon Man* from a script by Herman Raucher, starring Godfrey Cambridge.

Watermelon Man was based on a gimmick: a bigoted white insurance salesman wakes up one morning to discover he's turned Black. Van Peebles's direction was lackluster. The film is by turns dull and annoying. One has the sense that neither Van Peebles nor Cambridge was particularly happy bringing this fantasy to life. But as a "career move," *Watermelon Man* was smart. Van Peebles took the money he earned from the film and, with a $50,000 loan from Bill Cosby, was able to finance his next film entirely independently.

Sweet Sweetback's Baadasssss Song was immediately recognized as a major event in the renaissance of Black film when it was released in 1971. Melvin Van Peebles financed it, produced it, wrote and directed it, composed the music for it, and starred in it. It caused considerable controversy among Black critics and commentators, but it remains one of very few Black films from this decade to spring entirely from a Black artistic sensibility. Although this independent release doesn't appear on *Variety* charts, it grossed more than $10 million according to one educated estimate, thus becoming one of the most financially rewarding independent productions of all time. Since Van Peebles carefully orchestrated the marketing, advertising, and distribution, the major credit for the film's business success lies with him, too.

Sweet Sweetback is not an easy film to admire: it's violent, even sadistic, obscene, frenzied, painful. Critics who disliked the film condemned it for trading on a classic Black stereotype, the buck. On the surface, the film has all the most extreme elements of the most cynical Blaxploitation rip-offs. But Van Peebles, I think, is using these elements, commenting upon them.

The images of the film fall quite neatly into three classic categories, elemental actions that triangulate (and strangulate) ghetto life in the U.S.:

• People run. ("Keep this Nigger boy running," said the note in *Invisible Man*.)

• People stomp and kick and shoot and cut.

• People fuck. (They don't "make love," they don't "have sex." This is pure badass fucking.)

The narrative is linear, and boring as such. Sweetback (Van Peebles), who works in a brothel when the film begins, is finally moved to action, stomps a couple of cops unconscious, then begins running. He runs for the

Performers: Melvin Van Peebles as "Sweetback."

rest of the film. The movie reaches a high pitch almost before the credits begin and it stays there until shortly before the end. Even the gut-wrenching violence becomes boring; it is a commonplace of the world the film delineates.

The pain with which Van Peebles washes the screen is meant to be transmuted into anger by audiences, and then into political action. The film is dedicated to "All the Brothers and Sisters who have had enough of The Man." Does it succeed in this militant aim? Does any film? At the end, as Sweetback finally escapes to Mexico, leaving the carcasses of the hounds sent to rip him to shreds floating bloodily in the Rio Grande, we cheer, we are relieved. Then a set of titles appears on the screen: "*Watch Out. A Baadasssss Nigger is coming back to collect some dues.*" But it's hard to believe. Sweetback's unitary drama is so existentially rooted that it is difficult to see how his anger can work politically.

It probably can't. (Historically, it didn't.) But the film succeeds as a *cri de coeur*, an announcement that Black militancy has reached your neighborhood movie screen and that things will never be the same. Sweetback himself is a role model, one of the first. Sweetback teaches the lesson of survival. We might ask that he be more intellectually analytical. We might like John Shaft to be a more complicated, human character, too. And Leadbelly is certainly not a storybook hero. But these protagonists triumph in the short history of Black film because they are rooted in reality.

Van Peebles begins his spin-off book (there was also a record album) with a few phrases in French that bear repeating: "Sire, ceci n'est pas un ode à la brutalité que l'artiste aurait inventé, mais un hymne sorti de la bouche de la réalité. — *Incantation Traditionelle Du Moyenage.*"* Van Peebles is running a small game on us, but the point is well taken nevertheless. *Sweetback* is a morality tale of sorts: an image to be examined and discussed. Such a hymn of pain had no antecedents in Black film when Van Peebles made *Sweet Sweetback*, but it certainly could look to forerunners in the novel, most notably *Native Son* and *Invisible Man*. Like Ellison's ephemeral hero, Sweetback embarks upon an odyssey of terror and confusion, consciously learning the lessons intuited in childhood. It leads him underground—literally—into the sewers which were the refuge for Invisible Man. In theme, Sweetback is even closer to *Native Son*. The film clangs with anger and rage, like the frying pan Bigger Thomas hurls at the rat. Like Sweetback, Bigger ran until he could run no longer. Unlike Sweetback, he was caught. The difference between the two is the difference between the forties and the seventies. Existential freedom is no longer the main solace; now there is at least the possible dream of political freedom—not just freedom inside your head, but freedom in the world, as well.

Sweet Sweetback's Baadasssss Song thus situates itself squarely in a long and important tradition in Black American narrative art. The Sweetback character has been mimicked and repeated a number of times since, but never with such purity of purpose and such élan. Van Peebles bent the medium of film to his will. No one else has bent it so far or so well since.

Even if the film didn't succeed on this level, it would have been of historical interest for the way Van Peebles conceived and executed the project. In the introduction to the published script he described the analysis of the job he completed just before he began work on the script. To avoid "putting myself into a corner" and writing a film he wouldn't have been able to shoot, he made a list of "givens":[3]

1. NO COP OUT.
2. MUST LOOK AS GOOD AS ANYTHING CHUCK EVER DID.
3. ENTERTAINMENTWISE, A MOTHER FUCKER.
4. A LIVING WORKSHOP.
5. BREAD.
6. MONKEY WRENCHING.
7. UNKNOWNS AND VARIABLES:
   A. CALIBER OF ACTORS.
   B. CALIBER OF CREW.

---

*"Sire, this is not an ode to brutality that the artist has invented, but a hymn that comes from the mouth of reality."—*Traditional Medieval Prologue.*

The first rule dictated a victorious film, "a film where niggers could walk out standing tall instead of avoiding each other's eyes, looking once again like they'd had it." Rule 2 was a touchy point. It's a dilemma faced by any independent producer/director. As Van Peebles phrased it, "Hollywood polishes its product with such a great deal of slickness and expensive perfection that it ups the ante." He knew he was going to have to compete with studio films to gain an audience, and his film would have to look as good technically as theirs. As a Black filmmaker, intent on giving work to Blacks (point 4), he was in an especially difficult position, so he designed the script carefully so that he could shoot around it, if need be.

Van Peebles's analysis of the Hollywood entertainment machine (point 3) is so succinct and insightful that it could stand as the final word on the subject. "I had no illusion," he wrote, "about the attention level of people brainwashed to triviality." No better way to put it. He knew very well that even the slightest didacticism would mean empty theaters. He knew also that he was going to have to depend on whites for distribution and exhibition of the film: "The man has an Achilles pocket and he might go along with you if at least there is some bread in it for him. But he ain't about to go carrying no messages for you, especially a relevant one, for free."

He knew he would have very little money, and he also knew the media to be hostile (point 6), so he had better leave himself a margin for security, no matter how costly. As it happened, he later turned much of the hostility into useful, free publicity. "This movie rated 'X' by an all-white jury!" Finally, he had no idea how his cast and crew, more than half of whom were beginners and apprentices, would react under pressure. So he designed an extremely flexible script that would leave him room to correct for problems that came up on the set during the actual shooting.

Short as it is, this list is a well-nigh perfect analysis of the difficulties confronting the independent Black filmmaker. It explains the simplicity of the structure of the film as finally shot. What it doesn't explain is its vitality and passion. Van Peebles added to his list one "asset" and one "opportunity." The "Asset": "I kept asking myself," he wrote, "what could I do that Hollywood major studios couldn't. The thing that kept occurring to me was that I could delve into the Black community as they would never be able to do because of their cumbersome technology and their lack of empathy." Nothing describes *Sweetback*'s success (and the failure of so many Blaxploitation films) better.

The "opportunity" had to do with a basic lack, as Van Peebles saw it, in commercial filmmaking. "Most filmmakers," he noted, "look at a feature in terms of image and story. Effects and music...are strictly secondary considerations." He determined to build a scenario in which sound and music would be integral parts. The film is a "song" on purpose, and was conceived as such from the beginning. Van Peebles pecked out his musical themes on a piano, had them in his head while shooting. Years later, Steven Spielberg would construct *Close Encounters* in collaboration with composer John Williams. By that time, Hollywood had learned (or relearned) the Van Peebles rule.

The success of *Sweet Sweetback's Baadasssss Song* on both commercial and artistic levels has been unmatched in independent Black film since.

But what to do for an encore? It was evident from the calculations that went into the *Sweetback* project that Van Peebles wouldn't remain content to repeat himself. After he had breached the Hollywood fortress, beaten them at their own game, and still produced a film that was at least nominally relevant, what then? He was confronted with the same set of dilemmas that face every filmmaker who isn't content with engineering entertainment machines. On the evidence, Van Peebles was stymied.

He turned his attention to the stage. His musical *Ain't Supposed to Die a Natural Death* (with published script and original-cast album, of course) was as successful in its medium as *Sweetback* had been in film. Once again, Van Peebles redesigned the form to his own requirements. *Ain't Supposed to Die* is part cantata, part street blues, part talking poem. It is closer to the work of The Last Poets (who combine music, talking blues and other Black oral traditions in their performance poems) than it is to Rodgers and Hammerstein. It marked the coming of age of Black audiences on Broadway. They now form a significant part of the population New York theater depends on, rivaling surburban theater parties and tourists.

Another theater piece followed: *Don't Play Us Cheap* (1972). Van Peebles had actually made a film of it first, but it has never been released. Van Peebles next wrote, directed, and performed a couple of albums. In 1976 he was announced as director of *Greased Lightning*. He worked on the screenplay a bit, shot for a few weeks, then was replaced by Michael Schultz.

At about the same time, a television film Van Peebles had written appeared. *Just an Old Sweet Song*, directed by Robert Ellis Miller, and starring Cicely Tyson, Robert Hooks, and Beah Richards, concerned a Black family from Detroit who pay a visit to the South and decide to stay. The film showed enough promise to lead to a pilot—*Kinfolks*—with Hooks, Richards, and Madge Sinclair. *Kinfolks* was a product of MTM enterprises and directed by Fielder Cook. CBS did not pick up the series and the cast was released. Van Peebles may be acceptable as a writer for television; his scripts can be filtered through program practices offices, producers, directors, and editors. But it will be a long time before he will be allowed to direct. It won't be as easy for him to start his own television network as it was to build his own film production/distribution company.

Bill Gunn

Bill Gunn is almost unknown as a filmmaker. Only close friends and a few executives at Warner Brothers have seen his first film, *Stop* (1970), which the studio never chose to release. Only a few thousand people have seen his second film, *Ganja & Hess* (1973), which had a commercial run of only a week in New York before it was dumped by its distributor, the independent firm of Kelly-Jordan. Yet, in museum showings around the country, *Ganja & Hess* has over the past few years achieved an extraordinary reputation, especially among Black filmmakers. It is the great underground classic of Black film, and, I think, the most complicated, intriguing, subtle, sophisticated, and passionate Black film of the seventies. If *Sweet Sweetback* is *Native Son*, *Ganja & Hess* is *Invisible Man*. Some day it will take its rightful place in cinematheques and history books. Right now, it remains a valuable secret those who have seen it are eager to share with those who haven't.

Gunn started as an actor. In the early sixties he worked regularly on television in the minor and secondary parts open to Black actors, managing to save enough to finance a second career as a playwright and screenwriter. He wrote *The Landlord* (from a novel by Kristin Hunter), which was filmed in 1970 by Hal Ashby, with Diana Sands, Pearl Bailey, Lee Grant, and Beau Bridges. The story of a rich white boy who buys a Brooklyn tenement and gets involved with his Black tenants, *The Landlord* is a generally underrated crossover film.

Gunn shot *Stop* in Puerto Rico the same year. It is much more identifiably his own work, full of the mysteries and obsessions that give strange life to *Ganja & Hess* and the play *Black Picture Show*, which was produced in 1975 by Joseph Papp at Lincoln Center. In rough cut (the only form that now exists), *Stop* is difficult to judge without any exposure to Gunn's other work. That may, or may not, have been the reason Warner's decided to shelve the film. Gunn says they kept telling him, for months, that they loved the film and were only waiting for the right moment to send it into the theaters. But years have passed now, and it still doesn't seem to be the right time for *Stop*.

Almost before the credits have finished their cryptic roll in *Ganja & Hess*, you know you are watching an extraordinary film. Something about the "voice" of the film—its editing, camerawork, and point of view—tells you this experience will be unique. The film has a vitality that seems to broadcast itself. It comes alive as only masterworks do. Gunn had signed with Kelly-Jordan, a black and white production firm that had produced *Georgia, Georgia* from Maya Angelou's first screenplay. Hopes were bright for Jack Jordan and his partner. They had an exclusive contract with James Baldwin to film all his books. Meanwhile, Gunn was going to do a Black vampire film for them. What they got was considerably more than they bargained for.

Like the greatest films of the horror genre, *Ganja & Hess* taps hidden reservoirs in our collective unconscious for its power. But unlike most of those films, it doesn't think to emphasize the metaphor. Its terror is considerably closer to home than to Hollywood's Transylvania.

Dr. Hess Green (Duane Jones), an archaeological curator, reigns alone in a spacious Westchester Tudor mansion. He lives a quiet and introspective life of Bach and Mozart, fine wines and old books, interrupted only occasionally by his Draculan thirst for blood, which he usually slakes in a sensible way, by a trip to the nearest blood bank. His new assistant, George Meda (Gunn), a realistic foil to Hess's anthropological symbol, commits suicide. Like Green, he is more than half in love with easeful death. Ganja (Marlene Clark), Meda's widow, arrives and quickly proceeds to fall in love with Hess. Before long she too is vampirized. But even as Eros is about to triumph, Hess succumbs to Thanatos, committing the first recorded vampirean suicide by presenting himself before the cross in a rocking gospel church ceremony. Ganja lives on, carrying the curse.

This summary really gives you nothing of the flavor and mystery of the film. Blood lust is important to the film, true, but Gunn explains, "I wrote symbolically about blood *only* because everyone else writes about money. *Ganja & Hess* is really about the many addictions I've had in my life. There is something about my Blackness that I don't understand," Gunn concludes, "but that takes a major part of my time."[4] That, succinctly, is the subject of *Ganja & Hess*, the most introspective of Black films.

Gunn combines allusions to Black fundamentalist Christianity, African mythology and philosophy, drugs, sex, and the moneyed life in a strange brew that is rich with all kinds of transcendent meanings, for whites as well as Blacks. To convey this felt psychology, Gunn avails himself of an impressive arsenal of narrative techniques—straight documentary, high melodrama, dark ritual, and cool realism—each of which he handles with simple assurance. For this mix alone, *Ganja & Hess* is a notable film. Underlining and commenting upon the images and stimuli is an intriguing score by Sam Waymon, who also later wrote music for *Black Picture Show*. The collaboration is an important one.

Ganja & Hess confused its producers. They opened it in New York in April 1973 with the barest minimum of publicity. The film was met by expectably befuddled reviews from the major critics (except for James Murray's thoughtful appreciation in *The Amsterdam News*). After a week, just as word-of-mouth was beginning to draw audiences, the film closed. But it wasn't dead yet. Gunn himself presented it at Cannes that year, where it was chosen for showing by the Association of French Film Critics. It was

Marlene Clark in one of the elegant settings of *Ganja & Hess.*

screened there several times to stunned and enthusiastic audiences and was, according to Louis Marcorelles, head of the association, "the most popular film in the critics' week." At one screening, an audience of notoriously cynical film students jumped to their feet applauding, even though the film still had half an hour to run.

No word of this unusual triumph trickled back to the United States and Kelly-Jordan. In financial difficulties by this time, the production firm had sold the film to a company ironically called Heritage Enterprises. Fima Noveck, notorious film doctor, was hired to perform a vivisection on the film. He recut it, redubbed it, shot new scenes, and *Ganja & Hess* re-emerged as *Blood Couple*, which did get screened around the country. It bore little relationship to Gunn's film.

Ganja & Hess enjoyed one last reprieve. In December 1973, it was scheduled to be shown at the Museum of Modern Art (ironically, as part of "French Critics Week"). By now, word had circulated among the Black film community in New York. The auditorium was packed with people who realized they might never again have a chance to see this film. The response was overwhelming, the screening became a landmark event. Gunn was able to convince Kelly-Jordan to donate one print to the Museum. There is a rumor that another one exists. The negative, of course, is gone. For the last few years, that one exhibition print has been carefully projected at various museums and festivals. It has been damaged in the process, and may not be screened again until a duplicate can be made. But, someday, *Ganja & Hess* will rise.

207

The *Carwash* gang in the locker room: Grand Hotel from 9 to 5.

Michael Schultz

Several years younger than either Van Peebles or Gunn, Michael Schultz represents what may be a new wave of Black filmmakers operating within the Hollywood system. He worked first on the New York stage, directing productions of *The Song of the Lusitanian Bogey*, *Kongi's Harvest*, and *Does a Tiger Wear a Necktie?* He broke into film with *Cooley High* (1975) which most critics at the time described as a Black *American Graffiti*. It was set in the early sixties and did concern a group of high-school students, but the tone of Schultz's film was considerably different: it had a special Black vitality. This has become the one characteristic linking Schultz's otherwise disparate projects.

Carwash followed in 1976. It was one of the few thoroughly Black films of the post-1973 period, and it disproved the theory that Black films were no longer salable: *Carwash* had rentals of nearly $9 million, which put it near the top of the list of profitable Black films together with *Let's Do It Again* and *Lady Sings the Blues*. Simply plotted, *Carwash* gives us a day in the life of a group of characters who work at, visit, and hang around a Los Angeles auto laundry, and thereby breaks most of the rules in the Hollywood book. It doesn't focus on heroes, it presents a complex collective; it doesn't depend on action and tension, just the daily rhythms of work and life; it doesn't add white heroes for "crossover" potential; it doesn't even offer stars, although Richard Pryor does make a cameo appearance. In short, *Carwash*, judged by the rules, should have been a disaster. It most

208

Richard Pryor and Beau Bridges "integrate" a restaurant in *Greased Lightning,* ready to fight their way out.

certainly wasn't. Critic Joe Medjuck calls it "one of the rare American films in the René Clair tradition." As such, it is probably a more radical departure from narrative conventions than any recent Hollywood film, Black or white.

Schultz next worked with Richard Pryor on *Which Way Is Up?* (1977), an adaptation of the Lina Wertmüller film *The Temptation of Mimi* by Carl Gottlieb. Set in the milieu of California farm laborers, *Which Way Is Up?* did manage to present an attractive and realistic image of everyday life—Schultz used actors from Teatro Campesino rather than Hollywood extras—but Gottlieb would have been better advised to chuck the Wertmüller plot entirely rather than try to repair and translate it. *Which Way Is Up?* went off in too many directions at the same time. Perhaps the title is a result of hindsight.

Immediately after finishing shooting on *Which Way Is Up?* Schultz was called in to take over direction of *Greased Lightning* from Melvin Van Peebles. A biopic in the old Hollywood tradition, *Greased Lightning* (1977) presents the rather interesting story of Wendell Scott, the first Black stockcar driver to break the color bar in that quintessentially Southern sport. The film marked an important step for Richard Pryor to more dramatic roles, and the central relationships between Scott (Pryor) and his wife (Pam Grier) and Scott and his white friend (Beau Bridges, who seems to specialize in this sort of role) were considerably more sophisticated than such connections usually are in films of this sort. The script showed evident signs of having been doctored (both Van Peebles and Leon Capitano get screen credit, as well as original writers Kenneth Vose and Larry Du-Kore), but the Hannah Weinstein-Third World production survives, mainly due to Schultz's empathetic direction.

Greased Lightning tells a simple story, but a meaningful one. It's the sort of movie usually relegated to television. But it turned out to be the most financially successful Black film of 1977, disproving two shopworn Hollywood axioms in the process: that modest stories don't sell, and that films about sports don't sell.

Schultz next took on *Sergeant Pepper's Lonely Hearts Club Band*, a non-Black project evidently designed to mark his departure from the Hollywood ghetto. Parks had tried this before. Black directors like Mark Warren (*Laugh-In*) had been able to wangle a few non-Black film assignments in television. One of producer Robert Stigwood's pet musical exploitation projects, *Sergeant Pepper* was overshadowed in the summer of 1978 by Stigwood's *other* rock exploitation movie, *Grease*. Perhaps it was just as well. The raison d'être for the film, the music from the historic Beatles album, is sung and performed by the BeeGees and other equally unprepossessing beneficiaries of seventies-style hype-rock, which only serves to renew our admiration for the Liverpudlians of yore. The plot is a gassy contrivance. If Schultz, the director of *Carwash*, which was equally dependent on music, had had real control we might surmise that *Sergeant Pepper* would have looked radically different.

But we can still understand why Schultz took on the assignment. It looks now as if he will be the first Black American film director to earn the commercial respect of the Hollywood establishment. He will be able to work outside the cinematic ghetto to which almost all others have been consigned.

Schultz hasn't had a strong authorial hand in any of the films he's made so far. When they want to silence you, just making movies is winning. But he always manages to bring to his projects a friendly compassion for his characters and a likable understanding for their situations, qualities that are as rare as they are valuable. He seems to genuinely like the people he puts on the screen, and his enthusiasm is infectious. His is a talent that shouldn't be underestimated; it's low-key, it's modest, but it's an excellent base to build on. It may not be the stuff of which legends like *Ganja & Hess* get made; on the other hand, Schultz's films get seen.

It would be nice to conclude this very brief survey of Black film on a positive note. I would like to be able to tell you about the work of directors like Bill Crain (*Blacula*), Ivan Dixon (*Trouble Man*), Woodie King, Jr. (*The Long Night*), Wendell James Franklin (*The Bus Is Coming*), Mark Warren

More performers: Berry Gordy's 1976 production of *The Bingo Long Traveling All-Stars and Motor Kings* about a Black baseball team of the forties who learn to perform to earn a dollar might have worked better than it did if Gordy had taken over direction as he did with his earlier film, *Mahogany*. John Badham couldn't give focus to the film. The All-Stars (James Earl Jones, Billy Dee Williams, DeWayne Jessie, Sam "Birmingham" Brison, Jophrey Brown, and Tony Burton) enter town parading.

(*Come Back Charleston Blue*), Maya Angelou (*I Know Why the Caged Bird Sings*), and others. But for the most part, these directors have made only one or two films, usually within the strict rules of Blaxploitation, and they've had real trouble getting even that sort of assignment since 1974. Of the five directors whose work is discussed in some detail here, only Michael Schultz works regularly. Black film now exists more in theory than in reality.

While it's true that far more Blacks are working in American commercial film now than ever before, it's also true that none of them have any real clout, with the possible exception of Richard Pryor, who has certainly achieved stardom. Behind the camera, ten years after the Black revolution in cinema began, tokenism still rules.

Even in music, a field in which Blacks clearly excel outside of film, only Quincy Jones has an established reputation, having scored dozens of films since the mid-sixties. And even Jones has succeeded mainly because he has been able to produce the sort of tuneless jingles that characterize the great bulk of the contemporary Hollywood product. Blacks had better luck doing film music in the fifties, when at least the Modern Jazz Quartet used to get an occasional gig.

The situation in the seventies is best summed up by this curious fact:

211

Lady Sings the Blues, a film about one of the greatest Black musicians who ever lived, produced by the most successful Black music company of all time, starring one of the most popular contemporary Black singers, was scored by Michel Legrand.

The Black image in film has fared hardly better. The roles have multiplied perhaps tenfold, but the old stereotypes survive to be joined by new ones. The racism of the '70s and '80s is far more sophisticated than the racism of the fifties, but it's racism all the same. It may seem picayune to quibble with such obvious entertainments as *The Deep, New York, New York, Star Wars, Rocky,* and *Network*—certainly none of these films *mean* to be racist, and their writers and directors would no doubt be genuinely upset at the charge. Nevertheless, all the villains of *The Deep* are Black, and arch stereotypes at that. The villain of *Star Wars* is costumed in Black. (And, as we've noted earlier, George Lucas even thought it necessary to post-dub Darth Vader's dialogue using James Earl Jones's voice. It brings a touch of class to the film, no doubt, but that wasn't the point.) *Rocky* sets up a parody of Muhammad Ali for its not-so-great white hope to knock down, just as *Network* parodies Black militants. And *New York, New York,* a film supposedly about popular music in the late forties and early fifties, manages to avoid Black contributions almost entirely (except for one sequence, later cut from the film).

Now none of these films is consciously, actively racist (except perhaps *The Deep,* which seems calculated to profit from racist audience sentiments), but these little twists have a cumulative effect. The sum of them is excellent evidence of cultural attitudes toward Blacks. And while it might be argued that when they want to ignore you, just being on the screen is winning, that certainly isn't the whole truth, is it? Since Blacks don't fare very well in cinema for general audiences, there is still a demonstrable need for Black cinema. It even earns money for producers, but apparently it doesn't earn enough.

There are bright spots: the liberal tradition still survives in Hollywood. Every few years there's a film like *Brothers* (written and produced by Edward and Mildred Lewis, directed by Arthur Barron). Bernie Casey and Vonetta McGee do a superb job of re-creating screen images of two genuine heroes, George Jackson and Angela Davis. *Brothers* is a good film; one doesn't want to carp; but it would have been gutsier, livelier, funkier, and I think, would have significantly more meaning and would probably have been more profitable had it been written and directed by Blacks instead of whites.

Blue Collar represents an even more interesting line of development. It is the first film in a very long time with such unusual coordinates: it is not a Black film as such, but a general-interest film; yet two of three major

Vonetta McGee as a woman very much like Angela Davis; Bernie Casey as a man very much like George Jackson.

characters (Pryor and Yaphet Kotto) are Black, and take dominant roles; and while the script does not ignore their Blackness—it is an important element of the plot—race is clearly not the main issue, but a subsidiary one. *Blue Collar* is that very rare general-interest film in which Blacks take major roles simply because they would anyway in reality.

As logical as that might seem, the structure of a film like *Blue Collar* is still unique enough in seventies Hollywood to require comment. For a while there, between 1969 and 1973, the natives were restless. The system was cracking. But thanks in part to Black box-office dollars, it's been patched up. The studios have things under control. Not to worry. The people who make decisions are not rabid racists. They're probably all very nice men, hip, know the power handshake, and all that. The problem is, as Clayton Riley puts it, all things being equal, white executives prefer "to make stars of people who come from *our* tribe."[5]

That's why Black cinema is still necessary. And that's why it has been effectively censored.

7

The Importance of Being Funny
Comics and Comedians

What's Funny?
- A dozen people, two steamer trunks, a bed, and a manicurist's tray in a stateroom built for one short person.

    That's funny.
- "And three hard-boiled eggs."

    That's funny.
- W. C. Fields desperately trying to cope with the nasty blind man in *It's a Gift,* as the scourge of Fields's grocery shop wields his cane with testy abandon, and Bill begs him in his sweetest voice, "Oh, Mr. Muckle, honey . . . "

    Very funny.
- "Now, you take my wife . . . please? So I said to the girl with the wooden leg, Peg . . . So I asked my wife, '*How* did the car get into the *kitchen?!*' 'It was easy, I turned left at the dining room!'"

    Henny Youngman, king-of-the-one-liners, is funny.
- Woody Allen, on the *Tonight Show* in the late sixties, responding to a query whether or not he smoked grass, coming back quickly and brightly: "I do! But I don't inhale."

    Funny? Maybe. Certainly witty, humorous.
- Peter Sellers as Strangelove fighting his right arm, then bursting from his wheelchair as the bombs rain down, the truculent member shooting up in a triumphant fascist salute: "Mr. President! I can valk!!!" (Vera

Lynn on the soundtrack: "We'll meet again, don't know where, don't know when. . . .")

The scene is thrilling even now twenty years after the film was made (*especially* now, since we know the real Henry Kissinger). It's sublime, brilliant. But do we laugh? Is it "funny"? It goes beyond that.

The situation, the logic, the character, the delivery, the gag, the wit and irony—each of these touchstones has its comic roots in a different element, but they all elicit laughs from at least some of the people some of the time, so they're funny. What's funny is what you laugh at, and that tautology will have to suffice as a definition of the term for the time being.

Critics and pundits who have tackled the slippery subject of comedy have never been able to devise a more explicit definition of this physiological and psychological phenomenon, but most of them do seem to agree that, somehow, the sense of humor is a foundation upon which the American character is built.

There are some fairly convincing reasons for this. In the first place, the English language is easily the best in the world for puns, wordplay, and other comic linguistic twists: its vocabulary is twice the size of that of its nearest competitor; uniquely it has a double system of roots in the Germanic and Romance branches of Indo-European, which gives it enormous flexibility; and, most important, its rules have never really been successfully codified, a fact which provides speakers and writers with unusual freedom. Insofar as comedy is linguistic, the English language is the funniest in the world.

Then, too, the ethnic composition of the U.S. population has resulted in a fundamentally funny national culture. Italian-Americans, the second-largest nationality group in the U.S., have brought with them a fundamental Latin irony. Black Americans, the third-largest and most cohesive of U.S. ethnic groups, took certain ironic essentials of African philosophy and developed them into the even more elaborate Afro-American "Motherwit" which has proved a vital technique of psychological survival in a hostile environment. Similarly, Jews, who have had an influence on American culture out of all proportion to their numbers, have developed a comic vision necessary to the task of survival. (Yes, we've neatly sidestepped the dark Calvinist culture of America's two largest ethnic components, Anglo-Saxons and German-Americans; the rigid Protestant ethic is the chief reason we've had to turn to laughter.)

The very fact of the "melting pot" itself gave rise to ethnic humor: we eagerly laugh at each other (and sometimes at ourselves). Moreover, as residents of the New World and being relatively more democratic about such things than our Old World forebears, we tend to take culture in general far less seriously, in both senses of the word. One of our great successes, culturally, has been to blur the line which separates popular culture, which is essentially comic, from the elite culture of high moral seriousness. In America, the two merge, so that the entire spectrum of culture shows some comic aspects. From Mark Twain to Thomas Pynchon, from Vaudeville to sitcoms, from Chaplin, Keaton, and Lloyd to Allen, Mazursky, Ritchie, and Altman, the best American literature, theater, and cinema is vitally humorous.

This shouldn't be taken to mean that American culture is—how shall we put it—not so "high-minded" as other, more "serious" national cultures. Quite the opposite. As George Bernard Shaw was fond of demonstrating, comedy as a form handles ideas at least as well as tragedy, perhaps better. It may also be more psychologically effective, too. For half a century critics have been warning us of the death of tragedy; certainly that form no longer has the cathartic power it once did. But the relief and renewal that comes from the comic vision is just as powerful as it ever was, perhaps more so.

No wonder, then, that humor and comedy dominate and pervade what is best in American culture. Comedy is the best tool we have for analyzing, commenting upon, and perhaps controlling the world around us. Shaw used to say that life is a tragedy for those who feel, a comedy for those who think. The comic element gives a dimension of wisdom to narrative art. It's easy enough to sit around and tell sad stories of the death of kings. It's more difficult—and more rewarding—to put the death force to rout. The life force is comedic.

The Genre and the Style

The consensus now has it that American movies aren't as funny as they used to be. In a sense, this is true. On the one hand, other entertainment values besides humor vie in the marketplace, with increasingly profitable results. Challenging television, where comedy of a sort remains king, films now deal in sex and violence and spectacle, commodities that TV can't or won't allow itself to exploit. Consequently, comic performers tend to go into television rather than film, and comic writers follow them. There is some logic to this: since it's more efficient, comedy takes less time than competing dramatic forms. It's strong, but it's quick. Short, "small" films no longer seem profitable to most distributors and exhibitors, while the half-hour sitcom form is perfect for television.

Moreover, the style of comic performance has changed considerably since the thirties. The advent of sound film resulted in a mass migration of vaudeville and stage performers to Hollywood. They'd been practicing

Goin' Hollywood: George Burns and Gracie Allen in one of their first screen appearances—a short film circa 1930. At this time, Gracie still did ethnic accent humor, but as the transition from vaudeville to movies was completed she broadened her approach.

essentially theatrical, or "skit," routines for ten or twenty years on the circuits and they were more than ready to exploit the new medium. They were accompanied by an entire generation of Broadway playwrights —George S. Kaufman, Mae West, Ben Hecht, Charles MacArthur, and the rest—who had developed the American stage comedy to a high pitch. Theater has never been the same since they left. With this wealth of talent, no wonder early talkies were profoundly comic. Silent film had developed, early on, its own brand of visual slapstick humor. Now you could *hear* the jokes as well, and here were dozens of accomplished, trained comedians from vaudeville and the stage to tell them. Critics bemoan the lack of great comic actors now, but film itself has trained perhaps as many comic actors in the sixties and seventies as in the thirties; it's just that fewer have moved into film from outside.

The reason is simple: the vaudeville tradition has been replaced by the monologue, a form which is particularly apt for television, but doesn't work very well at all in the more elaborate dramatic structure of film. We can trace the monologue form back to Will Rogers and Robert Benchley, but Rogers's exceptionally valuable wit didn't work well in feature films, and Benchley had at his disposal the two-reeler, which has now disappeared.

Only Bob Hope of the early monologists managed to translate his stand-up persona into the idiom of feature films. Partly for this reason (and partly for his extraordinary mastery of the form) he has become a hero to contemporary monologists like Woody Allen and Dick Cavett.

Since the late 1950s, when the monologue began to supersede the skit as our preferred comic form, few practitioners of the art have been able to make the transition to film successfully. As his own director, Woody Allen has been able to project his persona both as author and performer. Bill Cosby's films are widely spaced. He certainly doesn't have the impact on the large screen, in character, that he does on the small screen, as himself. Richard Pryor has now joined this select group. He alone seems to be an actor—who can project character—as well as a monologist who projects a persona.

Mike Nichols and Elaine May have established careers as directors, but with one or two exceptions, they've had to leave behind the form of brilliant social satire they pioneered as performers in the fifties and early sixties. It's exceedingly difficult to maintain the commentator's persona in film.

Now that tastes have begun to shift back toward skit comedy, the transition from television to film may be easier for such comedians as Steve Martin, Martin Mull, and Chevy Chase, all of whom are equally at home in skit and monologue.*

A traditional vaudeville axiom makes a necessary differentiation between the comic, who says funny things, and the comedian, who says things funny. The monologists were comics for the most part: what they said was funnier than how they said it. To get the same effect, they would have to write and direct film. But at the same time they'd developed comic—or more properly, comedian—personas as integral parts of their acts, and these required that they also perform. Finally, there is a significant difference between telling things funny (or funny things) and showing them. The skit comedy of vaudeville fit the film medium quite well; monologues fit it not at all.

(When Woody Allen first became successful, he used to say, he rented a posh Fifth Avenue apartment and brought in a Swedish maid three days

---

*The form of monologue clearly isn't the only barrier that prevents television performers from enjoying equal success in film: witness Sid Caesar, a thoroughly practiced skit comedian who did brilliant work in TV in the fifties and has had regrettably few opportunities since to duplicate his success in movies.

The comic says funny things, the comedian says things funny, then there is the comedic personality who may do either, but whose main achievement is the projection of an ingratiating, humorous persona. Carole Lombard had one of the great comedic personalities of the thirties. Jill Clayburgh has some of the same talent now. Clayburgh as Lombard on the way to the studio commisary in *Gable and Lombard*.

a week. His mother saw the maid, and said, "what are you doing with this Swedish person? I could clean just as well for you and cheaper." So he fired the maid. And hired his mother. It worked out very well, for a while. But finally he had to let her go. She stole. When Allen tells this story, it's very funny. But it wouldn't be funny at all to watch it dramatized.)

In addition to the dichotomies between comic and comedian, telling and showing, we have to make a differentiation between comedy as genre and comedy as style. The comic style is thriving in the seventies. It hasn't been so healthy since Preston Sturges's heyday. But the genre of comedy seems paralyzed. There are only a handful of practitioners of it, and nine times out of ten they seem to think it necessary to reproduce the historical genre, to make a comedy about genre, as well as a genre comedy. So we are subjected to a continuing stream of spoofs and parodies, some of them better than others, but all of them essentially secondary material. Both Mel Brooks and Woody Allen have been victims of this obsession, although Allen seems to have conquered it recently. Occasional comedies by other directors—Mike Nichols's *The Fortune*, Peter Bogdanovich's *What's Up, Doc?*, even Elaine May's *A New Leaf*—also depend heavily on historical genres and historical settings. It's as if the straight comedy were a moribund form, its effects available only through the distance that nostalgia provides.

But this needn't be true, at least in theory. In the sixties, George Axelrod and Blake Edwards managed to devise comedies that had roots in their own generation. Axelrod as screenwriter provided some of the few bright spots of the fifties (*The Seven-Year Itch, Will Success Spoil Rock Hunter?*). He came out of television via Broadway. In the sixties, he wrote the screenplay for *Breakfast at Tiffany's*, the seminal romantic comedy of the generation, then collaborated with Richard Quine on two generally underestimated comedies that are aging well: *Paris When It Sizzles* (1963) and *How to Murder Your Wife* (1965). Interestingly, both had self-referential aspects. In the first, the hero is a screenwriter, in the second, a cartoonist: the arts are necessary plot elements. Axelrod himself started directing in 1966 with the cult success *Lord Love a Duck*, with Tuesday Weld. He also gave free rein to Walter Matthau in *The Secret Life of an American Wife* (1968). By this time the material was running thin.

Edwards, like Axelrod deservedly popular among film enthusiasts in the sixties, has managed to extend his career into the seventies. He directed *Breakfast at Tiffany's* (1961)* (and had written the fifties classic *Operation Mad Ball*, 1957, with Ernie Kovacs), and wrote *Notorious Landlady* (directed by Richard Quine, 1962) before hitting on the happy discovery of Peter Sellers as Inspector Clouseau in *The Pink Panther* (1963) and *A Shot in the Dark* (1964). *The Great Race* (1964) and *What Did You Do in the War, Daddy?* (1966) were other Edwards efforts in the mid-sixties. Each had its fans. After a string of more dramatic films, none of which had any great success, Edwards revived Clouseau for three profitable reprises in the seventies: *The Return of the Pink Panther* (1974), *The Pink Panther Strikes Again* (1976), and *The Revenge of the Pink Panther* (1978). These films received more attention than they deserved simply because they were judged to be effective and efficient comedies in a unique style at a time when everyone else in the field seemed to be trying to revive slapstick, screwball, or other ancient genres.

The Clouseau films work because they showcase Peter Sellers, generally regarded as the best comic actor of our generation, even if we take this statement more on faith than on evidence. Sellers, of course, was English, and most of the best film comedies of the last twenty years are also English, or have English components. After his string of Boulting

---

*Edwards is also responsible for *Days of Wine and Roses* (1962)—hardly a comedy—but along with *Breakfast at Tiffany's* a romantic touchstone for the college generation of the early sixties.

brothers comedies in the late fifties and early sixties, Sellers moved into international film. His work for Stanley Kubrick in *Lolita* (1962) and *Dr. Strangelove* (1963) is nothing short of magnificent, but he never managed to come up to that level again, with the possible exception of *Being There*.

Billy Wilder, a generation older than Blake Edwards, hasn't had much success in comedy in the seventies, but then his career stretches back to 1930. In the sixties, along with Edwards and Axelrod, he showed that contemporary comedy was both vital and possible in such films as *One, Two, Three* (1963), the controversial *Kiss Me Stupid* (1964), and the influential and relevant *The Fortune Cookie* (1966).* Wilder's *The Front Page* (1974) worked well enough, but it was the fourth time around for the Hecht–MacArthur story. *Fedora* (1979) received scant attention.

In this context we probably also have to mention Jerry Lewis. The French think he's a comic genius—perhaps because they're busy reading subtitles—and there are certainly occasional sparks of intelligence in his films. Whatever one thinks of his work, it's clear his career thrived in the sixties and came to a dead end in 1970 with *Which Way to the Front?*

There seems to be no really clear reason why straight comedy in a contemporary style is so rare in the 1970s. Axelrod, Wilder, and Edwards made it work in the sixties, and Edwards proved at least that the contemporary style was still serviceable in the seventies. We don't lack for comic actors or, perhaps more important, for comedians. Outside of film, comedy is healthy. Yet American filmmakers have shied away from any sort of comedy that doesn't rely on archaic models. The only answer seems to be the dominance in the seventies of the nostalgia craze. We seem to be ignoring our own time on purpose, and nowhere is this ignorance more evident or more hurtful than in comedy.

This is true abroad, too. By far the most accomplished and interesting of comic directors working in the English language in the sixties was Richard Lester. *A Hard Day's Night, Help!, The Knack, How I Won the War*, and *The Bed-Sitting Room* constitute a remarkable series of essays in comic styles, each with a pertinence and vividness that give them staying power. They improve with age (even if the last two were box-office failures). *A Funny Thing Happened on the Way to the Forum*, poorly reviewed when it was released in 1965, also gets better with each succeeding viewing. It is not only arguably the best musical of the sixties, but a

---

*Wilder is also responsible for the third film of the romantic triumvirate of the early sixties, *The Apartment* (1960).

remarkable catalogue of comic styles from Buster Keaton to Phil Silvers, Zero Mostel to Michael Crawford to Roy Kinnear. If we must revive the old comic styles, this is the way to do it: with the people who invented them. Yet Lester was unable to find a film to do for five years after *The Bed-Sitting Room* (1969), a financial disaster that experimented with the British Goon Show style of humor later to become successful in the varied persons of Monty Python's Flying Circus. When Lester did return to filmmaking in the mid-seventies, it was with historical comedies. (The less said about *The Ritz*, the one exception, the better.)

In both Britain and the United States, comedy has fared much better on television in the seventies. British film comedy, once a significant export commodity, seems to have died with British film, although the occasional "Carry On" or "Doctor" movie still reaches our shores, a reminder of times long past. Peter Cook and Dudley Moore, so promising in the sixties, seem to have faded rapidly, although they each still make occasional appearances. (Moore had a nice bit as Stanley Tibbets, the anxious sex hobbyist, in Colin Higgins's *Foul Play*, and scored big in Edwards's *10*.

The one bright spot in British comedy in the seventies (and it almost makes up for the wasteland that surrounds it) has been Monty Python, clearly the most inventive comics/comedians since Sid Caesar, Ernie Kovacs, and the generation of the fifties. The Pythons' unique blend of skits, wordplay, animation and other visual devices, echoes of the Music Hall tradition, and sheer social anarchy is breathtaking in its variety and acuity. The Pythons run the comedic gamut from bellylaugh to motherwit. Although their brilliant style of humor works best within the confines of the half-hour television show, their films—*And Now for Something Completely Different* (1971), *Monty Python and the Holy Grail* (1975), and *Jabberwocky* (1977)—work surprisingly well, and are added proof that a fresh, contemporary comic style is still possible in film.

In the United States, television comedy has thrived in the seventies. Yet almost without exception, none of the successful TV comedians— Mary Tyler Moore, Bob Newhart, Alan Alda, Norman Lear's crew—has been able to translate their art into filmic terms. Curiously—and this may be a significant sign of the true state of comedy in the seventies—the characteristic style of humor for the last five years in the United States has been the college wit perpetrated by the *National Lampoon-Saturday Night Live* axis. I have incontrovertible proof, Mr. Chairman, that this dangerous outbreak of sophomoric irreverence for our most sacred institutions has been instigated by a secret Canadian cabal. They have infiltrated this country with the sole aim of weakening our national moral

One of the secrets of comic success is accuracy. The more precise the parody the more effective it is. Classy Omega House men drink to the demise of animal house. They're a bit overdressed but the poses and the mugs are dead right. These men will grow up to be bankers. And models. Meanwhile, Animal House displays its existential lifestyle. (Bruce McGill, Tim Matheson, Peter Rigert, John Belushi, Thomas Hulce, Steven Furst, James Widdoes.) . . .

fibre by exposing us to silliness. This insidious gang of sneerers, lay-abouts, and coneheads* who look to their equally Canadian leader, the redolent Monty Hall, for inspiration, guidance, and perhaps a good deal behind door number three, seeks to reduce us to the level of helpless, giggling college girls.

To a large extent, they've succeeded, and we should be rather grateful for this rare relief from the samurai disco that was the seventies.

The majority of ex-*Lampoon* writers and several *Saturday Night Live* actors are now involved in filmmaking, but to date, only one of their various projects has reached American movie screens, *National Lampoon's Animal House* (1978), a perspicuous if self-conscious homage to the halls of ivy, circa 1962. The film is lackadaisical, but it is achingly precise. I should know. I vass dere, Sharlie.

While the *Lampoon-Saturday Night* axis looks as if it will enjoy a measure of success in film in the next few years, other, more creative comedians still remain outside the Hollywood domain. David Steinberg (also

---

*Lorne Michaels (producer of *Saturday Night Live*), Ivan Reitman (producer of *The National Lampoon Show*, where John Belushi and Gilda Radner first appeared, and of *Animal House*), Sean Kelly, Michel Choquette, Anne Beatts, Bruce McCall—all *Lampoon* alumni, Tony Hendra (well, he's English, but he *thinks* like a Canadian). There are probably many others. It's hard to identify them. They think they speak your language. They can be quickly identified, however, by their tortuous pronunciation of the word "about" or by the hollowness of their laughter when you make a Canuck joke, such as "Canada has two seasons: winter and July."

. . . If you doubt the veracity of *Animal House*, compare these snapshots from Alpha Tau Omega, Muhlenberg College, spring 1962, with the stills from the film. ATO fell somewhere in between Omega and animal house. The movie's plot has about as much coherence as a beer-soaked Senior Ball weekend. Its precision in evoking a nostalgic lifestyle accounted for its success.

Canadian) has been trying for several years now to find a way to transfer his unique brand of congenial commentary to the large screen. Robert Klein, a fine monologist live, or on Home Box Office (where his shows have met with success), takes an occasional film role. He should be remembered for his deathless burlesque of Peter Bogdanovich in *Hooper* (1978).

Albert Brooks, perhaps the most inventive American comic of the seventies, remains a cult figure. He has played at least one (noncomic) film role (the political operative in *Taxi Driver*), but his real reputation rests on the handful of short films he did for *Saturday Night Live* in 1975 and for his album, *A Star is Bought.*

As for Andy Kaufman, the less said about this conceptual-artist-masquerading-as-comedian the better, as Kaufman would be the first to admit, I'm sure, if he could only just get it out.

With so much of interest going on in comedy outside film, Hollywood's attempts at humoring us seem less and less important. Very few contemporary film comedies do not trade on our collective nostalgia for the old genres, so we are forced to seek the cinematic comic vision elsewhere in contemporary life. We look to comedy as style, rather than comedy as genre.

Maybe that's not such a bad thing after all. The influence of Hawks, of Capra, Lubitsch, and Preston Sturges survives in the work of a number of filmmakers who may not be as celebrated as the Whiz Kids, but nevertheless manage to keep on keeping on. Robert Altman has a tendency toward parody and pastiche of the old forms (see especially *The Long Goodbye*); somehow it works for him in the mélange of comic and dramatic elements which characterizes his style. John Cassavetes's work is

225

rooted in a profound understanding of the human comedy, even if the admittedly numerous people who don't enjoy his films can't feel it. Cassavetes is—on occasion—an American, working-class Lubitsch. Paul Mazursky has developed a gently satirical vision that's peculiarly apt for the 1970s. Michael Ritchie continues in the honorable tradition of Preston Sturges with a satirical style that's a little less humane, more biting, than Mazursky's. (More about these master filmmakers in Chapters 9 and 10.)

They are not alone. Much of the best work by other American directors in the seventies falls into the satiric, ironic tradition which runs from Capra and Sturges through Mazursky and Ritchie.

Two established directors who probably deserve better than they get from the critics are George Roy Hill and Herbert Ross. It's true that Hill's films are alternately sentimental (*Butch Cassidy*) and pretentious (*Slaughterhouse Five*). He can be sophomoric. But he is capable of more. *The World of Henry Orient* (1964) offered the unique spectacle of Peter Sellers upstaged by two teenage amateur actresses, Merri Spaeth and Tippy Walker, whom Hill handled with grace and affection. The film remains one of those rare American movies that treats children with intelligence and respect. Thirteen years later, Hill did a better than respectable job staging Nancy Dowd's rowdy, tough, yet subtly pointed satire of the contemporary sports business, *Slapshot*. And *The Sting*, despite its thoroughly derivative provenance, still works for audiences. Nostalgia, certainly; manipulative, yes; but nicely mounted.

Herbert Ross has become perhaps the most trustworthy metteur en scène of the seventies. *The Turning Point* may turn out to be just that for Ross, but up until now he has depended on screenwriters for the ultimate effect of his films. Given good material, he rises to the challenge, as he did in *Play It Again, Sam* (1972), written by and starring Woody Allen, and *The Sunshine Boys* (1975), arguably the quintessential Neil Simon movie, for better or worse. *The Seven-Percent Solution* (1976) was a leaden exercise, but the problem lay with Nicholas Meyer's script. Sigmund Freud meets Sherlock Holmes is an interesting idea, but Meyer worked it out mechanically, oblivious to potential resonances. Ross's most interesting film remains *The Last of Sheila* (1973), a workmanlike mounting of a fascinating and unusual script by Tony Perkins and Stephen Sondheim. Both are British crossword puzzle fans, and the film is a largely successful attempt to capture the wit and wordplay, logical and linguistic puzzles of those absorbing exercises on film. It comes as close to capturing the pure intellectual play of James Joyce's language as any other film ever made. (What other films have tried? Only the Marx Brothers movies; certainly not the films made of Joyce's novels.) Of course, most of this puzzlement,

Joan Hackett's elegant suicide attempt in *The Last of Sheila,* James Mason observing.

meant to puzzle, went over the heads of audiences. But it's there, never-theless: pure intelligence: the apotheosis of logos. Remarkable.

Mike Nichols and Elaine May, who together with Lenny Bruce, Mort Sahl, and Bob Newhart established styles of monologue that have been influential for twenty years, have been relative disappointments as film directors. Nichols seems to avoid comedy, as if afraid to be pigeonholed. *Catch-22* was an inflated homage that fell of its own weight. It had none of the testy, manic impatience of Heller's great novel. *The Graduate* had elements of satire, but they decorated the film, they weren't at the heart of its success. *The Fortune,* on the other hand, was underrated. Adrien Joyce's script had some interesting twists, and Warren Beatty and Jack Nicholson worked well together, but Stockard Channing dug a hole her co-stars couldn't fill. *The Day of the Dolphin* has already been dissected in Chapter 3. Nichols's one unarguable success has been *Carnal Knowledge,* from Jules Feiffer's screenplay (1971), one of the more important com-mentaries on lifestyles of the sixties and seventies, but more bitter than satiric.

May's *A New Leaf* (1971) manages, as none of Nichols's films has, to capture some of the atmosphere and wit of their brilliant routines together. But it floats out of time; it would have worked better in the twenties or thirties; it certainly doesn't connect with the seventies. *The Heartbreak Kid* (1973) does. May directed Neil Simon's script from Bruce Jay Friedman's story, and the confluence of three disparate comic sensibilities somehow works. The film is nasty, even cynical, but like *Carnal Knowledge* it's important despite this atmosphere because it attempts to deal with sexual politics. May's next film, *Mikey and Nicky* (1976), disappeared almost before it was released. Originally written for the stage by May, it tells the stories of some Cassavetes-like characters (played by Cassavetes and Peter Falk) without any of Cassavetes's flaky, self-indulgent humor. It looks like a conscientious attempt to exorcise a comic sensibility, akin in a way to Woody Allen's act of penance, *Interiors*. Why should May and Nichols both play so intently against their strengths? It's self-destructive, at the least. *

Screenwriters Robert Benton and David Newman first drew attention with *Bonnie and Clyde*, a film whose comic elements were overshadowed by its graphic violence. They worked on *What's Up, Doc?*, which seems to have been funnier as a script than it was as a film; Bogdanovich mounted it coldly and mechanically. Jay Cocks wrote that seeing the film was "like shaking hands with a joker holding a joy buzzer: the effect is both presumptuous and unpleasant." In this respect *What's Up, Doc?* is a model for most of the succeeding attempts to wring a few laughs out of ancient genres. But Newman and Benton are capable of much more, as the films they themselves have directed and their script (along with Leslie Newman) for *Superman* show.

Robert Benton was first to move into the director's chair. *Bad Company* (1972), about draft dodgers during the Civil War, created an unusually elegiac sense of period and established a valuable and intense relationship between audience and characters. David Newman's *Crazy American Girl* (1975) is an entirely different sort of film. It presents a set of hip American characters in France without the usual Benton/Newman humor and in a cinematic language that is essentially European. An interesting experiment, it was never released. Benton's *The Late Show* (1977) is a major film, if only because it gives us a commentary on the nostalgia for old genres, as its title indicates. Like *Bad Company*, it also creates an extraordinary empathy with its characters, and it exploits the talents of Lily Tomlin and Art Carney with fine style. Above all, it has a sense of the humanity of its people which is becoming increasingly rare. The film comes alive because Benton genuinely likes the people he's kidding, and he gives them enough room and time on the screen to describe themselves in attractive detail.

---

*Buck Henry is another underachiever from the fifties. He's written (*The Graduate*, *Catch-22*, and *The Day of the Dolphin*) three of Nichols's films, and Bogdanovich's *What's Up, Doc?*, which he cowrote with David Newman and Robert Benton.

We get the same pleasure in the human comedy from Howard Zieff and Jonathan Demme. After a successful career in commercials, Zieff's first feature was *Slither* (1973), a shaggy-dog road story that didn't get the attention it deserved. The script was written by W. D. Richter, who is also responsible for Bogdanovich's *Nickelodeon*, another film with a friendly sense of character. *Slither* played with the elements of a popular contemporary genre in a way that made some interesting comments on it. Dick Richards's *Rafferty and the Gold Dust Twins* (1975) dealt with similar elements. (Richards also came out of the advertising world. He and Zieff knew each other in New York in the sixties.) Zieff's second film, *Hearts of the West* (1975), from a script by Rob Thompson, dealt with the Hollywood of the early thirties. Again, a rather shaggy story (and likable for it), *Hearts of the West* succeeded where numerous other Old Hollywood films of the mid-seventies failed. Zieff's *House Calls* (1978), a calculated vehicle for Walter Matthau and Glenda Jackson, was altogether less interesting—a cloying comedy of middle age of the sort Melvin Frank specializes in.

Jonathan Demme cut his teeth on low-budget exploitation films, at least one of which—*Crazy Mama* (1975)—was of more than routine interest. Made on assignment from Roger Corman's New World Pictures (Julie Corman produced), *Crazy Mama* gives us Cloris Leachman and Ann Sothern as two-fifths of a five-generation band of female outlaws who travel down the road looking for money, fun, and adventure and in the process make some nice points about sexual politics. Women are the heroes here, and men are the querulous sidekicks; the effect of the role reversal is exhilarating. *Crazy Mama* is an offshoot of the minor "tough lady" genre Corman has been propagating for several years now. Other examples include Scorsese's *Boxcar Bertha* (1972), *Bloody Mama* (1971), which Corman directed himself, and Demme's own *Caged Heat* (1974). All of these films focus on active, aggressive outlaw women heroes, but *Crazy Mama* supersedes them by setting its women in a supportive, entirely female family context. For the first time here, Demme showed the strong sense of communality that marks his work. He hit his stride with his first A movie, *Citizen's Band* (*Handle with Care*) in 1977, from a script by Paul Brickman. Again, the human comedy controls the action. Demme gives us a chance to spend time with an unusually broad variety of contemporary American characters. Not much happens, but that's for the better. *Citizen's Band* is a film of character rather than action, and its affectionately drawn characters exist within a community that is reminiscent of Renoir's *Le Crime de M. Lange*. It's a deceptively ambitious film and a potential model for a new genre.

Renee Taylor and Joseph Bologna have been working along parallel

229

lines in their scripts for *Lovers and Other Strangers* (1970) and *Made for Each Other* (1971). Their middle-class comedies of manners are certainly far superior to more profitable essays in the style by Melvin Frank. James Frawley has directed two unusual films which share some of the same patterns of community, *Kid Blue* (1973), from a script by Edwin Shrake, a political western, and *The Big Bus* (1976), from a script by Fred Freeman and Lawrence J. Cohen, a surprisingly witty spoof of the disaster genre in which a giant bus stands in for more glamorous 747s and ocean liners.

Frawley's work is a little cooler and more analytical than the films by Benton, Zieff, Richards, Demme, Taylor, and Bologna, all of whom seem to be most interested in giving characters they like a framework in which to express themselves.

Moving further along the spectrum, we come to an area that is more explicitly satiric, and therefore more concerned with ideas, less interested in character. Ted Kotcheff spent the sixties and early seventies in England (*Life at the Top*, 1965) before returning to his native Canada for *The Apprenticeship of Duddy Kravitz* (1974) from Mordecai Richler's classic novel. Kotcheff certainly doesn't evince much sympathy or affection for his characters, but with the right actors he can achieve a certain balance. *Fun with Dick and Jane* (1977) was spotty, but it's so rare that we see any political content in a film that it deserves attention. Jerry Belson, from television, wrote the script for the film. His earlier efforts included Michael Ritchie's *Smile*. The scripts have similarities. *Smile* works significantly better because Ritchie enjoys the people he's filming; Kotcheff doesn't seem to share that affection. Kotcheff also guided *Who Is Killing The Great Chefs of Europe?* (1978, script by Peter Stone), a film that might have worked better if recipes had been included—although Robert Morley's talents nearly bring it off.

Ritchie's most ignored film has been *Prime Cut* (1972), written by Robert Dillon. It's a magnificent parody, with an unusually fresh and incisive point of view (which was perhaps one of the reasons the film was never allowed to find its audience). Dillon next wrote *99 44/100 % Dead*, a similarly wild and startling pastiche. The script was butchered mercilessly by John Frankenheimer, a director with no readily discernible sense of humor. Dillon gave up on the style. His next film (also for Frankenheimer—a gesture of contrition?) was the deadly serious *French Connection II*. Someday Dillon will find the right director, and the film that results will find its audience.

Another satirist whose quirky style has kept him from reaching a wider audience is novelist Thomas McGuane. The dialogue of his films is highly worked, allusive, and rhythmic—just the sort of qualities one might admire in a novel. As it is, people spend so much energy listening

Richard Castellano and Beatrice Arthur as the parents of the groom in *Lovers and Other Strangers*.

to McGuane's films, they don't quite watch them. Perhaps stronger directors might be able to correct the imbalance without diluting his very novelistic prose, but nevertheless, the McGuane voice is a little too precious: it calls too much attention to the teller at the expense of the tale. This may succeed in books, but it fails on the screen. *Missouri Breaks*, McGuane's original script for Arthur Penn (1976), is the least successful of his three films to date. Blame it on Brando's overacting. The film never seems to find out what it's about. *Rancho Deluxe* (1976), from a McGuane novel for Frank Perry, works much better, but audiences weren't prepared for the characteristic hip country folk of McGuane's world. *92 in the Shade*, which McGuane directed from his own novel (1976), is muddy and lackadaisical. Again the raw material is there, and it's intriguing, but McGuane is too supercilious. As director he simply compounds the problems he gives himself as screenwriter. If he cools off, and finds a strong enough director, he could produce some very effective cinematic satire.

If McGuane is a Juvenal of American movies, Terrence Malick is a Horace. On the basis of *Badlands*, which he wrote and directed in 1974, and *Days of Heaven*, which appeared four years later, Malick remains a director of potentially major talent. Like McGuane, he's fascinated by the American West. Like McGuane, he writes dialogue that approaches the condition of poetry in its intensity. But Malick is a more ambitious, less cynical writer, and his two films—especially *Days of Heaven*—stem

231

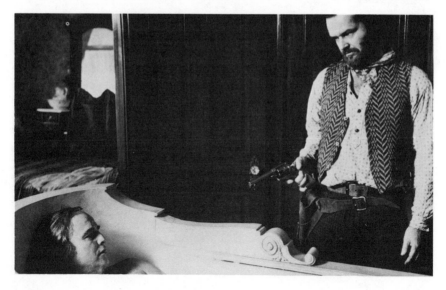

Jack Nicholson has the drop on Marlon Brando's epicene "regulator" in *Missouri Breaks.*

from a satirical vision that is more mythic than comic. By this point on the comedic continuum from slapstick shtik to high satire we have reached the point where the word "comedy" ceases to have any but theoretical significance. More on the mythopoeic films of Terrence Malick in Chapter 8.

The Sunshine Boys Make Movies:
Neil Simon, Mel Brooks, Woody Allen

A number of people made straight comedies in the seventies. Most of them, unexceptional, blow up television sitcom ideas to fill the big screen. Watching them is like looking at comic book art painstakingly projected by a football stadium flashcard section. There's little enough to them on the tube; on the big screen they evaporate. Bud Yorkin, former partner of Norman Lear, used to busy himself with this sort of material, while Lear attended to television. He directed Neil Simon's *Come Blow Your Horn* (1963) (Lear wrote the screenplay). He tried an *Inspector Clouseau* (1968), but with Alan Arkin instead of Peter Sellers. More recently, he's made *Start the Revolution Without Me* (1969), written by Lawrence J. Cohen, starring Gene Wilder, which had its moments, and *The Thief Who Came to Dinner* (1973), with Ryan O'Neal, which did not.

Carl Reiner, with long experience in television, has been more prolific, but no more successful in producing film comedies that appeal to anyone over the age of twelve. *Enter Laughing* (1967) at least had the benefit of being quasi-autobiographical. Other Reiner efforts include *Where's Poppa?* (1970), *Oh, God* (1977), and *The One and Only* (1978).

There are other occasional refugees from the verdant vineyards of the sitcom. The films almost always bomb. A good example is the witless, nasty, humorless film respected TV writers Gail Parent and Kenny Solms fashioned out of Parent's novel *Sheila Levine Is Dead and Living in New York* (1975, Sidney Furie, director). Meanwhile, the really talented television writers stick to their lasts—James Brooks and Allan Burns, for example, of the *Mary Tyler Moore* stable, or Larry Gelbart, who developed M*A*S*H for television.

Essentially, straight comedy in the '70s and '80s is ruled by the dominant troika of Neil Simon, Mel Brooks, and Woody Allen. Brooks and Allen are continually being pitted against each other in critics' Sunday thinkpieces. Simon, curiously, is usually left out of the discussion of Comedy Today, probably because he doesn't direct his own scripts and, unlike Brooks and Allen, he hasn't previously developed a comic persona as a performer. Yet, arguably his films succeed on several counts where the films of the former comics fail. Simon certainly is no Bernard Shaw, not even a Ben Hecht, but I think he's been unfairly maligned. He deals with contemporary people in contemporary situations, and he comes closer to wrestling modern anxiety to a draw than Allen does. Allen talks a lot about Angst but you never feel it. Simon's films, meanwhile, are always a bit off-putting precisely because of this core element of barely controlled hysteria. It's an unusual mix, comedy and deeply felt anxiety, and recollected in tranquillity twenty years from now, Neil Simon's plays and films will probably be more fairly judged.

The critical consensus now has it that Simon is facile, that his films follow safe paths without taking chances, that his plots are conventional, that he trades in anxiety, and that he depends far too much on one-liners. All of these criticisms are true to one extent or another. But then straight comedy is by nature formulaic, anxiety is a daring subject for a comic, and if he doesn't offer any cathartic conclusions, who among us has been able to deal with the emotion better? As for the one-liners (now you take his wife. Please!), they're a legitimate form. These aren't wholly effective excuses for Simon's failings, but they do help to mitigate the negative consensus.

Simon is, no doubt, facile. He has provided material—either stage plays or original screenplays—for at least one film per year since 1966. No other filmmaker, writer or director, comes close to that record. A number

The finga! the finga! George Burns and Walter Matthau, *The Sunshine Boys*. It's Simon's most coherent and most deeply felt film, but it is still fraught with anxiety.

of these films have been outright failures, but by my count Simon is batting over .500, a more than respectable average.

Simon's greatest problem—and he may never overcome it—is that unlike Allen or Brooks he can't or won't exert total control over his various projects. And he hasn't had good luck with directors. Teamed with hacks like Gene Saks (*Barefoot in the Park*, 1967; *Last of the Red Hot Lovers*, 1972), Jerry Paris (*The Star-Spangled Girl*, 1972), Melvin Frank (*Prisoner of Second Avenue*, 1975), or even Arthur Hiller (*The Out-of-Towners*, 1970; *Plaza Suite*, 1971), Simon doesn't have much of a chance. But Saks didn't do too much damage to Simon's most popular play, *The Odd Couple* (1968)—although some people think the television series was better—and more creative directors like Elaine May, Bob Fosse, and Herbert Ross are able to keep the Simon obsessions under better control and give his scripts some useful cinematic distance.

Fosse's film of *Sweet Charity* (1968, script by Peter Stone) remains one of the more interesting musicals of the last decade. Elaine May made *The Heartbreak Kid* her own film rather than Simon's (or Bruce Jay Friedman's). And Herbert Ross has guided two Simon scripts, one a play, the other an original, with taste and intelligence. *The Sunshine Boys* (1975) reprises Simon's most successful comic relationship from *The Odd Couple*: two friends who detest each other at the same time that they depend on each other. But now the relationship is set in a context—vaudeville—that is at the heart of Simon's world, and it gains added resonance from

234

Richard Dreyfuss and Marsha Mason find a Simonesque happiness in *The Goodbye Girl.*

this. *The Goodbye Girl* (1977) is seriously flawed. The Marsha Mason character is a throwback to pre-Monroe sexual politics. But the good nature and wit that Richard Dreyfuss and young Quinn Cummings bring to the other sides of this modern triangle go a long way to making up for the rather embarrassing Mason character. We pay so much attention to Dreyfuss and Cummings that Mason seems not to matter. For the first time in more than ten years, Simon is writing about characters this side of middle age, and that's refreshing too.*

With a good director, preferably handling an original script that avoids the stagy claustrophobia that afflicts too many of his filmed plays, Simon can produce sharp, relevant, contemporary character comedy. This happened with *California Suite* (1979, Herbert Ross). In the old Hollywood, with a studio head to answer to, he probably would have been regarded as a genius.

---

*Three times—once in the sixties, twice in the seventies—Simon has tried his hand at the prevailing comic formula, with middling success. *After the Fox* (1966), co-written with Cesare Zavattini and directed by Vittorio De Sica, attempted the madcap chase film that was popular at the time. *Murder by Death* (1976), directed by Robert Moore, was a shot at a genre spoof. It never took off. *The Cheap Detective* (1978), also directed by Moore, looked like a catalogue of the clichés of movie nostalgia—an embarrassingly unfunny movie.

Zero Mostel and a relatively calm Gene Wilder separated only by Kenneth Mars's expansive neo-Nazi gut in *The Producers*. "Springtime for Hitler and Germany!. . ."

Mel Brooks needs some discipline too. Over the past few years he has written, produced, and directed a series of genre spoofs which have earned a lot of money for the studios that financed them and distributed them. They are funny enough. There are always a couple of memorable scenes. But they're notably safe, unambitious projects. Eventually Brooks is going to run out of genres and be forced to take some interesting chances. He seems to retreat into second-rate spoofery, surrounding himself with singularly unfunny sketch actors like Harvey Korman and Dom De Luise who wouldn't have drawn more than an occasional forced chuckle in B movies of the thirties.

Each of these films manages an acceptable level of humor, and preteens think they're very funny. But one remembers the old Mel Brooks, who started out writing for Sid Caesar, one of the great comedians of the postwar period. In the sixties, when Brooks was doing talk shows, he was often advertised as the funniest man in the world. It was only a slight exaggeration. At his best, winging it with a talkshow host, Mel Brooks remains incomparable. He had developed a comic persona of unsurpassed vitality. He was always on, always able to inject the necessary dose of absurdity into a situation so that it came out funny. The main trouble with Mel's movies is that that persona isn't in them. He's gone Hollywood.

Nowhere is there a better illustration of the difference between the comic and the comedian. Brooks says things funny. When he isn't there to say them, or when he's trying to act a role he obviously doesn't fit, the joke falls flat. Brooks is urban. He's New York. To be even more specific, he's urban New York Jewish. He has vaudeville in his blood and chicken fat in his head. Mazel Tov! That's funny. What isn't funny is when Melvin Kaminsky tries to do goyische skits. Alfred Hitchcock! Now really, Mel. Come off it! You're about as effective dealing with Anglo-Saxon Catholic guilt as Hitch would be shooting *Funny Girl*.

Sheriff Cleavon Little encounters Count Basie in *Blazing Saddles*. Little and Harvey Korman meet with Governor Mel.

The best moments in Brooks's films almost all stem from his roots in Jewish humor. *The Producers* (1968), his first film, remains his most enjoyable overall because it deals with the New York entertainment world he knows and understands. Zero Mostel and Gene Wilder are perfect mirrors of the Brooks persona, and any film that can bring off a production number called "Springtime for Hitler" is a winner hands down. *The Producers* succeeds because it's properly manic and feverish, because it has faith in its own style and doesn't depend on spoofery, and because, like Gene Wilder, it's hysterical; it's hysterical and wet; it's hysterical, it's wet, and it's naked.

The Twelve Chairs (1970) attempted some historical rather than hysterical Jewish humor, and within limits it succeeds. Brooks's direction was a little ham-fisted—it got even heavier in successive films—but he had a good feeling for the Ilf and Petrov novel, and he had actors Ron Moody and Frank Langella. *The Twelve Chairs*, however, was too restrained for Brooks fans, and was a box-office failure. It set him back a couple of years.

With *Blazing Saddles* (1974), he found his niche. Andrew Bergman had written the treatment. Brooks, Bergman, Richard Pryor, Norman Steinberg, and Alan Ungar collaborated on the script. Pryor was supposed to play the lead. He might have injected the necessary evil gleam. But there was some talk of a drug problem, and Cleavon Little got the role of "Black Bart." Little was too rational and simply too attractive to energize the film. There also seem to have been major problems on the set. The original script reads much better than the finished film. A number of prize jokes have been left out, and those routines that survive move sluggishly. Yet the basic premise, the mockery of Black stereotypes, comes through, and the film made a lot of money.

Instead of developing the strength of *Blazing Saddles*—the ironic critique of stereotypes—Brooks took its superficial structure as a model for

237

his next three films. *Young Frankenstein* (1974), *Silent Movie* (1976), and *High Anxiety* (1977) are all rather thin spoofs of Hollywood genres and all essentially sophomoric, which, of course, has made them a big hit with the sophomores.

The basic technique in each, as it is with all spoofs, is to draw laughter from a recognition response. *High Anxiety,* a supposed paean to Hitchcock, is especially riddled with these cheap tricks. Brooks takes a shower. Someone enters the bathroom. The audience laughs. They aren't laughing because it's really funny. They're laughing to show each other that they catch the reference. It's the same sort of cackling one used to hear in sixties art-film houses when someone on the screen said "merde" and the subtitle translated "darn."

Yet each film has its moments. Marty Feldman injects some desirable manic intensity into *Young Frankenstein. Silent Movie,* the most varied of the three and the least pretentious, comes alive when Sid Caesar is on the screen; and Howard Morris, once a colleague of Caesar and Brooks, provides some much-needed depth of character for *High Anxiety.* Brooks is clearly hurt by the lack of comic acting talent. His two most interesting actors, Gene Wilder and Marty Feldman, have gone off on their own since *Young Frankenstein.* They now form a sort of school of Brooksian spoofery, but their own films—Wilder's *The Adventure of Sherlock Holmes' Smarter Brother* (1975) and *The World's Greatest Lover* (1977), Feldman's *The Last Remake of Beau Geste* (1977)—have precisely the same virtues, and the same flaws, as Brooks's movies.

Madeline Kahn has appeared in three of Brooks's six films and in the process developed a reputation as the reigning comic actress. (And why not? In the land of the unwitty . . .) She's done an equal number of spoofs for other directors, all of them equally semi-dull. Yet it is possible for a spoof to succeed, and to prove this we have only to look at Kahn's first film, George Coe, Sidney Davis, and Anthony Lover's brilliant *De Düve,* all of fifteen minutes long. It's a superb parody of Ingmar Bergman, touching base with every major Bergman film and capturing the cinematic essence of that style with lithe precision. Shot on location in verdant New Jersey, this pastiche of *Wild Strawberries, The Seventh Seal, Summer with Monika,* and a dozen other Bergman movies shows what Brooks, Wilder, and Feldman should be doing. It uses the humor of recognition, but it does much more. We laugh at it not only because we recognize English lurking in the fractured Swedish dialogue—such lines as "Düve-kocken. Eil veipen" and "Fallicken-symbol?" (this with the offer of a cigar) don't need subtitles—but also because it deals with human concerns as well as movie forms.

Mel Brooks is extraordinarily capable of making very funny movies

Death loses the badminton match in *De Düve.* "hoo kud saya? In de ensk, Ai meean, votska mättur? Fur de veekur en de strongur, de dumskahead en de smørtur ben al ask vun mit mir."

about people—people he knows—but he's chosen instead to concentrate on movies about movies, and not very insightful ones at that. Lover and Coe accomplish more in a cheap quarter of an hour than Brooks does in an expensive hour and a half.

Come on back to New York, Mel.

Woody Allen's never left the real city. Indeed, he has an abiding horror of the California southland, in which, as he puts it, "the only cultural advantage is that you can make a right turn on a red light." But if Brooks has gone Hollywood on us, Allen is in danger of going Stockholm. Constantly, in interviews, he bemoans the seeming unimportance of the films he's made. They're lightweight to him. He insists he wants to do Bergmanesque cinema—and he don't mean Düve parodies, either, but the real, heavy, Angst-laden thing. Until *Interiors*, we thought it was some sort of black humor. But despite that desperate mistake, Woody Allen remains clearly the most exciting comic filmmaker working in the United States. If he can't realize the value of his comedy, he'll make both Brooks's and Simon's apparently self-destructive tendencies look like Esalen ego massages.

Like Brooks and Simon, Allen started writing gags for television. Like Simon, he eventually moved to Broadway, but only for a brief time, and only after taking the plunge as a standup comedian himself. Like Brooks,

239

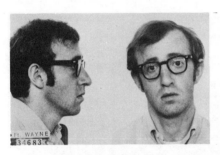 

Aside from verbal humor (which we can't illustrate) Allen's comic techniques fall into three categories:

Mugging: Convicted felon Virgil Starkwell (*Take the Money and Run*) and beauty pageant winner Miles Monroe (*Sleeper*) in representative Allen mug shots. The glasses, freckles and haircut add up to a simple caricature of the sort that could be (and is) successful in a comic strip. . . .

he made his reputation on talkshows. But whereas Simon seems never quite to get out from under his anxiety-ridden urban heritage, and Brooks battles his own guilt with savage glee, Allen has chosen to come to terms with his, to make it work for him. His sense of inferiority has become such a valuable comic took that one can almost understand his desire to make Swedishly serious films about love and death. Max von Sydow, crouching selflessly in the corner in *Shame* or *Hour of the Wolf* or *The Passion of Anna,* must be a personal hero for Stewart Allen Konigsberg, the short person from Brooklyn who conscientiously denied the regal splendor of his given last name and added a first that smacks of ventriloquists' puppets and crazed woodpeckers.

As a filmmaker, Woody Allen has had to confront many of the same problems as Mel Brooks. There has been an element of spoofery in all his films except *Annie Hall.* In general, he's been able to keep it under better control. His films are about people and ideas as well as movies. Like Brooks, too, he has had to deal with his own comedian's persona. But he started as an actor, and he has appeared in all his films so far (except *What's Up Tiger Lily?*, a success, and *Interiors,* a failure). As a result, his films are not only more cohesive than Brooks's but also—at least in my view—more authentic. One of the clearest signs of Allen's success is that he has been able to continue making movies on a regular schedule, mainly in New York, even though he has never had a blockbuster success the size of Brooks's *Blazing Saddles* or *Young Frankenstein.* Allen's films usually do very well in big cities, but that hasn't been enough to roll up huge box-office scores.

Allen wrote and appeared in Clive Donner's *What's New Pussycat?* (1965), probably the quintessential sixties comedy, full of wild action, with major stars, and generally evocative of the "swinging sixties." A

. . . **Concepts:** In prison Virgil works in the laundry. One day he finds a bra in the wash. Hmmn. . . . A simple sight gag. As a bank robber, Virgil's main failing was his penmanship. The teller can't read the note he hands him: "What's this? 'Gub?' What does that mean? 'I have a gub?'" . . .

year later, he bought rights to an unexceptional Japanese action movie, dubbed in his own English soundtrack (full of invective like "Heathen pig! Saracen dog! Spanish fly!"), and, quite surprisingly, made this hodgepodge work. It was an excellent object lesson in the power of the editor's art. In the late sixties, he played a James Bond (one of many) in *Casino Royale* and added a few bits to the chaotic script, and wrote his first Broadway play, *Don't Drink the Water* (1966). A second stage effort, *Play It Again, Sam* (1969), followed. At the same time he began to write for *The New Yorker*, producing humorous pieces in the Perelman vein.

His first directorial outing was *Take the Money and Run* (1969), in which he played the archetypal Allen bungler as crook. The film had a fresh, semidocumentary approach which set it immediately apart from the general comedic stream. Allen's films still benefit from this visual realism, much richer and more engaging than Brooks's glossy, glassy set constructions. *Take the Money and Run* worked as a showcase for the Allen comedy with which audiences had become familiar through his television appearances, but he was just beginning to discover how to translate the monologist's style into cinematic language. Again, the difference is between telling and seeing. During a prison sequence in *Take the Money*, our hero is sadistically sentenced to three days in a sweatbox, with an insurance salesman. Listening to this, you laugh; watching it, you say, "That's Funny."

Each of Allen's next three films had its experimental aspect. *Bananas* (1971, written with Mickey Rose) took the Allen schlemiel out of his native habitat, making him the unlikely hero of a South American revolution. Now the tenuous balance between visual and verbal jokes was further complicated by Woody's newly discovered interest in the art of film. He began sticking in parodic shots and scenes, such as the recrea-

241

. . . **Slapstick:** *Sleeper* is an essay in physical comedy. Miles struggles with banana and celery, the results of 21st-century fertilizers. Luna Schlosser (Diane Keaton) hitches a ride on Miles's deflated balloon suit.

tion of the famous *Potemkin* baby-carriage-on-the-steps sequence. Again, whatever laughter the scene elicits depends on recognition. Brooks moved further in this direction as his career progressed. Allen, conversely, discovered that the spoofery very often worked against the basic tone of his comedy. "Many times I've filmed terrific gags," he told an interviewer, "in a kind of arty way, but you always screw up the gag and you always cut it out of the picture."[1] As a result, he developed a strictly functional visual style, to focus attention on the gags.

Everything You Always Wanted to Know About Sex* (1972) offered some interesting structural possibilities. There was no way Allen could literally film David Reuben's successful pop psychology book. What he bought when he paid for the rights was really the title (which was what had made the book profitable anyway). Instead of attempting to construct a feature-length story on which to hang the gags, he decided to do a series of sketches instead. The advantages were obvious. Gag comedy works best in limited forms, and this structure allowed Woody to devise a number of disparate situations that wouldn't have all fit together in an extended narrative. The title was strong enough to provide shelter. If he had done any other film this way he very likely would have been criticized for stringing together a series of two-reelers and calling it a feature. But the publicity surrounding Reuben's book had been so extensive that Allen instead was praised for devising a novel way to film it.

The film is best remembered for two visual sequences, one, a giant marauding breast (which Woody finally captures in an equally capacious bra), and the last sequence, which presents us with an inside-the-body spectacle of male sexual function in the mode of a NASA moon shot. But

---

**But Were Afraid to Ask*

once again, the elaborate work that must go into constructing visualizations of these ideas detracts from their ultimate comic effect. Much more effective, I think, were the less ambitious gags: Gene Wilder as a shrink in love with a sheep, for instance, or a roomful of sex-starved cub scouts, milling, murmuring, and groaning—the door opens, we get the joke, the door closes. The first of these bits concentrates on character rather than visual fantasy, and Wilder is a master of controlled hysteria without peer. The cub-scout gag works well because it is such an efficient visual equivalent of a verbal joke.

Allen's film work is carefully thought out, and a close study of his films in sequence would make an excellent course in comic film technique. Each film has been measurably more efficient than its predecessor.

Sleeper (1973, written with Marshall Brickman) is Allen as sketch comedian in top form. By now, he had developed some elaborate ideas about what he could and couldn't do with the medium. There are still visual gags (the giant fruit, for example), but most of the comedy depends on the concept. The framework of futurism—Miles Monroe wakes up in 2173, wrapped in aluminum foil—allows him to build a rapid-fire string of comments on the world of 1973, each of which has added humor because it's phrased in the past tense.

Allen's first cut of Sleeper ran well over two hours. The release version lasts only eighty-three minutes. Most of the sequences that were cut (after viewings by test audiences) dealt with elaborate visual jokes. Two of them—Allen attempting to deal with an automatic kitchen; Allen attempting an escape from a top-floor window dangling by computer tape—were ruthlessly edited out because although they were funny enough by themselves, they interrupted the essential flow of the narrative.

Another problem—one which proves to be both universal and insoluble—is topicality. Humor depends on knowledge. The more you know, the easier it is to get the joke. The great popular comedians of film—Chaplin, Keaton, Lloyd, et al.—concentrated on the universal human condition. Everyone the world over was capable of getting the joke. But contemporary styles are far more topical. Mel Brooks might make bigger bucks with material that everyone in America can understand, but he's far funnier doing specifically ethnic, local humor.

Allen, to his credit (but not to his profit), has stuck much closer to his roots. His humor is not only more specifically intellectual, it's also geographically and sociologically precise. Miles Monroe, a health-food-store manager in Greenwich Village, gets into his Sleeper predicament when he enters St. Vincent's Hospital for minor surgery one day in 1973 and is frozen by mistake. This is mildly humorous, I suppose, to audiences in

Houston or Denver, but it has a special irony if, like me, you pass St. Vincent's every day. Once awake, Monroe discovers that the U.S. government was destroyed when a "man named Albert Shanker got hold of an H-bomb." This is not funny at all, unless you know the cranky, whining head of the New York United Federation of Teachers.

The more specific the comedy, the funnier it is, but the smaller the audiences to whom it appeals. For years, PBS avoided broadcasting the BBC's hit series *Monty Python's Flying Circus* because it was thought that American audiences wouldn't be able to fathom this sort of wonderfully precise British humor. Finally, the series was picked up by the Eastern Educational Network. (Easterners perhaps suffer from some useful Anglophilia.) But interestingly, the show had its first great success in Texas. There's an important lesson here. Specific comedy is a risk, no doubt. Every student of the art has a particular favorite comedian at whom nobody else laughs. But audiences are willing, in fact eager, to work to enjoy comedy. No other narrative form is so obviously participatory, which is why, on the one hand, we are burdened with laughtracks on sitcoms, and on the other, filmmakers must learn to leave calculated spaces for audiences to respond.

Love and Death (1975), Allen's sixth film, was a gift to himself. He was able to indulge his obsession with Great Literature and the Depressive European Sensibility. Because the film is distanced in time and place it is less directly funny than, say, *Sleeper,* but for anyone familiar with nineteenth-century Russian literature and knowledgeable about Allen's love of Bergmanesque Angst, the film works very well. Obviously, this is not the direction to take to find wide audiences, as Mel Brooks had discovered much earlier with *The Twelve Chairs.*

The most surprising fact about *Annie Hall* (1977) is that it took Woody Allen so long to make it. It is the most obvious and effective solution to all his esthetic problems; it's much closer in spirit to Allen's monologues and prose humor* than any of his previous films; and it marks a quantum jump for him as a filmmaker. Comedy as style is rightly superseding comedy as genre, and Allen's performance shtik—the persona he built on television and in night clubs—is neatly integrated into a classically structured, yet refreshingly contemporary narrative.

Annie Hall is autobiographical, but it's not so much about Woody and Diane Keaton as it is about Allen's confrontation with the goyische universe. As Annie (Diane Keaton, née Diane Hall) blurts out when

---

*Two volumes have been published: *Getting Even* (1971) and *Without Feathers* (1975).

244

they first meet: "You're what Grammy Hall would call a real Jew!" It's the premise of the film to follow.

A real Jew, as Allen and Marshall Brickman see him, is triangulated by the moral parable Allen/Alvy Singer, recounts in his opening monologue:

> Two women at a Catskill resort.
> First woman: "The food is terrible."
> Second woman: "Yes, and such small portions!"

There's no way to win. Gradually, the Jewish-gentile dichotomy becomes transmuted into the opposition between New York and Hollywood, which is the subject of many of the telling jokes in the film. Alvy Singer, quintessential New Yorker, has his roots in a culture in which the stuffy, constipated intellectual journals *Commentary* and *Dissent* have merged to become *Dissentary*, where Marshall McLuhan lurks behind movie-ad placards. Opposed to this is the city of angels, where "they don't throw their garbage away, they make it into television shows" and wheeler-dealers "take meetings." Woody/Alvy has his revenge by sneezing on the coke. But Alvy/Woody, when he later writes a play about his romance with Annie/Diane, decides it's the better part of valor to give it a happy ending, contrary to fact. California is fiction. New York is reality. You begin to see the sanity in Allen's obsession with European film. Life is real, life is earnest; it isn't always all that funny.

But that's precisely why we need comedy, even from a schlump like Woody, who doesn't own a car, or a mantra. Somebody has to be in charge of keeping things in perspective, and Woody Allen does the job exceedingly well.

And *this* is why Allen's long-threatened "serious" film, *Interiors* (1978), is so heartbreakingly disappointing. Coming from another filmmaker, *Interiors* might just have some mild excuses to make for itself. But coming from Woody Allen it looks like a violent act of self-mutilation, and those of us who greatly value his other films, books, plays, articles, and performances react instinctively against the rigid—nearly catatonic—strained seriousness of *Interiors* as if to a personal betrayal. We have depended on Allen for more than 15 years now as a champion against just this particular sort of bad-faith artiness and the midcult bourgeois sensibility from which it stems. Now, it seems, not only has Woody gone over to the enemy, but he's apparently been secretly enamored of the opposite camp during the very time we trusted him. (Writing in *Variety*, "Hege." noted, "Watching this picture, a question keeps recurring: what would Woody Allen think of all this? Then you remember he wrote and directed it.")

Clearly, from statements he has made in the past, Allen wanted an

Alvy Singer, Rob (Tony Roberts), and Annie (Diane Keaton), the semiautobiographical characters of *Annie Hall* caught on the wrong side of the playground fence.

opportunity to show he could be "serious" (just like the big fellas?). The question, as we noted earlier, lies in a definition of the word "serious." In once sense, it means "having import, earnest, sincere—dealing with important rather than trivial matters." To my mind, this is just what Allen's comedies—especially *Annie Hall*—have done. In the best sense of the word, he's been "serious" all along, like all great comedians.

But there seems to be a Pagliacci syndrome here. Woody has apparently seized on the secondary meaning of the word: "grave, sober." And the result is a film which fits the third definition of "serious": "causing anxiety, critical, dangerous," as for example in the sentence "He's in serious condition." Perhaps this linguistic string accounts for our own reaction against the film. The comic vision is too rare and vital to be so cavalierly dismissed, and if this is the sort of film a Woody Allen wants to make, we may all be in "serious" condition.

Even if it had been made by someone else—if it were, for example, Ingmar Bergman's first American film (and it is in a way), *Interiors* would be cause for concern. Allen's study in "beiges and earth tones" is the ultimate midcult American movie of the 1970s; it shares all of the failings of that bourgeois sensibility. For these reasons it has considerable historical significance. Fifteen years ago, when the reigning American cultural set was Philistine, *Interiors* wouldn't have been given a second thought by most critics, who would have dismissed it out of hand as some "egghead" nonsense. Now that the dominant cultural sensibility has reached the level of midcult—now that we all know about gourmet cuisine, study "films" rather than "movies" in college, and go to Europe regularly—now *Interiors* is not only acceptable, seeing it is a sign of our own seriousness (and therefore, our class). Gene Shalit, arbiter of movie taste for the powerful *Today* show, tearily proclaimed the film "A Masterpiece . . . a Work of Art."

On a technical level, *Interiors* is clearly well made, and this is a primary criterion of midcult criticism. More important, it is full of allusions and symbolism of the sort dear to every English teacher's heart. All the colors are muted browns, tans, and grays, see, except this one lady, Pearl, the life force in the film. She wears red. Get it? And her name, too, see, that's symbolic: she gleams, like, among the rest of these tortured people. And there are three sisters. . . . There was this play this Russian writer wrote about these people who could never get to Moscow, and *that* was called *Three Sisters*. And at the end there, where the three sisters, so nicely composed, are staring out the window at the sea (please be ready to talk about Sea Symbolism on Tuesday's exam), and one of them says, "The water's so calm," and the other replies, "Yes, it's very peaceful," and that's the last line of the play—I mean film . . . well, that's an allusion to . . . well, I know it's an allusion to something. I'll think of it. Just a moment.

In the age of midcult, this is what we are taught is art, and no doubt *Interiors* will get steady play on the high-school and college circuit.

As a drama the film fares no better than it does as an exercise in symbolism. Allen's waspy characters talk in overwritten paragraphs, with quotations, indented and single-spaced. The point isn't that this stagy dialogue isn't realistic. The point is that it's hard to take these people, you should forgive the expression, seriously. A long monologue by Renata (Diane Keaton) ends with this piece of arch philosophy:

> I can't seem to shake the real implication of dying. It's terrifying. The intimacy of it embarrasses me.

Fred (Richard Jordan) tells Flyn (Kristin Griffith):

> It's been such a long time since I made love to a woman I didn't feel inferior to.

This, just before he rapes her. Now *that's* funny.* Or it would be. In

---

*The tenuous possibility exists that *Interiors* was meant as a grand burlesque, a parody of cosmic proportions. Even if Allen didn't mean it as such, this remains by far the best way for audiences to view it. In twenty years, *Interiors* will certainly be regarded as ultra-camp.

another movie. One of the great successes of *Interiors* is that the actors, more often than not, actually bring these lines off without inciting fits of laughter in the audience.

No doubt such people as the writers Allen concerns himself with in *Interiors* do exist. All sorts of people exist. The question is, why choose to build a movie around such characters? There is an ethical problem here, too. Except for Pearl (Maureen Stapleton), Allen is merciless with his characters. He has designed them as perfect, finished neurotics. He gives them no room to act, to breathe. They can only think, and in thinking suffer. There is no sense of politics here; in fact, politics as a possibility of action is expressly denied: we hear that Fred is a filmmaker working on a film about politics, but the subject intentionally never comes into play.

Yes, *Interiors* is very much like a Bergman film, but in this case, imitation isn't the sincerest form of flattery. Allen's movie is so close to Bergman that it's eerie. *De Düve*'s affectionate parody made us feel closer to Bergman; Allen's deathly clone has the net effect of making it difficult even to treat Bergman with respect again: we'll always hear the ghosts of *Interiors* murmuring just off-screen.

The working title for *Annie Hall* was "anhedonia." A sad pun, the word means "absence of the feeling of pleasure in situations where it is normally present," which is a much better description of *Interiors* than of its sister film. Allen has spent more than twenty years in analysis trying to cope with this and other problems. It's to be hoped *Interiors* marks the end of that stage of his life and work.

Maybe it's not Woody who's anhedonic. Maybe it's the situation. This is why, all things being equal, the comic vision is more intelligent and wiser than the tragic, and in the end more useful and powerful. This is why it's important to be funny.

At the end of *Annie Hall,* Woody/Alvy comes on again to finish the monologue:

"Doc, my brother is crazy. He thinks he's a chicken."
The doc says, "Why don't you turn him in?"
"I would, but I need the eggs."
Life is crazy, irrational, and absurd.
But we keep going through it because
I guess most of us
need the eggs.

8

Myth, Reality, and Other Ways of Meaning

Arthur Penn's 1969 film *Alice's Restaurant* ends with a very unusual shot. The dream is over. Alice and Ray Brock's communal "church" of hippies, runaways, dropouts, and troubadours is splitting apart. The center cannot hold. Ray thinks the problem is location; like thousands of others of the sixties generation at the time, he wants to buy a farm. "If we'da just had a real place," he muses, "we'da all still been together . . . without buggin' each other . . . we'd all be some kind of family." Without saying anything, Alice knows better. Ray leaves, and Alice is left standing, pensive, at the doorway of their church in her wedding dress. She does not move. The camera begins to move back slowly, in an irregular, curving line, through the trees. The portrait of Alice is interrupted as tree trunks in the foreground pass between her and the camera. At the same time that the camera is tracking backward and a little sideways, cameraman Victor Kemper begins to zoom in on Alice. The size of the image of Alice therefore doesn't change. We don't move away from her geographically, or so it seems. But our perception of depth in the image frame changes. We are moving from an encompassing, deep-focus wide-angle shot of Alice, the church door, and the landscape to a flat, layered, shallow-focus long shot in which the image of Alice and the image of the out-of-focus trees exist in separate, distinct planes. Alice Brock has been extricated from the context of reality. She has become an icon, a symbol. She doesn't talk, she doesn't move; the camera stops moving eventually,

Alice (Pat Quinn) in wedding costume and Ray (James Broderick) out of focus in the Church.

holding this image of a woman left at the church doorstep at the end of a marriage at the end of an era. The last, stationary part of the shot might as well be a still, a freeze frame, but it's not. It's alive.

The shot, which lasts more than half a minute, is a brilliant example of how the language of pure film can create real meaning—in a way that words cannot—but it's something more as well. It's also an excellent model of the central cinematic relationship between myth and reality. The style of the film until this point has been basically realistic. Arlo Guthrie plays Arlo Guthrie, and Alice Brock has a minor role ("Alice" is played by Pat Quinn, and "Ray" by James Broderick). The screenplay, based on Arlo's talking blues "The Alice's Restaurant Massacree," is semifictional but has a number of documentary elements, and the film was shot for the most part where the original story, upon which Arlo fashioned his song, took place.

But Penn is not a filmmaker who is interested in simply capturing reality. He wants to make myths, he wants stories with solid meaning. Arlo's song was therefore a natural subject for him. It had quickly become the anthem of a generation. (Even now, it's played every Thanksgiving on one of the leading New York FM rock stations. Listening to it each year has become something of a religious celebration for refugees from the sixties.) At the end of the film, Penn has to forge a union of these two fundamental aspects, the realistic and the mythic. The long shot of Alice gradually lifts her out of the story and makes it clear cinematically

250

that, as cowriter Venable Herndon put it in his foreword to the published edition of the script: "Alice was the personification of the *anima* figure Jung speaks of, the clan matriarch, the sacred mother of the subconscious, the Yin force."[1] Herndon opposes his Alice figure to the "weight of so many Western centuries of patriarchally imposed guilt."

That's a bit heavy, perhaps, but certainly Alice, Ray, and Arlo do carry with them a weight of meaning beyond their own personalities. Alice Brock joins other archetypal Alices of the sixties and seventies—the Alice of the Jefferson Airplane's "White Rabbit," the Alice of *Alice Doesn't Live Here Anymore*—in the modern mythic pantheon. Arlo's story can now be seen as the second half of a multi-generational saga. His father Woody was apotheosized—and rightly so—a few years later with Hal Ashby's admiring *Bound for Glory*. There's no doubt that no matter how real they are (Arlo still sings, Alice has moved to Provincetown), the characters of the film are. mythic material.

Colloquially, we tend to oppose myth and reality. The phrase "that's a myth" suggests a statement is untrue, unreal. But in fact, myth and reality are closely interconnected. Real myths, those artistic evidences of our collective consciousness, spring directly from roots in reality, they heighten reality and condense it. In C. M. Bowra's phrase, "Myths bring the unknown into relation with the known." Myths carry meaning.

Clearly, the great American film tradition is comic. As a nation, we prize the elements of satire, irony, parody, and burlesque that go to make up comedy and work to analyze the phenomena that are its subjects. We also like a good joke. The textbooks usually oppose tragedy to comedy, but there is no real tragic form anymore, at least not in the classical sense of the term. Colloquially, a "tragedy" now is wholly arbitrary and accidental:

37 DIE IN TRAGIC BUS PLUNGE

the headline reads. This has nothing to do with admirable heroes falling from high estate to low through the workings of fate, the furies, or tragic flaws in personalities. So something called "drama" has replaced tragedy in the narrative arts. A "drama" is simply a work that isn't very funny, or ironic, or satiric. It's a comedy with the jokes left out. Very often—not always, but often—it's also rather ludicrous. The American liberal tradition of the "Serious Film" seems to be defined by subject matter that is intentionally maudlin. The films that fit this tradition are about cripples and outcasts, blind people and "Negroes," paraplegics and psychotics. Ironically, they try to elicit the same emotions—pity and fear—that Aristotle suggested were the roots of tragedy. But the Greek philosopher meant something quite different. The kind of pity we feel for the protagonists of American serious movies like *The Men; One Potato, Two*

Luke (Jon Voight) and Sally (Jane Fonda) after making love in *Coming Home*. The filmmakers may not have consciously intended it, but much of the attention that was paid to the film was the result of the love scenes and the other allusions to the paraplegic way of life.

Potato; or even *Coming Home* is the mawkish sort. We feel sorry for them, we don't experience cathartic empathy for them. And the fear we are subject to is not religious awe, but rather hypochondriacal anxiety or, in the case of psychotic protagonists like Travis Bickle in *Taxi Driver* or Jimmy Angelelli in James Toback's execrable *Fingers*, pure urban paranoia. In neither case do these emotions result in purgation.

But, thankfully, cripple and crazy movies aren't the only noncomedic films. Straight realism, more or less documentary, is also a strong American tradition and has been since the silent days, even if the history books tend to downplay its role in American cinema. A simple record of events and people has real value; it happens to be something film does exceptionally well. Moreover, as we've already suggested, realism sometimes reaches an artistic critical mass, at which point the record becomes transformed into myth.

All the great noncomic films, from *Scarface* and the Warner Brothers' gangster movies of the thirties, through such films noirs as Raoul Walsh's *White Heat* and Nicholas Ray's *Rebel Without a Cause* up to *2001: A Space Odyssey*, *The Godfather*, and even perhaps *Taxi Driver*, have pronounced mythic resonances. If they didn't start out with a consciousness of their mythic possibilities, they soon developed a sense of this important dimension.

Myth, then, is the opposite face of comedy. As comedy analyzes, myth synthesizes. Comedy is intelligent, myth is emotional. Both give us a needed intellectual distance from subject matter and theme, both help us to comprehend reality, but comedy separates us from reality, while myth brings us into communion with it—it "brings the unknown into relation with the known." Tragedy may be dead—may it rest in peace—but myth continues to offer psychological catharsis, by bringing us together in the celebration of reality and its lineaments.

Realism and Documentary

The raw material for this useful work of myth-building lies in reality. People only respond to the mythic nature of a story when they recognize the inherent truth of it. So realism as a film style is mythogenic—it generates myth. Again, this seems a contradiction of received opinion. Aren't myths "unreal"? Aren't they the work of the great expressionist individualist artists? Not really. Occasionally, the artist becomes the source of mythic power, but only when he is actually speaking for an entire society. The more direct path to myth is through the collective consciousness and a film is more likely to travel this path when the attention is focused sharply on the people and events in front of the camera, not the romantic "artiste" in back of it.

As a medium, film is supremely well equipped to record reality. Anthropologists have recognized its usefulness in this respect. An ethnographic description in prose is perforce filtered through the sensibility of the observer/writer, but a film record of, say, a fertility ceremony captures nuances of which the observer is very likely unaware. Those unseen elements exist on film; eventually observers of the *film* can gain the needed sophistication to see them.

Avant-garde film has put great store in this particular strength of the medium recently. In the mid-sixties, Andy Warhol learned to point the camera at a sleeping person or an office building, turn it on, and let it do its thing. The results were films like *Sleep* and *Empire*, many hours long, in which "nothing takes place but the place": a man sleeps, occasionally tossing and turning (of course!); the Empire State Building stands there. The angle doesn't change; the filmmaker doesn't intrude himself; film makes its closest approach to the asymptote of reality. Recently, Michael Snow, the Canadian experimental filmmaker, has extended this early Warholian esthetic to force emphasis on the relationship between reality and the camera (not the cameraman). Films like *Wavelength*, which consists of a forty-five-minute very slow zoom in across an empty loft, and *La Région Centrale*—a three-hour dithyrambic celebration of a northern

Quebec wasteland in which the camera revolves, pans, tilts, and swirls, but no human is seen—celebrate the material nature of reality. They are experimental only in the sense that they have been devised in order to see what their effect will be.

The aim of such structurally realist films is to make us see, if not necessarily to make us want to see. In a way, film validates reality, so that a filmed record of even the simplest and most commonplace of events invests them with greater significance than they would have on their own.

As a realist tool, film is most useful in making records, portraits, and analyses. We usually call this sort of film "documentary." For years, documentary film was severely limited by the unwieldy nature of the equipment. But in the late fifties and early sixties, important technical advances resulted in cameras and recorders that could go anywhere, and that produced sophisticated, flexible footage. The first filmmakers to take advantage of this new technological agility were those associated with Robert Drew. Richard Leacock, Donn Pennebaker, and the Maysles brothers, Al and David, became known as proponents of "Direct Cinema." This new style of documentary eschewed narration, ostensibly allowing its subjects to speak for themselves. But of course, all the while the filmmakers were making significant choices of what to film and what not to film, and they edited the footage, too. The result was vaguely misleading. The lack of a narrator brought viewer and subject closer together, but it also suggested that it was the subject who was in control of the film, which is clearly not the case.

Leacock has gone into teaching, Pennebaker has made a few music films in the seventies, but only the Maysles have really survived as creative forces with such films as *Gimme Shelter* (1971), *Grey Gardens* (1975) and *Running Fence* (1978). *Grey Gardens*, a portrait of two Long Island eccentrics, Edie Beale and her aged mother, points up some of the ethical problems involved in the Direct Cinema style. The Maysles crew spent a number of months with the Beale women and obviously a strong relationship developed between the filmmakers and the subjects of the film, yet the Maysles—still tied to the objective criterion of Direct Cinema—pay scant attention to this affective relationship. They don't show themselves actively participating in the film even though it's clear the Beales are playing to the camera and the Maysles behind it. This leaves viewers with a sense that the filmmakers have been condescending in their relationship with their subjects. *Grey Gardens* is a conversation, but we hear only one half of it.

The same is true for all examples of Direct Cinema, to a greater or

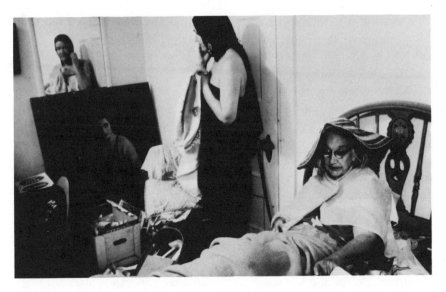

Little Edie and her mother Big Edie Bouvier Beale in *Grey Gardens*. They were not alone.

lesser extent, and the style has been enormously influential. Most standard television documentaries, for instance, follow the pattern.

Very few filmmakers have been able to use the style successfully. One is Frederick Wiseman, whose series of essays on various institutions for PBS (among them *Hospital*, 1970; *Primate*, 1974; *Welfare*, 1975; and *Meat*, 1976) have been among the most interesting accomplishments in documentary film in the seventies. Wiseman gets around the basic ethical problem in two ways: first, he shoots such an enormous amount of footage, literally living with the subjects of his films with the camera and sound recorder hardly ever turned off, that his subjects do come close to forgetting the presence of the machines and the people who operate them. More important, Wiseman manages to convey such a strong sense of his own feelings and prejudices through his editing that any viewer with the least sophistication "hears" his voice despite the lack of narration.

In a way, the rise of Direct Cinema in the sixties was anachronistic. At the same time that film journalists were striving for a new, supposedly selfless, objectivity, their brothers and sisters in print were developing the "New Journalism," which had as its premise the more sophisticated idea that there was really no such thing as pure objectivity and that therefore the most truthful journalism was the personal, participatory kind that clearly admitted the author's biases and his function within the story.

255

Gradually, film journalists and documentarians have come around to this point of view in the seventies, although the change hasn't been widely noted.

Emile De Antonio has always been a film essayist, making quite clear his own position on the subject, ever since his first film, *Point of Order* (1963), a condensation of kinescopes of the Army-McCarthy hearings of 1954. *Millhouse* (1971) did for Richard M. Nixon what the earlier film had done for Senator Joe, and earned De Antonio a highly prized position on the White House "enemies" list. *Painters Painting* (1972), the only film De Antonio has made about a nonpolitical subject, was an absorbing collection of interviews with American artists. *Underground* (1975, with Haskell Wexler and Mary Lampson) remains his most controversial film. An edited interview with members of the Weather Underground Organization, it presented added ethical problems in that one of the conditions for making the film was not to show the faces of Bernadine Dohrn and her associates, who were (and are), after all, fugitives. We see a lot of Haskell Wexler in a mirror, shouldering his camera, and shadows of the subjects, but Wexler, De Antonio, and Lampson all seem paralyzed. It's a Weather show, not a De Antonio essay.

Haskell Wexler, the premiere Hollywood cinematographer of the past ten years, has spent much of his time working in documentary film. His first nonfiction project was *The Bus* (1965), an effective document of the 1963 March on Washington. He is also responsible for *Nowsreel* (1969), *Brazil: A Report on Torture* and *Conversation With President Allende* (both 1971, both with Saul Landau), *Interviews with My Lai Veterans* (1971, with Joseph Strick), and *Introduction to the Enemy* (1974, with Jane Fonda and Tom Hayden) as well as *Underground*. All of these films are interesting in one way or another. The Brazil and Allende documents are especially meaningful historical and polemical records.

Wexler's greatest contribution so far, however, is most definitely *Medium Cool* (1969), a semifictional feature and a movie I have written about so many times in so many different contexts that I feel now somehow related to it. It has a lively underground reputation, but it was not widely seen on its release and hasn't received an unusual amount of play since. Yet it is clearly one of the most important American films of the 1960s, as much for *how* as for *what* it says.

Shot on location at the disastrous Democratic convention in 1968, *Medium Cool* gives us a relatively thin story involving a television news cinematographer (Robert Forster), his soundman (Peter Bonerz), a woman Forster meets who's moved to Chicago from Appalachia (Verna Bloom), and her son (Harold Blankenship). Forster is almost absurdly disconnected from the violence he films every day. About his only commentary on his work is an occasional expletive: "Jesus! I love to shoot film." He's naturally just as affectless in his private life. But as the highly charged political summer of 1968 proceeds, he gradually but irrevocably becomes politicized. This in turn opens him up to new emotions in his private life as well.

Forster's radicalization begins when he shoots a human-interest story about a Black cab driver who finds a large amount of money in his cab and turns it in. The filmmaker visits the cab driver a few days later only to discover that the television news story has proved nothing but headaches for him. The power of the medium to validate reality is extreme. "You put him on the six, the ten, *and* the twelve o'clock news," a Black militant challenges Forster, "then he be real." Forster's transformation is sealed when he finds out the FBI has been given free access to his station's newsfilm. He explodes, and quits.

Meanwhile, he has become involved with widow Verna Bloom through her son, Harold. The relationship is low-key, and all the more effective for it. Forster doesn't really do anything during the course of the movie. This isn't a film about action, but about passivity. But he does come alive, and he develops a commitment to the people around him; they're no longer simply subjects for his camera.

The film ends with a significant twist. After searching for and finding Verna and Harold in the midst of the debacle of the police riots surrounding the convention (remember? "The whole world is watching!"), Forster is driving slowly with them through a leafy park. His car, of a sudden, crashes and explodes. Some people stop to take a snapshot. Then the camera through which we, voyeurs as well, are viewing this scene pans slowly to the right to discover Haskell Wexler with *his* camera shooting the "tragedy." Haskell pans to his left, until his camera is looking directly at us.

It's a mutual accusation: *we all* are responsible for a society in which, when there's even a minor episode of violence, everybody turns to look for the camera. The film describes the dilemma, it doesn't offer a solution. But it gives new, ironic significance to the chant that symbolizes the violence surrounding the convention that, in effect, elected Nixon. The whole world is watching, indeed! And not doing very much about what it sees.

Wexler achieves this sharply ironic parable by weaving his scripted action seamlessly into the fabric of reality. More than a third of the film is straight documentary, although actors may appear in the foreground. In its image of the passive insurrection and active suppression that was Chicago '68, *Medium Cool* is an invaluable record. But it's only that. We weren't there. We didn't *do* anything. We are only watching. At one

Saul Landau's most recent film is *CIA: Case Officer* (1978), a portrait of ex-agent John Stockwell (second from left), seen here with the CIA-supported FLNA in Angola.

point, during a particularly gripping sequence, one of the crew shouts out on the soundtrack, "Watch out, Haskell! It's real!" But it isn't really. Not now. Now it's film. That's Haskell's dilemma, and ours.

As a genre, the political documentary attracted an understandably large number of independent filmmakers during the late sixties and early seventies. Saul Landau, in addition to the films he made with Haskell Wexler (cited above), was responsible for *Fidel* (1969) and *Robert Wall: Ex FBI Agent* (1973), among others. Cinda Firestone's *Attica*(1974) became one of the more widely circulated political documents of the seventies. The Newsreel collective did some interesting work in the late sixties, as did a large number of other groups of cooperative filmmakers working at the grass-roots level. (See *Street Scenes*, p. 153.) As the question of the relationship between filmmaker and subject grew in importance, several movements developed to put the subject, as it were, in the director's chair. The development of portable video equipment around 1970 was especially influential in this respect. In fact, as a field now, documentary must be broadened to include both video and film. Michael Shamberg and TVTV (Top Value TeleVision) were among the most prominent of video documentarists in the early seventies. The group finally broke up in 1977 due to an argument that stemmed from their first venture into network television, a quasifictional show done as a pilot for NBC that year. *The TVTV Show* developed such interesting satiric possibilities as the relationships between a television news team who set up accidents in order to film them; a typical video-addicted family who are happy to be held hostage as long as they can watch the show on TV; and a group of people who hang out in a bar devoted to TV singing old theme songs.

Vietnam had less influence than one might expect on documentary film in the late sixties and early seventies. Europeans dealt with the war more often than Americans, perhaps because U.S. television was flooded daily with images of the battlefield and the home front. Only Peter Davis's two films—*The Selling of the Pentagon* (1971), broadcast by CBS, and *Hearts and Minds* (1974)—had any real impact on thinking about the war, and the release of the latter film was so long delayed as to seriously lessen its influence. Yet it remains one of the most powerful nonfiction films ever made. *Hearts and Minds* is at once so deeply felt and so insistently rational that it almost transcends its subject, becoming a portrait of the national consciousness that will bear repeated viewings for years to come. It attempts to describe how we thought and how we felt about the war in Vietnam, and it comes surprisingly close to explaining how that crime came to be.

Certainly Davis, like Wexler and De Antonio, doesn't pretend to the specious objectivity of Direct Cinema. Most of the nonfiction filmmakers

Hearts and Minds remains an important film because of the attention it devoted to the emotion as well as the logic of the antiwar movement. Daniel Ellsberg's own ambiguous situation and the feelings it engendered in him serve as the centerpiece of the film.

who came to prominence in the seventies were devoted to a cinema that is more personal and passionate than seemingly objective. Coincidentally, the women's movement had a profound effect on nonfiction film in the seventies, too, perhaps because, ironically, women filmmakers were effectively excluded from participating in feature-film production for the most part.

In a documentary film festival in 1977, women won twenty-six out of thirty awards. It was a fair measure of their growing power in the nonfiction area in the mid-seventies. In this new wave of documentary talent are included Nell Cox (*A to B*, 1970), Amalie Rothschild (*Woo Who? May Wilson*, 1969; *Nana, Mom, and Me*, 1974), Julia Reichert (*Growing Up Female*, 1970), and Claudia Weill (*Joyce at 34*, 1973; *The Other Half of the Sky*, 1975, with Shirley MacLaine). Martha Coolidge (*David Off and On*, 1973; *An Old-Fashioned Woman*, 1974) began to move into features with *Not a Pretty Picture* (1976), a fictional film shot with documentary techniques that dealt with the kind of autobiographical subject favored by many of these filmmakers.

Claudia Weill was the first of the women documentarists to achieve commercial success with a fiction film. *Girl Friends* (1978) showed how inexpensive documentary techniques could combine with the realism inherent in nonfiction film to create an affecting portrait of a representative relationship.

Barbara Kopple's *Harlan County, U.S.A.* (1976) is probably the best-known example of the new, more personal style of nonfiction cinema.

Documentary approches: Like most women nonfiction filmmakers of the early seventies Martha Coolidge (here being comforted on the set of *Not a Pretty Picture* by alter ego Michele Manenti) chose an autobiographic approach, which eventually took on semifictional characteristics. The late seventies, in contrast, have been marked by a new interest in classic historical documentary. A striking example of this approach is *With Babies and Banners* (1978), directed by Lorraine Gray and produced by Anne Bohlen, Lyn Goldfarb, and Gray. Months of research unearthed remarkable historical footage of the Women's Emergency Brigade during the General Motors sitdown strike of 1937. This archival material was then counterpointed with sequences showing the women as they are today, forty years on.

Kopple lived and worked with coalminers and their families for more than a year while slowly putting together her very moving portrait of the people of Harlan County, Kentucky, memorialized in the thirties as "Bloody Harlan" and still a focal point of vital union struggle in the coal industry. The film worked for the miners as an analytical portrait of their own situation; it worked for general audiences by introducing them to the complex politics of the industry—and the people of Harlan County; and it also worked as a deeply human essay. Kopple's real-life people come through with unusual force and clarity, probably because they were so intimately involved in the making of the film. In a real sense, it's their film, not Kopple's, seen from their point of view, and this gives it a vitality and relevance it otherwise never could have achieved.

Harlan County, U.S.A., which situates a subjective truth in an historical context, shows just how far we've come from the tenets of Direct Cinema that were so influential in the early sixties. Direct Cinema worked best as a technique of portraiture. When it wasn't trying to objectify complex intellectual arguments but simply attempting to capture a personality on film it usually succeeded.* In this respect, the tradition still bears fruit. Jerry Bruck, Jr.'s, *I. F. Stone's Weekly* (1973) proved to be a reasonable and empathetic portrait of the highly respected journalist. William Miles's *Men of Bronze* (1977) is an invaluable and revealing essay on the struggle of the Black 15th Army Brigade in World War I, which is made especially effective through interviews with survivors.

But far more productive has been the development of the essay form in documentary. Like the prose essay, the film essay depends for its basic impact on our sense of the personality of its author. Marcel Ophuls, essentially an American filmmaker although he works in several languages with equal ease, has led the way here. His *The Sorrow and the Pity* (1969) must be regarded as the most influential nonfiction film of the last decade. *A Sense of Loss* (1973), about Northern Ireland, and *The Memory of Justice* (1976), concerning guilt and the holocaust, are equally complicated, subtle, thoughtful, and idiosyncratic investigations into human political situations. What makes these films come alive is our sense of Ophuls's own intelligence—questioning, condemning, and equivocat-

---

*It also worked well when it was used simply to record an event. Rock music and Direct Cinema forged a symbiotic relationship early on. D. A. Pennebaker's *Don't Look Back* (1966), *Monterey Pop* (1968), Michael Wadleigh's *Woodstock* (1970), and the Maysleses' *Gimme Shelter* (1971) all enjoyed uniquely profitable theatrical runs, but the focus here is on the music, the event, not the filmmaking. The most recent example of this has been Scorsese's *The Last Waltz* (1978).

ing, as he struggles with these knotty ethical dilemmas. Ophuls is far from being a polemical filmmaker. His essays aren't calls to action, and occasionally they suffer from an excess intellectual complexity. But Ophuls is always aware of the people behind the ideas, and he has proved once for all that film is measurably more effective in capturing this dimension of history than prose is. Second only to Jean-Luc Godard, Ophuls has shown that film is a valid medium of intellectual discourse.

He's not alone. Susan Sontag's *Promised Lands* (1973), for example, was a similarly complex, dense, informative record of the ambivalencies inherent in the intellectual structure of contemporary Israel. John Schott and E. J. Vaughn's *Deal* (1978), about the television show *Let's Make a Deal* and its impact, shows how Direct Cinema techniques can be used to build a convincing analysis. On the whole, however, the filmed essay of ideas has taken deeper root in Europe than in the United States. Orson Welles's *F for Fake* (1976) showed how the technique could be applied to lighter material.

American essays generally have been more interested in domestic sociology. PBS's *An American Family* (1973), produced by Craig Gilbert, shot by Alan and Susan Raymond, was a twelve-episode series which gained wide publicity. It's the best evidence yet of the ethical difficulties involved in nonfiction filming. The life of the Loud family was significantly altered by the shooting and by the release of the film, yet the filmmakers neither acknowledged nor analyzed this corollary of the Heisenberg Uncertainty Principle (that the observer must perforce alter that which he observes) as it applies to sociological filmmaking.

Six American Families, produced by Westinghouse television in 1976, written by Paul Wilkes, and shot by Wilkes, Mark Obenhaus, Bill Jersey, and Arthur Barron, was a much more sophisticated approach to similar subject matter, although it never received the attention lavished on its singular predecessor. Wilkes and the filmmakers worked with six different families in various parts of the country; Wilkes appears on camera; the relationship between the filmmakers and the subjects is not only admitted but becomes part of the subject matter; and, most important, the structure of each of the programs gives the families a chance to comment on the film as edited and shown. Not only do we get a better sense of the overall structure of each family (in much shorter time), we also begin to learn something about the process of turning people into characters.

Along with the work of Ophuls, Davis, and Sontag, *Six American Families* shows the enormous untapped potential in the filmed essay of ideas. It is likely to become one of the more important cinematic approaches of the 1980s.

The Mythos and the Ethos

Nonfiction films very seldom have mythic dimensions, although the best of them—films like *Harlan County, U.S.A.* or *The Sorrow and the Pity*—are certainly mythogenic. One of the prime functions of nonfiction, after all, is to demystify real people and events, and that aim goes directly contrary to the mythopoeic impulse. Conversely, fiction always more or less aims at the creation of myth. The mythos of a people is best transmitted through its art, after all.

The relationship between fiction and myth is so intimate in fact that most films that are generally considered important, from *Citizen Kane* to *2001: A Space Odyssey*, from *Gone with the Wind* to *The Godfather*, are obviously and strongly mythopoeic. The relationship between mythic content and the value of a film is almost tautological. Almost any movie worth discussing at length conveys the mythos. It's the driving force of film, and most other arts.

Yet the mythic content of a film can be the result of very different processes. On the one hand, the filmmakers start out with the idea of creating or transmitting myth; they work inductively to impose it on the material of the movie. The mythic element is supposed to be strong enough to carry the other elements of the film—character and plot, most obviously. The danger of course is that the film will turn out to be pretentious, specious, or pompous, as it so often does (although this isn't necessarily going to hurt it at the box office).

On the other hand, myth grows naturally out of close observation: if you've an interesting story to tell, with interesting people, and absorbing thematic material, myth will take care of itself. This is the deductive method of filmmaking. The problem is obvious: there's no way a filmmaker can plan such myths. They develop themselves. There's no guarantee. Yet the worst that can happen is that the film remains a modest record of events and people. Like an anthropological filmmaker you've captured a little of the ethos—values and lifestyles, in current jargon—even if you've missed the mythos—the distilled essence of values and historical experience that "brings the unknown into relation with the known."

Obviously, practical filmmaking isn't so clearly bifurcated. Anyone with a taste for myth certainly tries, at least, to root it in reality. It won't stand by itself. And the ethnographic filmmakers, on the other hand, supposedly concerned only with basic elements like plot and character, usually know well beforehand when they are onto something. Yet the differentiation is a useful one, I think. Very few of the mythmongers actually succeed in capturing myths of lasting value. (Orson Welles is the

263

great exception. He went hunting myths with a rare passion and brought more than his fair share back whole, vital, and influential.) Certainly, the more modest approach of the "ethnographers" is more appealing, and when it works it gives us myths that are much deeper-rooted, and therefore both longer-lasting and more resonant.

Myth for Myth's Sake

Of the group of contemporary filmmakers who put the mythic cart before the realistic horse, Arthur Penn stands as a model. Consistently, since his first film in 1958, *The Left-Handed Gun*, in which Paul Newman essayed the legend of Billy the Kid, Penn has aimed at producing movies with Meaning. *The Miracle Worker* (1962), the Helen Keller story from William Gibson's play, gave us a contemporary legend of liberally tragic and heroic dimensions that was much less maudlin than it might have been (or than dozens of films like it) because it concentrated on Annie Sullivan's job of teaching. François Truffaut had tried to acquire the rights to the play. He saw the power of this aspect of it, and later made his own essay on the teacher-student relationship, *The Wild Child*, a comparison of which with *The Miracle Worker* shows how such material can be handled with sentiment, but without sentimentality.

Penn's third film, *Mickey One* (1965), except for Woody Allen's *Interiors*, is the most pretentious film by a major American director in the last thirty years. Unbelievably murky and pointlessly symbolic, *Mickey One* presents Warren Beatty as Everyman As Stand-Up Comic Beset by Contemporary Cultural Angst and Political Paranoia. It's a film written in capital letters (by Alan Surgal), relieved only by the presence of Alexandra Stewart. Penn followed it up quickly with *The Chase* (1966), about an escaped convict, a sheriff, and a town. It was as theme-ridden as any of Penn's earlier efforts, but was redeemed slightly by having a narrative that was considerably more straightforward. Lillian Hellman wrote the screenplay from the portentous novel by Horton Foote.

By this time, Penn was in danger of losing his career. He seems to have survived by playing the role of Serious Artist in the Hollywood of the early sixties. This endeared him to the midcult critics (Judith Crist vastly admired *Mickey One*), and Hollywood grudgingly put up with him. His presence in the industry was a sign that the nay-sayers were wrong: Hollywood *was* hospitable to art (as long as it kept its place). And indeed Penn did serve as a model and hero for a generation of aspiring directors in the sixties.

Bonnie and Clyde (1967) did much to redress the balance for Penn. The film became an instant classic, studied and discussed in film classes for a decade after, and historically it served as the opening gun of the revolu-

The gangster archetype with a difference. The difference is Bonnie. (Warren Beatty and Faye Dunaway.)

tion for the young filmmakers waiting outside the Hollywood fortress. On examination, and with the benefit of hindsight, *Bonnie and Clyde* reveals the same attitude towards significance and meaning as Penn's earlier films, but it works much better, mainly because screenwriters Robert Benton and David Newman bring some much-needed humor into the claustrophobic Penn universe. Violence, too, is a key to its success both commercially and artistically. All four of Penn's previous efforts had been rooted in this sort of tension, but Penn hadn't been able to find an effective metaphorical release before. However, the final scene of *Bonnie and Clyde* worked, and worked well for audiences and critics alike. Slow-motion death in a hail of bullets soon became a cliché.

Looking back on Penn's early career now, we can see that for all his pretensions he nevertheless exhibited a kind of wall-eyed foresight. *The Left-Handed Gun* can be seen as a later example of the "adult western" of the fifties, in the *High Noon* tradition, or it can be seen as a forerunner of the new western of the seventies. *The Miracle Worker* is part Women's film from the forties, but it also looks forward to the new seriousness of the sixties and seventies we discussed earlier.

Mickey One, the most absurd of this group, is also the most prescient. It's the model for a string of paranoid fantasies that would become one of the major categories of myth in film in the late sixties and early seventies. Even *The Chase* has echoes of the future. It's pompous, but it is a chase film after all and one of the earlier examples of this popular late-sixties

265

genre. Its cast list—Brando, Jane Fonda, Redford, Duvall—looks more like the credits of a film made in 1976 than one that was released in 1966. Finally, *Bonnie and Clyde* gave us both Faye Dunaway and Gene Hackman, and became the model for a long string of imitations, including its own B-movie genre: outlaw couples on the run in the South.

I think *Alice's Restaurant* is Penn's most successful film. It won't surprise you to discover that it's also his least intentionally mythic. It tries to be about its people rather than their significance, despite the presence of Arlo and Woody. It's in a much lower key, less frenzied, than its predecessors. It wasn't appreciated much by Arlo's generation (and mine) when it was released. Neither was Antonioni's *Zabriskie Point*, which also wanted to capture the mythos of that generation. But now, we've forgotten or pay less mind to the little inaccuracies in these middle-aged views of the youth culture, and we can evaluate them from a longer perspective.

In the seventies, Penn attempted two large westerns, *Little Big Man* (1970) and *The Missouri Breaks* (1976), and one more essay in paranoia, *Night Moves* (1975). *Little Big Man*, from the Thomas Berger novel, tries to say something about white men and Indians, the Old West and our nostalgic memories of it, but once again Penn is hampered by his prodigious lack of humor, and that important dimension of the Berger novel doesn't make it to the screen. Robert Altman's *Buffalo Bill and the Indians* does this job better. *The Missouri Breaks*, an original script by Thomas McGuane, tries pretty much the same thing. There's no doubting McGuane's novel sensibility, but Penn allows Brando to ham it up embarassingly, and Jack Nicholson's smart work has no support. *Night Moves* works considerably better. If you have to do a film like this, this is the way to do it. Structurally the film isn't much different from its close cousin *Mickey One*. We are still in the land of simplistic significances for which crude characters are chopped to fit. But Gene Hackman, as the forlorn and frightened detective, brings some needed verisimilitude to the role (after all, he has specialized in it), and the relationship between the detective and his wife (Jennifer Warren) is of some interest. Bruce Surtees's photography and Michael Small's music also add to the impact of the film.

Although really fresh and new mythic significances are obviously hard to come by, there has been at least one new genre of the last twenty years that affords opportunities: the youth film, prefigured by Penn's *Bonnie and Clyde* and *Alice's Restaurant*. It lasted for only a brief time because the generation gap, which culturally set young people distinctly apart from their elders, lasted only a brief time. By the mid-seventies, the painful

266

The private-eye archetype with a twist: Harry Moseby (Gene Hackman) loses control of the situation in this very dark contemporary film noir. The character is a direct offshoot of Hackman's earlier portrayal of Harry Caul in *The Conversation* (see p. 341).

demographic bulge created by the war babies had moved on into early middle age and the youth film was superannuated. As critic Mitch Tuchman has described the last few trailing examples of the genre, "the films had all the earmarks of youth-market pictures—except, increasingly, youth." The genre had emerged from gangster movies like *Bonnie and Clyde*, and it shared the myth of the outsider with them. When there was no longer a significant youth rebellion to deal with, it was easy for the gangster genre and other established forms to serve as frameworks for the outsider myth once again.

To a large extent, the short history of the youth film is a history of BBS productions. Bert Schneider, the driving force behind BBS,* was the son of Abraham Schneider, longtime head of Columbia Pictures, and thus second-generation Hollywood. Schneider joined with Bob Rafelson in the mid-sixties to produce the television series *The Monkees*, a parody of the Beatles. When the series met its demise, he and Rafelson celebrated their "ripoff" with a film, *Head* (1968), which had moderate success.

Meanwhile Dennis Hopper and Peter Fonda (also second-generation Hollywood) had been working on a project for American International, the only producers to take the youth market seriously in the early and

---

*BBS: Bert Schneider, Bob Rafelson, Steve Blauner.

mid-sixties. *Easy Rider* started as an exploitation film and bears all the marks of that genre. When Fonda and Hopper ran into disagreements with AIP, they turned to Schneider, who agreed to produce the film. It was released in 1969; the youth film had come of age; it was to last less than three years.

Easy Rider was not a very interesting film to begin with, and has dated miserably since. It exhibits nearly all the self-centered faults of the contentiously mythic movie, and now seems to present a more wholly negative picture of the youth culture of the late sixties than films with more perspective like *Alice's Restaurant*. Basically a gangster film—two drug dealers take off in search of America on their laid-back motorcycles—it struck a responsive chord. The Fonda and Hopper characters were exploiters before the film begins; during it, they are notably passive victims; at the end, they are supercilious martyrs: not the stuff of which heroes are made, but somehow appealing to a generation that thought of itself as similarly put-upon. Curiously, the mythos that *Easy Rider* assiduously recommends is passive, even masochistic. Extraordinarily few of the successful youth films presented active heroes as role models. A perceptive observer of the evolving mythos in film might have guessed early on that the cultural "revolution," at least, was doomed to failure. These people obviously didn't really want to succeed; they simply wanted to wallow for a while in their temporary status as persecuted outsiders. *Easy Rider* ends with the arbitrary death of one of our heroes at the hands of evil rednecks. "You see?" the film seems to be saying, "What's the use?"

Most of the other BBS films follow a similar gestalt. *Five Easy Pieces* (1970), directed by Rafelson from a script by Adrien Joyce, raises the level of discourse socially but not intellectually. Bobby Dupee (Jack Nicholson) is a talented scion of the upper middle class (he can play classical piano on the back of a pickup truck in the middle of Texas traffic), but the poor fellow just doesn't know what to do with himself. *Five Easy Pieces* was exceptionally well received, both critically and popularly, when it was released, a fact which may raise some eyebrows now. At best, the film works as a not entirely conscious record of a common state of mind in the period around 1970: alienated self-pity.

BBS's last hit was *The Last Picture Show* (1971), directed by Peter Bogdanovich from the novel by Larry McMurtry. The same sentiments are reflected in *Last Picture Show* as in the earlier films—*où sont les neiges d'antan?* But they work better here, perhaps because McMurtry has provided an historical context and a wide range of characters who are well thought out. For once, the mythic resonances spring from a kind of reality.

268

Five Easy Pieces is about tensions: between the Northwest and the Southwest, between active and intellectual lives, between careers and existences. The poles are symbolized here: Jack Nicholson with Susan Anspach, Nicholson with Karen Black.

Three other BBS films released the same year were Jack Nicholson's *Drive, He Said*, from the novel by Jeremy Larner, Dennis Hopper's *The Last Movie*, and Henry Jaglom's *A Safe Place*. *Drive, He Said* puts the BBS characters in a college environment. Since that's where most of them were in real life, and since, like McMurtry, Larner has worked out his characters in greater detail, Nicholson's first effort as director is a rather interesting film. But it seems to have fallen between two stools. Middle-class college kids didn't want to watch themselves—they wanted exaggerated versions of themselves—so *Drive, He Said*, too realistic and not romantic enough, failed at the box office. An even greater failure on all counts was Jaglom's *A Safe Place*, puerile and grossly symbolic. BBS had reached its nadir.

One more fiction film followed: Rafelson's *The King of Marvin Gardens* (1972), from a script by Jacob Brackman. Nicholson plays an FM disk jockey, and since that particular profession was at the hot center of the youth culture, the concept seems potentially fruitful. The film opens with Nicholson doing a brilliantly parodic FM radio monologue—"I promised to tell you why I don't eat fish," a long shaggy-dog yarn that Nicholson takes particular relish telling in close-up. Then, of a sudden, it disappears. The disk jockey is taken out of context and sent to Atlantic City in winter to play out a symbolic but not very active charade with his gangster brother (Bruce Dern) in the city of Monopoly, a quintessential myth-for-myth's-sake ploy. The film deflates very quickly. The women are painfully stereotypical "chicks," as they were in most BBS movies. The misogyny of the youth films is one of the major signs (that should have been clearer to more of us sooner) that they were on the whole artificially mythic constructions rooted in romantic bad faith rather in the requisite understanding of the way we live now. There may have been an excuse for ignoring feminism (or simply real women, for that matter) in 1968; there certainly was none in 1972—which is not to say that the BBS filmmakers were alone in this respect. Far from it.[2]

By 1973, Schneider was deep into politics, and he took on production of Peter Davis's *Hearts and Minds*, a fact which almost redeems BBS, although some auteurists would argue that it is flawed by the same bad faith that characterizes *The King of Marvin Gardens* and *Easy Rider*. It was to be the last BBS film. Bert's father had been ousted from Columbia. (There were rumors of impropriety.) He was replaced by one David Begelman, who didn't like *Hearts and Minds* at all and smartly realized that the day of the youth film was over.

More promising were the films of Paul Williams, who was later friendly with many of the BBS group but whose films were produced (by Edward Pressman) separately. Along with Brian De Palma, he formed the East Coast branch of the new film culture.

His first film, *Out of It* (1969), was a rather charming homage to high school, jalopies, and beach dates set on Long Island. It predated *American Graffiti* by several years. *The Revolutionary* (1970) from a script by Hans Königsberger was altogether more ambitious. Of all the films about the youth rebellion it is the most thoughtful and complex. Königsberger and Williams put their revolutionary, Jon Voight, in a setting that is purposely unspecific. The point they are trying to make is that others had faced the same moral and political dilemmas in other times and other countries many times before. The sixties youth revolt was by no means unique. The film is vaguely Brechtian in that it clearly admits its relationship to ideas: the drama is obviously meant as a series of "teaching pieces" rather than moral parables, and the film thus shows considerable respect for its audience, besides being notably further advanced in its political thinking than any of its competitors.

Williams made one more youth film, *Dealing: Or the Boston-to-Berkeley Forty-Brick Lost-Bag Blues* (1972), from a novel by Michael Crichton and his brother. It, too, is noticeably superior to the general run of youth films. As *The Revolutionary* had taken mythic significance to its abstract extreme, so *Dealing* reduces the romantic mythos of the youth film to the level of verisimilitude: Douglas Crichton had lived in the world of the film, and Williams was not so far away from it himself, so the details ring true, and this makes the movie rather special.

By this time Williams appeared to have the potential to become one of the most interesting filmmakers of the seventies. But like a number of his Hollywood contemporaries he became involved in the Arica cult, and dropped out of filmmaking for several years, reappearing only in 1978 with *Nunzio*.

Ellen Barber, Robert F. Lyons, Joy Bang, and John Lithgow in *Dealing: Or the Boston-to-Berkeley Forty-Brick Lost-Bag Blues.*

While the BBS and Pressman-Williams production organizations formed the hot center of the youth-cult film, there was an interesting outer ring that deserves some attention, too. Like the youth filmmakers, these directors were working inductively with an insatiable taste for meaning and myth, but unlike the BBS group they did not get caught up in maudlin soul-searching.

Monte Hellman had been a journeyman director on B films for a while before gaining some underground notoriety for two strange westerns, *The Shooting* (1966) and *Ride the Whirlwind* (1967). *The Shooting* was produced by and starred Jack Nicholson (this was before he became a major box-office attraction through his role in *Easy Rider*) and was written by Adrien Joyce. *Two-Lane Blacktop* (1971), written by Rudolph Wurlitzer and Will Corry, was heralded in an *Esquire* cover story as "film of the year" before it opened. It bombed, perhaps because it didn't pander to youthful self-pity. It's egregiously mythic in intent, but somehow it works because it deliberately abstracts *Easy Rider* platitudes. Warren Oates and James Taylor and Dennis Wilson (two music stars) engage in a never-ending race from Southwest to Midwest with hardly a word spoken.

Michael S. Laughlin produced the film, as he had *The Christian Licorice Store* a year earlier. Clearly meant as a ripoff of a studio (Cinema Center) looking to cash in on the youth film trend, *Christian Licorice Store* afforded its filmmakers a number of pleasant, if not cinematically productive, opportunities: they got to throw a party for their Hollywood friends

271

Warren Oates, Dennis Wilson, Laurie Bird (back to camera), and James Taylor take a break in the cross-country race between Oates and the younger people that constitutes the plot of *Two-Lane Blacktop*.

(and film it), mosey around L.A. playing with the camera and Nagra, take a trip to Texas, and—best of all—meet with idol Jean Renoir at his home (and film it)! Director James Frawley moved on to more commercial comedies.

Writer Floyd Mutrux developed a highly idiosyncratic directorial style with two gutsy quasidocumentary films about the underside of Los Angeles street life, *Dusty and Sweets McGee* (1971) and *Aloha Bobby and Rose* (1975). Both fit the sentiments of the classic youth film, but their settings were in marked contrast. The latter, surprisingly, was a hit. This gave Mutrux the opportunity to move to larger budgets with *American Hot Wax* (1978), one of a series of late seventies nostalgic "youth" movies for a generation that was now all too rapidly approaching (and even passing) forty.

Sylvester Stallone's tour de force, *Rocky* (1976), also traded on the nostalgia for a simpler age that had simpler heroes. Set in the seventies, it's a fifties story that is unarguably ingratiating, mainly because of Stallone's obvious good humor. Director John Avildsen had prepared for this assignment with three earlier films—*Joe* (1970), *Save the Tiger* (1973), and *W. W. and the Dixie Dancekings* (1975)—that were all obviously meant to project myth and meaning, although of three contrasting sorts.

Ralph Bakshi has taken a much more cynical look at youth culture in his animated films. *Fritz the Cat* (1972), his first film, is still his most

Automania: *Two-Lane Blacktop* is only one of numerous recent films about the road and car culture. No one theme is more prominent or more pervasive in seventies movies. Here·is a small sampling: The massed gatherings of *Sugarland Express* (left) and *Convoy* (1978, right) suggest the power of the road. The ominous chases of *The Driver* (left) and *Slither* (right) build drama out of simple competition. In both *Grease* (left) and *Corvette Summer*, the car is offered as both artwork and symbol of adult power. *American Graffiti*'s endless cruises, which always centered around Mel's Drive-In, describe the social function of the road, an aspect of automania that reached an apotheosis in the *Citizen's Band* wedding by CB.

273

interesting, but *Heavy Traffic* (1973) and *Coonskin* (1975) are both violent, controversial images of the social chaos that gave birth to the sixties revolt. It still exists. Bakshi then moved into mythic fantasy—much less interesting on the evidence so far—with *Wizards* (1977), a soppy, thin-witted morality tale, and *Lord of the Rings* (1978).

John Korty, based in San Francisco, is certainly not in the Hollywood youth orbit, but his gentle, sometimes precious, legends of the sixties—*Crazy Quilt* (1966), *Funnyman* (1967), and *Riverrun* (1968)—are among the more interesting myth-dominated films in this category. Jerry Schatzberg's *Scarecrow* (1973), much admired in Europe, also fits this rather fey prescription. Korty later did more interesting, more controlled work in television—*The Autobiography of Miss Jane Pitman* (1973), for example. *Alex and The Gypsy*, from a script by Lawrence B. Marcus (1976), marked his return to the large screen with his myths still intact, but now rooted in a more vibrant reality.

Both Robert Altman (*Images*, 1973; *Three Women*, 1977) and to some extent Francis Coppola share the attraction to inductive, forced, mythic structure that characterizes the work of most of the filmmakers we've mentioned. Alan Rudolph's *Welcome to L.A.* (1977), produced by mentor Altman, shows that the self-serving pretension of the late sixties youth movie is still attractive to some filmmakers. James Toback's *The Gambler* (1974, directed by Karel Reisz) and *Fingers* (1978) are East Coast versions of mythic portentousness and self-serving signification.

Reisz, who directed *The Gambler*, did his best work in England. Like many other exiles from the U.K. he seems recently to have made a speciality of midcult importance. Other examples: John Schlesinger's *Midnight Cowboy* (1969) and *Day of the Locust* (1975); John Boorman's *Deliverance* (1972). *Who'll Stop the Rain* (1978) is Reisz's most recent contribution. Based on Robert Stone's well-received novel *Dog Soldiers*, this grand metaphor for America's Vietnam debacle loses something in the translation to the screen. We concentrate too much on the action at the expense of its mythic resonance. Like *Coming Home*, *Who'll Stop the Rain* is about echoes and aftermaths, and the reflected image of the war is often too faint.

During the last few years, an overlay of erstwhile mythic significance has become a valuable selling tool (or so many producers and directors think), and the result has been that a number of very small films have been invested with a grandiose importance the weight of which they can hardly bear. Irvin Kershner's *The Eyes of Laura Mars* (1978) is a perfect example of this ploy. At the center of the film is a very short, rather silly plot upon which is hung great gobs of would-be significance. Semioticians speak of a "sign" of communication composed of two equal halves:

Sylvester Stallone as "Johnny Kovak," the Jimmy Hoffa character in *F.I.S.T.*, talking with Senator Andrew Madison (Rod Steiger) as Max Graham (Peter Boyle) looks on: history as romance.

the "signifier" and the "signified". A film like *Laura Mars* is all signifiers that never connect with signifieds. Or to put it more poetically, full of sound and fury. Walter Hill's *The Driver* (1978) represents another face of this semiotic problem. Unlike Kershner's flatulent epic, Hill's movie is very conscious that its "signifiers" exist in and for themselves. Like some European films of this genre (especially Jean-Pierre Melville's later work), *The Driver* is something of an experiment in this way. It still may be pretentious, but it has a more interesting reason for being so. Then we have movies like *Heaven Can Wait* (1978), which are blithely and intentionally all myth and no meaning.

Many of Norman Jewison's films might fit in this category. Jewison clearly wants his films to be meaningful, but again, the meaning often seems pasted on, as in *F.I.S.T.* (1978), from a script by Joe Eszterhas that might have formed the basis for a truly interesting film about Jimmy Hoffa. Jewison and star/co-scenarist Sylvester Stallone goose the story with supposedly mythic touches that have an effect opposite to the one intended: because they are pasted on, they defuse the realistic basis of the film and therefore sap its energy.

Sydney Pollack is another director whose reach almost always exceeds his grasp. He shows a consistent commitment to middlebrow meaning, writ large. *They Shoot Horses, Don't They?* (1969) meant to make a statement about the Depression. *Jeremiah Johnson* (1972) was an elegy to

275

the frontier loner. *The Way We Were* (1973) attempted historical significance about the Blacklist period in the guise of an unlikely romance. *The Yakuza* (1975) introduced us to this highly stylized Japanese genre. *Bobby Deerfield* (1977), Pollack's most fatefully ambitious—and embarrassing—film to date, will undoubtedly become a camp classic. Race driver Al Pacino's mad, pointless romance with cancer victim Marthe Keller makes *Magnificent Obsession* look like a serious investigation into human emotions. It's hard not to find a little affection for a film in which the hero fondles the heroine's hair as they lie in bed after making love—and clumps come out. Despite such missteps, however, Pollack has done some interesting films when he works in strict collaboration: Robert Redford controlled *Jeremiah Johnson* and *Three Days of the Condor* (Pollack's best film); Paul Schrader (and his brother Leonard) wrote the script for *The Yakuza*.

The imposition of a mythic structure on the events and people of a film isn't always specious. A number of the films we've been discussing here are obviously pretentious to one degree or another, but we are dealing with a continuum, not discrete pigeonholes: one viewer's symbolist claptrap is another's cinematic epiphany. When the material itself is strongly mythic (usually in an historical context) the self-consciousness of a film often works in its favor, as in the Black classics *Sweet Sweetback*, *Ganja & Hess*, and *Leadbelly*; or *The Godfather*; or Robert Altman's genre films.

Hal Ashby's career presents an interesting case study. All of his films obviously aspire to mythic importance or something very much like it. I think it's clear that Ashby, like Penn, starts first with the mythic material, then works backward to discover a useful pattern in reality. But more often than not, Ashby brings it off because he seems to become more interested in his characters than their meaning once shooting begins.

His first film, *The Landlord* (1970), from a script by Bill Gunn, is good evidence of this. It's the people who come through here and make the message work. *Harold and Maude* (1974), written by Colin Higgins, became a cult object because of its egregiously eccentric characters. *The Last Detail* (1974), Darryl Ponicsan's novel adapted by Robert Towne, is more successful because its characters are less fey. In *Shampoo* (1975), Robert Towne and Warren Beatty's existential statement about the New Hollywood, set for some reason in 1968, myth begins to overtake reality. The characters work, their significance politically and culturally doesn't: it's too little, much too late.

Bound for Glory (1976, Robert Getchell's script) presents a separate case. Obviously, Woody Guthrie's biography presents enormous mythic potential, and Ashby, greatly aided by Haskell Wexler's stunning and

The road—and our fascination with it—started in the thirties. David Carradine as Woody Guthrie in *Bound for Glory* on Route 66.

stately photography, has fashioned a respectful tribute to Woody. But that's the problem: Woody himself would have made a gutsier, more irreverent film. The man is overtaken by the legend. *Coming Home* (1978) has problems too, but of a different nature. Jane Fonda and producer Jerome Hellman wanted to make a film about the home front during the Vietnam war. The script went through a succession of writers—Nancy Dowd first, Waldo Salt last. John Schlesinger dropped out and Ashby was brought in. Even during shooting, cast and crew were still hassling with the script. The characters grew in importance as the message faded, which isn't so bad, except that the message—or part of it—is still there. What's left is muddled. The characters don't come fully alive because we're aware of their theme-ridden roots, and the truncated message is simplistic. Had it been released in 1969 or 1970 it would have been extremely influential, but its insights had palled a decade later.

If Hal Ashby *induces* myth, Terrence Malick *deduces* it. If anything, his films have an even more persistent mythic aura than Ashby's, but it seems clear, at least to me, that Malick begins with the reality, then draws his impressively mythic material out of it. If a filmmaker wants to be consciously mythic this is obviously the modus operandi that will result in the most valid and affective movies. Yet of all the would-be Homers and Joyces working in American film today, Terrence Malick seems to be the only one who uses this sophisticated approach. In this

277

respect, his films are very much like Stanley Kubrick's* and even though he has only completed two (*Badlands*, 1974, *Days of Heaven*, 1978) he already has to be regarded as one of the most interesting American filmmakers of the 1970s.

A very sharply ironic retelling of the Charles Starkweather mass murders of the fifties, *Badlands* managed, without being heavy-handed, to say a lot about the way the media work to create role models. At the center of the film's ironic structure lay a curious amoral celebrityhood of the sort that has become a commonplace of the seventies. Malick investigated an interesting historical antecedent. The result was a film of some mythic weight which nevertheless managed to maintain its distance from the subject matter (which made it many times more effective than the straightforward, serious television docudramas about similar subjects). Malick's high satire depends on the carefully designed narration of his films. We are seeing one thing and hearing another and the tone of voice of the narrators tells us a great deal. It tells us how the character relates to her own story, and it therefore gives us an idea of Malick's position. The visuals alone might not.

This is (in both senses of the word) a tricky business, but Malick is clearly obsessed with this narrative idea, having used it in both his films. In *Badlands*, Sissy Spacek delivers the characterful running monologue, reading from her diary, which she has written in the only style she knows: the self-satisfied, almost humorous tone of voice of fan magazines. (Robert Altman later reprised this technique for *Three Women*. In that film it's Shelley Duvall who gets to keep the quaint diary.) *Badlands* was a critical success but did not do well financially. One of the reasons may just have been the irony of the film's irony: Malick wrote *Badlands* to within an inch of its life. The dialogue and the narration are so thickly allusive, so highly worked, that it was distracting.

Malick tones down this element in *Days of Heaven*. Linda Manz's narration is equally effective but much sparer. Like Spacek's it has a

---

*Although Stanley Kubrick was born in the Bronx and made his first films in this country, I don't regard him as a truly American director within the context of this book, which is why you haven't seen his name mentioned more often. Yet he looms in the background, his English-made movies quietly haunting those made by his former countrymen on native ground. *2001: A Space Odyssey* transcends all science-fiction films. *A Clockwork Orange* remains the ultimate comment on the sadomasochistic disco style of the seventies: it forecasts most of it accurately. And *Barry Lyndon*, while not directly relevant to the current American scene, is clearly a model of a sophisticated translation of an historical novel to the screen, a fascinating experiment in epic vision. *Days of Heaven* owes a lot to *Barry Lyndon*.

thrilling authenticity to it. If a young girl were talking to us in 1916 this is what it would sound like. It's also, excuse the expression, poetic: "I been thinkin' " Linda tells us, "what to do wit' my future. I could be a mud doctor. Check out the earth. Underneat'."

Visually, *Days of Heaven* is often literally breathtaking. Malick's im-

And still more legends of the road. . . Martin Sheen on a chain, with Sissy Spacek, his romantic chronicler, waiting for a plane in *Badlands*.

Brooke Adams in *Days of Heaven,* and the real stars of the film—the endless fields and the rickety machines.

ages are as obsessive as his dialogue. Few films since *2001* have utilized 70-mm filmstock to such advantage. The plot is almost an excuse for the images. The film has been criticized for just this, but I rather like Malick's insouciance. Here is a truly epic vision—of not much in particular. It's as if the writer/director had consciously decided after the poor reception of *Badlands* (which after all had enough social and cultural significance for at least two movies) to drain his film of elements that might be built into significance. It starts in one place, then quickly moves on to another. It stays there awhile, then comes to a dramatic but pointless conclusion. Then it goes on for a while longer. Then it stops finally almost in midsentence. It's as if Malick were saying, "Don't take any of this too seriously." The aim of *Days of Heaven* is not at all mythic, it's ethnographic. The film wants simply to show us what it was like, farming wheat, in the Texas panhandle, early in this century. What the combines looked like. How the people lived. How the wheatgrains and grasshoppers looked. What changes the seasons brought. Following current styles in historiography, *Days of Heaven* writes everyday life large. The less it is about, the more it is about.

"If You Want to Send a Message, Call Western Union"

That was the motto of the Old Hollywood and, to a large extent, it still holds. Meaning in film is perhaps best left to observers, and much of what we learn about our collective contemporary consciousness comes from an analysis of groups of films rather than individual masterworks. This is the coral theory of mythopoeia. The mythic reef builds up slowly but inexorably through the accretion of thousands of mythogenic bits and minimythic pieces. It's why genres are so important to studies of film and other popular culture.

Film is an aging art. Like the novel and painting, its best years are past. Nowhere is this more evident than in the generic self-consciousness that has dominated American movies in the seventies. Not having confidence in their own stories or the way they tell them (or not having any stories to tell), filmmakers in increasing numbers turn to the past for desperate inspiration. The straight remakes—*King Kong, Farewell, My Lovely, The Big Sleep, The Great Gatsby, The Front Page, Heaven Can Wait, Hurricane*—are invariably lesser films than their ancient models, although they occasionally come up with interesting twists, as in *A Star Is Born*, which shifted the locus of action from movies to rock. More intriguing are the numerous films that used elements of the old genres, sometimes even parody them, but also include a contemporary perspective.

The recent revival of private eyes is instructive. The genre was moribund through the late fifties and most of the sixties. Spies, on the James Bond model, were preferred to down-at-the-heels shamuses like Philip Marlowe or Sam Spade. Ross Macdonald's *Harper* was brought to the screen as a vehicle for Paul Newman in 1966. (William Goldman wrote the screenplay, Jack Smight directed.) But the contemporary setting and the contemporary character didn't have the moody style that was so important to detective stories in the forties. The true revival of the genre had to wait for Robert Towne's canny pastiche *Chinatown* (directed by Roman Polanski) in 1974. Towne revived the Marlowe/Spade type in a period setting, and gave Jack Nicholson's J. J. Gittes an historical mystery to investigate that had some contemporary relevance. Southern California water politics are still very interesting. Add John Huston (director of *The Maltese Falcon*) as the villain, and you have a film with very sharp resonances.

Dick Richards and David Zelag Goodman's remake of *Farewell, My Lovely* (1975) took the Huston trick one step further by casting Robert Mitchum as Marlowe, which connected the film with forties film noir in reality as well as in setting and style. This suggested—because Mitchum had of course aged—a historical context, and reminded us that Dick Powell was not a very felicitous choice for the first version of the Chandler novel.

While Coppola and Penn were experimenting with contemporary Angst-ridden private eyes in *The Conversation* and *Night Moves* (both with Gene Hackman), the most successful of the new versions of this old genre is probably Robert Benton's *The Late Show* (1977). Benton used an actor who could have (but didn't) play a similar role in the forties, Art Carney, and teams him with an actress, Lily Tomlin, who projects an image that's quintessentially seventies. The film then becomes a meditation on the relationship between the two decades as reflected in private-eye movies. Carney's Ira Wells may be over the hill, but he knows what the score is. In the opening credit sequence he is at work on his own detective novel, "Naked Girls and Machine Guns." He's hoping to cash in on the nostalgia craze for the forties.

The most popular and important American genre is undoubtedly the western. Its origins are lost in the pulp fiction of the mid-nineteenth century, movies and television have never strayed very far from it, and it has inspired Germans (Karl May) and Italians (Sergio Leone) as well. Once again, the most successful current examples of the genre are those that are clearly aware of their origins and manage to combine a contemporary attitude with an awareness of the qualities that made the style appealing years ago.

Westerns: Misogynist Gene Hackman and his mailorder bride Liv Ullmann in *Zandy's Bride,* a film noir western. Christopher Lloyd, Richard Bradford, and John Belushi as lawmen surround ne'er-do-well Jack Nicholson in *Goin' South,* a comedy Nicholson directed.

Don Siegel's *The Shootist* (1976), from the novel by Glendon Swarthout, is easily the most resonant of the seventies westerns, since it stars the ultimate hero of American western movies, John Wayne, and makes it clear that this film is going to continue to develop the persona Wayne had been at work on for more than forty-five years. The film opens with a montage of Wayne at various ages in other westerns.

Films like *Butch Cassidy and the Sundance Kid* have been highly popular, but they add little to our understanding of the mythic roots of the genre. They're appealing simply because they stick modern, irreverent stars in the western context. This makes for some nice clashes of mood, but it's rather mechanical. Thomas McGuane's *Missouri Breaks* tries the same trick, unsuccessfully, and his *Rancho Deluxe* (1975, directed by Frank Perry) reverses the equation by playing with no longer sacred Western myths in a modern setting.

Of more interest is Jan Troell's *Zandy's Bride* (from an old novel by Lillian Bos Ross), which disappeared without a murmur in 1974. The film is actually the third part of a magnificent trilogy that begins with *The Emigrants* and *The New Land,* a pair of films which trace the Swedish experience in emigrating to America. *Zandy's Bride* (which does not follow the same group of characters but does include one of the same actors, Liv Ullmann) takes the immigrant experience as far as it can go: the edge of the Pacific ocean. All three films are startlingly realistic. Troell's premise is the grandest American myth of all, but he conscientiously works against the mythic grain to show the reality of the immigrant experience; the myth takes care of itself.

A few years later *Roots* captured the national imagination, not only I think because it dealt with racial issues, but also because of its nominal subject matter. What could be more interesting to a nation that's rummaging feverishly in the old trunk where its cultural artifacts are stored

Westerns: There are more complex approaches to the genre, as well. Legends Wayne and Stewart in *The Shootist* refer to their own long histories in the film. Sometime director Alan Arkin plays a director in Howard Zieff's *Hearts of the West*. Jeff Bridges is the star of the early two-reel western movies that are the subject of the film.

than a film that begins to explain how we got to where we are? There's room for dozens more *Roots* and *Emigrants*, as feature films and as television series. It's rather remarkable that they aren't being made.

What is being made is a massive torrent of popular "entertainments," a large number of which seem to deal with a strictly limited number of themes. The most powerful cultural force operating in the seventies was definitely nostalgia; it's going to be impossible, twenty years hence, to revive the seventies; they have no style of their own. We see this best, in movies, in the rush to genre, but there are other evidences as well. Somehow, the fifties have become a unitary force. Preteens get crushes on the Fonz and the Sweathogs on television, characters one might have thought were aimed rather at their mothers. It's as if in the fifties we all went mad at sock hops for Frank Sinatra and Benny Goodman, rather than our own generationally rebellious heroes, Presley and company. More precisely, similar adolescent nostalgia for a time not known in the fifties would have yielded the curious spectacle of movie stars like James Dean and Sal Mineo achieving teenage acclaim because they were good at mimicking Fred Astaire or George Brent.

A fifties setting isn't actually necessary for a film to use the fifties mythos. *American Graffiti* was set nominally in 1962. Both *Mean Streets* and *Rocky* are vaguely contemporary even if the sentiments they project clearly belong twenty years earlier. *Saturday Night Fever*, the surprising box-office success of 1978, has roots in an ageless Brooklyn style that probably reached its peak in real life in the mid-fifties, just before the Dodgers left. Even the Hustle, the dance of the late seventies, looks to jaded eyes like imitation Lindy and Hokey Pokey. If *Saturday Night Fever* were at all ambitious, it might be about this curious communion between Dad's fifties and son's seventies. It's interesting to speculate to what extent the fifties craze is a result of aging fathers and mothers (who make

Laraine Newman plays a young woman in *American Hot Wax* whose career is reminiscent of Carole King's. Gary Busey is Buddy Holly with the Crickets (Don Stroud and Charlie Martin Smith) in *The Buddy Holly Story*.

the films and TV shows) forcibly imposing their own dream of youth on their children.

In film, fifties shtik was presaged by a very small, independent production (by Stephen Verona and Martin Davidson) called *The Lords of Flatbush,* starring two raw unknowns by the names of Sylvester Stallone and Henry Winkler. (See p. 103.) So far, only James Bridge's *September 30, 1955* (1978), which centers on Bridges's own recollection of his reaction to the news of the death of James Dean, has attemped to come to grips with this phenomenon historically. Floyd Mutrux's *American Hot Wax* (1978) managed to capture the gusto of the fifties urban lifestyle rather well. There have been dozens of these nostalgic evocations of the rock 'n' roll myths of the fifties in the past two years. They range from the brash comic-book style of the high-grossing *Grease*, which is more about our fantasies of a lost time than that time itself, to the quiet, likable, sensitive biography *The Buddy Holly Story* (directed by Steve Rash), which manages to touch us with a real understanding of what was important about the music of that period. This narrative of the short but productive life of one of the most influential popular musicians of the last thirty years is characterized by an intelligence which sets it apart from the general run of rock 'n' roll movies of the last few years.

The sixties have also become subject to film nostalgia. Early examples of the "rock" genre (as opposed to the "rock 'n' roll" genre) haven't yet captured the feel of the period. *Sergeant Pepper's Lonely Hearts Club Band* attempted a fantasy loosely hung on the Beatles music. It didn't work. *I Wanna Hold Your Hand* (Bob Zemeckis and Bob Gale) suffered from its rushed, cost-cutting production schedule. But *Hair* may do for the sixties what *Grease* did for the fifties. The one consolation in all this is that there's nothing after the sixties to distract our attention from the present tense.

Nostalgia isn't the only operating element of the seventies mythos,

There seems to be a certain relationship between the paranoia film and SM sexual fantasies. Here are two of the more reputable exercises in this style: Lenny Montana as Luca Brasi is garrotted in *The Godfather* after having his hand pinned to the bar with a knife. (The scene was cut from the television version.) Nazi dentist Laurence Olivier artistically creates an unneeded cavity in Dustin Hoffman's front tooth in *Marathon Man*. (If you aren't donto-phobic, it's rather droll. See also *Klute* below.

only the most pleasant. Fear and revenge also loom large as well and perhaps tell us more about the collective psyche than ankle bracelets and leather jackets.

Simple paranoia is responsible for the entire disaster genre as well as the seventies political thriller which was introduced by Alan Pakula's *The Parallax View* (1974). William Goldman's *Marathon Man* (1976), directed by John Schlesinger, was certainly the most elegant and extreme contribution to the genre, but neither these films nor lesser examples— Aldrich's *Twilight's Last Gleaming* (1977), Kramer's *The Domino Principle* (1977), Siegel's *Telefon* (1977)—do much except play with paranoia. Sydney Pollack's *Three Days of the Condor* (1976) goes a little further. Star Robert Redford finds himself caught in a pincers formed by two branches of the C.I.A. He escapes, logically, by going to the press. At the end of the film we are left with considerable doubt whether Redford's ploy will be successful: "How do you know they'll print it?" queries the C.I.A. operative. It's a very real question, and it involves us in the action of the film as a simpler ending would not have. *Condor* spends more time on politics than on paranoia, and that is as unique as it is intelligent.

We've already mentioned the more intellectual strain of paranoia, represented by the existential mysteries of *The Conversation* and *Night Moves*. Add *Rollerball* to this short list, which phrases a common futuristic political fear in a sports metaphor. Like most paranoid fantasies, it offers no hope: if James Caan can't beat the system, who can? Joseph Sargent's *The Forbin Project* (*Colossus*, 1970), written by James Bridges from a novel by D. F. Jones, is the model for blackly hopeless claustrophobic fear: master computers of the U.S. and U.S.S.R. begin talking

285

to each other. They decide to take over. Humans fight back. In the end, the computers have clearly won. There is no escape.

Of the more political contemporary paranoid fantasies, none has the wit of Alfred Hitchcock and Ernest Lehman's *North by Northwest* (1959), which not only forecast many of our later realized fears about the C.I.A.—"C.I.A.? F.B.I.? What's the difference? We're all in the same alphabet soup!"—but did so with an understanding of our ability to fight back. Similarly, the more elaborately psychological paranoid thrillers of the seventies aren't as 'thoughtful as the science-fiction classic of the 1950s *Forbidden Planet* (1956, directed by Fred M. Wilcox and written by Cyril Hume). There it's made clear that monsters are the creation of our own ids. Would that *The Exorcist* and the slew of supernatural horror films that have followed it in the seventies were as wise.

The passive paranoia myth, so common in seventies movies of all sorts, has an active companion in the revenge myth, which has been second in frequency for the last few years. Revenge is an inherent value of any cop film, and most private-eye stories. As a dramatic technique it goes back at least as far as *Hamlet*, but during the seventies it has taken on a new urgency. It's a common theme in Blaxploitation and, of course, basic to kung fu. It's also seen in A films: Clint Eastwood's *Dirty Harry* cycle and Phil Karlson's *Walking Tall* (1973) and its sequels established the style of bloody, righteous violence which dominates revenge films of the seventies. Both series came under strong criticism for what was presumed to be exploitation of violence, yet the censure seems to me to be class-oriented. The sentiments Harry Callahan and Sheriff Buford Pusser express may be crude, but they represent effective responses to an already violent world. Intellectual liberals prefer a more reasoned response, but their equivocations and analyses haven't come to grips with the problem Harry and Buford have. Until we have a workable political answer to a disintegrating, corrupt society, Callahan's Magnum 44 and Pusser's club will rule, for better or worse.

Anyway, middle-class liberals have had their own cycle of revenge films to compare with working-class *Dirty Harry* and *Walking Tall*. *Taxi Driver* combined revenge with psychotic paranoia, and it was generally applauded by the established critics. *Death Wish* (1974, written by Wendell Mayes, directed by Michael Winner) celebrated bourgeois vigilantism and was well received by filmgoers if not by some critics. Most Charles Bronson movies, in fact, trade on the same or similar sentiments. *Serpico* (1973), Sidney Lumet's staging of a very snide script by those masters of supercilious bad faith, Waldo Salt and Norman Wexler, recast the paranoia as fear of a corrupt police force and played on those fears without ever offering a more balanced and developed view of a real situation. All it added up to, eventually, was middle-class hippie revenge. Even feminists have been allowed a little revenge to get off on: David Rayfiel and Lamont Johnson's simplistic *Lipstick* (1976).

In the seventies, it seems, everyone was neurotically afraid of everyone else, and we all appeared to have a righteous desire, which movies eagerly fulfill, to beat up on, cut, kick, stomp, and blow away the supposed objects of our paranoia.

The mythic materials of paranoia and revenge, which certainly dominate American movies of the 1970s, are the clearest signs we have that all is not well in the Land of the Free and Home of the Brave, and that all of us—cops and addicts, private eyes and beautiful widows, crazy taxi drivers and middle-level executives, housewives, hookers, and journalists—are thoroughly alienated from a political, social, and cultural system that is either corrupt, moribund, ineffectual, or all of the above. As Paddy Chayefsky put it in *Network:* "We're mad as hell, and we're not going to take it anymore!"

But Chayevsky was perhaps indulging in a bit of wishful thinking in that second clause. No doubt we're mad. But we are taking it. Films that deal directly with political realities are as rare as they ever were. The collective rage is well expressed, as is the nostalgia for an earlier time, but seldom does a film confront the causes of that rage, and help to explain how we can deal with the situation. Chayefsky's own pair of jeremiads—*Hospital* (1971, directed by Arthur Hiller) and *Network* (1976, directed by Sidney Lumet)—begin with interesting premises, but quickly degenerate into rather cute fantasy. It's as if the business of confronting issues was too much for them; they retreat into abstract daydreams.

There are occasional exceptions, but we don't have a real political cinema yet. What we do have—and it results in many of the most engaging and interesting films of the last ten years—is what we might call a proto-political cinema, one that concerns itself with basic ideals of community, family, and sex relationships. It's cinema of domestic or sexual politics, if you like, and its aim in general is to try to describe what the present lineaments of the social contract are.

The Way We Live Now

John Cassavetes, Robert Altman, Francis Coppola, Michael Ritchie, and Paul Mazursky all investigate this topic, which is one main reason I see them as leaders of contemporary American film. They aren't alone, however. Gut emotions of paranoia and revenge may dominate the bulk of American moviemaking now, but there's a strong analytical intelligence running counter to this mainstream and it expresses itself in a variety of films.

Richard Lester's *Petulia* (1968) is very likely the model for this type of filmmaking. It wasn't especially popular at the time of its release, but its reputation has grown with each passing year, so that now it ranks third on our list of the ten best films of the last ten years. Lester was returning to the United States after fifteen years in Europe, and he saw as perhaps only an exile could see how the lifestyle of the late sixties had developed and where it was going. Filming in San Francisco in the midst of the summer of love in 1967, he had an uncanny sense of the impending failure of that ethos. With quick, deft strokes he and screenwriter Lawrence B. Marcus were able to sketch most of the major contradictions of the hip middle-class lifestyle of the late sixties: spuriously romantic and ultimately artificial. The hip people of *Petulia* idealize underclass experience so they won't have to confront class differences, just as they base their own relationships on romantic fictional models so that they can follow a cute script rather than actually living their lives out. Throughout the film Vietnam unobtrusively but insistently plays on the television set in the background. *Petulia* is about the death force that pervades and eventually triumphs over the summer of love. Lester and Marcus proved to be right, but in 1968 people didn't want to hear criticism of this sort.

Petulia is a superb example of the way in which an essentially realistic investigation can yield mythic resonances. We know *Petulia*'s people are real, and we respond immediately to Lester and Marcus's sharp perception of the way they operate. We get a tough, precise description of the ethos of a particular time and place; the irony the filmmakers provide raises this to the level of myth. Working deductively rather than inductively, the filmmakers abstract a commentary from a powerful collection of details. I suppose if we have to give a name to this style of filmmaking it would be called realism, but the esthetics aren't so important as the modus operandi: films like this have a powerful validity (which raises them above the level of the intentionally mythic movies discussed earlier) because they begin with real people leading real lives.

There were a number of films on this model around the time of *Petulia* and in the years that followed. Most of them dealt with middle-class family situations, it's true, but then remember that the vast majority of filmmakers and filmgoers are middle-class. Paul Mazursky's *Bob & Carol & Ted & Alice* provides a good companion piece to *Petulia*. Between them, they satirically triangulate West Coast lifestyles. Richard Brooks's *The Happy Ending* (1969) was well ahead of its time in its relatively thoughtful discussion of the predicament of a middle-aged housewife (Jean Simmons). Joan Didion's *Play It as It Lays* (1972), directed by

Frank Perry, was typically darker and more harshly satiric.

In New York, the film of domestic politics was a little more common. Frank Perry and Eleanor Perry directed and wrote *The Swimmer* (1968), *Last Summer* (1969), and *Diary of a Mad Housewife* (1970), uneven films but nevertheless ambitious. Irvin Kershner, who has had a spectacularly uneven career, directed *Loving* in 1970 (Don Devlin wrote the script from a J. M. Ryan novel). George Segal and Eva Marie Saint come close to providing the ultimate image of the suburban couple. (Kershner was less successful with *Up the Sandbox*, 1972, a vehicle for Barbra Streisand.) Bob Fosse's *Lenny* (1974) captured the urban atmosphere with rare precision.

Add to this list a number of films by Ritchie, Mazursky, and Cassavetes (on both coasts), and Coppola's early *The Rain People* (1969), and we have a pretty fair collection of films about sexual politics and domestic middle class lifestyles. It begins to become evident that such movies are often mildly feminist in orientation, which shouldn't be surprising. Any film that shows an interest in sexual politics must perforce be interpreted in feminist terms.

Domestic dramas often run the risk of lapsing into melodrama, and it must be admitted that a number of the films so far mentioned don't entirely successfully avoid this trap. Yet the issue of sexual politics is of such extreme importance in the '70s and '80s that we're grateful for any film that gives women a little room in which to operate. The vast majority of American movies during the last 15 years have violently restricted women to a handful of stereotypes.

The one genre that insists that women be accorded at least nominal equality is romance. Yet seventies love stories almost all follow the model of *Love Story* (1970): they're rather sadistic male fantasies in which the male hero is finally relieved of the feared responsibility of confronting women on a basis of equality by the convenient death of the love object. If she isn't killed, she's crippled, on the model of Bette Davis movies of the forties. In fairness, it must be noted that the perils that face women in romances aren't wholly the result of macho domination. If Davis was most popular when blind (*Dark Victory*) or neurotically dominated (*Now Voyager*) it was at least partially because women wanted to see her that way. Sadistic male fantasies find their comfortable match in masochistic female fantasies.

Even the recent "feminist" films are subject to this myth of morbidity. *Julia* (1977), from Lillian Hellman's story (Alvin Sargent wrote the script, Fred Zinnemann directed), presents us with a mysterious woman as hero who's fatefully attractive because she is sacrificed; we can cry for Julia, we don't have to deal with her. (Alvin Sargent must also be held

289

responsible for the script for *Bobby Deerfield*.)

Looking for Mr. Goodbar (1977), Richard Brook's version of Judith Rossner's novel, is an anti-romance that at least has the virtue of permitting a woman to play the active, dominant central role, but what is the moral of this story as Brooks tells it? Simply that women who take the same sexual liberties as men will pay with their lives.

Even if women aren't killed off in the last reel, they are almost universally presented as victims. This is true of the popular B-movie genre of women's prison films (*Caged Heat*), the occasional film by an independent woman director (Barbara Loden's *Wanda*, 1971; Joan Micklin Silver's *Hester Street*, 1975), and the popular "feminist" films (*Alice Doesn't Live Here Anymore*). The best of these—many of the B movies—at least present women who react against their victimization, but seldom does a woman get to play a hero instead of the stereotypical, passive, reactive heroine.

In this respect Alan Pakula's *Klute* (1971) is a film whose significance multiplies every year we get further away from it. Ignore for the moment the curious fact that the film is named for the secondary character, detective John Klute (Donald Sutherland), rather than for the character at the focal point of the movie, Bree Daniels. Jane Fonda dominates this filmed portrait of a women who as prostitute is both classic victim and psychological master of her situation. Screenwriters Andy and Dave Lewis usefully couch their resonant portrait of this archetypal woman in a mystery, but it's clear that the aim of the film is to investigate the complex personality of Bree Daniels, a character who reflects with specific verisimilitude the ultimate dilemma of womankind.

We haven't often matched the sensitivity and intelligence that *Klute* displays since. *Carnal Knowledge* met sexism head on, but it didn't suggest a way out. For the first thirty minutes *Coma* looks promising, then it sacrifices its woman hero. Only *The Turning Point* (1977, Herbert Ross, Arthur Laurents) and *Annie Hall*, recently, have allowed women to play central roles that are active and aggressive, but the former is often soapy, and concludes with a demeaning forced struggle between two women who should have been smarter, and the latter revolves around a character who is essentially a kook: she's in control mainly because Woody Allen/Alvy Singer is so weak.

In general American women and American romance in the seventies have been confined to the armed encampment between *The Other Side of the Mountain* and *The Other Side of Midnight*. The former is an outrageous sob story—the woman as cripple on the Bette Davis model—that is redeemed only by Marilyn Hassett's brilliant, forceful portrayal of Jill Kinmont, entirely devoid of self-pity. The latter is a howling romantic

Roy Scheider manhandles Jane Fonda in *Klute*.

cliché, but at least Marie-France Pisier's character has an opportunity for revenge. As we enter the eighties, that's about all women can expect American movies to give them.

Sexual politics aren't the only subject for essentially realist films about the way we live now. Scattered over the landscape of American movies in the seventies are a number of isolated, but very attractive individual films that don't fit particular categories but, when taken together, suggest a hopeful and potentially productive path for the future. In one way or another, they all deal with ideas of community, they describe elements of the social contract that keep us together, and sometimes they even tentatively suggest ways to renegotiate that timeworn agreement.

Altman's *Nashville* is a model: a film about disparate, isolated individuals who nevertheless depend on each other, even if they're not aware of their mutual interconnection. Jonathan Demme's *Citizen's Band* makes the social bonds clearer, as do most of Michael Ritchie's movies. Sidney Lumet's film of Mary McCarthy's novel *The Group* (1966) proved to be well ahead of its time. Lumet has enjoyed a promiscuously varied career and has probably made far too many movies for his own good, but at least two other New-York-oriented Lumet films bear mention: *Bye Bye Braverman* (1968), which has attained the status of a cult classic because it affectionately portrays the literary subculture, and *Dog Day Afternoon* (1975), from Frank Pierson's script which is a deservedly popular contemporary vision of the absurd dilemmas of life on the edge of American society, grotesquely if at times laughably distorted by the power of the

291

media to create a fictional reality that often seems more important than life as it's lived on the street.

Both Paul Williams and James Bridges have dealt intelligently with students' lives—another special case of the social contract—in *Dealing* (1972) and *The Paper Chase* (1973), respectively. Lamont Johnson's *The Last American Hero* (1973) and Michael Schultz's *Greased Lightning* (1977) are good examples of still more specific topics handled with some empathy and understanding. Sam Peckinpah's *Junior Bonner* (1972, his best film, I think) and Cliff Robertson's *J. W. Coop* (1972) provided interesting, if isolated, images of the world of rodeos. Philip Kaufman's *The White Dawn* (1974) suggests interesting possibilities in historical material.

Claudia Weill's *Girl Friends* (1978) stands as a model of how to make an absorbing movie out of the relationships of everyday life. Joan Micklin Silver's *Between the Lines* (1977) and Raphael D. Silver's *On the Yard* (1979) are equally sensitive portrayals of groups of people in interesting situations. The aim isn't visceral drama, it's intelligent—and friendly— description of the way we live. All three of these films, it's no surprise to discover, were independent East Coast productions.

Robert Mulligan is a notably underrated director who has often shown a particular taste for the geometry of human relationships, ever since *Love with the Proper Stranger* (1963). He also evinces a rare affection for his characters. These qualities combine with the passionate, melodramatic realism of Richard Price's novel to make *Bloodbrothers* (1978) one of the more unusual films of the last few years. This portrait of Italian-American working-class family life in the Bronx verges on maudlin exaggeration, but Mulligan's directorial kindness manages to keep the film under control.

This is a widely varied group of films, meant only to suggest the range for realist film. If there's one characteristic they share besides a basic concern for the relationship between an individual and the community, it is an abiding interest in how a job is done. To a large extent, character is defined by profession.

One filmmaker in the seventies has made a specialty of character defined by profession: Robert Redford. The films he has produced for himself reveal a continuing interest in how a certain kind of work is done that makes them more like each other than they are like other films by their directors. *Downhill Racer* (1969) and *The Candidate* (1972), both directed by Michael Ritchie, combine Ritchie's interest in competition with Redford's obsession with work. They remain perhaps the most knowledgeable movies about their respective subject professions— amateur sports and politics. *Jeremiah Johnson* (1972), directed by Sydney

Between the Lines had more interesting women in it than any six average films of the seventies including Lindsay Crouse (once again), Gwen Welles, and Jill Eikenberry.

Pollack, is less specific; it's a reprise of the pioneer role, abstracted to reveal the essential molding forces of that experience. Most important of the Redford-produced movies is of course *All the President's Men* (1976), which Alan Pakula directed from a script prepared by William Goldman. It's an important historical story, of course, but it gets much of its power because—under Redford's guidance—it makes it clear that Woodward and Bernstein, boy reporters, weren't acting out of any strong political convictions. They accomplished what they did because they were in love with their jobs as reporters, and they wanted to win this game. The film brilliantly depicts the obsessive, often boring groundwork of reporting: the endless interviews, the phone calls, the lists, the dead-end leads, the red herrings, and the ultimate dependence of all reporters on someone in the know eventually spilling the beans. Woodward and Bernstein aren't heroes at all in the old-fashioned image. The Watergate case wasn't cracked because two crusading journalists decided that it would be, but because these two reporters relentlessly fulfilled their parts in an ongoing process.

"Woodstein" may be the heroic myth of the seventies now, but the film's roots, like the real myth, lie in the day-to-day reality of work. A proper understanding of the way we live now stems from the effective portrayal of the material of everyday life. Movies capture this better than any other medium, and our sense of the mythos is nurtured and strengthened by our knowledge of the realistic ethos.

293

The China Syndrome (1979, directed by James Bridges)—the most pointed, and perhaps also the most influential political film of the last ten years—also centers on the character of an investigative reporter. In fact, so much attention is paid to Jane Fonda's role as an ambitious television news performer that it threatens to distract from the main business at hand. Producer-stars Fonda and Michael Douglas had no way of knowing, of course, that the near meltdown at Three Mile Island would take place only days after their movie was released. With hindsight we realize that *The China Syndrome*, despite the feverish and dramatic relevance of its subject, seems to want to melodramatize the logic of the anti-nuclear power movement.

It's as if the filmmakers were afraid that the environmental story they were telling wasn't exciting enough by itself. Ironically, Three Mile Island quickly proved this wasn't true.

Reality is often sufficient.

9

Who's Talking?
Cassavetes, Altman, and Coppola

Someone writes a book, you know who's talking to you. At its best, reading is a sophisticated form of conversation and the personality of the author is an essential part of the experience. Writers you like or admire are friends, in a way. They may not hear your end of the conversation, but, at least in theory they're aware of it.

As a medium, film seems to be a different matter entirely. So many individuals contribute to a movie, so many economic, industrial, sociological, and mythic forces operate to mold the eventual product, that often it seems as if films haven't any distinct parentage. Their authors are so numerous that movies often appear to be self-generating, as if each cinematic generation carried within itself the complete genetic pattern for the next.

They replicate like clones, or like asexual aphids. The little green bugs that suck the life out of roses and tomatoes need only one father a year to produce hundreds of duplicate generations. Similarly, the movies need only occasional progenitors, surviving quite well generation after generation with only the sustenance of the great nurturing financial mothers, the studios. Should one film thrive, it immediately becomes the template for a dozen others. The stream of replication doesn't stop until the ecology becomes so imbalanced that environmental economic laws of natural selection begin to work to kill off that profligate subspecies, only to replace it with another.

Biology—or perhaps biological economics—seems a better intellectual model for the study of film than any other naturalistically determinist system, better certainly than the sort of philosophical and esthetic arguments that characterize criticism of literature and the arts.

No one seems to be in charge here. Psychologically, this has resulted in the curious phenomenon of the auteur policy, the dominant cinematic critical principle since it was first phrased by the filmmaker/critics of the French New Wave more than twenty years ago. Strictly speaking, auteur policy describes the way things should be, not the way they are. Often, it looks like a desperate attempt to impose order on the otherwise happily anarchic ecological system of film.

Film will never be—and shouldn't be—as neatly personal and precise as, say, literature or painting. The singular value of movies is that they are wildly communal enterprises, more like building pyramids than writing private lyric poetry. As a critical theory, the auteur policy has resulted in some of the more absurd commentary on movies in recent years. What nonsense to think that the very strength of a personal style should be enough to make a director of interest. Yet, strictly considered as a policy—a plan—who can argue with auteurism? When filmmakers hide behind the impersonality of the medium, they lie whether they intend to or not. No matter how many people have a hand in the construction of a film, it's people who build it, not machines, not natural laws. And people should take the responsibility: it's a moral imperative, like signing letters to the editor.

I've tried to indicate the massive contributions of collaborators and technicians in previous chapters and to give a sense of the economic and cultural forces that mold movies. Nevertheless, it should also be clear that there are a number of dominant personalities in American film now. Moreover, we have to admit that by far the greatest number of really interesting and influential movies are the products of individual sensibilities. It's a very good feeling, sitting in the mass audience, to hear an individual voice in movies. So often all we hear is the creaking of the gears in the entertainment machine.

The five filmmakers who are the subjects of this and the next chapter were not selected as a pantheon (Andrew Sarris's term for the best and the brightest in his useful survey *American Cinema: Directors and Directions: 1929–1968*). They may yet turn out to be the major filmmakers of the seventies, and indeed a critical consensus seems to be developing in this direction,[1] but that's not the point. They're not important simply because they're auteurs with evident styles; they're important because of what they say, not how they say it. They are filmmakers I personally like hearing from. They aren't the only admirable filmmakers working in commercial

American film today. Far from it. Woody Allen, Alan Pakula, Haskell Wexler, and Bill Gunn are equally interesting, I think. Spielberg and Lucas, Nichols and Schultz, may get it together yet. Philip Kaufman, Jonathan Demme, James Bridges, Robert Benton, Terrence Malick, and others all have the potential to produce significant bodies of work in the eighties.

But in the late '70s, these five were at the "hot center" of American film. None of them except perhaps Cassavetes is particularly an innovator. Their films are traditional in form, but then that's the norm for the seventies. Three of them—Cassavetes, Altman, and Coppola—have been highly influential role models for the present generation. The other two—Ritchie and Mazursky—are well worth emulating. I have a feeling their influence will be felt acutely during the next five years. All of them have managed to turn the powerful engine of commercial film to work that's personal, intimate, intelligent—even wise.

John Cassavetes and the Mystique of the Actor

Here's a scene from *Minnie and Moskowitz*. Minnie Moore (Gena Rowlands) is having lunch with one Zelmo Swift (Val Avery), a sad, middle-aged man whose paunch is more obvious than his hip sideburns and mustache. The lunch date has been born out of sheer desperation. Each man in Minnie's life is more disappointing than the last. Poor Zelmo will prove to be no exception. He launches into a monologue that's as funny as it is sad. It's Cassavetes at his best:

ZELMO: Oh, I forgot to say that you're modest. There isn't one person out of a million people that would not smile when you're talking about them. Did you know that? When I was a kid I used to say, "You know, there's something about you"—and there would be immediate interest. How come you called me? Listen, when you called me, what made you call me? *Minnie can't answer.*
ZELMO: That's okay—I understand. Your bone structure's interesting, too. Your hair...the way you dress...the shape of your mouth...I would say that you're Slavic. Or Swedish. What are you?
MINNIE: I'm English.
ZELMO: Oh, English, of course. Minnie, I don't know what to say. I don't go out very often. I'm actually scared of women. I suppose you must be frightened of men, too. So I don't talk to them often...women. I say, "Hello," "hello, how are you?" But I'm very interested in the arts; the arts: ballet, opera, theater, concerts. I like poetry: Keats, Shelley, Byron, Shakespeare, Swinburne, Wordsworth...I like them. I've been reading since I'm twelve years old. I wear glasses now, I've read so much.
MINNIE: That's funny. I would have taken you for a businessman.
ZELMO: I hate business, Minnie, It's funny, 'cause I'm a fairly rich man, but

297

After his scene with Minnie, Zelmo (Val Avery) decks Moskowitz (Seymour Cassel) the parking lot attendant as Minnie (Gena Rowlands) looks on.

I hate making money. I don't know what to do with it. I get up in the morning, I ask myself, Zelmo, what am I gonna do with my money? I give it to charity, I give it to friends. I buy a big house, take a vacation—from what, I don't know? I'm not married anymore. I was married to a woman that was...a very rare woman, we had no children...it didn't last...not very long...I made a mistake on our wedding night...personal stuff, you know. You're very easy to talk to, Minnie. You look like you care about me. That's a terrific quality you have—a rare quality.

Zelmo's about to make his play. They haven't even ordered lunch yet. Minnie is flustered. She tries to put him off. So Zelmo jumps right into his confession:

Minnie, I got to tell you...my problem is that I have hair down my back, and on my chest, and down my arms...but not on my legs—my legs are very smooth. I don't know why I'm telling you this....

Minnie sticks it out for a few more embarrassed moments, then gets up to go. Zelmo is furious:

Always with blondes. They got some kind of Swedish suicide impulse in them. Took a girl out to lunch once—the next thing you know she wants me to kick her. I said—me kick you—for what? What's that supposed to be...something? (*he looks around and catches the waiter's attention*) Check—may I have the check, please?[2]

298

Vintage Cassavetes: it's anecdotal, in other words, representative but heightened and exaggerated for effect; the rhythms are brilliantly natural, contributing to the shock of recognition; and the speech is so thick with character you could cut it. Actors dream of bits like this. And acting, its art and craft, is the key to John Cassavetes's cinema. He started as an actor (he's a good one) and he still acts to make money to finance his own films. He seems to be more interested in the process of shooting a film than he is in the end result, and he designs his movies more often than not as attractive exercises for himself and his actor friends and relations.

Minnie and Moskowitz, A Woman Under the Influence, and *Opening Night* are constructed as showcases for his wife, Gena Rowlands. *Husbands, Minnie, A Woman Under the Influence*, and *The Killing of a Chinese Bookie* provide delectable roles for Cassavetes and buddies Peter Falk and Ben Gazzara (in *Husbands*), Seymour Cassel (*Moskowitz*), Falk again, and Gazzara again, respectively. There's usually a good bit part for the remarkable character actor (and quondam filmmaker) Timothy Carey, and John's and Gena's mothers show up with regularity, as do assorted kids and in-laws. Cassavetes's movies are family affairs; in fact they're like nothing so much as home movies, with all the problems and advantages thereof.

They go on too long, they're often too private and self-indulgent, they never seem to come to the point, they're loosely plotted—certainly leagues away from the intricately constructed Hollywood formula film—they don't seem to show much care for production values, and they tend to be repetitive. When Cassavetes finds an idea he likes, he'll run it into the ground. But they're also exhilaratingly verisimilitudinous—they're slices of life cut with precision enough for a biopsy; at their best they sing with pleasure in the craft of acting; and taken together they give us a rich portrait of contemporary sexual politics and its attendant anxieties that is unrivaled in the medium. They may be home movies, but these amateurs are professionals, workers who love their craft.

The result of this classically amateur provenance is that, as the critical cliché has it, people are either passionate devotees of John Cassavetes's movies, or they despise them. The key, I think, is how far you are willing to go to participate in this rather self-absorbed process. Cassavetes seems constitutionally incapable of playing to a broad audience. He makes movies for himself and his friends because that's all he knows how to do. What's surprising is that he has been able to find an audience large enough to support this ongoing project. He has, I think, because despite all the aforementioned crotchety difficulties one has with his movies, there is an essential humanism there that's undeniable. It's concentrated to make a sociological point in *A Woman Under the Influence*, and that's why that film has been his most widely seen and most financially remunerative. But it's available in any Cassavetes movie, for those who want to actively participate in the process. To do so, you have to give up a number of ideas about what a (commercial) movie should be—ideas about pace and construction and meaning—and learn to appreciate John's naturalistic rhythms.

Cassavetes's films may seem avant-garde: they are certainly the closest approach by commercial films to the so-called New American Cinema of personal art films. In the fifties, Cassavetes even used to hang out with Jonas Mekas, the prophet of the American avant-garde in the sixties and seventies, and a filmmaker who himself has a particular fondness for the home-movie style. But really, there isn't that much that's innovative about Cassavetes's cinema. He's not alone in what he's doing: Altman often gives his actors indulgent space in which to develop shtik. Other actors have directed similar films. Both Falk and Gazzara have done some television work. Timothy Carey, according to his friend Cassavetes, has been at work on a film called "The Little Old Ladies of Pasadena" for eight years now. The phenomenon has even spread abroad: Albert Finney's remarkable *Charlie Bubbles* bore some affinities to American actors' movies. In France, Pierre Barouh's exceptional *Ça Va, Ça Vient* (1970) captured a brighter atmosphere that was equally loose, realistic, and human.

Moreover, the shape of Cassavetes's actor-centered moodpieces was foreshadowed on the stage as early as Chekhov, a playwright who was entirely dependent on the talents and techniques of his actors, the Moscow Art Theater—as the two consecutive productions of *The Seagull*, one a failure, the second an enormous success, showed with the clarity of a laboratory experiment. Like Cassavetes's films, Chekhov's plays are about rather sad people—losers, if you like—who don't ever seem to get anywhere, but who enthrall audiences with their inaction, their self-centeredness, and their cosmically funny failures. The creation of pure atmosphere—and a rather lackadaisically maudlin one at that—has been legitimate ever since. Not only is Cassavetes not an innovator, but he can trace his roots straight to one of the grandfathers of the modern theater!

Perhaps that's part of the problem. His films are highly theatrical. There isn't one of them that couldn't be converted easily into a stage play. They take place almost exclusively in interiors. Except for *Minnie and Moskowitz*, lighter in tone than its companions, the number of outdoor scenes is so small that each of them is especially memorable: the Museum of Modern Art garden in *Shadows*, the driveway scene at the end of *Husbands* ("Ma! Dad's home! Boy, are *you* gonna get it!"), Nick Longhetti's somber romp with his kids on the beach after Mabel has been committed in *A Woman Under the Influence*. The actor/director took his cast and crew to London for an important sequence in *Husbands*—all we see is the inside of a hotel

The clan: With Cassel here are four members of the Cassavetes family, including Gena Rowlands, her mother Lady Rowlands, and John's mother Katharine Cassavetes.

room, a restaurant, and a couple of rainswept streets that could easily have been shot in New York.

Clearly, Cassavetes's people aren't outdoor folk. They don't thrive in the sunshine. They're interior characters in both senses of the word, and that seems more a theatrical trait than a cinematic characteristic. The director further emphasizes this with a very insouciant, almost sloppy mise en scène. Everything is organized around the actor and his work. Closeups are preferred. Most scenes are shot in long takes. Cassavetes's technique is to load the camera with as much film as it can carry, then turn it on and let the actors do their stuff. If a scene works in one take, he's not going to shoot it over again to get reverse angles and master shots. If a character's out of the frame, so be it. It's the words and delivery that are most important. *A Woman Under the Influence*, which takes place almost entirely in Nick and Mabel's house (a real location, not a set, of course), was shot essentially from two camera setups in the entrance hall. Cassavetes used a long lens to get in close to the action without disturbing the actors by the presence of the camera. About the only concession he makes to the art of the camera (as opposed to the art of the people in front of it) is to liven up a static scene occasionally with a handheld camera, which further in-

301

creases the claustrophobia so characteristic of his visual style.

At least in the theater, although we're confined to a room, we have the useful perspective of the tenth-row center (or the last row in the balcony). In John Cassavetes's theatrical cinema we're brought up on stage, into the heat of the verbal action. It's like sitting too close to the screen. It's disturbing. But so are the people we are watching, and so it fits, probably all too well, considering some of the criticism Cassavetes has come in for.

He enjoys shooting in restaurants and bars because those are the locations where people have nothing much to do but talk, and talk is at the center of his world—a universe of discourse. In fact, a better theatrical referent than Chekhov might be Harold Pinter. Both the filmmaker and the playwright deal with characters who at first appear from a comic perspective only to reveal in sharp and often poignant outbursts the violence and frustration which always lies just beneath the surface. Both take particular pleasure in the colors of speech—both are erstwhile actors who are very aware just what a pleasure it is to deliver monologues with wit and style—fun for the actors, certainly, and perhaps also for audiences. Pinter is more elegantly fey; Cassavetes is certainly more naturalistic, less symbolic, and elusive: that's to his credit. Neither cares very much where the piece is going; they just want to catch these actor/characters in the act of being. Existential? Yes, I'm afraid so. Both are eventually limited by their commitment to an essentially pessimistic worldview. But while Pinter's people take it out on each other, tyrannize each other, and kill, Cassavetes's people seldom do. If they hurt one another, and they do, it's not out of viciousness, but because they can't help themselves, much less each other.

Perhaps the ultimate Cassavetes movie is *Mikey and Nicky*, which isn't by Cassavetes at all. Elaine May had written the piece as a play expressly for friends Cassavetes and Falk. She filmed it in 1973, then went through a dithering process of editing that lasted years and got her involved in lawsuits with Paramount. The film was finally released—more precisely, dumped—in December 1976. It probably wouldn't have gained a very large audience anyway. The dark story of two Philadelphia lowlifes who get involved in a mutually self-destructive but classic film-noir plot, the film misses an essential element of Cassavetes style: the humor, the sense of play that works to balance our perception of his people, nearly all of whom lead lives of quiet desperation. (*Mikey and Nicky* is still a good film, by the way: markedly superior to the *Taxi Drivers* of the seventies which are equally humorless but entertain through false, hysterical superdramatics.)

There isn't a character in any Cassavetes film who isn't at base still adolescent. Maybe it's an inherent quality of actors, this childlike sense of play. It's certainly most evident when John and Ben and Peter clown around together in *Husbands*. Nevertheless, although he deals almost ex-

Mikey and Nicky, Cassavetes and Falk, on a Philadelphia bus in Elaine May's film.

clusively with middle-aged characters (*Shadows* and *A Child Is Waiting* are the exceptions), Cassavetes is never more than a good line drive from the schoolyard.

So what? The point is well taken: the child is father to the man, and most of us aren't very far away from those images of ourselves that we still idealize from high school or college. If we'd reached a real maturity, we'd be better able to deal constructively with wives and husbands and lovers and friends. But in general we can't, and that is what John Cassavetes's movies are all about. When Lelia has her first sexual experience in *Shadows,* her reaction is, "I didn't know it could be so awful." *Faces* is a harrowing closeup of the painfully slow disintegration of a marriage. Harry, Archie, and Gus of *Husbands* can't come to terms with their middle-aged selves or their wives: "Besides sex—and my wife's very good at it—I love you guys best," says Harry. You begin to understand the reasons for macho behavior, a shield against the world, a written role to play.

Minnie and Moskowitz provides an important contrast: at first, nobody in the film has any more luck with the opposite sex than Cassavetes's earlier characters, but these people, Minnie and Seymour, at least start single. The film is a true comedy: it ends with a very affecting marriage. If the troubles then begin, we don't know anything about them. In this context, *A Woman Under the Influence* is a much more humane film than it might at first appear to be. As destructive as it is, the relationship between Mabel and Nick at least is rooted in commitment, perhaps love, that is never re-

303

ally questioned, even if it also is never quite expressed.

Whatever position we take regarding Cassavetes' people—and sometimes you wish they could at least spend a holiday in a Robert Altman movie: they wouldn't feel out of place and they might even enjoy themselves—the fact remains that their writer/director's career has been exemplary. John Cassavetes is the one true hero of independent commercial cinema. Other filmmakers have made their own films, arduously, according to their own lights, and eventually got to show them in museums and perhaps a handful of art houses. This is true of the entire New American Cinema movement. Still others—Altman, Coppola, and now Lucas and Spielberg—have discovered a workable modus vivendi within the studio system, producing their own films (which look and feel a lot more like standard Hollywood product than Cassavetes's idiosyncratic work) and convincing the studios to distribute them through normal channels.

But only John Cassavetes has managed to continue producing and distributing his own movies in channels closely parallel to the commercial network. He has at least the chance of being seen by mass audiences, and that is unique.

How did he accomplish this? Let him describe it:

> In 1954 I was an assistant stage manager in New York and in the same year I finished my first film, *The Night Holds Terror.* In 1955 I acted in thirty-seven live television shows; in 1956 I did five; in 1957 I made three movies, including a good one called *Edge of the City.* At the end of 1957 we began filming a picture called *Shadows,* and that kept me busy until 1960. That was the year my wife had our first baby, and the year I did a TV series, followed by a quickie movie in Ireland. In 1961—that was a bad year—a lot of waiting. In 1962 I directed my first Hollywood film, then signed a big contract with the same studio for more punishment. In 1964 I left that studio and made my second Hollywood film, which wasn't exactly a Hollywood film to start with. In fact it had a chance of being a very good film. But somehow it became a Hollywood film under the guidance of Hollywood people... From 1964 to 1965 I stayed home, looked at trees, at my family, wrote several scripts, and learned patience. In 1965 I took a job running a company—a TV package company—in partnership with Screen Gems. After six months of that, I looked back at my accomplishments and I could find only two that I considered worthwhile—*Shadows* and *Edge of the City.* All the rest of my time had been spent playing games—painful and stupid, falsely satisfying and economically rewarding. Then at the end of 1965 *Faces* was born, out of friendships and mutual dissatisfactions.[3]

After four false starts, one in New York, three in Hollywood, Cassavetes was finally on the road to being a working filmmaker on his own terms.

Faces took three years to complete, but it was a success in its own terms and from then on Cassavetes could alternate between occasional juicy movie roles to make money (*The Dirty Dozen, Rosemary's Baby, Capone, Two-Minute Warning, The Fury*), most of them as a devilish villain, and work on his own films, which he has surprisingly managed to prepare, shoot, edit, and release every two years from 1970 to the present.

Shadows (1959) was an auspicious debut; in France the New Wave was just beginning; Antonioni and Fellini were making waves of their own in Italy; in Britain, the filmmakers of the Free Cinema movement were beginning to make features. The year 1959 was truly a watershed in world cinema, and John Cassavetes's *Shadows* served as the representative milestone in this country. Jonas Mekas memorialized the event in one of his *Village Voice* columns thirteen years later:

> The screening of John Cassavetes's *Shadows,* late in December 1958, be-
> came an occasion from which the rise of the New American Cinema is
> usually dated. I still remember the excitement some of us felt that late
> night, at the Paris theatre. We stood there, in the lobby, and we didn't
> want to leave. Independent film in America, known at that time as ex-
> perimental film, had been going strong since 1943, but it was beginning to
> need a fresh impulse. The screening of *Shadows* and, a few months later,
> *Pull My Daisy* (Robert Frank was there too, at the screening of *Shadows*)
> started moving the strange forces which grew and spread and exploded into
> what eventually became known as underground film.[4]

A few months after that wintery Rite of Spring, Cassavetes himself sounded the clarion in *Film Culture*, which was fast becoming the journal of the independent cinema movement. In an article entitled "What's Wrong with Hollywood" he wrote: "Hollywood is not failing. It has failed." He concluded that "the probability of a resurrection of the industry through individual expression is slim, for the men of new ideas will not compromise themselves to Hollywood's department heads. These artists have come to realize that to compromise an idea is to soften it, to make an excuse for it, to betray it."[5]

It's all the more ironic, then, that Cassavetes himself nevertheless attempted to go the Hollywood route. It set his filmmaking career back five years.

Shadows succeeded because, almost naively, it broke all the narrative rules of commercial filmmaking. It was largely improvised by a cast of unknowns that included Lelia Goldoni, Ben Carruthers, Hugh Hurd, and Rupert Crosse. It was shot in grainy black-and-white 16 mm, and it has the unmistakable rhythms of home-movie reality. Scenes go on as long as they

Rupert Crosse, Hugh Hurd and Lelia Goldoni in *Shadows*.

will, there's none of the cross-cutting of Hollywood's découpage classique that works to liven up a simple story. We have time to get to know these people, and if often it's too apparent that they are working at acting, there's something nevertheless charming and refreshing about this style. It's Brechtian, in a way, since it brashly admits its fiction. We know we're watching actors, not real people, and paradoxically that gives the film a riveting sense of reality. Jean-Luc Godard was doing something like this in France at the time. It's an attitude toward the underlying assumptions of filmmaking that's exceptionally modern. It's easy to understand why *Shadows* became a model for the new independent cinema (with which Cassavetes was never again associated): it strikes at the very foundations of the Hollywood dream movie. It's not entirely a conscious act of rebellion, but that makes it all the more likeable.

The story of *Shadows* involves a Black family, a brother and sister (Carruthers and Goldoni) who pass for white, and an older brother (Hurd), a jazz musician, who doesn't. Lelia dates white men, and her brothers' reaction to this forms the basic tension of the plot. Such a theme must have seemed avant-garde at the time, but it's not really the point of the film. Cassavetes was more interested in the interactions of his actor/ characters within each particular encounter. As he later put it talking to an interviewer, "I'm not really listening to dialogue. I'm watching to see if they're communicating something and expressing something....I'm just watching a conversation."[6] He captures these people on the wing. *Shadows* doesn't have the intensity that scripted dialogue would bring to later movies, but it survives very well as an almost unique slice of bohemian life in New York in the late fifties. As ethnography alone it's invaluable.

Too Late Blues (1961), which Cassavetes directed for Paramount, is an attempt to capture some of the same moods and themes in a standard commercial picture. Cassavetes acts in it along with Bobby Darin and Stella Stevens, and that really tells you all you need to know about the differences between the independent film and the studio film. Cassavetes considered it a failure, but to his surprise it led to a multi-picture contract with Paramount, a contract he broke almost immediately because he thought he'd have more freedom doing a film with producer Stanley Kramer.

A Child Is Waiting (1962), from a script by Abby Mann, starring Burt Lancaster and Judy Garland, uses some documentary techniques to investigate the world of retarded children. Most critics think it works pretty well, and judged against what we might regard as the standard Hollywood liberal film on the same subject, that's an arguable evaluation. But not from Cassavetes's viewpoint. Kramer took the film away from him and had it recut, and he now disowns it. Cassavetes sees it as a typically liberal Kramer tract whose point is that "retarded children are separate and alone and therefore should be in institutions with others of their kind. My film [before it was recut] said that retarded children could be anywhere, anytime, and that the problem is that we're a bunch of dopes, that it's our problem more than the kids'."[7]

After an abortive attempt at developing television series in association with Screen Gems, Cassavetes decided it might be worth the effort to try an entirely independent production along the lines of *Shadows*. Friend Maurice McEndree sifted through piles of screenplays Cassavetes had been writing and came up with "The Marriage," which John had originally intended as a stage play. It formed the basis for *Faces*. Another friend, Al Ruban, bought some secondhand equipment in New York and headed west. The cast they assembled was composed mostly of actors Cassavetes had worked with before, and friends. Actors also performed most of the technical jobs on the film. Shooting took five months in early 1966; editing took two years. The film was shot in 16 mm, which Cassavetes discovered was extremely difficult (at that time) to work with on the editing table. He spent much of his time repairing broken sprocket holes. None of the sound had been transferred to film during shooting because of the expense involved. Months later, Cassavetes and Ruban discovered that the soundtrack was seriously out of sync. "The next four months," Ruban recounts, "were spent cutting little pieces out of the sound, and adding to and subtracting from different places, trying to fit them to the action of the picture."

Lynn Carlin, one of the faces.

The first rough cut was in the neighborhood of six hours. Whole sequences had to be discarded, including one brilliant forty-minute scene in a bar and several major scenes that further developed the women's characters. Eventually, the film was whittled down to a potentially commercial length.* Yet one has the feeling that the film would work even better at its original length, since so much of its effect depends upon duration. Ingmar Bergman's not dissimilar *Scenes from a Marriage* exists in two versions, the television episodes and the feature-film synopsis. The longer version is clearly superior.

Exactly what Cassavetes demands from an audience is more obvious in *Faces* than in any of his other films. These people don't work in screen time, they work in real time. Force them into screen time with its neatly edited ellipses and thoughtful connections, and they become characters; leave them in real time, rough, sometimes boring, with idiosyncratic rhythms, disconcerting jumps, and inactive holes, and they tend to remain people. The effect of watching people rather than characters on the screen is startling, and I think, worth the effort films like these require. Filmmakers as disparate as Antonioni, Andy Warhol (in *Chelsea Girls,* his best film), and Jacques Rivette (*Out One, l'Amour fou*) have experimented with real time, and in every case, as with *Faces,* the result is sometimes maddening but eventually addictive. Once audiences understand the logic of this structure, they

---

* The original version is preserved in the published script.

become voyeuristically, hypnotically involved in the realistic action.

If most of these films, like *Faces* itself, tend to deal with relationships that are disintegrating, it is because breakdowns seem to lend themselves better to this lengthy treatment than constructive acts. It's a problem: form seems to dictate theme in this respect.

Beyond its experiments with time and acting, *Faces* also works well because it's one of very few American movies that deal with the central connection between middle-class lifestyles and the developing counterculture of the late sixties, and did so from the more complex point of view of the generation over thirty.

After the success of *Faces* (prizes at the Venice Film Festival, three Academy Award nominations, and a significant box-office gross), Cassavetes plunged into a series of films that confronted the same basic marital relationship from different angles. *Husbands* (1970) focuses intently on the "bustling, bravura ego" (as Cassavetes called it) of the men, ignoring the

Husbands pose in an early snapshot, argue in the street, and drink for twenty minutes of actual film time in a bar with Flemish lighting.

Cassavetes as director on the set with Rowlands and Falk in A *Woman Under the Influence*.

women almost entirely. Because Cassavetes, Falk, and Gazzara dominate it so, it seems a much more personal film than any of the others. It's certainly one of very few films about the suburban lifestyle of the American middle class, and valuable for that alone.

Minnie and Moskowitz (1972) provides a much-needed antidote to the neurotic atmosphere that pervades all of Cassavetes's other films. Minnie and Seymour aren't necessarily better adjusted than other characters in other films, they're just lucky enough to find themselves in a comedy on the way to a happy ending in marriage and family. (It should be remembered that although Cassavetes produced the film himself, it was made for distribution by Universal.)

Yet *Woman Under the Influence* (1974) could conceivably have started where *Minnie* left off. Nick is not all that different from his predecessor Seymour, and there's an understandable parallelism between the two Gena Rowlands roles. There's no denying the power of the film—it's by far the best portrait we have of the essential impossibility of the housewife's role, and it's a logically harrowing narrative of the painful neurosis that is so often the only response to that dilemma.

Yet by this time in Cassavetes's career we want more. *A Woman Under the Influence* is rare in its understanding of the dehumanizing forces of working-class life as well as sexist marriage patterns, but inasmuch as the film has a political dimension—it makes it clear that this neurosis isn't arbitrary; there are "influences" at work—it stops far too short. As Susan Schenker pointed out in a review of the film:

310

Cassavetes has purposefully designed the film without giving Mabel the slightest chance to explain herself. She has no girlfriend, no sympathetic listener to talk to, and so the deck is neatly stacked against her. It is important not to forget that Mabel is Cassavetes's invention...he hasn't given her any of her own resources to fight back with.[8]

This is a crucial point, I think. Cassavetes's films aren't documentaries, and the intimate relationship between him and his actors further suggests that we have a right to make claims for "character liberation." Schenker goes on to suggest, "Mabel needs to be left alone to work out her *own* problems for herself. She needs to be free of Nick for a while, and free of his friend (and her director) Cassavetes. Perhaps even, Gena should direct her own film next time."

The suggestion isn't entirely facetious. It became clear in Cassavetes's next two films after A Woman Under the Influence that he was locked in a bind of his own. No American writer/director knows more about the triangular relationship between character, acting, and reality. But finally, this isn't enough: the triangle becomes more and more constricting. *The Killing of a Chinese Bookie* (1976), with Gazzara as Cosmo Vitelli, a man squeezed by debts into committing a murder, was like *Mikey and Nicky* an attempt to work within a genre. It's Cassavetes's closest approach to contemporary film noir. *Opening Night* (1977) situates Gena Rowlands as Myrtle Gordon, an actress on the edge of a breakdown, and experiments with the relationship between the play-within-the film (entitled "The Second Woman"—are we supposed to complete the sentence—"Under the Influence"?) and Myrtle's neurotic reality.

Chinese Bookie has the excuse of genre. *Opening Night* has no excuse. Again, the performances are superb—Rowlands, Gazzara, Cassavetes, and Joan Blondell, who plays the author of "The Second Woman." But to what end? Like Ingmar Bergman, with whom he's often compared (*Opening Night* is certainly parallel with *Persona*, *A Woman Under the Influence* with *The Passion of Anna*, *Faces* with *Scenes from a Marriage*), Cassavetes eventually disappoints because he can't or won't extricate himself from this swampy delta of neurotic recrimination. He gives his actors enormous freedom, but he and his actors together team up to repress his characters. For people who go along with him, his films are emotionally draining experiences. But this isn't the only identifying characteristic of realism, as either style or attitude. People do learn to cope, sometimes even successfully; they don't always submit. Except for *Minnie and Moskowitz,* the most spirited of Cassavetes's movies, his characters are in search of a way to liberate themselves from their authors, both writer/director and actors. From *Faces* to *Opening Night*, Cassavetes operates as an artistic tyrant: characters, and fiction, don't have a chance against this champion of actors and

Timothy Agoglia Carey and Ben Gazzara in *The Killing of a Chinese Bookie*. . . .Familiar faces in *Opening Night*.

of a very precise (and often precious), limited reality. Like Bergman's, Cassavetes's films are stuck in the existential fifties. They haven't learned the truth of the sixties, that it is at least possible to take action, that passive suffering isn't the only legitimate response to psychological binds.

If Seymour Moskowitz had his way, I think, and could organize a characters' consciousness-raising session, Forst wouldn't be caught paralyzed on the staircase at the end of *Faces*, he'd walk out; Gus and his pals would have stayed in London at the end of *Husbands*; and Mabel would have realized that her family wasn't so healthy for her after all, despite their love. She would have established a life of her own, separate, no matter how difficult.

Robert Altman and the myth of the character

"An orgy for movie-lovers." That's the phrase Pauline Kael used to describe *Nashville* in her notorious pre-release panegyric for the film.* It's a perfect summary not only of that quintessential Altman movie, but of most of the eleven others he made during the 1970s. It's the ultimate critical metaphor for the work of the filmmaker who more than any other has

---

* Kael reviewed the film in a rough cut several months before it was released. Most other critics were angry that she had stolen a march on them, and the incident received considerable press coverage. She was criticized for judging an early version of the film. (Vincent Canby suggested the next step in this progression might be to review the final draft of the script.) It was also suggested that she was doing a friend a favor. Kael shared the film critic's chair at *The New Yorker* with Penelope Gilliatt, each of them writing six months, then taking six months off. *Nashville* was to be released during Gilliatt's tenure, and Kael wouldn't have had a chance to comment on the film. When all this brouhaha had cleared away, the fact remained that Pauline Kael had simply done her job as a reporter, bringing a newsworthy event to our attention as soon as she had the information rather than abiding by the stately rules of the critics' game.

come to represent for the majority of critics and cinephiles alike most of what's best in the new film style of the last ten years.

It's hard otherwise to get a critical handle on Altman. He doesn't have the obsessions of a Cassavetes or the popular bravura of the kids who direct blockbusters; he's not as sharply intelligent as, say, Ritchie or Mazursky, nor does he exhibit the brooding mythic preoccupations of a director like Coppola. He seems more relaxed than most people now making movies, as if the business were more an avocation than a calling, yet he's made more films in this decade than any pair of his rivals. Maybe he's more prolific because he has a healthy perspective on the art of film; he certainly has shown that he has the business well under control. He's half a generation older than any other director in the New Hollywood except John Cassavetes, and this may explain not only his winningly avuncular cinematic tone of voice but also his passion for shooting film—any type, any place. It's as if he were trying to make up for lost time. He started his feature-film career twice, once in the mid-fifties, once in the late sixties, sandwiching a respectable stint as a journeyman television director in between, and he was forty-five when M*A*S*H had its success. He was smart enough to husband his financial resources in such a way that that film bought him relative independence, and he has used it since to great effect. The result—Kael had it right—has been a real orgy of filmmaking. You can sense the pleasure he takes in doing the work. With Tom in Nashville, he can sing "I'm Easy." He simply loves to shoot film, and he packs as much cinema into each movie as it will hold.

The range of his films has been omnivorous. If there's a characteristic that unites the majority of them, it's an overall ambition to tackle every genre from science fiction (Countdown, 1968, Quintet, 1979) to period gangster (Thieves Like Us, 1974), from war film (M*A*S*H, 1970) to western (McCabe and Mrs. Miller, 1971; Buffalo Bill and the Indians, 1976), from psychological melodrama (That Cold Day in the Park, 1969) to musical (Nashville, 1975) to detective story (The Long Goodbye, 1973) to buddy movie (California Split, 1974). His three most personal projects have been symbolic fantasies: Brewster McCloud (1970), Images (1972), and Three Women (1977). The last two, the only scripts for which Altman is entirely responsible, are the most oblique, tendentious, and problematic. Left completely to his own devices, Altman would be much less interesting: stuffy, rather humorless, and not a little pretentious. He thrives, however, when he can collaborate with a screenwriter. Except for Ring Lardner, Jr., who had written the script for M*A*S*H before Altman got the assignment to direct it, he has worked with relatively unknown screenwriters and, except for Joan Tewkesbury, never more than once. He's curiously promiscuous in this respect, considering the reputation he has for having

The avuncular Altman on the set of *The Long Goodbye* with Nina van Pallandt and Elliott Gould.

developed a stock company of actors and a technical crew that is uniquely stable. He's been only slightly more faithful to a string of eminent cinematographers, having settled into a long-term relationship only recently with Paul Lohmann.

Yet, since M*A*S*H, every Altman film has been immediately identifiable as such, despite the wide range of settings and genres, despite the varied screenwriters, despite the fact that most of the films are based on novels. Partly, it's the sense of humor. More important, I think, it's the richness of the cinematic table he sets. Orgy indeed. He's not at all a thin man, and his gourmandise shows happily on the screen, as well. As Kael put it, "you don't get drunk on images, you're not overpowered—you get elated. . . . It's a pure emotional high, and you don't come down when the picture is over; you take it with you."[9]

As a consequence of this exhilarating approach to the medium, the whole of Altman's work is notably larger than the sum of its parts. Think of Altman-in-general and you're likely to get a warm glow, he's offered up so many goodies over the last nine years. Think of a particular film, however, and you become perplexed. *Nashville* comes exceeding close, but none of his other movies seems wholly satisfying; there are always critical problems.

M*A*S*H is a brilliant antiwar (and antiwar-*film*) satire—until about two-thirds of the way through, when it loses its aim and degenerates into horseplay. *Brewster McCloud* was an ambitious satire, but its targets were too broad: it started with the national anthem and worked its way up. *McCabe and Mrs. Miller* was a little too laid-back, *Images* too arch, *Buffalo Bill* too self-indulgent. You get the idea. If Altman's films are to be judged and evaluated, we'll end up with a reductive image of his career. I'm usually vaguely disappointed with an Altman film. One wants him to be more demanding of himself, not so self-indulgent, a little sharper and more pointed. If his films project a worldview, it's not a very interesting one. It almost seems calculated to play on contemporary hip cynicism. There are few winners in an Altman movie, despite their ironical point of view. Brewster falls to his death in the astrodome; McCabe gets his in the snow, almost as an afterthought; Bowie gets mowed down while Keechie watches screaming in slow motion at the climax of *Thieves Like Us*; *Nashville*'s aim is an assassination attempt; Buffalo Bill's defunct, and Millie, Willie, and Pinky, the *Three Women*, are reduced to catatonic stereotypes.

Yet none of this seems to matter, really. If the truth be told, Robert Altman is not the most thoughtful of filmmakers. He provides themes for his films almost against his will, often tacking on a set of scenes, music, or a soundtrack device after shooting is completed in order to comment on the action and provide a sense of unity where there really isn't any. His films are very much open rather than closed systems. They end only because they have to. In any particular movie, therefore, the sum of the parts is almost always greater than the whole. We may not learn as much from Altman's films as we might; yes, he lets his actors overdo it at times; some of his tricks are painfully obvious, and in general the films seem to have more panache than conviction. So what? With Altman, you remember the good bits: sounds, looks, shtiks, angles, correspondences, convergences, ironies, images: the raw material of moviemaking.

Altman himself seems to have a half-consciousness of this curious state of affairs. It's as if he didn't want audiences to spend much effort looking at the film as a whole. *Brewster McCloud* opens with a pre-credit sequence which introduces René Auberjonois's lecture on birds, which will thread itself through the movie, trying to tie up loose ends. It's a set piece, but it is also a self-conscious commentary. We see the M-G-M lion (who's lost his voice, presciently) as Auberjonois's first words are heard off-screen (it's a pun): "I forgot the opening line...," he says, then on-screen:

> Enough of that, Hobbs! Flight of Birds. Flight of Man. Man's similarity to Birds. Birds' similarity to Man... is the subject at hand. We will deal with them for the next hour or so and hope that we draw no conclusions. Elsewise the subject shall cease to fascinate us and, alas, another dream would be lost.[10]

Gruffly, impatiently, before the film even begins, there is a runthrough of

315

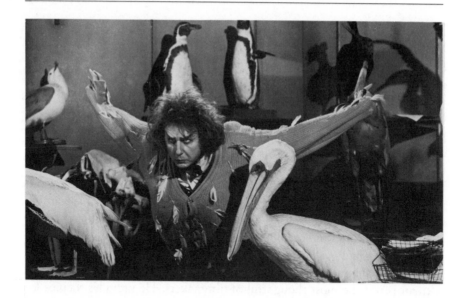

the critical stances toward its symbolism. They are rejected as supercilious, with the warning: "Draw no conclusions." Why? Robert Browning put Altman's esthetic principle this way: "What's come to perfection perishes." Altman has a distinct fear of finishing a work, not in the sense of ending it, necessarily, but rather of bringing it to full fruition, of realizing its implications. "Elsewise the subject shall cease to fascinate us." Altman has this childlike worry of losing the dream quality. Maybe it's a reaction to the high seriousness which weighs down so many films that pretend to the condition of Great Art. That's a rather healthy response, if it's true. More probably, it's a defense mechanism. Altman's most personal films, *Images* and *Three Women*, are both dreams, but not dreamy; they're too heavy for their own good. He doesn't trust himself on his own and, from the evidence, rightly so. He protects himself by playing with other people's scripts. Eventually they become very much his own movies, but this essentially reactive process allows him to add the ironic dimension that characterizes his best work: it's the basic stance of the critic, which is perhaps why he is so widely admired among film critics.

We can see this most clearly in his work with actors. All American directors have benefited tremendously from the exciting pool of acting talent that has developed since the mid-sixties; Altman more than most. Like Cassavetes, he has a high respect for their craft; unlike Cassavetes, he pushes them into character. The fictional nature of the people in Altman's movies is such a distillate of experience that his characters often verge perilously close on caricature. The style works only because of the thoroughly ironic context in which we see these creations.

Actors don't only act with Altman; they write. *Nashville* was a wildly collaborative effort. The cast indulged in their own professional orgy of songwriting, and the results are superb parodies of country music. The riveting focus of *Three Women* is certainly Shelley Duvall's archetypal Millie. Altman claims she wrote 80 percent of the dialogue herself. John Considine played a couple of good small roles for Altman, turned in a couple of outstanding performances in the Altman-produced *Welcome to L.A.* and *The Late Show*, then wrote the treatment for *A Wedding*. No wonder plots seem superfluous in Altman movies; character is clearly an obsession.

A list of the actors who have done especially good work in Altman films reads like an honor roll. He discovered Shelley Duvall in Houston for *Brewster McCloud*. He's the only director who's been able to utilize Elliott Gould's sloppy contemporary charm to full effect (in *M*A*S*H*, *The Long Goodbye*, and *California Split*). He's seen the dramatic potential of television comedians like Henry Gibson (Dr. Verringer in *The Long Goodbye* and Haven Hamilton in *Nashville*) and Lily Tomlin (Linnea Reese in *Nashville*). Among the leading actors who partly owe their reputations to him are Sally Kellerman, René Auberjonois, Keith Carradine, and Michael Murphy. Then there's the "stock company": John Schuck, Bert

This publicity still for *Nashville* identified all 24 actors and actresses, Altman later doubled the ante in *A Wedding*.

317

Remsen, Gwen Welles, Timothy Brown, Robert Doqui, and Geraldine Chaplin, among others. Interestingly, none of these people, nor any of the established actors—Donald Sutherland, Warren Beatty, Stacy Keach, George Segal, Karen Black, Sissy Spacek, for example—who have worked with him occasionally, project personas of great strength. Altman wants and needs outsiders, introverts, kooks.

Altman lovingly photographs these people. He knows very well how a performance can be deepened and enlarged by scenic context and cinematic technique. He uses more of the technical resources of contemporary film than any other major director. Cassavetes sets the camera up and lets the actors work. Altman is just as engaged behind the camera as his actors are in front of it. Diane Jacobs has a telling name for Altman's mise en scène; she calls it "actualism," to distinguish it from "realism." At first glance, it seems as if Altman's characters and their situations are realistic, but in each case they're distorted. We're watching actors, not people, and the actors are performing. Similarly, settings and situations appear within the limits of verisimilitude, but these are all very strong fictions—in fact, often commentaries upon previously existing fictions—and the teller is always a focus of attention with the tale. Always, there is an element of ironic distancing—elsewise, the subject shall cease to fascinate.

Robert Altman was born in Kansas City in 1925. His father was a successful insurance salesman. He was raised as a Catholic, took a college degree in mathematics, and saw service—according to the standard biography—in World War II as a bomber pilot. He returned to Kansas City and took a job making industrial films, and at the same time tried his hand at writing a couple of feature scripts. By 1957 he was able to put together his first feature, *The Delinquents*, which he wrote, produced, and directed. Tom Laughlin starred. It was released by United Artists. The same year, he and his friend and collaborator, George W. George, put together a documentary, *The James Dean Story*, for Warner Bros.

For the next ten years he busied himself in filmed television, directing episodes of such shows as *Alfred Hitchcock Presents*, *Bus Stop*, *Kraft Suspense Theatre*, *Bonanza*, and *Whirlibirds*. The New York-based directors of prestigious live television programs in the fifties may have been able to parlay their reputations on the small screen into feature careers with relative ease, but the journeyman directors of filmed episodes in Hollywood in the sixties had a much tougher time of it. There is no evidence that Altman accomplished anything of much value in his television work, but he seems to have been an independent sort. There is an apocryphal story that Hitchcock fired him after his second episode of the show because he had the temerity to reject a script. One of his projects, an hour-long show called

Once Upon a Savage Night, produced in 1964, was later padded and released as a theatrical film, *Nightmare in Chicago* (1969). But shows like *Bonanza* and *Whirlibirds* aren't what you might call major opportunities to show your stuff. (Are *McCabe* and *Brewster* reactions to the TV situation dramas?)

In 1967, ten years after his second feature, Altman put together his third, *Countdown*, a decent science-fiction movie for Warner Bros. (from a script by television writer Loring Mandel) that was eclipsed by the proteanly more ambitious *2001: A Space Odyssey* when it was released the next year. *Countdown* is not the stuff that cult reputations are made of—the plot involves a rather too serious race to the moon between Soviet and American spaceships—but it had a nice sense of technology and, as you might expect from Altman, a superb cast, which included James Caan, Robert Duvall, Joanna Moore, Barbara Baxley, Michael Murphy, and Ted Knight.

The born-again director followed up *Countdown* with another earnest genre exercise, *That Cold Day in the Park* (1969, script by Gillian Freeman from a novel by Richard Miles). An independent production, the film starred Sandy Dennis as a psychotic Canadian spinster who traps a young boy in her flat—sort of a reverse *Collector*. It is distinguished only by its superbly evocative location photography of rainy Vancouver (by Laszlo Kovacs) and the curious fact that John Garfield, Jr., played a small role.

After four movies and three career starts, Robert Altman was forty-five years of age and clearly not a good bet for impending directorial stardom, especially in the youth-oriented Hollywood of 1970. Then something akin to a miracle happened. Producer Ingo Preminger (brother of Otto) owned rights to a distinctly hip and irreverent script by Ring Lardner, Jr. (from a novel by Richard Hooker), but the project was in danger of self-destructing. Preminger had offered the script to more than a dozen directors before he turned in desperation to Robert Altman. Nothing in Altman's previous checkered career suggested he would do very well with satirical comedy. (Preminger has apparently said that if he had seen *That Cold Day in the Park*, which he hadn't, he never would have let Altman sign the contract.)

But *M*A*S*H* was a smash hit. It ranks number 22 on *Variety's* all-time list with net rentals to date of $36.7 million: a true blockbuster as well as stylistically a highly influential film. The television series which Larry Gelbart fashioned from it in 1972 has been one of the bright spots of the seventies, even if it is much more subdued than the movie. (A key to the difference is that the black-comic lyrics of the theme song, "Suicide Is Painless," aren't heard on TV.)

With an acumen that so far is unmatched in contemporary Hollywood, Altman converted the surprising success of *M*A*S*H* into solid financial and artistic independence. The whiz kids have since made movies that have grossed two, three, six times as much as M*A*S*H. In direct and telling contrast to Altman, they've often spent the money trying to top their early successes, or let it drain away through mismanagement. BBS is dead, Pressman-Williams disbanded, Coppola's American Zoetrope is paralyzed by the foolish expenses of *Apocalypse Now.* George Lucas's *Star Wars* corporations are probably generating such vast amounts of cash that he couldn't lose it all if he wanted to. But Altman remains a singular model for filmmakers who really prefer to make films, not money. His company, Lion's Gate, established just after M*A*S*H was completed, is a solid organization that has grown slowly and sensibly each year until it now offers Altman—and other filmmakers—a complete set of production facilities which on a small scale rival the studios of old. Lion's Gate lacks only sound stages, but since Altman has worked exclusively on location since *Brewster McCloud,* that's hardly a negative factor.

His success is all the more remarkable when one realizes that the nine films he has made since M*A*S*H have probably grossed together not very much more than that single blockbuster. He's been able to do this by sensibly keeping costs down—all of his films have cost under $2 million except *McCabe* ($3 million) and *Buffalo Bill* ($6 million)—and by plowing his own fees and salaries back into the company. Six of his ten films (*Brewster, Images, Thieves, Goodbye, Buffalo Bill* and *Three Women*) have yet to earn out their expenses, but this isn't a bad average in the Hollywood game.* To finance each film, Altman has used the leverage Lion's Gate provides to maintain control while using cash from every major studio except Universal (which doesn't much like coproductions). He's run into serious trouble only recently, in his association with Dino De Laurentiis, who recut *Buffalo Bill* and fired Altman from *Ragtime,* which was to be made from E.L. Doctorow's novel. This hurt especially because Doctorow's and Altman's styles and points of view seemed to mesh so well. It would have been Altman's first chance to collaborate with a peer.

Still, things have gone exceedingly well for a middle-aged director whose career might have been over ten years ago, and Lion's Gate is now able to support the work of other filmmakers, producing Alan Rudolph's *Welcome to L.A.* and Robert Benton's *The Late Show* in 1976, Rudolph's *Remember My Name* and Robert Young's *Rich Kids* in 1978. Altman has proved that it's not at all impossible to maintain some independence in contemporary Hollywood, if that is your true aim.

---

* For the films besides M*A*S*H which were profitable, *Variety* lists the following net rentals: *Nashville,* $8.6 million; *California Split,* $5 million; *McCabe and Mrs. Miller,* $4 million.

Paul Newman with Joel Grey and Harvey Keitel in the much maligned *Buffalo Bill and the Indians.*

In one way or another, all of Robert Altman's movies have reacted against the genre rules of the Old Hollywood. In this sense, his work provides the only real American parallel to the critical attitudes of the French New Wave. It's no surprise to discover that he is especially popular in France.

Brewster McCloud, his first independent project after M*A*S*H, announces this attitude with éclat. The film is a congeries of Hollywood references, from Margaret Hamilton, the old wicked Witch of the West, who finally gets to wear the red slippers here, to Michael Murphy's coolly witty parody of Steve McQueen's *Bullitt*. After a burlesque of the *Bullitt* car chase, the smartly turtlenecked "Frank Shaft" swerves off the road, careens down a hill, and settles squatly into a pond. Closeup of the steely, blue-eyed hero: one of his contacts has fallen out: the left eye is now distinctly and irrevocably brown. It's a small point; certainly most of the audience don't catch the joke; but it's typical of Altman's meticulous attention to detail. His films have an unusually rich fabric. It's as if he's cramming a lifetime's collection of cinematic ideas into an all too brief span. Sometimes it doesn't work; sometimes the effect is simply busyness. But on the whole, the density of Altman's movies provides their chief appeal. Audiences actively participate.

He's shot every film save one (*Thieves Like Us*) in Panavision to increase the potential area of the frame so that it can accommodate all these bits and pieces, and of course he's notorious for the thick, layered quality of his sound tracks. He boasts of throwing away his best lines. The Lion's Gate

321

eight-track Dolbyized recording system is the most sophisticated in the film business (even if it's of only average quality in the record business), and it has enabled him to get the precision of background noise and subtracks that add so much to his films. (Of course, most theaters aren't equipped to present the Altman soundtrack properly, which probably loses him audiences because his sound is so "muddy." It isn't his soundtrack that's unintelligible, it's the theater's system.)

Richard T. Jameson, one of the most perceptive film critics now writing, has a hobby of collecting little bits and pieces of movies that have impressed him over a year's time and publishing a straight list of them in the magazine he edits, *Movietone News*, every December. This collection of what Truffaut has called "privileged moments" has always impressed me as a very telling critical technique, even if it doesn't lead to grandiose judgments and timeless evaluations. Most of the true pleasure of movies lies in these privileged moments, and Altman's films have a much higher quotient than most. Peter Brook, who's worked both in theater and films, expresses this technique more theoretically: "What's the difference between a poor play [or film] and a good one?" he asks in his introduction to the published script of *Marat/Sade*:

> I think there's a very simple way of comparing them. A play in performance is a series of impressions: little dabs, one after another, fragments of information or feeling in a sequence which stir the audience's perceptions. A good play sends many such messages, often several at a time, often crowding, jostling, overlapping one another. The intelligence, the feelings, the memory, the imagination are all stirred. In a poor play, the impressions are well spaced out, they lope along in single file, and in the gaps the heart can sleep while the mind wanders to the day's annoyances and thoughts of dinner.[11]

By this critical calculus, Altman comes off very well indeed, "crowding, jostling, and overlapping" an orgy of "dabs."

They seem to me to fall into two general categories: the more practical technical cinematic devices he uses so well, and the more abstract effect the photography, sound, and acting have on our sense of the mythos, the societal pattern of values.

Here are a few samples from my own list of Altman's privileged moments:

• The flubbed movie announcements on the base p.a. system in M*A*S*H, ending with "Tonight's movie has been M*A*S*H. Follow the zany antics of our combat surgeons as they cut and stitch their way along the front lines, operating as bombs and bullets burst around them, snatching love and laughter between amputations and penicillin."

322

• The opium-smoky, green, flashed haze that suffuses the images of *McCabe and Mrs. Miller*, and spills over into the purposefully distant soundtrack as well, setting the hopeful settlement of Presbyterian Church in spacy historical perspective.

• The repetitive but always unfinished mock-torchy themesong of *The Long Goodbye*, which appears in the weirdest places, even in a doorchime.

• The breakfast of froot loops and beer in *California Split*, or Gwen Welles's cheerful offer of a lay in her froot-loopy panties, or Bert Remsen's transvestite shtik: "Like the dress? I had it made in Omaha. I just never had the balls to wear it!"

• The majestic 360°-plus pan that opens *Thieves Like Us* that tells the audience, according to Altman, "'This is the way it's gonna go. Don't anticipate — it's gonna go this way,'" or the slow-motion reaction shot as Keechie watches Bowie's death (but we don't) at the end of the film: a direct and telling criticism of the end of *Bonnie and Clyde*.

• Millie's magnificent magazine-spread apartment in *Three Women*, all yellow and violet, or her equally proper dinner party, featuring elegant goodies like pigs in blankets, Sau-Sea shrimp cocktail, chocolate-pudding tarts, and the pièce de resistance, Millie's special tuna casserole recipe: "First ya open all the cans and bottles..."

Nashville, of course, is a compressed compendium of such moments. It started out as an eight-hour rough cut (there was talk for a while of making it a television miniseries), and worked its way down slowly through six-, then four-hour versions, finally ending up at 161 minutes. It's Altman's most ambitious movie since *Brewster McCloud*, but I wouldn't put too much store in the meaning of *Nashville*. Hal Philip Walker's Replacement Party Campaign is rather jejune, and the assassination is simply a way to end the movie. The real success of *Nashville* lies in its multiple interstices.

Altman isn't very good at, or interested in, deep and lengthy investigations into character. In general, the more people an Altman movie contains, the better it is, with *Images* at the low end of the scale and *A Wedding* at the high end. His panoramic satire of the country-music scene, spread out over twenty-four major characters, works so well because his touch is gentle. He obviously likes the people in this film at the same time that he's aware of the ironies of their situation. So Barbara Jean (Ronee Blakley) can make a triumphant return from the burn center at the airport as the CBS reporter informs us that she was hurt "in a tragic accident involving a fire baton" and the Tricycle Man (Jeff Goldblum) is doing a magic trick for Sueleen Gay (Gwen Welles) and Wade (Robert Doqui) and

323

An Altman montage: various people drinking, eating, gambling, looking at babies and at funerals, running through the snow to no good end, having a good time in bed, and getting interviewed in *Brewster McCloud*, *That Cold Day in the Park*, *M*A*S*H*, *McCabe and Mrs. Miller*, *The Long Goodbye*, *Thieves Like Us*, *California Split*, and *Nashville*.

Sueleen can sing a song for him while L.A. Joan (Shelley Duvall) stands around anorexically in a tight tank top and multicolored platform clogs next to an arrow pointing at her on a sign that says "All persons must be screened for firearms" while Bill, Tom, and Mary check out their album display and Hal Philip Walker's soundtruck arrives, and various other people are doing various other things, and Barbara Jean collapses getting off the plane and is almost trampled by fans, and everybody leaves the airport in an unintentional caravan that includes a VW, a pickup, a Cadillac, a Rambler, The Tricyle Man, a limousine, and a camper, and a couch falls off a truck and causes a ten-car smashup, and Hal Philip Walker drones on about the national anthem, "composed by lawyers, anyway"—"Nobody knows the words, nobody can sing it, change it back to somethin' somebody can *sing*" — and Opal from the BBC (Geraldine Chaplin) — "I wish my cameraman had been here!"—takes the opportunity to interview Linnea Reese (Lily Tomlin) and discovers, to her disgust, that her children are deaf and dumb, and a party starts slowly on the highway as cans of beer are cracked open...This is the scene, or part of it, that greets Barbara Jean on her triumphant return to Nashville, and yet it doesn't at all detract from the moving drama of her breakdown later.

Thank you, Robert Altman, for cramming so much life into the limits of the screen and soundtrack and letting it overlap and jostle and crowd, and thank you for understanding the great, quiet funniness of it all.

There is, ultimately, an Altman theme behind all this. It's most apparent in the recent films—*Buffalo Bill*, *Nashville*, and *Three Women*—but it's clear, too, if you want to look for it, in the earlier films. It has to do with the very sea of images and sounds in which Altman plays so happily. Altman's people just don't fit. They try, sometimes desperately, like Millie, but it just doesn't work for them anymore. Only Brewster McCloud is a conscious rebel. His movie opens with a headline:

"AGNEW: SOCIETY SHOULD DISCARD SOME U.S. PEOPLE."

Brewster takes him seriously, and neatly disposes of some U.S. people he doesn't like before losing himself in a cockamamie dream of freedom through flight. All the other Altman characters more or less play at rebelling against the mythos, from the Mobile Army Surgical Hospital boys with their flip sense of humor to Janice Rule's painter Willie, morosely skulking around the desert painting painful if ultimately futile feminist symbols on the walls of empty swimming pools. McCabe thinks the American dream of the West is going to work for him. He's a bright-eyed entrepreneur. He gets his in the end. Elliott Gould's Marlowe is ungainly, out of place, and thirty years outside his time in a topless world. Keechie and Bowie have the continual model of the gangster myth accompanying them on the radio on their Southern voyages. It doesn't work any better than the private-eye myth or the western-hero myth or the bird myth.

California Split is refreshing because Charlie (Elliott Gould) and Bill (George Segal) are actually allowed to win in the end. But Bill has the last word: "Charlie, it don't mean a fucking thing." Like everybody else in *Nashville*, Albuquerque (Barbara Harris) is stoned on the mythos the media broadcast. "I know it sounds arrogant," she tells us, "but I'm on my way to Nashville to become a country singer. Or a star." If that doesn't work out, she figures she can always go into sales. She prefers trucks. The *Three Women* are, like Cathryn (Susannah York) in *Images*, among the most pitiable of Altman's characters. On his own, he seems to prefer an even darker vision of possibilities. In short, Altman's people are universally addicted to an American mythos, propagated by the media, not least of all film, to which their own reality never measures up. Altman doesn't seem to want to let them take action, and that is a major and unavoidable criticism of the theory of his work. It's especially evident—what else is new?—in his treatment of women. Millie, Willie, and Pinky ought to revolt: they deserve to get out of Altman's dream and into their own.

But somehow we don't really notice this essentially apolitical cynicism. The more people there are in an Altman film, the less likely we are to concentrate on its consequences. So, although *McCabe and Mrs. Miller*, *The Long Goodbye*, and *Thieves Like Us* are more unified and organized,

Sissy Spacek and Shelley Duvall prepare delectable Sau-Sea Shrimp cocktails and pigs-in-blankets in their charming yellow and lavender kitchen in the singles complex in *Three Women*. Gee, it looks good!

A Wedding: Muffin Brenner (Amy Stryker) and Dino Corelli (Desi Arnaz, Jr.) provide an excuse for a party—and a film with 48 major characters.

Altman's most attractive films are parties like *Brewster McCloud, California Split* and *Nashville. Buffalo Bill and the Indians, or Sitting Bull's History Lesson* is his only attempt so far to deal directly with the makers of the media mythos, and it is valuable for that.

Eventually, as in *Nashville*, the party winds up singing a song that's half an admission of defeat, half an ironic reminder that there's work to do:

It don't worry me.
It don't worry me.
You may say
That I ain't free.
But it don't worry me.*

The trouble with Altman's very enjoyable movies is that it do worry me.

---

* "It Don't Worry Me," words and music by Keith Carradine, copyright 1975 by American Broadcasting Music Co. and Lion's Gate Music and Easy Music. Reprinted with permission.

327

Francis Coppola:
The Stinky Kid as Mogul

Francis Coppola's money is more important than his movies. He has made some very good films, including two—perhaps three— great ones. But any discussion of his career has to begin with money. He was the first of the new generation of filmmakers to break into the business, the first to achieve remarkable financial success, and he has always viewed his career, as others have, in the context of this pioneering role. The *business* of film has been as important to him as the art for more than ten years now. He founded his first company, American Zoetrope, in 1969, even before he had any real cash. The millions he has earned from the *Godfather* films have simply raised the stakes tenfold. If Coppola can find a way to turn the rewards that occasionally accrue to directors in the new freelance Hollywood system into real power and freedom, he will revolutionize the industry. If he can't, he will have failed, in his own terms, no matter how much property he eventually owns, no matter how large his bank account.

For years, he stood alone. There were numerous actors who may have been as wealthy, but for the most part, they quietly invested their income and sat back to clip coupons (or worry about the fate of tax shelters). Since 1977, George Lucas, an old friend, has joined him in the ranks of multimillionaire filmmakers, and Steven Spielberg may not be far behind. Some of the pressure is off Coppola to make the money work in new ways, but there is still a personal commitment.

For years, he has been the singular role model for aspiring young writers and directors who think of themselves as outsiders, more intelligent and sensitive than the Hollywood establishment, who want to burrow into the industry to change it from within. If Coppola can't do it, then perhaps nobody can. Then the "Hollywood renaissance" has clearly failed.

The record, so far, is not promising. He moved to San Francisco in 1969 after a bitter experience with his first (and last) real Hollywood film, *Finian's Rainbow*, and established a small studio in a loft building there with perhaps $100,000 worth of cameras and equipment, and a dream of providing a home for young, independent directors. Warner Bros. nominally backed American Zoetrope, which produced only two films: Coppola's own *The Rain People* (1969), which was in production when the idea for the company was first conceived, and friend George Lucas's first feature, THX-1138 (1970).* As soon as the Warner executives took a look at that

---

* The nucleus of the Zoetrope group, loosely knit, consisted of Coppola, Lucas, John Milius, Willard Huyck and Gloria Katz, John Korty (who'd been making independent films in San Francisco for several years), Walter Murch, Carroll Ballard, Martin Scorsese, Hal Barwood, and Matthew Robbins.

cold intellectual exercise, they backed out. The youth-film boom had gone bust in the meantime. Coppola kept Zoetrope alive with his own money (the loft served as a set for *The Conversation* several years later), but it was crippled as a production organization.

His next step, under the aegis of Paramount, was the formation of the Directors Company with colleagues Peter Bogdanovich and William Friedkin, both, like Coppola, hot in 1972. The theory was apparently that if the studios wouldn't back untried directors like Lucas, they'd at least get behind filmmakers with demonstrated commercial clout. The Directors Company spawned three films—Coppola's *The Conversation* and Bogdanovich's *Paper Moon* and *Daisy Miller*—then folded.

By this time, Francis had his own cash to experiment with. No one knows quite how much he earned from the enormously successful first *Godfather* film, but the amount was certainly substantial. He had big plans. Through a network of variously named companies he invested heavily in San Francisco real estate, including a large mansion for himself and his family, an apartment house in the city, the Little Fox Theater (where he once intended to house a repertory company), a series of housing units in Mill Valley, north of the city (intended, one report has it, for writers and other associates), the Chateau Marmont hotel in Los Angeles, and part of Goldwyn Studios, in which he opened his own offices.

In 1974, he bought a large bloc of shares in Donald Rugoff's Cinema 5 distribution company, an influential force in the import market. In part, this was a gesture of support for Rugoff, who at the time was threatened with a takeover by a powerful domestic exhibition chain, but there was the obvious possibility that Coppola might eventually distribute his own films through Cinema 5. One of his own companies he named Coppola Cinema 7. He was well on his way to establishing an alternative to the restrictive studio distribution system.

At the same time, he became fascinated by other media, investing in television and radio, and most significantly in San Francisco's *City* magazine. He took control of the magazine early in 1975, and for six months showed up at the office daily. The circulation climbed by 50 percent, but by August was still losing money ($30,000 an issue, by some accounts). He lost interest and returned to filmmaking. Six months later he summarily closed the magazine. By early 1976 he was deeply involved in the *Apocalypse Now* project.

The film nearly became a self-fulfilling prophecy. Coppola had owned the John Milius script, which rephrases Joseph Conrad's *Heart of Darkness* in terms of the American experience in Vietnam, since 1967. Originally, George Lucas was supposed to direct it, perhaps in 16 mm to duplicate the effect of television news film. When Coppola embarked on the project himself in late 1975, the film was budgeted at $12 million. Estimates of its cost now range upwards of twice that amount. Although Coppola has been able to lay off most of that cost on distributors (United Artists paid $10 million for U.S. distribution rights; foreign rights may have brought in an equal amount), it has still been an obvious strain on his own financial resources. *City* magazine was first to go. It was followed quickly by other assets, including the shares in Cinema 5 and the Los Angeles offices. Real estate was mortgaged as well. No one yet knows how much. *Apocalypse Now* was plagued by disasters, both natural (a typhoon, an earthquake, dysentery) and man-made (quarrels with actors, outrageous cost overruns). It was clearly a quagmire of a film. Coppola was stuck in it for four years. He was obviously obsessed with it. According to Charles Higham, he told John Milius, "I've got to do this picture. I consider it the most important picture I will ever make. If I die making it, you'll take over, if you die, George Lucas will take over."[12]

It's a rather romantic attitude toward the business. After all, as Alfred Hitchcock once told one of his stars, "It's only a movie, Ingrid." Perhaps it does indicate a self-destructive streak. In 1975, when he was investing, Coppola told his associate Fred Roos, "I'll be broke and back to zero in a few years, so I might as well have fun." In any event, planned or not, *Apocalypse Now* has prevented any further thoughts of reforming the film industry.

In April 1977, just after his thirty-eighth birthday, Coppola found himself still in the Philippines, well into his second year of shooting on the film. He could look back on a fifteen-year career as director that included only seven films. He had nurtured a dream: instead of moguls and agents enforcing arbitrary decisions on serious filmmakers like himself, then gouging profits out of the product of the sweat of artists, he had envisioned a community of directors, writers, technicians, and actors, all pursuing honorable—and perhaps profitable—aims, making their own decisions, producing good movies, real ones, then plowing the cash back into more ambitious ventures. It would be an open, life-affirming industry, rather than the present closed, introverted, and reductive system.

It was a good idea, and it was possible, but somehow it never seemed to work. Now all seemed chaos, at least from the perspective Manila provided.

Coppola vented his anger and disappointment in a long memo, now famous, to his employees and associates back in the States. The prose is tortured, the tone anxious, but the gist of the message is clear: the dream is over. Coppola lays down new rules for his company, henceforth to be known only as American Zoetrope. The extravagances will have to stop. All expenditures must be allocated to budgetary lines. "I expect people to dress and behave as they would for any other company," he writes. "It is very important for me to dispel the seven-year ambience of a hippy hangout around the old American Zoetrope that attracted a certain group of young people anxious to work in the film business." Most important, after the current projects are completed (these include old classmate Carroll Ballard's *The Black Stallion* and *Hammett*, to be directed by Wim Wenders), American Zoetrope will be devoted wholly to the work of Francis Coppola. In other words, the scheme of a community of filmmakers has failed. One final item: henceforth "Francis Ford Coppola" will be referred to as "Francis Coppola." ("This comes from a statement I once heard which I feel is true: 'Never trust a man with three names.'")

The rather embarrassing memo was eventually leaked to *Esquire*, which published it several months later, without comment, as "Case Histories of Business Management: Hollywood Artistic Division." It's hard not to react to the memo facetiously. Coppola's apparent naiveté is remarkable, yet so was his position. He wanted to use his money to do real work. Other people in Hollywood have amassed similar sums (mainly actors). They haven't ended up writing memos like this one because they simply hired business managers who made safe investments. Yet it's hard to believe that the companies were so mismanaged that their losses could come close to matching Coppola's own investment in *Apocalypse Now*. It's as if he had planned that film to absorb the cash, to protect himself from having to deal with the responsibility that capital entailed.

In the most revealing paragraph of the memo, Coppola attempted to explain to the people working with him precisely what he thought his strategy with regard to money had been. "I am cavalier with money," he wrote,

> because I have to be, in order not to be terrified every time I make an artistic decision. Don't confuse that technique with the idea that I am infinitely wealthy. Many of you know that this is not true. Remember, the major studios and distributors have only one thing that a filmmaker needs: capital. My flamboyant disregard for the rules of capital and business is one of my major strengths when dealing with them. It evens the score, so to speak.[13]

It is an interesting theory, and in the land where people's competence is often judged by the class of car they drive, it has the ring of truth. Yet, certainly by 1977 Coppola no longer had to play by their rules. He was within reach of changing them dramatically, if he had husbanded his resources more carefully. Coppola was the first great financial success of the new Hollywood. He seems to have a self-destructive urge to be the first great financial failure, as well. It's almost as if he were embarrassed by the money

331

Families: Considering Francis Coppola's own background it is not surprising that the family life of the *Godfather* films is rendered with precision and compassion. Here, Vito's family in 1945 at Connie's first wedding.

he's made, as if it were a sign that he wasn't a serious artist. He hasn't yet been able to come to terms with the basic contradiction of commercial filmmaking, so he vacillates mercurially between the desire to make "personal" films, like *The Rain People* and *The Conversation*, and the urge to beat Hollywood at its own game, with movies like *The Godfather* and *Apocalypse Now*. It's a no-win situation: he hasn't been satisfied with the "personal" films and he seems to feel guilty about the money.

He can't really be condemned for the failures of the first American Zoetrope, the Directors Company, and the various companies that followed: at least he made the attempt. (Robert Altman is the only other filmmaker who has analyzed the dilemma similarly, and he has been more successful trying to deal with it.) But the reasons for the consistent underachievement of Zoetrope and its successors are, of course, of primary interest not only to George Lucas, Steven Spielberg, and other potential power centers in the industry, but also to a large number of less wealthy cinéastes who want desperately to decentralize the industry.

It's easy enough to ascribe the failure of the companies to bad business practices and perhaps an underlying self-destructive streak, but that's begging the question. The root of the problem appears to be psychological. In interviews, he has often alluded to the influence of his family, and indeed, if one theme unites his films from *You're a Big Boy Now* to *The Godfather*, it's certainly family. He often describes his father as a man embittered

Families: Michael's family in 1957 at his son's First Communion.

about the seeming failure of his own career. Carmine Coppola, a flautist for years with Toscanini's NBC Symphony, was always the interpreter, never the composer. "Our lives centered on what we all felt was the tragedy of his career," he told *Playboy*. "He was a very frustrated man . . . He felt that his own music never really emerged." Francis sometimes describes his own career using the musical metaphor. He thinks the real creative work in film lies with the writer. Perhaps 80 percent of the sum effect of a movie is clearly stated in the script. For Coppola, the director is simply the conductor, the interpreter of someone else's work. Even as a writer, he specialized in adaptations: hence the significance he attaches to *The Rain People* and *The Conversation*, his only two wholly original films. He made those films, he told Marjorie Rosen, "because I wanted more than anything to be a writer . . . . I finished and made those films more as a dare to myself to show myself that I could do it, that I could write original material. Anyone who's written knows how you doubt that."[14]

The mystique of the writer was further enhanced by the career of his older brother August, a professor of contemporary literature, a novelist, and a hero for Francis. Add to this Francis's experience of a year in bed with polio at the age of nine, and you have a good sense of the origins of his passive/aggressive personality. He thinks he eventually came to terms with this psychological dilemma. In 1975 he won three Oscars for adapting, directing, and producing *The Godfather, Part II*. (He had already won

two: for adapting *The Godfather* and for co-writing *Patton.*) More important, his father also won an Oscar (with Nino Rota) for the music for *Godfather II*—recognized at last. (His sister Talia Shire was nominated, but
didn't win that year.)

Psychologically, then, Coppola's career has served a dual function. He
has had to prove himself within his family's system of values; he has had to
be a success as well as an artist. In a way, he is less interested in actually
making films than in being a filmmaker. In 1975, he told Michael Goodwin:

> All my life, all I really wanted was to be a living member of *La Bohème*.
> My idea is to go up and write for three hours, then sit down in the
> cafe and tell funny stories about Proust to Mauriac, who is sitting next
> to me, then go over and see what's happening at the theater, drop down
> and see what the guys at the magazine are doing, have another cafe....
> That's the life I've always wanted to be part of, and since it doesn't exist
> I have set out on the totally naive, and maybe impossible, job of
> creating it. [15]

But then *Apocalypse* intervened. Back to the drudgery of filmmaking. His
wife, he says, is certain he gets involved in gargantuan, potentially futile,
projects simply to justify his anxiety. After every large project in the past,
he has told one interviewer or another that he's planning to quit for a
while, and just write. It never quite happens. He still claims that he works
at the typewriter three hours a day, from seven a.m. to ten, but not much
ever seems to come of it.

Francis Coppola was born in 1939 and grew up mainly on the North Shore
of Long Island, living first in Bayside, then Great Neck. He went to
Hofstra University, where he produced and directed student shows, and
enrolled in the U.C.L.A. film school in 1960. This was well before the influx of commercial talent at the film schools, and Coppola found himself
isolated and lonely. ("There was none of the camaraderie that I had im-
agined in high school in my *La Bohème* imagination.")[16] However, his directing teacher, Dorothy Arzner, did take an interest in him.

In 1962 Coppola won the Samuel Goldwyn award for an original
screenplay, "Pilma, Pilma," and decided to parlay his first credit into a
career. He went to work for Roger Corman as a Jack-of-all-trades. Knowing
no Russian, he invented dialogue for a Soviet film Corman had picked up
which was later released as *Battle Beyond the Sun* (1963), did the same for
another Russian film, *The Magic Voyage of Sinbad* (1963), and filled in as
dialogue director, assistant director, second-unit director, and script doctor
on a number of other Corman projects.

In Ireland on location with Corman, he hustled his way into directing *Dementia 13* (1963), the script of which he wrote in a few nights after getting a commitment from Corman for $20,000 and an equal amount from an English producer. The film, which featured Patrick Magee in a secondary role, received some decent reviews.

Back in the United States, having married one of his crew members on *Dementia 13*, Eleanor Neil, he parlayed his Samuel Goldwyn award into a job with Seven Arts productions. He adapted Carson McCullers's novel *Reflections in a Golden Eye*, then Tennessee Williams's *This Property Is Condemned*, as well as *Is Paris Burning?* and eight other scripts, most of which were never filmed. Those that were, he claims, bear little relation to his script drafts, even if he did receive screen credit (on *This Property Is Condemned* and *Is Paris Burning?*).

By the time he was twenty-four, Coppola was earning $1000 a week as a journeyman screenwriter. "I wanted to make a film so desperately," he later told Joe Gelmis, "that I saved all my money.

> And I had about $20,000 cash. I was really frustrated, because I could buy a Ferrari or I could buy a sailboat, but I couldn't make a film. So I decided I was going to risk it all on the stock market and either have $100,000 and make a film, or have nothing. I lost it, every penny of it. In one stock. Scopitone. That jukebox with the little films. Lost every penny of it.[17]

He survived by landing a job with Twentieth Century-Fox to write a film based on the life of General Patton. That script, too, went through a number of writers, but Coppola's original was revived by George C. Scott when the film was finally made in 1969.

In Paris while working on *Is Paris Burning?* he had amused himself nights by writing the first draft of *You're a Big Boy Now* from the novel by David Benedictus. When he was fired from Seven Arts he discovered they had appropriated the script to fulfill his contract. Somehow, he convinced them to let him direct it. He made $8000 for his work as writer and director, and the film had some mild success.

A *Bildungsfilm*, about a young boy from Great Neck (Peter Kastner) who moves into Manhattan on his own and discovers sex and independence, *You're a Big Boy Now* was a bit arch, but likeable nevertheless, especially for its charming score by John Sebastian and the Lovin' Spoonful. Critics compared it at the time to Richard Lester's *The Knack*, and it undoubtedly evinces some Lester influences, but Coppola showed some moderate style of his own. He's always been known as an actors' director. He convinced Geraldine Page, Rip Torn, and Julie Harris to participate. Karen Black and Tony Bill, unknowns, also had roles. In the end, the most important fact

Elizabeth Hartman as the unobtainable woman and Peter Kastner as the lovelorn kid in *You're a Big Boy Now.*

about *You're a Big Boy Now* is that it was made at all.

Coppola immediately decided not "to make the same mistake as a lot of guys—to suddenly get into projects over their head, films they didn't have complete control over." So he sat down to work on the screenplay for *The Conversation*. Three days into it, the phone rang: "Would you like to direct *Finian's Rainbow*?" It was a way to avoid the challenge of *The Conversation*, it was a fine musical in its time (the show was produced on Broadway in 1948), and as Coppola later admitted, it might be a project that would appeal to his father. Maybe he could shoot it on location, he thought. It would certainly be *interesting* to be involved in a big Hollywood movie. . . . Thus begins the continuing conflict between the "personal" and the "commercial" films, the ones he tells himself he wants to do, and the ones he actually enjoys doing. Coppola still hasn't admitted he's happier making the latter.

He didn't get to go to Kentucky to make the film. It was shot on Warners' back lot in Hollywood. Coppola wasn't at all satisfied with the production. The film was shot in twelve weeks at a cost of $3.5 million, not large by musical standards. It wound up competing with films like *Funny Girl* and *Star!* with budgets three times that. Hermes Pan, the choreographer hired at Fred Astaire's insistence, was fired, and Coppola had to stage the dances himself, knowing nothing about choreography. Surprisingly, Warners was pleased by the fine cut. They decided to make it a road show, blew it up to 70 mm—and cut off Fred Astaire's feet in the process.

Footless Fred Astaire with Petula Clark: "How are things in Glocca Morra? . . . "

No one had considered the change in aspect ratio. The film did not do well. But it remains an efficient and at times inspired staging of the Saidy-Harburg-Lane musical. It's useful to have a filmed record of it, especially with the participation of Astaire.

Coppola was depressed. "What I'm thinking of doing, quite honestly," he told an interviewer shortly after the film opened, "is splitting. I'm thinking of pulling out and making other kinds of films. Cheaper films. Films I can make in 16 mm."[18]

He took the money he had made from *Finian's Rainbow* and invested in $80,000 worth of equipment and a van. He had been an admirer of Shirley Knight's stage work for a long time. He convinced her to come along with him in the van to make a movie with James Caan and Robert Duvall. For five months, cast and crew wandered West by Northwest from New York to Wyoming shooting *The Rain People* (1969). Coppola had had the idea for the film as far back as 1960: a pregnant woman leaves her husband for no apparent reason. As a potential feminist statement, it was in conception far ahead of its time. But as the cast and crew kept moving on, the script changed. Natalie (Shirley Knight) meets a hitchhiker, "Killer" Kilgannon, along the way. Killer (Caan) is not all there; he's been injured in a football game. Gradually, the character of Killer increases in importance as that of Natalie decreases. There was nowhere to go with the premise, as long as Natalie was merely escaping. Killer becomes a surrogate for the child she is carrying. By the end of the film, she has "admitted" her commitment to

337

Robert Duvall stops Shirley Knight in *The Rain People*, a rather novel road film.

others, to Killer, to the child. Although she doesn't return to her husband, she has returned to the stereotypical trap of woman as protector and nurturer from which she was trying to escape.

"The way women have come out in my movies is very strange," he commented years later.[19] *You're a Big Boy Now* propagated the tired archetypes of women as smothering mother figures and dangerous vamps. *The Rain People* started well but got lost along the way. Women don't exist meaningfully in *The Conversation* (or, we might suppose, in *Apocalypse Now*) and are marginal figures in the *Godfather* films. For a filmmaker who has been so concerned with families, this is exceedingly strange. Perhaps one of the reasons Coppola has had such a hard time with his personal projects is that he has evidently shied away from domestic sexual politics, probably the most common subject of such films. Yet Kay's role in the *Godfather* films, especially *Part II*, should not be underestimated. Given the pervasively macho atmosphere of a Mafia story, Coppola worked to present the family from outsider Kay's point of view. Her revolt against Michael in *Part II* is one of the thematic hinges of that film, even if she does eventually return to beg forgiveness.

By 1970 Coppola had reached another of his periodic low points. Warners had canceled the American Zoetrope deal after the box-office failure of *The Rain People* and their first look at *THX-1138*. Coppola returned to screenwriting, knocking out a very faithful adaptation of *The Great Gatsby*. The film was meant as a vehicle for Ali McGraw, a gift from Robert Evans to the then current love of his life. But Coppola must have seen the auto-biographical implications in the great American novel of success from humble beginnings. When the film was finally released in 1974 (without McGraw, who'd moved on to another love story with Steve McQueen), Coppola griped in interviews about Jack Clayton's handling of his script. He was particularly upset at what Clayton had done with two scenes which he considered crucial. One of them was a long meeting between Daisy and Gatsby, which Coppola had written as an intense but unerotic discussion in the bedroom, with the actors seated far apart from each other. The scene didn't exist in the book but was obligatory for the film: the lovers had to be seen together. This is as close as Coppola has ever gotten to a love scene. Clayton broke up the tour de force into several pieces, and punctuated the last half of the film with them.

The other crucial scene in Coppola's opinion, also mishandled, in-volved Gatsby's father's arrival at the end of the film. Gatsby's common roots are revealed, but—as Coppola wrote it—in the context of his driving ambition. The little book in which he had written his childhood reso-lutions was to be the focal point. Coppola himself had once written to his mother, "Dear Mommy, I want to be rich and famous. I'm so discouraged. I don't think it will come true." Like Jay Gatsby, he seems even as a child to have been more concerned with the show of power than the uses of it.

Considering his commercial record up to this point, it's hard to under-stand why Paramount offered him the job of directing the film of Mario Puzo's very popular novel. For publication, it was suggested that a director with experience as a writer was needed. This is obvious nonsense. Maybe Evans sensed Coppola's capabilities. More likely, he was the only thinkable choice with an Italian surname. The producers were already having trouble with the Mafia and with Italian-American lobbying groups. A director named Coppola would (and did) take some of the heat off. Then too, Paramount never planned the film to be a blockbuster. It was supposed to be much less ambitious than it eventually turned out to be. Coppola had out-moguled the executives; most of the credit for the financial success of the film belongs to him.

Even during shooting, he was constantly rumored as about to be fired. Coppola says the studio was particularly exercised over three of his de-mands: (1) wanting to cast Brando; (2) wanting to cast Pacino; (3) insist-ing on a period setting and location work in Sicily. Of course, these are three of the very reasons the film was as profitable as it was.

The Godfather is arguably the most important American film of the 1970s (especially if both parts are considered together) not only because it struck a deep, mythic chord in most Americans, but also because it demonstrated clearly that a highly popular film need not be superficial, that art and commerce need not be antithetical. But Coppola didn't necessarily see it this way.

He immediately used the financial freedom the film brought him to return to "personal" filmmaking. The first draft of the script for *The Conversation* (1974) had been completed six years previously, before Watergate was even conceivable. Shooting began in late 1972 when the dimensions of the great scandal weren't yet clear to most people. But the film wasn't released until the height of the Watergate crisis: it undoubtedly gained added resonance from its unforeseen historical context. It was extraordinarily well received critically, but not a popular success. Coppola thinks he knows why. "*The Conversation*, although it had some sense of social responsibility, made people feel crummy," he told Mike Goodwin. ". . . in the end the guy didn't break out."

He's put his finger on the problem. *The Conversation* is a magnificent technical achievement. Coppola accomplishes what Godard was saying in the early seventies that he wanted to do: he liberates sound from the tyranny of the image. This is a film to listen to first, to watch second. At the same time it is a brilliantly accurate delineation of one of the more important elements of the national mythos of the seventies: the destruction of privacy. On the level of commodity, it is the ultimate in paranoia movies. But it only describes this situation; it doesn't explain what can be done about it. It gives us a trapped rat as hero. Harry Caul, bugger extraordinary, is Gene Hackman's most complex role, but it's narrowly introverted. "The guy didn't break out." Coppola, just then discovering politics, didn't understand until after the film was completed that it had to work in relationship to an audience, on a political level. "That's why I'm looking at a lot of Frank Capra these days," he noted. Capra's heroes may be naive, but they are active. If Coppola had *The Conversation* to do over, it's pretty sure Harry Caul wouldn't be at the focus of the film.

Part of the reason the film does present the negative, static portrait that it does is that even as he finished shooting he didn't know where the story was going. As was his habit on other films, he shot many takes of each scene, but he also shot alternative story-line developments. Rushing off to begin work on *Godfather II*, he left the editing to Walter Murch, who had done sound for all of Coppola's films (including *American Graffiti*) since *The Rain People*. Murch, together with Coppola's brother-in-law David Shire (who is credited with the music for the film), is responsible for the fascinating soundtrack of *The Conversation*. As editor he managed to stitch together the disparate footage into a semblance of a story.

Like *The Rain People*, Coppola's only other original script, *The Conversation* then appears to have been an open-ended concept rather than a fully thought-out story. It begins to become clear just why Coppola has a fear of

The Conversation: Harry Caul (Gene Hackman) crouched under a bathroom sink next to the toilet listening . . . . and watching in Union Square through a one-way mirror.

writing. To his credit, he has insisted in interviews since that Walter Murch should be considered a co-author of the film, but the film's credits don't reflect this. If it's true, they should.

When Coppola signed to do a sequel to *The Godfather,* a number of critics charged him with selling out to commercial pressures. Coppola defended himself by noting that Charlie Bluhdorn, head of Gulf + Western, had promised him much more control the second time around, that he was going to have an opportunity to do many of the things he had wanted to do, but couldn't, in the first film, that he had a scheme for the film that would make it possible later to intercut both parts to make one six-hour movie (which eventually happened), and, finally, that he was going to use the opportunity to make a very expensive film directed to a mass audience that was at the same time personal.

To a surprising extent Coppola succeeded in these multiple ambitions. *The Godfather, Part II* realized $30 million in net rentals for Paramount in the United States alone, an extraordinary figure for a film which tells two separate stories both of which depend for their full impact on the audience's familiarity with a previous film—moreover, it is a film a third of which is in Italian with English subtitles. This is not the stuff of which commercial blockbusters are made, but Coppola brings it off. The film depends on and extends the significance of *The Godfather.* It is also a more intellectual, less active and violent treatment of the themes the first film introduced. It's not clear how much of the script Francis wrote and how much Mario Puzo contributed, but at least half the film—the saga of Michael after the death of his father—goes significantly beyond where Puzo's novel left off.

Audiences responded to *The Godfather* for a number of reasons. Certainly it is a masterpiece of the gangster genre, but that fact alone accounts for the popularity of neither the book nor the film. It is simply the foundation on which Puzo and Coppola build. There have been numerous books

341

and movies about the Mafia within the last ten years. None of them has approached the success of *The Godfather*. What Puzo understood—what Coppola wisely heightened—was the attraction of the family aspect of the film. Quite simply, *The Godfather* has the force that it does because it is the story of a father and sons. The title tells you that. The film is about an immigrant generation for whom the streets of America really were paved with gold. Their victims understand the choice that the Corleone family has made, and there is never a sense that they begrudge them their power. A given of the film, never explicitly stated, is that there is no other way to realize the American dream. If Vito gets richer, it is at someone else's expense. *Così fan tutti*. His business may be slightly more violent than other people's but not all that much. Consider the wars in the coalfield of the thirties; consider the sweatshops of the teens. As Rap Brown put it, "Violence is as American as cherry pie."

The drama that Vito and his sons—especially Michael—enact at home was played out in a million households after World War II, as the more pragmatic generation of the fifties took over from those who at least paid lip service to the dream.* Audiences responded deeply to this aspect of the film, I believe. *The Godfather* looked like an action saga. It wasn't. It was really a film about relationships and connections: between men and women, between fathers and sons, between "business" and "personal" lives. Vito's tragedy is that he separates them; Michael's, that he can't. No film that begins with a wedding sequence half an hour in length, returns repeatedly to family scenes, and climaxes with a magnificent, privileged moment between grandfather and grandson (Vito's death among the tomato vines) can really be supposed to be primarily about gangsters.

The Godfather, Part II expands upon these themes and deepens them. Vito's immigrant experience, which constitutes nearly half the film, was left out of the first film because it is not very melodramatic. It's inclusion here makes the context of the immigrant life relevant. It helps us to understand the choices made by an older Vito in the first film. Most of *Part II* deals with Michael's story. A good guess is that the expansion of Kay's role in the second film was Coppola's decision rather than Puzo's. Coppola had held on to the scenes between Michael and Kay (few of which really advance the action) in the first part. Here, he forces the relationship into an archetype of the fifties marriage. Kay is literally imprisoned in the family compound; most women—Natalie, for example—were metaphorically sequestered. The pain was no less real. It's no accident that Diane Keaton

---

* Since the fifties, a third generation, more like the first than the second, has come to the fore. Neither *Godfather* film deals with it. Part III, already announced, may.

Father and sons: Don Vito (Marlon Brando) with Michael (Al Pacino), Sonny (James Caan), and Fredo (John Cazale).

looks like Shirley Knight here.

The Godfather, Part II also pays a great deal more attention to the parallelism between the Family business and business at large. What's good for the Corleones is good for America. As Michael puts it to the senator, "We're both part of the same hypocrisy." Hyman Roth's carving of the birthday-cake Cuba is daringly brash as a symbol, but it works, because that is in fact what happened.* It's important that Coppola doesn't take a liberal, accusative attitude here. We're all part of the same hypocrisy. He's spoken of himself, perhaps facetiously, as identifying with Michael: both of them begin with ideals, then find themselves caught in a web of tradition that turns them into parodic duplicates of the older generation they despised. By casting Roger Corman and other Hollywood figures as senators, and Lee Strasberg as Hyman Roth, Coppola makes the connection.

Cinematically, both *Godfather* films are remarkable. Coppola is by no means a *film*maker, the way Cassavetes and Altman are. He makes movies, and thus we tend not to pay attention to his mise en scène. We shouldn't. He obviously wants us to concentrate on the mythic dimensions of his movies, not their cinematography and montage, not even their acting. Nevertheless, as a cinéaste Coppola can hold his own against any rivals. He takes real chances, artistically, and he succeeds. Gordon Willis's

---

* With fine irony, the Cuban sequences were shot in the Dominican Republic, a partly owned subsidiary of Gulf+Western.

First generation: Vito (Robert De Niro).   **Second generation:** Michael.

Third generation: Michael with Anthony (James Gounaris), who clearly will take center stage in *The Godfather, Part III*.

cinematography for both films manages to capture both the harsh light of southern Italy and the brown shadows of the American forties in direct contradiction to the sort of high-key lighting we would ordinarily expect in a film meant to attract massive audiences. Visually, both films really are private and personal.

This quality extends to the mise en scène. Coppola has a special distaste for closeups, preferring to set his actors in broad visual contexts for the most part. This too causes him to sacrifice some immediately visceral power for more atmospheric, intelligent ends.

He has always been known as a fine director of actors. What else is new? Every successful contemporary director depends prodigiously on actors' talents, but Coppola uses them in a unique way. He doesn't give us actors *qua* actors (like Cassavetes), nor does he lavish them with thick character (like

Altman). Rather, he forces their energy into developing the mythic values of the story line. I think it's a more sophisticated approach than either Cassavetes's or Altman's. Again, like the mise en scène, it sacrifices some immediate effect for a long-term goal.

In order to develop this sense of a lived story, Coppola invited Brando and the other main actors of *The Godfather* to dinner one night and asked them to improvise. Before long, they were a real family, each younger actor playing for the favors of Brando. For the second film, he locked the cast in the Lake Tahoe family compound for the day. Soon they were visiting each other and trading recipes.

We can see why Brando was essential to *The Godfather*. No other actor (who could play a seventy-year-old Italian immigrant) carries with him such a weight of personal myth.

Coppola also showed an unparalleled attention to detail in the practical mise en scène of the *Godfather* films. It wasn't necessary. He would have got by with less. A few of us recognize the rightness of a car with wooden bumpers in 1945. If the marquee of Radio City Music Hall *hadn't* advertised *The Bells of St. Mary's* that Christmas, thousands in the audience would have caught it. But it certainly wasn't necessary to re-create the wooden toll booths that guarded Long Island's Jones Beach in the forties. How many viewers would have missed them? Francis Coppola, who grew up in Great Neck, for one. (James Monaco, who was raised in Little Neck, for another.)

Meticulous attention to period detail is, at the least, nostalgic. Coppola makes something more of it here. He re-creates times and places that many of us half remember. In the process he helps us to integrate the experience of our own pasts.

Similarly, a significant, if minor, reason for the films' success with audiences is their evocation of the forties and fifties. Coppola knows that what the world knows as tomato sauce Americans with Italian backgrounds call "gravy," and that the first thing you do upon entering the kitchen is to dip a piece of bread in the slowly simmering pot, as Sonny does when he goes to see his mother to break the news that Pop has been shot.

These thousands of details eventually add up to a powerful and affecting authenticity which measurably moves audiences, even if it doesn't call attention to itself. This profound—even reverent—reconstruction of a common past, together with an understanding of the inherent dilemmas of American family life that approaches tragic dimensions, and a political perspective that thoroughly dissects the myth of the American Dream and demonstrates with painful clarity that "we are all undesirables," makes *The Godfather* (both parts—all seven hours ot it) the most significant American film since *Citizen Kane*. Charles Foster Kane and Vito Andolini Cor-

345

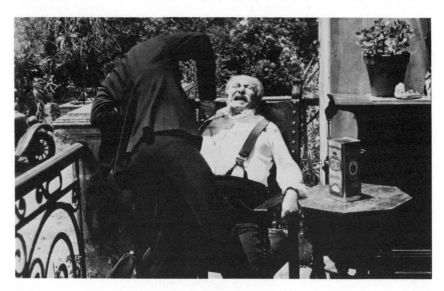

E chisto è per ti! Vito (De Niro) avenges his father's death with a knife to the heart of Don Ciccio (Giuseppe Sillato).

leone, separated by thirty years, are brothers. Together they explain a great deal about this country—more than most books, more than most songs. They are the best evidence of the extraordinary power of the medium of film.*

Apocalypse Now, which finally premiered in August, 1979, after an unusual "work-in-progress" screening at Cannes the previous May, wants

---

* Coppola's promised extended version of *The Godfather* was broadcast by NBC in November 1977. *Mario Puzo's The Godfather: The Complete Novel for Television* (to give it its proper monicker) was stretched out over four evenings and advertised as nine hours in length. Excluding commercials, the program actually ran seven hours and fourteen minutes, several minutes of which were taken up with repeated credits each evening. The two films released theatrically add up to six hours, fifteen minutes. Something less than an hour of footage was added to the television show, approximately nine scenes. Most of them are minor and don't add much to the narrative. We learn how Hyman Roth got his name. Hyman Suchowsky's favorite hero was Arnold Rothstein. We also see a short sequence that was a favorite of Coppola's. As a young man, Vito visits a man named Agostino Coppola, who sells guns and whose little son plays the flute. The episode was part of the Coppola family lore. The Family's antagonism toward Jack Woltz, the Hollywood producer, is given stronger motivation. Vito kills Don Ciccio's henchmen as well as the don himself (which probably weakens that extraordinary scene). Most of the additions are to the De Niro sequences of Part II, which in this version come first. Busy with *Apocalypse Now*, Coppola left the editing of the television version to Barry Malkin.

E chisto . . . Michael avenges his father in a shabby restaurant in the Bronx.

very much to surpass *The Godfather* films as a mythic statement. With roots in Joseph Conrad's *Heart of Darkness*, and pointed references to Jessie L. Weston's *From Ritual to Romance* and Sir James Frazer's *The Golden Bough*, this 70-mm Dolby stereo magnum opus certainly makes no secret of its ambitions. Not since *Cleopatra* has an American movie received such voluminous publicity during the long years of production. It would have been nearly impossible for the ultimate experience of the film to come close to the hype which had preceded it.

Admittedly, *Apocalypse Now* is an admirable technical achievement which certainly expresses "the horror, the horror" (as Marlon Brando's Walter Kurtz puts it) of the direct experience of the Vietnam war. But despite the references to literary antecedents and the critically widely-noted theme of patricide, the movie—like its nominal narrator Martin Sheen's Captain Willard—has no moral foundation from which to judge the psychedelic terrors of the war.

Coppola has not avoided the trap that awaits any filmmaker who tries to deal with the historical horrors of the twentieth century: by picturing the war he makes it comprehensible, almost acceptable, perhaps even entertaining. With a narration just this side of Mickey Spillane, *Apocalypse Now* prefers to see Vietnam as a psychotropic aberration rather than a political crime.

Perhaps this view is the result more of a special sort of cinematic hubris rather than any intellectual decision. The medium seems to have such

347

unlimited power that you think simply to picture reality is somehow to explain it. Coppola is not unaware of this seductive logic. In what may be the most telling scene of the film we see Francis himself staging an attack on a village. Crouching next to the camera, he directs the "cast": "*Don't* look at the camera! Just keep moving! *Look* like you're fighting!" As filmmakers from Alain Resnais to Richard Lester and Stanley Kubrick have understood, the only way to get leverage on a subject like this is through irony.

Part of the problem with *Apocalypse Now* is its own grandiosity. It's a fairly simple story, simply told. It should have been finished in a year or two, not four. Much more elaborate war films are made nearly as well much more quickly. No film could fulfill such limitless ambitions. More important, however, is Coppola's choice to focus on the visceral experience of the war rather than its political context. No doubt the former is more entertaining, more "cinematic"—that's the problem. We need to understand how it happened, not re-experience it.

Francis Coppola may recover quickly from the obsession of *Apocalypse Now*. For years now, he has been planning a film called "Tucker," much smaller, much less grandly ambitious, and in the end probably a lot more important.

Preston Tucker was an inventor, perhaps a con man, who built a car with many safety devices in the 1940s. As Coppola explained the story to Susan Braudy:

> American products used to be the best in the world. "Tucker" is about that period in American history when making the best car became irrelevant. Detroit destroyed Tucker. Car companies preferred making profits.[20]

A bit like movie companies today, perhaps.

> I like him because he feels human, the lovable American con man, the used-car salesman with his heart in the right place. In his way he was a charlatan. He wore those brown and white pointy shoes, and he was handsome and good with the ladies. He talked fast. He was a little stinky. Some people say I identify with him. . . .

10

Who's Talking?
Ritchie and Mazursky

Once upon a time people woke up in the morning and went to work, came home and ate, raised their children, loved, hated, laughed and cried, caught the circus as it came through town, and lived their lives as best they could. Once upon a time, people lived in communities. The job was at the end of town, the stores along the way, the church around the corner, and if you were too sick to go to the doctor, the doctor dropped by your place. Once upon a time, people played baseball or football because it was fun and skiied down a mountain to get to the other side and nobody but nobody ever saw a play except maybe some of the rich folk.

Then, oh maybe fifty or sixty years ago, things started changing. Rapidly. First there were the picture newspapers, then radio and the movies, and finally television. It was no longer enough to say you were having beans for supper. Now there were umpteen kinds of beans. Choices had to be made. Raising children became a difficult art, an advanced science. How your mother ever did it, I'll never know. Lucky we have experts now. People started spending less time living their own lives and more and more time watching other people live theirs. Your great-grandfather counted himself lucky if he got to go to the big city to see a show once a year. Now, most of us spend an average of 2500 hours every year watching staged realities on the tube, and another dozen or two at the movies. It's become increasingly harder just to live a life; now you have to create it. There are thousands upon thousands of insistent models suggesting new ways, better ways, more successful ways to do it. Your grandfather had a life, maybe. You don't. You have a lifestyle.

How can you match your puny, colorless, haphazard existence against the well-shaped, dramatic, meaningful stories of the people on the television and at the movies? Well, you can't. You'll never live up to their image of you. But you try: you buy what they buy, you do what they do, you think what they think. Somehow it doesn't come out the same way when you do it. It's not real. It's only valid when they do it. But you can't stop thinking about it. Run off to Vermont to stick spouts in unsuspecting maple trees, install a woodburning fireplace, and eat only what you can grow. Go ahead. They're way ahead of you. The point is that the media have made us a supremely self-conscious society. For a while a few years ago, some of us thought we could drop out. We can't drop out. Dropping out is part of the model. It's like *not* thinking about elephants.

The media culture isn't necessarily a bad thing. Its self-consciousness, after all, is highly intellectual. Lifestyles (as opposed to lives) are matters of ideas, opinions, knowledge, judgment, and decision, and that can't be so wrong, at least theoretically. The examined life is worth living. But more and more it seems to have got out of hand. Everyone's a star, and psychologists talk about "lifescripts" and "games people play." Fiction is rampant. Someone gets shot on the street, everyone turns to look for the cameras. There's no *there* there anymore, as Dorothy Parker once said. (Gertrude Stein said it of Oakland, too.) The arbitrariness of the media culture is reflected in the architectural organization of our lives, too. We used to live in towns; they weren't planned, they were hodge-podges, but they worked. With the freedom the automobile offered, we were able to impose a logic on this experience: we stretched the units of the town out along the linear highways. We still had nostalgia for the old village: shops on the highways still affect names that suggest they are more than just individual units in an endless uniform line: "Car City," "Christmas Town," "Food Village." The lines got too long, so we curled them in upon themselves and called them shopping centers. But something was still missing.

The mall was born. The shops were organized along a central pathway. In the middle is a focus, where people can meet and eat, talk, and just hang out together. We had rebuilt the nineteenth-century town, although in a more convenient location (out of town), and covered over, so it won't rain, and the trees don't lose their leaves because they're rubber trees or live oaks. Everything looks much better. It looks like it should. It looks like TV. It looks like California.

Now, everyone knows all about this lifestyle culture. Critics have been

350

issuing jeremiads about it for many years—they're part of the style of it. There is nothing you can do about self-consciousness on this scale without performing a collective frontal lobotomy. So perhaps the best thing is simply to settle back and enjoy the immense humor of it as we sink slowly, slowly into the vast, warm, fictional sea . . . until eventually—as it will—it covers us over and none of us is real anymore and we're all actors or characters, our lives written out for us by people with more talent, and staged by designers who know their business, and bright young directors with brilliant futures.[1]

This is the world that two of the best and brightest (if not the youngest) of them—Michael Ritchie and Paul Mazursky—gently analyze and satirize in their films. Consider the possibilities.

Michael Ritchie the Ironist

Michael Ritchie's films are deceptively simple. He comes on as a relaxed, often charming and jovial storyteller. As a result, it is only recently that critics have started talking about his work seriously. Yet behind the unpresumptuous facade, there is a cinematic intelligence as complex as any operating in America today. Ritchie has continued the work Haskell Wexler began in *Medium Cool*: the analysis of the intricate relationship between media fiction and lived reality. But he has done it with an awareness of the high comedy of the human condition, and that is an equally important component of his style. Like most of his contemporaries, he's also struggling quietly with the tyrannical forms bequeathed to us by the genres of the thirties and forties, but he doesn't confront them head-on like Cassavetes, or parody them like Altman; he burrows from within, using the forms for his own purposes while he comments on them at the same time.

His six films to date represent a range of subtle approaches to the problem of the relationship of film and reality, from the near-documentary style of *Downhill Racer* (1969) and *The Candidate* (1972), via the detour of burlesque in *Prime Cut* (1972), his most unusual film, to the progressively more straightforward entertainments of *Smile* (1975), *Bad News Bears* (1976), and *Semi-Tough* (1977). Ritchie's first four films were marginal enterprises, barely returning their investments or failing outright, as in the case of *Smile*. *Bad News Bears* and *Semi-Tough*, in contrast, have been major financial successes of the last few years. They've established Ritchie finally as a bankable director.

There are those who consider these two films less ambitious works than their predecessors; certainly they are more candidly aimed at mass audiences. But Ritchie has never thought of himself as a coterie director. He

351

For *The Candidate*, Ritchie and his associates staged an authentic campaign. Robert Redford's face was all they needed to draw crowds.

also has looked toward large audiences for his films even if he didn't always get them. And his most recent work is of a pattern with his earlier films. The new films are cut from the same cloth, but the shape is smarter. It's worth pointing out, too, that both *Downhill Racer* and *The Candidate*, which established Ritchie's earliest reputation, were Robert Redford productions and, as Ritchie puts it, "very much ruled by Redford's sensibilities. If you see *All the President's Men*, the strengths and the drawbacks of that film are very similar to the strengths and drawbacks of *The Candidate* or *Downhill Racer*."[2] In this context, we've only had "pure Ritchie" to judge from recently. His own voice is considerably warmer, more insouciant, than the Redford-influenced tone of the first two films.

What Redford likes to do is show how things work. *Downhill Racer* is simply the best film ever made about the world of high-powered sports, just as *The Candidate* is arguably the most perspicacious film we have about campaigning, and *All the President's Men* is a fine evocation of the job of the working journalist. Ritchie likes the latter Redford production, but his reservations about it are instructive. He wishes, he told me, that the film had spent more time on the personalities of Woodward and Bernstein. He wanted to see them bumble more (as they did in real life). He thinks the film would have had more resonance if we knew that our heroes had almost been fired for incompetence, and that they were so desperate to get the story that they made several serious errors along the way.

Ritchie directing *The Candidate*.

Similarly, he thinks *The Candidate* is flawed because Bill McKay's wife is treated so offhandedly. If he had it to do over again, he would expand that relationship considerably. But Redford isn't very interested in this aspect of things. He is clearly, from the evidence of these three films, intent on explaining in detail how the job is done; character is secondary.

Ritchie has a parallel interest in how institutions and individuals function within society, but he also wants to know how people live their lives—or their lifestyles—off the job. The irony is the same, but the attitude toward the people is more gentle. From David Chapellet in *Downhill Racer* to Billy Clyde Puckett and Shake Tiller in *Semi-Tough*, none of Ritchie's characters is essentially likable; he makes them so. He probes every weakness, and there's hardly a scene in a Ritchie film that doesn't have at least one satiric point to it. Moreover, the points are sharp, but Ritchie applies them with empathy. Ritchie *likes* the butts of his jokes, and that's important.

Conversely, his ironic touch may seem outrageously broad at times, but it is always firmly rooted in reality. The "Exhausted Rooster" ceremony, for example, that the Jaycees perform in *Smile* may look like a very broad joke indeed, but Ritchie simply duplicated one he'd observed. Jaycees who saw the film laughed a little, but a group of them in Norfolk, Virginia, after a screening, could come up to him afterwards and say, " 'Wow, that was terrific. You know we do our Exhausted Rooster Cere-

Redford and Gene Hackman in *Downhill Racer*. David Chapellet learns to smile for the cameras.

mony a little differently, but from now on we're going to do it the way they do it in the film.' "[2] Most people do know how fictitious their lives have become. They're not stupid. As Big Bob Freelander (Bruce Dern) says in *Smile* after telling his story about how he once had a date with Liz Taylor, but she didn't show up, "You just learn to expect a little less from life."

The Liz Taylor story is crucial. Many of Ritchie's characters are vaguely disappointed with their lives: they don't measure up to the American Dream, birthright of all consumers, that the media present. This is especially true of *Smile*, in which the score of contestants strive brightly and earnestly to fit the image of Young American Miss while their elders more or less learn to come to terms, expecting a little less from life. But even the honchos of *Semi-Tough* are desperately and breathlessly trying to stay au courant with the latest lifestyle self-improvement plan. And the Little League—the name tells you this—of *Bad News Bears* is only a small copy of the Big League: it forces kids to play all too seriously at being adults. Walter Matthau's boozy, irascible Morris Buttermaker at least lets the Bears off the hook at the end of the film. Adults don't have that option.

A number of Ritchie's films have dealt with the other half of the media connection. David Chapellet and Bill McKay (both played by Robert Redford) learn to manipulate the media to their own advantage in *Downhill Racer* and *The Candidate*. Billy Clyde Puckett (Burt Reynolds) and

Shake Tiller (Kris Kristofferson) aren't bad at the game either in *Semi-Tough*. Gene Hackman's Mary Ann (*Prime Cut*) is a metaphor for the media baron: "I give 'em what they want," says Mary Ann, the meat-packer who deals in drugs and girls, "things to stick in their arm and things to rub their belly with."

Mary Ann aside, Ritchie's characters are often knowledgeable. They aren't victims of the system and so they don't fit the common patterns of seventies movies. They can win. The victories may by Pyrrhic, but the struggle continues.

Ultimately, what's most interesting about Ritchie's movies is that he can create such real, dimensional, identifiable characters within a form that is at least ironic and more often fully satiric. Irony and satire are objective. They focus the main attention on the teller of the tale and his point of view. They are meant to draw conclusions, to analyze. It's not often that characters have much of a chance to defend themselves, as it were, in such forms. Michael Ritchie has developed a style that is a remarkable fusion of identifiable realism and commentative irony. He's able to bring it off mainly because he has a highly sophisticated sense of the function of realism in film.

Downhill Racer, *The Candidate*, and *Smile* were all shot with semidocumentary techniques. The first film was shot on location during the amateur ski season in Europe; dialogue is minimal (it was often written the night before); it's the feel that Ritchie captures of the business of sports that makes the film so successful. When local politicians saw the turnout for the parade Ritchie staged for Robert Redford/Bill McKay they told the star all he had to do was name his office. They'd get him elected for real. The pageant in *Smile* works so well because Ritchie staged a real one. None of the contestants knew who would win and the audience had paid $2.50 each to watch. They weren't there to see a movie; they were there to see a beauty pageant. All the "talent" routines the girls do were copied from life, even including the "Rotting Maggots of Death" poem.

In a way, this technical realism may work counter to Ritchie's best commercial interests. He comes too close to the truth. This is most evident with *Smile*, his problem child. The tone of the film seems too broadly burlesque. Exhausted Roosters kissing a chicken's ass? "Rotting Maggots of Death" in the middle of a Beauty pageant? Audiences felt uncomfortable with the film. People especially dislike the teenage peeping toms, yet most men can remember similar experiences, or they knew kids like that when they were fifteen. Verisimilitude is sometimes embarrassing. *The Candidate* worked the other way, forecasting Jerry Brown's campaign and election in California several years before it actually took place. (Ritchie says Brown himself loves the film. "He wanted to buy time on it when it was shown on TV during the campaign, but his advisors talked him out of it at the last minute, pointing out to him that people might misunderstand.")

At times maybe Ritchie comes off a bit bushy-tailed. His naive wonder at this brave new world isn't necessarily shared by mass audiences. In recent films he has retreated from his characteristic stance a little. He thins out the mass of satiric detail, as in *Bad News Bears*, or he forces the film into a more traditional star-centered narrative form, as in *Semi-Tough*. Yet the point of view is still brightly incredulous. Ritchie takes such active pleasure in the absurdity that surrounds him that it's hard not to join him.

Michael Ritchie was born in Wisconsin and grew up in Berkeley, where his father taught psychology at the university. He studied history and literature at Harvard and picked up a "track record" early with his production of Arthur Kopit's first play, *Oh Dad, Poor Dad, Momma's Hung You in the Closet and I'm Feelin' So Sad*. Doors opened. He was offered and accepted a job as assistant producer to Robert Saudek on the *Omnibus* television series in the early sixties. Other series followed: *Profiles in Courage*, then directorial assignments including episodes of *The Man from UNCLE*, *Dr. Kildare*, *The Big Valley*, and *Felony Squad*. He directed the pilot for *The Outsider* and more than a dozen episodes of *Run for Your Life*, including one (his best, he says) by Adrien Joyce. He didn't get on well with the Hollywood television establishment. This all occurred before youth had become a badge of merit, and his age was against him. He also developed a habit of doing things differently, which wasn't at all appreciated. At the same time, he was working on industrials and documentaries (sometimes with the Maysles brothers), and one suspects this experience was at least as important to his development as a filmmaker as the bread-and-butter fiction series.

Robert Redford saw one of Ritchie's television films and hired him immediately to direct *Downhill Racer*. Paramount thought of it mainly as an exploitation product for ski buffs, and rushed production in order to get it into distribution for the winter season. But audiences discovered the film had a lot more going for it than snow and schusses and, despite Paramount's best efforts, *Downhill Racer* has become a repertory classic.

Ritchie's first feature bears some of the vestiges of his television career. It's a very tight film, cool in tone. The images are closely cropped, and the editing is sharp and efficient. The story, too, seems initially like a made-for-TV melodrama, but working with screenwriter James Salter, Ritchie has turned it into something much more interesting. It's an extraordinary evocation of the rhythms and feel of competitive skiing. It's a film of felt truths, an assured collage of images and sounds, each of which contributes to our immediate experience of the locales and the people. To increase the verisimilitude, Ritchie de-dramatizes the action. His characters are only semi-articulate anyway, so this becomes a story of looks and gestures rather than words. The judicious mixture of professionals and nonprofessionals also adds considerably to the truth of the film. (*Smile*, *The Candidate*, and *Bad News Bears* would benefit from this technique as well.) In effect, the film is acted cinéma vérité.

The style fits the theme. If there's a classic antagonist in the movie, it's not the mountain, not even the other skiers, it's journalism. David Chapellet is a crotchety, selfish loner—eminently dislikable—but the television commentators seem to have no trouble turning him into a modest, shy, All-American hero fit for public consumption. And he hates them for it. Television monitors and microphones are all over *Downhill Racer*, and the film even develops a technical critique of television sports coverage.

The film is more complex than it looks. But eventually it's successful because at it's center there is an interesting network of relationships between people—icy, perhaps, but nonetheless real. Chapellet goes home to Idaho Springs, Colorado, one summer and visits his dad, who's even more tight-lipped than David. They stare at each other across the kitchen. David tries to explain: "I'll be famous. I'll be a champion." Pause. Dad replies: "World's full of 'em." David hops in the old Chevy to cruise down main street looking for the girl he left behind. He finds her. They make love in the back seat. After, the girl tells David of her plans for the future. (She has a chance to go to school in Denver to become a dental technician.) His response is a blank look. A pause. Then—"Say, you got any more of that gum?" Enough said.

After *Downhill Racer*, Ritchie spent most of 1970 working on an adaptation of William Bradford Huie's *Three Lives for Mississippi*, about the 1964 assassination of Chaney, Goodman, and Schwerner. Nobody was interested. It was the first of a number of projects that never got off the ground and which, because they weren't shot, have contributed to the impression of Ritchie as a director obsessed with sports and competition. He's not, really; he's interested, yes, but not compulsive about it. It's just turned out that these are the only films he's been allowed to make.

In direct contrast to Cassavetes, Altman, Coppola, and most of the filmmakers of the New Hollywood, Ritchie has never tried to set himself up in business. I once asked him why. "The danger really is," he replied, "that you have to have enormous risk capital in order to have the project far enough along so that you can command your own deal. You have to do what Kubrick did, which is to spend two or three years assembling an organization that can supervise distribution. I'd rather make movies."

In 1971, Ritchie took on the assignment of directing Paddy Chayefsky's *Hospital*, He did not get along well with the playwright-turned-filmmaker. Chayefsky fired him a few weeks before shooting was to begin. "On the rebound," he took *Prime Cut*, Robert Dillon's quirky and ingenious screenplay. He shot the film during the late summer of that year, racing the wheat harvest north through the Midwest to Saskatchewan. Cinema Center Films, CBS's quondam production unit, was in the process of going out of business by this time, but they nevertheless took enough interest in *Prime Cut*, one of their last films, to "seriously reshape" Ritchie's cut.

The Candidate, which had been in development for more than a year, was shot on location in northern California in the winter of 1971-72. Ritchie and Redford had full control of the film. Warner Bros. picked it up only after it was completed.

Ritchie then spent a year on what he calls a "contemporary ghost story," "The Stone Carnation," which was to be made for Playboy Productions. It was canceled. Next, he turned to the development, with Stanley Elkin, of an ambitious original screenplay, "The Art of War," which followed the career of photographer Robert Capa from the Spanish Civil War to his death in Indochina in 1954. The film would have cost at least $5 million. Columbia cancelled.

In late 1973 and early 1974 Ritchie was working on a screenplay of the book *Ten-Second Jailbreak* by *Ramparts* writers Bill Turner and Warren Hinkle, which recounts the true story of an escape from a Mexican prison several years ago. Ritchie saw it as a kind of "Watergate black comedy." Charles Bronson was hired. Charles Bronson didn't see it that way. Ritchie left. He had been working on *Smile* for some time with writer Jerry Belson. He was able to convince David Picker to finance the film. *Smile* got made, in August and September of 1974.

By the time it was released, Ritchie had (luckily) already signed to direct *Bad News Bears*, a film that happened very quickly in the summer of 1975. After *Bears* returned $25 million in rentals (far more than Ritchie's previous four films combined), he had no worries. But it had been close. If *Smile* had failed before *Bears* began, chances are very good it would never have been made, certainly not with Ritchie. Shooting *Smile*, Ritchie and his cast used to joke that they had something for everyone—adults, teenagers, children. But if a film full of unknown—but nubile—teenage girls bombs, who in his right mind would take a chance on a movie full of equally unknown but even younger boys? (Tatum O'Neal doesn't even do a high kick.) Commercial folly, obviously. *Bad*

News Bears was the fourth most profitable film of the year and has already resulted in two sequels.*

To be fair, Ritchie's film bears little resemblance to the draft script Paramount's executives first saw. That one was obviously commercial. Bill Lancaster had designed it that way. He knew he couldn't sell a film about baseball. According to Ritchie, the character of Buttermaker was much younger, and spent most of his time having an affair with the wife of the coach of the other team. "The kid on the motorcycle [Kelly] was selling hard drugs, and *his* mother had an affair with the councilman who set up the team. When the kid found out about the affair, he stole the councilman's Mercedes and there was a mad police chase. . . . "

Ritchie's relationships with his screenwriters have always been intimate. He never takes screen credit himself, but it's clear he has a major effect on the final version of the shooting script. As time goes on, he seems to be more in control of the preparation of script. *Smile* was his own conception. Jerry Belson was hired to execute it. *Bad News Bears* was entirely rewritten after Ritchie came into the project. *Semi-Tough* owes very little to Dan Jenkins's book. Ritchie developed the core of the film after reading Adam Smith's *Powers of Mind* and hired Walter Bernstein to write the story. The writers, for their part, consistently win awards. Bill Lancaster won the Writers Guild Award for *Bad News Bears;* Jerry Belson was nominated for the same award; Jeremy Larner won an Oscar for *The Candidate;* and Walter Bernstein received a Writers Guild nomination for *Semi-Tough.*

Early on in *The Candidate*, professional political manager Marvin Lucas (Peter Boyle) sits down with shaggy-haired lawyer and vaguely radical activist Bill McKay and makes what turns out to be a convincing argument for getting involved in electoral politics. "You're happy? O.K., clams are happy. You saved some trees, you got a clinic opened. Does that make you feel good? Meanwhile Jarmon sits on his committees and carves up the land, the oil, the taxes. . . . " Lucas has phrased the essential political dilemma for activists in the early seventies: electoral politics is cooptative and ultimately severely compromising. But "street" politics seems futile.

In some ways *The Candidate* is a companion piece to *Downhill Racer*. Both Redford films deal with a highly competitive situations, both de-

---

*Paramount approved Ritchie for the film, he told me, "because they had just seen *Smile* and they'd seen the kids talking dirty and they figured, well, he can direct kids talking dirty. They don't look much beyond your last project."

The Candidate: Bill McKay and opponent Crocker Jarmon (Don Porter) in a television debate . . . McKay with campaign manager Marvin Lucas (Peter Boyle). . . . McKay with his father John, a former governor (Melvyn Douglas) . . . and with his wife Nancy (Karen Carlson). This last shot is from a sequence that was cut from the film. Ritchie now wishes he'd done more with the relationship between McKay and his wife. [Still courtesy Michael Ritchie.]

velop an interesting tension between cinéma vérité and acted fiction, both work well to capture particular atmospheres. The relationships among the characters are similar: Redford is again a performer with a coach (two of them this time, in fact) who has equal troubles with the media and women. But *The Candidate* is a much more ambitious film. It was intended as a political instrument. Ritchie, Redford, and Larner wanted the film to be seen by delegates to the Democratic National Convention in 1972. They hoped it would have some small effect.

It's doubtful that it did. It poses a meaningful dilemma, and does so with fine precision. But it doesn't at all suggest a way out of the quandary. At the end of the film, Bill McKay is left almost cowering in a sterile white hotel room. He turns to his mentor and manager and inquires plaintively, "What do we do now?" What is to be done? Neither the candidate nor *The Candidate* seems to have any idea.

Yet as a portrait of the mechanics of the media-dominated electoral process in which the political operatives' main work is to establish a semifiction that is eminently salable, the film is nothing less than brilliant. It shows how very rewarding Ritchie's cinéma-vérité technique can be in certain situations.

Most of the filmmakers had worked in political compaigns (real ones) recently. Larner had been a speechwriter for Eugene McCarthy. Ritchie shot film for John Tunney. So *The Candidate* is packed with insights into the process. Its details ring with accuracy. Many of the characters are sharp caricatures of real political kingmakers: Allen Garfield's Klein is a dead ringer for David Garth. Peter Boyle's Lucas has touches of Richard Goodwin and Richard Aurelio (manager of a former political star named John Lindsay who turned to acting after he left politics). Crocker Jarmon (Don Porter) spoofs Senator and former song-and-dance man George Murphy (who turned to politics after he left acting). McKay himself is part Jerry Brown, part John Tunney; his physical resemblance to Robert Kennedy struck many people as spooky. Even some minor characters are recognizable—one of McKay's aides, for example, is a double for Jeff Greenfield, who was a speechwriter for both Kennedy and Lindsay.

On another level, we can't forget that Melvyn Douglas, who plays McKay's former-governor father (Pat Brown), is married to Helen Gahagan Douglas, who once ran for the Senate from California. She was beaten by a Red-baiting, shifty-eyed young congressman with a perpetual five-o'clock shadow who later cheated his way to even higher office. The network of relationships between the real world and the media world in *The Candidate* is complex indeed.

Yet as truthful as it is, *The Candidate* is still marred by the attitude it projects. In most of Ritchie's films, the distance irony creates is useful as well as attractive. But here, dealing with a concrete political situation, we want answers, or at least the attempt at them. "What do we do now?" We didn't answer that question at all satisfactorily in 1972. And we still haven't.

Prime Cut is Ritchie's most unusual film. The reason is Robert Dillon's unique sense of humor. If Cinema Center's release version is only a poor copy of the Ritchie-Dillon original, nevertheless this is as close as the writer has ever come to seeing his particular brand of black comedy on the screen. Ritchie clearly understands what's going on in Dillon's head.

Nick Devlin (Lee Marvin), a natty Irish gangster from Chicago, is sent to Kansas City, in the heart of the heartland, to corral the newly independent and uppity Mary Ann (Gene Hackman), a meatpacker-gangster who does a healthy business in drugs and girls on the side. Devlin rescues one of the girls (Sissy Spacek) from Mary Ann's scientifically run flesh pens. (This is what happens in the producer's version; in Ritchie's original cut he simply took her, almost against his will, as collateral.) Finally, Nick has a classic shootout with Mary Ann, shoots him in the groin, and refuses to finish him off. (In the producer's version, he also rescues the little girls from the "orphanage" where they are being trained.)

The film makes magnificently sardonic connections between the macho myths of the Hollywood gangster genre, capitalist consumption psychology, and sexism, and it does so with a very subtle and reasonable sense of humor. The Cinema Center people, in their release cut of the film, worked hard to attenuate these strengths. They injected the love story and the happy ending. (Ritchie's cut ended with a mock-samurai confrontation between Hackman and Marvin after which Marvin stepped out into a vast field of sunflowers surrounding the barn as the 4-H band played and the credits rolled.) In his cut, according to Ritchie, "the tone of cold irony was more pervasive and the black comedy much stronger."

Yet there's still enough of this left that audiences can see what Dillon and Ritchie were up to. In France and England, *Prime Cut* has become a cult movie. Eventually, it will be rediscovered here as well.

You can see what the film might have been in the centerpiece sequence which remains intact: a fine homage to *North by Northwest*. Marvin and Spacek are hiding from Mary Ann's henchmen in the elephant-eye-high wheat. Suddenly a fat-faced grinning farm boy in a giant reaper-baler appears from nowhere and begins bearing down on them. There is no escape in the wide-open spaces. He cuts wide swathes through the waving wheat. Marvin and Spacek panic. They're about to be harvested. Just then, in the nick of time, Marvin's men arrive in their big-city Cadillac to save the harried couple. They ram the huge car smack into the mouth of the reaper-bailer and the country devours the city as the machine dutifully chews up the Cadillac, bales it neatly, and drops it out the back in clanking turds. *Prime Cut*, even cut primly by producers running scared, remains the most ambitious movie about American genres of the seventies, and for those who know it, one of the best.

Smile and *Bad News Bears* are very similar films. Why one was an enormous success and the other a box-office failure is difficult to tell. It may just be the preteen audience has a $30-million clout. They were attracted to *Bad News Bears* while *Smile* apparently held little interest for them.

Both films are gentle studies of suburban small-town lifestyles. Both have episodic structures. Both study groups of kids and hang their plots on contests. *Smile* is more elaborate and more insightful, but its greater ambition can't alone explain its financial failure.

We spend most of our time in *Smile* with the thirty-three teenage contestants in the film's semi-real Young American Miss beauty pageant, and although several of them are exceptionally funny, Ritchie never

Prime Cut: Lee Marvin comforts Sissy Spacek just after they have escaped a fate worse than death. The reaper/baler has almost finished digesting the Cadillac.

exploits them, which is what sets *Smile* apart from other, more simplistic satires of middle-class America. Elsewhere in Santa Rosa, the all-American town that had once served as the peaceful setting for Hitchcock's *Shadow of a Doubt*, life goes on. People make the best of things. All except Andy Di Carlo, that is. Andy (Nicholas Pryor) makes little brass and plastic trophies for a living, the kind that clutter the mantelpieces of millions of amateur bowlers and Little League managers throughout the country. Andy has begun to drink heavily. He is approaching his thirty-fifth birthday, which means he'll have to undergo the Bears Club's Exhausted Rooster Ceremony, a kind of ritual admission of impotence and humility before the gods of youth. Nobody else has the slightest idea why Andy's so cranky. His wife, Brenda (Barbara Feldon), is annoyed at what she calls his "sarcasm and self-pity."

We follow these people during the pageant week. Along the way there are several shaggy-dog episodes. "Little Bob" Freelander is caught trying to photograph the girls in their dressing room—he has orders from his junior-high classmates for a dozen Polaroid nudes. He is sentenced to see a psychiatrist. Andy survives his ceremony, takes a futile pot shot at his wife, but only wings her. She shows up for the last night of the pageant with her arm in an impeccably tailored sling. The girls rehearse their hearts out, learn to rub vaseline on their teeth, sing the songs, do their skits, and take revenge on one particularly ambitious contestant. The winners are chosen, and as we leave beautiful Santa Rosa, the city is

363

Smile: Big Bob Freelander (Bruce Dern) and Brenda Di Carlo (Barbara Feldon) discuss the pageant . . . . the girls arrive . . . . the girls rehearse . . . . and Tommy French (Michael Kidd), the choreographer of the show, comforts Doria Houston, Miss Anaheim (Annette O'Toole) after a nasty fall as her roommate the naive Miss Antelope Valley (Joan Prather) massages her leg.

getting back to normal. Big Bob is back at the car lot, Brenda's on the mend, the winners of the pageant are learning how to endorse products, and Andy? Andy is lost in the backwash, an anomaly in small-town U.S.A., where everything is for the best in this best of all possible worlds, and people have learned to expect a little less from life. *Smile* has a surprisingly elegiac tone.

The myth of the American Dream survives in the person of the Young American Misses, but there's just a hint of a rising new consciousness. Miss Antelope Valley (Joan Prather), who has been the primary focus of interest among the contestants, is just slightly more skeptical than the other girls. At one point she turns to her roommate and suggests that perhaps beauty pageants are a little demeaning. Miss Anaheim (Annette O'Toole) replies: "Boys get money for making touchdowns, why shouldn't girls get money for being cute?" There is a pause, as Miss Antelope Valley works this out in her own sloe-eyed way, then: "Yeah, but maybe boys *shouldn't* get money for playing football." The light dawns, slowly but inevitably; *Smile* has the patience to wait for it.

The Bad News Bears is a much simpler film. Like its successor, *Semi-Tough*, it's a star movie. Walter Matthau cost $750,000, Tatum O'Neal $350,000, and as a result, *Bears* cost three times as much as *Smile* to bring to the screen. In financial terms it was worth it. The stars guaranteed that Paramount would sell the film initially. Gradually, the word of mouth built among the preteen set; the rest is history.

The film doesn't have the resonance of *Smile* or Ritchie's earlier films. It spends a great deal more time telling a good yarn than investigating the social and mythic matrix from which that yarn is spun. But it is ambitious in its way. Ritchie and Lancaster took a considerable chance focusing intently on the kids of the Little League team. The film works as well as it does because it presents these kids accurately and realistically. It is the ultimate anti-Disney movie and young people responded to it with understandable passion. Once again, Ritchie found himself drawing vital performances out of nonactors through a combination of cinéma vérité and script, and this technique works as well as it did in the past. Maybe it's carping to ask *Bad News Bears* to do more—it's surely the best film about and for children in many years, and we need more like it—but one can't help thinking that it would be nice if *Bears* extended itself a bit further, into family and school, for example. If it had, it would have been a more reflective film. It also would then have been slower-paced. And it wouldn't have been so popular.

Ritchie thinks each successive movie he has made has been better than its predecessor. If the films are judged solely as products, it's hard to argue with him. *Semi-Tough* has an even slicker gloss to it than *Bad News Bears:* more stars, more action, quicker pacing—zip, zip, zip, it's the closest

Morris Buttermaker (Walter Matthau) lectures his team. Some of them even listen.

The Semi-Tough triangle: Barbara Jane Bookman, the owner's daughter (Jill Clayburgh), with Billy Clyde Puckett (Burt Reynolds) and Shake Tiller (Kris Kristofferson) in the apartment they all share.

thing we have to a really modern screwball comedy. It's also colder and less amenable than, say, *Smile* or *The Candidate*. If Ritchie has lost some feeling as he has moved further away from the realism of his earliest films, he has, conversely, picked up a stronger sense of entertainment. I suppose it was inevitable.

Ritchie calls *Semi-Tough* "*Philadelphia Story*, except it's about two jocks." As a genre film it works magnificently. It is by far Ritchie's funniest movie. It is not a critique of merchandised sports and consciousness groups. It begins where criticism leaves off. Like Barbara Jane's publishing friend, it assumes the absurdities as givens. It couldn't possibly conceive of a world organized differently. The editor wants Billy Clyde to think about doing a sports book, not like the usual ripoffs—you know, honest, forthright, let it all hang out—"The real *truth*! What drugs the players take . . . how the games are fixed." Like that. Are there more homosexuals on offense or defense? What about orgies? All within the bounds of good taste, of course.

The movie begins with a game and ends with a game and returns to the field once in a while in the middle, but, as Ritchie has pointed out, it's not really about sports. And that fits. Sports isn't about sports anymore, either. It's about doing commercials for condoms on cable TV and groupies and consciousness-raising and getting your ass traded to Seattle—or Tampa Bay—when you cross the owner. The film thoroughly

Keith Carradine as the young American director with Monica Vitti, the wife of the Italian producer, in *An Almost Perfect Affair*, shot partially on location in Cannes during the 1978 film festival. A slow-paced rather private affair, the film was unsuccessful.

catalogues all the with-it self-help therapies and it is especially good on est (BEAT in the film). It's ingenious and pointed throughout, but somehow it doesn't stick. All the jokes are in the right places with the right targets and they work within the limits of the film. The relationship between Jill Clayburgh's Barbara Jane and her two goofy roommates is all too uniquely contemporary. There isn't a dead moment in the film. (The wedding at the end is thin and sloppy, but carried off with enough energy to fool you long enough.) But . . . .

Maybe *Semi-Tough* is too loud. Ritchie's speaking in a professional voice here. He's very good at it, but he's performing. His films used to speak in a more personal tone. There were hesitancies, small private jokes, digressions, and a sense of wonder. Sometimes he lost his train of thought for a moment. But there *was* a train of thought. Now he's cleaned up his act. He's much more entertaining to a greater number of people. But those of us who knew him when miss the less confident, more tentative timbre of his earliest films. He's not likely to get it back, any more than the rest of us are likely to escape from lifestyles back to lives. "Believing is shit," Friedrich Bismarck (the Werner Erhard character) tells us. "Being is where it's at." We've all got trouble with our Movagenic backspace and we'd better get pelfed before it's too late. Try to confront these lunacies and you get a response like Friedrich's: "Thank you. I acknowledge that." Might as well make movie-movies.

367

Paul Mazursky the Satirist

One of the first books of serious film criticism I ever read (this was back in the early sixties when "films" came from Europe; only "movies" were made here) was a little volume printed on delicate paper in 8-point type by the Wisconsin Film Society Press entitled, ambitiously, *Classics of the Film*. It was full of high seriousness, and that impressed me. Writing about movies and quoting Keats? Hmmn. Somewhere in the middle there was a prodigious article in defense of Bela Lugosi ("Be-la Lu-go-si. What these often mispronounced syllables evoke!") The author was evidently deeply and personally pained by the ignominy to which, he fully believed, this magnificent artist had been consigned by a gruff and uncaring world. By the second paragraph, awed by the seeming impossibility of the task before him the apologist for the macabre Hungarian was ready to concede. "In many ways," he wrote, "Bela Lugosi is a difficult figure. Perhaps one must take him *con amore* or not at all.'

I couldn't read on. I underlined those sentences. I put asterisks next to them. I typed them out on a little card and hung it above my desk. Never before, I thought, had the ultimate futility of criticism been so sublimely expressed. I had visions of masses of serious students of film in the future collectively approaching the benighted actor *con amore*. (Or not at all.) Be-la Lu-go-si.

Years later, that absurd critical dictum finally makes some sense. Here we are, confronted with Paul (né Irwin) Mazursky, an aging, long-haired kid from Brownsville, Brooklyn, who has made some very interesting movies in the last ten years. In many ways, he too is a difficult figure. Perhaps we should take him *con amore* or not at all.

Paul Mazursky's movies are simple and direct. There are no complex underlying theories here involving the mystique of the actor (as in Cassavetes's exercises), no tricky interplay between character and genre (as with Altman). Mazursky isn't madly ambitious to be an auteur of the first magnitude (or frightened that he may not make it) like Francis Coppola, and although he has some of the same sense of humor that sets Michael Ritchie's films apart, there isn't the same complicated set of motives in Mazursky's work that there is in Ritchie's. With Mazursky's films, what you see is what you get, and you either respond to it with admiration, even *con amore*, as I do, or you do not.

Mazursky is rather sensitive to criticism. (Or, more precisely, he's more openly responsive to it.) He has no particular personal reason to be, since his films are generally well received. But the people whom his films are about are people he knows, people he is clearly fond of, and he seems genuinely disappointed when people who watch and write about his

368

movies don't respond in the same way to them. Ask him why he didn't do this or did do that, and he's likely to counter a little too quickly, "Are you talking about a picture you would like to see or the picture you saw?"[3] And he's right, of course. Most criticism involves a kind of egoistic attack on art: the critic pushes here, pulls there, trying hard to rework the film (or book or play) into his own image. This is fine, as long as the film was meant as the opening statement in a dialectic between author and audience, but it doesn't work at all with films like Paul Mazursky's. As Wordsworth put it, "We murder to dissect."

Mazursky is rightly very protective of his people. They are resilient (which is one of their most admirable qualities) but nevertheless fragile. He himself has just taken satiric liberties with them. Maybe he feels a little guilty. He wants us to laugh, of course, but he also wants us to like them. We should leave them alone, now, let them breathe a little. Everyone in a Mazursky film is made to look at least a little bit foolish, but there is never a tone of ridicule. Quite the contrary. The most valuable quality of Mazursky's movies is the profound hum of the life force that courses through them. They are exhilarating, invigorating, affirmative. Fools that they show us to be, they celebrate us.

This doesn't wash well when judged by contemporary critical standards. A movie that ends with cast and crew wandering in a Las Vegas parking lot while Dionne Warwick sings "What the world needs now is love, sweet love" on the soundtrack? Another about a crusty but lovable old man *and his cat*! A third about a man who so loves his wife that he'll die if he can't have her back, that ends with a sublime reunion in Venice with a baby about to be born and the band playing the love theme from *Tristan und Isolde* in the background? Insupportable! No wonder the pundits approach Mazursky's work gingerly, if at all.

But he brings it off, I think. He's just as aware as, say, Cassavetes that what we now prefer to call relationships are often painful and unfulfilling. He knows as well as Michael Ritchie that our current social contract is absurd. But he takes such evident pleasure in our sillinesses, and he's so genuinely fond of his wonderfully foolish people, that his satire is therapeutic. He makes us believe in possibilities. Like victims of slapstick, Mazursky's characters don't quite seem to realize they've been bopped, kicked, slapped, and knocked over. They stick with you. They keep on keeping on, often grinning all the way. They know "we need the eggs." Mazursky's world is Woody Allen's without fear. He manages a proper balance between the death force and the life force, and his sense of that balance comes startlingly close to real wisdom.

In this respect, Mazursky's films are noticeably traditional. Not only because they avoid cinematic pyrotechnics to focus more intently on

Harry (Art Carney) and Tonto with Harry's son the California swinger (Larry Hagman).

characters and story, but more important, because they echo the American satiric sensibility that stretches back to Will Rogers, Chaplin, and even Mark Twain. Not to put too fine a point on it, but if Cassavetes is the American Bergman (an invidious comparison, but not inaccurate), then Mazursky is our Fellini. I've often thought, only half-jokingly, that the main problem with Bergman's characters was their environment—if only they'd take a vacation, go visit Fellini's people. Likewise, there are very few characters in American films of the seventies, from Travis Bickle to Nick and Mabel Longhetti, who wouldn't benefit greatly from a visit to a Mazursky movie. At the very least, they'd learn to take themselves considerably less seriously. My point is that it's relatively easy for a filmmaker to portray the death force rampant—it is so overwhelmingly present in our lives; all the evidence points to its imminent triumph. It's much harder to suggest convincingly that the life force still exists—harder and also more accurate.

Richard Corliss has called Mazursky "the Horace with a Heart of Gold." The reference to the Latin satirist is well taken. Yes, Mazursky is an affectionate critic in the Horatian mold. There's little of the bitterness of Juvenal here (or the nastiness of Preston Sturges, for that matter). But the "Heart of Gold" business is misleading. Mazursky's no Pollyanna. His films include their fair share of selfishness, broken marriages, pomposity, bad faith, failure, and suicide. However, you just never seem to put much weight on these negative factors because, in the first place, Mazursky regards them—almost insouciantly—as givens of our situation, and in the second, he makes it very clear that life goes on. We allow such positive statements in our music (o-bla-di, o-bla-da)—but of course that's what music's for, to make you feel good. We don't take too kindly to them in our films, which are now meant to be serious works of art and therefore, like respectable tragedy, should deal in death—or at least cripples and losers. Mazursky, evidently, has no truck with that theory.

Mazursky was born and raised in Brooklyn, moved to California when live television dried up in New York in 1959, and managed to accommodate himself to the West Coast lifestyle. Several years ago he moved back to New York (while still maintaining his place in L.A.) and now tries to spend at least half the year here. Why? In L.A., he told me, "you lose track of people. You see studio people, show business people, sun worshipers, the whole scene—some very decent people, some fine people—but you don't see the mob. If you have no need for seeing the mob then you have no conflict, but if you have a need, then you gotta come here. That's all there is to it."

This coastal dichotomy has ruled all his films. The first four were about California Southland lifestyles seen through the surprised eyes of the Easterner. The last two have been set in New York. *Harry and Tonto*, the transitional film, gives us a bridge in the form of a coast-to-coast odyssey. The difference between Los Angeles and New York for Mazursky is the difference between the all-too-imminent future, and the past, which is quickly receding. When his characters need roots, as they do in *Blume in Love* and *An Unmarried Woman*, they find them in Europe. L.A., conversely, is a perpetual state of what another kid from Brooklyn calls High Anxiety. New York is the fulcrum.

When he is in New York, Mazursky lives around the corner from me. The neighborhood is part of Greenwich Village but it doesn't fit the cliché image. There are some nice townhouses (Mazursky's), some old apartment houses (mine), good shops, some light industry, a famous bar or two, even some offices. It is an unusual mix, and it works well. We don't have to drive to malls to hang out. I met Mazursky in a local coffee shop to ask him some of the standard questions. We started off trading news about a mutual friend, a man of eighty-two whom we both admire. After a lifetime in the corporate world of suburbia, Le. Gravier returned to the city twenty years ago to get back into the stream. He fills his time with books and plays, helps run a recycling center, is on the board of his block association and trustee of an avant-garde repertory theater. His daughter lives in Florida; Le. gets bored in the sun. He's not only beaten the lifestyles, he's got a working truce with the death force. He's a hero.

Mazursky played Stephen Blume's uptight law partner in *Blume in Love*.

Paul would make a movie about him, but he already has.

Mazursky discovered acting at Brooklyn College ("Actor! Fantasy time! Get out of the ghetto"), where he starred in a production of *He Who Gets Slapped*, which he later took to Manhattan for a short run. Howard Sackler saw him in it and asked him to meet Stanley Kubrick—almost as young as Mazursky, but from the Bronx—who was preparing his first feature, *Fear and Desire*. Paul got the role, and his first ticket to the coast, "on an unscheduled airline out of Newark." He finished the part, returned to New York, acted in *Hello Out There*, the Saroyan play, at the fabled Provincetown Playhouse, started hanging out in the Village, and eventually directed a review (also at the Provincetown) called *Kaleidoscope*, which was "greeted with an incredibly bad set of reviews." (*Fear and Desire* was no winner either.)

He played Willie Loman. He played Undershaft in Shaw's *Major Barbara*. He made money working in a health-food restaurant, later recreated for *Next Stop, Greenwich Village*. One of the other guys working behind the counter knew John Cassavetes. Cassavetes tipped him that they were "looking for tough guys for this film out in Hollywood." Paul went to the casting session, answered the questions like a hood ("in a Fonz accent"), lied about his past credits, got the role in *Blackboard Jungle*, and found himself on a plane back to L.A. (The entire film was shot in Hollywood.)

Then he returned to New York ("I didn't like it there. It was awful") for one more try at the theater. He did a lot of live television. "The essential story of my career," he summarizes, "is that I started out wanting to play Hamlet, et cetera, and the work I began getting was juvenile delinquents, because that's what I looked like. In my mind I could have played great roles. I still think I could have. I really think I'm a good actor. I wasn't getting any. So I started doing a nightclub act." It was funny. He played the Bon Soir in New York, the Gate of Horn in Chicago, eventually the hungry i in San Francisco.

When live television began to dry up in New York, he finally gave in to the lure of the opposite coast and moved with his wife and child to L.A. By this time, he was writing his own nightclub routines. He continued the television acting, and started writing television scripts, "never selling them. I would look at the show on TV—*Route 66*, whatever it was—I'd write one and try to sell it. No way. I couldn't sell it. Very little encouragement."

Then some people he'd met in Chicago who called themselved *Second City* arrived for a tour. They got booked into New York, but wanted to keep the West Coast company going. "They called me, and I, with a man named Larry Tucker who had been a nightclub owner in New York—a big, fat, funny guy—we sort of teamed and took over the West Coast *Second City*." Soon they were improvising their own material. When *Second City* closed, they opened *Third City*, then other reviews.

At the same time, Mazursky was edging closer to film. He coproduced and costarred in a production of Genet's *Deathwatch*, which then was filmed, with Vic Morrow doing the directing. There was a very funny short called *Last Year at Malibu*. Then he and Tucker were hired as writers for the Danny Kaye television show. They stayed four years, the entire run of the show.

It was during this period, making a good living, that Mazursky started thinking of himself more as a writer than an actor. He tried his hand at movie scripts. He wrote a couple that didn't sell (including one he's still fond of called "H-Bomb Beach Party"). Then Tucker and he wrote *I Love You, Alice B. Toklas* (1968) and sold it to Warner Bros. with themselves as coproducers. Mazursky nearly directed the film as well, but got into "a squabble" with star Peter Sellers and backed down in favor of Hy Averback.

Mazursky still likes the film, "but it isn't me. It wasn't my vision of what I really saw the hippies as. After all, it was the first movie made in the United States about somebody dropping out and smoking grass!" Averback's direction is flat: the characters come out caricatures, but the film still has its moments. As it turned out, it didn't matter much because Warner Bros. "was terrified of its Jewishness. They were terrified of the

Bob & Carol share a hash pipe while Alice & Ted look on disapprovingly. (Natalie Wood & Robert Culp & Dyan Cannon & Elliott Gould.)

dope. They were terrified of everything. They released it with bookings right behind it."

Mazursky resolved to keep full control of any film he wrote. When he went to Mike Frankovich with the script for *Bob & Carol & Ted & Alice* (1970) somewhat later, the producer asked him why he wanted to direct. "Because that's the way it's gonna be," Mazursky told him. He ran through his credits, and concluded, "That's enough to direct a movie. Based on my experiences as an actor, the guys who directed me couldn't direct traffic—with a few wonderful exceptions." Frankovich said, "O.K., let's do it." The film eventually brought in net rentals close to $20 million and made Mazursky himself a lot of money. He didn't have to worry again. Part of the reason he has been able to do his own films his own way ever since is that he's been careful. "I kept enough of it," he points out, "to have what's notoriously called 'fuck-you money.' So when *Harry and Tonto* was turned down fourteen times, which it was, I was still there for the fifteenth time."

Mazursky and Tucker's next film, *Alex in Wonderland* (1971), was a financial disaster (Mazursky's only one, so far). It got caught in a change of management at M-G-M and was dumped only a few days after the final cut was completed and just before Christmas—in second-rate houses. When the critics caught up with the film (there were no advance screenings), they found it pretentious. They did, however, ironically recognize Mazursky-the-actor. He came in second, for his protrayal of Hal Stern, the producer, in the New York Critics Circle vote for best supporting actor.

Alex doesn't quite have the satirical distance of *Bob & Carol & Ted & Alice*, which is what may have thrown the critics off, but it remains the best movie there is about contemporary Hollywood. Mazursky has tried to buy back the rights to the film several times since in order to re-release it. It's as relevant today as it was seven years ago. But the studio won't sell. *Alex* is condemned to the timeless night of the living dead that awaits all tax write-offs.

This gives even more credence to Mazursky's great scene as Hal Stern, the producer who offers Alex money, paintings, trips to Europe, you name it—"just do for me!" I asked Mazursky to summarize his view of the business which, after all, has done rather well by him:

> Stupidity reigns! In any other business, acting the way they do, they'd fold immediately. Hollywood can survive all of that with one hit. That's what you gotta remember. Secondly, you gotta remember that the people running it very often—particularly in the last decade—don't know anything about movies. So that you begin to think then about Jack Warner and Sam Goldwyn and Harry Cohn as intellectual giants . . . because they would say things about story, content, conflict, drama, and they had emotions still from the streets from their own lives, whereas these guys—*mostly*—were deal-makers. And are. And that's it.

Alex's Wonderland: Alex (Donald Sutherland) spends half his time in the real world and half in fantasy. Real: his wife (Ellen Burstyn) and kids; Hal Stern (Paul Mazursky) the solicitous producer. Fantasy: a carriage ride with Jeanne Moreau, a visit with Fellini.

Ironically, the deal-makers offered Mazursky plenty of work after the failure of *Alex in Wonderland*. I thought that was curious. He explained: "Let's say you've made *Bob & Carol* so they know you can make a biggie. And then you make *Alex*, and they say, 'Boy, are we lucky! He got it out of his system! Now he'll go back and be a good guy again.'"

About this time he and Tucker parted, amicably he says. Instead of taking on directing assignments of other people's films, he took some of his "fuck-you money" and went first to Rome for six months with his wife and family, then to England. He came back and spent three months trying to sell *Harry and Tonto*. One producer told him, "I don't want to see a movie about my father." Another said simply, "I don't see the lines around the block." (He was wrong: the film eventually netted close to $5 million.) At least a dozen others turned him down. He began to think maybe he was fooling himself. He wondered if he should take one of the assignments that had been offered. He actually said yes to one, figuring, "I dunno. Maybe I can turn this thing around." Then he called them back the next morning and said, forget it, "I'm gonna write another script."

Blume in Love (1973) was ready in six weeks. "They read the script and we made a deal in ten minutes. They wanted me to use Ali McGraw, someone like that. . . ." He politely ignored the suggestion.

Blume in Love, made for Warner Bros., did all right financially, but it certainly set no records. Mazursky didn't care, because he'd discovered Alan Ladd at Twentieth Century–Fox, a production executive who likes to make interesting movies as well as money and has financed Mazursky's last three films, and come out well ahead on the deal.

On the whole, Paul Mazursky has had less trouble getting his films made within the system than the great majority of personal filmmakers. One big reason, of course, is the success of *Bob & Carol*. "One blockbuster takes care of you for a long time," he says. Another is that he knows how not to waste money. He avoids major box-office stars, who can treble the cost of a film immediately: he has an eye for good actors who are affordable. All his films have been made for $2 million or less (*Harry* cost only $1 million) except his most recent, *An Unmarried Woman*, which cost $2.3 million. "If somebody else made it," he points out, "it would have cost five." Add a couple of big stars, multiply by twenty-five percent studio overhead, and "right away it's four point eight."

There have been Mazursky projects that haven't made it to the screen. "Uncle Sam's Wild West Show," (a script by Venable Herndon) and "Chateau Hollywood," both about Alex's wonderland. But on the whole, this has been Mazursky's decision rather than the moguls'. His films are cheap enough so they don't represent huge gambles, and they

Blume in Love and Elmo in love. With Nina. (Susan Anspach, George Segal, Kris Kristofferson). Compare *Semi-Tough*, p. 366.

are close enough to what Hollywood knows so that they don't seem artistically rebellious. It's nice to know someone like this ·can operate with relative freedom within the present system, but it's not necessarily comforting to a younger director, unless, of course, he's had his blockbuster.

If you rearrange the order of Paul Mazursky's 6½ movies slightly, you begin to see that they are all parts of more or less the same story. Two of them are quasi-autobiographical; two develop parallel fantasies: they describe ways in which Mazursky's life—or one like it—might have developed (but didn't). Two provide a more general context, and the remaining film forecasts the future. You can understand, then, Mazursky's reluctance to take on assignments. He wants only to use people, ideas, and feelings that he knows from personal experience and observation.

In this sense his films are better seen as essays than constructed fictions. A Mazursky film never tells a great story: myth isn't part of his sphere of interest. What it does do is comment insightfully for a couple of hours on the way we live now (or in one case, the way we lived then). The plot structure is never very strong: After a while, the film simply comes to an end. Along the way, Mazursky has had the chance to comment broadly on manners and morals, attitudes and lifestyles. These are familiar essays about the ethos of the United States in the sixties and

377

seventies, and the perspective the films provide, one hopes, enables us to deal with our own lives a little more intelligently. Their aim then is essentially moral (in a very unpresumptuous way), and Mazursky's own authorial voice is an important element: nobody wants to see essays by impersonal, omniscient narrators.

There are two important corollaries to this approach. First, there is and must be a pervasive self-consciousness to films like these. Unlike Michael Ritchie, who makes films similar in tone but about other types of people, Mazursky sticks almost exclusively to the professional, more or less intellectual middle class he knows so well. His characters are lawyers, film directors, college professors, psychiatrists, actors, stockbrokers, artists, and social workers. This is the self-conscious class—the people who support the awareness movement, who may even know the difference between lives and lifestyles, although—in Mazursky's films—few of them ever transcend the latter to realize the former, authentically. (In contrast, Ritchie's people are athletes, politicians, car salesmen and children: these are notably not the cadres of the self-consciousness movement.) Because they think about the quality and style of their lives, Mazursky's people share his own general critical stance. They aren't objects of his films (like Ritchie's characters) so much as subjects. This accounts for much of the good feeling that his films project: we're all in this together: filmmaker, characters, audience. (Clearly, the majority of Mazursky's films are directed to a specific audience. They're not very entertaining if you don't know at least a little about these middle-class attitudes and concerns.)

I think you can see the second corollary coming. It is the direct result of the first: if Mazursky is going to stay with people like this, his films are going to be forced into a fairly narrow range of interests. He's well aware of this problem. Alex (like Mazursky at the time) finds himself with real power—the result of the success of his first film. He's paralyzed about his next movie. He should use this power to do good, he thinks, and make a film about the Black revolution, or ecology, or something else political. But he can't. All he really knows is himself. Mazursky's decision (he made a film about the difficulty of making a film, in part) is in a way courageous; it admits limitations. You can't do everything, so do what you do well, he seems to be telling himself, and what you do well is observe with useful precision and pleasant humor the condition of the professional class of which you are a part.

Part of the problem here is the California lifestyle culture that compartmentalizes existence. Blume and his wife met at a rally for farmworkers, but it's only in artificial situations like that that they have any contact at all with the world outside their class. When Mazursky moved

East (cinematically as well as geographically) the purview of his films broadened considerably. *Harry and Tonto, Next Stop, Greenwich Village*, and *An Unmarried Woman* are still about the people he knows but now in a much broader context. Are they more "realistic," then? Not really. It would have been noticeably untruthful to take Bob & Carol or Alex & Beth or even Blume & Nina out of their socially isolated boxes. And the urban environment of New York isn't the ultimate solution to this problem. *Harry* and *Next Stop* had greater ranges not only because of their settings but also because they dealt with people much younger and much older than Mazursky, which provided an added perspective. When he returned to his own generation in the new Eastern setting in *An Unmarried Woman*, the difficulties cropped up again.

Watching the film for the first time, I was a little annoyed at Erica. It's difficult to feel much sympathy for a woman whose erring husband obviously earns and spends more than a hundred thousand a year, whose main dilemma at the end of the film is whether to spend the summer in Vermont or move into a gorgeous old brownstone. I asked Mazursky about this and he shot back, "Oh. You wanted her to be poor, huh?" "Not poor," I said, "you know, more like people I know and like, more like me." There was only the briefest pause for consideration and I had to add, "Yes, poor, I guess."

But of course if Erica had been "more like us," she wouldn't have found herself in this difficulty in the first place. She wouldn't find her main emotional outlet with the ladies who lunch at "1/5"; she would have been into consciousness-raising years ago. This is the dilemma Mazursky confronts. He's aware of it. At the end of *An Unmarried Woman*, Erica—not overwhelmed by, but coping with, the huge painting Saul has given her—walks the streets, eventually merging into the background. In the foreground in the final freeze frame are two purposeful, interesting women from obviously quite another class. It's the barest hint, but quite suggestive, of the ultimate artificiality of Erica's position.

Within this admittedly narrow world, Mazursky covers the territory very well, and with surprising symmetry. *Next Stop, Greenwich Village* gives us the introduction to this life, *Alex in Wonderland* presents a portrait of the artist in midlife crisis (these are the two semi-autobiographical films); and *Harry and Tonto*, which Mazursky wrote when he turned forty and could suddenly understand, he says, what it would be like to be seventy, forecasts the end. *Bob & Carol & Ted & Alice* is his broadest investigation of the lifestyle culture. (Since it's the most general, it's no surprise it was the most popular.) *I Love You, Alice B. Toklas* had been a kind of preparatory essay for *Bob & Carol*. These films provide the context.

379

Mazursky's best films—*Blume in Love* and *An Unmarried Woman*—present complementary but opposing meditations on the same fearful fantasy: What happens if you lose your partner? The contrast in logic between the two films is interesting. *Blume*, from Mazursky's own point of view, is blatantly romantic: if Blume can't have Nina back, he'll die. He doesn't want to die, so therefore he will have her back. Q.E.D. Erica, in contrast, hurt just as much by separation as Blume, copes. The reason is simple: she loses Martin, but she gains a sense of herself. There's a new balance. Blume has no such luck. It's an index of the basic inequity of marriage. *An Unmarried Woman* is dedicated to Mazursky's wife, Betsy (who has recently reported in interviews that after raising two children, she is now trying to rebuild a career for herself).

Couples are very important in Mazursky films, even when they are metaphorical, as in *Harry & Tonto*. Almost alone among his contemporaries, Mazursky takes it for granted that the natural state is marriage, and that single people are anomalies. The titles tell us this. What's striking about *An Unmarried Woman* is that she *is* (unmarried); almost immediately she finds another mate at least as good as the last. Her real problem isn't her divorce from Martin, it's keeping her proper distance from Saul. In this respect, Mazursky is certainly an incurable romantic. But a lot of the strength of his films comes from this understanding—so deep-rooted it's taken for granted—that no man is an island. There's an underlying sense of community in Mazursky's movies, even if it is most often expressed in its basic unit: the family. Given the chance, his people immediately form into groups, as in *Next Stop, Greenwich Village*. Blume discovers he likes Elmo, Nina's lover, quite a lot, Ted and Carol and Bob and Alice (reading from left to right) find themselves in bed together at the end of their movie, and then mixing with cast and crew. Alex has visions of Fellinian circus groupings in his film, Harry naturally punctuates his cross-country trip with visits to his children (who aren't doing too well it must be said), and Erica has her lunch group. People are trying to extend the bonds, but it isn't easy.

Mazursky only has two kinds of titles, and if they don't announce the group, they announce the situation, which is usually a dilemma. Alex is in wonderland, Blume is in love; Larry Lapinsky and friends are in the Village and Erica is in transit. The structure of Mazursky's movies is classically simple: he sets up relationships between his people, puts them in the context of a situation, then sits back to see what happens. In terms of plot, this is subtly realistic and refreshing. Mazursky's movies never seem plot-ridden; his characters don't have to get anywhere in particular. The most pointed and dramatic ending of any of the six is Blume's reunion with Nina and child in Venice, but this is phrased in such a way that it might as well be Blume's fantasy. It doesn't really matter. Life goes on.

Within these situations, Mazursky tends to cast actors-as-people rather than actors-as-characters or actors-as-actors. With a few very minor exceptions (notably himself, Shelley Winters, Ellen Burstyn, and his psychiatrist, Donald F. Muhich), Mazursky never uses the same people twice. In this respect, he's looking for a documentary realism. Like everyone else who's any good, he has high respect for the actor's craft, and he works well with actors. But he'd rather cast them to type than experiment with the interrelationships among actor, persona, and character that his contemporaries find so absorbing. He adds occasional nonprofessionals to the cast to increase this documentary feel. Shrinks are played by shrinks, people from the art world appear in *An Unmarried Woman*, teacher Herbert Berghof played a role in *Harry and Tonto* and later showed up as a character in *Next Stop, Greenwich Village* (in which "Herb's" wife is played by the writer Helen Hanft).

Even the professionals are often put in a position from which they can't calculate responses. "It's very easy for good actors to get results, to indicate and do very good glib things," Mazursky says. "But it is very hard for them and for the director to trust or delve deeply and take the time; especially when you are shooting and time becomes money. . . ." Casting to type helps. So does loosening the restraints of plot. For the final bed scene in *Bob & Carol* Mazursky refused to indicate a direction. He knew he would have a shot of the four of them in bed, but he purposely didn't write the scene out. The actors "were very weird and very giggly and very strange. It was real; it was happening to them. I am to this day curious as to what would have happened had I just let the camera roll on forever. I don't know, we probably would have had *Deep Bob and Carol*. We would have made a lot more money."

In his own way, Paul Mazursky is trying to get in touch with feelings every bit as much as Esalen-soaked Bob and Carol are. He wants to find out why people do what they do. Those of us in the middle class all have that aim, now, for better or worse (and it's hard to criticize self-awareness), but there was a time when that particular cultural value was the province of a strict minority.

Next Stop, Greenwich Village show us the roots of the self-consciousness culture in the Bohemia of actors and writers, painters and playwrights the Village symbolized for everyone in the fifties. Mazursky pins down the coordinates of that influential subculture with magnificent precision. In those days, the thing was to be honest, authentic—like Brando. Larry Lapinsky and his friends work hard at it, but for the most part they just

The Greenwich Village gang just after one of Anita's periodic suicide attempts. (Ellen Greene, Dori Brenner, Lois Smith, Christopher Walken, Antonio Fargas, Lenny Baker).

dig themselves deeper into poses (which is what we were all afraid of before we learned to live with and love lifestyles). The characters are all perfect archetypes of young Village Bohemia. Robert is the icy poet, just published in *Sewanee Review*, the closet sadist who plays the Truth game. "Underneath that pose," Larry tells him later, "is just more pose," which is just what we used to say about people like Robert who pretended to be more authentic than the rest of us. Bernstein's gay aristocrat is the model for the camp revolution of the sixties. Anita's periodic suicide attempts provide the most dramatic pose. Everyone enjoys attending them, until she decides to make one authentic. Add Sarah, the Jewish Princess, Connie, everybody's best friend, an acting teacher as role model, and Larry Lapinsky's sketch of the artist as a young man, and you have all the elements of Village life in the fifties. *Next Stop* is a quiet film, but an important historical essay. It should be shown on double bills with *Shadows*.

By the time Mazursky started making movies, this cultural style was spreading rapidly. *Bob & Carol* nailed it down years before other filmmakers were ready to deal with Esalen and its imitators. Since Mazursky knows where these people are coming from, the film has an added validity. Bob and Carol are so ingenuously involved in their absurd voyage of self-discovery that it takes on the dimensions of a quest. *Alex in Wonderland* provides a companion piece: we see the situation from the point of view of the artist who wants to capture it. Alex has a professional reason to control experience that most of Mazursky's characters do not, but all of them—except perhaps Harry, now that he's at the end of his life—want that control. As Mrs. Cramer (Shelley Winters), the wife of a shrink tells her divorce lawyer, Stephen Blume: "I hope the plane crashes! I don't want him to die. I want *her* to die!" Most of all, "I want the Jaguar!" That's the basic level of control. At a more sophisticated level, we have Erica's newfound independence.

In between, there's Blume, perhaps Mazursky's most attractive character because he combines elements of total, open vulnerability—"Love is a miracle. It's like a birthmark. You can't hide it"—with a sublimely obsessive regard for his own power to control his destiny. It isn't that he won't take no for an answer—he is constitutionally incapable of hearing the question. He's slept with his secretary, Gloria. His wife has walked in on them. She does not react with Bob's flustered equanimity when he finds Carol with the tennis pro and offers him a drink in his own bedroom. She's angry. Gloria has to go. Blume breaks it to her gently. He sleeps with her again, then:

BLUME: Gloria, there's something I have to tell ya.
GLORIA: You're pregnant.
BLUME: Christ, this is hard!
GLORIA: Go ahead, I'm a big girl.
BLUME: (*Sighs.*) You're fired.
GLORIA: You son of a bitch!
Cut.

That kind of gloriously self-assured posing will be redoubled later in *An Unmarried Woman* when Martin, gravely upset, starts bawling on a street in Soho. Erica is shook, vulnerable. What's the matter? Martin blurts it out (you can see he's written his own script): "I'm in love with somebody else!" He breaks into beautiful sobs. Erica, of course, is overwhelmed. Martin: "Oh, Gawd! I don't wanna hurt you! . . . I met her at Bloomingdale's, for Christ's sake!" Erica makes a try at a comeback: "You tell Patti [their daughter] that you're sorry. Is she a good lay?" She walks off down the street with her mouth half-open, then grabs a lamppost and vomits.

Mazursky's at his best trying to comprehend what people do to other people when they feel they have to do it—either because they're just plain selfish or because they think this is the right move in their life-script, or because they're bored. He's most serious about this in *An Unmarried Woman*, which could easily have become a film not very far away in tone from *A Woman Under the Influence* (both Mabel and Erica dance *Swan Lake* in their dreams). But his most exhilarating film remains

An Unmarried Woman: Erica (Jill Clayburgh) with her husband Martin (Michael Murphy), with her daughter Patti (Lisa Lucas), with her lovers Saul and Charlie (Alan Bates and Cliff Gorman), and—just for a moment—alone in Soho just after she's heard Martin's leaving her.

Blume in Love, perhaps because it sees the same dilemma, but from his own point of view. The last scene of that film, as Blume rushes toward his pregnant wife in the Piazza San Marco, says it all.

All around him are lovers, including the formerly fictional Tadzio and Aschenbach. The theme from *Tristan und Isolde* swells majestically to a major chord as they embrace. "I'm not your wife, Blume," she says. She's in labor. *"Dov'è il ospedale?"* Blume inquires hurriedly of the waiter. "I don' unnerstond," replies *il cameriere*. "She's not my wife, she's the mother of my child." The balance redressed. The camera follows them as Nina repeats quietly, "I'm not your wife, Blume." Then the camera leaves them alone as they pass a man and a woman. The man looks past a column to another man, the camera pans back to the column, then up to the building. The music stops and we are left with street sounds and the voices of children and the stones of Venice.

Art moves, and it helps. Mazursky thinks that last sequence very risky. "I wanted to do something on the verge of corn, yet with tongue in cheek, or whatever, and still move you." He does.

In Mazursky's mind (for us it would happen later) Harry has already discovered the realities: his first son's family, on Long Island, is a nest of anxieties; his daughter, Shirley, in Chicago, can't make a marriage work and doesn't get on very well with her dad, either; his second son, Eddie (Larry Hagman), on the Coast, is a failure, breaks down, and cries. Even Jessie (Geraldine Fitzgerald), his ancient paramour, doesn't know who he is. No wonder Tonto takes on such significance for him.

But there's another reality. Well, maybe it's not a reality—call it parareality. It happens in movies, it happens in fantasy. Blume succeeds this way. At the end of Erica's story, she's struggling with art in reality, lugging the aerodynamic canvas Saul has imposed on her down the mean streets, and it looks like she'll make it. These are wildly affirmative images, and it takes courage to make them. On the verge of corn, they move us.

One of the more successful elements of An Unmarried Woman is the subtle, quirky, resonant relationship between Erica and her daughter, Patti (Lisa Lucas). It comes to a head when Saul comes to dinner. Patti's very nervous. She comes on to Saul. She talks about things she shouldn't: "Relax. I know that you and Saul are lovers." By the end of the scene, however, mother and daughter are at the piano singing.

Mazursky hasn't done much with children yet. Alex's daughter suggested he make a movie about her, but he didn't take her up on it. Nina does talk to her unborn child: "If you're a boy kid," she tells it, "you'd better learn to respect women. And if you're a girl kid, I'm gonna teach you to respect yourself." This is about as far as he's gone with children. They don't have the self-consciousness his characters have so far required.

But he has been working for a while on a modern version of The Tempest. The play holds obvious attractions for a man who has two daughters, and who is also a filmmaker, and thus a magus himself. (If he can't play Hamlet, he'll play Prospero.) The Tempest is about power—particularly artistic power—and about the self-consciousness of the intellectual adult and the innocence of children. It abstracts the essence of a Mazursky movie. "O brave new world that has such people in't."

The director has a first draft of this proposed film but is unhappy with it. Maybe the reason has to do with the lesson of the play. What Miranda teaches her father is to let go. That isn't easy for Mazursky's obsessive characters. And it certainly presents a dilemma to the filmmaker himself. But maybe it is necessary to learn to relax control—intellectually over our own lives and lifestyles and emotionally over the other people in them. Mazursky's people are going to have to learn to say with Prospero:

Now my charms are all o'erthrown,
And what strength I have's mine own,
Which is most faint.

385

Amore in Venezia.

Harry Coombs knows this already. The others will learn as they grow.

Paul Mazursky, I think, understands Prospero's abdication theoretically, but hasn't yet been able to put it into practice. The great value of his films has been their lack of authorial pretension. Once he invents them, he lets his people alone. But he's getting to the point where they are going to be a little wiser than they have been, and therefore the tone of a typical Mazursky film is going to change. You can already see this happening in *An Unmarried Woman*. Erica illustrates that you don't have to be hiply foolish to lose a husband. There's far less comedy of manners here, the satiric distance has shortened. We're drawing closer to the characters, empathizing more.

These six movies about various people coping are excellent models for the future of American filmmaking. They are in no sense avant-garde, but to be avant-garde in the next ten years is to be anachronistic. We've passed that period of artistic history. The values of Mazursky's movies remain, however: subtle, restrained craft but in the service of modest insight. We need a lot more movies like these. They improve with age. They're organic, alive—like wine. They do more than satirically delineate the ethos. They come close to capturing human nature on the screen. Sentimental? You decide. There's a movable line between honest sentiment and false sentimentality. Like Blume in love in Venice in fantasy perhaps one must take Mazursky *con amore*.

11

The Fourth Estate

Begelmania

In October 1977, Columbia Pictures announced that David Begelman, head of film and television operations at that studio, was taking a leave of absence and that "unauthorized financial transactions" were being investigated. Within weeks, the so-called "Begelman affair" had grown to extraordinary proportions as newspapers and magazines across the country picked up on what looked to be the Hollywood Watergate. The attention paid to David Begelman's peccadilloes seemed out of all proportion to his "crimes." He had forged checks amounting to perhaps as much as $61,000. This was not petty larceny, of course, but neither was it a corporate crime of the first magnitude. As a number of industry observers noted at the time (few paid attention to them), a similar event in another industry would never have garnered headlines.

Even within the film industry, there were far bigger journalistic fish to fry. Joel Dolkart, former counsel for Gulf + Western Industries, was convicted at about the same time of embezzling $2.5 million from two law firms that did business with G + W. In January 1978, at the height of the Begelman affair, Dolkart's three-year sentence was commuted to five years' probation, ostensibly because he was cooperating with a Securities and Exchange Commission investigation of Gulf + Western. Yet neither Dolkart nor the far more significant SEC investigation received a fraction of the attention in the media that was devoted to Begelman.

The rather sad story of this successful studio executive caught with his hand in the till received the extensive press coverage that it did not because of any intrinsic value but because it seemed emblematic of an ethical malaise in Hollywood. Even though Begelman was clearly suffering from emotional problems, somehow it seemed that we finally had proof that the golden city of entertainment was run by crooks and other shady characters. In one of the most informative and analytical pieces to appear on the Begelman affair, Lucian K. Truscott IV put the finger on the financial eminence grise of Columbia Pictures, Herbert Allen, a New York investment banker.[1] Truscott referred to Herbert Allen's father, Charlie Allen, as "a man who could be said to richly deserve the title 'Godfather of the New Hollywood.'" Allen & Co. took umbrage at this cinematic metaphor and sued *The New York Times* for libel. (The suit was eventually settled out of court.) Truscott's article tried to make it clear that although check forgery might not be commonplace in Bel Air and Beverly Hills, other shady financial practices were. An industry in which a potential investment of, say, $1 million could result in an eventual profit twenty or fifty times that amount had naturally drawn high-stakes gamblers in international finance. (Allen's own controlling interest in Columbia in 1978 was probably worth twenty times his initial investment five years earlier, for example.)

Truscott quoted "an important Hollywood figure with excellent Wall Street credentials" as saying:

> For the past 25 years, there has been a constant flow of mob money, pure blue sky, phony tax shelters, public promotion of boiler room stock, bucket shop paper, off-shore funny money... Every kind of money you can imagine finding its way into films. I have personally sat down at a table where 22 different men representing 22 different kinds of money, signed to finance a single movie. . . . Columbia hasn't been any better or any worse than the other studios. . . . For years, the attitude has been: don't ask questions, just sign. . . .[2]

Other reporters picked up on these general ethical problems. Articles appeared which detailed bribes made by television producers to network programmers, shady loans to studio executives (perhaps to cover heavy gambling losses), bribes to studio executives from theater owners for preferential treatment, payoffs to union officials, expense-account padding, the practice of "block booking," in which a theater owner is forced to take an unprofitable film along with a profitable one, and the curious fact that studio executives who get fired often leave with lucrative independent production contracts (as did David Begelman himself).*

---

* In June 1978 Begelman was fined $5000 by a California Superior Court judge and sentenced to three years' probation for having allegedly stolen $40,000 from Columbia Pictures. He was also required to produce a film, as part of his punishment. It will be a short documentary on the evils of the drug "angel dust"; Begelman will have to show it to high-school students and prisoners. The film is expected to cost $35,000, thus making up the difference between the fine and the theft.

While journalists and a number of readers waxed moralistic over these revelations, most professional observers of the business scene—together with anyone who has had experience in business, from aerospace to the garment trade—hardly raised an eyebrow. These financial sins of Babylon-on-the-Pacific are duplicated every day in numerous other industries. That doesn't make such practices right, of course, but it certainly does make them understandable. A studio executive, for example, called on the carpet by a congressional investigator for accepting a lucrative production deal from his own former associates, might rightly feel persecuted, knowing that this same congressman might be in line, should he lose an election, for a post with a major industrial organization doing significant business with the government.

In this regard, the Begelman affair and the surrounding furor over Hollywood business practices does actually resemble Washington's Watergate affair. Like that earlier, long-running media circus, the Hollygate Scandals of 1978 diverted our attention away from real political and economic problems toward more colorful but much less significant minor infractions of rules that are respected in the real capitalist world more in the breach than in the observance.

No doubt Richard Nixon had committed several thoroughly impeachable acts during his tenure: the invasion of Cambodia and the "Cointelpro" plan, for example, both seem clear contraventions of the Constitution. He wasn't impeached for these offenses, however, but rather for covering up dirty tricks. Nixon was not altogether wrong to feel unjustly persecuted for doing only what others had done before him—even if he did evince a singularly amoral gusto the others had lacked.

Similarly, the media furor over the case of poor David Begelman seems to me to be beside the point. Cashing a few forged checks makes a colorful story, especially if the perpetrator is a high-level Hollywood mogul.* But this is "human interest" material; it has no real significance. Neither do occasional bribes, "offshore funny money," and various and sundry other shady deals. What *is* significant about the New Hollywood is its conglom-

---

* With Freddie Fields, Begelman ran a top talent agency of the sixties. With Alan Hirschfield, president of Columbia until he too was ousted in July 1978, Begelman shares responsibility for the biggest Hollywood financial success story of the seventies. In just a few years, he and Hirschfield completed a brilliant rescue of the sick sister of the major studios, turning a company that lost more than $60 million five years ago into a profit-making enterprise in two years and by 1978 wiping out a bank debt that had exceeded $100 million.[3] Considering the magnitude of this accomplishment, it's a little easier to understand why the Columbia board of directors was loath to see Begelman suspended. A lot can be forgiven for $100 million.

389

erate economic structure. This structure literally defines the limits of possibilities in the industry. It is not illegal. It is not immoral. Most important, it is not dramatic. As a result, it doesn't get much coverage. But it affects our lives profoundly. And the so-called New Hollywood, despite numerous cosmetic changes, will not undergo a real and lasting Renaissance until that conglomerate economic structure is radically altered or outlawed entirely.

For the purposes of discussion, let's define a "conglomerate" as a financial organization which owns and operates a number of widely diversified companies in various industries. Within the film world, the degree of conglomeration varies from the giant Gulf + Western Industries, Inc. only 6 percent of whose 1977 revenues were realized from Paramount film and television operations, to Twentieth Century-Fox Film Corporation, still an undiversified company committed to film (as its name indicates), 73 percent of whose 1977 revenues stemmed from film and television sales.

The term "conglomerate" is used rather loosely in economic journalism these days, largely because the conglomerates themselves present a bewildering variety of structures. Gulf + Western no doubt fits anyone's definition of the term, with lucrative interests in almost every area of the economic spectrum from manufacturing, consumer and agricultural products (the corporation owns significant acreage in the Dominican Republic), financial services, and apparel products to paper and building products, automotive replacement parts (the company's original business), theatrical and television films, and book publishing. Warner Communications, Inc., however, may not fit the strictest definition of the term. As diversified as WCI is, the company is nevertheless strongly focused on interrelated media activities which feed off each other. Even its toys-and-games division fits into the total scheme, since many of its products are electronic and eventually may be sold as adjuncts to home television entertainment.

Yet Warners is still thought of by most people as a film company with interests in other areas, and this is far from the truth. In 1977 only 22 percent of WCI's revenues came from theatrical films, while more than twice as much was realized from records and music publishing, an industry which WCI, along with CBS, thoroughly dominates.[4]

The chart on p. 392 outlines the basic industrial commitments of the six major film distributors (and their conglomerate owners). The chart on p. 393 shows how those six companies divvied up film revenues during the period 1975–77, when the film industry was beginning to reverse the long-term downward trend in popularity that began with the advent of television in the late forties. It's interesting that no single company or pair of companies dominates the industry very long; none of the companies has placed first in domestic rentals two years in a row, for example. Compared with other media industries, film is slightly less centralized. WCI and CBS, control perhaps as much as 70 percent of the recording industry. CBS, RCA, and ABC, of course, monopolize television.

In the end it is not so important whether a particular film company is thoroughly conglomerated or not. It is the psychology of contemporary conglomerate business rather than the fact of it that is vitally significant. As we noted in Chapter One, the brilliant American economist Thorstein Veblen made the important differentiation more than seventy-five years ago between what he termed "industrialists" who were, he thought, essentially interested in the products they produced, and "businessmen" who were, Veblen conjectured, primarily concerned not with products but with profits. Veblen saw the U.S. economic system shifting from control by the industrialists to control by the businessmen. The conglomerate phenomenon of the last fifteen years is simply the ultimate sign that this shift has been completed.

The film industry, once colorful, romantic, and in Veblen's terms a little out of date, has been one of the last to go under. For Veblen, this transfer of power posed serious dangers, and the situation that pertains in the media industries now suggests that we have yet to heed his warning.

In Veblen's terms, an "industrialist" making widgets (or movies) clearly wants to make a profit, both to continue in business and for the sake of the profit itself. But Veblen's industrialist is also intimately concerned with the product he makes. If he is in the widget business, he wants to make the best widgets he knows how: he has an ego investment in widgets, and he also equates better widgets with a higher share of the widget market, which in turn means more revenue. A "businessman" for Veblen does not have a personal emotional or psychological investment in widgets. Working for a publicly-owned corporation rather than a privately-held company, the "businessman" is primarily and perhaps solely concerned with the accountant's profit-and-loss statement. The businessman is a pure capitalist. If, for example, the widget industry has an average rate of return on investment of, say, 15 percent, while the electronics industry returns an average of perhaps 30 percent, the businessman will liquidate his holdings in widgets and put the resultant liquid capital to work in electronics.

The industrialist is concerned with profit as opposed to loss. The businessman is more interested in profit as opposed to higher profit.

To return to movies from widgets, we have the example of Metro-Goldwyn-Mayer, once the largest, most profitable, and most prestigious of Hollywood studios. The company was effectively liquidated in the late sixties by Las Vegas real-estate magnate Kirk Kerkorian. Twelve years later

391

Conglomerate Media Revenues

Conglomerate	Film Company	(Percentage of total revenues from)		
		Theatrical Film	Film & TV	All Media
Columbia Pictures Industres, Inc.	Columbia	39%	66%	81%
Gulf + Western Industries, Inc.	Paramount	4	6	11
MCA Inc.	Universal	24	60	70
Transamerica Corporation	United Artists	10(est.)	12(est.)	15
Twentieth Century-Fox Film Corporation	Fox	63	73	96
Warner Communications, Inc.	Warner Bros.	22	31	87

SOURCE: Annual reports for 1977.

it was reorganized, acquired United Artists, then effectively liquidated that venerable company.

No true conglomerate has so far liquidated a film studio in this way, but the profit-and-loss psychology still pertains. It must if annual reports are to keep investors happy. Warner Bros. is now part of a conglomerate wholly devoted to media industries, as we have already noted. Yet Warners film operations constitute a relatively small part of Warner Communications, Inc., revenues and profits. In the strictest business sense, Warners—like its five competitors—was in far better economic health in the late seventies than it was before it joined the conglomerate. Diversification tends to even out the notorious hills and valleys in the year-by-year graph of film-company profits. During 1976 and 1977 Warners film operations realized before-tax profits equal to about 15 or 16 percent of yearly revenues, which seems like a fair ratio.

Yet the point can be made that sophisticated business practices—which make the annual reports look so much more attractive to investors—also result in a situation in the film industry (and other media industries, for that matter) that looks very much like profit-gouging.

Let's continue with the example of Warner Bros. (although any one of the other five studios could also serve to illustrate this point). In 1976, the company realized before-tax profits of $42 million from the production, financing, and distribution of 12 films. Had half of that profit been recirculated into film production, Warners would have been able to produce, finance, and distribute at least six more films in 1976—and an even larger number if the cash had been used for leverage, as it usually is. This would have meant that Warners would have sponsored 50 percent more movies that year. Fifty percent more directors, actors, screenwriters, and techni-

Domestic Distribution Market Shares: 1975–78

Company	1978 Rank/Share*		1977 Rank/Share*		1976 Rank/Share*		1975 Rank/Share*	
20th Century-Fox	3	13.4%	1	19.5%	3	13.4%	2	14.0%**
United-Artists***	6	10.3%	2	17.8%	2	16.2%	5	10.7%
Warner Bros.	4	13.2%	3	13.7%	1	18.0%	6	9.1%**
Universal	2	16.8%	4	11.5%	4	13.0%	1	25.1%
Columbia	5	11.6%	4	11.5%	6	8.3%	3	13.1%
Paramount	1	23.8%	6	10.0%	5	9.6%	4	11.3%
Buena Vista	7	4.8%	7	5.6%	7	6.7%	7	6.0%
American International	8	1.4%	8	3.4%	8	3.8%	8	3.4%

SOURCE: *Variety*

(Based on films in release during the calendar year which generated film rentals in the U.S. and Canada of at least $1,000,000. This is an estimated ranking of major distributors by their top-grossing films in terms of rentals, not box office receipts.)

Notes: *Total domestic market shares do not add to 100%; residual amount accounted for by smaller distributors.
**In 1975 rankings, Fox was given all domestic rentals on "The Towering Inferno" though Warners as partner received half of them.
***United Artists includes, since 1974, all domestic MGM rentals.

cians would have had the chance to contribute. Half again as many viewers might have been drawn to these films that were never made. It should be remembered, too, that these "extra" films might themselves very well have made profits. In 1977, a year in which Warners released fourteen films, using the same ratios, the company could have made at least nine more films than it did by reinvesting some of its profits: a 64 percent increase. The result for the two years would have been equal to the addition of a seventh major studio/distributor.*

The financial health of the film industry in the late seventies was bought at the expense of movies themselves. Although the trend now shows some signs of reversing, throughout the seventies the six major distributors, each year, reduced the number of films made and distributed. One result has been that the share of the total film audience each year represented by the ten highest-grossing films is increasing *three times faster* than the size of that total audience. In other words, increasingly we are all going to see the same ten movies.

The "businessmen" of the New Hollywood have, in a sense, "desaturated" the film market, and the result has been higher profits all around and safer gambles on each individual film made. This is very good for business, not so good for filmmakers and filmgoers. In another industry— cosmetics or detergents, for example—such desaturation might be admira-

---

* It should also be remembered that these release lists include a number of "pickups"—films Warners did not initially finance—and that of those they did finance, most were coproductions.

393

ble and welcome, but film is not only an industry, it is, more important, a medium of communication. We have no way of knowing what films have been sacrificed to a stable profit curve.

A significant part of the "product problem" during the last fifteen years has been the result of blockbuster psychology. When we look at the huge profits that have been realized from eight-figure productions like *Jaws*, *Star Wars*, and *Close Encounters* we quickly draw the conclusion that the profit a film makes must be related directly to the size of its budget. Yet this is misleading.

In the first place, blockbusters are essentially a conservative and cautious strategy. It may seem like a tremendous gamble to invest $20 or $30 million in a film, but in fact very few blockbusters actually lose money: the size of the budget—and the mass psychology that it creates among exhibitors and audiences—almost guarantee that the film will break even. Although Dino De Laurentiis's *King Kong* was judged a box-office failure, the producer came out of the affair relatively unscathed. Before the film opened he had covered most of his costs with advance sales of distribution rights.

Conversely, even when a blockbuster is highly successful it is—in relative terms—a rather lacklustre performer, in investment terms. Any film, no matter what it cost to produce, stands an equal chance to make big money. Hits remain unpredictable. Fully half the films among the top ten highest-grossing movies of all time on the *Variety* list had average budgets. (The others could be considered blockbusters.) Indeed, a couple of them (*One Flew Over the Cuckoo's Nest*, *Rocky*) were made on veritable shoestrings.

The fact is that small films are, on the face of it, better investments than large films, assuming you have a modicum of faith in the talents of the filmmakers. *Star Wars*, produced on a medium-sized blockbuster budget, is in absolute terms the industry's most profitable film of all time. Yet, *Star Wars* has returned only $10 for every dollar invested while *American Graffiti*, for example—a small film produced on an even smaller budget—has so far returned $50 in rentals for every dollar invested in production. Which film would you have preferred to have invested in? Dollar-for-dollar, Lucas's earlier film was five times more profitable than his blockbuster.

The conclusion we must draw from these numbers is clear. The conglomerate film world is, paradoxically, not so interested in making a lot of money as in breaking even, or earning a small profit to keep the sales curve stable. The blockbuster strategy doesn't make you rich; it simply means more cash flow, and unsophisticated observers are excited by that, just as they might be thrilled by all the bells and alarums on a pinball machine (or a mother ship). Increasing the number of films produced by the American film industry each year (and consequently decreasing the size of the average budget) not only benefits filmmakers and filmgoers, it might also strengthen the profitability of the industry.

In their defense, studio executives I have spoken with suggest that the problem isn't quantity at all but quality. From their point of view this is undoubtedly a factor. Studio executives today, with very few exceptions, act as arbiters—traffic cops. They do not have the creative power or impulse of their predecessors, the moguls of the Old Hollywood. It is up to others to initiate projects and put together packages. Studio executives must wait in most instances until these potential movies are brought to them for approval. This apparent lack of quality, however, also seems to me to be a direct result of the business practices of the New Hollywood.

The structure of the New Hollywood is radically different from the system that helped to make the American film industry dominant worldwide in the thirties and forties. Gone are the studio factories that processed entertainment for the American and world markets on an assembly-line basis, with writers, directors, players, and technicians under long-term contract ready to jump into a project on a week's notice. The mass-production industrial techniques of the Old Hollywood have been replaced by a system that looks more like a pre-Industrial Revolution cottage industry than anything else.

This, too, made much sense from the businessman's strict-accounting point of view. Why tie up large amounts of capital in sound stages, processing equipment, and regular salaries for contract players and creative personnel when you could find others to put up the cash necessary for the economic infrastructure of the industry? At one time, when there was a high studio overhead to meet each week, films shot on location were prohibitively expensive. But once location shooting proved that it could attract audiences, the sound stages were either closed (the back lots were more valuable as real-estate developments) or rented out on an ad hoc basis. Technical personnel were no more expensive hired by the week than they had been on yearly contracts. Actors and actresses might cost a good deal more as freelancers than they did as clock-punching employees, but the producers enjoyed the freedom of choice this new system gave them as much as the creative people did.

The great problem with a cottage industry of this size is simply that it doesn't permit for an orderly development of talent. There is no longer an industry-sponsored training ground for writers, directors, actors, and others. When the system first began to break down in the early sixties the disappearance of the apprentice—journeyman—master chain was applauded, and rightly so. It meant young people could jump into filmmak-

395

The United States Film Box Office: 1946-77

(in $ billions, actual and adjusted to 1946 ticket prices)

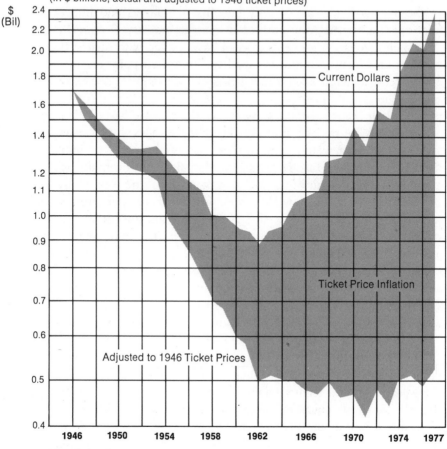

Chart: *Variety*; Data: MPAA

ing without serving a twenty-year apprenticeship. Yet now we are feeling the lack of just such a system. As Mike Medavoy, executive vice president of Orion Pictures, puts it, "There's a lack of talent in all areas. This is a business with a shortage of manpower. There's no place to train anyone."[5]

Medavoy may be exaggerating slightly—certainly there has never before been a larger reservoir of acting talent to draw on. And film schools during the last fifteen years have taken up some of the slack in training "creative" personnel (thus, by the way, shifting the expense of such training from the studios that will eventually profit from it to the individuals and the society that support such schools). Yet in terms of the key creative/administrative jobs in the film business—writer, producer, and director—what Medavoy says seems true. Ironically, the lack of training is most apparent in the business end of film, which is one of the reasons so many former agents now find themselves in key positions in the industry. (The other reason for the rise to power of the agent is simply that these are the people best situated to put together the ad hoc packages the new cottage industry of film now requires.) The lack of training may also be the reason that, with very few exceptions, vice presidents in charge of production at the six studios move in and out of office with metronomic regularity.

The latest generation of production execs—all under thirty-three—took office in 1978. The group included Donald Simpson, thirty-two, vice president in charge of production at Paramount; Paula Weinstein, thirty-two, vice president for production at Fox; Mark Rosenberg, thirty, vice president for production at Warners; Thom Mount, twenty-nine, executive vice president in charge of production at Universal; and Claire Townsend, twenty-six, vice president in charge of production at United Artists (formerly, for a few months, vice president for creative affairs at Fox). A number of these people came to the film industry with vaguely New Left backgrounds from the sixties, which led several commentators to muse that a *new* New Hollywood was about to be born. The personnel may have changed, but the structure hasn't. As long as studio presidents have to answer to conglomerate boards of directors, as long as executives in charge of production simply pass on projects others have developed, it's unlikely that much will change.

The New Constellation

Undoubtedly the most promising development of the late seventies was the creation early in 1978 of Orion Pictures Corporation by five former executives of United Artists. Arthur Krim, Robert Benjamin, Eric Pleskow, William Bernstein, and Mike Medavoy made up the entire top-level management of UA before they quit in January 1978 because of individual and collective disagreements with conglomerate owner Transamerica. So strongly had the company been identified with these men that in effect they took "United Artists" with them when they left, leaving behind only the name, the backlist, and the corporate superstructure, which quickly began to disintegrate once they had left. Krim and Benjamin had founded the modern United Artists company when they took control of the almost bankrupt organization from Charlie Chaplin and Mary Pickford (the only surviving founders) in 1951. They were clearly the elder statesmen of Hollywood in the 1970s. Pleskow and Bernstein also had long histories with the company. Only Medavoy was a relative newcomer, having joined as executive vice president in charge of production in 1974 after a very successful career as an agent associated with many of the directors and writers who now constitute the New Hollywood. The five had worked closely as a team, and United Artists as a result of their efforts had achieved a significant reputation among directors, writers, actors, and independent producers for a degree of taste and honesty unmatched by the other studios. United Artists had always been run differently from Warners, M-G-M, Paramount, and the others. It never owned its own physical plant, nor did it maintain producers and technicians on staff. It was a clearing house and a distribution service for independent producers and, as such, served as a model for the sixties and seventies versions of the other traditional studios.

Unlike Paramount, Fox, and the others, UA under Krim and Benjamin was headquartered in New York rather than Hollywood, and this locale perhaps determined the studio's independent reputation. It undoubtedly reinforced it. During the twenty-six years that Krim and Benjamin managed United Artists, the company's films won ten Academy Awards for best picture. In their last year there, UA set an industry record in rentals. The final three years of the Krim-Benjamin-Pleskow regime saw UA win best-picture honors three times in a row, with One Flew Over the Cuckoo's Nest, Rocky, and Annie Hall. No wonder, then, that sixty-three filmmakers, including Robert Altman, François Truffaut, and Stanley Kubrick, took out an advertisement in the trade papers questioning "the wisdom of the Transamerica Corporation in losing the talents of these men...."[6] No wonder, too, that in less than two months after leaving UA, the five men were able to establish their own company with a reported $100 million credit line. The money comes from a consortium of banks and Warner Communications, Inc. in a complicated arrangement in which WCI apparently has only strictly limited control over financing. The major bank behind Orion is known to be the First National Bank of Boston.

United Artists had been acquired by Transamerica, a conglomerate basically devoted to insurance and financial services (they also run an airline), in 1967 by mutual consent. For their part, Krim and Benjamin expected, as did other studio heads who joined the conglomerate bandwagon in the late sixties, to realize in the association a source of ready cash, always a problem in the mercurial film business, and a certain financial stability and respectability. They probably also were attracted by the opportunity to cash out while still maintaining control of their company. Transamerica, like other conglomerates shopping for Hollywood studios, was undoubtedly attracted more by the glamour of owning an entertainment company than by the financial possibilities.

By the late seventies, it had become clear to the UA managers that they had given up more than they got. Whatever stock they held in the conglomerate parent was affected not at all by United Artists' excellent market performance during the last few years, which is not surprising considering that even in a year it broke industry records UA contributed only 10 or 11 percent of the revenues of Transamerica as a whole. Eric Pleskow, former president of UA and current president of Orion, insists that Transamerica never exerted any control over UA's production decision-making process.[7] The conglomerate's strict business practices did, however, annoy the Orion quinciumvirate. Apparently, the last straw as far as Pleskow was concerned was TA's refusal to allow Pleskow to pay Medavoy as much as he was clearly worth in Hollywood terms. Transamerica's rules put a ceiling on salaries and stock options—admirable enough in the corporate world, but ironically galling to the men who had built UA into what it was. There was some talk about Medavoy's company car, as well. Transamerica had rules about that, too. In Hollywood, where you are what you drive, this may have seemed an insupportable burden.

At first, Krim thought he could devise a parallel, spinoff corporation with more independence from the conglomerate that would allow him to compensate his executives in the manner he thought proper. But this was impossible. When the five (and other, secondary executives) resigned, only the shell of UA was left. All five men were courted by the other major distributors, but it became clear to them that they had enough clout collectively so that they wouldn't have to work for anyone but themselves. It was clear to the banks, if not Transamerica's corporate leadership, that the major assets of United Artists, its executives, were now free agents and a substantial line of credit was quickly forthcoming.

More important, Orion, as the new company was named,* made an arrangement with Warners to use the distribution structure of that company while still maintaining complete control over advertising, publicity, distribution, and booking for their films. This unprecedented deal made it possible for Orion to enter the market immediately as the full equal of the six established major studios. If they had had to make the considerable investment necessary to match distribution facilities it would have taken perhaps twice as much cash to get started and several years at least before they were in a position to challenge the "giants."

The significance of this new structure shouldn't be underestimated. For

---

* Pleskow, Medavoy, and the others explain the choice of their corporate name as a matter of numerology: "Orion is a five-main-star constellation," Medavoy is quoted as saying. But of course Orion has seven main stars, which may lead astronomy-minded observers to conjecture on the identity of the two so far silent partners. Mythology-minded prognosticators will remember that Orion hunted after giants and slew them, and that he was born from a bullhide upon which the gods had urinated, both of which observations seem to fit, and that he was slain either by Artemis or a scorpion.

the first time, one of the six major channels through which the great majority of films reach the public is being operated on a rental basis. Orion, apparently, maintains full control over the distribution of its films while paying Warners only the standard 30–40 percent distribution fee. Independent producers have long used United Artists and the other distributors to get their product to the public. But never before has an independent organization been able to maintain control over the marketing process.

Warners' production executives, as opposed to their distribution personnel, were understandably exercised about this arrangement. In effect, Warner Communications, Inc. was setting up a full-fledged independent quasi-studio to compete with the Warner Bros. production arm for the distribution facilities of the company.* Since Orion clearly had at least as much expertise in film production as any of its older competitors, since it was to use the full facilities of one of these companies as if they were its own, and since through its personnel Orion would have no trouble attracting independent producers, directors, and actors to its fold, the success of the company seemed well-nigh assured.

For years, Hollywood's major studios had been moving toward concentration on distribution, leaving the business of production to independents, but never before had the line between the two functions been so clearly drawn. In political and cultural terms we may very well not need more than six distribution channels, as long as these channels are open on an equal basis to be used by more numerous producer-distributors like Orion. In late 1979, the Ladd Company, formed by Alan Ladd, Jr., and associates, established a similar relationship with Warners.

For their part, the conglomerate owners of the so-called "studios," the distribution companies, might very well like to see this come to pass. They may lose some control over the number of films released each year (although it would be easy for them to set limits on the quantity of films their companies would handle from independents), but they would be relieved of the considerable gamble of actually producing (or working in tandem with independent production companies, as they often do now). They could concentrate their full financial resources on the two most profitable areas of the film production process—investment and distribution. When

---

* Orion Pictures *Corporation*, wholly owned by the five principals, also operates Orion Pictures *Company* as a joint venture with Warners, so the latter company stands to gain from investments in Orion films as well as from distribution from them, but it is not yet clear what the precise relationship will be between the Corporation and the Company.

a particular project seemed worthy, they could throw in for a few dollars with the production company. In any event, they would realize at least the standard 30 to 40 percent distribution fee with a minimal investment of capital.

The industry has, as we have already noted, been moving in this direction for several years now. One of the reasons Orion's deal may have seemed attractive to Warner Communications executives is that Warner Bros. was in considerable chaos for at least two years prior to the founding of Orion. (They weren't losing money, just not producing very many films.) It was much easier to develop a relationship with Krim and company than to set WB's house in order, and the concept of housing two production companies fits well with conglomerate philosophy.

Most of the financial news in Hollywood at the end of the seventies was made by independents. Robert Stigwood, whose main expertise is records, has had considerable success with *Saturday Night Fever* and *Grease*. Mel Simon, formerly a shopping-center developer, has entered the film business with an extensive string of projects (including *Tilt*, *The Stuntman*, and *The Runner Stumbles*). Alex Winitsky and Arlene Sellers, an independent production team who have hitherto maintained a low profile, had six films in production as of late 1978 (including *The Lady Vanishes*, *Cuba*, and *Dynasty*), a schedule that competes with that of some studios. There are numerous other independents who would welcome the chance to rent the distribution facilities of the six majors without having to give up essential control of advertising and booking.

Within the next few years we are likely to see a further fractioning of the American film industry as the studios continue to retreat to the safest economic levels. By artificially reducing the number of films available to the public in the mid-seventies, these organizations may have paved the way for independent challenges. As it stands now, independent producers have the potential to compete with studio productions. They can't fully realize that potential as long as the distribution arms of the conglomerates maintain full power, policing the crucial channels to the public. If, however, the Orion arrangement with Warners is duplicated, that control will break down, and the monopoly that the studios have effectively exerted over the art and industry of American film for more than fifty years will break down with it.

What Is to Be Done?

The Orion model offers some interesting possibilities, but in itself it is not a solution to Hollywood's problems. While a substantial increase in the number of independent producers with control over the exploitation of their own films would be very welcome, there is no guarantee that those companies would not more or less quickly metamorphose into duplicates of the conglomerated studios which gave rise to them. Market forces will, after all, still operate even if the number of potential customers for a film project is sixty rather than six. Orion's own slate of films for its first full year of operation is at best unadventurous.

Our basic aim must be, in Veblen's terms, to shift the economic focus of the film industry back to product, away from profit. This, of course, is no easy matter in late capitalist society, but let me try to indicate some of the ways I think it might be done.

First, it is necessary to realize that the problems of the film industry are not unique. Increasingly, the media—both print and nonprint—must be seen as a whole. In recordings, television, and radio, as well as in newspapers, books, and magazines, the trend during the late sixties and seventies has been to further concentration of ownership in a conglomerate setting where the medium itself and the information it conveys are seen only as means toward the end of stable, ever-growing profits. Six film companies effectively control American movies. Three companies (the networks) exert an even more forceful monopoly over television. Two of these companies (CBS and RCA) together with the film companies (WCI in particular) thoroughly dominate the recording industry. Newspaper chains are acquiring properties at an unprecedented rate. Even the book-publishing industry, long a refuge for "industrialists," in Veblen's term, devoted to product even strangely at the expense of profit, has been subject in recent years to more than 300 mergers and acquisitions.

Rather than try to fight this increasing centralization, let us use the model of Orion, Warners, and the film industry to restructure these industries while maintaining the kind of centralized distribution which is economically useful. There is nothing wrong with having only six film-distribution companies (which is after all twice the number of television companies) as long as we all have equal and free access to their facilities.

But how to achieve that ideal? Gulf + Western, Coca-Cola, MCA, WCI, and the others are not likely to look kindly on any attempt to meddle with what they must consider their own corporate freedom to finance and distribute any films they please.

The first step must be to rethink our social definition of the media, including film. Since the Middle Ages the concept of the Fourth Estate has existed in common law. The press was separated from the three vested estates of clergy, nobility, and commons and protected from their interference for very good reasons. The concept of the fourth estate had a profound effect on the drafting of the U.S. Bill of Rights. But whereas it was sufficient in the eighteenth century and earlier to set newspapers apart from the old estates of clergy, nobility, and commons, we now must recognize that the medium of the press has been joined and in some cases even superseded by the new media, including film and television. Whether we think of a particular medium as essentially devoted to news or to entertainment, we now have to recognize that all media perform both those functions. The "fictions" of movies, for example, often convey more information and a greater sense of experienced truth than a straightforward press report. The concept of the Fourth Estate now must be rephrased to separate all news/entertainment media (for they all perform both functions) from business, government, and social/educational/religious institutions—the contemporary equivalents of the old estates.

Over the years, numerous laws relating to broadcasting and the other print media have suggested that the concept of the Fourth Estate still has some juridical power. However, never has the situation been restated clearly. As a result, the media have become intimately intertwined with just those new estates they should be inviolably separate from.

The FCC's recent rulings in regard to cross-ownership in the news media between television stations and newspapers point in this direction, but they deal only with relationships *within* the media. It is far more important to outlaw "cross-ownership" between business and the media—just the sort of conglomerate relationship that now dominates the Hollywood structure.

In the best of all possible worlds we would simply pass laws declaring media companies off limits to other businesses, and vice-versa. *The New York Times* would have to give up its paper mills, Gulf + Western would have to divest itself of Paramount and Simon & Schuster (although it could keep Madison Square Garden, the New York Knickerbockers and the Dominican Republic), Columbia would lose its pinball-machine company, and Fox would be forced to bid adieu to Aspen Skiing Corporation and its beautiful mountains. Paramount, Simon & Schuster, Columbia, Fox, and the other new orphans would thus be forced to succeed or fail on their own terms entirely within their own media industries. We might even be so bold as to eliminate cross-ownership *within* the media world, in which case MCA would have to admit that it was primarily a television company and spin off its movie operations and G. P. Putnam's Sons, Warners would have to make the not so difficult choice between movies and records (certainly they would have no compunctions about selling their book-publishing and magazine-distribution companies), and Fox would have to get out of the film processing business.

The force of such a reorganization would be to refocus the corporate energies of each of these new entities on the business at hand, whether it be movies, newspapers, television, records, books, magazines, or radio. Of course, this of itself doesn't guarantee better movies (or books, or records).

It does, however, assure us that never again would a major company like M-G-M be liquidated simply in order to use its capital in more profitable enterprises, and it does suggest that entrepreneurial energies would be kept within each particular medium. If anyone is going to get rich in this newly independent Fourth Estate he is going to have to do it by making movies, not Coca Cola, or newspapers, not building products.

Legally enforcible independence for the media companies would, I think, at least increase the various energy levels. But it certainly wouldn't make it impossible for profit-gouging to continue. We would have moved from a conglomerate business psychology back to a corporate one, but we would not yet have achieved the goal of industry we're after.

In order to do this it will be necessary to restructure corporate philosophy (and its legal apparatus) to include the concept of a fair profit limit. This would have the effect of keeping whatever profits are generated by particular media industries within the industries themselves so that they can contribute to the capital structure of those industries. (I'm not suggesting that we limit profits by taxing companies heavily, rather that we insist that a certain amount of "gross profit" be reinvested in the company rather than taken out in dividends, or wasted, from an industrial point of view, on acquisitions.)

Now, clearly, neither of these radical reorganizations is likely to occur soon. Over a period of, say, ten years, we might, through the application of antitrust laws, have some success enforcing the independence of media companies from other businesses, government, and institutions, but we are not likely to be able to prohibit cross-ownership within the media world successfully, and we are certainly not going to be able to force the media to accept limits on the amount of profit that can be taken out of the industries.

In strictly economic terms, the media industries are not particularly large or influential,* but they do, after all, control the media through which we might hope to discuss these modest proposals. It seems most likely that this sort of reorganization will have to wait for a general application of antitrust principles to all conglomerate business structures. That, in turn, will probably have to wait until we are able to introduce into the

---

*In the high-power corporate world, media companies are very small fry. For example: the total revenues from all media industries, print and nonprint, including advertising, were smaller than the revenues of a single oil company in 1977. (Both Shell and Exxon exceeded the level of the media industries.) The *profits alone* of the Seven Sister oil companies were significantly larger than the *total revenues*, in 1977, of both the film and television industries taken together! Of course, the importance of media industries lies in their social function, not their economic status.

economic structure of the United States some basic principles of industrial democracy.

In the meantime (and it will probably be a very long time) there are some reformist measures that can and should be taken. The Kennedy government's investment tax credit of the early sixties offers a model. Suppose, for example, that reinvestments in the film industry were taxed at a different rate from profits and that, in addition, reinvestments in the film industry per se were taxed less heavily than investments by film conglomerates in Caribbean real estate, Coca-Cola bottling plants, banks or Las Vegas gambling franchises? This is not impossible, assuming that the concept of the Fourth Estate can be revived in the public imagination and revised to include all the media. And the result should be at least mildly beneficial: the more money that was directed back into film production, the more films would be made, the more films made, the greater the chance for minority representation in American film culture.

We can't collectively legislate *better* films; we may be able to legislate *more* films.

At the same time, we should not lose sight of the basic implication of the concept of the Fourth Estate: that is, that the companies that control our channels of communication bear a public trust and must be forced to answer for it. It seems entirely too optimistic to suggest public control of the channels of film distribution, especially when we consider the history of the broadcasting industry during the last fifty years. Originally, stations were licensed to use the public airwaves in the public interest. In the early thirties it was assumed that radio (and television) stations would allow access to their distribution networks to a variety of programmers. In a sense, they were to act as "common carriers," like the telephone system, open to all. In the beginning, they did. But as we know, this conception of broadcasting was soon superseded as the networks took full control of their programming.

If we refuse to control broadcasting, which uses a limited, clearly public medium to distribute its product, how can we ever think to control commercial film distribution? Yet the investment in a film-distribution network dwarfs the investment necessary to set up a television network. It would be nice to think that anyone was free to enter into competition with Universal, Paramount, Warners, and the others, but that freedom is deceptive. It cost Orion $100 million simply to go into partnership with Warners. (They don't, in the end, have their own distribution system; they simply have an agreement to use someone else's.) Few of us can put our hands on that sort of ready cash. And the Orion story is unique, anyway. The conclusion that must be drawn is that the distribution systems operated by the six major "studios" constitute a de facto public communications network which should therefore be brought under law as soon as possible. It is time to recognize the studios as common carriers.

We are confronted with an American film industry that, primarily because of the intricacies of its economic structure, is not as responsive as it must be to the many currents of American culture. Contrary to popular belief, Hollywood is not America. But if we're not careful, it might become so.

• We must realize in law that movies (and other media) constitute our Fourth Estate and therefore must be guaranteed inviolate financial independence from business, government, and other social institutions.

• We must recognize that film distribution companies, like other media companies, bear a public trust as members of the Fourth Estate and must be held accountable for it.

In order to achieve these aims it is going to be necessary to restructure the film industry so that:

• distribution companies operate as common carriers, allowing independent and equal access to the channels of communication entrusted to them;

• production companies are confronted with a tax structure such that it is more profitable for them to reinvest the profits generated by movies within the film industry rather than outside it.

If we can accomplish these modest aims, then the American movie *business* is going to become once again an *industry,* independent of outside control, responsible only to itself and its future, and accountable to us. Then it would really be time for a Hollywood Renaissance—our own cultural revolution.

Let a thousand movies bloom.

12

THE 1980s:
The People
and the Movies

A list of the people who make movies in 1984 looks surprisingly like a list of people who made movies five years ago. The most remarkable development of the 1980s is that there has been so little development.

There are a few new arrivals. Lawrence Kasdan's name comes to mind first. He has scored in several different areas. He's written successful scripts for blockbusters *Raiders of the Lost Ark* and *Return of the Jedi*. He has written a pleasant romantic comedy (*Continental Divide*), and he has directed two notable films: *Body Heat* (a stylish film noir) and *The Big Chill*.

The Big Chill received considerable attention from critics and public in 1983 because it dealt with a generation that doesn't get much attention in films: people in their mid to late thirties who were on the trailing edge of the sixties generation. As pleasant as it was, *The Big Chill* was still sort of a *Four Seasons* for younger people.

The second name people most often come up with when asked to name a new director of the early eighties is John Sayles. Sayles has had an interesting career as novelist, commercial screenwriter (*Piranha*, and others of that sort), and independent filmmaker. So far, he's best known for *Return of the Secaucus Seven* (1979), the progenitor of Kasdan's more popular *Big Chill*.

The team of Bob Gale and Robert Zemeckis still hasn't been able to jolt the public imagination, although critics were fond of *I Wanna Hold*

407

JoBeth Williams, Kevin Kline, William Hurt, and Glenn Close at their reunion in *The Big Chill*.

Your Hand (1977) and *Used Cars* (1980). Zemeckis and Gale must also admit to having written the screenplay for *1941*.

Albert Brooks, the "comedian's comedian," turned to directing with *Real Life* and *Modern Romance*. The first was an interesting experiment, the second was a quietly important film about a type of character who's really unique to the '70s and '80s: the not-very-intelligent man or woman who's been educated by the media to have far more psychological sensitivity than anyone needs—or he can handle. Brooks is worth watching, if he gets another chance.

Robert Towne, the screenwriting eminence grise of the 1970s, got a chance to direct with *Personal Best* (1982), an unusual and insightful movie about competitive track and field.

James L. Brooks, one of the creators of *The Mary Tyler Moore Show*, moved to feature films with *Starting Over* (1980), a sharp and witty essay that had many of the same humorous qualities Brooks had contributed to the Moore show. (He wrote and produced *Starting Over*, Alan Pakula directed.) Brooks followed this with the surprise hit of late 1983, *Terms of Endearment*, his directorial debut, from the Larry McMurtry novel. It is this sort of solid melodrama for which the early eighties will be best remembered.

Jim Henson returned to film after 15 years with two ingenious vehicles for his classic puppets, *The Muppet Movie* (1979) and *The Great Muppet Caper* (1982), as well as an ambitious attempt at feature animation,

Jim Henson surrounded by Fraggles, his most recent creation.

The Dark Crystal (1982). The first was a popular success, *The Muppet Caper* was a much more accomplished film (and a musical with five times as many memorable tunes as *Annie*), but it failed to find an audience.

Steve Gordon made an auspicious directorial debut with *Arthur*, a funny, old-style movie which solidified Dudley Moore's new-found popularity. Sadly, it was also Gordon's last film. He died shortly after.

Andy Bergman turned from writing to directing with *So Fine* (1982) which disappeared all too soon.

* * * * *

None of the directors who are featured in *American Film Now* have made great strides during the last five years. It has been a period of consolidation, at best. Some have managed to keep their heads above water, most have lost ground during the last five years.

Woody Allen has rebounded from the disaster of *Interiors*. *Manhattan* was as good an Allen film as we can expect to find these days, very much on the order of *Annie Hall*. *Stardust Memories*, his attempt at Fellini, was of less interest. Another misstep—*A Midsummer Night's Sex Comedy* (1982)—was followed by the more ambitious *Zelig* (1983) and *Broadway Danny Rose* (1984)—Allen again at the top of his form. None of these films stand out as particular landmarks, but it's good to know there will be a Woody Allen movie every year.

409

Neil Simon, certainly one of the most prolific screenwriters ever.

Allen received a lot of critical attention for *Zelig*, mainly because of its unusual technique, combining live action with historical footage. Carl Reiner had done the same sort of thing a year earlier with the Steve Martin vehicle *Dead Men Don't Wear Plaid*. Allen did it better, but the interesting thing is that two of our leading comedians, both with roots in the 1950s, find it appropriate in the 1980s to wrap themselves in the films of the 1940s.

Mel Brooks had run out of genres to caricature by 1979 and started to flounder. *The History of the World, Part I* was a disappointment even to Brooks's fans: crass and sloppy. But Brooks rebounded in excellent form with *To Be Or Not To Be* in 1983. Yes, it's a remake. Yes, the Lubitsch original is preferable. But the film gave Brooks a platform to be himself and do his inimitable shtik in a way he hadn't been able to do since *The Producers*. I don't even mind if he reprises "Springtime for Hitler," an "hommage" to Alan Johnson, who had choreographed that scene in *The Producers* and who directed *To Be Or Not To Be* for Brooks. The presence of Anne Bancroft is another sign that the eighties may be good years for Mel Brooks. She's worth twice the sum of the entire group of actors he used in the seventies and wisely jettisoned before *To Be Or Not To Be*.

Neil Simon has continued apace. His assembly-line production for the last 20 years now takes on the proportions of the extraordinary. Simon films can be criticized for seeming glib but it doesn't really matter. He's

The redoubtable Anne Bancroft and the undoubtable Mel Brooks played actors in *To Be Or Not to Be.*

put his finger on a moment of contemporary anxiety and he's not going to let go. So be it.

Of all the recent Simon films, *I Ought to Be in Pictures,* based on the play and directed by Herbert Ross, stands out. It has the best role for a young woman in years—a role that Dinah Manoff relishes. It showcases Ann-Margret as an admirable, intelligent woman—a role she's never been allowed to play before. It gives Walter Matthau something to do besides slouch. It has a number of telling lines about contemporary Hollywood. And, most important, it's free of the shrill anxiety that hurts so many other Simon movies.

Allen, Brooks, Simon, and Carl Reiner all came out of live television in the fifties. Finally, in 1982, someone made a good film about that Golden Age. Brooks produced Norman Steinberg's script of *My Favorite Year,* but Richard Benjamin directed.

Since 1979, new American film comedy has been dominated not so much by directors, but by actors. Interestingly enough, those actors, like their predecessors, almost all had their training and their early success in television—most of them on *Saturday Night Live.*

By the summer of 1981, actors like John Belushi and Bill Murray were the hottest box office draws in the country—the result of TV's extraordinary power to create celebrity. Steve Martin, Chevy Chase, and Dan Aykroyd weren't far behind. Of that group with its roots in seventies TV, only Martin Mull hasn't yet been able to score with popular au-

411

Steve Martin in *The Jerk.*

diences. While the films these people have made usually make money, most of them have been unremarkable products. The whole seems often to be less than the sum of the parts.

Probably the collaboration of Steve Martin and Carl Reiner comes closest to fulfilling expectations: but even *Dead Men Don't Wear Plaid* and *The Man With Two Brains* can't build the energy necessary to transcend skit humor. Maybe that type of comedy simply doesn't work in film.

On television, *Saturday Night Live* stumbled after the original cast graduated, but was able to recover somewhat when Eddie Murphy and Joe Piscopo joined up. Murphy has already been able to translate TV success into film, most notably with *48 Hours* (1983).

More interesting has been the saga of SCTV. Second City Television, an ensemble composed of Canadians and Americans, had been in syndication for several years before NBC decided to pick it up for network distribution in the fall of 1981. The actors and writers of this exceptional troupe made a brilliant ensemble. Rick Moranis's and Dave Thomas's sketch in which Woody Allen and Bob Hope play golf together tells you more about the changes the American soul has undergone during the last 50 years than any five movies I can think of. Joe Flaherty, Eugene Levy, Andrea Martin, Catherine O'Hara, and John Candy can be equally incisive at their best.

Moranis and Thomas were the first to make the jump to feature film with *Strange Brew* (1983). They too were unable to transcend skit humor and they didn't find their audience. Meanwhile, the remainder of the troupe took their act off late-night network and moved to prime-time cable as the featured drawing-card of HBO's second service, Cinemax.

It's of more than passing interest that for sixty years, since the vaudevillians took over radio, successive waves of America's best comedians have nearly all been members of loose-knit "families" of entertainers. In the thirties and forties, it was Burns and Allen, and Benny, and Fred Allen: the vaudevillians. In the fifties, nearly everybody who was anybody worked for Max Liebman, Sid Caesar, and *Your Show of Shows*. Those who didn't—Mike Nichols and Elaine May, for example—started with the Second City troupe. In the sixties two hot spots flashed briefly: the Smothers Brothers and *Laugh-In*. Only Goldie Hawn and Lily Tomlin survived. In the seventies, Second City, in its Canadian incarnation, proved fruitful once again.

In the eighties, these "families" are as often real as metaphorical. Murray, Aykroyd, and Belushi all have brothers in the business. Reiner's son Rob has been a television star. Brooks and Bancroft are working together. Their young son Max made his debut in *To Be Or Not To Be*.

Left to its own devices, without the help of television or the stage, American film doesn't seem to be able to come up with very much in the way of comedy.

The best it can offer seems to be pastiches like *Airplane!*, a good-natured collection of sophomoric jokes from the 1950s. In the same vein, but more sophisticated, was 1982's *Young Doctors in Love*, the product of the TV sensibility of Paramount producer Garry Marshall, director of the film.

* * * * *

During the past few years, John Cassavetes has produced one of his most interesting—and most widely seen—films, *Gloria*. But he seems to have lost the impetus for independent production and has spent more time acting than directing during the 1980s. Most of the roles he has played have been caricatures of Rosemary's husband.

Pauline Kael is right when she claims Cassavetes has a very difficult personality on film, and it's a little surprising that he has survived for as long as he has. The only interesting acting job he has done in five years or more was for Paul Mazursky in *Tempest* (1982), an indulgent, elaborate film that failed immediately in the U.S. but was a surprising hit with European audiences.

If the "auteur" theory ever had any validity, *Tempest* torpedoes it.

413

Cartoon touchups of Robin Williams and Shelley Duvall as made-up for *Popeye*.

Here's a long-time Mazursky project which Cassavetes invades and thoroughly dominates. *Tempest* has all the rhythms and concerns—and even quirks—of a Cassavetes-directed film. In the struggle between actor-director and director-actor, the actor wins. There's a moral lesson here.

Like so many filmmakers from the seventies, Robert Altman has also found himself in the middle of a dark wood where the straight way is lost. *Quintet* (1978) was certainly his worst film, pretentious with no redeeming social importance. *A Perfect Couple* (1979), was one of his best, quirky and humorous in a very particular Altman way, with all his tricks of character, perhaps a bit precious, but vital nevertheless. It never found an audience.

Health (1980) was shelved for years and released only perfunctorily thereafter. By 1981 Altman was forced to sell Lion's Gate Studios and go to work for other people. *Popeye* (1980), a studio production, was really rather an interesting movie, given the constraints under which it must operate, but certainly not the sort of product that can get the kids to line up three times during the summer. Altman's only other productions to date have been films of stage plays: *Come Back to the Five and Dime, Jimmy Dean, Jimmy Dean* (1982) and *Streamers* (1982).

Francis Coppola has continued to provide most of the off-screen drama in Hollywood during the early 80s. As usual, his role as a businessman

414

Matt Dillon continued his eighties version of James Dean in *Rumble Fish*. Nicholas Cage, Vincent Spano, and Christopher Penn assist.

is of considerably more interest than his role as an artist. In 1980, he purchased the old Hollywood General Studios, full of bright plans to return to the thrilling days of yesteryear when men were men, starlets were starlets, and everybody punched a clock at the studio gate. There was also a lot of talk about a studio devoted to the well-being of its artistic employees.

The result of all of this was a vastly inflated budget for a film called *One From the Heart*, which, when released in the spring of 1981, lasted only a few days longer than *Heaven's Gate*.

It's hard to figure what Coppola must have been thinking about. At a budget approaching $30 million, there seems to have been no chance at all that *One From the Heart* would ever make its money back. Clearly he had honestly mortgaged himself to the hilt for this one and within two months after the debacle of *One From the Heart*, Zoetrope Studios, as it was then called, was up for sale—just two years after Coppola had purchased it.

Meanwhile, Coppola the artist was hard at work on other films. His versions of the S. E. Hinton novels for young adults, *The Outsiders* (1982) and *Rumble Fish* (1983), were equally disappointing: too much operatic energy lavished on very small, fragile stories.

By late 1983, Coppola seemed to be back in *Godfather* form again, at work on *Cotton Club*, the kind of grand, ambitious mythic project that had served him well in the past. After a few weeks of shooting, he was

415

way over budget.

As a producer, Coppola has fared little better. Carroll Ballard's *The Black Stallion* (1979) deserved the success it received: a nicely done classic romance. Robert Dalva's sequel, *The Black Stallion Returns* (1983), was nice too. It takes some courage these days to make films children and adults can watch. Wim Wenders's *Hammett*, released finally in 1982, was a disaster from every point of view, and Caleb Deschanel's *The Escape Artist* (1981) also failed at the box office.

In choosing to direct the films of the Hinton novels Coppola may have been trying to recapture the success of *The Black Stallion* himself, but he simply didn't have the sensibility to communicate that sort of story. Meanwhile, Carroll Ballard went on to direct a very interesting film for Disney, *Never Cry Wolf* (1983).

For a director who has managed to produce at least one of the greatest American films of all time (*The Godfather*), it's hard to see why Coppola continues to work at cross-purposes to his own best interests. He seems to be driven by a desire to appear to live a life that's more dramatic than those of his characters.

After somehow having survived the financial storms of the early eighties, the impresario found himself producing and directing an elaborate historical musical drama for Orion Pictures late in 1983 and on into 1984. After ten weeks of shooting, the financiers called in outside accounting help. The production had run stupendously over budget.

It is only a matter of time before some ambitious young producer in Hollywood gets $40 million backing for the great blockbuster of the eighties: "The Francis Ford Coppola Story."

Michael Ritchie released *An Almost Perfect Affair* in 1979, his least successful film to date. It was an attempt at an in-joke for filmmakers about the Cannes Film Festival and no one got it. He then moved on to a blockbuster production, *The Island*, exactly the sort of film he'd assiduously avoided for the previous 12 years. That was equally unsuccessful and Ritchie fell into the doldrums. He snapped back nicely in 1983 with *The Survivors* pairing Walter Matthau and Robin Williams in a story by Michael Leeson. The result was a film with some bite and the classic, gently Ritchie wit: his best since *Smile*. But nobody came.

Robin Williams moved on, collecting directors. In a brief but exciting film career he has worked with Robert Altman, George Roy Hill (*The World According to Garp*), Michael Ritchie, and Paul Mazursky (*Moscow on the Hudson*).

Mazursky himself has suffered fewer setbacks than most of the other filmmakers featured in the first edition of this book.

416

Willie and Phil with Ray Sharkey, Margot Kidder, and Michael Ontkean.

Willie and Phil, his 1980 film, never found its proper audience and didn't make much money, but it remains one of the very few movies that have attempted to come to grips with the way we lived our lives these last 20 years. Twenty or 30 years from now *Willie and Phil* is going to be one of the movies people will be most eager to see from that strange period—the late 70s and early 80s.

Tempest was a project Mazursky had been working on for over ten years. It finally came to fruition in 1982. It combined a lot of his old interests with some new attempts at style. At least it showed you could still be ambitious over 50. *Tempest* is a longish, indulgent character study, stunningly photographed in 70 mm, but with rather little drama to sustain it through more than two hours. It is precisely the kind of European filmmaking that has never succeeded on American screens. Mazursky deserves some sort of recognition for such chutzpah. (His hero Fellini might call it "sprezzatura.")

And what about the "whiz kids"? Most submerged below the noise level in the early eighties.

Peter Bogdanovitch released what is arguably his best film, *Saint Jack,* and then followed it with what is equally arguably his worst film, *They All Laughed.*

Billy Friedkin went for the sociological shock effect, once again, with *Cruising,* a film that was more notable for the demonstrations outside the movie theatres than for what happened on screen inside. It's mo-

417

Al Pacino and Carmine Stipo as the bartender in a tableau from *Cruising*.

Robert De Niro as a convincing Jake La Motta in *Raging Bull*.

vies like this that make critics dust off words like "execrable."

Martin Scorsese slowed down a bit. *Raging Bull* (1980) was probably as good as any Scorsese film. *The King of Comedy* (1982) had an interesting premise and Jerry Lewis and Robert De Niro, but not much else.

418

Indiana Jones (Harrison Ford) joined the contemporary mythology in *Raiders of the Lost Ark*. A lot depends on the snap-brim fedora and the crooked smile.

Meanwhile, Brian De Palma got himself in trouble with the film students and cineastes.

By 1981, *Saturday Night Live* could joke about a De Palma film called "The Clams":

> "Once again, as he does every year, Brian De Palma has ripped off Alfred Hitchcock and found a job for his wife."

De Palma would call this an "hommage." Critics, however, were rightfully concerned that scenes in De Palma's 1981 *Blow-out* were uncomfortably close to scenes in another film—*Prince of the City*—on which De Palma had worked for a while.

Do the shower scene from *Psycho* (he has), and you can call it an hommage; do a scene from a film which hasn't been released as you shoot and it's quite another matter.

Dressed to Kill (1980) was De Palma's *Psycho* showcase for Angie Dickinson. *Scarface* (1983), a more direct and obvious remake, received some good notices, despite trouble with the ratings board over its graphic violence. Probably De Palma's best movie of the last five years, however, is the one he made with film students at Sarah Lawrence College—*Home Movies* (1979).

George Lucas (who quit directing after *Star Wars*) joined with Steven Spielberg and Lawrence Kasdan for *Raiders of the Lost Ark*, one of the most popular films of recent years and probably the ultimate whiz kid movie. With great elan, they summarized all of the cliches and much of the fun of the 1930s and 40s Hollywood Saturday morning serials.

A whole new generation was exposed to this genre with *Raiders*. If you're in your 50s, you saw the antecedents of *Raiders* in the movies on Saturday mornings. If you're in your 30s, you saw those same films re-run on television in the early 1950s. And if you're in your teens—well, you probably think *Raiders of the Lost Ark* is an invention.

As producer, George Lucas quietly dominates Hollywood today. Coppola may appear to be the mogul of the eighties, and certainly acts with the panache associated with that role, but Lucas is the real power. His films continue to dominate *Variety's* list of highest-grossing films of all time, his Lucasfilm company has made significant contributions to film technology as well. Any child in America today owes much of his personal folklore to Lucas's various reincarnations of old Hollywood themes in the *Star Wars* series and *Raiders of the Lost Ark*. Lucas has, on occasion, produced other, smaller films, by the way. For the record: *More American Graffiti* (B. W. L. Norton, 1979), *Twice Upon a Time* (John Korty, 1983).

Spielberg working alone is equally capable of striking a responsive chord at the box office, as 1982's *E.T.* showed quite well. He can also bomb out as *1941* (1979) demonstrated. As producer he has a mixed record: some attractive films by Zemeckis and Gale and Michael Apted (*Continental Divide*) and at least one money-maker: *Poltergeist* (1982, directed by Tobe Hooper).

And Black American filmmakers?

Certainly the most direct evidence of our political paralysis these past ten years is the situation of Black filmmakers in—and out of—Hollywood. Ossie Davis, Bill Gunn, Gordon Parks, and the others still wait for an opportunity to join the American film industry. Meanwhile they continue working in other arts—see especially Bill Gunn's recent novel *Rhinestone Cowboy*, about Blacks and movies.

Each year, the situation gets slightly but inevitably worse. Actors don't even have the opportunities they had in the mid-seventies to work in white films. Richard Pryor is a star. Eddie Murphy is a star. Lou Gossett won an Oscar. Michael Jackson is a celebrity. The list ends there.

To a film scholar, perhaps one of the more interesting developments of the early 80s has been the unremarked death of the auteur policy. Partly this was a result of a number of commercial disasters—Michael Cimino's

Gene Wilder and Richard Pryor were known as a successful comedy team after *Silver Streak*. Here they are in *Stir Crazy*.

Heaven's Gate was the primary example. Mainly it was the result simply of a lack of talent. If the directors can't direct, well then, other people will. And they have been, with increasing regularity during the last few years.

A number of actors have followed in the footsteps of Orson Welles. Paul Newman had tried this occasionally in the early 70s. Robert Redford won an Academy Award for *Ordinary People* (1981) his very serious middle-class drama, starring Mary Tyler Moore. The next year Warren Beatty won for a much more interesting film, *Reds*. Alan Alda, much too nice a fellow and much too aware of his niceness, continues to exploit that cute persona in fairly successful films like *The Four Seasons*. Richard Benjamin did a credible job on *My Favorite Year* and *Racing With the Moon*, and Burt Reynolds does at least as well when he directs his films as when he doesn't. He seems to know it doesn't matter.

More important, no matter who directs a film these days, it seems, the stars seem to have more of an artistic impact. Directors may get their name above the title, but audiences aren't paying attention to it. Although I'm sure there are numerous film students around the country who do so, I find it hard to imagine serious filmgoers being intent on following the careers of, say, John Landis, Hal Needham, or John Badham.

Landis and Badham, by the way, have taken up much of the slack left by the relative inactivity of the original whiz kids. Landis earned his spurs

421

directing Ivan Reitman's production of *National Lampoon's Animal House* (1978)—the one film of the last 8 years that really set a trend: kids capers. He followed that with the overblown and overbudget *Blues Brothers* (1980), based on a thin *Saturday Night Live* TV skit. Then came *An American Werewolf in London* (1981); and *Trading Places* (1983), again with TV stars. Then he ran into serious legal problems over the deaths of several actors during the filming of *Twilight Zone* (1983). He may be best known today to some Americans as the "director" of Michael Jackson's *Thriller* video—the first "director" to be so credited.

Badham rattled around after *Saturday Night Fever* (1977) with *Dracula* (1979) and *Whose Life Is It Anyway?* (1981) before striking paydirt in 1982-83 with *Blue Thunder* and the nicely timed kids computer thriller-caper *WarGames*.

While the not-so-young auteurs have been stumbling, a number of the old hands have revived. Here is a quick overview: Blake Edwards has returned to form with three rather financially successful films, *10*, *S.O.B.*, and *Victor/Victoria*, and a raft of Pink Panthers.

S.O.B. was a heartfelt satire, and a direct result of his trials with the Hollywood system of the seventies. *10* presented the kind of sexual fantasy we thought went out with Jayne Mansfield. Yet *10* was able to turn the talented veteran Dudley Moore into one of the top box office stars of 1981, a considerable accomplishment. *Victor/Victoria* traded on the new-fangled interest in transvestitism that also supported the highly overrated *Tootsie* and *La Cage Aux Folles*.

Martin Ritt contributed one of the more resonant myths of '79 and '80 with *Norma Rae*, a movie whose politics weren't up to its emotions. And Sidney Lumet, who remains probably the most underrated American director now working has added to his list two perfect New York movies: *Just Tell Me What You Want* and *Prince of the City*: sharp, witty, and gutsy. Lumet's *The Verdict* (1982) gave Paul Newman his best role in 20 years.

Other veterans weighed in with heavyweight literary works: George Roy Hill's *The World According to Garp* (1982), Alan Pakula's *Sophie's Choice* (1983). These are the sort of "meaningful," literary projects that Hollywood's liberals used to do in the late forties. Ulu Grosbard's *True Confessions*, released about the same as *Body Heat* in the fall of 1981, also caught that forties tone with great elegance.

Gerundive titles were quite popular in the late '70s and early '80s. Hal Ashby's *Being There*, Peter Yates's *Breaking Away*, and Alan Pakula's *Starting Over* all in various ways touched a collective nerve.

Mike Nichols returned after a long absence with *Silkwood* (1983), a rare

Meryl Streep and Kurt Russell in Mike Nichols's *Silkwood* (1983).

attempt at political statement somehow overcome with melodrama.

Howard Zieff finally found financial success with *Private Benjamin* (1980), which somehow appealed to audiences and became a television series. Herbert Ross's best work in the eighties was the curious Steve Martin vehicle, *Pennies From Heaven*, an interesting idea that probably worked better when it was a television series.

These are movies for grown-ups and as the population bell-curve ages, we can expect to see even more of them, despite the domination of the 13-24-year-old consumer in the marketplace. Add to this list the recent work of the Roberts: Benton's *Kramer vs. Kramer*, Young's *Rich Kids*, and Fosse's *All That Jazz*.

Of all the veterans, Sydney Pollack has probably made the most significant progress in the early eighties. He had always maintained a low profile in comparison to his younger colleagues, and continues, as he has for fifteen years, to work in close collaboration with stars like Robert Redford and Paul Newman.

Yet, since 1978, Pollack has directed three influential movies. *The Electric Horseman* (1979) put Fonda and Redford, the two leading Hollywood politicos, together for the first time. *Absence of Malice* (1981) gave Paul Newman a chance to do something with guts again. And *Tootsie* (1982) showcased the incorrigible Dustin Hoffman as a literal prima donna (after many years of figurative practice in that role).

It's one of the strange signs of the times of the 1980s that *Tootsie* was

Streep and Hoffman in *Kramer vs. Kramer.* Streep and Allen in *Manhattan.*

regarded as some sort of feminist tract.

Perhaps the oddest Hollywood sensibility right now belongs to Peter Hyams. His films are never treated seriously by the critics, but they now comprise an eclectic list: *Capricorn One* (1978) suggested that Hollywood knew more about outer space than NASA did. *Hanover Street* (1979) was a brash attempt to make a World War II romance and take it seriously. *Outland* (1981) was a stylish Sci-Fi Western, made with great economy. More than most directors working today, Hyams has particular ideas and tastes.

As the director's star wanes, producers come to the fore again. David Puttnam, who won a Best Picture Academy Award in 1982 for the rather mild *Chariots of Fire* (a thoroughly British production), has been instrumental during the last few years in getting jobs for fellow Britons in Hollywood. Adrian Lyne's *Foxes* and Alan Parker's *Fame* are the two most interesting. Both are seminal. *Fame* showed there were new and interesting opportunities in musical films. Lyne later set styles and fashions with *Flashdance* (1983). Let us not forget, either, the impact of Ridley Scott's calculating *Alien* (1980). It's interesting that such American genres have been so well-served by British filmmakers.

Tony Bill (actor turned producer) had an auspicious directing debut with *My Bodyguard* (1980), proving that you can make intelligent funny movies for kids. Bill followed this with another nice, small film, *Six Weeks* (1982).

Producer Rob Cohen (*The Wiz, Thank God It's Friday*) turned to directing with *A Small Circle of Friends* (1980).

Ivan Reitman rose to a position of some considerable prominence in the Hollywood establishment mainly as a result of *National Lampoon's Animal House*, but also for his direction of *Meatballs* and *Stripes*. As the inventor of the kids caper movie Reitman can lay claim to being the first

424

Burt Lancaster and Susan Sarandon in Louis Malle's *Atlantic City*.

real innovator in American film since Stanley Kubrick.

Jane Fonda's and Bruce Gilbert's IPC production unit has done some of the most noteworthy movies of the last few years, including *The China Syndrome* and *9 to 5*, to say nothing of *On Golden Pond*.

Two movies don't make a new wave, but it might just be that James Bridges, who's been around for quite some years, will be one of the more interesting directors to watch in the 1980s. *The China Syndrome* (1979), was certainly the most harrowing and affective political melodrama in quite some time. And *Urban Cowboy*, a year later, also caught the mood of the country.

On the basis of *Citizen's Band* and *Melvin and Howard* (1980), Jonathan Demme also bears attention in the coming years.

Foreigners have had more of an opportunity in the American film industry too, as movies have become increasingly international. Milos Forman's *Hair* captured the '60s spirit, and his *Ragtime* (produced by an Italian and filmed mainly in England) has got to be one of the great American movie myths of all time—and the only attempt to deal with the Black experience on that level of popularity.

Another immigrant, Louis Malle, gained some measure of popularity with *Atlantic City* and *My Dinner With Andre*.

Costa-Gavras made an effective transition to American film with *Missing*. Costa-Gavras still has the power to excite and inform, something

425

that cannot be said of so many of his European contemporaries of the 1960s.

Meanwhile, the British invasion of Hollywood has been so thorough that it can almost be said that the two national industries have merged. It is no accident that British produced and directed films have won Best Picture Academy Awards two years running in the mid-eighties. Most of the blockbusters of the last seven years have used at least some British technical talent as Americans have become major clients of the British studios. At the same time, a significant number of British directors have settled in Hollywood, and actors like Michael Caine, Dudley Moore, Peter Cook, Lynn Redgrave—and even Sir John Gielgud—have eased their way into the American mainstream.

Not far behind are the Australians. Mel Gibson may yet become an American star and Bruce Beresford's U.S. directorial debut—*Tender Mercies* (1983), with Robert Duvall—proved an extraordinary essay, both dramatically and cinematographically: a real celebration of American character and the American landscape.

Except for an occasional political melodrama like *Missing* or *Silkwood*, filmmakers in the early eighties have been rather incapable, it seems, of producing movies with any public mythic resonance. The most popular films—more *Star Wars* episodes, *Raiders of the Lost Ark*—simply rehash the myths of the thirties and forties, as we've noted. But there have been a few (less popular) movies in the last five years that strike responsive chords.

Three stand out: *Ragtime* managed to highlight the theme that was all but lost in the pyrotechnics of the novel. There hasn't been such a poignant evocation of the American racial dilemma since *Invisible Man* and it's difficult to think of any competition on film. Beatty's *Reds* combined romance with politics, old-fashioned Hollywood melodrama with documentary in a way that hasn't been done before. *Reds* is a first step to beginning to understand how we got to where we are politically, now that the twentieth century is dragging to a close. Philip Kaufman's unusual *The Right Stuff* is also remarkable for what it shows us about the erratic course of the American soul these past twenty years.

There's still room for more films about the '60s. We haven't yet figured out what happened then that made things so different since then. Rob Cohen's *Small Circle of Friends* (1980) like John Sayles's *Return of the Secaucus Seven* was an attempt to figure out just what happened. Arthur Penn's *Four Friends* (1981), from a script by Steven Tesich, was a striking evocation of the period. It stays in the mind. Barry Levinson's *Diner* (1981) probably comes closest to a precise reproduction of after high-school life

Ragtime: the mythic panorama includes Evelyn Nesbit (Elizabeth McGovern), the beginnings of the movies (Mandy Patinkin), the Golden Age of Hollywood (James Cagney) and the Black experience in America (Howard E. Rollins as Coalhouse Walker).

in the late fifties, early sixties. Call it an East Coast *American Graffiti.*

* * * * *

Perhaps the most telling comment on the state of American film in the
mid-eighties is contained in this press release issued in January, 1984:

> In 1960, Roger Corman produced and directed a quickie
> called *The Little Shop of Horrors.* The shooting schedule in-
> cluded two days and one night. The budget was about $15,000.
> Noting well the success of the off-broadway musical inspired by
> that movie, producer Steven Spielberg has announced that he
> will remake the cult classic and has signed director Martin
> Scorsese to the project. The film is budgeted at $20 million.
> Spielberg has also signed singing star Michael Jackson for the
> title role in his new version of Peter Pan.

427

13

The 1980s:
The Power
and the Money

In 1981 for the first time, film revenues from cable television— including pay-cable services—exceeded revenues from theatrical film rentals. By 1983 revenues from video tapes and video discs were also climbing rapidly. There, in brief, is the essence of the Hollywood experience in the early '80s.

In the '50s, the film industry had come to grips with the television industry by avoiding it. The two media grew up separately. And it wasn't until ten years later that the new owners of the Hollywood studios discovered that they could produce just as efficiently and profitably for television as for cinema screens. In the '80s, the challenge of discs, tapes, cable, and satellite (collectively called "homevideo") will not be so easy to avoid. Films lend themselves much more directly to homevideo than they do to broadcast television.

Revenues for the film studios from cable TV have already increased drastically. If you're a film producer now, you look first at the amount of money you can expect to make from sales of foreign rights, next at cable and broadcast television rights and only finally do you consider the revenues that might accrue from theatrical film rental. But as HBO/Cinemax, and Showtime/The Movie Channel fees increase, network rental fees decrease. The networks have felt the effect of the ca-

TV stars: John Ritter in *Hero at Large*, Goldie Hawn in *Private Benjamin*.

ble revolution, and feature films that have appeared on pay-cable are clearly not as valuable to NBC, CBS, and ABC as they once were.

This is what worries film producers: in the long run (by 1990) it's clear that total dollar revenues from all sources of distribution, both new and old, will increase significantly. In the short run, however, over the next two years, it's not at all clear what the effect of the new structure will be.

Perhaps partly in anticipation of this new entertainment bonanza, and perhaps simply to avoid the shame and ignominy that attached to the Begelman fiasco of 1977, film executives during the past few years have been paying themselves pretty nice salaries. In September of 1981 Columbia Pictures announced that Frank Price, its chairman at that time, had signed a four-year contract that was almost certain to earn him more than ten million dollars. If you're slow with arithmetic, that comes out to 2.5 mil per year. This is what we call a pretty nice salary. Back in 1977 when David Begelman found it somehow necessary to cash other people's checks, the poor fellow was earning only a few hundred thousand a year.

Price was not alone. Most of the major studio executives routinely earn more than a million a year now and even third- and fourth-level executives are up in the multi-hundred-thousand-dollar range.

All of this began back in 1978 when Alan Ladd, Jr., earned close to two million simply because of a bonus clause in his contract that gave him 1.5% of 20th Century-Fox's net profits. You'll remember that 1977 was the year of *Star Wars*, the most profitable movie ever made.

Is it any wonder then that in the early '80s Hollywood was shaken by a series of strikes? In the summer of 1980, the Screen Actors Guild hit the sidewalks, costing the industry perhaps as much as fifty million dollars a week during their lengthy strike. In the spring of '81 the Writers Guild attempted the same sort of action with less success.

By the summer of '81, the Directors Guild had decided not to strike.

430

You can make a movie without writers; there are plenty of scripts lying on the shelf. You can make a movie without directors; producers would love to have a chance to fill in. But you can't make a movie without actors.

The ostensible reason for the strikes was to gain a share of homevideo revenues. Both the writers and the actors remembered acutely their battle during the early 1960's to gain a significant share of television residual rights and they were intent on avoiding the same mistake with homevideo. However, behind all of this there must have been some motivation from the knowledge that the executives in the industry, many of them in their late 20's or early 30's, were earning even more than the highest paid journeymen actors and writers.

Then, too, everyone in Hollywood is learning in the early '80s that although there might be a lot of money in film for those who can find it, the industry as a whole was a lot less lucrative than others one might point to.

Computers, for example.

Star Wars remains the most profitable film of all time (although *E.T.* outranks it in studio revenues), with total revenues hovering somewhere near the five-hundred-million-dollar mark. Space Invaders, a video arcade game which is not unlike *Star Wars*, easily exceeded that revenue figure. And Pac Man, 1982's entry in the video arcade market, set a record with revenues in excess of one billion dollars. (Then the roof fell in on the video arcade market. In 1983 it was only 150% as large as the feature film market.)

The conglomerate owners of the studios can read these numbers as well as you or I. For years now, Warner Communications Industries has been more interested in its Atari Computer division than in its movie and television divisions. The obvious reason? Until the disaster of 1983, Atari had contributed most of Warner Communications Industries' profit margin each quarter. During the early '80s other studios rushed to catch up with WCI. Unless they could place a successful bid for Apple Computers or Radio Shack, they didn't have much of a chance, for the real action was in computers, not the associated media of homevideo.

Throughout the early 1980s journalists increasingly looked north to "Silicon" Valley (and away from the movie industry in the San Fernando Valley) in search of interesting personalities and stories. By 1984, for many people the computer industry had replaced the film industry as a subject of daily gossip and news. The eyes of the world were increasingly focused on towns called Cupertino and Sunnyvale (not Hollywood and Burbank).

431

This scene from *Fame* is known as "46th Street Jam." Fifty years ago it would have been choreographed much more neatly (and without the vitality) by Busby Berkeley.

MCA, Inc. found this out to its chagrin when videodiscs did not develop as quickly as projected. In early '82, MCA and IBM, partners in the Discovision laser videodisc operation, decided to sell out to co-partner Pioneer Electronics.

Meanwhile, smaller fish in the industry were trying to swallow larger fish, as during 1980 and '81 everyone made an attempt to purchase the two remaining independent studios, Columbia and 20th Century-Fox.

Coca Cola was the successful suitor for Columbia. (There is no truth to the rumor that the soft-drink company's purchase of the studio was the result of a misinterpretation of some message about a Colombian coke deal.)

With the help of silent partner Mark Rich, Marvin Davis, a Denver oil man, purchased 20th Century-Fox, thereby "saving it" from the hands of rapacious conglomerates. From Davis's actions so far it seems he understands that the real value of Fox is in its backlist and its real estate. Most Hollywood observers expect him to sell the latter at a very significant profit and sit on the former while paying scant attention to contemporary film production.

Early in 1980, real estate mogul Kirk Kerkorian discovered after nine years that in fact he really did want to be in the movie business and MGM, of which he owns a major portion, split itself into two companies—MGM Film Company and MGM Real Estate. David Begelman signed on with MGM in January 1980 at a salary of $500,000. He

432

Shirley MacLaine finally won an Oscar in 1984 for her performance in *Terms of Endearment*. (Here she is with up-and-coming Debra Winger.) More than any other actress, MacLaine has shown unusual staying power, remaining a leading star from age 20 to 50.

had paid his penance. His tenure lasted a short time, as the musical chairs game Hollywood executives play increased its tempo markedly during the early eighties.

MGM Film Company embarked on an ambitious schedule of production and was soon deeply in debt. As of this writing, despite several successful films in 1983, they have yet to pull out of the red.

Meanwhile, the debacle of *Heaven's Gate* so shocked the corporate managers of Transamerica that they immediately put United Artists on the block. In a complicated case of conglomerates chasing their own tails, MGM, formerly a customer of United Artists, bought out UA. Within a year, the two companies had merged into MGM-UA. Little more than a year later, the old UA was effectively dissolved, although the name remains.

Founded more than 60 years ago by Mary Pickford, Douglas Fairbanks, D. W. Griffith, and Charlie Chaplin, UA had a long and distinguished history in the '60s and '70s. Arthur Krim and Eric Pleskow and crew had led United Artists to a position of leadership in the industry. Michael Cimino, with the great help of UA managers, and executives in the Transamerica tower, managed to destroy all this in a matter of months.

The map of Hollywood business relationships now is tortuous and complicated. Tandem/TAT (Norman Lear's organizations) acquired AVCO

433

Dan Aykroyd and Eddie Murphy in *Trading Places* (here with Jamie Lee Curtis and Denholm Elliott).

Embassy. The executives of Orion Pictures (formerly the executives of United Artists) bought Filmways early in 1982, and merged it into Orion. By the summer of 1982, there were no real independent Hollywood studios aside from Walt Disney. In the spring of 1984, even Disney came under attack from the buyout artists.

Late in 1980, four of the six Hollywood studios had attempted to meet the challenge of HBO by forming their own pay-cable television network: Premiere. In August of 1980, the Justice Department brought suit against Columbia Pictures, MCA, Paramount, and 20th Century-Fox (together with Getty Oil) charging them with restraint of trade. Within six months Premiere was dead and Time Inc.'s HBO was free to monopolize the pay-cable television industry.

Studios regrouped in an attempt to gain a foothold in the new electronic distribution network. Paramount quietly went into homevideo distribution, manufacturing and marketing videocassettes of its movies and joining Time Inc. and MCA Inc. as partners in USA Network, an advertiser-supported cable channel. Columbia Pictures organized joint ventures with four other companies including HBO, Bell and Howell, RCA, and Gaumont. The deal with HBO seemed to provide as much as 25% of the financing for Columbia motion pictures during 1982 and 1983.

Warner Communications Inc., the studio best situated to take advantage of the new media, formed joint ventures with American Express

Company, a ready source of the huge amount of cash that all the rest of us decide not to carry with us. Universal has arrangements with Oak Industries Inc., an operator of over-the-air pay-TV and with the British company Thorn EMI Ltd.

Even Walt Disney has an arrangement with Westinghouse Electric Corporation. The deal includes some one hundred million to be spent producing programs for family entertainment channels during the next four years. CBS Cable had a deal with Fox and distribution contracts with MGM, Metromedia, and the USA Network, before its rapid demise.

ABC had arrangements with Getty Oil's Entertainment and Sports Programming Network, the Hearst Corporation, and Westinghouse. In 1983, the television networks pulled out of cable even more quickly than they had entered it a year earlier. CBS Cable and RCTV (a joint venture of Rockefeller Center and RCA) disappeared and ABC's ARTS network was merged with an outside service. (In early 1984, RCA also dropped its money-losing videodisc operation.)

Meanwhile, in late 1983 the film companies tried once again to mount some competition to HBO as Warner's The Movie Channel was merged with Showtime and Warner Bros., Paramount, MCA, Viacom (owner of Showtime), and American Express were brought into the deal to support the new company. When Showtime/The Movie Channel came into existence it had 6.3 million subscribers compared with HBO/Cinemax's 11 million. One of its first deals reportedly guaranteed Paramount $500 million for exclusive first rights to Paramount films over the next few years.

Not to be outdone, HBO has been increasing its own film production schedule. It got into production in 1982. By early 1984 it had decided to compete directly with its supplier/competitors in theatres, as well as on the home screen. The lines were drawn. Meanwhile, the movie companies were trying to persuade the networks to compete directly with HBO for first-run television rights. This seems the one serious threat to the continued dominance of Time Inc.'s pay cable operation in the marketplace.

No one yet knows where the profit centers will be in the new media of the '80s and therefore everyone is intent upon making as many connections as possible in order to hedge their bets.

The net result of all of this hurrying and scurrying is good, I think. From the filmmakers' point of view, the number of channels for distribution has increased drastically even during the last three years, and promises to expand further during the next few years.

More important, the independent identity of theatrical feature film is being compromised at every turn. Increasingly in the future we will think of film (and that means television and all forms of video and audio entertainment as well), more the way we think of books. Books are a general category that include fiction and non-fiction, entertainment and information—all sorts and varieties of communication. In the past we have tended to separate a feature film from all other kinds of sounds and images. This will no longer be possible in the future.

Even the artistic doldrums offer hope. We're simply observing a state of transition. For the last 75 years, the theory of the "New" has dominated art, and that includes film: that theory is just about dead.

At this juncture, we should probably say something about developments in film culture in the 1980s. Probably. Except that there haven't been any developments. The same critics hold sway—although most people are much less interested in what they say. The same theories are taught in the schools—although enrollments have leveled off, or declined. With the single exception of David McClintick's wonderful book about the Begelman scandal, the same sorts of books are written about the same topics.

In the future we will look at these products—films, disks, tapes, broadcasting—with a more jaundiced eye, and that, paradoxically, is good for filmmakers as well as film viewers.

What all the media moguls tend to ignore is the very real possibility that audiences have reached a saturation point. That it may no longer be possible to consume ever more and more media, whether it's print or non-print, video or film, audio or satellite.

We may all take tomorrow off collectively and go to the beach, or the woods, or the mountains. And never come back.

After all, it was only a movie.

The Data

Critics and Critical Choices
The Best Films of the Decade

From an historian's point of view, perhaps the most significant fact about American cinema in the 1970's is that "movies" have metamorphosed quietly but surely into "film." As little as ten years ago, "movies" were still regarded as mass entertainment, of some sociological or political significance perhaps, but certainly beneath serious consideration by nearly all academics and scholars. Now, the situation is drastically different. Film study in colleges and universities has experienced an explosive growth during the seventies—and this at a time when numerous other departments of academia were retrenching.

The industry itself is still very much a business—even more concerned with profit-and-loss and the manipulation of consumers than it was in the thirties or forties. The nature of American cinematic entertainment hasn't really changed all that much. But our attitude toward it has. We are now much more interested in the cultural context of the film experience. We take "movies"— from *Grease* to *Interiors,* from *Macon County Line* to *A Woman Under the Influence*—much more seriously. They may still operate as entertainment machines, but now we are much more interested collectively in finding out just how those machines do what they do, who makes them, and for what purposes. In part, this shift in attitude has been the result of a shift in social function. As television became the prime mass medium of communication and entertainment, "film" was forced up the intellectual scale a bit. In order to survive as a business and medium separate from TV it had to adopt a new image for itself as a more intelligent and complicated art. It wasn't necessary that the products of this art actually raise the intellectual ante (although it could be argued that they have in the seventies). It was sufficient only that our approach to the medium change.

The differentiation between film and television isn't the only reason for the shift. Just as important has been a general change in cultural attitudes which began in the mid-sixties and developed rapidly in the seventies: we no longer make as many invidious comparisons between "high art" and "popular culture" as we once did. We tend toward a more holistic approach to films, books, plays, comics, television, music, and painting. We are beginning to understand now that, for example, a movie seen by fifty million people is just as culturally significant and perhaps just as artistically admirable as, say, a "serious" novel read by a hundred thousand people.

We can trace this new acceptance of popular culture back to the mid-sixties and the rise of rock music. Once the academic journals began gingerly to test the waters with nervous essays on the musicology of The Beatles, the dam broke. If rock 'n roll, once the bête noire of teachers and other guardians of the elite culture, was now an acceptable subject of study, could movies be far behind? On the whole, this new unified and eclectic approach to our culture must be considered a major and historic advance in the intellectual life of the United States. We may still separate classes politically and economically, but we are moving toward a real and valuable cultural populism—and movies are in the vanguard of this revolution. For all its flaws, American film is now perhaps the one art that spans most class divisions in the U.S., and thus perhaps helps to unify the disparate economic and cultural groups that make up this country.

Parallel with the growth of this new cultural populism has been the rise of a new tradition of film criticism. More people are writing more interestingly about movies in the 1970s than ever before. The vitality of the new criticism, together with the unusual celebrity that now attaches to some of its most respected practitioners, remains a good index of the real significance of contemporary movies in the U.S. cultural matrix.

Although there had always been a strain of intelligent American film criticism,* such attitudes did not become widespread until the very late sixties. The careers of three contemporary critics are landmarks in this respect. Andrew Sarris began writing for the then underground Village Voice in the late fifties. He proselytized for the French "auteur" policy of the Cahiers du Cinéma critics that forced attention on directors, who had

---

*Even before 1920 the poet Vachel Lindsay and the psychologist Hugo Münsterberg had written seminal and still remarkably insightful books about movies as an art and cultural activity. In the thirties, Otis Ferguson and Harry Alan Potamkin wrote intelligently for small magazines. In the forties, James Agee and Robert Warshow championed film and popular culture. (Ferguson, Potamkin, Agee, and Warshow all died young.) In the fifties, Manny Farber and Parker Tyler, among others, became cult leaders. In the early sixties, Dwight Macdonald (from politics) and Stanley Kauffmann (from literature) helped to raise the level of discussion.

hitherto been regarded simply as hired hands at the film factories. It was a necessary first step in the maturation process of American film criticism. Pauline Kael developed an opposite tack, from a West Coast perspective. Whereas Sarris had been most effective explaining the "art" of film, Kael continued to insist on the popular nature of movies. Considering the history of the American film industry, this was not only a necessary corrective, but an approach of simple logic. Kael is at her best describing the gut experience of movies. John Simon, the third of our seminal seventies critics, has established a position closer to Sarris than to Kael (although he would be outraged to hear it put that way). The most conservative of contemporary critics, he continues to insist on "standards"—rules by which accomplishments can be strictly judged. As a theorist, Simon seems reactionary. As a practical observer, he is often perspicacious. But his real significance in the spectrum of contemporary film criticism rests with his understanding of the position of the critic as an independent, active persona in the drama of the cinematic experience. Over the years, he has developed certainly the strongest and perhaps the most enticing character as the critic/curmudgeon, ranting about failures far more often than quietly discussing successes.

Although his work as a critic is generally unknown in this country, Richard Roud, an ex-Bostonian who now lives in Paris and has written regularly on film for *The Guardian* of London for many years, must be included in this group of seminal influences. Roud is not only the most widely intelligent of the four—a critic who brings an admirable sense of sanity to his work—but he is also the director, since its founding in 1963, of the New York Film Festival and thus has had a profound influence on the development of cinematic taste during the last fifteen years in the U.S.*

---

*There is some statistical proof of this influence. Judged by the survey which served as the basis for the lists below, Roud's New York Film Festival premiered: 59 percent of the European films cited in the poll, including four of the six that led the list, 47 percent of the films that lead the Third World list; and, most surprising, since the Festival has very little choice among domestic films, 16 percent of the top American movies. Roud is limited by distribution practices to little more that 20 percent of all American films released in any one year, so the real percentage of Festival choices among the top films in the survey would if adjusted approach 80 percent.

WHAT'S THE SCORE? THE BEST OF THE DECADE

Early in 1978, while I was at work on this book, I decided it would be interesting to survey a number of the world's leading film critics to find out what they thought were the best films of the decade. "Ten-best" lists, long a staple of movie reviewing, obviously don't permit a really intelligent discussion of either the art or the industry of film, yet taken with a little humor, they do show us something about current critical tastes.

The Rules of the Game were relatively simple: for the purposed of the survey, the decade ran from 1 January 1968 through 31 December 1977. World-premiere dates decided eligibility. This seemed a more logical period in film history than the strict chronology of the seventies. 1968 was a watershed year (in both the U.S. and Europe) in both politics and film—a better starting point, it seemed, than the arbitrary year 1970.

Critics were asked to choose ten films (no more, no less) in American and European categories, and five in the Third World category.*

Choosing twenty of the world's best film critics was, of course, an even more personal and idiosyncratic business than choosing the world's best films. Certain names suggested themselves immediately, both for the recognized quality of their work and their obvious influence. Vincent Canby, Molly Haskell, Stanley Kauffmann, Gene Moskowitz, Andrew Sarris, and Richard Schickel fit this description. (Penelope Gilliatt, Pauline Kael, Richard Roud, and John Simon were invited, but declined, due to long-standing antipathies to ten-best lists.) I also wanted to indicate a range of the most interesting younger critics working in the late seventies. Peter Biskind, Richard Corliss, Jan Dawson, Stephen Farber, Michael Goodwin, Diane Jacobs, Janet Maslin, Frank Rich, and Clayton Riley all write for general-interest as well as specialized magazines. Each of them has established an interesting critical persona during the last few years. Finally, I wanted to extend the boundaries of the often claustrophobic world of film criticism by inviting several writers who aren't weekly or monthly critics to participate. François Truffaut is the world's premiere filmmaker-as-critic. Scholars Peter Cowie and David Thomson have demonstrated an acuity and a breadth of interest that suggested their inclusion here. Greil Marcus is best known for his literary and music criticism but has also written about film on a regular basis. Richard T. Jameson,

---

*Only American films are discussed in detail here, though European and Third World tastes were also polled. The complete survey was published in *Take One*, July 1978, and readers are referred there for further details.

editor of *Movietone News*, is, like his magazine, something of a cult object: not widely known, but highly respected.*

In keeping with the spirit of enterprises like ten-best lists, let me point out that one of the pleasures of such games is the mathematical cat's cradle to which statistics give rise. For example: If we assign a numerical value to inclusion on a list, we can sum up the total value of each critic's choices. The ideally accurate evaluator of American films of the past decade would thus present us with ten-best list whose "Accuracy Quotient" was 78, since that is the sum of the votes received by the ten highest-ranking films overall. (The European top score would be 58, and the combined sum 136.) The chart on p. 420 shows how our critics faired, judged against each other. Vincent Canby, Molly Haskell, and Frank Rich had the highest Accuracy Quotients for the American list, while Diane Jacobs took honors in the European field. What this means is that if you want to know how these twenty critics feel, on the average, about European movies but you only have time to read one of them, Jacobs is your choice. In the combined scores, Jacobs and Rich were clearly ahead of the pack. Their success is all the more surprising when we realize the remarkable fact that their combined ages do not together exceed the retirement age for the average film critic.

On the other hand (and there is always another hand, statistically speaking), critics with the lowest Accuracy Quotients naturally and inevitably (and conversely) have the highest "Originality Quotients." Kauffmann and Truffaut score unusually high in the American category. (A perfect Originality Quotient would be 10—representing ten single films absolutely no one else had chosen.) The two are joined by Moskowitz and Biskind in the European list. Truffaut just edges out Kauffmann in the combined scores. (I particularly like Kauffmann's lists, but that is a matter of individual judgment, not scientific evaluation.)

Substract O.Q.s from A.Q.s and you then have an index of some sort of ineffable balance between conformity and idiosyncrasy. Biskind and Dawson were dead on the mean for American films, Riley for European films, and Corliss for combined scores (although he was way off in separate categories, an example of the sort of difference my physics teacher used to define between accuracy and precision).

But enough of this. Here are the results:

---

*Since 1978, Jan Dawson and Gene Moskowitz have died, but all the others are still writing. More important, no new critics have made reputations that would suggest their inclusion here—unless you count the TV stars: Gene Siskel, Roger Ebert, Leonard Maltin, etc.

THE FILMS

Thirteen American films qualified in the top rank (with 5 or more votes apiece). The strong showings of *The Godfather* and *Nashville* were no surprise, but is is interesting to note that *Petulia*'s cult reputation has built over the years into a remarkable third-place finish in our poll. *Annie Hall*'s strength is notable as well. (Critics voted before Woody Allen's Oscar coup.) *Badlands, McCabe and Mrs. Miller*, and *Barry Lyndon* also showed unexpected strength.

Among the American runners-up (those films with more than 2 votes), *Blume in Love* and *The Man Who Would Be King* are perhaps surprises. Also unusual is Alan Pakula's strong showing with two films in the top 21. Judged according to the list, he thus joins the ranks of Altman, Coppola, Scorsese, and Kubrick (each of whom also directed two top-ranked films.)

Adding up the total number of votes received by each director we find Altman leading with 21 votes (for 6 films) with Coppola close behind: 18 votes for 3 films.* Scorsese garnered 13 votes (3 movies). Richard Lester, a surprisingly strong finisher, won 11 votes (3 films), as did Stanley Kubrick (2 films). Alan Pakula and Sam Peckinpah were close behind with 9 votes each (for 3 films each), and Woody Allen also won 9 (all for *Annie Hall*).

Other American directors with five or more votes include George Lucas (7 for 2), Roman Polanski (7 for 2), Don Siegel (6 for 4), Steven Spielberg (5 for 4), John Schlesinger (5 for 2), John Huston (5 for 2), Bob Rafelson (5 for 2), Paul Mazursky (5 for 2), and Terrence Malick (5 for 1): a potential pantheon for the seventies.

---

*In the chart, *The Godfather* is treated as a single film in two parts, since most of our critics regarded it that way. Eleven critics voted for one or both parts of the film, eight voted for the opus as a whole, two for the first part, and four for Part II. If the films had been ranked separately, *Godfather II* would have been tied with *Nashville*.

The Best American Films Of The Decade
The Leaders: More than 5 votes each

The Godfather (14)	1971-74	Coppola
Nashville (12)	1975	Altman
Petulia (9)	1968	Lester
Annie Hall (9)	1977	Allen
Mean Streets (7)	1973	Scorsese
2001: A Space Odyssey (6)	1968	Kubrick
The Wild Bunch (6)	1969	Peckinpah

5 votes each

American Graffiti	1973	Lucas
Badlands	1973	Malick
Taxi Driver	1976	Scorsese
McCabe and Mrs. Miller	1971	Altman
Chinatown	1974	Polanski
Barry Lyndon	1975	Kubrick

4 votes each

Blume in Love	1973	Mazursky
The Conversation	1974	Coppola
Midnight Cowboy	1969	Schlesinger
All the President's Men	1976	Pakula

3 votes each

The Man Who Would Be King	1975	Huston
Klute	1971	Pakula
Five Easy Pieces	1970	Rafelson
The Last Picture Show	1971	Bogdanovich

2 votes each

The Shootist	1976	Siegel
One Flew Over the Cuckoo's Nest	1975	Forman
Fat City	1972	Huston
Beyond the Valley of the Dolls	1970	Meyer
The Parallax View	1974	Pakula
Rosemary's Baby	1968	Polanski
Sweet Sweetback's Baadasssss Song	1971	Van Peebles
Ganja & Hess	1973	Gunn
Harlan County, USA	1976	Kopple
Pat Garrett and Billy the Kid	1973	Peckinpah
The Night of the Living Dead	1968	Romero
The King of Marvin Gardens	1972	Rafelson
Madigan	1968	Siegel
Alice's Restaurant	1969	Penn
Star Wars	1977	Lucas
Deliverance	1972	Boorman
Close Encounters of the Third Kind	1977	Spielberg

The Best European Films Of The Decade
The Leaders: More than 5 votes each

My Night at Maud's (7)	1968	Rohmer
Scenes from a Marriage (7)	1973	Bergman
Claire's Knee (60)	1970	Rohmer
The Conformist (6)	1970	Bertolucci
Amarcord (6)	1973	Fellini
The Sorrow and The Pity (6)	1971	Ophuls

5 votes each

Lancelot du lac	1974	Bresson
The Mother and the Whore	1973	Eustache
The Discreet Charm of the Bourgeoisie	1972	Buñuel
Le Boucher	1970	Chabrol
The Passenger	1975	Antonioni

The Best Third World Films Of The Decade
The Leaders: 4 or more votes each

Memories of Underdevelopment (6)	1968	Gutierrez Alea	(Cuba)
The Hour of the Furnaces (5)	1968	Grupo Cine Liberacion (Fernando Solanas, Octavio Getino)	(Argentina)
The Harder They Come (4)	1973	Perry Henzell	(Jamaica)
Lucia (4)	1969	Humberto Solas	(Cuba)
Distant Thunder (4)	1973	Satyajit Ray	(India)

3 votes each

A Touch of Zen	1975	King Hu	(Hong Kong)
Antonio Das Mortes	1969	Glauber Rocha	(Brazil)
The Battle of Chile	1973-6	Equipo Tercer Año (Patricio Guzman)	(Chile)
Days and Nights in the Forest	1970	Satyajit Ray	(India)

Critics' Lists: The Best American Films 1968-1977

PETER BISKIND
1. The Godfather
2. Jaws
3. The Godfather, Part II
4. Annie Hall
5. Pat Garrett and Billy the Kid
6. Klute
7. Night of the Living Dead
8. Midnight Cowboy
9. The French Connection
10. Chinatown

VINCENT CANBY
1. 2001: A Space Odyssey
2. Alice's Restaurant
3. True Grit
4. The Wild Bunch
5. Mean Streets
6. Nashville
7. Milestones
8. Annie Hall
9. Star Wars
10. The Godfather

RICHARD CORLISS
1. Petulia
2. Blume in Love
3. Carnal Knowledge
4. Beyond the Valley of the Dolls
5. Badlands
6. The Parallax View
7. Alice Doesn't Live Here Anymore
8. The Conversation
9. The Way We Were
10. Schoolgirl

PETER COWIE
1. The Godfather
2. Five Easy Pieces
3. 2001: A Space Odyssey
4. Deliverance
5. Midnight Cowboy
6. American Graffiti
7. A Woman Under the Influence
8. Annie Hall
9. Play Misty for Me
10. Fat City
Preferential order.

JAN DAWSON
1. McCabe and Mrs. Miller
2. Mean Streets
3. David Holzman's Diary
4. Zabriskie Point
5. Annie Hall
6. The King of Marvin Gardens
7. Le Vieux Pays, ou Rimbaud est Mort
8. Inserts
9. Nashville
10. Night of the Living Dead

STEPHEN FARBER
1. Petulia
2. The Wild Bunch
3. Five Easy Pieces
4. Deliverance
5. American Graffiti
6. Badlands
7. The Conversation
8. Nashville
9. Dog Day Afternoon
10. Carrie

MICHAEL GOODWIN (with Naomi Wise)
1. Coogan's Bluff
2. 2001: A Space Odyssey
3. Petulia
4. The Last Movie
5. The Last Picture Show
6. Mean Streets
7. The Legend of Lylah Clare
8. The Texas Chainsaw Massacre
9. Beyond the Valley of the Dolls
10. The Shootist

MOLLY HASKELL
1. Nashville
2. Petulia
3. Barry Lyndon
4. Blume in Love
5. Annie Hall
6. All the President's Men
7. The Godfather I, II
8. Klute
9. Faces
10. Madigan
11. Mean Streets

DIANE JACOBS
1. American Graffiti
2. Annie Hall
3. Badlands
4. The Godfather
5. Harry and Tonto
6. The Man Who Would Be King
7. McCabe and Mrs. Miller
8. Mean Streets
9. Midnight Cowboy
10. Smile

RICHARD T. JAMESON
1. 2001: A Space Odyssey
2. Petulia
3. The Wild Bunch
4. Topaz
5. Performance
6. The Private Life of Sherlock Holmes
7. Chinatown
8. The Parallax View
9. Nashville
10. The Man Who Would Be King

STANLEY KAUFFMANN
1. Close Encounters of the Third Kind
2. The Conversation
3. Desperate Characters
4. Harlan County, U.S.A.
5. The Hired Hand
6. Midnight Cowboy
7. Mikey and Nicky
8. Payday
9. Wanda
10. The Wild Bunch

GREIL MARCUS
1. The Godfather, Part II
2. The Godfather
3. Thieves Like Us
4. The Man Who Would Be King
5. Across 110th Street
6. The Autobiography of Miss
   Jane Pittman
7. McCabe and Mrs. Miller
8. Spend It All
9. Mean Streets
10. Chinatown

JANET MASLIN
1. Nashville
2. Taxi Driver
3. Bad Company
4. Blume in Love
5. September 30, 1955
6. The Last American Hero
7. Annie Hall
8. Rosemary's Baby
9. Dirty Harry
10. Sugarland Express

GENE MOSKOWITZ
1. American Graffiti
2. Easy Rider
3. The Wild Bunch
4. The Shootist
5. One Flew Over the Cuckoo's Nest
6. The Godfather, Part II
7. Fat City
8. Taxi Driver
9. Duel
10. Nashville

FRANK RICH
1. Alice's Restaurant
2. Badlands
3. Barry Lyndon
4. The Godfather, Part II
5. McCabe and Mrs. Miller
6. The Memory of Justice
7. Nashville
8. Petulia
9. Taxi Driver
10. 2001: A Space Odyssey
Alphabetical order.

CLAYTON RILEY
1. Sweet Sweetback's Baadasssss Song
2. The Long Goodbye
3. Chinatown
4. Julia
5. Ganja and Hess
6. The Godfather
7. The Conversation
8. Taxi Driver
9. Harlan County, U.S.A.
10. The Fortune

ANDREW SARRIS
1. Petulia
2. Love Among the Ruins
3. Three Women
4. The Passenger
5. Barry Lyndon
6. All the President's Men
7. Nashville
8. McCabe and Mrs. Miller
9. Annie Hall
10. Madigan

RICHARD SCHICKEL
1. American Graffiti
2. Badlands
3. Barry Lyndon
4. Five Easy Pieces
5. The Godfather, I and II
6. Klute
7. M*A*S*H
8. Nashville
9. The Wild Bunch
10. Star Wars

DAVID THOMSON
1. Chinatown
2. Close Encounters of the Third Kind
3. The Godfather, I and II
4. The King of Marvin Gardens
5. The Last Picture Show
6. Mean Streets
7. Nashville
8. Pat Garrett and Billy the Kid
9. Taxi Driver
10. Trash

FRANCOIS TRUFFAUT
1. Rosemary's Baby
2. The Honeymoon Killers
3. Johnny Got His Gun
4. The Last Picture Show
5. Rio Lobo
6. One Flew Over the Cuckoo's Nest
7. All the President's Men
8. Family Plot
9. F for Fake
10. Annie Hall
Chronological order.

JAMES MONACO
1. Petulia
2. Medium Cool
3. The Godfather
4. Blume in Love
5. Hearts and Minds
6. Nashville
7. Downhill Racer
8. All the President's Men
9. 2001: A Space Odyssey
10. Barry Lyndon
Sweet Sweetback's Baadasssss Song and Ganja and Hess appeared on Third-World list.

The Quotients

ORIGINALITY QUOTIENT

American List		European List		Combined Score	
Kauffmann	23	Moskowitz	19	Truffaut	48
Truffaut	25	Truffault	23	Kauffmann	49
Corliss	30	Biskind	24	Corliss	63
Goodwin	33	Kauffmann	26	Biskind	65
Riley	37	Schickel	29	Goodwin	66
Maslin	37	Monaco	29	Riley	67
Marcus	38	Canby	29	Moskowitz	69
Biskind	41	Riley	30	Marcus	69
Dawson	41	Marcus	31	Dawson	72
Cowie	47	Dawson	31	Maslin	77
Farber	48	Sarris	32	Cowie	80
Jameson	49	Corliss	33	Farber	82
Moskowitz	50	Goodwin	33	Schickel	85
Sarris	53	Cowie	33	Sarris	85
Thomson	53	Haskell	33	Monaco	86
Jacobs	54	Farber	34	Jameson	89
Schickel	56	Maslin	40	Canby	89
Monaco	57	Thomson	40	Thomson	93
Canby	60	Jameson	40	Haskell	96
Haskell	63	Rich	43	Jacobs	103
Rich	64	Jacobs	49	Rich	107
Perfect Accuracy	78		58		136

ACCURACY QUOTIENT

Who's Who

PETER BISKIND is editor of *American Film* Magazine.

VINCENT CANBY is the film critic for *The New York Times* and occasional novelist.

RICHARD CORLISS writes about film for *Time* and is editor of *Film Comment*.

PETER COWIE edits *International Film Guide* and is author of books on Scandinavian cinema and general world cinema.

JAN DAWSON was a prolific freelance critic and journalist.

STEPHEN FARBER has written for a wide variety of publications.

MICHAEL GOODWIN AND NAOMI WISE are San Francisco-based freelancers.

MOLLY HASKELL is former film critic for *New York* and author of *From Reverence to Rape: The Treatment of Women in the Movies*.

DIANE JACOBS is a freelance critic and author of *Hollywood Renaissance*.

RICHARD T. JAMESON is editor of Seattle Film Society's magazine *Movietone News* and teaches film at the University of Washington.

STANLEY KAUFFMANN is film critic for *The New Republic* and author and editor of numerous books on film.

GREIL MARCUS lives in Berkeley, is author of *Mystery Train: Images of America in Rock 'n' Roll Music*, and writes about books for *Rolling Stone*.

JANET MASLIN currently writes about film for *The New York Times*.

GENE MOSKOWITZ, based in Paris, was *Variety's* "Mosk." and thus one of the most quoted film critics in the business.

FRANK RICH is currently film and television critic for *Time*. He previously wrote for the *New York Post* and *New Times*.

CLAYTON RILEY is a freelance writer and playwright with a wide range of interests, including film. He has written for numerous publications including *The New York Times*, *The Village Voice*, *Amsterdam News*.

ANDREW SARRIS is film critic for *The Village Voice*, author of many books on film, and teaches at Columbia.

RICHARD SCHICKEL writes about film, has produced television series on movies, and has written numerous books about movies.

DAVID THOMSON teaches film and is author of the indispensable *Biographical Dictionary of Film*.

FRANÇOIS TRUFFAUT describes himself this way: "Je suis metteur en scène de cinéma."

Ten Major Filmographies

Here are fairly complete and accurate filmographies to date for the ten most dominant filmmakers discussed in *American Film Now*. Only lack of space prohibits inclusion of perhaps a dozen more directors whose work is interesting or influential—Hal Ashby, Sidney Lumet, Terrence Malick, Bill Gunn, Mel Brooks, and others.

I'm indebted to Sharon Boonshoft, Diane Jacobs, and Peter Cowie (editor of the *International Film Guides*) upon whose filmographical prowess I have partly drawn.

WOODY ALLEN

1966   WHAT'S UP TIGER LILY?
Script: Allen, Frank Buxton, Len Maxwell, Louise Lasser, Mickey Rose, Julie Bennett, Bryna Wilson (all of whom dubbed the film).
Direction: Allen.
Photography (Eastmancolor, scope): uncredited.
Editing: Richard Krown.
Music: The Lovin' Spoonful.
Production conception: Ben Shapiro.
Cast: Tatsuya Mihashi (*Phil Moskowitz*), Miyi Hana (*Terri Yaki*), Eiko Wakabayashi (*Suki Yaki*), Tadao Nakamura (*Shepherd Wong*), Susumu Kurobe (*Wing Fat*), Woody Allen, The Lovin' Spoonful, China Lee (*themselves*).

Produced by Reuben Bercovitch and Allen for Benedict. 79 min. [This is a re-edited, dubbed version of *Kagi No Kagi* ("Key of Keys"), Japan, 1964. Script: Hideo Ando. Direction: Senkichi Taniguchi. Photography: Kazuo Yamada.]

1969   TAKE THE MONEY AND RUN
Script: Allen, Mickey Rose.
Direction: Allen.
Photography (Technicolor): Lester Shorr.
Editing: Paul Jordan, Ron Kalish.
Music: Marvin Hamlisch.
Art Direction: Fred Harpman.

Cast: Woody Allen (*Virgil Starkwell*), Janet Margolin (*Louise*), Marcel Hillaire (*Fritz*), Jacquelyn Hyde (*Miss Blair*), Lonny Chapman (*Jake*), Jan Merlin (*Al*), James Anderson (*Chain Gang Warden*), Howard Storm (*Fred*), Mark Gordon (*Vince*), Micil Murphy (*Frank*), Minnow Moskowitz (*Joe Agneta*), Nate Jacobson (*Judge*), Grace Bauer (*Farmhouse Lady*), Ethel Sokolow (*Mother Starkwell*), Henry Leff (*Father Starkwell*), Don Frazier (*psychiatrist*), Mike O'Dowd (*Michael Sullivan*).

Produced by Charles G. Joffe for Palomar Pictures. 85 min.

1971   BANANAS
Script: Allen, Mickey Rose.
Direction: Allen.
Photography (DeLuxe Color): Andrew M. Costikyan.
Editing: Ron Kalish.
Music: Marvin Hamlisch.
Production Design: Ed Wittstein.

Cast: Woody Allen (*Fielding Mellish*), Louise Lasser (*Nancy*), Carlos Montalban (*General Emilio M. Vargas*), Natividad Abascal (*Yolanda*), Jacobo Morales (*Esposito*), Miguel Suarez (*Luis*), David Ortiz (*Sanchez*), Tene Enriquez (*Diaz*), Jack Axelrod (*Arroro*), Howard Cosell, Roger Grimsby, Don Dunphy (*themselves*), Charlotte Rae (*Mrs. Mellish*), Stanley Ackerman (*Dr. Mellish*), Dan Frazer (*priest*), Martha Greenhouse (*Dr. Feigen*), Axel Anderson (*tortured man*), Tigre Perez (*Perez*), Baron De Beer (*British Ambassador*), Arthur Hughes (*Judge*), John Braden (*prosecutor*), Ted Chapman (*policeman*), Dorothi Fox (*J. Edgar Hoover*), Dagne Crane (*Sharon*), Ed Barth (*Paul*), Nicholas Saunders (*Douglas*), Conrad Bain (*Semple*), Eulogio Peraza (*interpreter*), Norman Evans (*Senator*), Robert P. Connell (*first FBI man*), Robert Dudley (*second FBI man*), Marilyn Hengst (*Norma*), Ed Crowley, Beeson Carroll (*FBI Security men*), Allen Garfield (*man on cross*), Princess Fatosh (*snake rite lady*), Dick Callinan (*cigarette commercial man*).

Produced by Jack Grossberg for Rollins and Joffe Productions. 81 min.

1972   EVERYTHING YOU ALWAYS WANTED
        TO KNOW ABOUT SEX *
        *But Were Afraid to Ask
Script: Allen, from the book by David Reuben.
Direction: Allen.
Photography (DeLuxe Color): David M. Walsh.
Editing: Eric Albertson.
Music: Mundell Lowe.
Production design: Dale Hennesy.

Cast: Allen (*Victor/Fabrizio/The Fool/Sperm*), John Carradine (*Dr. Bernardo*), Lou Jacobi (*Sam*), Louise Lasser (*Gina*), Anthony Quayle (*King*), Tony Randall (*operator*), Lynn Redgrave (*Queen*), Burt Reynolds (*switchboard*), Gene Wilder (*Dr. Ross*), Jack Barry (*himself*), Erin Fleming (*Girl*), Elaine Giftos (*Mrs. Ross*), Toni Holt (*herself*), Robert Q. Lewis (*himself*), Heather Macrae (*Helen*), Sidney Miller (*George*), Pamela Mason (*herself*), Regis Philbin (*himself*), Titos Vandis (*Milos*), Stanley Adams (*stomach operator*), Oscar Beregi (*Brain Control*), Alan Caillou (*fool's father*), Dort Clark (*Sheriff*), Geoffrey Holder (*sorcerer*), Jay

Robinson (*priest*), Ref Sanchez (*Igor*), Don Chuy (*football player*), Baruch Lumet (*Rabbi Baumel*), Tom Mack (*football player*), Robert Walden (*Sperm*), H. E. West (*Bernard Jaffe*).

Produced by Charles H. Joffe for United Artists (A Jack Robbins/Charles H. Joffe/Brodsky/Gould production). 87 min.

1973   SLEEPER

Script: Allen, Marshall Brickman.

Direction: Allen.

Photography (DeLuxe Color): David M. Walsh.

Editing: O. Nicholas Brown, Trudy Ship.

Music: Allen, with The New Orleans Funeral and Ragtime Orchestra and The Preservation Hall Jazz Band.

Production design: Dale Hennesy.

Art direction: Dianne Wager.

Cast: Allen (*Miles Monroe*), Diane Keaton (*Luna Schlosser*), John Beck (*Erno Windt*), Mary Gregory (*Dr. Melik*), Don Keefer (*Dr. Tryon*), Don McLiam (*Dr. Agon*), Bartlett Robinson (*Dr. Orva*), Chris Forbes (*Rainer Krebs*), Marya Small (*Dr. Nero*), Peter Hobbs (*Dr. Dean*), Susan Miller (*Ellen Pogrebin*), Lou Picetti (*MC*), Brian Avery (*Harold Cohen*), Spencer Milligan (*Jeb*), Spencer Ross (*Sears Swiggles*), Jessica Rains.

Produced by Jack Grossberg for Jack Rollins and Charles Joffe Productions. 88 min.

1975   LOVE AND DEATH

Script and direction: Allen.

Photography (DeLuxe Color): Ghislain Cloquet.

Editing: Ralph Rosenblum, Ron Kalish.

Music: S. Prokofiev.

Art direction: Willy Holt.

Cast: Allen (*Boris Grushenko*), Diane Keaton (*Sonja Volonska*), Georges Adel (*Old Nehamkin*), Frank Adu (*Drill Sergeant*), Edmond Ardisson (*Priest*), Feodor Atkine (*Mikail*), Albert Augier (*Walter*), Yves Barsacq (*Rimsky*), Lloyd Battista (*Don Francisco*), Jack Berard (*General Lecoq*), Eva Bertrand (*woman in hygiene class*), George Birt (*Doctor*), Yves Brainville (*Andre*), Gerard Buhr (*servant*), Brian Coburn (*Dmitri*), Henry Coutet (*Minskov*), Henry Czarniak (*Ivan*), Despo Diamantidou (*Mother*), Sandor Eles (*second soldier*), Luce Fabiolle (*grandmother*), Florian (*Uncle Nikolay*), Jacqueline Fogt (*Lyudmila*), Sol L. Frieder (*Voskovec*), Olga Georges-Picot (*Countess Alexandrovna*), Harold Gould (*Anton*), Harry Hankin (*Uncle Sasha*), Jessica Harper (*Natasha*), Tony Jay (*Vladimir Maximovich*), Tutte Lemkow (*Pierre*), Jack Lenoir (*Krapotkin*), Leib Lensky (*Father Andre*), Ann Lonnberg (*Olga*), Roger Lumont (*first baker*), Alfred Lutter III (*young Boris*), Ed Marcus (*Raskov*), Jacques Maury (*second*), Patricia Crown, Narcissa McKinley (*cheerleaders*), Aubrey Morris (*fourth soldier*), Denise Peron (*Spanish countess*), Beth Porter (*Anna*), Alan Rossett (*guard*), Shimen Ruskin (*Borslov*), Persival Russel (*Berdykov*), Chris Sanders (*Joseph*), Zvee Scoolar (*father*), C. A. R. Smith (*Father Nikolay*), Fred Smith (*soldier*), Bernard Taylor (*third soldier*), Clément-Thierry (*Jacques*), Alan Tilvern (*sergeant*), James Tolkan (*Napoleon*), Hélène Vallier (*Madame Wolfe*), Howard Vernon (*General Levêque*), Glenn

Williams (*first soldier*), Jacob Witkin (*Sushkin*).

Production by Charles H. Joffe for Jack Rollins and Charles H. Joffe Productions. 85 min.

1977   ANNIE HALL
Script: Allen, Marshall Brickman.
Direction: Allen.
Photography: Gordon Willis.
Sound mixer: James Sabat.
Editing: Ralph Rosenblum.
Art direction: Mel Bourne.
Costumes: Ruth Morley.
Songs: "Seems Like Old Times" (Carmen Lombardo, John Jacob Loeb), "It Had To Be You" (Isham Jones, Gus Kahn).

Cast: Allen (*Alvy Singer*), Diane Keaton (*Annie Hall*), Tony Roberts (*Rob*), Carol Kane (*Allison*), Paul Simon (*Tony Lacey*), Colleen Dewhurst (*Mom Hall*), Shelley Duvall (*Pam*), Janet Margolin (*Robin*), Christopher Walken (*Duane Hall*), Donald Symington (*Dad Hall*), Helen Ludlam (*Grammy Hall*), Marshall McLuhan (*himself*), Jonathan Munk (*Alvy, age 9*), Mordecai Lawner (*Alvy's dad*), Joan Newman (*Alvy's mom*).

Produced by Charles H. Joffe for Jack Rollins-Charles H. Joffe Productions/United Artists. Executive producer: Robert Greenhut. 94 min.

1978   INTERIORS
Script and Direction: Allen.
Photography: Gordon Willis.
Editing: Ralph Rosenblum.
Production design: Mel Bourne.
Costumes: Joel Schumacher.

Cast: Kristin Griffith (*Flyn*), Marybeth Hurt (*Joey*), Richard Jordan (*Frederick*), Diane Keaton (*Renata*), E. G. Marshall (*Arthur*), Geraldine Page (*Eve*), Maureen Stapleton (*Pearl*), Sam Waterston (*Mike*).

Produced by Charles H. Joffe for Jack Rollins-Charles H. Joffe Productions/United Artists. Executive producer: Robert Greenhut. 93 min.

1979   MANHATTAN

Allen has also written scripts for *What's New, Pussycat?* (1965), and *Play It Again, Sam* (1972, based on his play). As an actor, he has also appeared in *What's New, Pussycat?*, *Play It Again, Sam*, and *The Front* (1976). His play *Don't Drink the Water* was filmed in 1969 without his participation.

ROBERT ALTMAN

1957   THE DELINQUENTS
Script and direction: Altman.
Photography: Charles Paddock (or Harry Birch).
Editing: Helene Turner.

Music: Bill Nolan Quintet Minus Two.
Song: Bill Nolan, Ronnie Norman ("The Dirty Rock Boogie"), sung by Julia Lee.
Art direction: Chet Allen.

Cast: Tom Laughlin (*Scotty*), Peter Miller (*Cholly*), Richard Bakalyn (*Eddy*), Rosemary Howard (*Janice*), Helene Hawley (*Mrs. White*), Leonard Belove (*Mr. White*), Lotus Corelli (*Mrs. Wilson*), James Lantz (*Mr. Wilson*), Christine Altman (*Sissy*), George Kuhn (*Jay*), Pat Stedman (*Meg*), Norman Zands (*Chizzy*), James Leria (*Steve*), Jet Pinkston (*Molly*), Kermit Echols (*barman*), Joe Adleman (*station attendant*).

Produced by Altman (Imperial Productions) for United Artists. 72 min.

1957　THE JAMES DEAN STORY
Script: Stewart Stern.
Direction: Altman, George W. George.
Photography: twenty-nine various cameramen (stills: Camera Eye Pictures).
Music: Leith Stevens.
Song: Jay Livingston, Ray Evans.
Production design: Louis Clyde Stoumen.
Narrator: Martin Gabel.

Cast: Marcus, Ortense and Markie Winslow (*Dean's aunt, Uncle and cousin*), Mr. and Mrs. Dean (*his grandparents*), Adeline Hall (*his drama teacher*), Big Traster, Mr. Carter, Jerry Luce, Louis de Liso, Arnie Langer, Arline Sax, Chris White, George Ross, Robert Jewett, John Kalin, Lew Bracker, Glenn Kramer, Patsy d'Amore, Billy Karen, Lille Kardell (*his friends*), Officer Nelson (*highway patrolman*).

Produced by Altman and George W. George for Warner Bros. 83 min.

1968　COUNTDOWN
Script: Loring Mandel, from the novel by Hank Searls.
Direction: Altman.
Photography (Technicolor, Panavision): William W. Spencer.
Editing: Gene Milford.
Music: Leonard Rosenman.
Art direction: Jack Poplin.
Set decoration: Ralph S. Hurst.

Cast: James Caan (*Lee*), Robert Duvall (*Chiz*), Joanna Moore (*Mickey*), Barbara Baxley (*Jean*), Charles Aidman (*Gus*), Steve Ihnat (*Ross*), Michael Murphy (*Rick*), Ted Knight (*Larson*), Stephen Coit (*Ehrman*), John Rayner (*Dunc*), Charles Irving (*Seidel*), Bobby Riha Jr. (*Stevie*).

Produced by William Conrad (Productions) for Warner Bros. 101 min.

1969　NIGHTMARE IN CHICAGO
Script: Donald Moessinger, from the novel *Killer on the Turnpike* by William P. McGivern.
Direction: Altman.
Photography (color): Bud Thackery.
Music: Johnny Williams.

Cast: Charles McGraw, Robert Ridgely, Ted Knight, Philip Abbott, Barbara Turner, Charlene Lee, Arlene Kieta.

Produced by Altman for Roncom/Universal. 81 min. [This was a release version of the TV movie *Once Upon a Savage Night*, expanded with out-takes from an original 54 min. to 81 min. The shorter version was first televised on 2 April 1964.]

1969   THAT COLD DAY IN THE PARK

Script: Gillian Freeman, from the novel by Richard Miles.
Direction: Altman.
Photography (Eastmancolor): Laszlo Kovacs.
Editing: Danford Greene.
Music: Johnny Mandel.
Art Direction: Leon Erickson.
   Cast: Sandy Dennis (*Frances Austen*), Michael Burns (*The Boy*), Susanne Benton (*Nina*), Luana Anders (*Sylvie*), John Garfield Jr. (*Nick*).
   Produced by Donald Factor and Leon Mirell for Factor-Altman-Mirell Films. 115 min.

1970   M*A*S*H

Script: Ring Lardner Jr., from the novel by Richard Hooker.
Direction: Altman.
Photography (DeLuxe Color, Panavision): Harold E. Stine.
Editing: Danford B. Greene.
Music: Johnny Mandel.
Song: Johnny Mandel and Mike Altman ("Suicide Is Painless").
Art Direction: Jack Martin Smith, Arthur Lonergan.
Set Decoration: Walter M. Scott, Stuart A. Reiss.
   Cast: Donald Sutherland (*Hawkeye Pierce*), Elliott Gould (*Trapper John McIntyre*), Tom Skerritt (*Duke Forrest*), Sally Kellerman (*Major Hot Lips*), Robert Duvall (*Major Frank Burns*), Jo Ann Pflug (*Lt. Dish*), Rene Auberjonois (*Dago Red*), Roger Bowen (*Col. Henry Blake*), Gary Burghoff (*Radar O'Reilly*), David Arkin (*Sgt. Major Vollmer*), Fred-Williamson (*Spearchucker*), Michael Murphy (*Me Lay*), Kim Atwood (*Ho-Jon*), Tim Brown (*Corporal Judson*), Indus Arthur (*Lt. Leslie*), John Schuck (*Painless Pole*), Ken Prymus (*Pfc. Seidman*), Dawne Damon (*Capt. Scorch*), Carl Gottlieb (*Ugly John*), Tamara Horrocks (*Capt. Knocko*), G. Wood (*General Hammond*), Bobby Troup (*Sgt. Gorman*), Bud Cort (*Private Boone*), Danny Goldman (*Capt. Murrhardt*), Corey Fischer (*Capt. Bandini*), J.B. Douglas, Yoko Young.
   Produced by Ingo Preminger for Aspen/Twentieth Century-Fox, 116 min.

1970   BREWSTER McCLOUD

Script: Brian McKay (uncredited), Doran William Cannon.
Direction: Altman.
Photography (Metrocolor, Panavision): Lamar Boren, Jordan Cronenweth.
Editing: Lou Lombardo.
Music: Gene Page.
Songs: Francis Scott Key, Rosamund Johnson and James Weldon Johnson, John Phillips, Sung by Merry Clayton, John Phillips.
Art Direction: Preston Ames, George W. Davis.
   Cast: Bud Cort (*Brewster McCloud*), Sally Kellerman (*Louise*), Michael

Murphy (*Frank Shaft*), William Windom (*Haskel Weeks*), Shelley Duvall (*Suzanne Davis*), Rene Auberjonois (*lecturer*), Stacy Keach (*Abraham Wright*), John Schuck (*Lt. Alvin Johnson*), Margaret Hamilton (*Daphne Heap*), Jennifer Salt (*Hope*), Corey Fischer (*Lt. Hines*), G. Wood (*Capt. Crandall*), Bert Remsen (*Douglas Breen*), Angelin Johnson (*Mrs. Breen*), William Baldwin (*Bernard*), William Henry Bennet (*band conductor*), Gary Wayne Chason (*camera shop clerk*), Ellis Gilbert (*butler*), Verdie Henshaw (*Feathered Nest Sanatorium manager*), Robert Warner (*camera shop assistant manager*), Dean Goss (*Eugene Ledbetter*), Keith V. Erickson (*Prof. Aggnout*), Thomas Danko (*color lab man*), W.E. Terry Jr. (*police chaplain*), Ronnie Cammack (*Wendell*), Dixie M. Taylor (*nursing home manager*), Pearl Coffey Chason (*nursing home attendant*), Amelia Parker (*nursing home manageress*), David Welch (*Breen's son*).
Produced by Lou Adler (Adler-Phillips/Lion's Gate) for M-G-M. 105 min.

1971   McCABE AND MRS. MILLER
Script: Altman, Brian McKay, from the novel *McCabe* by Edmund Naughton.
Direction: Altman.
Photography (Technicolor, Panavision): Vilmos Zsigmond.
Editing: Lou Lombardo.
Music: Leonard Cohen.
Production design: Leon Ericksen.
Art Direction: Phillip Thomas.
   Cast: Warren Beatty (*John McCabe*), Julie Christie (*Constance Miller*), Rene Auberjonois (*Sheehan*), Hugh Millais (*Dog Butler*), Shelley Duvall (*Ida Coyle*), Michael Murphy (*Sears*), John Schuck (*Smalley*), Corey Fischer (*Mr. Elliott*).
Produced by David Foster, Mitchell Brower for Warner Bros. 121 min.

1972   IMAGES
Script and direction: Altman (with passages from "*In Search of Unicorns*" by Susannah York).
Photography (Technicolor, Panavision): Vilmos Zsigmond.
Editing: Graeme Clifford.
Music: Johh Williams (with sounds by Stomu Yamash'ta).
Art direction: Leon Ericksen.
   Cast: Susannah York (*Cathryn*), Rene Auberjonois (*Hugh*), Marcel Bozzuffi (*René*), Hugh Millais (*Marcel*), Cathryn Harrison (*Susannah*), John Morley (*Old Man*).
Produced by Tommy Thompson for Lion's Gate Film/The Hemdale Group. 101 min.

1973   THE LONG GOODBYE
Script: Leigh Brackett, from the novel by Raymond Chandler.
Direction: Altman.
Photography (Technicolor, Panavision): Vilmos Zsigmond.
Editing: Lou Lombardo.
Music: John Williams.
   Cast: Elliott Gould (*Philip Marlowe*), Nina van Pallandt (*Eileen Wade*), Sterling Hayden (*Roger Wade*), Mark Rydell (*Marty Augustine*), Henry Gibson (*Dr. Verringer*), David Arkin (*Harry*), Jim Bouton (*Terry Lennox*), Warren

461

Berlinger (*Morgan*), Jo Ann Brody (*Jo Ann Eggenweiler*), Steve Coit (*Detective Farmer*), Jack Knight (*Mabel*), Pepe Callahan (*Pepe*), Vince Palmieri (*Vince*), Pancho Cordoba (*doctor*), Enrique Lucero (*Jefe*), Rutanya Alda (*Rutanya Sweet*), Tammy Shaw (*dancer*), Jack Riley (*piano player*), Ken Sansom (*colony guard*), Jerry Jones (*Dectective Green*), John Davies (*Detective Dayton*), Rodney Moss (*supermarket clerk*), Sybil Scotford (*real estate lady*), Herb Kerns (*Herbie*).

Produced by Jerry Bick (Lion's Gate Films) for United Artists. 111 min.

1974 THIEVES LIKE US

Script: Calder Willingham, Joan Tewkesbury, Altman, from the novel by Edward Anderson.
Direction: Altman.
Photography (color): Jean Boffety.
Editing: Lou Lombardo.
Visual consultant: Jack DeGovia.
Radio research: John Dunning.

Cast: Keith Carradine (*Bowie*), Shelley Duvall (*Keechie*), John Schuck (*Chicamaw*), Bert Remsen (*T-Dub*), Louise Fletcher (*Mattie*), Ann Latham (*Lula*), Tom Skerritt (*Doc Mobley*), Al Scott (*Capt. Stammers*), John Roper (*Jasbo*), Mary Waits (*Noel*), Rodney Lee Jr. (*James Mattingly*), William Watters (*Alvin*), Joan Tewkesbury (*lady in train station*), Eleanor Matthews (*Mrs. Stammers*), Pam Warner (*woman in accident*), Suzanne Majure (*Coca-Cola girl*), Walter Cooper and Lloyd Jones (*sheriffs*).

Produced by Jerry Bick and George Litto for United Artists. 123 min.

1974 CALIFORNIA SPLIT

Script: Joseph Walsh.
Direction: Altman.
Photography (Metrocolor, Panavision): Paul Lohmann.
Editing: Lou Lombardo.
Production design: Leon Ericksen.

Cast: Elliott Gould (*Charlie Waters*), George Segal (*Bill Denny*), Ann Prentiss (*Barbara Miller*), Gwen Welles (*Susan Peters*), Edward Walsh (*Lew*), Joseph Walsh (*Sparkie*), Bert Remsen ("*Helen Brown*"), Barbara London (*lady on the bus*), Barbara Ruick (*Reno barmaid*), Jay Fletcher (*robber*), Jeff Goldblum (*Lloyd Harris*), Barbara Colby (*receptionist*), Vince Palmieri (*first bartender*), Alyce Passman (*go-go girl*), Joanne Strauss (*mother*), Jack Riley (*second bartender*), Sierra Bandit (*woman at bar*), John Considine (*man at bar*), Eugene Troobnick (*Harvey*), Richard Kennedy (*used-car salesman*), John Winston (*tenor*), Bill Duffy (*Kenny*), Mike Greene (*Reno dealer*), Tom Signorelli (*Nugie*), Sharon Compton (*Nugie's wife*), Arnold Herzstein, Marc Cavell, Alvin Weissman, Mickey Fox and Carolyn Lohmann (*Californie Club poker players*), "Amarillo Slim" Preston, Winston Lee, Harry Drackett, Thomas Hal Phillips, Ted Say, A.J. Hood (*Reno poker players*).

Produced by Altman and Joseph Walsh (Won World/Persky Bright/Reno) for Columbia. Executive producers: Aaron Spelling, Leonard Goldberg. 109 min.

1975 NASHVILLE

Script: Joan Tewkesbury.

Direction: Altman.
Photography (Color, Panavision): Paul Lohmann.
Editing: Sidney Levin, Dennis Hill.
Political Campaign: Thomas Hal Phillips.
Songs: "200 Years" (lyrics by Henry Gibson, music by Richard Baskin), "Yes, I Do" (lyrics and music by Richard Baskin and Lily Tomlin), "Down to the River" (lyrics and music by Ronee Blakley), "Let Me Be the One" (lyrics and music by Richard Baskin, "Sing a Song" (lyrics and music by Joe Raposo), "The Heart of a Gentle Woman" (lyrics and music by Dave Peel), "Bluebird" (lyrics and music by Ronee Blakley), "The Day I Looked Jesus in the Eye" (lyrics and music by Richard Baskin and Robert Altman), "Memphis" (lyrics and music by Karen Black), "I Don't Know If I found It in You"(lyrics and music by Karen Black), "For the Sake of the Children" (lyrics and music by Richard Baskin and Richard Reicheg), "Keep a Goin'" (lyrics by Henry Gibson, music by Richard Baskin and Henry Gibson), "Swing Low Sweet Chariot" (arrangements by Millie Clements), "Rolling Stone" (lyrics and music by Karen Black), "Honey" (lyrics and music by Keith Carradine), "Tapedeck in his Tractor (The Cowboy Song)" (lyrics and music by Ronee Blakley), "Dues" (lyrics and music by Ronee Blakley), "I Never Get Enough" (lyrics and music by Richard Baskin and Ben Raleigh), "Rose's Cafe" (lyrics and music by Allan Nicholls), "Old Man Mississippi" (lyrics and music by Juan Grizzle), "My Baby's Cookin' in Another Man's Pan" (lyrics and music by Jonnie Barnett), "One, I Love You" (lyrics and music by Richard Baskin), "I'm Easy" (lyrics and music by Keith Carradine), "It Don't Worry Me" (lyrics and music by Keith Carradine). "Since You've Gone" (lyrics and music by Garry Busey), "Trouble in the U.S.A." (lyrics and music by Arlene Barnett), "My Idaho Home" (lyrics and music by Ronee Blakley).

Cast: David Arkin (Norman), Barbara Baxley (Lady Pearl), Ned Beatty (Delbert Reese), Karen Black (Connie White), Ronee Blakley (Barbara Jean), Timothy Brown (Tommy Brown), Keith Carradine (Tom Frank), Geraldine Chaplin (Opal), Robert Doqui (Wade), Shelley Duvall (L.A. Joan), Allen Garfield (Barnett), Henry Gibson (Haven Hamilton), Scott Glenn (Pfc. Glenn Kelly), Jeff Goldblum (Tricycle Man), Barbara Harris (Albuquerque), David Hayward (Kenny Fraiser), Michael Murphy (John Triplette), Allan Nicholls (Bill), Dave Peel (Bud Hamilton), Cristina Raines (Mary), Bert Remsen (Star), Lily Tomlin (Linnea Reese), Gwen Welles (Sueleen Gay), Keenan Wynn (Mr. Green), James Dan Calvert (Jimmy Reese), Donna Denton (Donna Reese), Merle Kilgore (Trout), Carol McGinnis (Jewel), Sheila Bailey and Patti Bryant (Smokey Mountain Laurel), Richard Baskin (Frog), Jonnie Barnett, Vassar Clements, Misty Mountain Boys, Sue Barton, Elliott Gould and Julie Christie (themselves).

Produced by Altman (ABC Entertainment) for Paramount. Associate producers: Robert Eggenweiler, Scott Bushnell. Executive producers: Martin Starger, Jerry Weintraub. 161 min.

1976   BUFFALO BILL AND THE INDIANS, OR
        SITTING BULL'S HISTORY LESSON
Story and script: Alan Rudolph, Altman, based on the play Indians by Arthur Kopit.
Direction: Altman.
Photography: Paul Lohmann.

Music: Richard Baskin.
Production design: Tony Masters.
Editing: Peter Appleton, Dennis Hill.
Sound: Jim Webb, Chris McLaughlin (Lion's Gate 8-track).
Re-recording mixer: Richard Portman.
Sound editor: Richard Oswald.
Costumes: Anthony Powell.

Cast: Paul Newman (*the Star*), Joel Grey (*the Producer*), Kevin McCarthy (*the Publicist*), Harvey Keitel (*the Relative*), Allan Nicholls (*the Journalist*), Geraldine Chaplin (*the Sure Shot*), John Considine (*the Sure Shot's Manager*), Robert Doqui (*the Wrangler*), Mike Kaplan (*the Treasurer*), Bert Remsen (*the Bartender*), Bonnie Leaders (*the Mezzo-Contralto*), Noelle Rogers (*the Lyric Coloratura*), Evelyn Lear (*the Lyric Soprano*), Denver Pyle (*the Indian Agent*), Frank Kaquitts (*the Indian*), Will Sampson (*the Interpreter*), Ken Krossa (*the Arenic Director*), Fred N. Larsen (*the King of the Cowboys*), Jerry and Joy Duce (*the Cowboy Trick Riders*), Alex Green and Gary MacKenzie (*the Mexican Whip and Fast Draw Act*), Humphrey Gratz (*the Old Soldier*), Pat McCormick (*the President of the United States*), Shelley Duvall (*the First Lady*), Burt Lancaster (*the Legend Maker*). With people from the Stoney Indian Reserve.

Produced by Robert Altman for Dino De Laurentiis Corporation/Lion's Gate Films, Inc./Talent Associates Norton Simon, Inc. United Artists. Executive Producer: David Susskind. Filmed entirely on the Stoney Indian Reserve, Alberta, Canada. 118 min.

1977   THREE WOMEN
Script: Altman.
Direction: Altman.
Photography: Chuck Rosher.
Editing: Dennis Hill.
Sound: Jim Webb, Chris McLaughlin (Lion's Gate 8-track).
Sound editing: David M. Horton, Bill Phillips.
Art direction: James D. Vance.
Visual consultant: J. Allen Highfill.
Music: Gerald Busby.
Murals: Bodhi Wind.
Re-recording mixer: Richard Portman.

Cast: Shelley Duvall (*Millie Lammoreaux*), Sissy Spacek (*Pinky Rose*), Janice Rule (*Willie Hart*), Robert Fortier (*Edgar Hart*), Ruth Nelson (*Mrs. Rose*), John Cromwell (*Mr. Rose*), Sierra Pecheur (*Ms. Bunweill*), Craig Richard Nelson (*Dr. Maas*), Maysie Hoy (*Doris*), Belita Moreno (*Alcira*), Leslie Ann Hudson (*Polly*), Patricia Ann Hudson (*Peggy*), Beverly Ross (*Deidre*), John Davey (*Dr. Norton*).

Produced by Robert Altman for Lion's Gate Films, Inc. Twentieth Century-Fox. 124 min.

1978   A WEDDING
Script: John Considine, Patricia Resnick, Allan Nichols, Altman, from a story by
    Considine and Altman.
Direction: Altman.
Photography (Panavision): Charles Rosher.

Editing: Tony Lombardo.
Sound: Jim Webb, Chris McLaughlin, Jim Bourgeois, Jim Stuebe (Dolby).
Re-recording: Richard Portman.
Assistant director: Tommy Thompson.
Sound editing: Sam Gemette, Hal Sanders.
Painting of "Bride for the People": Sally Benton.
Music: John Hotchkis, sung and played by the Choir of St. Luke's Episcopal
    Church, Evanston, Illinois, the Chicago Brass Ensemble, Ruth Pelz (organ).
Song: "Bird on a Wire" by Leonard Cohen.
Bridal consultant: Carson, Pirie, Scott & Co., Chicago.

Cast: The Groom's Family: Lillian Gish (*Nettie Sloan*), Ruth Nelson (*Beatrice Sloan Cory*), Ann Ryerson (*Victoria Cory*), Desi Arnaz, Jr. (*Dino Corelli, the groom*), Belita Moreno (*Daphne Corelli*), Vittorio Gassman (*Luigi Corelli*), Nina Van Pallandt (*Regina Corelli*), Virginia Vestoff (*Clarice Sloan*), Dina Merrill (*Antoinette Sloan Goddard*), Pat McCormick (*Mackenzie Goddard*), Luigi Proietti (*Little Dino*).

The Bride's Family: Carol Burnett (*Tulip Brenner*), Paul Dooley (*Snooks Brenner*), Amy Stryker (*Muffin Brenner, the bride*), Mia Farrow (*Buffy Brenner*), Dennis Christopher (*Hughie Brenner*), Mary Seibel (*Aunt Marge Spar*), Margaret Ladd (*Ruby Spar*), Gerald Busby (*David Ruteledge*), Peggy Ann Garner (*Candice Ruteledge*), Mark R. Deming (*Matthew Ruteledge*), David Brand, Chris Brand, Amy Brand, Jenny Brand, Jeffrey Jones, Jay D. Jones, Courtney MacArthur, Paul D. Keller III (*the Ruteledge children*).

The Corelli House Staff: Cedric Scott (*Randolph*), Robert Fortier (*Jim Habor, gardener*), Maureen Steindler (*Libby Clinton, cook*).

The Wedding Staff: Geraldine Chaplin (*Rita Billingsley*), Mona Abboud (*Melba Lear*), Viveca Lindfors (*Ingrid Hellstrom*), Lauren Hutton (*Flo Farmer*), Allan Nicholls (*Jake Jacobs*), Maysie Hoy (*Casey*), John Considine (*Jeff Kuykendall*), Patricia Resnick (*Redford*), Margery Bond (*Lombardo*), Dennis Franz (*Koons*), Harold C. Johnson (*Oscar Edwards*), Alexander Sopenar (*Victor*).

The Friends and Guest: Howard Duff (*Dr. Jules Meecham*), John Cromwell (*Bishop Martin*), Bert Remsen (*William Williamson*), Pamela Dawber (*Tracy Farrell*), Gavan O'Hirlihy (*Wilson Briggs*), Craig Richard Nelson (*Capt. Reedley Roots*), Jeffry S. Perry (*Bunky Lemay*), Marta Heflin (*Shelby Munker*), Lesley Rogers (*Rosie Bean*), Timothy Thomerson (*Russell Bean*), Beverly Ross (*Nurse Janet Schulman*), David Fitzgerald (*Kevin Clinton*), Susan Kendall Newman (*Chris Clinton*).

The Musicians: Ellie Albers (*Gypsy Violinist*), Tony Llorens (*at the piano-bar*), Chuck Banks' Big Band with Chris La Kome (*in the ballroom*).

Produced by Robert Altman for Lion's Gate Films, Inc. Twentieth Century-Fox. Executive producer: Tommy Thompson. Filmed on location in the suburbs of Chicago. 124 min.

1978   QUINTET

Altman wrote the story for *Bodyguard* (1948) with George W. George. He Has produced Alan Rudolph's *Welcome to L.A.* (1977), Robert Benton's *The Late Show* (1977), Rudolph's *Remember My Name* (1978), and Robert Young's *Rich Kids* (1979).

JOHN CASSAVETES

1960   SHADOWS
Script and direction: Cassavetes.
Photography (16mm): Erich Kollmar.
Editing: Len Appelson, Maurice McEndree.
Music: Charles Mingus (saxophone: Shafi Hadi).
   Cast: Lelia Goldoni (*Lelia*), Ben Carruthers (*Ben*), Hugh Hurd (*Hugh*), Anthony Ray (*Tony*), Rupert Crosse (*Rupe*), Tom Allen (*Tom*), Dennis Sallas (*Dennis*), David Pokitellow (*David*).
   Produced by Maurice McEndree-Cassel. 81 min.

1961   TOO LATE BLUES
Script: Cassavetes, Richard Carr.
Direction: Cassavetes.
Photography: Lionel Lindon.
Editing: Frank Bracht.
Music: David Raksin.
Art direction: Tambi Larsen.
   Cast: Bobby Darin (*John "Ghost" Wakefield*), Stella Stevens (*Jess Polanski*), Everett Chambers (*Benny Flowers*), Nick Dennis (*Nick*), Rupert Crosse (*Baby Jackson*), Vince Edwards (*Tommy*), Val Avery (*Frielobe*), J. Allen Hopkins (*Skipper*), James Joyce (*Reno, the barman*), Marilyn Clark (*Countess*), Allyson Ames (*Billie Gray*), June Wilkinson (*girl at bar*), Cliff Carnell (*Charlie, the saxophonist*), Seymour Cassel (*Red, the bassist*), Dan Stafford (*Shelley the drummer*), Richard Chambers (*Pete, the trumpet player*).
   Produced by Cassavetes for Paramount. 103 min.

1962   A CHILD IS WAITING
Script: Abby Mann, from his own story.
Direction: Cassavetes.
Photography: Joseph LaShelle.
Editing: Gene Fowler Jr.
Music: Ernest Gold.
Production design: Rudolph Sternad.
   Cast: Burt Lancaster (*Dr. Matthew Clark*), Judy Garland (*Jean Hansen*), Gena Rowlands (*Sophie Widdicombe*), Steven Hill (*Ted Widdicombe*), Bruce Ritchey (*Reuben Widdicombe*), Gloria McGehee (*Mattie*), Paul Stewart (*Goodman*), Lawrence Tierney (*Douglas Benham*), Elizabeth Wilson (*Miss Fogarty*), Barbara Pepper (*Miss Brown*), John Marley (*Holland*), June Walker (*Mrs. McDonald*), Mario Gallo (*Dr. Lombardi*), Frederick Draper (*Dr. Sack*).
   Produced by Stanley Kramer (Larcas Productions) for United Artists. 104 min.

1968   FACES
Script and direction: Cassavetes.
Photography: Al Ruban.
Editing: Al Ruban, Maurice McEndree.
Music: Jack Ackerman.
Song: Charles Smalls ("Never Felt Like This Before").

Art direction: Phedon Papamichael.

Cast: John Marley (*Richard Forst*), Gena Rowlands (*Jeannie Rapp*), Lynn Carlin (*Maria Forst*), Fred Draper (*Freddie*), Seymour Cassel (*Chet*), Val Avery (*McCarthy*), Dorothy Gulliver (*Florence*), Joanne Moore Jordan (*Louise*), Darlene Conley (*Billy Mae*), Gene Darfler (*Jackson*), Elizabeth Deering (*Stella*), Dave Mazzie, Julie Gambol.

Produced by Maurice McEndree. 130 min.

1970 HUSBANDS

Script and direction: Cassavetes.
Photography (DeLuxe color): Victor Kemper.
Sup. editing: Peter Tanner.
Art direction: Rene D'Auriac.

Cast: Ben Gazzara (*Harry*), Peter Falk (*Archie*), John Cassavetes (*Gus*), Jenny Runacre (*Mary Tynan*), Jenny Lee Wright (*Pearl Billingham*), Noelle Kao (*Julie*), Leola Harlow (*Leola*), Meta Shaw (*Annie*), John Kullers (*Red*), Delores Delmar (*Countess*), Peggy Lashbrook (*Diana Mallabee*), Eleanor Zee (*Mrs. Hines*), Claire Malis (*Stuart's wife*), Lorraine McMartin (*Annie's mother*), Edgar Franken (*Ed Weintraub*), Sarah Felcher (*Sarah*), Antoinette Kray ("*Jesus Loves Me*"), Gwen Van Dam (*Jeannie*), John Armstrong ("*Happy Birthday*"), Eleanor Gould ("*Normandy*"), Carinthia West (*Susanna*), Rhonda Parker (*Margaret*), Joseph Boley (*minister*), Judith Lowrey (*Stuart's grandmother*), Joseph Hardy ("*Shanghai Lil*"), K.C. Townsend (*barmaid*), Anne O'Donnell (*nurse*), Gena Wheeler (*nurse*), David Rowlands (*Stuart Jackson*).

Produced by Al Ruban for Columbia. 154 min.

1971 MINNIE AND MOSKOWITZ

Script and direction: Cassavetes.
Photography (Technicolor): Arthur J. Ornitz, Alric Edens, Michael Margulies.
Editing: Fred Knudtson.
Music: Bo Harwood.

Cast: Gena Rowlands (*Minnie Moore*), Seymour Cassel (*Seymour Moskowitz*), Val Avery (*Zelmo Swift*), Tim Carey (*Morgan Morgan*), Katherine Cassavetes (*Sheba Moskowitz*), Elizabeth Deering (*girl*), Elsie Ames (*Florence*), Lady Rowlands (*Georgia Moore*), Holly Near (*Irish*), Judith Roberts (*wife*), John Cassavetes (*husband*), Jack Danskin (*Dick Henderson*), Eleanor Zee (*Mrs. Grass*), Sean Joyce (*Ned*), David Rowlands (*Minister*).

Produced by Al Ruban for Universal. 115 min.

1974 A WOMAN UNDER THE INFLUENCE

Script and direction: Cassavetes.
Photography: Mitch Breit, Chris Taylor, Bo Taylor, Merv Dayan, Caleb Deschanel.
Editing: Tom Cornwell, Elizabeth Bergeron, David Armstrong, Sheila Viseltear.
Music: Bo Harwood.
Art direction: Phedon Papamichael.

Cast: Peter Falk (*Nick Longhetti*), Gena Rowlands (*Mabel Longhetti*), Matthew Cassel (*Tony Longhetti*), Matthew Laborteaux (*Angelo Longhetti*), Christina Grisanti (*Maria Longhetti*), Katherine Cassavetes (*Mama Longhetti*), Lady

Rowlands (*Martha Mortensen*), Fred Draper (*George Mortensen*), O.G. Dunn (*Garson Cross*), Mario Gallo (*Harold Jensen*), Eddie Shaw (*Doctor Zepp*), Angelo Grisanti (*Vito Grimaldi*), James Joyce (*Bowman*), John Finnegan (*Clancy*), Hugh Hurd (*Willie Johnson*), Leon Wagner (*Billy Tidrow*), John Hawker (*Joseph Morton*), Sil Words (*James Turner*), Elizabeth Deering (*Angela*), Jacki Peters (*Tina*), Elsie Ames (*Principal*).

Produced by Faces International Films (Sam Shaw). 155 min.

1976   THE KILLING OF A CHINESE BOOKIE
Script and direction: Cassavetes.
Photography: Fred Elmes, Mike Ferris.
Editing: Tom Cornwell.
Music: Bo Harwood.
Production design: Sam Shaw.

Cast: Ben Gazzara (*Cosmo Vitelli*), Timothy Agoglia Carey (*Flo*), Azizi Johari (*Rachel*), Meade Roberts (*Mr. Sophistication*), Seymour Cassel (*Mort Weil*), Alice Friedland (*Sherry*), Donna Gordon (*Margo*), Robert Phillips (*Phil*), Morgan Woodward (*John the Boss*), Virginia Carrington (*Betty*), John Red Kullers (*Eddie Red*), Al Ruban (*Marty Reitz*), Soto Joe Hugh (*Chinese bookie*), Haji (*Haji*), Carol Warren (*Carol*), Derna Wong Davis (*Derna*), Kathalina Veniero (*Annie*), Yvette Morris (*Yvette*), Jack Ackerman (*musical director*).

Produced by Al Ruban for Faces Distribution Corp. 135 min.

1977   OPENING NIGHT
Script and direction: Cassavetes.
Photography: Al Ruban.
Sound: Bo Harwood.
Editing: Tom Cornwell.
Mixing: Bill Varney.
Art direction: Brian Ryman.
Costumes: Alexandra Corwin-Hankin.
Music: Bo Harwood. Arranged and conducted by Booker T. Jones.

Cast: Gena Rowlands (*Myrtle Gordon*), John Cassavetes (*Maurice Aarons*), Ben Gazzara (*Manny Victor*), Joan Blondell (*Sarah Goode*), Paul Stewart (*David Samuels*), Zohra Lampert (*Dorothy Victor*), Katherine Cassavetes (*Vivian*), Lady Rowlands (*Melva Drake*), Laura Johnson (*Nancy Stein*), John Tuell (*Gus Simmons*).

Produced by Al Ruban for Faces Distribution. Executive producer: Sam Shaw. Associate producer: Michael Lally. 144 min.

Cassavetes has also acted in the following films: *Taxi* (1953), *The Night Holds Terror* (1955), *Crime in the Streets* (1956), *Edge of the City/A Man Is Ten Feet Tall* (1957), *Affair in Havana* (1957), *Saddle the Wind* (1958), *Virgin Island* (1958), *The Webster Boy* (1962), *The Killers* (1964, made for TV), *The Devil's Angels* (1967), *The Dirty Dozen* (1967), *Rosemary's Baby* (1968), *Gli intoccabili/Machine Gun McCain* (1968) *Roma come Chicago/Bandits in Rome* (1968), *If It's Tuesday, This Must be Belgium* (1969), *Capone* (1975), *Two-Minute Warning* (1976), and *The Fury* (1978).

468

FRANCIS COPPOLA

1961   TONIGHT FOR SURE
Script: Jerry Shaffer, Coppola.
Direction: Coppola.
Photography: Jack Hill.
Editing: Ronald Waller.
Music: Carmine Coppola.
Art direction: Al Locatelli.
Produced by Coppola. c. 75 min.

1963   DEMENTIA 13
Script and direction: Coppola.
Photograhphy: Charles Hannawalt.
Editing: Stewart O'Brien.
Music: Ronald Stein.
Art direction: Albert Locatelli.
    Cast: William Campbell (*Richard Haloran*), Luana Anders (*Louise Haloran*),
Bart Patton (*Billy Haloran*), Mary Mitchell (*Kane*), Patrick Magee (*Justin Caleb*),
Eithne Dunn (*Lady Haloran*), Peter Reed (*John Haloran*), Karl Schanzer (*Simon*),
Ron Perry (*Arthur*), Derry O'Donovan (*Lillian*), Barbara Dowling (*Kathleen*).
    Produced by Phil Feldman (Seven Arts) for Warner-Pathé. 97 min.

1967   YOU'RE A BIG BOY NOW
Script: Coppola, from the novel by David Benedictus.
Direction: Coppola.
Photography (Eastmancolor): Andy Laszlo.
Editing: Aram Avakian.
Music: Bob Prince.
Songs: John Sebastian (sung by The Lovin' Spoonful).
Art direction: Vassele Fotopoulos.
Choreography: Robert Tucker.
    Cast: Peter Kastner (*Bernard Chanticleer*), Elizabeth Hartman (*Barbara
Darling*), Geraldine Page (*Margery Chanticleer*), Julie Harris (*Miss Thing*), Rip
Torn (*I.H. Chanticleer*), Tony Bill (*Raef*), Karen Black (*Amy*), Michael Dunn
(*Richard Mudd*), Dolph Sweet (*Policeman Francis Graf*), Michael O'Sullivan
(*Kurt Doughty*).
    Produced by Phil Feldman (Seven Arts) for Warner-Pathé. 97 min.

1968   FINIAN'S RAINBOW
Script: E.Y. Harburg, Fred Saidy, based on their musical play (music: Burton
    Lane; lyrics: E.Y. Harburg).
Direction: Coppola.
Photography (Technicolor, Panavision, presented in 70 mm): Philip Lathrop.
Editing: Melvin Shapiro.
Music direction: Ray Heindorf.
Production design: Hilyard M. Brown.
Choreography: Hermes Pan.
    Cast: Fred Astaire (*Finian McLonergan*), Petula Clark (*Sharon McLonergan*),

469

Tommy Steele (*Og*), Don Francks (*Woody*), Barbara Hancock (*Susan the Silent*), Keenan Wynn (*Judge Billboard Rawkins*), Al Freeman Jr. (*Howard*), Brenda Arnau (*Sharecropper*), Avon Long, Roy Glenn, Jerster Hairston (*Passion Pilgrim Gospellers*), Louis Silas (*Henry*), Dolph Sweet (*Sheriff*), Wright King (*district attorney*).

Produced by Joseph Landon (Warner Bros./Seven Arts). for Warner-Pathé. 144 min.

1969   THE RAIN PEOPLE
Script and direction: Coppola.
Photography (Technicolor): Wilmer Butler.
Editing: Blackie Malkin.
Music: Ronald Stein.
Art direction: Leon Ericksen.

Cast: James Caan (*Kilgannon*), Shirley Knight (*Natalie*), Robert Duvall (*Gordon*), Marya Zimmet (*Rosalie*), Tom Aldredge (*Mr. Alfred*), Laurie Crews (*Ellen*), Andrew Duncan (*Artie*), Margaret Fairchild (*Marion*), Sally Gracie (*Beth*), Alan Manson (*Lou*), Robert Modica (*Vinny*).

Produced by Bart Patton and Ronald Colby (Coppola Company Presentation) for Warner Bros./Seven Arts. 101 min.

1972   THE GODFATHER
Script: Mario Puzo, Coppola, Based on the novel by Puzo.
Direction: Coppola.
Photography (Technicolor): Gordon Willis.
Editing: William Reynolds, Peter Zinner, Marc Laub, Murray Solomon.
Music: Nino Rota (conducted by Carlo Savina).
Production design: Dean Tavoularis.
Art direction: Warren Clymer.

Cast: Marlon Brando (*Don Vito Corleone*), Al Pacino (*Michael Corleone*), James Caan (*Sonny Corleone*), Richard Castellano (*Clemenza*), Robert Duvall (*Tom Hagan*), Sterling Hayden (*McClusky*), John Marley (*Jack Woltz*), Richard Conte (*Barzini*), Diane Keaton (*Kay Adams*), Al Lettieri (*Sallozzo*), Abe Vigoda (*Tessio*), Talia Shire (*Connie Rizzi*), Gianni Russo (*Carlo Rizzi*), John Cazale (*Fredo Corleone*), Rudy Bond (*Cuneo*), Al Martino (*Johnny Fontane*), Morgana King (*Mama Corleone*), Lenny Montana (*Luca Brasi*), John Martino (*Paulie Gatto*), Salvatore Corsitto (*Bonasera*), Richard Bright (*Neri*), Alex Rocco (*Moe Greene*), Tony Giorgio (*Bruno Tattaglia*), Vito Scottia (*Nazorine*), Tere Livrano (*Theresa Hagen*), Victor Rendina (*Philip Tattaglia*), Jeannie Linero (*Lucy Mancini*), Julie Gregg (*Sandra Corleone*), Ardell Sheridan (*Mrs. Clemenza*), Simonetta Stefanelli (*Apollonia*), Angelo Infanti (*Fabrizio*), Corrado Gaipa (*Don Tommasino*), Franco Citti (*Calo*), Saro.Urzi (*Vitelli*).

Produced by Albert S. Ruddy (Alfran Productions) for Paramount. 175 min.

1974   THE CONVERSATION
Script and direction: Coppola.
Photography (Technicolor): Bill Butler.
Editing: Walter Murch, Richard Chew.
Music: David Shire.

Production design: Dean Tavoularis.
Technical advisers: Hal Lipset, Leo Jones.
Cast: Gene Hackman (*Harry Caul*), John Cazale (*Stan*), Allen Garfield (*Bernie Moran*), Frederic Forrest (*Mark*), Cindy Williams (*Ann*), Michael Higgins (*Paul*), Elizabeth MacRae (*Meredith*), Harrison Ford (*Martin Stett*), Mark Wheeler (*receptionist*), Teri Garr (*Amy*), Robert Shields (*Mime*), Phoebe Alexander (*Lurleen*), Robert Duvall (*The Director*).
Produced by Coppola and Fred Roos (Coppola Company) for Paramount. 113 min.

1974   THE GODFATHER Part II
Script: Coppola, Mario Puzo, from the novel by Puzo.
Direction: Coppola.
Photography (Techniclolor): Gordon Willis.
Editing: Peter Zinner, Barry Malkin, Richard Marks.
Music: Nino Rota (conducted by Carmine Coppola).
Production design: Dean Tavoularis.
Art direction: Angelo Graham.
Cast: Al Pacino (*Michael Corleone*), Robert Duvall (*Tom Hagen*), Diane Keaton (*Kay Adams*), Robert De Niro (*Vito Corleone*), John Cazale (*Fredo Corleone*), Talia Shire (*Connie Corleone*), Lee Strasberg (*Hyman Roth*), Michael V. Gazzo (*Frankie Pentangeli*), G. D. Spradlin (*Senator Pat Geary*), Richard Bright (*Al Neri*), Gaston Moschin (*Fanucci*), Tom Rosqui (*Rocco Lampone*), B. Kirby Jr. (*young Clemenza*), Frank Sivero (*Genco*), Francesca De Sapio (*young Mama Corleone*), Morgana King (*Mama Corleone*), Mariana Hill (*Deanna Corleone*), Leopoldo Trieste (*Signor Roberto*), Dominic Chianese (*Johnny Ola*), Amerigo Tot (*Michael's bodyguard*), Troy Donahue (*Merle Johnson*), John Aprea (*young Tessio*), Joe Spinell (*Willi Cicci*), Abe Vigoda (*Tessio*), Tere Livrano (*Theresa Hagen*), Gianni Russo (*Carlo Rizzi*), Maria Carta (*Vito's mother*), Oreste Baldini (*Vito Andolini, as a boy*), Giuseppe Sillato (*Don Francesco*), Mario Cotone (*Don Tommasino*), James Gounaris (*Anthony Corleone*), Fay Spain (*Mrs. Marcia Roth*), Harry Dean Stanton (*first FBI man*), David Baker (*second FBI man*), Carmine Caridi (*Carmine Rosato*), Danny Aiello (*Tony Rosato*), Carmine Foresta (*Policeman*), Nick Discenza (*barman*), Father Joseph Medeglia (*Father Carmelo*), William Bowers (*Senate Committee chairman*), Joe Della Sorte, Carmen Argenziano, Joe Lo Grippo (*Michael's buttonmen*), Ezio Flagello (*impresario*), Livio Giorgi (*tenor in "Senza Mamma"*), Kathy Beller (*girl in "Senza Mamma"*), Saveria Mazzola (*Signora Colombo*), Tito Alba (*Cuban President*), Johnny Naranjo (*Cuban translator*), Elda Maida (*Pentangeli's wife*), Salvatore Po (*Pentangeli's brother*), Ignazio Pappalardo (*Mosca*), Andrea Maugeri (*Strollo*), Peter La Corte (*Signor Abbandando*), Vincent Coppola (*street salesman*), Peter Donat (*Questadt*), Tom Dahlgren (*Fred Corngold*), Paul B. Brown (*Senator Ream*), Phil Feldman (*first Senator*), Roger Corman (*second Senator*), Yvonne Coll (*Yolanda*), J.D. Nichols (*attendant at brothel*), Edward Van Sickle (*Ellis Island doctor*), Gabria Belloni (*Ellis Island nurse*), Richard Watson (*custom's official*), Venancia Grangerard (*Cuban nurse*), Erica Yohn (*governess*), Theresa Tirelli (*midwife*), and James Caan (*Sonny Corleone*).
Produced by Francis Coppola (A Coppola Company Production) for Paramount. 200 min.

1977   MARIO PUZO'S THE GODFATHER:
           THE COMPLETE NOVEL FOR TELEVISION
A television version of the two *Godfather* films in four episodes re-edited by Barry
Malkin, including footage which did not appear in the theatrical release versions
of the films. Broadcast by NBC 12, 13, 14, 15 November 1977. Part one: 1:34:
part two: 1:31: part three: 1:34, part four: 2:25. Total running time 7:14.

Coppola apparently also directed two other "nudie" films besides *Tonight for Sure*
in the early sixties or late fifties. Other credits include: *Come On Out* (1961), a
compilation of three films which he wrote and directed: "Pilma, Pilma" an
unproduced screenplay which won a Samuel Goldwyn award in 1962; *Battle
Beyond the Sun* (1963), the English-dubbed version of the Russian film *Nebo Zowet*
(1959), for Roger Corman.
     Working for Corman, he also served as assistant director on *The Premature
Burial* (1962), dialogue director on *The Tower of London* (1962), sound man and
second unit director on *The Young Racers* (1963), associate producer and uncredited second unit director on *The Terror* (1962).
     As screenwriter, Coppola is responsible in whole or in part for the scripts of the
following films: *This Property Is Condemned* (1966), *Paris, brule-t-il?/Is Paris
Burning?* (1966), *Patton* (1970), *The Great Gatsby* (1974). He also collaborated on
Reflections in a Golden Eye (1967) and is credited with at least two unproduced
scripts: "The Disenchanted" and "The Fifth Coin."
     As producer, through his company, American Zoetrope, Coppola is respon-
sible for George Lucas's *THX-1138* (1971) and *American Graffiti* (1973).

BRIAN DE PALMA

(1963)   THE WEDDING PARTY
Script and direction: Wilfred Leach, Cynthia Munroe, and De Palma.
Photography (black & white): Peter Powell.
Sound: Betsy Taylor.
Editing: De Palma.
Mixing: Jim Townsend.
Costumes: Ellen Rand.
Music: John Herbert McDowell.
     Cast: Jill Clayburgh (*bride*), Charles Pfluger (*groom*), Valda Setterfield (*Mrs.
Fish*), Raymond McNally (*Mr. Fish*), Jennifer Salt (*Phoebe*), John Braswell (*Rev.
Oldfield*), Judy Thomas (*organist*), Sue Ann Converse (*nanny*), Robert De Niro
(*Cecil*), William Finley (*Alistair*), Klaus R. Kollmar, Jr. (*Jean-Claude/Hindu/
Klaus*).
     Produced by Leach, Munroe, and De Palma for Ondine Productions. Released
April 1969 by Powell Productions Plus. Shot on location on Shelter Island, N.Y.
and in Jim Thorpe, Pa., Summer 1963. 90 min.

1968   MURDER A LA MOD
Script and direction: De Palma.
Photography (black & white): Jack Harrell.
Sound: Robert Fiore.
Editing: De Palma.
Music: John Herbert McDowell.
   Cast: Margo Norton (*Karen*), Andra Akers (*Tracy*), Jared Martin (*Christopher*), William Finley (*Otto*), Ken Burrows (*Wiley*), Lorenzo Catlett (*policeman*), Jennifer Salt, Melanie Mander, Laura Rubin, Laura Stevenson (*"birds"*).
   Produced by Ken Burrows for Aries Documentaries. Shot in New York, Summer 1967. Released April 1968. 80 min.

1968   GREETINGS
Script: Charles Hirsch, De Palma.
Direction: De Palma.
Photography: Robert Fiore.
Sound: Charles Ritts, Jeffrey Lesser.
Editing: De Palma.
Costumes: "Chuck Shields" (Hirsch).
Music: The Children of Paradise.
   Cast: Jonathan Warden (*Paul Shaw*), Robert De Niro (*Jon Rubin*), Gerrit Graham (*Lloyd Clay*), Richard Hamilton (*pop artist*), Megan McCormick (*Marina*), Bettina Kugel (*Tina*), Jack Cowley (*photographer*), Jane Lee Salmons (*model*), Ashley Oliver (*Bronx secretary*), Melvin Margulies (*Rat magazine vendor*), Cynthia Peltz (*divorcee*), Peter Maloney (*Earl Roberts*), Ruth Alda (*Linda*), Ted Lescault (*bookstore manager*), Mona Feit (*mystic date*), M. Dobish (*TV cameraman from Vietnam*), Richard Landis (*Ex-GI at party*), Carol Patton (*Blonde at party*), Allen Garfield (*smut peddler*), Sara-Jo Edlin (*nymphomaniac*), Roz Kelly (*photographer*), Ray Tuttle (*TV news correspondent*), Tisa Chiang (*Vietnamese girl*).
   Produced by Charles Hirsch for West End Film. Released December 1968 by Sigma III. Shot in New York, Spring 1968. MPAA rating: X. 88 min.

1970   DIONYSUS IN 69
Direction: De Palma (with Robert Fiore, Bruce Rubin).
A documentary film of the play directed by Richard Schechner, based on material
   from *The Bacchae* by Euripedes, trans. William Arrowsmith.
Photography: Robert Fiore and De Palma.
Sound: Bruce Rubin.
Editing: De Palma and Bruce Rubin.
Mixing: Jim Townsend.
   Cast: The Performance Group: Remi Barclay, Samuel Blazer, John Bosseau, Richard Dic, William Finley, Joan MacIntosh, Vicki May, Patrick McDermott, Margaret Ryan, Richard Schechner, William Shephard, Ciel Smith.
   Produced by De Palma, Fiore, and Rubin. Shot in New York, Fall 1969. Released March 1970. MPAA rating: X. 90 min.

1970   HI, MOM!
Script: De Palma, from a story by De Palma and Charles Hirsch.
Direction: De Palma.

Photography: Robert Elfstrom.
Editing: Paul Hirsch.
Art direction: Peter Bocour.
Music: Eric Kaz.

Cast: Robert De Niro (*Jon Rubin*), Allen Garfield (*Joe Banner*), Lara Parker (*Jeannie Mitchell*), Jennifer Salt (*Judy Bishop*), Gerrit Graham (*Gerrit Wood*), Peter Maloney (*pharmacist*), Charles Durning (*superintendent*), Abraham Goren (*pervert*),Nelson Peltz (*playboy*), Floyd Peterson (*newscaster*), William Daley. "Be Black Baby!" troupe: Buddy Butler, David Connell, Milton Earl Forrest, Carolyn Craven, Joyce Griffin, Kirk Kerksey. "Be Black Baby!" audience: Ruth Alda, Carol Vogel, Beth Bowden, Joe Stillman, Joe Fields, Gene Elman, Paul Milvy.

Produced by Charles Hirsch for Sigma III. Shot in New York, Spring 1969. Released April 1970. 87 min.

1972   GET TO KNOW YOUR RABBIT
Script: Jordan Crittenden.
Direction: De Palma.
Photography: John Alonzo.
Editing: Peter Colbert.
Sound: Robert Miller.
Art direction: William Malley.
Music: Jack Elliott.
Prestidigitation adviser: H. Blackstone, Jr.

Cast: Tom Smothers (*Donald Beeman*), John Astin (*Mr. Turnbull*), Suzanne Zenor (*Paula*), Samantha Jones (*Susan*), Allen Garfield (*Vic*), Katharine Ross (*the Terrific-Looking Girl*), Orson Welles (*Mr. Delasandro*), Hope Summers (*Mrs. Beeman*), Jack Collins (*Mr. Reese*), George Ives (*Mr. Morris*), Robert Ball (*Mr. Weber*), M. Emmet Walsh (*Mr. Wendel*), Helen Page Camp (*Mrs. Wendel*), Pearl Shear (*Flo*), Timothy Carey (*Cop*), Charles Lane (*Mr. Beeman*), Larry D. Mann (*Mr. Seager*), Jessica Myerson (*Mrs. Reese*), Anne Randall (*stewardess*), Bob Einstein (*police officer*), King Moody (*TV reporter*), Judy Marcione (*Miss Parsons*).

Produced by Steve Bernhardt and Paul Gaer. Warner Bros. Associate producer: Robert Birnbaum. 93 min.

1973   SISTERS
Script: De Palma and Louisa Rose, from a story by De Palma.
Direction: De Palma.
Photography: Gregory Sandor.
Sound: Russell Arthur.
Editing: Paul Hirsch.
Mixing: Dick Vorisek.
Production design: Gary Weist.
Music: Bernard Herrmann.
Assistant director: Ann Hopkins.

Cast: Margot Kidder (*Dominique/Danièle*), Jennifer Salt (*Grace Collier*), Charles Durning (*Joseph Larch*), William Finley (*Dr. Emile Breton*), Lisle Wilson (*Philip Wood*), Dolph Sweet (*detective*), Barnard Hughes (*magazine editor*), Mary

Davenport (*Mrs. Collier*).

Produced by Edward Pressman for Pressman-Williams. Released by AIP, April 1973. Shot on Staten Island, N.Y., Spring 1972. 93 min.

1974   THE PHANTOM OF THE PARADISE
Script: De Palma.
Direction: De Palma.
Photography: Larry Pizer.
Production design: Jack Fisk.
Music: Paul Williams.
Editing: Paul Hirsch.
Sound editor: Dan Sable.
Sound mixer: Al Grammaglia, Magno Sound Inc.
Music Supervision: Michael Arciaga, Jules Chaikin.
Special effects: Greg Auer.

Cast: Paul Williams (*Swan*), William Finley (*Winslow, the Phantom*), Jessica Harper (*Phoenix*), George Memmoli (*Philbin*), Gerrit Graham (*Beef*), Jeffrey Comanor, Archie Hahn, Harold Oblong (*the Juicy Fruits, the Beach Bums, the Undead*), Gene Gross (*Warden*), Harry Calvert (*night watchman*), Ken Carpenter, Sam Forney (*stage hands*), Leslie Brewer, Celia Derr, Linda Larimer, Roseanne Romine (*Surfgirls*), Nydia Amagas, Sara Ballantine, Kristi Bird, Cathy Buttner, Linda Cox, Jane Deford, Bibi Hansen, Robin Jeep, Deen Summers, Judy Washington, Susan Weiser (*dancers*), Janet & Jean Savarino (*singing twins*), Keith Allison (*country & western singer*), Bobby Birkenfeld (*guy*), Sandy Catton & Friends (*Black singers*), William Donovan, Scott Lane, Dennis Olivieri, Adam Wade (*reporters*), Nancy Moses, Diana Walden (*back-up singers*), Sherri Adeline (*girl in ticket line*), Carol O'Leary (*Betty Lou*), Marty Bongfeld, Coleen Crudden, Bridgett Dunn (*Mini-boppers*), William Shephard (*rock freak*), Andrew Epper, Jim Lovelett (*Winslow's doubles*), Steven Richmond, James Gambino (*Swan's doubles*).

Produced by Edward Pressman for Pressman-Williams. Twentieth Century-Fox. Executive producer: Gustave Berne. 91 min.

1976   OBSESSION
Script: Paul Schrader, from a story by Schrader and De Palma.
Direction: De Palma.
Photography (Technicolor Panavision): Vilmos Zsigmond.
Editing: Paul Hirsch.
Art direction: Jack Senter.
Sound editing: Dan Sable.
Sound mixing: David Ronne.
Special effects: Joe Lombardi.
Music: Bernard Herrmann, performed by the National Philharmonic Orchestra and the Thames Choir.
Visual Consultant: Anne Pritchard.
Portraits: Barton De Palma.

Cast: Cliff Robertson (*Michael Courtland*), Genevieve Bujold (*Elizabeth Courtland/Sandra Portinari*), John Lithgow (*Robert La Salle*), Sylvia "Kuumba" Williams (*Judy*), Wanda Blackman (*Amy Courtland*), Patrick McNamara (*third kidnapper*), Stanley J. Reyes (*Inspector Brie*), Nick Krieger (*Farber*), Stocker Fontelieu (*Dr. Ellman*), Don Hood (*Ferguson*), Andrea Esterhazy (*D. Annunzio*), Thomas Carr (*paper boy*), Tom Felleghy (*Italian businessman*), Nella Simoncini Barbieri (*Mrs. Portinari*), John Creamer (*Justice of the Peace*), Regis Cordic (*newscaster*), Loraine Despres (*Jane*), Clyde Ventura (*ticket agent*), Fain M. Gogrove (*secretary*).

Produced by George Litto and Harry N. Blum. A George Litto Production. Columbia. Executive producer: Robert S. Bremson. Filmed on location in New Orleans and Italy. 98 min.

1976   CARRIE
Script: Lawrence D. Cohen, based on the novel by Stephen King.
Direction: De Palma.
Photography (Technicolor, Panavision): Mario Tosi.
Editing: Paul Hirsch.
Music: Pino Donaggio.
Art direction: William Kenny, Jack Fisk.
Costumes: Rosanna Norton.
Special effects; Gregory M. Auer.
Sound mixing: Bertil Halberg.
Sound editing: Dan Sable.
Stunt coordinator: Richard Weiker.

Cast: Sissy Spacek (*Carrie*), Piper Laurie (*Margaret White*), Amy Irving (*Sue Snell*), William Katt (*Tommy Ross*), John Travolta (*Billy Nolan*), Nancy Allen (*Chris Hargenson*), Betty Buckley (*Miss Collins*), P. J. Soles (*Norman Watson*), Sydney Lassick (*Mr. Fromm*), Stefan Gierash (*Mr. Morton*), Priscilla Pointer (*Mrs. Snell*), Michael Talbot (*Freddy*), Doug Cox (*the Beak*), Harry Gold (*George*), Noelle North (*Frieda*), Cindy Daly (*Cora*), Dierdre Berthrong (*Rhonda*), Anson Downes (*Ernest*), Rory Stevens (*Kenny*), Edie McGlurg (*Helen*), Cameron De Palma (*boy on bicycle.*).

Produced by Paul Monash. United Artists. Associate producer: Louis Stroller. 98 min.

1978   THE FURY
Script: John Farris.
Direction: De Palma.
Photography: Richard H. Kline.
Music: John Williams.
Production design: Bill Malley.
Costumes: Theoni V. Aldredge.
Editing: Paul Hirsch.
Art direction: Richard Lawrence.
Sound editing: Dan Sable.
Special effects: A. D. Flowers.

Cast: Kirk Douglas (*Peter*), John Cassavetes (*Childress*), Carrie Snodgress (*Hester*), Charles Durning (*Dr. Jim McKeever*), Amy Irving (*Gillian*), Fiona Lewis (*Susan Charles*), Andrew Stevens (*Robin*), Carol Rossen (*Dr. Ellen Lindstrom*), Rutanya Alda (*Kristen*), Joyce Easton (*Mrs. Bellaver*), William Finley (*Raymond*), Jane Lambert (*Vivian Nuckells*), Sam Laws (*Blackfish*), J. Patrick

McNamara (*Robertson*), Alice Nunn (*Mrs. Callahan*), Melody Thomas (*LaRue*), Hilary Thompson (*Cheryl*), Patrick Billingsley (*Lander*), J.P. Bumstead (*Greene*), Barry Cullison ((*Chase #1 driver*), Jack Callahan (*DeMasi*), Dennis Franz (*Bob*), Anthony Hawkins (*Chase #1 shotgun*), Michael O'Dwyer (*Marty*), Feliz Shulman (*Dr. Ives*), Albert Stevens (*Arab Prince*), Anne Brunk (*Deborah*), Eva Cadet (*woman*), John Roche (*drunk*), Gordon Jump (*Nuckells*), Eleanor Merriam (*Mother Nuckells*), Harold Johnson (*garbage man*), Wayne Dahmer (*Nelson*), Joe Finnegan (*man*), Katheleen Francour (*Betsy*), Daryl Hannah (*Pam*), Laura Innes (*Jody*), Clair Nelson (*Dr. Becker*), Peter O'Connell (*Dr. Conn*), Al Wyatt (*security agent driver*), Douglas J. Stevenson (*houseboy*), Mickey Gilbert, Hanns Manship, Marland Proctor (*CIA agents*), Marshall Colt, Roberta Feldner, Stephen Johnson, Robin Marmor (*technicians*), Michael Copeland, Alfred Tinsley (*tough youths*), Tom Blair (*Top Guy #1*), Gunnar Lewis (*Top Guy #2*).

Produced by Frank Yablans for Frank Yablans Presentations, Inc. Twentieth Century-Fox. Executive producer: Ron Preissman. Associate producer: Jack B. Bernstein. 118 min.

De Palma has also made a couple of short films, the most notable of which is *Woton's Wake* (1963, 28 min.), and a documentary, *The Responsive Eye* (1965).

GEORGE LUCAS

1970   THX 1138
Script: Lucas, Walter Murch, from a story by Lucas.
Direction: Lucas.
Photography: Dave Myers, Albert Kihn.
Editing: Lucas.
Sound: Lou Yates, Jim Manson.
Sound montages: Walter Murch.
Production design: Michael Haller.
Costumes: Donald Longhurst.
Stunts: Jon Ward, Duffy Hamilton.
Titles and animation: Hal Barwood.
Music: Lalo Schifrin.
   Cast: Robert Duvall (*THX*), Donald Pleasence (*SEN*), Pedro Colley (*SRT*), Maggie McOmie (*LUH*), Ian Wolfe (*PTO*), Sid Haig (*NCH*), Marshall Efron (*TWA*), John Pearce (*DWY*), Johnny Weissmuller, Jr., Robert Feero (*chrome robots*), Irene Forrest (*IMM*), Claudette Bessing (*ELC*).
   Produced by Francis Ford Coppola and Lawrence Sturhahn for American Zoetrope. Associate producer: Ed Folger. Warner Bros. 95 min./88 min.

1973   AMERICAN GRAFFITI
Script: Lucas and Gloria Katz & Willard Huyck.
Direction: Lucas.
"Visual consultant" (photography): Haskell Wexler.
Editing: Verna Fields, Marcia Lucas.

Sound montage and re-recording: Walter Murch.
Design consultant: Al Locatelli.
Art direction: Dennis Clark.
Costumes: Aggie Guerard Rogers.

Cast: Richard Dreyfuss (*Curt*), Ronny Howard (*Steve*), Paul Le Mat (*John*), Charlie Martin Smith (*Terry*), Cindy Williams (*Laurie*), Candy Clark (*Debbie*), Mackenzie Phillips (*Carol*), Wolfman Jack (*disc jockey*), Harrison Ford (*Bob Falfa*), Bo Hopkins, Manuel Padilla, Jr., Beau Gentry (*the Pharaohs*).

At the Sock Hop: Flash Cadillac and the Continental Kids (*Herby and the Heartbeats*), Kathy Quinlan (*Peg*), Tim Crowley (*Eddie*), Terry McGovern (*Mr. Wolfe*), Jan Wilson, Kay Ann Kemper, Caprice Schmidt. At the Drive-In (Mel's Burger City): Jane Bellan (*carhop*), Joe Spano (*Vic*), Chris Pray (*Al*), Susan Richardson (*Judy*), Donna Wehr (*Carhop #2*). On the Streets with John: Jim Bohan (*policeman*), Ron Vincent (*Jeff Pazzuto*), Fred Ross (*Ferber*), Jody Carlson (*girl in Studebaker*), Cam Whitman (*ballroom girl*), John Bracci (*gas station attendant*). On the Streets with Curt: Debbie Celiz (*Wendy*), Lynne Marie Stewart (*Bobbie*), Ed Greenberg (*Kip Pullman*), Suzanne Somers (*blonde in T-bird*). On the Streets with Terry: Gordon Analla (*Bozo*), Lisa Herman (*girl in Dodge*), Debralee Scott (*Falfa's girl*), Charles Dorsett (*man at accident*), Stephen Knox (*kid at accident*). On the Streets with Steve: Bob Pasaak (*Dale*). At the Liquor Store: Joseph Miksak (*man*), George Meyer (*bum*), William Niven (*clerk*), James Cranna (*thief*). In the Alley: Del Close (*man*), Charlie Murphy (*old man*), Jan Dunn (*old woman*), Johnny Weissmuller, Jr. (*Badass #1*). At the Amusement Arcade: Scott Beach (*Mr. Gordon*), Al Nalbandian (*Hank*).

Produced by Francis Ford Coppola for Lucasfilm Ltd./Coppola Company. Universal. Co-producer: Gary Kurtz. Filmed in Marin and Sonoma counties and completed at American Zoetrope Studios, San Francisco. 110 min.

1977   STAR WARS
Script: Lucas.
Direction: Lucas
Photography: Gilbert Taylor.
Production design: John Barry.
Editing: Paul Hirsch, Marcia Lucas, Richard Chew.
Costumes: John Mollo.
Art direction: Norman Reynolds, Leslie Dilley.
Music: John Williams, performed by the London Symphony Orchestra.
Special Photographic effects supervisor: John Dykstra.
Special production and mechanical effects supervisor: John Sears.
Production supervisor: Robert Watts.
Sound mixing: Derek Ball.
Supervising sound editor: Sam Shaw.
Special dialogue and sound effects: Ben Burtt.
Sound editing: Robert R. Rutledge, Gordon Davidson, Gene Corso.
Advertising/publicity supervisor: Charles Lippincott.
Minature and optical effects unit supervisor: George E. Mather.
Composite optical photography: Robert Blalack (Praxis).
Matte artist: P. S. Ellenshaw.

Planet and satellite artist: Ralph McQuarrie.
Effects illustration and design: Joseph Johnston.
Additional spacecraft design: Colin Cantwell.
Chief model maker: Grant McCune.
Animation and rotoscope design: Adam Beckett.
Assistant editor (opticals): Bruce Michael Green.

Cast: Mark Hamill (*Luke Skywalker*), Harrison Ford (*Han Solo*), Carrie Fisher (*Princess Leia Organa*), Peter Cushing (*Grand Moff Tarkin*), Alec Guinness (*Ben Obi-Wan Kenobi*), Anthony Daniels (*C3PO*), Kenny Baker (*R2-D2*), Peter Mayhew (*Chewbacca*), David Prowse (*Lord Darth Vader*), James Earl Jones (*voice of Darth Vader, uncredited*), Phil Brown (*Uncle Owen Lars*), Shelagh Fraser (*Aunt Beru Lars*), Jack Purvis (*Cheif Jawa*).

Rebel Forces: Alex McCrindle (*General Dodonna*), Eddie Byrne (*General Willard*), Drewe Henley (*Red Leader*), Dennis Lawson (*Red Two/Wedge*), Garrick Hagon (*Red Three/Biggs*), Jack Klaff (*Red Four/John "D"*), William Hootkins (*Red Six/Porkins*), Angus McInnis (*Gold Leader*), Jeremy Sinden (*Gold Two*), Graham Ashley (*Gold Five*).

Imperial Forces: Don Henderson (*General Taggi*), Richard le Parmentier (*General Motti*), Leslie Schofield (*Commander #1*).

Produced by Gary Kurtz for Lucasfilm, Ltd. Twentieth Century-Fox. Filmed in Panavision, Technicolor, and Dolby on location in Tunisia, Tikal National Park, Guatemala, Death Valley National Monument, California, and EMI Elstree Studios, Borehamwood, England. Post-production completed at American Zoetrope, San Francisco. 121 min.

George Lucas also directed *The Electronic Labyrinth*, a short film which is an early version of *THX 1138*, as well as numerous other student films.

PAUL MAZURSKY

1969   BOB & CAROL & TED & ALICE
Script: Mazursky, Larry Tucker.
Direction: Mazursky.
Photography (Technicolor): Charles Lang.
Editing: Stuart H. Pappe.
Music: Quincy Jones.
Art direction: Pato Guzman.

Cast: Natalie Wood (*Carol*), Robert Culp (*Bob*), Elliott Gould (*Ted*), Dyan Cannon (*Alice*), Horst Ebersberg (*Horst*), Lee Bergere (*Emelio*), Donald F. Muhich (*psychiatrist*), Noble Lee Holderreal Jr. (*Sean*), K.T. Stevens (*Phyllis*), Celest Yarnall (*Susan*), Greg Mullavey (*group leader*).

Produced by Larry Tucker (A Frankovich production) for Columbia. 105 min.

1970   ALEX IN WONDERLAND
Script: Mazursky, Larry Tucker.

Direction: Mazursky.
Photography (Metrocolor): Laszlo Kovacs.
Editing: Stuart H. Pappe.
Music: Tom O'Horgan.
Production design: Pato Guzman.

   Cast: Donald Sutherland (*Alex*), Ellen Burstyn (*Beth*), Meg Mazursky (*Amy*), Glenna Sergent (*Nancy*), Viola Spolin (*mother*), Federico Fellini and Jeanne Moreau (*themselves*), André Philippe (*André*), Michael Lerner (*Leo*), Joan Delaney (*Jane*), Neil Burstyn (*Norman*), Leon Frederick (*Lewis*), Carol O'Leary (*Marlene*), Paul Mazursky (*Hal Stern*), Moss Mabry (*Mr. Wayne*).

   Produced by Larry Tucker for M-G-M. 109 min.

1973   BLUME IN LOVE

Script and direction: Mazursky.
Photography (Technicolor): Bruce Surtees.
Editing: Donn Cambern.
Music and songs: Kris Kristofferson, Bob Dylan, Richard Wagner, Van Morrison, Zelma and Otis Redding, Carole King, Carosone, Amilcare Ponchielli, Giocchino Rossini, Rudolf Sieczynski, Wolfgang Amadeus Mozart, etc.
Production design: Pato Guzman.

   Cast: George Segal (*Stephen Blume*), Susan Anspach (*Nina Blume*), Kris Kristofferson (*Elmo*), Marsha Mason (*Arlene*), Shelley Winters (*Mrs. Cramer*), Donald F. Muhich (*analyst*), Paul Mazursky (*Hellman*), Erin O'Reilly (*Cindy*), Annazette Chase (*Gloria*), Shelley Morrison (*Mrs. Greco*), Mary Jackson (*Louise*), Ed Peck (*Ed Goober*), Jo Morrow (*bar hostess*), Gigi Ballista (*old man*), Ian Linhart (*young boy*), Mario Demo (*Venice waiter*), Erika Von Kessler (*girl at party*), Dennis Kort (*boy at party*), Judy Ann Elder (*Lulu*), Carol Worthington (*Annie Goober*), Lou Gottlieb (*party guru*), Ray Schmidt (*party guest*), Virginia Dension (*Yoga leader*).

   Produced by Mazursky for Warner Bros. Associate producer: Tony Ray. 116 min.

1974   HARRY AND TONTO

Script: Mazursky, Josh Greenfeld.
Direction: Mazursky.
Photography (DeLuxe color): Michael Butler.
Editing: Richard Halsey.
Music: Bill Conti.
Art direction: Ted Haworth.

   Cast: Art Carney (*Harry Coombs*), Ellen Burstyn (*Shirley*), Chief Dan George (*Sam Two Feathers*), Geraldine Fitzgerald (*Jessie*), Larry Hagman (*Eddie*), Arthur Hunnicutt (*Wade*), Phil Burns (*Burt*), Joshua Mostel (*Norman*), Melanie Mayron (*Ginger*), Dolly Jonah (*Elaine*), Herbert Berghof (*Rivetowski*), Avon Long (*Leroy*), Barbara Rhoades (*happy hooker*), Cliff DeYoung (*Burt Jr.*), Lou Guss (*Dominic*), Mike Nussbaum (*old age home clerk*), Rene Enriquez (*grocery clerk*), Michael McCleery (*mugger*), Rashel Novikoff (*Mrs. Rothman*), Sybil Bowan (*old landlady*), Michael Butler (*hitchhiker*).

   Produced by Mazursky for Twentieth Century-Fox. (Associate producer: Tony Ray.) 115 min.

1976   NEXT STOP, GREENWICH VILLAGE
Script and direction: Mazursky.
Photography (Color, Panavision): Arthur Ornitz.
Editing: Richard Halsey.
Production design: Philip Rosenberg.
   Cast Lenny Baker (*Larry Lapinsky*), Ellen Green (*Sarah*), Shelley Winters (*Mom*), Mike Kellin (*Pop*), Christopher Walken (*Robert*), Dori Brenner (*Connie*), Antonio Fargas (*Bernstein*), Lois Smith (*Anita*), Lou Jacobi (*Herb*), Helen Hanft (*Herb's wife*), John Ford Noonan (*Barney*), Rashel Novikoff (*Mrs. Tupperman*), Joe Madden (*Jake the Poet*), Joe Spinnell (*Cop*), Rochelle Oliver (*Doctor*), Michael Egan (*Herbert*), Gui Andrisano (*Marco*), Denise Galik (*Ellen*), Carole Manferdini (*Southern girl*), Jeff Goldblum (*Clyde*), John C. Becher (*Sid Weinberg*), Rutanya Alda (*party person*).
   Produced by Mazursky and Tony Ray for Twentieth Century-Fox. 110 min.

1978   AN UNMARRIED WOMAN
Script and direction: Mazursky.
Photography: Arthur Ornitz.
Production design: Pato Guzman.
Editing: Stuart H. Pappe.
Music: Bill Conti.
Costumes: Albert Wolsky.
Production manager: Terry Donnelly.
Mixing: Arthur Piantadosi.
Contributing artists: Robert Bechtle, Frank Bramblett, John Chamberlain, John Clem Clarke, Colette, Robert Cottingham, John Deandrea, Porfirio Didonna, Marilyn Gelfman Pereira, Ralph Goings, H. N. Han, Yan Hsia, Paul Jenkins, John Kacere, Lila Katzen, Tony King, E. J. Kresnar, Marsha Liberty, Toshio Odate, Peter Saari, John Salt, Andy Warhol, "with special thanks to Paul Jenkins."
   Cast: Jill Clayburgh (*Erica*), Alan Bates (*Saul*), Michael Murphy (*Martin*), Cliff Gorman (*Charlie*), Pat Quinn (*Sue*), Kelly Bishop (*Elaine*), Lisa Lucas (*Patti*), Linda Miller (*Jeannette*), Andrew Duncan (*Bob*), Daniel Seltzer (*Dr. Jacobs*), Matthew Arkin (*Phil*), Penelope Russianoff (*Tanya*), Novella Nelson (*Jean*), Raymond J. Barry (*Edward*), Ivan Karp (*Herb Rowan*), Jill Eikenberry (*Claire*), Michael Tucker (*Fred*), Chico Martinez (*Cabbie*), Clint Chin (*Chinese waiter*), Ken Chapin (*man at bar*), Tom Elios (*ice vendor*), Karen Ford (*executive secretary*), Alice J. Kane (*waitress*), Paul Mazursky (*Hal*), Pamela Meunier (*hat-check girl*), Donna Perich (*Sophie*), Vincent Schiavelli (*man at party*), John Stravinsky (*bartender*), Ultra Violet (*Lady MacBeth*).
   Produced by Paul Mazursky and Tony Ray for Twentieth Century-Fox. Filmed on location in New York. 124 min.

Mazursky also wrote, with Larry Tucker, the screenplay for *I Love You, Alice B. Toklas!* (1969, Hy Averback).

MICHAEL RITCHIE

1969   DOWNHILL RACER
Script: James Salter, based on the novel "The Downhill Racers" by Oakley Hall.
Direction: Ritchie.
Photography (Technicolor): Brian Probyn.
Editing: Nick Archer.
Music: Kenyon Hopkins.
Art direction: Ian Whitaker.
  Cast: Robert Redford (*David Chappellet*), Gene Hackman (*Eugene Claire*), Camilla Sparv (*Carole Stahl*), Joe Jay Jalbert (*Tommy Erb*), Timothy Kirk (*D. K. Bryan*), Dabney Coleman (*Mayo*), Jim McMullan (*Johnny Creech*), Oren Stevens (*Tony Kipsmith*), Karl Michael Vogler (*Machet*), Rip McManus (*Bruce Devore*), Jerry Dexter (*Ron Engel*), Tom J. Kirk (*Stiles*), Robert Hutton-Potts, Heini Schuler, Peter Rohr, Arnold Alpiger, Eddie Waldburger, Marco Walli.
  Produced by Richard Gregson for Wildwood International/Paramount. 101 min.

1972   PRIME CUT
Script: Robert Dillon.
Direction: Ritchie.
Photography (Technicolor, Panavision): Gene Polito.
Editing: Carl Pingatore.
Music: Lalo Schifrin.
Art direction: Bill Malley.
  Cast: Lee Marvin (*Nick Devlin*), Gene Hackman (*Mary Ann*), Angel Tompkins (*Clarabelle*), Gregory Walcott (*Weenie*), Sissy Spacek (*Poppy*), Janit Baldwin (*Violet*), William Morey (*Shay*), Clint Ellison (*Delaney*), Howard Platt (*Shaughnessy*), Les Lanhom (*O'Brien*), Eddie Egan (*Jake*), Therese Reinsch (*Jake's girl*), Bob Wilson (*Reaper Driver*), Gordon Signer (*Brockman*), Gladys Watson (*Milk Lady*), Hugh Gillin Jr. (*clerk*), P. Lund (*Mrs. O'Brien*), David Savage (*Ox-Eye*), Craig Chapman (*Farmer Bob*), Jim Taksas (*Big Jim*), Wayne Savagne (*Freckle Face*).
  Produced by Joe Wizan for Cinema Center Films. 86 min.

1972   THE CANDIDATE
Script: Jeremy Larner.
Director: Ritchie.
Photography (Technicolor): Victor J. Kemper, John Korty.
Editing: Richard A. Harris, Robert Estrin.
Music: John Rubinstein.
Songs: John Rubinstein, David Colloff.
Production design: Gene Callahan.
  Cast: Robert Redford (*Bill McKay*), Peter Boyle (*Marvin Lucas*), Don Porter ("*Crocker*" *Jarmon*), Allen Garfield (*Howard Klein*), Karen Carlson (*Nancy McKay*), Quinn Redeker (*Rich Jenkin*), Morgan Upton (*Wally Henderson*), Michael Lerner (*Paul Corliss*), Kenneth Tobey (*Starkey*), Melvyn Douglas (*John J. McKay*).
  Produced by Walter Coblenz (a Redford/Ritchie production) for Warner Bros. 110 min.

1975   SMILE
Script: Jerry Belson.
Direction: Ritchie.
Photography (DeLuxe Color): Conrad Hall.
Editing: Richard Harris.
Music: popular songs.
Pageant Music: Daniel Orsborn (lyrics: Ritchie).
Additional music: Leroy Holmes.
Choreography: Jim Bates.
    Cast: Bruce Dern (*"Big Bob" Freelander*), Barbara Feldon (*Brenda DiCarlo*), Michael Kidd (*Tommy French*), Geoffrey Lewis (*Wilson Shears*), Nicholas Pryor (*Andy DiCarlo*), Colleen Camp (*Connie Thompson/"Miss Imperial County"*), Joan Prather (*Robin Gibson/"Miss Antelope Valley"*), Denise Nickerson (*Shirley Tolstoy/"Miss San Diego"*), Annette O'Toole (*Doria Houston/"Miss Anaheim"*), Maria O'Brien (*Maria Gonzales/"Miss Salinas"*), Melanie Griffith (*Karen Love/ "Miss Simi Valley"*), Kate Sarchel (*Judy Wagner/"Miss Modesto"*), Titos Vandis (*Emile Eidleman*), Dennis Dugan (*Logan*), William Traylor (*Ray Brandy*), Eric Shea (*"Little Bob" Freelander*), Adam Reed (*Freddy*), Brad Thompson (*Chuck*), Paul Benedict (*Orren Brooks*), Dick McGarvin (*Ted Farley*), Helene Nelson (*Jo Ann Marshall*), Caroline Williams (*Helga*), George Skaff (*Dr. Malvert*).
    Produced by Ritchie for United Artists. 113 min.

1976   THE BAD NEWS BEARS
Script: Bill Lancaster.
Direction: Ritchie.
Photography (Movielab Color): John A. Alonzo.
Editing: Richard A. Harris.
Music: Jerry Fielding (adapted from Bizet's "Carmen").
Production design: Polly Platt.
    Cast: Walter Matthau (*Morris Buttermaker*), Tatum O'Neal (*Amanda Whurlizer*), Vic Morrow (*Roy Turner*), Joyce Van Patten (*Cleveland*), Ben Piazza (*Councillor Bob Whitewood*), Jackie Earle Haley (*Kelly Leak*), Alfred W. Lutter (*Ogilvie*), Brandon Cruz (*Joey Turner*), Chris Barnes (*Tanner Boyle*), Erin Blunt (*Ahmad Abdul Rahim*), Gary Lee Cavagnaro (*Engelberg*), Quinn Smith (*Timmy Lupus*), Scott Firestone (*Regi Tower*), David Pollock (*Rudi Stein*), David Stambaugh (*Toby Whitewood*), Brett Max (*Jimmy Feldman*), Jaime Escobedo (*José Agilar*), George Gonzales (*Miguel Agilar*), Timothy Blake (*Mrs. Lupus*), Bill Sorrells (*Mr. Tower*), Shari Summers (*Mrs. Turner*), Joe Brooks (*Umpire*), George Wyner (*White Sox Manager*), David Lazarus (*Yankee*), Charles Matthau (*Athletic*), Maurice Marks (*Announcer*).
    Produced by Stanley R. Jaffe for Paramount. 103 min.

1977   SEMI-TOUGH
Script: Walter Bernstein, based on the novel by Dan Jenkins.
Direction: Ritchie.
Photography: Charles Rosher, Jr.
Production design: Walter Scott Herndon.
Editing: Richard Harris.
Music: Jerry Fielding.

Songs by Gene Autry.
Costumes: Theoni V. Aldredge.
Mixing: Barry Thomas, Richard Portman.
Stunt coordinator: Hal Needham.

Cast: Burt Reynolds (*Billy Clyde Puckett*), Kris Kristofferson (*Shake Tiller*), Jill Clayburgh (*Barbara Jane Bookman*), Robert Preston (*Big Ed Bookman*), Bert Convy (*Friedrich Bismark*), Roger E. Mosley (*Puddin*), Lotte Lenya (*Clara Pelf*), Richard Masur (*Phillip Hooper*), Carl Weathers (*Dreamer Tatum*), Brian Dennehy (*T. J. Lambert*), Mary Jo Catlett (*Earlene*), Joe Kapp (*Hose Manning*), Ron Silver (*Vlada*), Jim McKrell (*McNair*), Peter Bromilow (*interpreter*), Norm Alden (*Coach Parks*), Fred Stuthman (*Minister*), Janet Brandt (*dressmaker*), William Wolf (*fitter*), Jennifer Shaw (*stewardess*), Kevin Furry (*Puddin, Jr.*), Ava Roberts (*Puddin's wife*), Melonie Magruder (*Linda*), Michelle Griffin (*little girl*), Mark Franklin (*Attendant Tom*), Mary Rae Hoskins, Charlotte Stanton, Niki Flacks, Rose Pearson (*BEAT women*), Thom Phillips, Hugh Gorrian (*BEAT men*), Mickey Caruso (*Curtis*), Edward Jones, Kevin Grady, Tim Guy (*football players*), Dick Schaap, Lindsay Nelson, Paul Hornung (*themselves*).

Produced by David Merrick for United Artists. Shot on location in Dallas and Miami. 108 min.

1979　TAKE TWO

MARTIN SCORSESE

1969　WHO'S THAT KNOCKING AT MY DOOR?
Script and direction: Scorsese (additional dialogue by Betzi Manoogian).
Photography: Michael Wadleigh, Richard Coll, Max Fisher.
Editing: Thelma Schoonmaker.
Art direction: Victor Magnotta.

Cast: Zina Bethune (*the young girl*), Harvey Keitel (*J.R.*), Anne Collette (*young girl in dream*), Lennard Kuras (*Joey*), Michael Scala (*Sally Gaga*), Harry Northup (*Harry*), Bill Minkin (*Iggy*), Phil Carlson (*the guide*), Wendy Russell (*Gaga's small friend*), Robert Uricola (*the armed young man*), Susan Wood (*Susan*), Marissa Joffrey (*Rosie*), Catherine Scorsese (*J. R.'s mother*), Victor Magnotta and Paul De Bionde (*waiters*), Saskia Holleman, Tsuai Yu-Lan and Marieka (*dream girls*), Martin Scorsese (*gangster*), Thomas Aiello.

Produced by Joseph Weill, Betzi Manoogian and Haig Manoogian (Trimrod) for release by Joseph Brenner Associates. 90 min. Earlier versions known as *Bring on the Dancing Girls* (1965) and *I Call First* (1967). Also released as J.R.

1972　BOXCAR BERTHA
Script: Joyce H. Corrington, John William Corrington, from the book *Sister of the Road* by Boxcar Bertha Thompson as told to Ben L. Reitman.
Direction: Scorsese.
Photography (DeLuxe color): John Stephens.
Editing: Buzz Feitshans.
Music: Gib Guilbeau, Thad Maxwell.

Cast: Barbara Hershey (*Bertha*), David Carradine (*Bill Shelley*), Barry Primus (*Rake Brown*), Bernie Casey (*Von Morton*), John Carradine (*H. Buckram*

Sartoris), Victor Argo and David R. Osterhout (The McIvers), "Chicken" Holleman (Michael Powell), Grahame Pratt (Emeric Pressburger), Harry Northup (Harvey Hall), Ann Morell (Tillie), Marianne Dole (Mrs. Mailer), Joe Reynolds (Joe), Gayne Rescher and Martin Scorsese (brothel clients).

Produced by Roger Corman for American International. 88min.

1973   MEAN STREETS

Script: Scorsese, Mardik Martin.
Direction: Scorsese.
Photography (Technicolor): Kent Wakeford.
Editing: Sid Levin.

Cast: Harvey Keitel (Charlie), Robert De Niro (Johnny Boy), Amy Robinson (Teresa), David Proval (Tony), Richard Romanus (Michael), Cesare Danova (Giovanni), Victor Argo (Mario), George Memmoli (Joey Catucci), Lenny Scaletta (Jimmy), Jeannie Bell (Diane), Murray Mosten (Oscar), David Carradine (drunk), Robert Carradine (the young assassin), Lois Walden (Jewish girl), Harry Northup (Vietnam veteran), Dino Seragusa (old man), D'Mitch Davis (black cop), Peter Fain (George), Julie Andelman (girl at party), Robert Wilder (Benton), Ken Sinclair (Sammy), Catherine Scorsese (woman on the landing), Martin Scorsese (Shorty, the killer in the car).

Produced by Jonathan T. Taplin (Taplin—Perry—Scorsese) for Warner Bros. 110 min.

1974   ALICE DOESN'T LIVE HERE ANYMORE

Script: Robert Getchell.
Direction: Scorsese.
Photography (Technicolor): Kent Wakeford.
Editing: Marcia Lucas.
Original music: Richard LaSalle.
Production design: Toby Carr Rafelson.

Cast: Ellen Burstyn (Alice Hyatt), Kris Kristofferson (David), Alfred Lutter (Tommy), Billy Green Bush (Donald), Diane Ladd (Flo), Lelia Goldoni (Bea), Lane Bradbury (Rita), Vic Tayback (Mel), Jodie Foster (Audrey), Harvey Keitel (Ben), Valerie Curtin (Vera), Murray Moston (Jacobs), Harry Northup (Joe and Jim's bartender), Mia Bendixsen (Alice aged 8), Ola Moore (old woman), Martin Brinton (Lenny), Dean Casper (Chicken), Henry M. Kendrick (shop assistant), Martin Scorsese and Larry Cohen (diners at Mel and Ruby's), Mardik Martin (customer in club during audition).

Produced by David Susskind and Audrey Maas for Warner Bros. 112 min.

1976   TAXI DRIVER

Script: Paul Schrader.
Direction: Scorsese.
Photography (color): Michael Chapman.
Editing: Marcia Lucas, Tom Rolf, Melvin Shapiro.
Music: Bernard Herrmann.
Art direction: Charles Rosen.

Cast: Robert De Niro (Travis Bickle,), Cybill Shepherd (Betsy), Jodie Foster (Iris), Harvey Keitel (Sport), Peter Boyle (Wizard), Albert Brooks (Tom),

Leonard Harris (*Charles Palantine*), Diahne Abbott (*concession girl*), Frank Adu (*angry black man*), Vic Argo (*Melio*), Gino Ardito (*policeman at rally*), Garth Avery (*Iris's friend*), Harry Cohn (*cabbie in Bellmore*), Copper Cunningham (*hooker in cab*), Brenda Dickson (*soap opera woman*), Harry Fischler (*dispatcher*), Nat Grant (*stick-up man*), Richard Higgs (*tall Secret Service man*), Beau Kayser (*soap opera man*), Vic Magnotta (*Secret Service photographer*), Robert Maroff (*Mafioso*), Norman Matlock (*Charlie T*), Bill Minkin (*Tom's assistant*), Murray Moston (*Iris's timekeeper*), Harry Northup (*doughboy*), Gene Palma (*street drummer*), Carey Poe (*campaign worker*), Steven Prince (*Andy, gun salesman*), Peter Savage (*the John*), Martin Scorsese (*passenger watching silhouette*), Robert Shields (*Palantine aide*), Ralph Singleton (*TV/interviewer*), Joe Spinell (*personnel officer*), Maria Turner (*angry hooker on street*), Robin Utt (*campaign worker*).

Produced by Michael and Julia Phillips (Bill/Phillips production) for Columbia. 112 min.

1977   NEW YORK, NEW YORK
Script: Earl Mac Rauch, Mardik Martin, from a story by Rauch.
Direction: Scorsese.
Photography: Laszlo Kovacs.
Production design: Boris Leven.
Original songs by John Kander and Fred Ebb ("Theme From *New York, New York*," "There Goes the Ball Game," "But the World Goes 'Round," "Happy Endings.")
Musical supervisor and conductor: Ralph Burns.
Choreography: Ron Field.
Supervising film editors: Irving Lerner, Marcia Lucas.
Editing: Tom Rolf, B. Lovitt.
Costumes: Theadora Van Runkle.
Hair designs for Liza Minnelli: Sydney Guilaroff.
Sound editing: Michael Colgan, James Fritch.
Saxophone solos: Georgie Auld.
Executive in charge of production: Hal W. Polaire.
Cast: Liza Minnelli (*Francine Evans*), Robert De Niro (*Jimmy Doyle*), Lionel Stander (*Tony Harwell*), Barry Primus (*Paul Wilson*), Mary Kay Place (*Bernice*), Georgie Auld (*Frankie Harte*), George Memmoli (*Nicky*), Dick Miller (*Palm Club owner*), Murray Moston (*Horace Morris*), Lenny Gaines (*Artie Kirks*), Clarence Clemons (*Cecil Powell*), Kathi McGinnis (*Ellen Flannery*), Norman Palmer (*desk clerk*), Adam David Winkler (*Jimmy Doyle, Jr.*), Dimitri Logothetis (*desk clerk*), Frank Sivera (*Eddie di Muzio*), Diahnne Abbott (*Harlem club singer*), Margo Winkler (*argumentative woman*), Steven Prince (*record producer*), Don Calfa (*Gilbert*), Bernie Kuby (*Justice of the Peace*), Selma Archerd (*wife of Justice of the Peace*), Bill Baldwin (*announcer in Moonlit Terrace*), Mary Lindsay (*hatcheck girl in Meadows*), Jon Cutler (*musician in Frankie Hart's band*), NickyBlair (*cab driver*), Casey Kasem (*D. J.*), Jay Salerno (*bus driver*), William Tole (*Tommy Dorsey*), Sydney Guilaroff (*hairdresser*), Peter Savage (*Horace Morris' assistant*), Gene Castle (*dancing sailor*), Louie Guss (*Fowler*), Shera Danese (*Doyle's girl in Major Chord*), Bill McMillan (*D. J.*), David Nichols (*Arnold Trench*), Harry Northup (*Alabama*), Marty Zagon (*manager of South Bend ballroom*), Timothy Blake (*nurse*), Betty Cole (*charwoman*), De Forest Covan (*porter*), Phil Gray (*trombone

player in Doyle's band), Roosevelt Smith (*bouncer in Major Chord*), Bruce L. Lucoff (*cab driver*), Bill Phillips Murry (*waiter in Harlem club*), Clint Arnold (*trombone player in Palm Club*), Richard Alan Berk (*drummer in Palm Club*), Jack R. Clinton (*bartender in Palm Club*), Wilfred R. Middlebrooks (*bass player in Palm Club*), Jake Vernon Porter (*trumpet player in Palm Club*), Nat Pierce (*piano player in Palm Club*), Manuel Escobosa (*fighter in Moonlit Terrace*), Susan Kay Hunt, Teryn Jenkins (*girls at Moonlit Terrace*), Mardik Martin (*well-wisher at Moonlit Terrace*), Leslie Summers (*woman in black at Moonlit Terrace*), Brock Michaels (*man at table in Moonlit Terrace*), Washington Rucker, Booty Reed (*musicians at hiring hall*), David Armstrong, Robert Buckingham, Eddie Garrett, Nico Stevens (*reporters*), Peter Fain (*greeter in Up Club*), Angelo Lamonea (*waiter in Up Club*), Charles A. Tamburro, Wallace McClesky (*bouncers in Up Club*), Ronald Prince (*dancer in Up Club*), Robert Petersen (*photographer*), Richard Raymond (*railroad conductor*), Hank Robinson (*Francine's bodyguard*), Harold Ross (*cab driver*), Eddie Smith (*man in bathroom at Harlem club*).

Produced by Irwin Winkler and Robert Chartoff for United Artists. Associate producer: Gene Kirkwood. 155 min. (originally).

1978   THE LAST WALTZ
Direction: Scorsese.
Photography: Michael Chapman, Laszlo Kovacs, Vilmos Zsigmond, David Myers, Bobby Byrne, Michael Watkins, Hiro Narita.
Editing: Yeu-Bun Yee, Jan Roblee.
Production design: Boris Leven.
Concert producer: Bill Graham.
Concert music production: John Simon. (Audio production: Rob Fraboni.)
Music editor: Ken Wannberg.
Treatment and creative consultant: Mardik Martin.
The performers in order of appearance: Ronnie Hawkins, Dr. John, Neil Young, The Staples, Neil Diamond, Joni Mitchell, Paul Butterfield, Muddy Waters, Eric Clapton, Emmylou Harris, Van Morrison, Bob Dylan, Ringo Starr, Ron Wood.
Poems by Michael McClure, Sweet William Fritsch, Lawrence Ferlinghetti.
Interviewer: Scorsese.
The Band: Rick Danko (bass, violin, and vocal), Levon Helm (drums, mandolin, and vocal), Garth Hudson (organ, accordion, saxophone, and synthesizers), Richard Manuel (piano, keyboards, drums, and vocal), Robbie Robertson (lead guitar and vocal).

Produced by Robbie Robertson for United Artists. Executive producer: Jonathan Taplin. Filmed on location at Winterland Arena, San Francisco, November 1976, and M-G-M Studios, Culver City, and Shangri-La Studios, Malibu, thereafter. 119 min.

short and medium-length films:
1963   WHAT'S A NICE GIRL LIKE YOU
          DOING IN A PLACE LIKE THIS?
Script and direction: Scorsese.   Music: Richard Coll   (lyrics by Sandor Reich). Players: Zeph Michaelis (*Harry*), Mimi Stark (*His wife*), Sarah Braverman (*Psychoanalyst*), Fred Sica (*Friend*), Robert Uricola (*The singer*).
Produced for the Cinema Dept. of New York University. 9 min. (16 min.)

1964   IT'S NOT JUST YOU, MURRAY. Script: Scorsese and Mardik Martin. Direction: Scorsese. Photography (16mm): Richard Coll. Editing: Eli Bleich. Art Direction: Lancelot Braithwaite, Victor Magnotta. Players: Ira Rubin (*Murray*), Sam DeFazio (*Joe*), Andrea Martin (*the wife*), Catherine Scorsese (*the mother*), Robert Uricola (*the singer*), Bernard Weisberger, Victor Magnotta, Richard Sweeton, John Bivona, Mardik Martin, Richard Coll, Martin Scorsese. Produced by the Cinema Dept. of New York University. 15 min.

1967   THE BIG SHAVE. Script and direction: Scorsese. Photography (color, 16mm): Ares Demertzis, Music: Bunny Berigan. Player: Peter Bernuth. Sponsored by the Cinémathèque Royale de Belgique. 6 min.

1974   ITALIANAMERICAN. Script: Mardik Martin, Larry Cohen. Direction: Scorsese. Photography (16mm, color): Alex Hirschfeld. Editing: B. Lovitt. Players: Catherine, Charles and Martin Scorsese, Produced by Saul Rubin and Elaine Attias. 48 min.

1978   AMERICAN BOY: A PROFILE OF STEVEN PRINCE. Treatment: Mardik Martin, Julia Cameron. Direction: Scorsese. Photography: Michael Chapman. Editing: Amy Jones, Bertram Lovitt. Sound: Darin Knight. Song: "Time Fades Away" by Neil Young. People in the room: Steven Prince, Martin Scorsese, George Memmoli, Mardik Martin, Julia Cameron, Kathy McGinnis. Produced by Bertram Lovitt for New Empire Films/Scorsese Films. Executive producers: Ken and Jim Wheat. 55 min.

Scorsese has also worked on commercials (G.B., 1968) and on the screenplay for *Obsessions* (1968, Pim de la Parra). He was replaced on *Honeymoon Killers* (1969) by Leonard Kastle. He was assistant director and supervising editor for *Woodstock* (1969) and associate producer/supervising editor for *Medicine Ball Caravan* (1971). He served as supervisor of montages for *Elvis on Tour* (1972) and as supervising editor for *Unholy Rollers* (1973, Vernon Zimmerman.) He was post-production director on *Street Scenes 1970* (New York Cinetracts Collective).

In 1977, Scorsese directed the stage musical *The Act*, with Liza Minnelli (originally titled "In Person" and "Shine It On"). Gower Champion later took over direction.

STEVEN SPIELBERG

1971   DUEL
Script: Richard Matheson.
Direction: Spielberg.
Photography: Jack A. Marta.
Editing: Frank Morriss.
Music: Billy Goldenberg.
Production design: Robert S. Smith.
   Cast: Dennis Weaver (*David Mann*), Tim Herbert (*station attendant*), Charles Seel (*old man*), Eddie Firestone (*cafe owner*), Shirley O'Hara (*waitress*), Gene Dynarski (*man in cafe*), Lucille Benson (*Snakorama lady*), Alexander Lockwood (*old man in car*), Amy Douglass (*lady*).
   Produced by George Eckstein for Universal television. Later released theatrically abroad. First broadcast ABC, 20 November 1971. 74 min/90 min.

1973   SUGARLAND EXPRESS
Script: Hal Barwood, Matthew Robbins, from a story by Spielberg.
Direction: Spielberg.
Photography: Vilmos Zsigmond.
Editing: Edward M. Abroms, Verna Fields.
Production design: Joseph Alves.
Sound: John Carter, Robert Hoyt.
Music: John Williams.
   Cast: Goldie Hawn (*Lou Jean Poplin*), Ben Johnson (*Capt. Tanner*), Michael Sacks (*Officer Slide*), William Atherton (*Clovis Poplin*), Gregory Walcott (*Officer Mashburn*), Harrison Zanuck (*Baby Langston*), Steve Kanaly, Louise Latham, A. L. Camp, Jessie Lee Fulton, Dean Smith, Ted Grossman, Bill Thurman, Kenneth Hudgins, Buster Daniels, Jim Harrell, Frank Stegall, Roger Ernest, Guich Kooch, Merrill L. Connally, Gene Rader, Gordon Hurst, George Hagy, Big John Hamilton.
   Produced by Richard D. Zanuck and David Brown. Universal. Shot on location in Texas in Panavision and Technicolor. 110 min.

1975   JAWS
Script: Peter Benchley, Carl Gottlieb from Benchley's novel.
Direction: Spielberg.
Photography: Bill Butler.
Production design: Joseph Alves, Jr.
Editing: Verna Fields.
Music: John Williams.
Live shark footage filmed by Ron and Valerie Taylor.
Underwater photography: Rexford Metz.
Special effects: Robert A. Mattey.
Sound: John R. Carter, Robert Hoyt.
Camera operator: Michael Chapman.
   Cast: Roy Scheider (*Brody*), Robert Shaw (*Quint*), Richard Dreyfuss (*Hooper*), Lorraine Gary (*Ellen Brody*), Murray Hamilton (*Vaughn*), Carl Gottlieb (*Meadows*), Jeffrey C. Kramer (*Hendricks*), Susan Backlinie (*Chrissie*), Jonathan Filley (*Cassidy*), Ted Grossman (*estuary victim*), Chris Rebello (*Michael Brody*), Jay Mello (*Sean Brody*), Lee Fierro (*Mrs. Kintner*), Jeffrey Voorhees (*Alex Kintner*), Craig Kingsbury (*Ben Gardner*), Dr. Robert Nevin (*medical examiner*), Peter Benchley (*interviewer*).
   Produced by Richard D. Zanuck and David Brown for Universal. Filmed on location in Martha's Vineyard. 124 min.

1977   CLOSE ENCOUNTERS OF THE THIRD KIND
Script and direction: Spielberg.
Photography: Vilmos Zsigmond.
Special photographic effects: Douglas Trumbull.
Music: John Williams.
Additional photography: William A. Fraker, Douglas Slocombe, John Alonzo, Laszlo Kovacs.
Production design: Joe Alves.
Editing: Michael Kahn.

Technical adviser: Dr. J. Allen Hynek.
Realization of extraterrestrial: Carlo Rambaldi.
Music editing: Kenneth Wannberg.
Supervising sound effects editor: Frank Warner.
Supervising dialogue editor: Jack Schrader.
Production sound mixer; Gene Cantamessa.
Special mechanical effects: Roy Arbogast.
Photography—photographic effects: Richard Yuricich.
Matte artist: Matthew Yuricich. (UFO photography: Dave Stewart.)
Chief modelmaker: Gregory Jein.
Animation supervision: Robert Swarthe.
Optical photography: Robert Hall.
Effects unit project manager: Robert Shepherd.

    Cast: Richard Dreyfuss (*Roy Neary*), François Truffaut (*Claude Lacombe*), Teri Garr (*Ronnie Neary*), Melinda Dillon (*Jillian Guiler*), Cary Guffey (*Barry Guiler*), Bob Balaban (*David Laughlin*), J.Patrick McNamara (*project leader*), Warren Kemmerling (*Wild Bill*), Roberts Blossom (*farmer*), Philip Dodds (*Jean Claude*), Shawn Bishop (*Brad Neary*), Adrienne Campbell (*Silvia Neary*), Justin Dreyfuss (*Toby Neary*), Lance Hendricksen (*Robert*), Merrill Connally (*team leader*), George Dicenzo (*Major Benchley*).

    Produced by Julia Phillips and Michael Phillips for Columbia/EMI. Associate producer: Clark Paylow. Shot in Panavision, Dolby. 130 min.

1979   1941

Spielberg has directed numerous television episodes. His short film, *Amblin'* was made in 1969. In 1977 he produced *I Want to Hold Your Hand* (Bob Zemeckis). In addition to *Duel*, his made-for-television movies include:

1971   SOMETHING EVIL. Script: Robert Clouse. Direction: Spielberg. Photography: Bill Butler. Editing: Allan Jacobs. Art direction: Al Heschong. Music: Wladimir Selinski. Special effects: Logan Frazee. Cast: Sandy Dennis (*Marjorie Worden*), Darren McGavin (*Paul Worden*), Ralph Bellamy (*Harry Lincoln*), Jeff Corey (*Gehrmann*), Johnny Whittaker (*Stevie Worden*), John Rubinstein (*Ernest*), David Kapp (*John*), Laurie Hagen (*Beth*), Sandy and Debbie Lampert (*Laurie Worden*), Herb Armstrong (*Mr. Schiller*), Margaret Avery (*Irene*), Norman Barthold (*Mr. Hackett*), Sheila Barthold (*Mrs. Hackett*), Lois Battle (*Mrs. Faraday*), Bella Bruck (*Mrs. Gehrmann*), Lynn Cartwright (*secretary*), John J. Fox (*sound man*). Produced by Alan J. Factor for Bedford Productions. First telecast 21 January 1971. c. 75 min.

1973   SAVAGE
Script: Mark Rogers, William Link, Richard Levinson, from a story by Rogers. Direction: Spielberg. Cast: Martin Landau (*Paul Savage*), Barbara Bain (*Gail Abbott*), Barry Sullivan (*Jud Stein*), Louise Latham (*Maureen Stern*), Pat Harrington (*Russell*), Susan Howard (*Lee Reynolds*), Dabney Coleman (*Ted Seligson*), Paul Richards (*Philip Brooks*), Michele Carey (*Alison Baker*). Produced by Paul Pierson for Link & Levinson Productions/Universal. First telecast on NBC 31 March 1973.

FILMOGRAPHIES
1979-1984

WOODY ALLEN

1979   MANHATTAN
Script: Woody Allen, Marshall Brickman
Photography: Gordon Willis
Production design: Mel Bourne
Costumes: Albert Wolsky
Editing: Susan E. Morse
Music: George Gershwin
    Cast: Woody Allen (*Isaac Davis*), Diane Keaton (*Mary Wilke*), Michael Murphy (*Yale*), Mariel Hemingway (*Tracy*), Meryl Streep (*Jill*), Anne Byrne (*Emily*), Karen Ludwig (*Connie*), Michael O'Donoghue (*Dennis*), Victor Truro, Tisa Farrow, Helen Hanft, Bella Abzug (*Party Guests*), Gary Weis (*Television Director*), Kenny Vance (*Television Producer*), Charles Levin, Karen Allen, David Rasche (*Television Actors*), Damion Sheller (*Willie Davies*), Wallace Shawn (*Jeremiah*), Mark Linn Baker (*Shakespearean Actor*), Frances Conroy (*Shakespearean Actress*), Bill Anthony, John Doumanian (*Porsche Owners*), Ray Serra (*Pizzeria Waiter*).
    Produced by Robert Greenhut, Jack Rollins, and Charles Joffe for United Artists. 96 mins. black and white.

1980   STARDUST MEMORIES
Script: Woody Allen
Photography: Gordon Willis
Editing: Susan Morse
Production design: Mel Bourne
Art director: Michael Molly
Costumes: Santo Loquasto
    Cast: Woody Allen (*Sandy Bates*), Charlotte Rampling (*Dorrie*), Marie-Christine Barrault (*Isobel*), Jessica Harper (*Daisy*), John Rothman (*Jack Abel*), Amy Wright (*Shelley*), Helen Hanft (*Vivian Orkin*), Daniel Stern (*Actor*), Tony Roberts (*Tony*), Anne DeSalvo (*Sister*), Gabrielle Strasun (*Charlotte Ames*), Bob Maroff (*Jerry Abraham*), Leonardo Cimino (*Sandy's analyst*), Robert Munk (*Sandy as a Boy*), Ken Chapin (*Sandy's Father*), Jaqui Safra (*Sam*), Andy Albeck, Robert Friedman, Douglas Ireland, Jack Rollins (*Studio executives*), Howard Kissel

(*Sandy's Manager*), Max Leavitt (*Sandy's Doctor*), Renee Lippin (*Sandy's Press agent*), Sol Lomita (*Sandy's Accountant*), Irving Metzman (*Sandy's Lawyer*) Dorothy Leon (*Sandy's Cook*).

Produced by Jack Rollins, Robert Greenhut, and Charles Joffe for United Artists. 84 min.

1982   A MIDSUMMER'S NIGHT SEX COMEDY
Script: Woody Allen
Photography: Gordon Willis
Editing: Susan E. Morse
Production design: Mel Bourne
Music: conducted by Eugene Ormandy
Cast: Woody Allen (*Andrew Hobbs*), Mia Farrow (*Ariel Weymouth*), Jose Ferrer (*Professor Leopold Sturgis*), Julie Hagerty (*Dulcy Ford*), Tony Roberts (*Dr.Maxwell Jordan*), Mary Steenburgen (*Adrian Hobbs*), Adam Redfield (*Studen Foxx*), Moise Rosenfeld (*Mr. Hayes*), Timothy Jenkins (*Mr. Thomas*), Kate McGregor-Stewart (*Mrs. Baker*).

Produced by Robert Greenhut, Charles H. Joffe for Orion. Distributed by Columbia-EMI-Warner. 88 min.

1983   ZELIG
Script: Woody Allen
Photography: Gordon Willis
Editing: Susan E. Morse
Production design: Mel Bourne
Music: Dick Hyman
Cast: Woody Allen (*Leonard Zelig*), Mia Farrow (*Dr. Eudora Fletcher*), Garrett Brown (*Actor Zelig*), Stephanie Farrow (*Sister Meryl*), Will Holt (*Rally Chancellor*), Sol Lomita (*Martin Geist*), John Rothman (*Paul Deghuee*), Deborah Rush (*Lita Fox*), Marianne Tatum (*Actress Fletcher*), Susan Sontag, Irving Howe, Saul Bellow, Bricktop, Dr. Bruno Bettelheim, Professor John Morton Blum.

Produced by Charles Joffe, Robert Greenhut, Jack Rollins for Orion Pictures and Warner Brothers. 84 min.

1983   BROADWAY DANNY ROSE
Script: Woody Allen
Photography: Gordon Willis
Production design: Mel Bourne
Costumes: Jeffrey Kurland
Music: Dick Hyman
Editing: Susan E. Morse
Cast: Woody Allen (*Danny Rose*), Mia Farrow (*Tina Vitale*), Nick Apollo Forte (*Lou Canova*), Milton Berle, Sandy Baron, Corbett Monica, Jackie Gayle, Morty Gunty, Will Jordan, Howard Storm, Jack Rollins (*Themselves*), Craig Vandenburgh (*Ray Webb*), Herb Reynolds (*Barney Dunn*).

Produced by Robert Greenhut and Charles H. Joffe for Orion Pictures. 86 min. Black and white.

492

ROBERT ALTMAN

1979   A PERFECT COUPLE
Script: Robert Altman
Assistant directors: Bill Cosentino, Tommy Thompson
Photography: Edmond Koons
Music: Tom Pierson
Editing: Tony Lombardo
Art Direction: Leon Ericson
   Cast: Paul Dooley (*Alex Theodopoulos*), Marta Heflin (*Sheila Shea*), Titos Vandis (*Panos Theodopoulos*), Belita Moreno (*Eleousa Theodopoulos*), Henry Gibson (*Fred Bott*), Dimitra Arliss (*Athena*), Allan Nicholls (*Dana "115"*), Ann Ryerson (*Skye "147"*), Poppy Lagos (*Melpomeni Bott*), Dennis Franz (*Costa*), Margery Bond (*Wilma*), Mona Golabek (*Mona*), Susan Blakeman (*Penelope Bott*), Melanie Bishop (*Star*), Fred Bier (*1/2 of Imperfect Couple*), Jette Seear (*1/2 of Imperfect Couple*).

1980   POPEYE
Script: Jules Feiffer
From character of: E. C. Segar
Production manager: Frederick Muller
Unit coordinator: David Levy
Photography: Giuseppe Rotunno
Camera: Gianfranco Trasunto, Lorenzo Battaglia
Sound: Robert Gravenor
Set decoration: Jack Stephens
Wardrobe supervisor: John Hay
Costumes: Scott Bushnell
Art: Alfredo Tiberi
Supervising editor: Tony Lombardo
Music and lyrics: Harry Nilsson
Stunt coordinator: Roberto Messina
   Cast: Robin Williams (*Popeye*), Shelly Duvall (*Olive Oyl*), Ray Walston (*Poopdeck Pappy*), Paul Dooley (*Wimpy*), Wesley Ivan Hurt (*Swee' Pea*), Paul L. Smith (*Bluto*), Richard Libertini (*Geezil*), Donald Moffat (*The Taxman*), MacIntyre Dixon (*Cole Oyl*), Roberta Maxwell (*Nana Oyl*), Donovan Scott (*Castor Oyl*), Allan Nicholls (*Roughhouse*), Bill Irwin (*Ham Gravy the Old Boyfriend*), Robert Fortier (*Bill Barnacle the Town Drunk*), David McCharen (*Harry Hotcash the Gambler*), Sharon Kinney (*Cherry his Moll*), Peter Bray (*Oxblood Oxheart the Fighter*), Linda Hunt (*Mrs. Oxheart his Mom*), Geoff Hoyle (*Scoop the Reporter*), Wayne Robson (*Chizzelflint the Pawnbroker*), Larry Pisoni (*Chico the Dishwasher*), Carlo Pellegrini (*Swifty the Cook*), Susan Kingsley (*La Verne the Waitress*), Michael Christensen (*Splatz the Janitor*), Ray Cooper (*Preacher*), Noel Parenti (*Slick the Milkman*), Karen McCormick (*Rosie the Milkmaid*), John Bristol (*Bear the Hermit*), Julie Janney (*Mena Walfleur*), Patty Katz (*Mina Walfleur*), Diane Shaffer (*Mona Walfleur*) Nathalie Blossom (*Blossom Walfleur*), Dennis Franz (*Spike*), Carlos Brown (*Slug*), Ned Dowd (*Butch*), Hovey Burgess (*Mort*), Robert Messina (*Gozo*), Pietro Torrisi (*Bolo*), Margery Bond (*Daisy*), Judy Burgess (*Petunia*), Sandra MacDonald (*Violet*), Eve Knoller (*Min*), Peggy Pisoni (*Pickelina*),

493

Barbara Zegler (*Daphne*), Paul Zegler (*Mayor Stonefeller the Official*), Pamela Burrell (*Mrs. Stonefeller*), David Arkin (*Mailman, Policeman*), Klaus Voormann (*Von Schnitzel the Conductor*), Doug Dillard (*Clem the Banjo Player*), Van Dyke Parks (*Hoagy the Piano Player*), Stan Wilson (*Oscar the Barber*), Roberto Dell'Aqua (*Chimneysweep*), Valerie Velardi (*Cindy the Drudge*).

Produced by C. O. Erickson (executive producer), Robert Evans, Scott Bushnell (associate producer) for Walt Disney Productions, Paramount Pictures. 114 min.

1980   HEALTH
Script: Frank Barhydt, Paul Dooley, Robert Altman
Photography: Edmond Koons
Sound: Bob Gravenor
Editing: Dennis M. Hill
   Cast: Glenda Jackson, Carol Burnett, James Garner, Lauren Bacall, Dick Cavett, Paul Dooley, Henry Gibson.
   Produced by Lion's Gate for Twentieth Century-Fox. 102 min.

1982   COME BACK TO THE FIVE AND DIME JIMMY DEAN, JIMMY DEAN
Script: Robert Graczyk
Direction: Robert Altman
Photography: Pierre Mignot
Editing: Jason Rosenfeld
Art direction: David Gropman
   Cast: Sandy Dennis (*Mona*), Cher (*Sissy*), Karen Black (*Joanne*), Sudie Bond (*Juanita*), Kathy Bates (*Stella May*), Mark Patton (*Joe Qualley*).
   Produced by Jerry Chester, Peter Newman (executive producers), Scott Bushnell, Mark Goodson and Sandcastle 5 for Viacom. 109 minutes.

1982   STREAMERS
Altman also produced *Remember My Name* (Alan Rudolph, 1978) and *Rich Kids* (Robert Young, 1979).

JOHN CASSAVETES

1980   GLORIA
Script: John Cassavetes
Production Manager: Steve Kestsern
Photography: Fred Schuler
Music: Bill Conti
Art Direction: Rene D'Auriac
Costumes: Peggy Farrell, Emmanuel Ungaro
   Cast: Julie Carmen (*Jeri Dawn*), Tony Knesich (*First Gangster*), Gregory Cleghorne (*Kid in elevator*), Buck Henry (*Jack Dawn*), John Adames (*Phil Dawn*), Lupe Garnica (*Margarita Vagas*), Jessica Castillo (*Joan Dawn*), Tom Noona (*Second Gangster*), Ronald Maccone (*Third Gangster*), George Yudzevich (*Heavy-set Man*), Gena Rowlands (*Gloria Swenson*), Gary Klar (*Irish Cop*), William E. Rice

(*TV Newscaster*), Michael Proscia (*Uncle Joe*), John Finnegan (*Frank*), Gaetano Lisi (*Mister*), Val Avery (*Sill*), Ferruccio Hrvatin (*Aldo*).
Produced by Sam Shaw for Columbia Pictures. 111 min.

Cassavetes also acted in *The Fury* (De Palma, 1977), *Brass Target* (John Hough, 1978), *Whose Life Is It, Anyway?* (John Badham, 1981), *Tempest* (Paul Mazursky, 1982), *The Incubus* (John Hough, 1982).

FRANCIS FORD COPPOLA

1979   APOCALYPSE NOW
Script: John Milius
Photography: Vittorio Storaro (*Technicolor*)
Production Manager: Barrie Osborne
Production design: Dean Tavoularis
Art Director: Angelo Graham
Set Decorator: George Nelson
Editing: Richard Marks
Special effects: Joseph Lombardi, A. D. Flowers
Music: Carmine Coppola
   Cast: Martin Sheen (*Capt. Benjamin*), Marlon Brando (*Col. Walter E. Kurtz*), Robert Duvall (*Lt. Col. Bill Kilgore*), Fred Forrest (*Hicks the "Chef"*), Sam Bottoms (*Lance*), Albert Hall (*Chief Phillips*), Larry Fishburne (*"Clean"*), Dennis Hopper (*Photo-journalist*), Harrison Ford (*Col. Lucas*), G. D. Spradlin (*General Corman*), Jerry Ziesmer (*Civilian*), Scott Glenn (*Capt. Richard Colby*), Bo Byers (*MP Sergeant*), Ifugao people of Banaue, Phillippine Islands.
   Produced by Fred Roos, Tom Sternberg, Gary Frederickson and Omni Zoetrope for United Artists.

1981   ONE FROM THE HEART
Script: Francis Coppola, Armyan Bernstein
Photography: Vittorio Storaro, Ronald V. Garcia (Metrocolor)
Editing: Arne Goursaud, Rudi Fehr, Randy Roberts
Production design: Dean Tavoularis
Music: Tom Waits
   Cast: Frederic Forrest (*Hank*), Teri Garr (*Frannie*), Nastassia Kinski (*Leila*), Raul Julia (*Ray*), Lainie Kazan (*Maggie*), Harry Dean Stanton (*Moe*).
   Produced by Fred Roos, Mona Skager, Armyan Bernstein, Bernard Gersten and Gary Frederickson for Zoetrope Studios. 101 min.

1982   THE OUTSIDERS
Script: Kathleen Knutsen Rowell
Photography: Stephen H. Burum (Panavision)
Editing: Anne Goursaud
Music: Carmine Coppola
Production design: Dean Tavoularis
Sets: Gary Fettis
Costumes: Marge Bowers

Sound: Jim Webb (Dolby)
   Cast: C. Thomas Howell (*Ponyboy Curtis*), Matt Dillon (*Dallas Winston*), Ralph Maccio (*Johnny Cade*), Patrick Swayze (*Darrel Curtis*), Rob Lowe (*Sodapop Curtis*), Diana Lane (*Cherry Valance*), Emilio Estevez (*Two-Bit Matthews*), Tom Cruise (*Steve Ranle*), Leif Garrett (*Bob Sheldon*), Glenn Withrow (*Tim Shepherd*), Tom Waits (*Buck Merrill*).
   Produced by Fred Roos, Gray Frederickson for Warner Bros. 91 min.

1983   RUMBLEFISH
Script: S. E. Hinton
Photography: Stephen H. Burum
Editing: Barry Malkin
Sound: David Parker
Production designer: Dean Tavoularis
Music: Stewart Copeland
   Cast: Matt Dillon (*Rusty James*), Mickey Rourke (*Motorcycle Boy*), Diane Lane (*Patty*), Dennis Hopper (*Father*), Diana Scarwid (*Cassandra*), Vincent Spano (*Steve*), Nicolas Cage (*Smokey*), Christopher Penn (*BJ*), Larry Fishburne (*Midget*), William Smith (*Patterson*).
   Produced by Fred Roos and Doug Claybourne for Universal Pictures. 94 min.

1984   COTTON CLUB

Coppola also produced *The Black Stallion* (Carroll Ballard, 1979), *The Escape Artist* (Caleb Deschanel, 1982), *Hammett* (Wim Wenders, 1982), and *The Black Stallion Returns* (Robert Halva, 1983).

BRIAN DE PALMA

1979   HOME MOVIES
Script: Robert Harders, Gloria Norris, Kim Anbler, Dana Edelman, Stephen LeMay, Charles Loventhal
Photography: James Carter
Editing: Corky Ohara
Art direction: Tom Sugal, Rachel Feldman
Sound: Rick Waddel
Music: Pino Donaggio
   Cast: Kirk Douglas (*Dr. Tuttle*), Nancy Allen (*Kristine*), Keith Gordon (*Denis*), Gerrit Graham (*James*), Vincent Gardenia (*Dr. Byrd*), Mary Davenport (*Mrs. Byrd*), Captain Haggerty (*Captain*).
   Produced by De Palma, Jack Temchin and Gil Adler for S L C Films. 90 min.

1980   DRESSED TO KILL
Script: Brian De Palma
Photography: Ralf Bode
Editing: Jerry Greenberg
Music: Pino Donaggio
Costumes: Ann Roth

Production design: Gary Weist
Set Decorator: Gary Brin
Sound: John Bolz, Peter Ilardi
  Cast: Michael Caine (*Dr. Elliott*), Angie Dickinson (*Kate Miller*), Nancy Allen (*Liz Blake*), Keith Gordon (*Peter Miller*), Dennis Franz (*Detective Marino*), David Margulies (*Dr. Levy*), Ken Baker (*Warren Lockman*), Brandon Maggart (*Cleveland Sam*), Susanna Clemm (*Betty Luce*), Fred Weber (*Mike Miller*).
  Produced by Samuel Arkoff, Fred Caruso, and George Litto and Cinema 77 for Filmways Pictures. 105 min.

1981   BLOWOUT
Script: Brian De Palma
Photography: Vilmos Zsigmond (Technicolor)
Music: Pino Donaggio
Editing: Paul Hirsch
Production Design: Paul Sylbert
  Cast: John Travolta (*Jack*), Nancy Allen (*Sally*), John Lithgow (*Burke*), Dennis Ranz (*Manny Karp*), Peter Boyden (*Sam*), Curt May (*Frank Donohue*), Ernest McClure (*Jim*).
  Produced by George Litto for Filmways. 107 min.

1983   SCARFACE
Script: Oliver Stone
Photography: John A. Alonzo (Technicolor)
Editing: Jerry Greenberg
Music: Giorgio Moroder
Art direction: Ed Richardson
  Cast: Al Pacino (*Tony Montana*), Steven Bauer (*Manny Ray*), Michelle Pfeiffer (*Elvira*), Mary Mastrantonio (*Gina*), Robert Loggia (*Frank Lopez*), Miriam Colon (*Mama Montana*), Murray F. Abraham (*Lomar*), Paul Shenar (*Alejandro Sosa*), Harris Yulin (*Bernstein*), Angel Salazar (*Chi Chi*).
  Produced by Louis A. Stroller, Peter Saphier, and Martin Bregman for Universal Pictures. 169 min.

GEORGE LUCAS

Produced: *More American Graffiti* (B. W. L. Norton, 1979), *The Empire Strikes Back* (Irvin Kershner, 1980), *Raiders of the Lost Ark* (Steven Spielberg, 1981), *Twice Upon a Time* (John Korty, 1983), *Return of the Jedi* (Richard Marquand, 1983).

PAUL MAZURSKY

1980   WILLIE & PHIL
Script: Paul Mazursky
Photography: Sven Nykvist
Music: Claude Bolling

Editing: Donn Cambern
Production design: Pato Guzman
Sound: Dennis Maitland
    Cast: Michael Ontkean (*Willie Kaufman*), Margot Kidder (*Jeannette Sutherland*), Ray Sharkey (*Phil D'Amico*), Jan Miner (*Mrs. Kaufman*), Tom Brennan (*Mr. Kaufman*), Julie Bovasso (*Mrs. D'Amico*), Louis Guss (*Mr. D'Amico*), Kathleen Maguire (*Mrs. Sutherland*), Kaki Hunter (*Patti Sutherland*) Kristine DeBell (*Rena*), Alison Cass Shurpin (*Zelda Kaufman No. 4*), Christine Varnai (*Zelda Kaufman No. 3*), Natalie Wood (*Herself*), Ed Van Nuys (*Official Clerk*).
    Produced by Paul Mazursky and Tony Ray for Twentieth Century-Fox. 116 min.

1982   TEMPEST
Script: Paul Mazursky, Leon Capetanos
Photography: Don McAlpine
Editing: Donn Cambern
Music: Stomu Yamashta
Production designer: Pato Guzman
Costumes: Albert Wolsky
    Cast: John Cassavetes (*Phillip*), Gena Rowlands (*Antonia*), Susan Sarandon (*Aretha*), Vittorio Gassman (*Alonzo*), Raul Julia (*Kalibanos*), Molly Ringwald (*Miranda*), Sam Robards (*Freddy*), Paul Stewart (*Phillip's Father*), Jackie Gayle (*Trin*), Tony Holland (*Sebastian*), Jerry Hardin (*Harry Gondorf*), Lucianne Buchanan (*Dolores*).
    Produced by Paul Mazursky, Steven Bernhardt, Pato Guzman for Columbia Pictures. 140 min.

1984   MOSCOW ON THE HUDSON

Mazursky also acted in *A Man, A Woman, and a Bank* (Noel Black, 1979), *A History of the World, Part I* (Mel Brooks, 1981).

MICHAEL RITCHIE

1979   AN ALMOST PERFECT AFFAIR
Script: Walter Bernstein
Photography: Henri Decae
Editing: Richard A. Harris
Art direction: Willy Holt
Music: Georges Delerue
    Cast: Keith Carradine (*Hal*), Monica Vitti (*Maria*), Raf Vallone (*Freddie*), Christian DeSica (*Carlos*), Dick Anthony Williams (*Jackson*), Henri Garcin (*Lt. Montand*), Anna Maria Horsford (*Amy Zon*).
    Produced by Terry Carr for Paramount Pictures. 93 min.

1980   THE ISLAND
Script: Peter Benchley
Photography: Henri Decae

Editing: Richard A. Harris
Production design: Dale Hennesy
Music: Ennio Morricone
   Cast: Brad Sullivan (*Stark, Pilot*), John O'Leary (*1st Doctor*), Bruce McLaughlin (*2nd Doctor*), Jimmy Casino (*3rd Doctor*), Suzanne Astor (*Mrs. Ellen Burgess, Susan Bredhoff (Kate)*), Reg Evans (*"Jack the Bat"*), Steve Gladstone (*Pirate*), David Hart (*Attendant*), Cary Hoffman (*Mr. Burgess*), Robert Salmi (*Ship's Captain*), William Schilling (*Baxter, the Gunsmith*), Stewart Steinberg (*Hiller, Maynard's Editor*), Bob Westmoreland (*Charter Boat Captain*), Mark Westwood (*Coast Guardsman*), Michael Caine (*Blair Maynard*), David Warner (*Jean-David Nau*), Angela Punch McGregor (*Beth*), Dudley Sutton.
   Produced by Richard Zanuck and David Brown for Universal. 114 Min.

1980   DIVINE MADNESS
Script: Jerry Blatt, Bette Midler, Bruce Vilance
Photography: William A. Fraker
Editing: Glenn Farr
Music: Tony Berg, Randy Kerber
Art direction: Albert Brenner
   Cast: Bette Midler (*The Divine Miss M*), Jocelyn Brown (*A Harlette*), Ula Hedwig (*A Harlette*), Diva Gray (*A Harlette*), Irving Sudrow (*Head Usher*), Tony Berg (*Band Vocalist*), Jon Bonine (*Band Vocalist*), Joey Carbone (*Band Vocalist*), Randy Kerber (*Band Vocalist*).
   Produced by Michael Ritchie, Jeffrey Howard, and the Ladd Company and Warner Bros. for Columbia-EMI-Warner. 93 min.

1983   THE SURVIVORS
Script: Michael Leeson
Photography: Billy Williams
Editing: Richard A. Harris
Music: Paul Chibara
Art direction: Jay Moore
   Cast: Walter Matthau (*Sonny Paluso*), Robin Williams (*Donald Quinelle*), Jerry Reed (*Jack Locce*), James Wainwright (*Wes Huntley*), Kristen Vigard (*Candice Paluso*), Annie McEnroe (*Doreen*).
   Produced by Howard Pine and William Sackheim with Rastar Productions for Columbia. 102 min.

MARTIN SCORSESE

1980   RAGING BULL
Script: Paul Schrader, Mardik Martin
Photography: Michael Chapman
Editing: Thelma Schoonmaker
Art direction: Alan Manser, Kirk Axtell, Sheldon Haber
   Cast: Robert De Niro (*Jake La Motta*), Cathy Moriarty (*Vickie La Motta*), Joe Pesci (*Joey La Motta*), Joseph Bono (*Guido*), Lori Anne Flax (*Irma*), Charles Scorsese (*Charlie, man with Como*), Don Dunphy (*Himself*), Bill Hanrahan (*Eddie Ea-*

gan), Rita Bennet (*Emma, Miss 48s*), James V. Christy (*Dr. Pinto*), Ernie Allen (*Comedian*), Michael Badaluccio (*Soda Fountain Clerk*), Paul Forrest (*Monsignor*), Peter Savage (*Jackie Curtis*), Joe Malanga (*Bodyguard*), Eddie Mustafa Muhammad (*Billy Fox*).

Produced by Irwin Winkler and Robert Chartoff for United Artists. 129 min.

1982 KING OF COMEDY
Script: Paul D. Zimmerman
Photography: Fred Schuler
Editing: Thelma Schoonmaker
Sound: Les Lazarowitz
Music: Robbie Robertson
Production Designer: Boris Leven
    Cast: Robert De Niro (*Rupert Pupkin*), Jerry Lewis (*Jerry Langford*), Diahnne Abbott (*Rita*), Sandra Bernhard (*Masha*), Shelley Hack (*Cathy*), Tony Randall (*Himself*), Ed Herlihy (*Himself*), Lou Brown (*Bandleader*), Margo Winkler (*Receptionist*).

Produced by Robert Greenhut, Arnon Milchan for Twentieth Century Fox. 101 min.

STEVEN SPIELBERG

1979 1941
Script: Robert Zemeckis, Bob Gale
Photography: William A. Fraker
Editing: Michael Kahn
Music: John Williams
Art director: William F. O'Brien
Production design: Dean Edward Mitzner
    Cast: Dan Ackroyd (*Sergeant Tree*), Ned Beatty (*Ward Douglas*), John Belushi (*Wild Bill Kelso*), Lorraine Gary (*Joan Douglas*), Murray Hamilton (*Claude*), Christopher Lee (*Von Kleinschmidt*), Tim Matheson (*Birkhead*), Mifune Toshiro (*Commander Mitamura*), Warren Oates (*Maddox*), Treat Williams (*Sitarksi*), Nancy Allen (*Donna*), Eddie Deezen (*Herbie*), Bobby DiCicco (*Wallly, Diane Kay* (*Betty*), John Dandy (*Foley*), Slim Pickens (*Hollis Wood*), Robert Stack (*General Stilwell*), Elisha Cook (*Patron*), Patti Lupone (*Lydia Hedberg*).

Produced by John Milius, Buzz Feitshans, Janet Healy, Michael Kahn for Universal. 118 min.

1981 RAIDERS OF THE LOST ARK
Script: Lawrence Kasdan
Photography: Douglas Slocombe and Paul Beeson
Production design: Norman Reynolds
Art direction: Leslie Dilley
Editing: Michael Kahn
Music: John Williams
Special effects: Peter Dawson
    Cast: Harrison Ford (*Indiana Smith*), Karen Allen (*Marion Ravenwood*), Paul

Freeman (*Belloq*), Ronald Lacey (*Tont*), John Rhys-Davies (*Sallah*), Denholm Elliot (*Marcus Brody*), Alfred Molina (*Satipo*), Wolf Kahler (*Dietrich*), Anthony Higgins (*Gobler*), Vic Tablian (*Barranca, Monkey Man*), Don Fellows (*Col. Musgrove*), William Hootkins (*Major Eaton*), Bill Reimbold (*Bureaucrat*), Fred Sorenson (*Jock*), Patrick Durkin (*Australian Climber*), Christopher Frederick (*Otto*), Tutte Lemkow (*Imam*), Ishaq Bux (*Omar*), Kiran Shah (*Aou*), Souad Messaoudi (*Fayah*), Terry Richards (*Arab Swordsman*), Steve Hanson (*German Agent*), George Harris (*Katanga*).

Produced by Frank Marshall, George Lucas, Howard Kazanjian and Robert Watts, by Lucasfilm Ltd. for CIC. 115 min.

1982   E.T., THE EXTRA-TERRESTRIAL
Script: Melissa Mathison
Photography: Allen Daviau
Editing: Carol Littleton
Music: John Williams
Production designer: James D. Bissell
Creator of E.T.: Carlo Rambaldi
    Cast: Dee Wallace (*Mary*), Henry Thomas (*Elliot*), Peter Coyote (*Keys*), Robert MacNaughton (*Michael*), Drew Barrymore (*Gertie*), K. C. Martel (*Greg*), Sean Frye (*Steve*), Tom Howell (*Tyler*), Erika Eleniak (*Pretty Girl*), David O'Dell (*Schoolboy*), Frank Toth (*Policeman*), Richard Swingler (*Science Teacher*), Robert Barton (*Ultra Sound Man*), Michael Darrell (*Van Man*).

Produced by Steven Spielberg and Kathleen Kennedy for Universal Pictures.

1983   TWILIGHT ZONE: THE MOVIE Sequence 2
Script: Josh Rogan, Richard Matheson
Photography: Allen Daviau
Editing: Michael Kahn
Set design: William Teegarden, Jackie Carr
    Cast: Scatman Crothers (*Mr. Bloom*), Bill Quinn (*Mr. Conroy*), Martin Garner (*Mr. Weinstein*), Selma Diamond (*Mrs. Weinstein*), Helen Shaw (*Mrs. Dempsey*), Murray Matheson (*Mr. Agee*), Peter Brocoo (*Mr. Mute*), Priscilla Pointer (*Miss Cox*), Tanya Fenmore (*Young Mrs. Weinstein*), Evan Richards (*Young Mr. Agee*), Laura Mooney (*Young Mrs. Dempsey*), Christopher Eisenmann (*Young Mr. Mute*), Richard Swingler (*Mr. Grey Panther*), Alan Haufrect (*Mr. Conroy's Son*), Cheryl Secher (*Daughter-in-Law*), Elsa Raven (*Nurse 2*).

Produced by Kathleen Kennedy for Warner Brothers.

Spielberg also produced *I Wanna Hold Your Hand* (Robert Zemeckis, 1977), *Used Cars* (Robert Zemeckis, 1980), *Continental Divide* (Michael Apted, 1981), *Poltergeist* (Tobe Hooper, 1982), and *Twilight Zone: The Movie* (1983). He acted in *The Blues Brothers* (John Landis, 1980).

Reading About
American Film Now
A Guide

With the growth of film magazines in the 1970s and the renewed interest in the glamorous business of Hollywood among the general-interest magazines, the amount of print now devoted to movies each year is considerable. The following list is highly selective. It concentrates on interviews and general articles which have appeared in the specialized journals. In general, these focus more on information and analysis and less on personality and gossip than the mass-market magazines. Specific reviews of films are listed only if they were newsworthy at the time. You might also want to check the collections of reviews published regularly by such critics as Pauline Kael and Andrew Sarris.

There are very few books on American Film in the 1970s. In English only two—Diane Jacobs's *Hollywood Renaissance* and Lynda Myles's *Movie Brats* deal specifically and extensively with this period. Included in the "General" section of this list are a number of interesting recent critical books that touch tangentially on the past decade.

Scripts of recent American films are also hard to come by. Even the admirable French series L'Avant-Scène has published relatively few titles. (They are listed under appropriate categories.) On the other hand, spin-off exploitations— novelizations and "on-the-set" journalistic reports—are very common. (Only a few of the more interesting ones have been listed here.)

Readers interested in continuing to follow the developing American film scene should be aware of the range of journals now devoted to serious and popular appreciation of the movies.

American Film publishes general articles on film and television, including long interviews. *Cineaste* specializes in a political approach to movies. *Film Comment* covers the business as well as the art. *Millimeter* is basically a filmmakers' journal, but almost always has articles of general interest. Their interviews with various professionals are useful. *Sight and Sound*, the venerable British publication, often comments on the American scene.

The list that follows is divided into eight major categories: General, The Business, The Craft, Film Culture and Criticism, Issues, Genres, Major Directors, and Other Filmmakers.

502

General

BOOKS

Balio, Tino, ed. *The American Film Industry.* Madison: University of Wisconsin Press, 1976. See especially Thomas Guback's contribution.

Blumenberg, Hans C., Peter Figlestahler, Hans Peter Kochenrath, et al. *New Hollywood.* Munich: Carl Hauser Verlag, 1976.

Braudy, Leo. *The World in Frame: What We See in Films.* New York: Doubleday & Co., 1977.

Fadiman, William. *Hollywood Now:.The Industry, the Agent, the Director, the Star, the Writer, the Producer, the Future.* With a foreword by Irving Wallace. New York: Liveright, 1972.

Jacobs, Diane. *Hollywood Renaissance: Altman, Cassavetes, Coppola, Mazursky, Scorsese, and Others.* New York: A.S. Barnes & Co., 1977.

Louis, Theodore and Jean Pigeon. *Le Cinéma américain d'aujourd'hui.* Paris: Seghers, 1975.

Madsen, Axel. *The New Hollywood.* New York: Crowell, 1975.

Monaco, James. *How to Read a Film.* New York: Oxford University Press, 1977. Includes commentary on contemporary films.

Sklar, Robert, *Movie-Made America: A Cultural History of American Movies.* New York: Random House, 1975. A few comments on the contemporary scene.

Thomson, David. *America in the Dark: Hollywood and the Gift of Unreality.* New York: William Morrow and Co., 1977. Some commentary on contemporary films.

————.*A Biographical Dictionary of Film.* New York: William Morrow and Co., 1976. Brilliant analyses of star personas. Essential reading.

Toeplitz, Jerzy. *Hollywood and After: The Changing Face of Movies in America.* Chicago: Henry Regnery Company, 1974. Some interesting analysis of Hollywood economics.

ARTICLES:

Sarris, Andrew. "After *The Graduate*," *American Film*, July-August 1978.

Williams, Tony, et al. "American Cinema in the 70s," *Movie* 25 (Winter 1977/78).

The Business

BOOKS:

Balio, Tino. *United Artists.* Madison: University of Wisconsin Press, 1976.

Dunne, John Gregory. *The Studio.* New York: Farrar, Straus, & Giroux, 1969.

Guber, Peter. *Inside The Deep.* New York: Bantam Books, 1977.

Sylbert, Paul. *Final Cut: The Making and Breaking of a Film.* New York: Seabury Press.

ARTICLES:

American Film Institute. "Dialogue on Film: Sue Mengers," *American Film*, November 1976.

Byron, Stuart. "Don Rugoff: Ballyhoo With a Harvard Education," *Film Comment*, May-June 1975.

————."The Movie-House Game," *New York*, 27 March 1978.

Chernow, Ron. "The Perils of the Picture Show: Fade-Out on an Era," *New York*, 22 August 1977.

Cohen, Mitchell. "Head to Gardens via Easy Rider: The Corporate Style of BBS," *Take One* 3:12 (November 1973).

Collins, Lisa. "Selling the Movies," *Take One*, August 1976.

Cook, Bruce. "Producers and Publishers: The Book Brothers," *American Film*, April 1978.

Gordon, David. "Why the Movie Majors Are Major," *Sight and Sound*, Autumn 1973.

Harmetz, Aljean. "Orion's Star Rises In Hollywood," *New York Times*, 19 April 1978.

Hennessee, Judith Adler. "Gross Behavior: How To Get Your Percentage Back," *Action*, January-February 1978.

Lewis, Richard Warren. "The Selling of the Deep," *New York Times*, 3 July 1977.

Lindsey, Robert. "The New Tycoons of Hollywood," *New York Times Magazine*, 7 August 1977.

Monaco, James. "Dan Talbot, Film Distributor," *Take One* 4:2 (March 1974).

————. "Donald Rugoff: Mining Silver From the Silver Screen," *Changes*, February 1975.

————. "Stealing the Show: The Piracy Problem. Special Report," *American Film*, July-August 1978.

Ruby, Michael, and Martin Kasindorf. "Inside Hollywood,"*Newsweek*, 13 Feb.1978.

Vallely, Jean, "In the Office of Alan Ladd Jr.", *Esquire*, 11 April 1978.

Willeford, Charles. "From Cockfighter to Born to Kill," *Film Quarterly*, Fall 1975. On the metamorphosis of a film project.

THE BEGELMAN AFFAIR:

Dager, Nick. "A Begelman Bibliography," *Take One*, May 1978. Survey of press reaction.

Kasindorf, Jeannie. "Begelman Babylon," *New York*, 6 February 1978.

McClintick, David. "Slow Fade Out: At Columbia Pictures, A Hollywood Scandal Has Lingering Effects," *Wall Street Journal*, 30 January 1978.

Orth, Maureen. "After Begelman: The Whiz Kids Take Over," *New York*, 12 June 1978.

Tobias, Andrew. "The Fall, Rise and Fall of David Begelman," *Esquire*, March 1978.

Truscott, Lucian K., IV. "Hollywood's Wall Street Connection," *New York Times Magazine*, 26 February 1978.

The Craft

BOOKS:

Brosnan, John. *Movie Magic: The Story of Special Effects in the Cinema.* New York: New American Library, 1976.

Corliss, Richard, ed. *The Hollywood Screenwriters.* New York: Avon Books, 1972. Some material on contemporary screenwriters.

ARTICLES:

Bilowit, William. "A Montage of Feature Film Editors Discuss Their Craft," *Millimeter*, September 1978.

Blalack, Robert. "*Star Wars*' Effect on the World of Special Effects," *Millimeter*, April 1978.

Corliss, Mary, and Carlos Clarens. "Designed for Film: The Hollywood Art

Director," *Film Comment*, May-June 1978.

Farber, Stephen. "On Screenwriters" *New Times*, 19 September 1975.

Maliga, John, "Post Production Sound Systems," *Millimeter*, May 1978.

Rivlin, Robert. "Special Effects: How They Entered Our System and Where They're Headed," *Millimeter*, September 1977.

Schreger, Charles, Jonathan Rosenbaum, Elisabeth Weis. "The Second Coming of Sound," *Film Comment*, September-October 1978.

Sharples, Win, Jr., Elias Savada, Ruth Lissak, and Jay Wertz, eds. "Prime Cut: The Work of the Film Editor," *Film Comment*, March-April 1977.

Thomson, David. "The Art of the Art Director: Designing the Film," *American Film*, February 1977.

Film Culture and Criticism

BOOK:

Murray, Edward. *Nine American Film Critics*. New York: Ungar, 1975. Articles on Kael, Sarris, Simon.

ARTICLES:

Cook, Bruce. "Bob and Pauline: A Fickle Affair," *American Film*, December-January 1978. Altman and Kael relationship.

Monaco, James. "Furthermore: One Hand Washes the Other," [*More*], September 1975. On film criticism.

————. "Bringing Up The Baby with the Movie Camera," *Take One* 4:12 (December 1975). On the situation in film academia.

————. "What's the Score? The Best of the Decade," *Take One*, July 1978.

Rosen, Marjorie. "Critics and the Politics of Superlatives, *Millimeter*, April 1976.

Sarris, Andrew, and Robin Wood. "Film Criticism in the Seventies," *Film Comment*, January-February 1978.

Taylor, John Russell. "The Critic as Superstar," *Sight and Sound*, Summer 1976.

Tuchman, Mitch. "Pauline Kael, the Desperate Critic," *Take One*, Nov. 1977.

Issues

BOOKS:

Bogle, Donald. *Toms, Coons, Mulattoes, Mammies, & Bucks: An Interpretive History of Blacks in American Films*. New York: Viking Press, 1973.

Cripps, Thomas, *Slow Fade to Black: The Negro in American Film, 1900-1942*. New York: Oxford University Press, 1977.

————. *Black Film as Genre*. Bloomington: Indiana University Press, 1977.

Haskell, Molly. *From Reverence to Rape: The Treatment of Women in the Movies*. New York: Penguin Books, 1974.

Mellen, Joan. *Women and Their Sexuality in the New Film*. New York: Horizon Press, 1973.

————. *Big Bad Wolves: Masculinity in the American Film*. New York: Pantheon, 1977.

Monaco, James. *Celebrity: Who Gets It, How They Use It, Why It Works*. New York: Delta Books, 1978. A collection of essays by a variety of writers.

————. *Media Culture: The People, The Products, The Power*. New York: Delta Books, 1978. A collection of essays by various writers, including "Who Owns the Media?" an appendix of data on media economics.

Murray, James. *To Find an Image: Black Films from Uncle Tom to Superfly.* Indianapolis: Bobbs-Merrill Company, Inc., 1973.

Patterson, Lindsay, ed. *Black Films and Filmmakers.* New York: Dodd, Mead & Company, 1975.

Rosen, Marjorie. *Popcorn Venus: Women, Movies, and the American Dream.* New York: Coward, MacCann, & Geoghegan, 1973.

Vogel, Amos. *Film as a Subversive Art.* New York: Random House, 1974.

ARTICLES:

Baldwin, James. "Growing Up with the Movies: White Screen in Harlem," *American Film,* May 1976.

Cineaste. Special Issue: Radical American Film. 5:4.

Kael, Pauline. "The Current Cinema: Fear Of Movies," New Yorker, 25 September 1978.

Kleckner, James, et al. "Television Censorship and the Movies," *Take One* 4:10 (June 1975).

Monaco, James. "Looking for Diane Keaton," *Take One,* November 1977.

Sklar, Robert. "A Woman Directs in Hollywood!" *American Film,* July 1977.

Take One. Special Issue. Women in Film. 3:2 (February 1972).

Zito, Stephen. "Women Directors In Search of a Hit," *Action,* March-April 1978.

Genres

BOOKS:

French, Philip. *Westerns.* New York: Oxford University Press, 1977.

Kaminsky, Stuart M. *American Film Genres: Approaches to a Critical Theory of Popular Film.* New York: Dell Publishing Co., 1974.

Melton, Hollis. *A Guide to Independent Film and Video.* New York: Anthology Film Archives, 1976.

Sitney, P. Adams. *Visionary Film: The American Avant-Garde.* New York: Oxford University Press, 1974.

ARTICLES:

Bogdanovich, Peter. "The B-Movie As Art," *Take One* 3:4 (June 1972).

Copeland, Roger. "When Films 'Quote' Films, They Create a New Mythology," *New York Times,* 25 September 1977.

Friedkin, William. "Anatomy of a Chase," *Take One* 3:6 (October 1972).

Henderson, Brian. "Romantic Comedy Today: Semi-Tough or Impossible?" *Film Quarterly,* Summer 1978.

Hyatt, Richard. "Haeee! Gung Fu Movies: A Primer," *Take One* 3:12 (November 1973).

Jameson, Richard T. "Son of Noir," *Film Comment,* November-December 1974.

Kael, Pauline. "The Current Cinema: The Street Western," *New Yorker,* 25 February 1974.

Kawin, Bruce. "Me Tarzan, You Junk," *Take One,* March 1978. The emergence of the paranoia film.

Morthland, John. "Porn Films: An In-Depth Report," *Take One,* 4:4 (July 1974).

Rosenbaum, Jonathan, Jonas Mekas, and Robert Sklar. "Aspects of the Avant Garde," *American Film,* September 1978.

Schwartz, Nancy, and Richard Corliss. "TV Films, Telefilm U.," *Film Comment,* March-April 1975.

Schrader, Paul "Notes On Film Noir," *Film Comment*, Spring 1972.
———. "Yakuza-Eiga," *Film Comment*, January-February 1974.
Smith, Julian. "What Mad Pursuit: Car Culture in Film," *American Film*, September 1976.
Thomson, David. "The Discreet Charm of *The Godfather*," *Sight and Sound*, Spring 1978.

Major Directors

WOODY ALLEN

BY ALLEN:
Allen, Woody. *Quoi de neuf, Pussycat?* L'Avant-Scène 59 (1966) (*What's New, Pussycat?*)
———and Marshall Brickman. *Annie Hall.* L'Avant-Scène 198 (Dec. 1977).
———. *Without Feathers.* New York: Warner Paperback, 1975.
———. *Getting Even.* New York: Vintage, 1977.
BOOKS ABOUT ALLEN:
Adler, Bill and Jeffrey Feinman. *Woody Allen: Clown Prince of American Humor.* New York: Pinnacle, 1975.
Lax, Eric. *Woody Allen: On Being Funny.* New York: Charterhouse, 1975.
ARTICLES ABOUT ALLEN:
Allen, Woody. "Woody Allen on Love and Death," *Esquire*, July 1975.
Drew, Bernard. "Woody Allen Is Feeling Better," *American Film*, May 1977.
Gilliatt, Penelope. "Profiles: Woody Allen," *New Yorker*, 4 February 1974.
Halberstadt, Ira. "Scenes From A Mind," *Take One*, November 1978.
Maltin, Leonard. "Take Woody Allen. . . Please!" *Film Comment*, March-April 1974.
Mamber, Stephen. "Woody Allen Interview," *Cinema* (Beverly Hills), Winter 1972-73.
Rich, Frank. "Woody Allen Wipes the Smile off His Face," *Esquire*, May 1977.
Trotsky, Judith. "The Art of Comedy: Woody Allen and Sleeper,"*Filmmakers Newsletter*, Summer 1974.
Way, Gregg. "Woody Allen: Together Again for the First Time," *Movietone News* 51 (August 1976).
Weiner. Bernard. "The Wooden Acting of Woody Allen," *Take One*, 3:7 (Dec. 1972).

ROBERT ALTMAN

BOOKS:
Kass, Judith M. *Robert Altman, an American Innovator.* New York: Popular Library, 1978.
McClelland, C. Kirk. *On Making a Movie: Brewster McCloud.* New York: New American Library, 1971.
ARTICLES:
American Film Institute. Robert Altman. *Dialogue on Film* 4:5 (February 1975).
Byrne, Connie, and William O. Lopez. "Nashville—an Interview 'Documentary,'" *Film Quarterly*, Winter 1975-76.
Ciment, Michel, and Bertrand Tavernier. "Entretien avec Robert Altman," *Positif*, February 1973.

————and Michael Henry. "Entretien avec Robert Altman (de *The Long Good-bye à Thieves Like Us*)," *Positif,* February 1975.

Dawson, Jan. "Robert Altman Speaking," *Film Comment,* March-April 1974.

Dempsey, Michael. "Altman: The Empty Staircase and the Chinese Princess," *Film Comment,* September-October 1974.

Gardner, Paul. "Altman Surveys Nashville and Sees Instant America," *New York Times,* 13 June 1975. Interview.

Jameson, Richard T., and Kathleen Murphy. "'They Take On Their Own Life... Robert Altman Interviewed," *Movietone News,* September 1977.

Kael, Pauline. "Coming: Nashville," *New Yorker,* 3 March 1975.

Marcus, Greil. "Ragtime and Nashville: Failure-of-America Fad," *Village Voice,* 4 August 1975.

Michener, Charles. "Robert Altman Interviewed," *Film Comment,* September-October 1978.

Reid, Max. "The Making of California Split," *Filmmakers Newsletter,* October 1974. Interview.

Rosenbaum, Jonathan. "Improvisations and Interactions in Altmanville," *Sight and Sound,* Winter 1975.

Rosenthal, Stuart. Robert Altman," *International Film Guide* 1975.

Tarantino, Michael. "Movement as Metaphor: *The Long Goodbye,"* *Sight and Sound,* Spring 1975.

Wicker, Tom. "Nashville: Dark Perceptions in a Country Music Comedy," *New York Times,* 15 June 1975.

Wood, Robin. "Smart-Ass and Cutie-Pie: Notes Toward an Evaluation of Altman," *Movie* 21 (Autumn 1975).

JOHN CASSAVETES

BY CASSAVETES:

Cassavetes, John. *Shadows.* L'Avant-Scène 197 (December 1977).

————.*Faces.* New York: New American Library, 1970.

————.*Minnie & Moskowitz.* Los Angeles: Black Sparrow Press, 1973.

————."What's Wrong with Hollywood,"*Film Culture,* April 1959.

ABOUT CASSAVETES:

American Film Institute. John Cassavetes, Peter Falk. *Dialogue on Film* 4 (1972).

Degener, David. "Director Under the Influence," *Film Quarterly,* Winter 1975.

Higham, Charles. "The Family That Films Together May Win Oscars Together," *New York Times,* 6 April 1975. Interview.

Jacobs, Diane. "John Cassavetes," *International Film Guide* 1976.

Loeb, Anthony, ed. *A Conversation with John Cassavetes.* Chicago: Columbia College. March 1975. Pamphlet.

McNally, Judith. "A Woman Under the Influence: An Interview with John Cassavetes," *Filmmakers Newsletter,* January 1975.

Mekas, Jonas. "Movie Journal," *Village Voice,* 23 December 1971.

Stabiner, Karen. "Cassavetes: Hollywood's Loner," *Mother Jones,* May 1976.

FRANCIS COPPOLA

BY COPPOLA:

Coppola, Francis. *Conversation Secrète,* L'Avant-Scène 152 (November 1974). Photographs, filmography, interview (*The Conversation*).

BOOK ABOUT COPPOLA:
Johnson, Robert K. *Francis Ford Coppola*. Boston: Twayne Publishers, 1978.
ARTICLES ABOUT COPPOLA:
Aigner, Hal, and Michael Goodwin. "The Bearded Immigrant From Tinsel Town," *City* (San Francisco), 12-25 June 1974.
Braudy, Susan. "Francis Ford Coppola: A Profile," *Atlantic*, August 1976.
Coppola, Francis. "Case Histories of Business Management: Hollywood Artistic Division," *Esquire*, November 1977. (The memo discussed in Chapter 9.)
Cowie, Peter. "Francis Ford Coppola," *International Film Guide* 1976.
De Palma, Brian. "The Making of *The Conversation*," *Filmmakers Newsletter*, May 1974. Interview.
Farber, Stephen. "Coppola and *The Godfather*," *Sight and Sound*, Autumn 1972. Article and interview.
Higham, Charles. "Director's Guild Winner: Francis Ford Coppola," *Action*, May-June 1973.
————."Coppola's Vietnam Movie Is a Battle Royal," *New York Times*, 15 May 1977.
McBride, Joseph. "Coppola, Inc.: The Director as Godfather," *American Film*, November 1975.
Murray, W. "Francis Ford Coppola," *Playboy*, July 1975. Interview.
Rosen, Marjorie. "Francis Ford Coppola, Interviewed," *Film Comment*, July-August 1974. (On Gatsby.)

BRIAN DE PALMA

Bartholomew, D. "De Palma of the Paradise," *Cinefantastique* 4:2 (1975).
Brown, Royal S. "Considering De Palma," *American Film*, July-August 1977.
Coates, J. "The Making of *Phantom of the Paradise*," *Filmmakers Newsletter*, February 1975. Interview.
Gelmis, Joseph. "Brian De Palma," in *The Film Director As Superstar*. New York: Doubleday & Co., 1970.
Kael, Pauline. "Current Cinema: The Curse," *New Yorker*, 22 November 1976.
Margulies, E. "Brian De Palma," *Action*, September-October 1974. Interview.
Pressman, Edward R., et al. "Brian De Palma, American Anarchist," special section of *Cinemabook* 1:2 (Winter 1977).
Rubinstein, R. "The Making of *Sisters*," *Filmmakers Newsletter* September 1973. Interview.

GEORGE LUCAS

Lucas, George, Gloria Katz, Willard Huyck. *American Graffiti*. New York: Grove Press, 1973.
Farber, Stephen. "George Lucas: The Stinky Kid Hits the Big Time," *Film Quarterly*, Spring 1974.
Lubow, Arthur, and Terry Curtis Fox. "The *Star Wars* War," *Film Comment*, July-August 1977.

PAUL MAZURSKY

American Film Institute. Paul Mazursky, *Dialogue on Film* 4:2 (November 1974).
Corliss, Richard. "The New Hollywood: Paul Mazursky: The Horace with the Heart of Gold," *Film Comment*, March-April 1975.

Fox, Terry Curtis. "A Mazursky 'Woman,'" *Film Comment*, March-April 1978. Interview.

Kael, Pauline. "The Artist as a Young Comedian," *New Yorker*, 2 February 1976. (*Next Stop, Greenwich Village*.)

Pasquariello, N. "Paul Mazursky: The Four-Year 'Overnight' Success of *Harry & Tonto*," *Millimeter*, May 1975.

————."Paul Mazursky Discusses *Next Stop, Greenwich Village*," *Filmmakers Newsletter*, April 1976.

MICHAEL RITCHIE

BOOK:

Bahrenburg, Bruce. *Filming "The Candidate."* New York: Warner Paperback Library, 1972.

ARTICLES:

American Film Institute. "Dialogue on Film: Michael Ritchie," *American Film*, November 1977. Interview.

Jacobs, Diane. "Michael Ritchie: Satire with a Semi-Tough Smile," *Film Comment*, November-December 1977

Monaco, James. "Realist Irony: The Films of Michael Ritchie," *Sight and Sound*, Summer 1975. .

PAUL SCHRADER

BY SCHRADER:

Schrader, Paul. *Transcendental Style in Film: Ozu, Bresson, Dreyer.* Berkeley: University of California Press, 1972.

————."Notes On Film Noir," *Film Comment*, Spring 1972.

————."Yakuza-Eiga," *Film Comment*, January-February 1974.

ABOUT SCHRADER:

Crowdus, Gary, and Dan Georgakas. "Blue Collar: An Interview with Paul Schrader," *Cineaste* 8:3.

Goodwin, Michael. "'Suppose We Talk About Screenwriting. I Mean, That's What I Do,'" *Village Voice*, 6 September 1976. Interview with Paul Schrader.

Thompson, Richard. "Screenwriter: Paul Schrader Interviewed," *Film Comment*, March-April 1976.

MARTIN SCORSESE

American Film Institute. Martin Scorsese. *Dialogue on Film* 4:7 (April 1975).

Belie, C. "Alice n'est plus ici et Mean Streets," *Ecran*, July/August 1975. Interview.

Bell, Arthur. Shooting with Scorsese—Ready When You Are Paisan," *Village Voice*, 18 August 1975.

Bobrow, Andrew C. "The Filming of *Mean Streets*: An Interview with Martin Scorsese." *Filmmakers Newsletter*, January 1974.

Carducci, M. "Martin Scorsese," *Millimeter*, May 1975.

Ciment, Michel, and M. Henry. "Entretien avec Martin Scorsese," *Positif*, June 1975.

Flatley, Guy. "Martin Scorsese's Gamble," *New York Times Magazine*, 8 February 1976.

Gardner, Paul. "Martin Scorsese," *Action*, May-June 1975.

Goldstein, Richard, and Mark Jacobson. "Martin Scorsese Tells All: Blood and Guts Turns Me On!" *Village Voice*, 5 April 1976.

Goodman, Mark. "Tripping with Martin Scorsese," *Penthouse*, May 1977.

Henry, Michael. "La Passion de Saint Martin Scorsese," *Positif*, June 1975.

Howard, Steve. "The Making of *Alice Doesn't Live Here Anymore*: An interview with Director Martin Scorsese," *Filmmakers Newsletter*, March 1975.

Kaplan, Jonathan. "New York, New York: Martin Scorsese Interviewed," *Film Comment*, July-August 1977.

Macklin, F. Anthony. "It's a Personal Thing for Me," *Film Heritage* 10:3 (1975). Interview.

Rosen, Marjorie. "The New Hollywood: Martin Scorsese," *Film Comment*, March-April 1975. Interview.

STEVEN SPIELBERG

BY SPIELBERG:

Spielberg, Steven. *Close Encounters of the Third Kind.* New York: Dell Publishing Co., 1977.

BOOK ABOUT SPIELBERG:

Gottlieb, Carl. *The Jaws Log.* New York: Dell Publishing Co., 1975.

ARTICLES ABOUT SPIELBERG:

American Film Institute. Spielberg/Barwood & Robbins/Zsigmond On *Sugarland Express. Dialogue on Film* 3:7 (July 1974).

————.Dialogue on Film: Steven Spielberg. *American Film*, September 1978.

Cumbow, Robert C. "The Great American Eating Machine: Steven Spielberg's *Duel, The Sugarland Express*, and *Jaws*," *Movietone News* 52 (October 1976).

Helpern, David. "At Sea with Steven Spielberg," *Take One* 4:10 (June 1975).

Jacobs, Diane. "An Interview with Steven Spielberg," *Millimeter*, Nov. 1977.

Kroll, Jack. "Close Encounters with Spielberg," *Newsweek*, November 21, 1977.

Maslin, Janet. "Spielberg's Journey from Sharks to the Stars," *New York Times*, 15 December 1977.

Margolis, Herbert, and Craig Modderno. "Steven Spielberg," *Penthouse*, February 1978. Interview.

Tuchman, Mitch. "Spielberg's Close Encounter," *Film Comment*, January-February 1978. Interview.

Other Filmmakers
DIRECTORS

BOOKS:

Gelmis, Joseph. *The Film Director as Superstar.* New York: Doubleday & Company, 1970. Interviews with De-Palma, Cassavetes, Corman, Coppola, Penn, Lester, Nichols, and Kubrick, among others.

Koszarski, Richard, ed. *Hollywood Directors, 1941-1976.* New York: Oxford University Press. 1977. Including Frankenheimer, Penn, Corman, Friedkin, Ritchie.

McCarthy, Todd, and Charles Flynn, eds. *Kings of the Bs: Working Within the Hollywood System.* New York: E. P. Dutton Co., 1975. Articles on Roger Corman and others.

Schuth, H. Wayne. *Mike Nichols*. Boston: Twayne Publishers, 1978.

Van Peebles, Melvin. *Sweet Sweetback's Baadasssss Song*. New York: Lancer Books, 1971.

ARTICLES:

American Film Institute. William Friedkin. *Dialogue on Film* 3:4 (February-March 1974).

———."Dialogue on Film: Sydney Pollack," *American Film*, April 1978.

———.Paul Williams. *Dialogue on Film* 6 (1972).

Atkins, Thomas R. "American Institutions: The Films of Frederick Wiseman," *Sight and Sound*, Autumn 1974.

Atlas, Jacoba. "Mel Brooks: The Film Director as Fruitcake," *Film Comment*, March-April 1975.

Andrews, Nigel. "Sam Peckinpah: The Survivor and the Individual," *Sight and Sound*, , Spring 1973.

Crowdus, Gary. "Filming in Harlan—An Interview with Barbara Kopple and Hart Perry," *Cineaste* 8:1 (Summer 1977).

Denby, David. "Bogdanovich—Will *Nickelodeon* Be His Last Picture Show?," *New York Times*, 30 January 1977.

Jameson, Richard T. "The Pakula Parallax," *Film Comment*, Sept.-Oct. 1976.

Kaminsky, Stuart M. "Don Siegel," *Take One* 3:4 (June 1972). Interview.

Kehr, Dave. "The B Movie Is Alive and Well . . . ," *Film Comment*, September-October 1977.

Nichols, Bill. "Fred Wiseman's Documentaries: Theory and Structure, *Film Quarterly*, Spring 1978.

Salvato, Larry. "Monte Hellman," *Millimeter*, July-August 1975.

Shepard, Thom. "Beyond the 'Black Film': An Interview with Gordon Parks," *Cineaste* 8:2.

Thomsen, Christian B. "An Interview with Monte Hellman," *Take One* 4:2 (March 1974).

Viertel, Jack, and David Colker. "The *New* New Hollywood," *Take One*, September 1978. Six new directors: Jeremy Paul Kagan, Claudia Weill, John Badham, Robert Zemeckis, Randall Kleiser, John Landis.

Zito, Stephen. "Bakshi among the Hobbits," *American Film*, September, 1978.

PRODUCERS

American Film Institute. "Dialogue on Film: David Brown and Richard Zanuck," *American Film*, October 1975.

———."Dialogue on Film: Irwin Winkler and Robert Chartoff," *American Film*, December-January 1977.

Collins, Allan. "New World Pictures," *Take One* 2:12 (October 1971).

Medjuck, Joe. "The Further Adventures of Ivan Reitman," *Take One*, 1978.

Salvato, Larry. "Roger Corman," *Millimeter*, December 1975.

———."Julia Phillips," *Millimeter*, September 1976.

———, and Dennis Schaefer. "Alan Ladd, Jr.," *Millimeter*, March 1977. Interview.

Stamelman, Peter. "Mike Medavoy," *Millimeter*, September 1976.

———."Producer Frank Yablans on *The Other Side of Midnight*," *Millimeter*, May 1977.

WRITERS

SELECTED SCRIPTS:

Feiffer, Jules. *Carnal Knowledge.* New York: Noonday, 1971.

Fonda, Peter, and Dennis Hopper. *Easy Rider.* New York: New American Library. 1969.

Goldman, William. *Butch Cassidy and the Sundance Kid.* New York: Bantam, 1969.

Herndon, Venable, and Arthur Penn. *Alice's Restaurant.* New York: Doubleday & Company, 1969.

Pinter, Harold. *Le Dernier Nabab.* L'Avant-Scène 192 (1977). (*The Last Tycoon.*)

Wexler, Norman. *Joe.* New York: Avon, 1970.

ARTICLES:

American Film Institute. "Dialogue on Film: Robert Towne," *American Film,* December 1975.

————."Dialogue on Film: Neil Simon," *American Film,* March 1978.

Gross, Larry. "Benton and Newman," *Millimeter,* October 1976.

Rivlin, Michael. "Elaine May," *Millimeter,* October 1975.

Thompson, Richard. "In the American Grain: An Interview With Robert Getchell," *Sight and Sound,* Summer 1976.

Warren, Madeline and Robert Levine. "Gloria Katz and Willard Huyck: Graffiti Kids Get Lucky," *Film Comment,* March-April 1975. Interview.

CINEMATOGRAPHERS, EDITORS, MUSICIANS, AND ACTORS

American Film Institute. Cinematographer Conrad Hall. *Dialogue on Film* 3:1 (October 1973).

————.Cinematographers Laszlo Kovacs/Vilmos Zsigmond. *Dialogue on Film* 4:1 (October 1974).

————."Dialogue on Film: Verna Fields," *American Film,* June 1976.

Baffer, Christopher. "Ralph Rosenblum," *Millimeter,* March 1977.

Cook, G. Richardson. "Michael Small," *Millimeter,* September 1975. Interview.

Epstein, Renee. "An Interview with Haskell Wexler," *Sight and Sound,* Winter 1975-76.

Kilday, Gregg. "The Cutting Edge of Verna Fields," *Action,* Jan.-Feb. 1978.

Prince, David, Peter Lehman, et al. "Film Editing: An Interview with Dede Allen," *Wide Angle* 2:1 (1977).

Taubin, Amy. "Days of a Cameraman: An Interview with Nestor Almendros," *Soho Weekly News,* 14 September 1978.

Taylor, John Russell. "Profession: Actor: An Interview with Jack Nicholson," *Sight and Sound,* Summer 1974.

Salvato, Larry, and Dennis Schaefer. "Laszlo Kovacs: Budapest to Beverly Hills," *Millimeter,* December 1976.

Schaefer, Dennis, and Larry Salvato. "An Interview with Vilmos Zsigmond," *Millimeter,* November 1977:

Shedlin, Michael. "Haskell Wexler," *Take One* 3:6 (October 1972).

Wu, Ying Ying. "Ellen Burstyn Talks," *Take One,* March 1977.

Some Notable Books
Published Since 1978:

Brosnan, John. *Future Tense: The Cinema of Science Fiction.* New York: St. Martin's Press, 1979.

Brown, Les. *Les Brown's Encyclopedia of Television.* New York: New York Zoetrope, 1982.

Cagin, Seth and Philip Dray. *Hollywood Films of the Seventies: Sex, Drugs, Violence, Rock 'n' Roll and Politics.* New York: Harper & Row, 1984.

Clark, Frank P. *Special Effects in Motion Pictures.* New York: Society of Motion Picture and Television Engineers, 1982.

Coppola, Eleanor. *Notes.* New York: Simon and Schuster, 1979.

Georgakas, Dan and Lenny Rubinstein. *The Cineaste Interviews on the Art and Politics of the Cinema.* Chicago: Lake View Press, 1983.

Giannetti, Louis. *Masters of the American Cinema.* Englewood Cliffs, N.J.: Prentice-Hall, 1981.

Goldman, William. *Adventures in the Screen Trade: A Personal View of Hollywood and Screenwriting.* New York: Warner Books, 1983. Highly recommended.

Haun, Harry. *The Movie Quote Book.* New York: Harper & Row, 1983.

Hoberman, J. and Jonathan Rosenbaum. *Midnight Movies.* New York: Harper & Row, 1983.

Insdorf, Annette. *Indelible Shadows: Film and the Holocaust.* New York: Vintage Books, 1983.

Jacobs, Diane. *But We Need the Eggs: The Magic of Woody Allen.* New York: St. Martin's Press, 1982.

Klotman, Phyllis R. *Frame by Frame: A Black Filmography.* Bloomington: Indiana University Press, 1979.

Kolker, Robert Phillip. *A Cinema of Loneliness: Penn, Kubrick, Coppola, Scorsese, Altman.* New York: Oxford University Press, 1980.

Lees, David. *The Movie Business.* New York: Random House, 1981.

Lipton, Lenny. *Independent Filmmaking.* New York: Scribner & Sons, 1983.

Macek, Carl. *The Art of Heavy Metal: Animation for the Eighties.* New York: New York Zoetrope, 1981.

Maltin, Leonard. *T.V. Movies: 1983-1984 Edition.* New York: New American Library, 1983.

Mast, Gerald. *The Comic Mind: Comedy and the Movies.* Chicago: University of Chicago Press, 1979.

McClintick, David. *Indecent Exposure: A True Story of Hollywood and Wall Street.* New York: William Morrow, 1982. Highly recommended.

McCreadie, Marsha. *Women on Film: The Critical Eye.* New York: Praeger Publishers, 1983.

Pye, Michael. *The Movie Brats: How the Film Generation Took Over Hollywood.* New York: Harper & Row, 1979.

Rosenbaum, Jonathan. *Moving Places: A Life at the Movies.* New York: Harper and Row, 1980.

Samuels, Stuart. *Midnight Movies: A Revealing Look at America's Most Popular Cult Movies.* New York: Macmillan, 1983.

Sitney, P. Adams. *Visionary Film: The American Avant-Garde: 1943-1978.* New York: Oxford University Press, 1979.

Speed, Carol. *Inside Black Hollywood.* Holloway, 1980.

Squire, Jason. *The Movie Business Book.* Englewood Cliffs, N.J.: Prentice-Hall, 1983.

Steinberg, Cobbett. *Reel Facts: The Movie Book of Records (updated).* New York: Random House, 1982.

Taylor, Geoffrey. *Paul Mazursky's Tempest.* New York: New York Zoetrope, 1982.

Thompson, David. *Overexposures: The Crisis in American Filmmaking.* New York: Quill, 1981. Highly recommended.

Wasko, Janet. *Movies and Money: Financing the American Film Industry.* Norwood, N.J.: Ablex Publishing, 1982.

Wicking, Christopher and Tise Vahimagi. *The American Vein: Directors and Directions in Television.* London: Talisman Books, 1979.

Yacowar, Maurice. *Loser Take All: The Comic Art of Woody Allen.* New York: Ungar, 1979.

References

Chapter 1: Properties and Packages

1. "Planning to Rob a Bank as Research, Writer Is Slain," *The New York Times*, 21 July 1978.
2. For more information on Guber's marketing strategy, see Richard Warren Lewis's "The Selling of *The Deep*," *The New York Times*, 3 July 1977.

Chapter 2: Products and Profits

1. For more complete data on conglomerates in the media, see "Who Owns the Media?" in my book *Media Culture* (New York: Delta books, 1978) and the revision and update of that essay which appeared in *Take One*, November 1978.
2. *The New Yorker*, 5 August 1974.

Chapter 3: The Entertainment Machine

1. For more, see *The New Wave* (New York: Oxford University Press, 1976).
2. See "The language of Film: Signs and Syntax," Chapter 3 of *How to Read a Film* (New York: Oxford University Press, 1977).

Chapter 4: The People Who Make Movies

1. For a brilliant analysis of the role of star personas in Hollywood, see David Thomson's *A Biographical Dictionary of Film* (New York: William Morrow & Co. 1975).
2. New York: A.S. Barnes and Co., 1977.
3. For a good description of the decline and fall of the late sixties generation, see Bo Burlingham's "Politics Under the Palms," in *Media Culture*, pp. 62-90.
4. For a good description of the contemporary independent producer's curious dilemma, see Robert Alan Aurthur's "Harry Makes a Movie," in *Media Culture*, pp. 142-49.
5. For more on editors, see Win Sharples, Jr., and others "Prime Cut: 75 editors' filmographies and supporting material," *Film Comment*, March-April 1977.

Chapter 5: The Whiz Kids

1. *A Biographical Dictionary of Film*, p. 52.
2. *Dialogue on Film*, February-March 1974, p. 4.
3. "It's a Personal Thing with Me: An Interview with Marty Scorsese," *Film Heritage*, June 1975, p. 15.
4. "Screenwriter: *Taxi Driver*'s Paul Schrader," interviewed by Richard Thompson, *Film Comment*, March-April 1976.
5. I'm indebted for a number of these correlations to Ron Diamond.

6. "George Lucas: The Stinky Kid Hits the Big Time," *Film Quarterly*, Spring 1974, p. 9.
7. "Close Encounters with Steven Spielberg," *Film Comment*, January-February 1978, p. 50.
8. "Spielberg's Journey from Sharks to Stars,"*The New York Times*, 18 December 1977.
9. See Schrader's interview with Richard Thompson in *Film Comment*, March-April 1976, for more.
10. "Notes on Film Noir," *Film Comment*, Spring 1972.

Chapter 6: The Black Film (and the Black Image)

1. *To Find an Image*, p. xiv.
2. See Cripps's excellent *Slow Fade to Black*, pp. 370-73, for more details on the writing of *Casablanca*.
3. *Sweet Sweetback's Baadasssss Song: The Story and the Journal* (New York: Lancer Books, 1971).
4. Conversation with the author.
5. Conversation with the author.

Chapter 7: The Importance of Being Funny

1. Quoted in "The Art of Comedy: Woody Allen and *Sleeper,*" by Judith Trotsky, *Filmmakers Newsletter*, Summer 1974.

Chapter 8: Myth, Reality, and Other Ways of Meaning

1. Venable Herndon and Arthur Penn, *Alice's Restaurant* (New York: Doubleday & Co., 1970), p. 10.
2. For a telling portrait of the group of hip but aging filmmakers of which BBS formed the nucleus, see Bo Burlingham's "Politics Under the Palms."

Chapter 9: Who's Talking? Cassavetes, Altman, and Coppola

1. Diane Jacobs's critical survey, *Hollywood Renaissance*, discusses these five plus Martin Scorsese.
2. *Minnie and Moskowitz* (Los Angeles: Black Sparrow Press 1971), pp. 46-48.
3. *Faces*, introduction, (New York: New American Library. 1970), p. 7.
4. *The Village Voice*, 23 December 1971.
5. *Film Culture*, April 1959, pp. 4-5.
6. Joseph Gelmis, *The Film Director as Superstar* (New York: Doubleday & Co., 1970), p. 84.
7. Gelmis, p. 78.
8. Susan Schenker. "A Woman Under the Influence,"*Take One*, March 1975.
9. "Coming: *Nashville*," *The New Yorker*, 3 March 1975, p. 79.
10. C. Kirk McClelland, *Brewster McCloud: On Making A Movie* (New York: New American Library, 1971).
11. Peter Weiss, *Marat/Sade*, (New York: Atheneum, 1965), Introduction.
12. "Coppola's Vietnam Movie Is a Battle Royal," *New York Times*, 15 May 1977.
13. *Esquire*, November 1977, pp. 190-96.
14. "Francis Ford Coppola Interviewed," *Film Comment*, July-August 1974.
15. Hal Aigner and Michael Goodwin, "The Bearded Immigrant From Tinseltown," *City* magazine, 12 June 1974, pp. 30-41.
16. Marjorie Rosen, "Interview with Francis Coppola," *Film Comment*, July-August 1974.

17. Quoted in Gelmis.
18. Quoted in Gelmis.
19. Quoted in Aigner and Goodwin.
20. Susan Braudy, "Francis Ford Coppola: A Profile," *Atlantic*, August 1976.

Chapter 10: Who's Talking? Ritchie and Mazursky

1. If, as I do, you like the rhythms of this last sentence, you may be interested to know they're not my own. They belong to E. B. White. See his piece "The Decline of Sport," in *Media Culture*.
2. All quotations from conversations with the author.
3. All quotations from conversations with the author.

Chapter 11: The Fourth Estate

1. Lucian K. Truscott IV, "Hollywood's Wall Street Connection," *The New York Times Magazine*, 26 February 1978.
2. Truscott, p. 53.
3. *Variety*, 5 October 1977.
4. For more information see "Who Owns the Media?" in *Media Culture* and *Take One*, November 1978.
5. Conversation with the author.
6. Quoted in Aljean Harmetz's "Orion's Star Rises in Hollywood," *The New York Times*, 19 April 1978.
7. Conversation with the author.

Index

Note: For the sake of concision, passages more than a page in length are identified here only by their initial page numbers. Most extended commentaries are noted in the table of contents.

C

H

O

P

S

T

U

V

W

Credits

CREDITS

AMERICAN FILM NOW
by James Monaco

Line editing: John Thornton
Additional editing: James Raimes, David Emblidge
Research: Sharon Boonshoft
Maps and graphs: David Lindroth
Editorial assistance: Peter Lebensold, Sharon Boonshoft
Copy editing: Ted Johnson
Layout: Kay Susmann
Layout assistance: Al Weisser, Susan Rivoir
Computer index supervision: Robert Monaco
Production and design: New York Zoetrope
Photoengraving and postproduction:
    Publishers' Preparation Department, Inc., Levittown, Pa.
Oxford University Press liaison: John Shinkarick
Reprographic Services: Jerry Wortman, Village Copier
Agent: Virginia Barber
Stills: New York Zoetrope, and Movie Star News, Cinemabilia, and The
    Museum of Modern Art/Film Stills Archive
Acknowledgements:
    For interviews: Thanks to Ossie Davis, Brian De Palma, Bill Gunn,
Paul Mazursky, Mike Medavoy, Eric Pleskow, Michael Ritchie, and
Melvin Van Peebles.
    For information: Thanks to Carol Carey, Mary Corliss, Bob Frederick,
Mike Goodwin, Pamela Hedley, Mike Hutner, Pauline Kael, Mike
Kaplan, Bill Kenly, Wynn Loewenthal, Eileen Noon, Clayton Riley,
Margaret Ross, and Ann Thompson.
    For permissions: Syd Silverman (*Variety*), Peter Lebensold (*Take One*).

American Film Now is set in a phototype version of Goudy Old Style, 11/13 points. Designed in 1915 by Frederic W. Goudy, the most influential of early twentieth-century American type designers, Old Style was modeled on a few letters Goudy had copied from a portrait by Hans Holbein. In "oldstyle" typefaces the various elements of the individual letters are of relatively uniform weights so that the design is approximately the same color throughout, which makes oldstyle typefaces generally very readable. Goudy was a printer as well as a designer who operated his own press for many years—a craftsman in the nineteenth-century mold.

The display type for the chapter titles of *American Film Now* is Americana. "Who's Who" is set in Helvetica Condensed.

American Film Now was printed and bound by Vail-Ballou Press, Inc., Binghampton, N.Y.

The End